Algorithmic Languages and Calculi

IFIP – The International Federation for Information Processing

IFIP was founded in 1960 under the auspices of UNESCO, following the First World Computer Congress held in Paris the previous year. An umbrella organization for societies working in information processing, IFIP's aim is two-fold: to support information processing within its member countries and to encourage technology transfer to developing nations. As its mission statement clearly states,

> IFIP's mission is to be the leading, truly international, apolitical organization which encourages and assists in the development, exploitation and application of information technology for the benefit of all people.

IFIP is a non-profitmaking organization, run almost solely by 2500 volunteers. It operates through a number of technical committees, which organize events and publications. IFIP's events range from an international congress to local seminars, but the most important are:

- the IFIP World Computer Congress, held every second year;
- open conferences;
- working conferences.

The flagship event is the IFIP World Computer Congress, at which both invited and contributed papers are presented. Contributed papers are rigorously refereed and the rejection rate is high.

As with the Congress, participation in the open conferences is open to all and papers may be invited or submitted. Again, submitted papers are stringently refereed.

The working conferences are structured differently. They are usually run by a working group and attendance is small and by invitation only. Their purpose is to create an atmosphere conducive to innovation and development. Refereeing is less rigorous and papers are subjected to extensive group discussion.

Publications arising from IFIP events vary. The papers presented at the IFIP World Computer Congress and at open conferences are published as conference proceedings, while the results of the working conferences are often published as collections of selected and edited papers.

Any national society whose primary activity is in information may apply to become a full member of IFIP, although full membership is restricted to one society per country. Full members are entitled to vote at the annual General Assembly, National societies preferring a less committed involvement may apply for associate or corresponding membership. Associate members enjoy the same benefits as full members, but without voting rights. Corresponding members are not represented in IFIP bodies. Affiliated membership is open to non-national societies, and individual and honorary membership schemes are also offered.

Algorithmic Languages and Calculi

IFIP TC2 WG2.1 International Workshop on Algorithmic Languages and Calculi 17–22 February 1997, Alsace, France

Edited by

Richard S. Bird

Computing Laboratory
Oxford University
Oxford
UK

and

Lambert Meertens

CWI
Amsterdam
The Netherlands

Published by Chapman & Hall on behalf of the International Federation for Information Processing (IFIP)

CHAPMAN & HALL

London · Weinheim · New York · Tokyo · Melbourne · Madras

Published by Chapman & Hall, 2–6 Boundary Row, London SE1 8HN, UK

Chapman & Hall, 2–6 Boundary Row, London SE1 8HN, UK

Chapman & Hall GmbH, Pappelallee 3, 69469 Weinheim, Germany

Chapman & Hall USA, 115 Fifth Avenue, New York, NY 10003, USA

Chapman & Hall Japan, ITP-Japan, Kyowa Building, 3F, 2-2-1 Hirakawacho, Chiyoda-ku, Tokyo 102, Japan

Chapman & Hall Australia, 102 Dodds Street, South Melbourne, Victoria 3205, Australia

Chapman & Hall India, R. Seshadri, 32 Second Main Road, CIT East, Madras 600 035, India

---

First edition 1997

Printed in Great Britain by Athenæum Press Ltd, Gateshead, Tyne & Wear

ISBN 0 412 82050 1

A catalogue record for this book is available from the British Library

∞ Printed on permanent acid-free text paper, manufactured in accordance with ANSI/NISO Z39.48-1992 and ANSI/NISO Z39.48-1984 (Permanence of Paper).

CONTENTS

PREFACE

This book contains the papers presented at the IFIP Working Conference on Algorithmic Languages and Calculi, held in Bisschoffsheim, Alsace, on February 17–19, 1997. The conference was sponsored by IFIP Technical Committee 2 and organised in cooperation with Working Group 2.1 on Algorithmic Languages and Calculi, whose 50th meeting was held immediately afterwards.

For a number of years the inspiration of WG 2.1 has been to seek to develop a theory of algorithmics, comprising notations and calculi appropriate for rigorous yet elegant methods of program development. The following papers reflect this inspiration in a variety of ways. Together, they provide a state-of-the-art overview of ongoing research in the field, as well as its application to the production of practical software. There are derivations both of individual programs and classes of algorithms, a number of which are conducted in a point-free style using equational and inequational reasoning in a relational calculus. There are presentations of general program-transformation schemes, descriptions of implemented systems for carrying out transformations automatically (or semi-implemented systems for semi-automatic transformations), and explorations of the use of categorical concepts in the specification and design of general systems. Overall, the papers attest to continuing progress in our ability to improve conceptual clarity, to increase notational simplicity, and to tackle progressively harder problems. All this is made possible by striving for mathematical abstraction and unification.

The papers are recorded in the order they were presented at the conference, and are interleaved with edited transcripts of four short discussion sessions.

The editors are grateful to the members of the Program Committee and the reviewers for their careful work, and to the Organising Committee for providing a stimulating environment for the conference. They would also like to thank Doug Smith, chairman of WG 2.1, for providing much useful information, and Aileen Parlane of Chapman & Hall for general support in the preparation of this book.

Amsterdam, April 1997

Richard Bird
Lambert Meertens

PROGRAMME COMMITTEE

D.R. Smith, Palo Alto, USA (Chair)
J-P. Finance, Nancy, France (Co-Chair)

R. Back, Turku, Finland
R. Backhouse, Eindhoven, The Netherlands
T. Coquand, Goteborg, Sweden
H. Ehrig, Berlin, Germany
M.S. Feather, Pasadena, USA
J. Gibbons, Auckland, New Zealand
D. Gries, Ithaca, USA
A.M. Haeberer, Rio de Janeiro, Brazil
R. Hehner, Toronto, Canada
L.G.L.T. Meertens, Amsterdam, The Netherlands
B. Möller, Augsburg, Germany
C. Morgan, Oxford, UK
F. Orejas, Barcelona, Spain
R. Paige, New York, USA
H. Partsch, Ulm, Germany
P. Pepper, Berlin, Germany
D. Sannella, Edinburgh, UK
M. Sintzoff, Louvain-la-Neuve, Belgium
W. Turski, Warsaw, Poland

Dynamic programming: a different perspective

Sharon Curtis
Oxford University Computing Laboratory
Parks Road, Oxford, UK. OX1 3QD
sharon@comlab.ox.ac.uk

Abstract

Dynamic programming has long been used as an algorithm design technique, with various mathematical theories proposed to model it. Here we take a different perspective, using a relational calculus to model both problems and their solutions obtained from dynamic programming. This approach serves to shed new light on the different styles of dynamic programming, representing them by different search strategies of the tree-like space of partial solutions.

Keywords

dynamic programming, optimization problems, relational calculus

1 INTRODUCTION AND HISTORY

Dynamic programming is an algorithm design technique for solving many different types of optimization problem, applicable to such diverse fields as operations research (Ecker and Kupferschmid, 1988) and neutron transport theory (Bellman, Kagiwada and Kalaba, 1967).

The mathematical theory of the subject dates back to 1957, when Richard Bellman (Bellman, 1957) first popularized the idea, producing a mathematical theory to model multi-stage decision processes and to solve related optimization problems. He was also the first to introduce the idea of the *Principle of Optimality*:

> "An optimal policy has the property that whatever the initial state and initial decision are, the remaining decisions must constitute an optimal policy with regard to the state resulting from the first decision."

This he presented as the essential condition that such an optimization problem had to satisfy for the dynamic programming technique to be applicable. (Morin (1982) subsequently showed that this is a sufficient but not necessary condition.)

The early standard formalizations of dynamic programming as applied to combinatorial optimization problems concerned *discrete decision processes*, which are a set of strings of decisions (or *policies*) and a cost function on policies. These were modelled as automata by Shreider (1961), and further extended to *sequential decision processes* (discrete decision processes with an added cost structure imposed) by Karp, Held and others (Karp and Held, 1962 and 1967; Elmaghraby, 1970; Ibaraki, 1973). These structures model the problem itself, then the solution is obtained by checking that the principle of optimality applies, and producing the relevant *functional equation*, a recursion equation giving a recipe for the actual computer program. The method of solution was either via *tabulation* of the values of the function concerned, or by direct application of the functional equation, using the technique of *memoization* to avoid computing the same subproblem twice.

The method of performing the computation is little addressed in the early literature, although Bonzon did explore a particular theory for executing particular types of tabulation (Bonzon, 1970).

More recent research has considered the method of computation more fully, and also alternative formulations of the Principle of Optimality. Mitten (1964) considered a Monotonicity Assumption and more recently, Morin (1982) presented more recent work on this, connecting it to the Principle of Optimality.

Also, in line with recent trends concerning data structures, Helman (Helman and Rosenthal, 1985; Helman, 1986; Helman, 1989) has reworked traditional dynamic programming using trees rather than just strings, and specifically separating the ideas of problem structure and computation. Further work by de Moor (de Moor, 1992; Bird and de Moor 1992, 1996) has extended the theory of data structures used within dynamic programming to initial datatypes.

In this paper, dynamic programming will be presented from a different angle, more similar to a technique already in existence that involves keeping several candidate partial solutions at each stage of the algorithm, and discarding unnecessary ones. This is a summary of work from Curtis (1996). Helman's strategy of separating structure from computation will be exercised, but we will generalize from both Helman and de Moor's work, as the datatypes used are not restricted to initial datatypes.

A calculus of relations will be used to model both optimization problems and the computation of their solutions. A simple imperative-style loop operator will model the construction of feasible solutions to a solution, similar to a discrete decision process. The computation of an optimal solution will also be modelled using a relational loop, and the relationship of this particular style of dynamic programming towards other more traditional styles will be investigated.

This work is more abstract than previous approaches, exploring the subject from a higher level.

And as every walker knows, if you take a high level route, you get a much better view.

2 THE *LIM* MODEL

Firstly, we briefly review the operators needed, before going on to examine the structure of dynamic programming problems and their solutions.

2.1 Preliminaries

A relation $R : A \leftarrow B$ is a subset of $A \times B$, and we will use the shorthand xRy (or sometimes $x \xleftarrow{R} y$) for $(x, y) \in A \times B$.

The intersection, union and converse operators, $\cap, \cup, ^\circ$ respectively, have their usual meanings, and relational composition $\cdot$ will be from right to left, in a similar style to functional programming. The universal properties for $\cap$ and $\cup$ are as follows:

$$P \cup Q \subseteq R \;\equiv\; P \subseteq R \,\wedge\, Q \subseteq R \tag{1}$$

$$P \subseteq Q \cap R \;\equiv\; P \subseteq Q \,\wedge\, P \subseteq R \tag{2}$$

Converse distributes over $\cup$ and $\cap$, which also distribute over each other. Composition distributes over $\cup$, and converse has the following property:

$$(P \cdot Q)^\circ \;=\; Q^\circ \cdot P^\circ \tag{3}$$

The left and right quotient operators are defined by the following universal properties:

$$R \cdot S \subseteq T \;\equiv\; R \subseteq T/S \tag{4}$$
$$R \cdot S \subseteq T \;\equiv\; S \subseteq R\backslash T, \tag{5}$$

and are called quotients because of the following cancellation laws:

$$R/S \cdot S \subseteq R \tag{6}$$
$$R/(S \cdot T) \cdot S \subseteq R/T \tag{7}$$
$$R/S \cdot S/T \subseteq R/T \tag{8}$$

(and similarly for \). A relation f is a function if $f \cdot f^\circ \subseteq id$ and $id \subseteq f^\circ \cdot f$, where id is the identity relation. Functions interact with quotients with the following rules:

$$R/S \cdot f \;=\; R/(f^\circ \cdot S) \tag{9}$$
$$f \cdot R/S \;=\; (f \cdot R)/S. \tag{10}$$

The projection functions *outl* and *outr* return the left and right element of an ordered pair, respectively. The product operator $\times$ is such that if $R : A \leftarrow B$ and $S : C \leftarrow D$ then $R \times S : A \times C \leftarrow B \times D$ and

$$(a, c)(R \times S)(b, d) \;\Leftrightarrow\; aRb \;\wedge\; cSd. \tag{11}$$

Products interact with the projection functions as follows:

$$outl \cdot (R \times S) \subseteq R \cdot outl, \tag{12}$$
$$outr \cdot (R \times S) \subseteq S \cdot outr. \tag{13}$$

Note that the precedences of the operators introduced so far are (from loosest to tight binding): $\cup, \cap, \times, \cdot, /, \backslash, ^\circ$.

The converse of the membership relation $\in$ is denoted by $\ni$, and the power transpose operator Λ applied to a relation R yields a function returning the set of elements relating by R to the input, also defined by the following equivalence:

$$f = \Lambda R \;\Leftrightarrow\; \in \cdot f = R. \tag{14}$$

A useful property known as Λ-cancellation is the following:

$$\Lambda R \cdot R^\circ \subseteq \ni. \tag{15}$$

A related operator is E, which returns a function defined as follows:

$$(\mathsf{E}R)X \;=\; \{y \mid \exists x \bullet yRx\}. \tag{16}$$

It satisfies the following properties:

$$\begin{aligned} \mathsf{E}R &= \Lambda(R \cdot \in) && (17)\\ \in \cdot\, \mathsf{E}R &= R \cdot \in && (18)\\ \mathsf{E}R \cdot \tau &= \Lambda R, && (19) \end{aligned}$$

where τ applied to x returns $\{x\}$. The powerset operator P relates two sets of elements as follows:

$$\mathsf{P}R \;=\; \in\backslash(R\cdot\in) \;\cap\; (\ni\cdot R)/\ni \qquad (20)$$

That is, $X(\mathsf{P}R)\,Y$ precisely when every element of X is related by R to an element of Y, and vice-versa.

The following two operators are subsets of the identity relation: $dom\,P$ corresponds to those elements in the domain of P, and vice-versa for $notdom\,P$:

$$\begin{aligned} dom\,P &= \{(x,x) \mid \exists y \bullet yPx\} && (21)\\ notdom\,P &= \{(x,x) \mid \neg\exists y \bullet yPx\}. && (22) \end{aligned}$$

Properties concerning these operators that we will need are

$$\begin{aligned} dom\,P \;\cup\; notdom\,P &= id && (23)\\ Q \cdot notdom\,(P\cdot Q) &\subseteq notdom\,P \cdot Q && (24)\\ notdom\,(P\cdot Q) \cdot Q^{\circ} &\subseteq Q^{\circ} \cdot notdom\,P && (25)\\ notdom\,P \cdot dom\,P &= \emptyset && (26)\\ notdom\,P \subseteq notdom\,Q \;&\equiv\; dom\,Q \subseteq dom\,P && (27) \end{aligned}$$

The operator min is used for taking a minimum with respect to a relation:

$$min\,R \;=\; \in \;\cap\; R/\ni\,. \qquad (28)$$

In words, $x(min\,R)X$ precisely when $x \in X$ and for all $y \in X$, xRy. For a reflexive relation R, we also have that

$$min\,R \cdot \ni \;=\; R. \qquad (29)$$

A universal property concerning minima is the following:

$$P \subseteq min\,R \cdot \Lambda Q \;\equiv\; P \subseteq Q \;\wedge\; P \cdot Q^{\circ} \subseteq R \qquad (30)$$

2.2 The Problem Structure

To specify an optimization problem formally, the feasible solutions to the problem and the criterion for optimality must both be expressed.

For expressing the choice of an optimal solution, we use the min operator. This yields slightly more generality than non-relational formalisms: the use of a relation $min\,R$ can be used to minimize or maximize a cost function, for example $R = f^{\circ} \cdot \geq \cdot f$, but more general orderings can also be used, such as the lexicographical ordering.

To express relationally the feasible solutions to a problem, we will use the following notion of limits. The operator *lim T* is defined to be the least solution X of

$$X \;=\; notdom\ T \ \cup\ X \cdot T. \tag{31}$$

This gives a relational model of a simple loop with guard *dom T* and loop body T. That is, *lim T* does T until it can do so no more, and then stops. Some useful properties of *lim* (that are easily derived from previous laws) are as follows:

$$lim\ T \cdot notdom\ T \;=\; notdom\ T \tag{32}$$
$$lim\ T \cdot dom\ T \;=\; lim\ T \cdot T \tag{33}$$
$$lim\ T \cdot T \;\subseteq\; lim\ T. \tag{34}$$

Also, the rule for least fixpoints gives the following useful property:

$$lim\ T \subseteq Q \quad \Leftarrow \quad notdom\ T \ \cup\ Q \cdot T. \tag{35}$$

We will use the limit operator to model both the specification of feasible solutions to a problem, and the dynamic programming computation of an answer.

Optimization problems expressed in their most general form can be specified relationally as follows:

$$min\ R \cdot \Lambda\, G.$$

In this specification, we call the relation G the *generator* as it generates a single feasible solution from the input. Thus $\Lambda\, G$ generates the set of all possible feasible solutions, and *min R* then selects a best one according to the relation R. We will use limits to generate feasible solutions:

$$min\ R \cdot \Lambda\,(lim\ T).$$

The use of a simple loop to generate feasible solutions is similar to earlier work on automata, although not quite like discrete decision processes, as we are not restricted to the datatype of strings for completed solutions (policies). Helman and Rosenthal (1985) and de Moor (1992) have both considered more general datatypes, trees and more general initial datatypes, respectively. De Moor uses relational catamorphisms and anamorphisms as generators; these are relational versions of the *fold* operator of functional programming, and their converses. Although this is an elegant theory, the use of non-initial datatypes is not covered. The *lim* operator is not restricted to any particular datatype.

2.3 Searching the Space of Partial Solutions

One simple way to solve the above specification is to execute it directly: that is, by enumerating all possible feasible solutions with $\Lambda(lim\ T)$, then selecting an optimal solution using *min R*. This is not at all efficient. Dynamic programming is a strategy that aims to reduce the amount of computation necessary, and we will consider this aim in the context of searching the space of partially-completed feasible solutions.

We first consider how the completed solutions to the problem are generated. The following diagram represents an example of how feasible solutions are built up from the input:

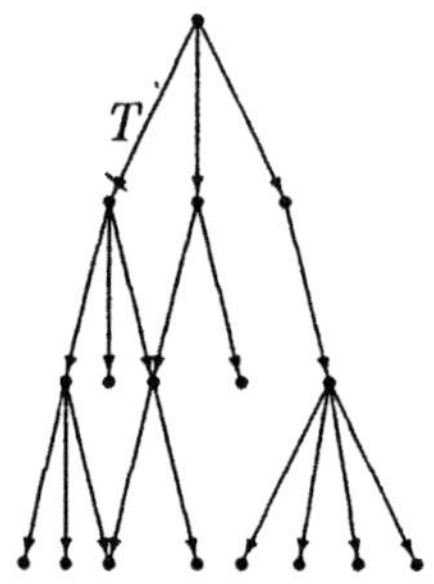

Each node represents a partial solution. The node at the top represents the input, and for each node, the set of its children is the set given by ΛT applied to that node. Thus each arrow represents a possible application of T. The diagram is tree-like, but technically not a tree as some of the nodes may coincide. The completed solutions are the leaves (that is, nodes with no children), corresponding to partial solutions that are not in the domain of T.

The above tree of partial solutions may also be likened to a diagram of an automaton representing a discrete decision process, with the nodes representing states, and T the transition predicate. The policies (Bellman's terminology for completed solutions) would be the strings corresponding to the paths from the root to the leaves. Policies correspond to the complete history of decisions made, whereas our partial solutions are more general, and can contain this information and more; also they can use more general datatypes than strings and other initial datatypes (Malcolm, 1990).

The straightforward implementation of the specification would involve generating all the leaves of the tree from the input. In order to see how we might reduce the amount of computation, we consider how the set of completed solutions might be generated from the input.

We use a relational operator that takes a set of partial solutions and moves one step closer to the set of completed solutions. This operation we will call *sprouting*:

$$sprouts\ T \quad = \quad cup \cdot (\mathsf{E}T \cdot \mathsf{P}\,(dom\ T) \times id) \cdot luni^{\circ} \tag{36}$$

where

$$luni\,(x, y) \quad = \quad x \cup y, \ \text{ if } x \neq \{\} \ \wedge \ x \cap y = \{\} \tag{37}$$

$$cup\,(x, y) \quad = \quad x \cup y \tag{38}$$

Translating the above into English, *sprouts* T takes the input set, takes some uncompleted partial solutions out of the set, applies T in all possible ways to them, then adds these new partial solutions back into the set, doing nothing to the unchosen solutions apart from retaining them.

Consider the following example, by way of illustration. Suppose the input set of partial solutions are those circled in the diagram

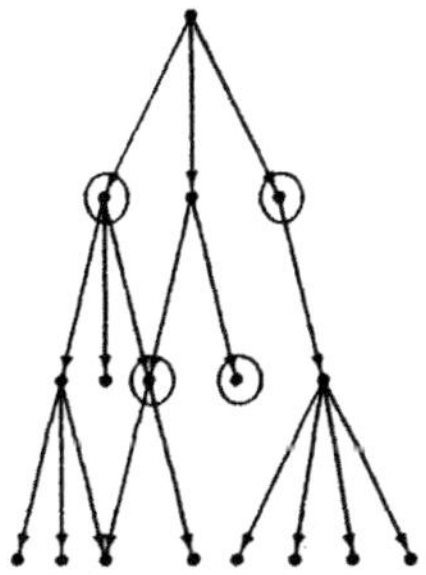

Sprouting just the left-most node would result in the set of partial solutions represented by the circled set in

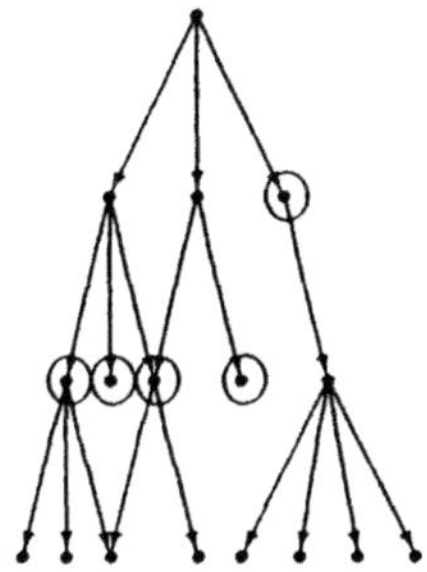

Properties of the relations mentioned above that will be used in equational reasoning are the following:

$$\in \cdot \, sprouts\ T \subseteq T \cdot \in \cup \in \tag{39}$$
$$\in \cdot \, luni = \in \cdot \, outl \cup \in \cdot \, outr \tag{40}$$
$$cup \cdot outl^{\circ} \subseteq \ni / \ni \tag{41}$$
$$cup \cdot outr^{\circ} \subseteq \ni / \ni \tag{42}$$

We will also use more particular styles of sprouting. The relation *allsprouts* sprouts every possible uncompleted solution, and leaves completed solutions alone:

$$allsprouts\ T = \mathsf{E}(T \cup notdom\ T) \cdot dom\,(T \cdot \in). \tag{43}$$

The relation *sprout* T sprouts a single uncompleted solution:

$$sprout\ T = cup \cdot (\Lambda T \cdot dom\ T \times id) \cdot lcons^{\circ}, \tag{44}$$

where

$$lcons\,(x, y) = \{x\} \cup y, \text{ if } x \notin y. \tag{45}$$

Straightforward calculation can be used to show that

$$allsprouts\ T \subseteq sprouts\ T \tag{46}$$
$$sprout\ T \subseteq sprouts\ T. \tag{47}$$

To continue the gardening theme, after sprouting some fresh partial solutions, we want to retain the ones that might lead to a best solution, and remove ones that we know are worthless. The gardening terminology for removing unwanted plants that have sprouted is *thinning*, and that is exactly what we shall be doing.

The following relation thins a set with respect to a preorder S:

$$thin\, S \;=\; \in\backslash\in \;\cap\; (\ni \cdot S)/\ni. \tag{48}$$

That is, a subset of the original is returned, so that every member of the original set has something S-ier than it in the subset.

So we will use a relation S to compare partial solutions to decide which are definitely going to result in a better final solution. This *comparison relation* is similar to Helman's notion of *dominance relations.* To prove correctness, we will be using a variation of the Monotonicity Assumption (Mitten, 1964). Often two partial solutions will be incomparable, which is why we do a thinning rather than taking a minimum.

2.4 Dynamic Programming

Using the concepts of thinning and sprouting as explained above, we will model a dynamic programming step by the relation

$$D \;=\; thin\, S \cdot sprouts\, T.$$

Here a set of partial solutions is maintained, and *sprouts* T performs some amount of construction on these, that is, it applies T to some of the partial solutions. The relation S is a comparison relation which can indicate whether a partial solution is worse than another, and the relation $thin\, S$ removes some of the worse partial solutions. The entire algorithm is

$$min\, R \cdot lim\, D \cdot \tau,$$

thus τ puts the input into a singleton set, then $lim\, D$ repeats the dynamic programming step until all the partial solutions are completed, and then an optimum is selected using $min\, R$. The statement of the dynamic programming theorem is as follows:

Theorem 1
Let

$$M \;=\; min\, R \cdot \Lambda\, lim\, T$$
$$D \;\subseteq\; \in\backslash\in \cdot sprouts\, T,$$

where R is a preorder on the set of completed solutions represented by notdom T. Suppose also that the following conditions are satisfied:

(i) $dom\,(T \cdot \in) \subseteq dom\, D$

(ii) $D \cdot \ni \cdot (lim\, T)^\circ \subseteq \ni \cdot (lim\, T)^\circ \cdot R.$

Then

$$min\, R \cdot lim\, D \cdot \tau \subseteq M.$$

Proof
See the appendix. □

The definition of the relation D is slightly different to that mentioned above; D is not given precisely, but instead is merely restricted to containment in $\in\backslash\in \cdot$ *sprouts* T, which does include *thin* S · *sprouts* T. There is no need to force D to be equal to *thin* S · *sprouts* T, as condition (ii) of the theorem ensures that any thinning performed is appropriate. Most algorithms that have been derived from this theorem do use $D =$ *thin* S · *sprouts* T, although one algorithm suggested by a colleague of mine, Jesús Ravelo, required the more general format.

Condition (i) simply states that it is possible to perform a dynamic programming step D whenever there is still an uncompleted solution within the set of partial solutions maintained: that is, the algorithm does not stop prematurely.

The final condition (ii) is the one ensuring correctness. Translated into English, it says that given a set X of partial solutions so far, then if a partial solution $x \in X$ is completed in some way, and the dynamic programming step D is performed on X to obtain Y, then there is a partial solution in Y which can be completed to yield a completion at least as good as the completion of x. That is, D does not throw away a partial solution necessary for optimality.

This last condition is a difficult one to prove directly, and so the following lemmas give results which reduce it to a monotonicity condition, making the proofs much easier. (The lemmas are proved in the appendix.)

Lemma 1
Condition (ii) of Theorem 1 holds, provided that S is a relation such that

$$D \subseteq \mathit{thin}\, S \cdot \mathit{sprouts}\, T \tag{49}$$
$$\mathit{lim}\, T \cdot S^{\circ} \subseteq R^{\circ} \cdot \mathit{lim}\, T. \tag{50}$$

This reduces the necessary proof condition to $\mathit{lim}\, T \cdot S^{\circ} \subseteq R^{\circ} \cdot \mathit{lim}\, T$. In English, if a partial solution x is worse with respect to S than another y, that is $x \xleftarrow{S} y$, then for any completion of x there is always a better completion of y.

This condition can be simplified further to a monotonicity condition, of the form $S \cdot T^{\circ} \subseteq T^{\circ} \cdot S$, indicating that a better partial solution at one stage can be constructed one step further using T to result in a better partial solution at the next stage. However not all partial solutions take the same number of steps to completion, and thus making appropriate modifications to allow for the domain of T, we have the following:

Lemma 2
The condition $\mathit{lim}\, T \cdot S^{\circ} \subseteq R^{\circ} \cdot \mathit{lim}\, T$ holds, provided that:

$$\mathit{dom}\, T \cdot S \cdot T^{\circ} \subseteq T^{\circ} \cdot S \tag{51}$$
$$\mathit{notdom}\, T \cdot S \cdot T^{\circ} \subseteq S \tag{52}$$
$$S \cdot \mathit{notdom}\, T \subseteq (\mathit{lim}\, T)^{\circ} \cdot R. \tag{53}$$

The first condition is the monotonicity assumption for uncompleted solutions. The second says that a completed solution better than a partial solution remains better if you complete the partial solution. The final condition says that if a partial solution is better than a completed solution, there is a way to complete the partial solution so that it remains better with respect to R.

Lemma 3
The condition $lim\ T \cdot S^\circ \subseteq R^\circ \cdot lim\ T$ *holds, provided that:*

$$dom\ T \cdot S \cdot T^\circ \subseteq T^\circ \cdot S \quad (54)$$
$$notdom\ T \cdot S \cdot notdom\ T \subseteq R \quad (55)$$
$$S \cdot notdom\ T = notdom\ T \cdot S. \quad (56)$$

This is similar to the previous lemma, with conditions slightly altered for those problems which are compared at the same stage of development. Then the second condition says that S respects R on completed solutions, and the third says that if S is comparing one completed solution with another solution, the other is completed too. These are a little easier to prove for suitable problems.

We will use the above lemmas in the following examples, and the examples will be used as motivation to discuss aspects of this particular style of dynamic programming.

3 EXAMPLES AND DISCUSSION

3.1 *0-1 Knapsack Problem*

The well-known 0-1 Knapsack problem concerns a thief ransacking a safe containing various items of given weights and values. The thief has to maximize the total value of the haul, subject to the total weight being less than some maximum capacity C.

We will assume two functions *wgt* and *val* to give the weight and value, respectively, of items in the safe. Partial solutions will be the weight and value of the packing so far, together with the list of items not yet considered. Possible packings can be generated using the following relation:

$$\begin{array}{rcl} (w, v, is) & T & (w, v, i : is) \\ (w + wgt\ i, v + val\ i, is) & T & (w, v, i : is), \text{ if } w + wgt\ i \leq C. \end{array}$$

The input takes the form $(0, 0, ss)$, where ss is the list of items in the safe initially. The second line corresponds to the selection of item i, and the first corresponds to its rejection. Defining R by

$$(w_1, v_1, []) \ R \ (w_2, v_2, []) \equiv v_1 \geq v_2,$$

the problem is specified as $min\ R \cdot \Lambda\, lim\ T$.

To solve this problem with dynamic programming, we need a comparison relation S which says when one partial solution will definitely be better than another. A reasonable S to choose is the following

$$(w_1, v_1, is) \ S \ (w_2, v_2, is) \equiv v_1 \geq v_2 \ \wedge \ w_1 \leq w_2.$$

Translated into words, this says that a partial solution is better if it is more valuable and lighter.

We now use Lemma 3, which is suitable for problems such as this, where completed solutions are all constructed from the same number of T steps.

To check the first condition,

$$dom\ T \cdot S \cdot T^{\circ} \subseteq T^{\circ} \cdot S,$$

suppose that

$$(w_1, v_1, i : is) \xleftarrow{S} (w_2, v_2, i : is) \xrightarrow{T} (w_2, v_2, is),$$

where item i is rejected, then

$$(w_1, v_1, i : is) \xrightarrow{T} (w_1, v_1, is) \xleftarrow{S} (w_2, v_2, is).$$

Alternatively, if i is accepted, so that

$$(w_1, v_1, i : is) \xleftarrow{S} (w_2, v_2, i : is) \xrightarrow{T} (w_2 + wgt\ i, v_2 + val\ i, is),$$

then as $w_1 \leq w_2$, $w_1 + wgt\ i \leq w_2 + wgt\ i$ and so

$$(w_1, v_1, i : is) \xrightarrow{T} (w_1 + wgt\ i, v_1 + val\ i, is) \xleftarrow{S} (w_2 + wgt\ i, v_2 + val\ i, is).$$

The second and third conditions follow directly from the definition of S.

Thus we know that dynamic programming is applicable to this problem. We can implement this algorithm as the standard method for solving this problem: the maximum possible thinning is done at each stage (often a good strategy), and the maximum possible sprouting is done using *allsprouts* T at each stage.

Using functional programming the set of partial solutions can be kept as an ordered list of partial solutions, ordered by decreasing value and weight. Then at each stage the sprouting and thinning is implemented by a simple merge and purge operation on two lists (one representing the choice of the next object, one representing the rejection of the next object), that also removes solutions worse with respect to S. Then when the solutions are completed, the most valuable packing is at the head of the list.

3.2 Use of the Recursion Equation

In the example above, it was shown that dynamic programming was a possible technique to use for solving the problem, but the algorithm given by the theorem is still considerably abstract, and there is still considerable freedom of implementation. This is the trade-off that happens with such a theorem. As we will see, many different sorts of dynamic programming algorithms are covered by this theorem. However, this generality abstracts away from the actual implementation.

The thinning and sprouting method is an illustration of the common dynamic programming method that keeps a set of potential candidates. Let us compare this to a recursive algorithm obtained directly from the functional equation corresponding to the problem. Let $P_C(is)$ be the value of the best packing subject to weight capacity C, from a sage with items is. Then the recursion equation is

$$\begin{array}{rcll} P_C([\,]) & = & 0 & \\ P_C(i : is) & = & P_C(is), & \text{if } wgt\ i > C \\ & = & \bigsqcup\{P_C(is), val\ i + P_{C-wgt\ i}(is)\}, & \text{otherwise.} \end{array}$$

If this were to be implemented directly (using memoization, say, to avoid the computation of similar results), the movement of the computation across the space of partial solutions would result in a depth-first search across the tree. This is in contrast to the "candidates" method described above, which performs a breadth-first search, searching all partial solutions at one level at the same step.

3.3 *The Paragraph Formatting Problem*

We will consider a simple form of the sort of paragraph formatting problem considered by Knuth and Plass (1981). Given is a list of words, to be formatted into as neat a paragraph as possible, by inserting suitable line breaks in a list of words.

A paragraph is a list of lines, each line being a list of words. It must also fit onto the paper, and thus has a maximum line width W. For a simple measure of neatness, we define the *whitespace* of a line as its length subtracted from W; the untidiness of a paragraph is then the sum of the squares of the whitespaces of every line except the last, and we wish to minimize this.

To formally specify the problem, we first construct paragraphs using the limit operator. There are several ways by which line breaks can be added to a list of words: one simple way is to add them sequentially starting with the first line. Thus we define

$$(ls +\!\!+ [l], y)\ T\ (ls, l +\!\!+ y), \qquad \text{if } 0 < linelength\ l \leq W.$$

The input takes the form $([\,], ws)$ where ws is the list of words to be formatted. The above definition assumes that the line length of an empty line is 0, and that non-empty lines have length greater than 0. Note that the function *linelength* is left undefined: the definition will depend on the words and font chosen, and is not important for what follows.

With the following definitions

$$\begin{array}{rcl} whitespace\ l & = & W - linelength\ l \\ whites\ ls & = & sum\,(map\,(square \cdot whitespace)\ ls) \\ untidiness\ (ls +\!\!+ [l]) & = & whites\ ls, \end{array}$$

we can now define R to be

$$(ls_1, [\,])\, R\, (ls_2, [\,]) \;\equiv\; untidiness\ ls_1 \leq untidiness\ ls_2.$$

The problem of formatting paragraphs is now specified as $min\ R \cdot \Lambda\, lim\ T$.

To solve the problem by dynamic programming, we need to find a comparison relation S to compare partial paragraphs. Once lines at the beginning of the paragraph are chosen, they do not subsequently change, so an obvious choice for S is to compare the untidiness of the already chosen lines. Furthermore, if the paragraphs are not completed, then the last lines of the partial paragraphs can be compared too.

Hence we define

$$\begin{array}{ll} (ls_1, y)\, S\, (ls_2, y), & \text{if } \mathit{whites}\ ls_1 \le \mathit{whites}\ ls_2 \ \wedge\ y \ne [\,] \\ (ls_1, [\,])\, S\, (ls_2, [\,]), & \text{if } (ls_1, [\,])\, R\, (ls_2, [\,]). \end{array}$$

To prove that S is a valid choice, we use Lemma 3. Note that (ls, y) is in the domain of T precisely when y is non-empty. First we need that $\mathit{dom}\ T \cdot S \cdot T^{\circ} \subseteq T^{\circ} \cdot S$. If

$$(ls_1, l \mathbin{+\!\!+} y) \xleftarrow{\ S\ } (ls_2, l \mathbin{+\!\!+} y) \xrightarrow{\ T\ } (ls_2 \mathbin{+\!\!+} [l], y),$$

then from the definitions of T and S, we have that

$$(ls_1, l \mathbin{+\!\!+} y) \xrightarrow{\ T\ } (ls_1 \mathbin{+\!\!+} [l], y) \xleftarrow{\ S\ } (ls_2 \mathbin{+\!\!+} [l], y).$$

The second and third conditions for Lemma 3 trivially follow from the definition of S.

We now know that S is a suitable relation to thin partial solutions with, but an algorithm is still a long way off, as sprouting and thinning can be done in many possible ways. Usually doing the maximum possible amount of thinning is a good idea, as there is no reason to retain useless partial solutions. However there is a good reason to be careful what sort of sprouting we perform. Suppose there is a "bad" partial solution (one destined to be thinned eventually), and a partial solution that is better with respect to S is not yet available, because it is not yet developed to that stage. Sprouting the bad partial solution is unnecessary computation, and instead sprouting less developed partial solutions is a better strategy.

So for this problem, the partial solutions to be sprouted at each stage are the ones with the most words left to place. Hence at each stage we want to sprout the partial solution (ls, y) for which y is longest. The partial solutions could be kept in a list in descending order of the length of their second component. Then just the head of the list is sprouted at each stage. If the result of the sprout is put into a similarly ordered list, then the thinning can be performed by a linear merging and purging operation on the two lists. If there are n words in the original list, and partial solutions are kept labelled with their white space usage, the result is an $O(n^2)$ algorithm. □

3.4 Sub-problems

Intrinsic to the main idea of dynamic programming is that the solution to any sub-problem is only calculated once. Either tabulation or memoization may be used to implement this idea, so that when the solution to one sub-problem is calculated, using the formula given by the recursion equation, the solutions to its own sub-problems are already entered in the table. Thus the solution to one sub-problem may be used many times over in the entire computation.

Using the *lim* model, the situation is reversed: instead of partial solutions sharing the result of the computation to a sub-problem, as in the standard model, worse partial solutions (with respect to the comparison relation) are discarded, leaving only those better solutions to remain, to be completed.

Note that in the *lim* model, sub-problems are not present explicitly. They are represented by portions of the construction which remains to be done to partial solutions, in order to complete them.

For illustration, consider the two partial solutions of the above paragraph formatting problem:

(["`I remember the time I knew what happiness was;`"],"`Let the memory live again.`")
(["`I remember`","`the time I knew what happiness was;`"],"`Let the memory live again.`")

The first is better with respect to the S above, and thus the second may be discarded. The first partial solution (or another better than it) will remain in the current set of partial solutions, and will eventually (unless discarded on account of a better solution) have its remaining word list "`Let the memory live again.`" processed.

3.5 *The String Edit Problem*

The string editing problem concerns the transformation of one string into another, using as few operations as possible. This has many applications: the number of operations required is called the *edit distance* or Levenshtein distance (see Levenshtein, 1966, or Wagner and Fischer, 1974) between the two strings, and can be used for spell-checking, speech recognition, and comparison of DNA sequences (see Galil and Giancarlo, 1989 for example). Sankoff and Kruskal's book (1983) is the comprehensive reference on the subject.

We will consider the following edit operations on strings: adding, deleting, or retaining a character. If the editing is carried out from left to right of the given word, then a partial solution can be represented by a triple (es, u, v), where es is the list of edits done so far, u is the remainder of the word that we are transforming, and v is the remainder of the word required. An edit step can be performed by the relation T:

$$\begin{array}{lll} (es +\!\!\!+ [Ret\ c], u, v) & T & (es, c : u, c : v) \\ (es +\!\!\!+ [Add\ c], u, v) & T & (es, u, c : v) \\ (es +\!\!\!+ [Del\ c], u, v) & T & (es, c : u, v). \end{array}$$

As it is desired to find the shortest list of edit operations possible, we define

$$(es_1, [\,], [\,])\, R\, (es_2, [\,], [\,]) \;\equiv\; \#es_1 \leq \#es_2.$$

The problem can now be specified as $min\ R \cdot \Lambda\, lim\ T$, with the input $([\,], w_1, w_2)$, with w_1 being the given word, and w_2 being the required word.

In order to use dynamic programming for this problem, we need a comparison relation S to determine when one partial solution is better than another. One obvious choice for S is that if two partial solutions are at the same stage with respect to the remaining input, then the one which has used fewest edit operations so far must be better. Hence we define

$$(es_1, u, v)\, S\, (es_2, u, v), \quad \text{if} \quad \#es_1 \leq \#es_2$$

We need to prove that this is a suitable choice of S. Using Lemma 3, the first condition required is that $dom\, T \cdot S \cdot T^{\circ} \subseteq T^{\circ} \cdot S$, and we must consider all three possibilities that T° might perform on the left hand side. If

$$(es_1, c : u, c : v) \xleftarrow{S} (es_2, c : u, c : v) \xrightarrow{T} (es_2 +\!\!+ [Ret\ c], u, v),$$

then from the definitions of T and S,

$$(es_1, c : u, c : v) \xrightarrow{T} (es_1 +\!\!+ [Ret\ c], u, v) \xleftarrow{S} (es_2 +\!\!+ [Ret\ c], u, v).$$

For the second possibility, if

$$(es_1, c : u, v) \xleftarrow{S} (es_2, c : u, v) \xrightarrow{T} (es_2 +\!\!+ [Del\ c], u, v),$$

then from the definitions of T and S, we have that

$$(es_1, c : u, v) \xrightarrow{T} (es_1 +\!\!+ [Del\ c], u, v) \xleftarrow{S} (es_2 +\!\!+ [Del\ c], u, v),$$

and the third case is symmetrical to this one. The second and third conditions of Lemma 3 follow trivially from the definition of S.

We have yet to decide on an actual algorithm. Again, the consideration that least-developed partial solutions should be sprouted first applies.

Hence at each stage we want to sprout the partial solutions for which there is most unprocessed input. Thus we do not wish to sprout a partial solution (es_1, u, v) if there is another partial solution $(es_2, u' +\!\!+ u, v' +\!\!+ v)$ in the set, with at least one of u' and v' non-empty. One way to implement this strategy is to at each stage sprout the partial solutions with minimal $\#u + \#v$.

3.6 Tabulation

The tabulation of results from the solving of sub-problems is one of the most important techniques in dynamic programming. However, the use of limits to construct feasible solutions has resulted in an abstraction away from the structures of the optimization problems, so there is no longer a notion of sub-problem.

However, the table can be still seen in this method of dynamic programming. The table is an embedding into the partial space of solutions, and often the computation of the dynamic programming algorithm will mimic the steps taken to construct the table.

To illustrate this embedding, we consider an example of a computation for the above String Edit problem. The word Cih is to be changed into Caph, and this diagram shows the partial solutions that are considered during the execution of the algorithm. The arrows represent applications of T, $Ret\ x$ is abbreviated by x,

Add x by $\overrightarrow{x}$ and *Del* x by $\overleftarrow{x}$. The partial solutions marked with a cross are those which get discarded from the thinning process.

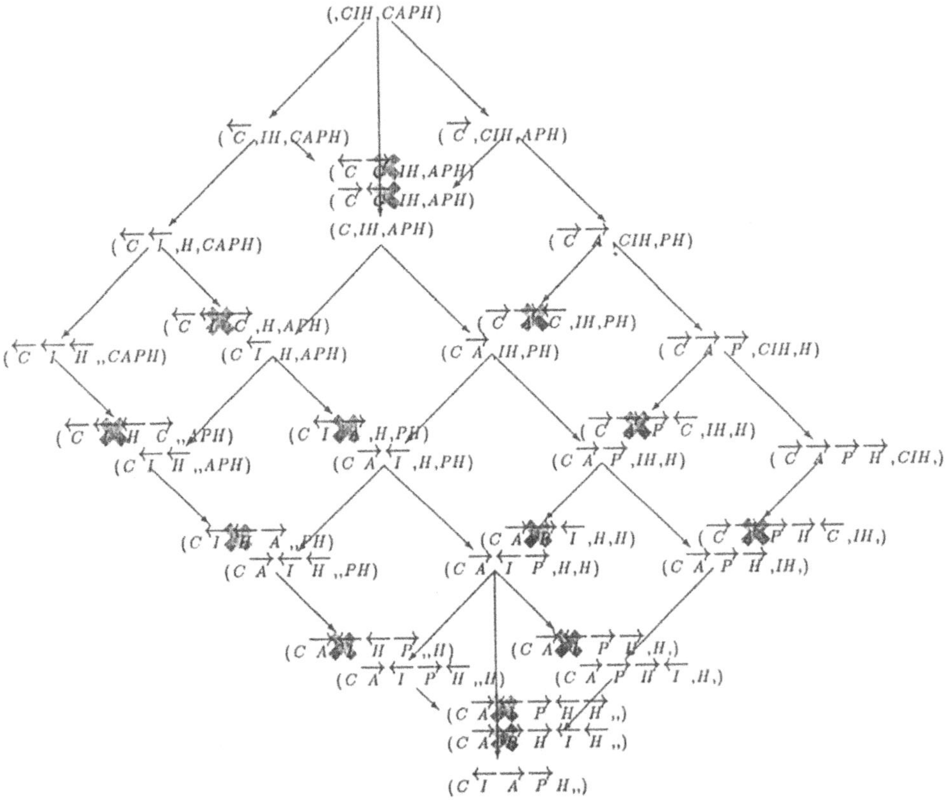

Looking just at the arrows, the embedding of a rectangular structure can clearly be seen within the space of partial solutions. This structure corresponds to that of the table used to solve this problem with the standard dynamic programming algorithm.

One other consideration that is vital in the formal development of imperative programs is the termination of loops, and this has not yet been addressed.

When performing a loop *lim P*, it might be thought that a suitable requirement would be that *lim P* is total. Certainly this is necessary, but it is not sufficient. The totality of a relation only says that it is possible to produce a result, but does not guarantee that a result will be produced. The calculus of relations does not model termination accurately.

In practice, for each individual example, it has always been straightforward to check that the loop terminates, by using the well-known method of variants.

4 CONCLUSIONS

In this paper, we have seen a fresh way of looking at dynamic programming: while other views take the functional equation approach, with the Principle of Optimality, here we have chosen to use a monotonicity condition. The choice of which computation to avoid has been based on "which is better so far", not "what have we left to do".

The theorem presented here gives a very abstract view of a dynamic programming algorithm, best viewed as a search through the space of partial solutions, eliminating some branches from consideration. Using the traditional recursive method in this way results in a depth-first search of the space, while the method of keeping potential candidates results in a breadth-first search.

The high level abstraction of the algorithm gives freedom to do either of these search approaches, or a different search strategy entirely. Many possibilities can be explored, even with different approaches to the same problem. In the examples given here, simple search strategies of "sprout all" or "sprout the least developed" have been used, and the comparison relations chosen have been very straightforward, the obvious naive choices. The exploration of more sophisticated comparison relations is a fun pastime, stretching partway into the theory of branch-and-bound algorithms, resulting in many different algorithms, even variations on well-known algorithms for common problems.

The huge variety of possibilities for dynamic programming algorithms is not, I think, seen as clearly in the traditional approach based on the functional equation, nor even in recent approaches which focus on using the data structure inherent in the problem. Concentrating on data structures can lead to elegant algorithms, but this sometimes misses the possibility of alternative algorithms inspired by lateral thinking.

The work presented here is by no means practical: the theory is still very abstract and the actual program is a long way off. There is still a great deal of freedom of implementation, and the theory does not even begin to address efficiency considerations, although the use of data refinement is touched upon in Curtis (1996).

Nevertheless, this is a fresh approach, which reveals insight into this interesting subject, and it opens up possibilities for exploration of different dynamic programming algorithms for optimization problems.

APPENDIX: PROOFS

Proof of Theorem 1 (using definitions as in the theorem):
Let $M' = \mathit{min}\, R \cdot \mathsf{E}\, \mathit{lim}\, T$. Then

$$\begin{array}{ll} & \mathit{min}\, R \cdot \mathit{lim}\, D \cdot \tau \subseteq M \\ \equiv & \quad \{\text{definition, (19)}\} \\ & \mathit{min}\, R \cdot \mathit{lim}\, D \cdot \tau \subseteq \mathit{min}\, R \cdot \mathsf{E}\, \mathit{lim}\, T \cdot \tau \\ \Leftarrow & \quad \{\text{monotonicity, definition}\} \\ & \mathit{min}\, R \cdot \mathit{lim}\, D \subseteq M' \\ \equiv & \quad \{(5)\} \\ & \mathit{lim}\, D \subseteq \mathit{min}\, R \backslash M' \\ \Leftarrow & \quad \{(31), (35)\} \\ & \mathit{notdom}\, D \cup \mathit{min}\, R \backslash M' \cdot D \subseteq \mathit{min}\, R \backslash M' \\ \equiv & \quad \{(1), (5)\} \end{array}$$

$$
\begin{array}{ll}
& min\, R \cdot notdom\, D \subseteq M' \\
& \quad \wedge\ min\, R \cdot min\, R \backslash M' \cdot D \subseteq M' \\
\Leftarrow & \quad \{\text{assumption, (27)}\} \\
& min\, R \cdot notdom\, (T \cdot \in) \subseteq M' \\
& \quad \wedge\ min\, R \cdot min\, R \backslash M' \cdot D \subseteq M' \\
\Leftarrow & \quad \{(6)\} \\
& min\, R \cdot notdom\, (T \cdot \in) \subseteq M' \\
& \quad \wedge\ M' \cdot D \subseteq M' \\
\equiv & \quad \{(17), (30)\} \\
& min\, R \cdot notdom\, (T \cdot \in) \subseteq lim\, T \cdot \in \\
& \quad \wedge\ min\, R \cdot notdom\, (T \cdot \in) \cdot \ni \cdot (lim\, T)^\circ \subseteq R \\
& \quad \wedge\ M' \cdot D \subseteq lim\, T \cdot \in \\
& \quad \wedge\ M' \cdot D \cdot \ni \cdot (lim\, T)^\circ \subseteq R
\end{array}
$$

The first of these inequalities can be shown as follows:

$$
\begin{array}{ll}
& min\, R \cdot notdom\, (T \cdot \in) \\
\subseteq & \quad \{(28\} \\
& \in \cdot\, notdom\, (T \cdot \in) \\
\subseteq & \quad \{(24)\} \\
& notdom\, T \cdot \in \\
\subseteq & \quad \{(31)\} \\
& lim\, T \cdot \in.
\end{array}
$$

The second inequality proceeds thus

$$
\begin{array}{ll}
& min\, R \cdot notdom\, (T \cdot \in) \cdot \ni \cdot (lim\, T)^\circ \\
\subseteq & \quad \{(25)\} \\
& min\, R \cdot \ni \cdot notdom\, T \cdot (lim\, T)^\circ \\
= & \quad \{\text{reflexivity, (29)}\} \\
& R \cdot notdom\, T \cdot (lim\, T)^\circ \\
= & \quad \{(32)\} \\
& R \cdot notdom\, T \\
\subseteq & \quad \{(22)\} \\
& R.
\end{array}
$$

The third inequality is shown as follows

$$
\begin{array}{ll}
& M' \cdot D \\
= & \quad \{\text{definition}\} \\
& min\, R \cdot \mathsf{E}\, lim\, T \cdot D \\
\subseteq & \quad \{28\} \\
& \in \cdot\, \mathsf{E}\, lim\, T \cdot D \\
= & \quad \{(18)\}
\end{array}
$$

$$
\begin{array}{ll}
& lim\ T \cdot \in \cdot D \\
\subseteq & \{\text{definition of } D\} \\
& lim\ T \cdot \in \cdot \in\backslash\in \cdot sprouts\ T \\
\subseteq & \{(6)\} \\
& lim\ T \cdot \in \cdot sprouts\ T \\
\subseteq & \{(39)\} \\
& lim\ T \cdot (T \cdot \in\ \cup\ \in) \\
= & \{\text{distribution of union over composition}\} \\
& lim\ T \cdot T \cdot \in\ \cup\ lim\ T \cdot \in \\
\subseteq & \{(34), \text{idempotence of union}\} \\
& lim\ T \cdot \in,
\end{array}
$$

and the final inequality can be proved as follows:

$$
\begin{array}{ll}
& M' \cdot D \cdot \ni \cdot (lim\ T)^\circ \\
\subseteq & \{\text{assumption,(3)}\} \\
& M' \cdot \ni \cdot (lim\ T)^\circ \cdot R \\
= & \{\text{definition, (17), (3)}\} \\
& min\, R \cdot \Lambda(lim\ T \cdot \in) \cdot (lim\ T \cdot \in)^\circ \cdot R \\
\subseteq & \{(15)\} \\
& min\, R \cdot \ni \cdot R \\
\subseteq & \{(29), \text{transitivity of preorders}\} \\
& R.
\end{array}
$$

□

Proof of Lemma 1:

$$
\begin{array}{ll}
& thin\, S \cdot sprouts\ T \cdot \ni \cdot (lim\ T)^\circ \\
\subseteq & \{\text{claim}\} \\
& thin\, S \cdot (\ni\ \cup\ \ni/\ni \cdot \Lambda T \cdot dom\ T) \cdot (lim\ T)^\circ \\
\subseteq & \{(48)\} \\
& (\ni \cdot S)/\ni \cdot (\ni\ \cup\ \ni/\ni \cdot \Lambda T \cdot dom\ T) \cdot (lim\ T)^\circ \\
\subseteq & \{\text{union, (6), (8)}\} \\
& \ni \cdot S \cdot (lim\ T)^\circ \\
& \quad \cup\ (\ni \cdot S)/\ni \cdot \Lambda T \cdot dom\ T \cdot (lim\ T)^\circ \\
= & \{(31), (33)\} \\
& \ni \cdot S \cdot (lim\ T)^\circ \\
& \quad \cup\ (\ni \cdot S)/\ni \cdot \Lambda T \cdot T^\circ \cdot (lim\ T)^\circ \\
= & \{(15),(6)\} \\
& \ni \cdot S \cdot (lim\ T)^\circ\ \cup\ \ni \cdot S \cdot (lim\ T)^\circ \\
= & \{\text{idempotence, assumption}\}
\end{array}
$$

$$\ni \cdot (lim\ T)^\circ \cdot R$$

The claim is that $sprouts\ T \cdot \ni \subseteq \ni \cup \ni/\ni \cdot \Lambda T \cdot dom\ T$ and is proved

$$
\begin{array}{ll}
& sprouts\ T \cdot \ni \\
= & \quad \{(36)\} \\
& cup \cdot (\mathsf{E}T \cdot \mathsf{P}domT \times id) \cdot luni^\circ \cdot \ni \\
= & \quad \{(40);(3)\} \\
& cup \cdot (\mathsf{E}T \cdot \mathsf{P}domT \times id) \cdot (outr^\circ \cdot \ni \cup outl^\circ \cdot \ni) \\
= & \quad \{\text{distribution of union}\} \\
& cup \cdot (\mathsf{E}T \cdot \mathsf{P}domT \times id) \cdot outr^\circ \cdot \ni \\
& \ \cup\ cup \cdot (\mathsf{E}T \cdot \mathsf{P}domT \times id) \cdot outl^\circ \cdot \ni \\
\subseteq & \quad \{(12),(13)\} \\
& cup \cdot outr^\circ \cdot \ni \ \cup\ cup \cdot outl^\circ \cdot \mathsf{E}T \cdot \mathsf{P}domT \cdot \ni \\
\subseteq & \quad \{(41),(42)\} \\
& \ni/\ni \cdot \ni \ \cup\ \ni/\ni \cdot \mathsf{E}T \cdot \mathsf{P}domT \cdot \ni \\
\subseteq & \quad \{(6),(20),(5)\} \\
& \ni \ \cup\ \ni/\ni \cdot \mathsf{E}T \cdot \ni \cdot dom\ T \\
= & \quad \{(9),(3),(18)\} \\
& \ni \ \cup\ \ni/(\ni \cdot T^\circ) \cdot \ni \cdot dom\ T \\
\subseteq & \quad \{(7)\} \\
& \ni \ \cup\ \ni/T^\circ \cdot dom\ T \\
= & \quad \{(15),(3),(9)\} \\
& \ni \ \cup\ \ni/\ni \cdot \Lambda T \cdot dom\ T
\end{array}
$$

□

Proof of Lemma 2

$$
\begin{array}{ll}
& lim\ T \cdot S^\circ \subseteq R^\circ \cdot lim\ T \\
\equiv & \quad \{(4)\} \\
& lim\ T \subseteq (R^\circ \cdot lim\ T)/S^\circ \\
\Leftarrow & \quad \{(31),(35)\} \\
& notdom\ T \cup (R^\circ \cdot lim\ T)/S^\circ \cdot T \subseteq (R^\circ \cdot lim\ T)/S^\circ \\
\equiv & \quad \{(1\} \\
& notdom\ T \subseteq (R^\circ \cdot lim\ T)/S^\circ \\
& \ \wedge (R^\circ \cdot lim\ T)/S^\circ \cdot T \subseteq (R^\circ \cdot lim\ T)/S^\circ \\
\equiv & \quad \{(4),(3)\} \\
& S \cdot notdom\ T \subseteq (lim\ T)^\circ \cdot R \\
& \ \wedge (R^\circ \cdot lim\ T)/S^\circ \cdot T \cdot S^\circ \subseteq R^\circ \cdot lim\ T \\
\equiv & \quad \{\text{assumption}\} \\
& (R^\circ \cdot lim\ T)/S^\circ \cdot T \cdot S^\circ \subseteq R^\circ \cdot lim\ T
\end{array}
$$

$$
\begin{array}{ll}
\equiv & \{(23), \text{distribution of union}\} \\
& (R^\circ \cdot \mathit{lim}\ T)/S^\circ \cdot T \cdot S^\circ \cdot \mathit{dom}\ T \subseteq R^\circ \cdot \mathit{lim}\ T \\
& \ \wedge (R^\circ \cdot \mathit{lim}\ T)/S^\circ \cdot T \cdot S^\circ \cdot \mathit{notdom}\ T \subseteq R^\circ \cdot \mathit{lim}\ T \\
\Leftarrow & \{\text{assumptions}, (3)\} \\
& (R^\circ \cdot \mathit{lim}\ T)/S^\circ \cdot S^\circ \cdot T \subseteq R^\circ \cdot \mathit{lim}\ T \\
& \ \wedge (R^\circ \cdot \mathit{lim}\ T)/S^\circ \cdot S^\circ \subseteq R^\circ \cdot \mathit{lim}\ T \\
\Leftarrow & \{(6)\} \\
& R^\circ \cdot \mathit{lim}\ T \cdot T \subseteq R^\circ \cdot \mathit{lim}\ T \\
& \ \wedge R^\circ \cdot \mathit{lim}\ T \subseteq R^\circ \cdot \mathit{lim}\ T \\
\Leftarrow & \{\text{monotonicity}; (31), (35)\} \\
& \mathit{true}.
\end{array}
$$

□

Proof of Lemma 3: this is a corollary of Lemma 2. For the second condition,

$$
\begin{array}{ll}
& \mathit{notdom}\ T \cdot S \cdot T^\circ \\
= & \{\text{assumption}\} \\
& S \cdot \mathit{notdom}\ T \cdot T^\circ \\
= & \{(26)\} \\
& \emptyset \\
\subseteq & \{\text{empty relation}\} \\
& S.
\end{array}
$$

For the third condition,

$$
\begin{array}{ll}
& S \cdot \mathit{notdom}\ T \\
= & \{\text{property of coreflexives}\} \\
& S \cdot \mathit{notdom}\ T \cdot \mathit{notdom}\ T \\
= & \{\text{assumption}\} \\
& \mathit{notdom}\ T \cdot S \cdot \mathit{notdom}\ T \\
= & \{\text{property of coreflexives}\} \\
& \mathit{notdom}\ T \cdot \mathit{notdom}\ T \cdot S \cdot \mathit{notdom}\ T \\
\subseteq & \{\text{assumption}\} \\
& \mathit{notdom}\ T \cdot R \\
\subseteq & \{(31)\} \\
& (\mathit{lim}\ T)^\circ \cdot R.
\end{array}
$$

□

REFERENCES

Bellman, R., Kagiwada, H. and Kalaba, R. (1967), Dynamic programming and an inverse problem in transport theory. *Computing*, 2:5–16.

Bellman, Richard E. (1957), *Dynamic Programming.* Princeton University Press.

Bird, R. S., and de Moor, O. (1993), From dynamic programming to greedy algorithms. In B. Möller, H. Partsch, and S. Schuman, editors, *Formal Program Development*, volume 755 of *Lecture Notes in Computer Science*, pages 43–61.

Bird, R. S., and de Moor, O. (1996), *The Algebra of Programming.* Prentice Hall.

Bonzon, P. (1970) Necessary and sufficient conditions for dynamic programming of combinatorial type. *Journal of the ACM*, 17(4):675–682.

Curtis, Sharon (1996), *A Relational Approach to Optimization Problems.* PhD thesis, Oxford University Computing Laboratory, Wolfson Building, Parks Rd, Oxford, UK, OX1 3QD. Available by FTP from `ftp.comlab.ox.ac.uk` in `pub/Documents/techpapers/Sharon.Curtis/thesis.ps.gz`.

Ecker, Joseph G. and Kupferschmid, Michael (1988) *Introduction to Operations Research.* John Wiley and Sons.

Elmaghraby, Salah E. (1970), The concept of "state" in discrete dynamic programming. *Journal of Mathematical Analysis and Applications*, 29:523–557.

Galil, Z., and Giancarlo, R. (1989), Speeding up dynamic programming with applications to molecular biology. *Theoretical Computer Science*, 64:107–118.

Held, Michael and Karp, Richard (1962), A dynamic programming approach to sequencing problems. *SIAM Journal for Applied Mathematics*, 10:196–210.

Helman, Paul (1986), The principle of optimality in the design of efficient algorithms. *Journal of Mathematical Analysis and Applications*, 119:97–127.

Helman, Paul (1989), A common schema for dynamic programming and branch and bound algorithms. *Journal of the ACM*, 36(1):97–128.

Helman, Paul and Rosenthal, Arnon (1985), A comprehensive model of dynamic programming. *SIAM Journal on Algebraic and Discrete Methods*, 6(2).

Ibaraki, T. (1973), Solvable classes of discrete dynamic programming. *Journal of Mathematical Analysis and Applications*, 43:642–693.

Karp, Richard M. and Held, Michael (1967), Finite-state processes and dynamic programming. *SIAM Journal of Applied Mathematics*, 15(3):693–718.

Knuth, D. E. and Plass, M. F. (1981), Breaking paragraphs into lines. *Software — Practice and experience*, pages 1119 – 1184.

Levenshtein, V. I. (1966), Binary codes capable of correcting deletions, insertions and reversals. *Soviet Physics-Doklady*, 10(8):707–710.

Malcolm, G. R. (1990), *Algebraic Data Types and Program Transformation.* PhD thesis, Groningen University.

Mitten, L. G. (1964), Composition principles for the synthesis of optimal multistage processes. *Operations Research*, 12.

Moor, O. de (1992), Categories, relations and dynamic programming. D.Phil. thesis. Technical Monograph PRG-98, Computing Laboratory, Oxford.

Morin, T. L. (1982), Monotonicity and the principle of optimality. *Journal of Mathematical Analysis and Applications*, 86:665–674.

Sankoff, David and Kruskal, Joseph B., editors. (1983), *Time warps, string edits and macromolecules: the theory and practice of sequence comparison.* Addison-Wesley, Reading, Mass.

Shreider, Yu. A. (1961), Automata and the problem of dynamic programming. *Problems of Cybernetics*, 5:31–48.

Wagner, Robert A. and Fisher, Michael J. (1974), The string-to-string correction problem. *Journal of the Association for Computing Machinery*, 21(1):168–173.

BIOGRAPHY

Dr. Sharon Curtis received her doctorate in 1996 from the University of Oxford, and has been a lecturer at St. Hugh's College, Oxford since 1994. Her current research interests include the formal exploration and development of algorithms, amongst other areas of theoretical computer science.

Calculating With Pointer Structures

Bernhard Möller
Institut für Informatik, Universität Augsburg
Universitätsstr. 14, D-86135 Augsburg, Germany.
email: `moeller@uni-augsburg.de`

Abstract

Based on the algebra of relations and maps we present some techniques for safe manipulation of pointer structures, with a special emphasis on tree-like structures. We investigate sufficient criteria for preservation of substructures under selective updating. The approach is illustrated with some simple examples.

Keywords

Pointer structures, sharing, destructive updating, program transformation, relational calculus

1 INTRODUCTION

Although pointer algorithms are very error-prone they lie at the very heart of many implementations. Yet they have received surprisingly little attention in work on formal derivation and verification of programs. If they are treated, mostly formulas from predicate logic are used, which tend, however, to be very complex and unwieldy. First attempts at a more algebraic approach were presented in our previous previous work (Berger et al. 1991, Möller 1991–1993). However, the calculation steps there were still comparatively small, and even simple algorithms had somewhat lengthy derivations.

The present paper generalizes that approach and develops additional techniques for calculating safe pointer implementations of operations that are specified at an abstract functional level. As usual, pointer level and abstract level are related via an abstraction function. We investigate the particular class of *reasonable* abstraction functions that depend only on the reachable part of the overall store. This allows reducing many questions about changes in a data structure to an analysis of the changes in reachability. Hence the treatment becomes independent of particular data structures such as lists or trees. As a result, we are able to prove the relevant properties once and for all and to condense the derivations considerably, which brings us closer to the goal that simple algorithms should have simple derivations.

2 RELATIONAL NOTATION

Our prominent mathematical tool will be binary relations by which we model the directed graph underlying a pointer structure and describe accessibility and sharing. Given a set X we denote its power set by $\wp(X)$. Now the set of all *binary relations* between sets M and N is $M \leftrightarrow N \stackrel{\text{def}}{=} \wp(M \times N)$. We use the notations $R : M \leftrightarrow N$ and $R \in M \leftrightarrow N$ synonymously.

By $\mathsf{dom}R$ and $\mathsf{ran}R$ we denote domain and range of $R : M \leftrightarrow N$. The *converse* $R^{\smile}$: $N \leftrightarrow M$ of R is given by $R^{\smile} \stackrel{\text{def}}{=} \{(y,x) : (x,y) \in R\}$. The *image* of set $L \subseteq M$ under R is $R(L) \stackrel{\text{def}}{=} \{y : \exists\, x \in L : (x,y) \in R\}$.

Particularly for analyzing the reachable part of a pointer structure we shall use the *domain restriction* of R to a subset $L \subseteq M$ given by $L \bowtie R \stackrel{\text{def}}{=} R \cap L \times N$. Dually, the *range restriction* of R to a subset $L \subseteq N$ is $R \bowtie L \stackrel{\text{def}}{=} R \cap M \times L$. Useful properties are

$$\begin{array}{rclrcl} \mathsf{dom}(L \bowtie R) & = & L \cap \mathsf{dom}R\,, & \mathsf{dom}(R \bowtie L) & = & R^{\smile}(L) \\ \mathsf{ran}(L \bowtie R) & = & R(L)\,, & \mathsf{ran}(R \bowtie L) & = & L \cap \mathsf{ran}R\,. \end{array} \tag{1}$$

This implies $L \subseteq \mathsf{dom}R \Rightarrow \mathsf{dom}(L \bowtie R) = L$.

The *composition* $R\,;S : M \leftrightarrow P$ of two relations $R : M \leftrightarrow N$ and $S : N \leftrightarrow P$ is defined as $R\,;S \stackrel{\text{def}}{=} \{(x,z) : \exists\, y \in N : (x,y) \in R \wedge (y,z) \in S\}$. Left and right neutral elements for R w.r.t. this operation are provided by I_M and I_N, where for a set P one defines the *identity relation* $I_P : P \leftrightarrow P$ by $I_P \stackrel{\text{def}}{=} \{(x,x) : x \in P\}$. The index $_P$ will be omitted when P is clear from the context.

As usual, R^+ and R^* are the transitive and the reflexive transitive closures of relation R.

Relation $R \subseteq M \times N$ is called a *(partial) map* if each element of M is in relation with at most one element from N, i.e., if $(x,y) \in R \wedge (x,z) \in R \Rightarrow y = z$. This can be expressed more concisely as $R^{\smile}; R \subseteq I_N$. We write $R : M \leadsto N$ to indicate that R is a map.

For further notions and laws concerning relations consider e.g. Schmidt, Ströhlein (1993).

3 A MODEL OF POINTER STRUCTURES

3.1 Stores and Pointer Structures

A pointer structure consists of a set of records connected by pointers. Let $\mathcal{A}$ be a set of *records* (represented, say, by their initial addresses). We assume a distinguished element $\diamond \in \mathcal{A}$ which plays the role of nil in Pascal or NULL in C, i.e., serves as a terminal pseudo-node for the underlying graph. The elements of $\mathcal{A}\backslash\{\diamond\}$ are called *proper* records. Let, moreover, $(\mathcal{N}_j)_{j \in J}$ be a family of sets of *node values*, such as integers or Booleans.

Then a *record scheme* consists of a non-empty set K of *selectors* each with a type $\mathcal{A} \to \mathcal{A}$ or $\mathcal{A} \to \mathcal{N}_j$ for some $j \in J$. Given such a record scheme, a *store* is a family $S = (S_k)_{k \in K}$ of partial maps such that

1. $S_k : \mathcal{A} \rightsquigarrow \mathcal{A}$ if k has type $\mathcal{A} \to \mathcal{A}$,
2. $S_k : \mathcal{A} \rightsquigarrow \mathcal{N}_j$ if k has type $\mathcal{A} \to \mathcal{N}_j$,
3. $\diamond \notin recs(S)$,

where $recs(S) \stackrel{\text{def}}{=} \bigcup_{k \in K} \text{dom} S_k$ is the set of records allocated in S.

A store may be viewed as a labeled directed graph: the selectors are the arc labels and S_k is the set of arcs labeled by k. We record these sets separately to be able to model updating along single selectors adequately. The requirement that the S_k be maps serves to model the uniqueness of selection in records. By the third requirement, in a store, $\diamond$ is not related to anything and hence cannot be "dereferenced". This implies that there can be no $\diamond$ record in the "interior" of a pointer structure; if present, $\diamond$ terminates the structure at that point. The relational operations are extended componentwise to stores.

As an example of a record scheme consider a single set $\mathcal{N}$ of node values and three selectors l, v, r with types $l : \mathcal{A} \to \mathcal{A}$, $v : \mathcal{A} \to \mathcal{N}$ and $r : \mathcal{A} \to \mathcal{A}$. Then a binary tree store BT consists of three partial maps $BT_l : \mathcal{A} \rightsquigarrow \mathcal{A}$, $BT_v : \mathcal{A} \rightsquigarrow \mathcal{N}$ and $BT_r : \mathcal{A} \rightsquigarrow \mathcal{A}$, where BT_l and BT_r give the roots of the left and right subtree, if any, of a node, whereas BT_v returns the node value.

Frequently we want to abstract from the node values of the records and consider just their interrelationship through the pointers, since this is the only source of problems in pointer algorithms. Given a store $S = (S_k)_{k \in K}$, this is modeled by the binary *access relation* $[S] \subseteq \mathcal{A} \times \mathcal{A}$ given by

$$[S] \stackrel{\text{def}}{=} \bigcup_{k \in J} S_k \ ,$$

where $J \subseteq K$ is the set of all selectors k of type $\mathcal{A} \to \mathcal{A}$. In the graph view, this operation "forgets" the arc labels. For instance, the access relation for a binary tree store BT is $[BT] \stackrel{\text{def}}{=} BT_l \cup BT_r$.

Store S is *closed* if $\text{ran}[S] \subseteq recs(S) \cup \{\diamond\}$. This means that there are no "dangling references" to addresses not allocated in S. Equivalently, S is closed if $\text{ran}[S] \backslash recs(S) \subseteq \{\diamond\}$. One may wonder why closedness was not built into our definition of store. This is because non-closed stores will frequently be used in constructing larger stores from smaller ones.

Let now $\mathcal{S}$ denote the set of all stores for a given record scheme. The set of *entries* to pointer structures is $\mathcal{A}^+$, the set of all non-empty finite lists of elements of $\mathcal{A}$. We choose lists rather than sets or bags of entries, since in pointer algorithms both order and multiplicity of entries may be relevant.

Now a *pointer structure* is an element of $\mathcal{P} \stackrel{\text{def}}{=} \mathcal{A}^+ \times \mathcal{S}$. For convenience we introduce the functions

$$\begin{aligned} ptr(s, S) &\stackrel{\text{def}}{=} s \ , \\ sto(s, S) &\stackrel{\text{def}}{=} S \ , \\ recs(s, S) &\stackrel{\text{def}}{=} recs(S) \ . \end{aligned}$$

In denoting lists of entries we separate the elements by commas. So a pointer structure will be written in the form $x_1, \ldots, x_n, S$ with entries $x_1, \ldots, x_n$ and store S.

As an example, we define an operation for the allocation of new records. Let $\mathcal{V} \stackrel{\text{def}}{=} \prod_{k \in K} \mathcal{V}_k$ be the set of possible records, where $\mathcal{V}_k = \mathcal{N}_j$ if selector k has type $\mathcal{A} \rightarrow \mathcal{N}_j$ and $\mathcal{V}_k = \mathcal{A}$ otherwise. Then the relation $newrec \in (\mathcal{P} \times \mathcal{V}) \leftrightarrow \mathcal{P}$ is given by

$$(m, T) \in newrec(p, v) \stackrel{\text{def}}{\Leftrightarrow} m \notin recs(p) \cup \{\diamond\} \wedge T = sto(p) \cup N \ ,$$

where $N \stackrel{\text{def}}{=} \{(m, v_k)\}_{k \in K}$ is the (generally non-closed) store assigning the components of v to the newly allocated record address m. In our examples the set K of selectors will be finite. We shall assume a fixed linear order on it and write elements of $\mathcal{V}$ as ordered tuples.

3.2 Reachability and Sharing

In a pointer structure $(s, S) \in \mathcal{P}$ we can follow the pointers from the entries s to other records. This is modeled by the set

$$reach(s, S) \stackrel{\text{def}}{=} [S]^*(\text{set}\, s) \ ,$$

where set s is the set of elements occurring in $s \in \mathcal{A}^+$.

Associated with this is the *reachability relation* $\vdash : \mathcal{P} \leftrightarrow \wp(\mathcal{E})$ given by

$$p \vdash L \stackrel{\text{def}}{\Leftrightarrow} reach(p) \cap \text{set}\, L \neq \emptyset \ ,$$

where $\text{set}\, L = \bigcup_{s \in L} \text{set}\, s$. So this relation holds iff some record in the entries in L is accessible from the entries of p. For singleton set L we will omit the set braces.

Moreover, we introduce a unary predicate *sharing* on $\mathcal{P}$ by setting

$$sharing(n_1, \ldots, n_k, S) \stackrel{\text{def}}{\Leftrightarrow} \bigvee_{i=1}^{k} \bigvee_{j=i+1}^{k} reach(n_i, S) \cap reach(n_j, S) \not\subseteq \{\diamond\} \ .$$

So a pointer structure shows sharing iff a proper record is reachable from two of its entries. Note that this predicate is independent of the order of the entries n_i but not of their multiplicity. So if a record occurs twice in a list of entries, there will be sharing, as expected.

Using this, we can, for instance, characterize pointer structures that are "independent of their surroundings" in the sense that the only pointers into their reachable part originate in that part itself. In pointer structure $(s, S) \in \mathcal{P}$ there is no sharing with records outside $reach(s, S)$ if $\forall\, n \in \mathcal{A} : sharing(n, s, S) \Rightarrow (s, S) \vdash n$.

The reachable set abstracts too much from the actual contents of the store in a pointer structure. Therefore we characterize additionally that part of store S that is reachable from s by the restriction

$$from(s, S) \stackrel{\text{def}}{=} (s,\ reach(s, S) \bowtie S) \ ,$$

i.e., the substructure in which only the contents of records reachable from the entries s are kept. The restriction is again taken componentwise, i.e., for all $k \in K$. Note that, for $L \subseteq \mathcal{A}$, we have $L \bowtie [S] = [L \bowtie S]$ and $[S] \bowtie L = [S \bowtie L]$. From the definitions it is immediate that

Lemma 1 *For any store S we have $reach(\diamond, S) = \{\diamond\}$ and $from(\diamond, S) = (\diamond, \emptyset)$.*

Moreover, we have the following properties of *reach* and *from* (see the Appendix for the proof):

Lemma 2 *1.* $from(s, S) = from(s, T) \Rightarrow reach(s, S) = reach(s, T)$.
2. $from(s, from(s, S)) = from(s, S)$ (Idempotence).
3. $(s, S) \not\models recs(T) \Rightarrow from(s, S \cup T) = from(s, S)$ (Localization I).

4 POINTER IMPLEMENTATIONS

4.1 Reasonable Abstraction Functions

We now consider implementations of abstract objects of some set $\mathcal{O}$ by pointer structures in such a way that each object is represented by a pointer structure $(n, S) \in \mathcal{P}$ with a single entry $n \in \mathcal{A}$. As usual (see e.g. Hoare (1972)), the relation between abstract and concrete levels is established by a partial abstraction function $F : \mathcal{A} \times \mathcal{P} \rightsquigarrow \mathcal{O}$ such that F is surjective. We do not need the more general concept of a linking invariant between abstract and concrete level. To allow representations of *tuples* of abstract objects, we extend F to a partial function $F : \mathcal{P} \rightsquigarrow \mathcal{O}^+$ on arbitrary pointer structures by setting

$$F(n_1 \cdots n_k, S) \stackrel{\text{def}}{=} F(n_1, S) \cdots F(n_k, S) \ .$$

As usual, F induces an equivalence relation $\sim$ on $\mathcal{P}$ by

$$p \sim q \stackrel{\text{def}}{\Leftrightarrow} F(p) = F(q) \ .$$

Note that the image set $F(p) = \emptyset$ for $p \notin \text{dom}F$. So all pointer structures that do not represent an element of $\mathcal{O}$ are equivalent under $\sim$.

Since the pointer representation of an abstract object should be essentially determined by the entries to the structure, we say that an abstraction function is *reasonable* if for all $p, q \in \mathcal{P}$ we have

$$from(p) = from(q) \Rightarrow p \sim q \ .$$

This seemingly simple concept is the key idea that makes our treatment work uniformly and independently of particular data structures such as lists or trees. It allows us to reduce questions about the changes a selective updating effects to a much simpler analysis of the changes in reachability. In particular, we can use the well-established relational calculus for that analysis.

From the definitions and Lemma 2.2. we have immediately

Corollary 3 *For any reasonable abstraction function F, we have $F(p) = F(from(p))$, i.e., $p \sim from(p)$.*

A sufficient criterion for reasonableness (see the Appendix for the proof) is

Lemma 4 *If for all s, S, T we have $reach(s, S) \bowtie S = reach(s, S) \bowtie T \Rightarrow F(s, S) = F(s, T)$, then F is reasonable.*

4.2 Implementation of Operations

As usual (see e.g. Hoare (1972)), the general pattern for transferring operations from abstract level to pointer level is as follows.

Consider an operation of type $\mathcal{O}^n \leadsto \mathcal{B}$ that leads into a set $\mathcal{B}$ of "external" values such as integers or Booleans. We define an *implementation relation* $OPOI \in (\mathcal{P} \leadsto \mathcal{B}) \leftrightarrow (\mathcal{O}^n \leadsto \mathcal{B})$ by setting

$$pg\ OPOI\ g \overset{\text{def}}{\Leftrightarrow} pg = F\,;g\ .$$

So the implementation pg has to mimic the specification g faithfully. Note the implicit use of the extended abstraction function F for the representation of tuples in $\mathcal{O}^n$.

For operations of type $\mathcal{O}^n \leadsto \mathcal{O}$ we are more liberal and allow the implementation to be non-deterministic, i.e., a relation rather than a map. This is reasonable, since different concrete objects may represent the same abstract object. A typical non-deterministic operation at the pointer level is *newrec* as defined in Section 3.1. Our notion of implementation will be parameterized by additional requirements on the implementing relation, such as preservation of certain aspects of the store. Such requirements are again formulated as relations between "old" and "new" pointer structures. Hence our *implementation relation* has type $POI : (\mathcal{P} \leftrightarrow \mathcal{P}) \to ((\mathcal{P} \leftrightarrow \mathcal{P}) \leftrightarrow (\mathcal{O}^n \leadsto \mathcal{O}))$ and is defined by

$$pf\ POI(req)\ f \overset{\text{def}}{\Leftrightarrow} pf\,; F = F\,; f \wedge pf \subseteq req\ .$$

Here req is the additional requirement, examples of which will be given later. The unconstrained relation $POI(ALL)$, where $ALL \overset{\text{def}}{=} \mathcal{P} \times \mathcal{P}$ is the universal relation, leaves complete freedom for realizing pf by copying or by re-use of relevant parts of its argument p. In particular, it does not exclude indirect side-effects on parts of p that point into the reachable part $from(p)$.

However, one frequently is interested in implementations that change as little as possible. We therefore want to give stronger specifications that guarantee that changes take place only in the relevant reachable part or outside the current store, i.e., on "new" records. To this end we define the set

$$noreach(p) \overset{\text{def}}{=} recs(p) \backslash reach(p) = recs(p) \backslash recs(from(p))\ .$$

For closed S, the set $noreach(s, S)$ does not contain records outside the set $recs(S)$ of allocated records. It is the set of all records that are not reachable from the entries s and hence should better be left alone by changes to S. Note that $n \in noreach(p) \Rightarrow p \not\vdash n$.

Now we can define two constraining relations $loc, pres \in \mathcal{P} \leftrightarrow \mathcal{P}$ by setting

$$p\ loc\ q \stackrel{\text{def}}{\Leftrightarrow} noreach(p) \bowtie sto(p) = noreach(p) \bowtie sto(q)\ ,$$
$$p\ pres\ q \stackrel{\text{def}}{\Leftrightarrow} noreach(p) \subseteq noreach(q)\ .$$

So loc requires that the part of the store that is unreachable in p is left untouched in q; by our definition this does, however, not exclude adding new records to the store.

However, loc also holds if in the "modified" structure q there are pointers into $noreach(p)$. So records that were unreachable in p may become reachable by the modification and hence accessible for subsequent modification. This potential source of problems for updates in q through $ptr(p)$ is excluded by postulating $pres$.

Now we can work with the strengthenings $POI(loc)$, $POI(pres)$ or even $POI(loc \cap pres)$ of $POI(ALL)$. They all still admit implementation by copying and by re-use.

4.3 Development Strategy

To calculate a pointer implementation pf of $f : \mathcal{O}^n \rightsquigarrow \mathcal{O}$, we start with the expression $f(F(p))$ and try to transform it by equational reasoning into an expression $F(E)$ such that $F(E) = f(F(p))$ and E does not contain F. Then we can define pf by setting $pf(p) \stackrel{\text{def}}{=} E$ and are sure that $pf\ POI(ALL)\ f$ holds. Design decisions are reflected by the particular choice of the applied equations and generally result in a reduction of nondeterminacy. For implementations of operations $g : \mathcal{O} \rightsquigarrow \mathcal{N}$ we may, more directly, start with the expression $g(F(p))$ and transform it in such a way that F is eliminated from it.

One design goal is to keep changes to a minimum. This has two aspects:

- preserve the entries to pointer structures, if possible;
- implement changes to single record components by selective updating, if possible.

We shall see these goals influence our example derivations. In particular, they will motivate the introduction of strengthened requirements as additional invariants.

5 OVERWRITING POINTER STRUCTURES

5.1 Overwriting, Selecting and Updating

An essential operation on stores is their selective updating. To describe this we define the operation of *overwriting* one relation with another one (see also e.g. Pepper, Möller (1991), Hehner (1993) and Spivey (1994) for the special case of maps). Given relations $R, S : M \leftrightarrow N$, we define the relation $R \mid S : M \leftrightarrow N$ (pronounced "R onto S") by

$$R \mid S \stackrel{\text{def}}{=} R \cup \overline{\mathsf{dom} R} \bowtie S\ ,$$

where $\overline{\mathsf{dom} R}$ is the complement of $\mathsf{dom} R$. Hence $(x,y) \in R \mid S \Leftrightarrow (x,y) \in R \vee (x \notin \mathsf{dom} R \wedge (x,y) \in S)$. Thus, $R \mid S$ results from S by changing the values associated with the "arguments" from M according to the prescription of R (if any). For example, if S is a map then $\{(x,y)\} \mid S$ "updates" S to make y the value corresponding to x. One has

$$\mathsf{dom}(R \mid S) = \mathsf{dom}R \cup \mathsf{dom}S \; . \tag{2}$$

We use the convention that $\mid$ binds stronger than all set-theoretic operations. The set $M \leftrightarrow N$ forms a monoid under $\mid$ with $\emptyset$ as its neutral element. Moreover, the set of $M \leadsto N$ of maps is a submonoid of $M \leftrightarrow N$. Finally, for maps S, T we have the property

$$S \subseteq T \Rightarrow S \mid T = T \; . \qquad \text{(Annihilation)} \tag{3}$$

For further properties see Möller (1993b).

Consider now two stores S and T over the same record scheme. The *overwriting* $T \mid S$ is again defined componentwise. For pointer structure p and store S we set

$$S \mid p \stackrel{\text{def}}{=} (ptr(p), S \mid sto(p)) \; .$$

From (2) it follows that $recs(S \mid p) = recs(S) \cup recs(p)$. Moreover, Lemma 2.3. tells us that overwriting outside the substructure belonging to some entries does not change that substructure:

Corollary 5 $p \not\vdash recs(S) \Rightarrow from(S \mid p) = from(p)$ (Localization II).

In selective updating only one of the component maps of a store is overwritten properly. A store which models the update along selector k is $(x \stackrel{k}{\mapsto} y)$ given by

$$\begin{aligned} (x \stackrel{k}{\mapsto} y)_k &\stackrel{\text{def}}{=} \{(x,y)\} \; , \\ (x \stackrel{k}{\mapsto} y)_j &\stackrel{\text{def}}{=} \emptyset \qquad \text{for } j \neq k \; . \end{aligned}$$

To ease the notation and to keep with traditional programming languages, we introduce an operation $\_.\_ := \_ : \mathcal{P} \times K \times \mathcal{P} \to \mathcal{P}$ for selective updating. For selector k of type $\mathcal{A} \to \mathcal{A}$ and pointer structures (n, S) and (m, T) with $n, m \in \mathcal{A}$ we define

$$(n, S).k := (m, T) \stackrel{\text{def}}{=} (n, (n \stackrel{k}{\mapsto} m) \mid T) \; .$$

If k has type $\mathcal{A} \to \mathcal{N}_j$ and $x \in \mathcal{N}_j$ we set

$$(n, S).k := x \stackrel{\text{def}}{=} (n, (n \stackrel{k}{\mapsto} x) \mid S) \; .$$

Moreover, we define the selection operation $\_.\_ : \mathcal{P} \times K \leadsto (\mathcal{A} \cup \bigcup_{j \in K} \mathcal{N}_j)$ by

$$(n, S).k \stackrel{\text{def}}{=} (S_k(n), S)$$

if k has type $\mathcal{A} \to \mathcal{A}$ and $S_k(n)$ is defined

$$(n, S).k \stackrel{\text{def}}{=} S_k(n)$$

if k has type $\mathcal{A} \to \mathcal{N}_j$. Otherwise $(n, S).k$ is undefined. When using selections as arguments, undefinedness is assumed to propagate according to the strictness of relational semantics.

Selection and updating interact as expected:

Lemma 6 *1.* $ptr(p.k := q) = ptr(p)$.
2. $(p.k := p.k) = p$.
3. $j : \mathcal{A} \to \mathcal{N}_j \wedge j \neq k \Rightarrow (p.k := q).j = p.j$.

Proof. 1. is immediate from the definition.
2. We only treat the case of a selector $k : \mathcal{A} \to \mathcal{A}$.

$$\begin{array}{ll} & (n, S).k := (n, S).k \\ = & \quad \{\!\!\{ \text{ definition of selection } \}\!\!\} \\ & (n, S).k := (S_k(n), S) \\ = & \quad \{\!\!\{ \text{ definition of updating } \}\!\!\} \\ & (n, (n \overset{k}{\mapsto} S_k(n)) \mid S) \\ = & \quad \{\!\!\{ \text{ by annihilation (3), since } (n \overset{k}{\mapsto} S_k(n)) \subseteq S \}\!\!\} \\ & (n, S)\ . \end{array}$$

3. is proved similarly.
□

Again we have localization properties, which are immediate from Corollary 5 and the definitions:

Corollary 7 *Let* $n \overset{\text{def}}{=} ptr(p)$ *and* $r \overset{\text{def}}{=} (n, sto(q))$. *Then*

1. $q \not\vdash n \Rightarrow from((p.k := q).k) = from(q)$.
2. $j \neq k \wedge r.j \not\vdash n \Rightarrow from((p.k := q).j) = from(r.j)$.

We note how selection and updating interact with the *noreach* set:

Lemma 8 *1. For arbitrary p and all selectors j we have* $noreach(p) \subseteq noreach(p.j)$, *i.e.,* p *pres* $p.j$.
2. $noreach((n, S).k := (m, T)) = noreach(m, \overline{\{n\}} \bowtie T)$.

Proof. The first property is straightforward from the definitions, whereas the second one additionally needs Corollary 5 of Möller (1993b). □

So far we have considered only selections that involve a single selector. However, one also wants to consider longer selection paths. To this end we extend the selection notation to words $u \in K^*$, where K is the set of selectors. To smoothen the notation, concatenation on K^* will be denoted by . while ε denotes the empty word. We define inductively, for $k \in K$ and $u \in K^*$,

$$\begin{aligned} p.\varepsilon &\stackrel{\text{def}}{=} p\,, \\ p.(k.u) &\stackrel{\text{def}}{=} (p.k).u \text{ if } k \text{ has type } \mathcal{A} \to \mathcal{A} \text{ or } u = \varepsilon. \end{aligned}$$

In all other cases the selection is undefined. We have

Lemma 9 $p.(u.v) = (p.u).v$.

Proof. If $v = \varepsilon$, the claim is trivial. For $v \neq \varepsilon$ we use induction on u. The base case $u = \varepsilon$ is again trivial. For the induction step we calculate

$$\begin{aligned} & p.(k.u.v) \\ = \;& \{\!\!\{ \text{ definition of . since } v \neq \varepsilon \Rightarrow u.v \neq \varepsilon \}\!\!\} \\ & \begin{cases} (p.k).(u.v) & \text{if } k \text{ has type } \mathcal{A} \to \mathcal{A} \\ \text{undefined} & \text{otherwise} \end{cases} \\ = \;& \{\!\!\{ \text{ induction hypothesis for } u \}\!\!\} \\ & \begin{cases} ((p.k).u).v & \text{if } k \text{ has type } \mathcal{A} \to \mathcal{A} \\ \text{undefined} & \text{otherwise} \end{cases} \\ = \;& \{\!\!\{ \text{ definition of . and image } \}\!\!\} \\ & \begin{cases} ((p.k).u).v & \text{if } k \text{ has type } \mathcal{A} \to \mathcal{A} \\ \text{undefined} & \text{otherwise} \end{cases} \\ = \;& \{\!\!\{ \text{ definition of . } \}\!\!\} \\ & (p.(k.u)).v\,. \end{aligned}$$

□

For that reason we shall omit the parentheses and write simply $p.u.v$ for the composite selection $p.(u.v)$.

5.2 Overwriting and Abstraction

For pointer implementations that use selective updating it usually is important that the updates work locally. This can be established using the following localization property which is immediate from Corollary 5:

Corollary 10 *For any reasonable abstraction function F we have*

$$p \not\,\downarrow recs(S) \Rightarrow S \mid p \sim p \qquad \text{(Localization III).}$$

From Corollary 7 we obtain

Corollary 11 *Assume that abstraction function F is reasonable and let $n \stackrel{\text{def}}{=} ptr(p)$ and $r \stackrel{\text{def}}{=} (n, sto(q))$. Then*

1. $q \not\vdash n \Rightarrow (p.k := q).k \sim q$.
2. $j \neq k \wedge r.j \not\vdash n \Rightarrow (p.k := q).j \sim r.j$.

6 ACYCLIC STORES AND FORESTS

6.1 Basic Properties

We have seen that many properties depend on the absence of sharing. This is guaranteed by forests, which are therefore of special interest. For their characterization we need two notions about binary relations. A relation $R : M \leftrightarrow N$ is *acyclic* iff $R^+ \cap I = \emptyset$. Hence R is acyclic iff no element is reachable from itself via a non-empty path. R is *injective* iff $R ; R^\smile \subseteq I$, i.e., iff no two distinct elements have a common successor under R.

Corollary 12 *If $Q \subseteq P$ and P is acyclic or injective, then so is Q.*

Proof. All operations involved in the characterizations of these notions are monotonic w.r.t. inclusion. □

These notions are carried over to stores as follows. A store S is called *acyclic* if $\lfloor S \rfloor$ is acyclic, and *injective* if $\lfloor S \rfloor \bowtie \overline{\{\diamond\}}$ is injective. This means that no two different records point to the same *proper* record or, equivalently, that the underlying directed graph has maximal in-degree 1, except perhaps at the pseudo-record $\diamond$. Finally, S is called a *forest* if it is acyclic and injective.

We now state several auxiliary properties of binary relations.

Lemma 13 *Let R be an injective binary relation. Then R^* is upwards locally linear, i.e.,*

$$R^* ; (R^*)^\smile \subseteq R^* \cup (R^*)^\smile .$$

For the proof see the Appendix.

Lemma 14 *Let R be an acyclic binary relation. Then*

1. $R^\smile \cap R^* = \emptyset$.
2. *If R is injective then* $R^\smile ; R \cap R^+ = \emptyset \wedge R^\smile ; R \cap (R^+)^\smile = \emptyset$.
3. $\overline{I} \cap R^* = R^+$.
4. *If R is injective then* $R^\smile ; R \cap \overline{I} \subseteq \overline{R^* ; (R^*)^\smile}$.

For the proof see the Appendix. It should be noted that Lemmas 13 and 14 hold in all abstract relation algebras as well. We can exploit these properties for acyclic stores or forests to show strong separation properties which will allow localization of side effects:

Lemma 15 *1. Let S be injective. Then for all $x, y \in \mathcal{A}$ we have*

$$sharing(x, y, S) \Rightarrow ((y, S) \vdash x \vee (x, S) \vdash y) .$$

2. *Let S be acyclic and assume $y \in [S]^+(x)$. Then $(y, S) \not\vdash x$.*
3. *Let S be acyclic and assume $y \in [S]^+(x)$. Then $\forall\, z \in \mathcal{A} : \neg\, sharing(z, x, S) \Rightarrow \neg\, sharing(z, y, S)$.*
4. *Let S be a forest and y, z two distinct successors of x under $[S]$, i.e., assume $y, z \in [S](x) \wedge y \neq z$. Then $\neg\, sharing(x, y, S)$.*
5. *Let S be a forest and assume $y \in [S](x)$. Then*

$$noreach(y, S) = noreach(x, S) \cup \{x\} \cup \bigcup_{z \in [S](x) \setminus \{y\}} reach(z, S) .$$

Proof. 1. We have $sharing(x, y, S)$ iff $(x, y) \in [S]^* ; [S]^{*\smile} = [S]^* ; [S]^{\smile *}$. Now we may apply Lemma 13.
2. is immediate from acyclicity.
3. The assumption implies $reach(y, S) \subseteq reach(x, S)$. Now the claim follows by monotonicity.
4. is immediate from Lemma 14.4.
5. Set $L \stackrel{\text{def}}{=} noreach(x, S) \cup \{x\} \cup \bigcup_{z \in [S](x) \setminus \{y\}} reach(z, S)$. We prove the claim by showing that $reach(y, S) \cup L = recs(S)$ and $reach(y, S) \cap L = \emptyset$. We have

$$\begin{array}{ll} & reach(y, S) \cup L \\ = & \quad \{\!|\text{ set theory }|\!\} \\ & noreach(x, S) \cup \{x\} \cup \bigcup_{z \in [S](x)} reach(z, S) \\ = & \quad \{\!|\text{ fixpoint property of } \_^* \;|\!\} \\ & noreach(x, S) \cup reach(x, S) \\ = & \quad \{\!|\text{ definition of } noreach \text{ and set theory }|\!\} \\ & recs(S) \end{array}$$

and

$$\begin{array}{ll} & reach(y, S) \cap L \\ = & \quad \{\!|\text{ distributivity }|\!\} \\ & (reach(y, S) \cap noreach(x, S)) \;\cup\; (reach(y, S) \cap \{x\}) \;\cup \\ & \quad \bigcup_{z \in [S](x) \setminus \{y\}} (reach(y, S) \cap reach(z, S)) \;. \end{array}$$

The first summand is $\emptyset$ by definition of *noreach*, the other two are $\emptyset$ by 2. and 4.
□

So far we have considered only stores. A pointer structure (n, S) is called *acyclic*, *injective* or a *forest* if the store of its reachable part $from(n, S)$ is acyclic, injective or a forest, respectively.

6.2 Composition of Forests

Next we investigate how acyclicity and injectivity propagate through union:

Lemma 16 *Consider relations $R, S : M \leftrightarrow N$.*

1. *If $R \cup S$ is acyclic then so are R and S.*
2. *If R and S are acyclic and $\mathsf{ran}R \cap \mathsf{dom}S = \emptyset$ then $R \cup S$ is acyclic as well.*
3. *$R \cup S$ is injective iff R and S are injective and $R\,;S^{\smile} \subseteq I$.*

For the proof see the Appendix. Again this also holds in all abstract relation algebras. Now we obtain

Corollary 17 *Consider $(m,T) \in newrec((n,S),v)$ and $N \stackrel{\text{def}}{=} \{(m,v_k)\}_{k\in K}$.*

1. *If S and N are acyclic and $\mathsf{ran}[N] \cap \mathsf{dom}[S] = \emptyset$ then (m,T) is acyclic as well.*
2. *If S is injective and $[S]\,;[N]^{\smile} \subseteq I$ then (m,T) is injective as well.*

For the proof of 2. note that N is always injective.

6.3 Forests and Updating

We are now in the position to formulate the strong preservation properties for updating acyclic structures and hence forests.

Corollary 18 *Assume that p is acyclic and $u \neq \varepsilon$. Then*

1. *$from((p.k := p.u).k) = from(p.u)$.*
2. *$j \neq k \Rightarrow from((p.k := p.u).j) = from(p.j)$.*

If, moreover, F is a reasonable abstraction function, then

3. *$(p.k := p.u).k \sim p.u$.*
4. *$j \neq k \Rightarrow (p.k := p.u).j \sim p.j$.*

Proof. This is an application of Corollaries 7 and 11. In this particular case we have $r = p$ and the preconditions are satisfied by Lemma 15. □

Another, although not so important, property is

Corollary 19 *If S is closed and S and T are acyclic then $S \mid T$ is acyclic as well.*

Proof. We have $S \mid T = S \cup R$ where $R = \overline{\mathsf{dom}[S]} \bowtie T$. Using the criterion from Lemma 16.2. we obtain

$$\begin{array}{ll} & \mathsf{ran}[S] \cap \mathsf{dom} R \\ = & \quad \{\!\!\{ \text{ by (1) } \}\!\!\} \\ & \mathsf{ran}[S] \cap \overline{\mathsf{dom}[S]} \cap \mathsf{dom} T \\ \subseteq & \quad \{\!\!\{ \text{ since } S \text{ is closed } \}\!\!\} \\ & \{\Diamond\} \cap \mathsf{dom} T \\ = & \quad \{\!\!\{ \text{ definition of store } \}\!\!\} \\ & \emptyset. \end{array}$$

□

Moreover, from Lemma 16 we obtain

Corollary 20 *Let* $r = (p.k := q)$ *and set* $n \stackrel{\text{def}}{=} ptr(r) = ptr(p)$ *and* $R \stackrel{\text{def}}{=} \overline{\{n\}} \bowtie sto(r) = \overline{\{n\}} \bowtie sto(q)$.

1. *If* $ptr(q) \notin \{n\} \cup \mathsf{dom}[R]$ *and* R *is acyclic, then* r *is acyclic as well.*
2. *If* R *is acyclic and* $n \notin \{ptr(q)\} \cup sto(q)(\overline{\{n\}})$, *then* r *is acyclic as well.*
3. r *is injective iff* $ptr(q) \notin \mathsf{ran}[R]$ *and* R *is injective.*

Proof. 1. Immediate from Lemma 16.2.
2. Immediate from Lemma 16.2.
3. Set $m \stackrel{\text{def}}{=} ptr(q)$. Then $[(n \stackrel{k}{\mapsto} m)] ; [R]^{\smile} = \{(n,m)\} ; [R^{\smile}]$ is contained in I iff $\{(n,m)\} ; [R]^{\smile} = \emptyset$, which is equivalent to $m \notin \mathsf{ran}[R]$. The remainder is clear from Lemma 16.3. and injectivity of $\{(n,m)\}$.
□

Finally, we give a stronger criterion for acyclicity of overwritten structures:

Lemma 21 *Consider* $r \stackrel{\text{def}}{=} (n,S).k := (m,T) = (n,(n \stackrel{k}{\mapsto} m) \cup R)$ *where* $R \stackrel{\text{def}}{=} \overline{\{n\}} \bowtie T$. *Then* r *is acyclic iff* R *is acyclic and* $(m,R) \not\vdash n$.

Proof. Set $S \stackrel{\text{def}}{=} (n \stackrel{k}{\mapsto} m) \cup R$.
($\Rightarrow$) By Corollary 12, R is acyclic. Suppose $n \in reach(m,R)$. Then by monotonicity also $n \in reach(m,S)$ and hence $m[S]^{*}n[S]m$, a contradiction.
($\Leftarrow$) Suppose S is cyclic. Since R is acyclic, every cycle in S must involve the only arc of $(n \stackrel{k}{\mapsto} m)$. Choose a cycle of minimal length, say $l[S]^{*}n[S]m[S]^{*}l$. By minimality then already $l[R]^{*}n$ and $m[R]^{*}l$. But then $m[R]^{*}n$, i.e., $(m,R) \vdash n$, a contradiction. □

7 POINTER IMPLEMENTATION OF BINARY TREES

7.1 Abstract Trees

The set $\mathcal{T}$ of *binary trees* with elements of $\mathcal{N}$ as nodes is defined inductively as the least set $\mathcal{X}$ with

$$\varepsilon \cup \mathcal{X} \times \mathcal{N} \times \mathcal{X} \subseteq \mathcal{X} ,$$

where ε now also denotes the empty tree and $\_ \times \_ \times \_$ is the ternary cartesian product. A non-empty tree, i.e., an element of $\mathcal{T} \times \mathcal{N} \times \mathcal{T}$, will be denoted as triple $\langle l, x, r\rangle$ with left subtree $l \in \mathcal{T}$, node $x \in \mathcal{N}$ and right subtree $r \in \mathcal{T}$.

7.2 An Abstraction Function

Let now $\mathcal{P}$ denote the set of all pointer structures over the record scheme for binary trees, as discussed in Section 3.1. The abstraction function $tree : \mathcal{P} \rightsquigarrow \mathcal{T}$ constructs the tree reachable from a record in a store. For $n \in \mathcal{A}$ we set

$$tree(n, B) \stackrel{\text{def}}{=} \begin{cases} \varepsilon & \text{if } n = \diamond , \\ \langle tree(B_l(n), B), B_v(n), tree(B_r(n), B)\rangle & \text{if } n \neq \diamond . \end{cases}$$

In the case where a cycle is reachable from n in B, this recursion is non-terminating. In a strict underlying semantics this means that the value of $tree(n, B)$ is undefined, whereas in a non-strict setting the value of $tree(n, B)$ is an infinite tree corresponding to an unwinding of the subgraph reachable from n in B. Since we are working in a relational setting, the strict interpretation is relevant here. So from now on we shall assume that *tree* is used only for acyclic pointer structures. Note, however, that *tree* also works for non-forests, i.e., dags: it copies the abstract trees that correspond to shared substructures.

The recursion pattern is typical of an *unfold operation* or *anamorphism* (see Meijer et al. (1991), Bird (1996)). A thorough investigation of this connection is left to subsequent papers.

Using the selection notation from Section 5.1, the definition of *tree* can be simplified to

$$tree(p) \stackrel{\text{def}}{=} \begin{cases} \varepsilon & \text{if } ptr(p) = \diamond , \\ \langle tree(p.l), p.v, tree(p.r)\rangle & \text{otherwise} . \end{cases}$$

We have (see the Appendix for the proof)

Lemma 22 *The abstraction function tree is reasonable.*

7.3 Search

We now calculate pointer implementations of a number of sample operations. First we treat the operation *elem* : $\mathcal{N} \times \mathcal{T} \to \mathbb{B}$ that tests whether an element occurs in a binary search tree over a totally ordered set $\mathcal{N}$ of node values. It is recursively defined by

$$\begin{aligned} elem(x,\varepsilon) &= \mathsf{false}\ , \\ elem(x,\langle l,y,r\rangle) &= \begin{cases} \mathsf{true} & \text{if } x = y\ , \\ elem(x,l) & \text{if } x < y\ , \\ elem(x,r) & \text{if } x > y\ . \end{cases} \end{aligned}$$

For a derivation of this recursive version from an implicit specification via the multiset of elements contained in a tree see Dosch, Möller (1997).

According to our general scheme from Section 4, the pointer implementation *pelem* is then specified by

$$pelem(x,p) = elem(x, tree(p))\ ,$$

where we assume that p is acyclic to ensure definedness of $tree(p)$. The goal is now to calculate a direct recursion for *pelem*.

For the case that $ptr(p) = \Diamond$ we have $tree(p) = \varepsilon$ and hence

$$pelem(x,p) = \mathsf{false}\ .$$

Otherwise we calculate

$$\begin{aligned} & pelem(x,p) \\ = \quad & \{\!\!|\ \text{unfold definitions of } pelem \text{ and } tree\ |\!\!\} \\ & elem(x, \langle tree(p.l), p.v, tree(p.r)\rangle) \\ = \quad & \{\!\!|\ \text{unfold definition of } elem\ |\!\!\} \\ & \begin{cases} \mathsf{true} & \text{if } x = p.v \\ elem(x, tree(p.l)) & \text{if } x < p.v \\ elem(x, tree(p.r)) & \text{if } x > p.v \end{cases} \\ = \quad & \{\!\!|\ \text{fold definition of } pelem\ |\!\!\} \\ & \begin{cases} \mathsf{true} & \text{if } x = p.v \\ pelem(x, p.l) & \text{if } x < p.v \\ pelem(x, p.r) & \text{if } x > p.v\ . \end{cases} \end{aligned}$$

The requirement that the argument structure be acyclic ensures that the implementation is as undefined as the specification. The recursion by itself will terminate if the searched element is found before a cycle is entered.

Of course, this derivation was easy, since no updating and hence no questions of sharing arose. We have presented it merely to show the notions at work as a preparation for the next example.

7.4 Insertion

Next we treat the operation $ins : \mathcal{N} \to (\mathcal{T} \leadsto \mathcal{T})$ that inserts an element into a binary search tree. It is recursively defined by

$$
\begin{aligned}
ins(x)(\varepsilon) &= \langle \varepsilon, x, \varepsilon \rangle , \\
ins(x)(\langle l, y, r \rangle) &= \begin{cases} \langle ins(x)(l), y, r \rangle & \text{if } x \leq y , \\ \langle l, y, ins(x)(r) \rangle & \text{if } x > y . \end{cases}
\end{aligned}
$$

Consider again Dosch, Möller (1997) for a derivation of this recursive version from an implicit specification.

Using our general scheme from Section 4 we specify a general pointer implementation *pins* by requiring, for all $x \in \mathcal{N}$, that $pins(x)\ POI(ALL)\ ins(x)$, i.e., $pins(x)\ ;\ tree = tree\ ;\ ins(x)$ and want to find a direct recursion for $pins(x)$.

The derivation will exhibit the need for a strengthening of ALL to allow application of our updating laws; this will lead to an additional invariant.

Again we assume that the argument p is acyclic to ensure definedness of $tree(p)$. For the case that $ptr(p) = \diamond$ we have $tree(p) = \varepsilon$ and hence $tree(pins(x)(p)) = \langle \varepsilon, x, \varepsilon \rangle$. According to the definitions of *tree* and *newrec* and Corollary 17 this can be achieved by choosing

$$pins(x)(p) = newrec(p, \langle \diamond, x, \diamond \rangle)$$

in this case.

For $ptr(p) \neq \diamond$ we only treat the subcase $x \leq p.v$, the other one being symmetric. We calculate

$$
\begin{aligned}
& ins(x)(tree(p)) \\
= \quad & \{\!\!\{ \text{ unfold definition of } tree \}\!\!\} \\
& ins(x)(\langle tree(p.l), p.v, tree(p.r) \rangle) \\
= \quad & \{\!\!\{ \text{ unfold definition of } ins \}\!\!\} \\
& \langle ins(x)(tree(p.l)), p.v, tree(p.r) \rangle \\
= \quad & \{\!\!\{ \text{ fold with specification of } pins(x) \}\!\!\} \\
& \langle tree(pins(x)(p.l)), p.v, tree(p.r) \rangle .
\end{aligned}
$$

The aim now is to find for certain $q' \in pins(x)(p.l)$ a pointer structure q such that this expression is equal to $tree(q)$. According to our general aim of making do with minimal change we try to choose $q \overset{\text{def}}{=} (p.l := q')$. Since p is assumed to be acyclic, we have by Lemma 15 that $ptr(p) \in noreach(p.l)$. If we therefore additionally require $q'\ loc\ p.l$, Corollary 11 tells us that $q.l \sim q'$, $q.v = p.v$ and $q.r \sim p.r$. Then we may continue

$$
\begin{aligned}
& \langle tree(q'), p.v, tree(p.r) \rangle \\
= \quad & \{\!\!\{ \text{ as just explained } \}\!\!\} \\
& \langle tree(q.l), q.v, tree(q.r) \rangle
\end{aligned}
$$

$$= \quad \{\!\![\text{ fold definition of } tree \,]\!\!\}$$
$$tree(q) \ ,$$

so that we may choose $pins(x)(p) = q$ in this case. It is easily checked, using Lemma 8, that p *loc* q again, so that the additional invariant is preserved. Moreover, the above base case establishes *loc*. Altogether we obtain the recursion

$$\begin{aligned} pins(x)(p) = \text{if } & ptr(p) = \diamond \\ & \text{then } newrec(p, \langle \diamond, x, \diamond \rangle) \\ & \text{else if } x \le y \text{ then } p.l := pins(x)(p.l) \\ & \qquad\qquad \text{else } p.r := pins(x)(p.r) \text{ fi fi} \end{aligned}$$

which satisfies $pins(x)$ $POI(loc)$ $ins(x)$.

7.5 Rotation

When considering balanced search trees such as AVL trees one uses tree rotations. We consider left rotation $lrot : \mathcal{T} \rightsquigarrow \mathcal{T}$, specified by

$$lrot(\langle l, x, \langle m, y, r \rangle \rangle) = \langle \langle l, x, m \rangle, y, r \rangle \ .$$

Using our general scheme from Section 4 we specify a localized pointer implementation *plrot* by requiring *plrot* $POI(ALL)$ *lrot* and want to find an explicit version of *plrot*.

Again we assume that the argument p is acyclic to ensure definedness of $tree(p)$. We have

$$\begin{aligned}
& lrot(tree(p)) \\
= \quad & \{\!\![\text{ unfold definition of } tree \text{ twice }]\!\!\} \\
& lrot(\langle tree(p.l), p.v, \langle tree(p.r.l), p.r.v, tree(p.r.r) \rangle \rangle) \\
= \quad & \{\!\![\text{ unfold definition of } lrot \,]\!\!\} \\
& \langle \langle tree(p.l), p.v, tree(p.r.l) \rangle, p.r.v, tree(p.r.r) \rangle \rangle \\
= \quad & \{\!\![\text{ defining } u \stackrel{\text{def}}{=} p.r \,]\!\!\} \\
& \langle \langle tree(p.l), p.v, tree(u.l) \rangle, u.v, tree(u.r) \rangle \rangle \\
= \quad & \{\!\![\text{ defining } q \stackrel{\text{def}}{=} p.r := u.l \text{ and using Corollary 18 and Lemma 21 }]\!\!\} \\
& \langle \langle tree(q.l), q.v, tree(q.r) \rangle, u.v, tree(u.r) \rangle \rangle \\
= \quad & \{\!\![\text{ fold definition of } tree \,]\!\!\} \\
& \langle tree(q), u.v, tree(u.r) \rangle \rangle \\
= \quad & \{\!\![\text{ defining } w \stackrel{\text{def}}{=} u.l := q \text{ and using Corollary 18 and Lemma 21 }]\!\!\} \\
& \langle tree(w.l), w.v, tree(w.r) \rangle \rangle \\
= \quad & \{\!\![\text{ fold definition of } tree \,]\!\!\} \\
& tree(w) \ .
\end{aligned}$$

So we may choose

$$\begin{array}{l} plrot(p) \; = \\ \quad \mathsf{let}\; u = p.r \\ \qquad\quad q = (p.r := u.l) \\ \quad \mathsf{in}\;\; u.l := q\;. \end{array}$$

The derivation has shown that here we do not need a strengthening of ALL, i.e., no additional invariant. Note that the intermediate pointer structure q is not injective and hence not a forest, but still acyclic, so that our laws apply.

8 CONCLUSION AND OUTLOOK

The chosen abstraction seems adequate, as the fairly concise derivations in the examples show. It is encouraging that to a large extent the treatment is independent of the particular data structures involved.

The approach also covers the examples of in-situ concatenation and reversal of lists dealt with in Möller (1991–1993) and makes the derivations considerably shorter. We have to omit these examples here for lack of space and note only that the predicate *sharing* now replaces the one called *disjoint* in our earlier approaches.

It remains to integrate the approach with the general theory of unfold operations or anamorphisms (see Meijer et al. (1991), Bird (1996)). The proof of Lemma 22 leads us to conjecture that every anamorphic abstraction function is reasonable.

Although our notions were defined for general pointer structures, in the examples we have concentrated on tree-like structures. However, many seemingly cyclic structures such as doubly-linked lists or even threaded trees behave as forests when selection is considered along a certain subclass of links only. Preliminary studies indicate that our results for forests can be carried over to these structures. Moreover, recent work (Möller 1997) shows that the techniques extend in a simple way to properly cyclic structures.

Acknowledgements I am grateful to Jules Desharnais and Walter Dosch for valuable remarks on drafts of this paper. This research was partially sponsored by Esprit Working Group 8533 *NADA — New Hardware Design Methods.*

9 APPENDIX: PROOFS

Proof of Lemma 2.

1. Let $T \stackrel{\text{def}}{=} reach(s, S) \bowtie S$. We first show $reach(s, S) = \mathsf{set}\, s \cup \mathsf{ran}[T]$.

$$\begin{array}{ll} & \mathsf{set}\, s \cup \mathsf{ran}[T] \\ = & \{\!\!\{ \text{ definition of } T \text{ and } (1) \}\!\!\} \\ & \mathsf{set}\, s \cup [S](reach(s, S)) \\ = & \{\!\!\{ \text{ definition of } reach \}\!\!\} \end{array}$$

$$\begin{array}{ll}
& \mathsf{set}\ s \cup [S]([S]^\bullet(\mathsf{set}\ s)) \\
= & \quad \{\kern-0.3em[\ \text{recursion for } _^\bullet\ ]\kern-0.3em\} \\
& [S]^\bullet(\mathsf{set}\ s) \\
= & \quad \{\kern-0.3em[\ \text{definition of } \mathit{reach}\ ]\kern-0.3em\} \\
& \mathit{reach}(s, S)\ .
\end{array}$$

From this the claim is immediate.

2. Set $(s, T) \stackrel{\text{def}}{=} \mathit{from}(s, S)$. We first show that $\mathit{reach}(s, T) = \mathit{reach}(s, S)$. The inclusion $\subseteq$ follows from $T \subseteq S$ and monotonicity of $\_^\bullet$. For the other inclusion we show more generally $\forall\, T \subseteq \mathit{reach}(s, S) : [S]^\bullet(T) \subseteq [T]^\bullet(T)$ by fixpoint induction on the continuous predicate $PP(X) \stackrel{\text{def}}{\Leftrightarrow} \forall\, T \subseteq \mathit{reach}(s, S) : X(T) \subseteq [T]^\bullet(T)$ and the functional $\tau : X \mapsto I \cup [S]\,;X$ associated with the recursive definition of $\_^\bullet$. The induction base $PP(\emptyset)$ is trivial. For the induction step we calculate, assuming $PP(X)$:

$$\begin{array}{ll}
& \tau(X)(T) \\
= & \quad \{\kern-0.3em[\ \text{distributivity, and definition of image and composition}\ ]\kern-0.3em\} \\
& T \cup X([S](T)) \\
\subseteq & \quad \{\kern-0.3em[\ PP(X), \text{ and } T \subseteq \mathit{reach}(s, S) \Rightarrow [S](T) \subseteq \mathit{reach}(s, S)\ ]\kern-0.3em\} \\
& T \cup [T]^\bullet([S](T)) \\
= & \quad \{\kern-0.3em[\ T \subseteq U \Rightarrow R(T) = (U \bowtie R)(T)\ ]\kern-0.3em\} \\
& T \cup [T]^\bullet([T](T)) \\
= & \quad \{\kern-0.3em[\ \text{definition of image and composition and distributivity}\ ]\kern-0.3em\} \\
& (I \cup [T]^\bullet\,; [T])(T) \\
= & \quad \{\kern-0.3em[\ \text{fixpoint property of } _^\bullet\ ]\kern-0.3em\} \\
& [T]^\bullet(T)\ .
\end{array}$$

Now we have

$$\begin{array}{ll}
& \mathit{from}(s, T) \\
= & \quad \{\kern-0.3em[\ \text{definition of } \mathit{from}\ ]\kern-0.3em\} \\
& (s, \mathit{reach}(s, T) \bowtie T) \\
= & \quad \{\kern-0.3em[\ \text{definition of } T\ ]\kern-0.3em\} \\
& (s, \mathit{reach}(s, T) \bowtie (\mathit{reach}(s, S) \bowtie S)) \\
= & \quad \{\kern-0.3em[\ \text{because } \mathit{reach}(s, T) = \mathit{reach}(s, S)\ ]\kern-0.3em\} \\
& (s, \mathit{reach}(s, S) \bowtie (\mathit{reach}(s, S) \bowtie S)) \\
= & \quad \{\kern-0.3em[\ \text{idempotence of restriction}\ ]\kern-0.3em\} \\
& (s, \mathit{reach}(s, S) \bowtie S) \\
= & \quad \{\kern-0.3em[\ \text{definition of } \mathit{from}\ ]\kern-0.3em\} \\
& \mathit{from}(s, S)\ .
\end{array}$$

3. See Möller (1993a), Corollary 3.

Proof of Lemma 4. Suppose that $from(s,S) = from(s,T)$. By Lemma 2.1., we have $reach(s,S) = reach(s,T)$ $(*)$.
Now we obtain

$$\begin{array}{ll} & (s, reach(s,S) \bowtie S) \\ = & \quad \{\!\mid \text{definition of } from \mid\!\} \\ & from(s,S) \\ = & \quad \{\!\mid \text{assumption} \mid\!\} \\ & from(s,T) \\ = & \quad \{\!\mid \text{definition of } from \mid\!\} \\ & (s, reach(s,T) \bowtie T) \\ = & \quad \{\!\mid \text{by } (*) \mid\!\} \\ & (s, reach(s,S) \bowtie T)\ . \end{array}$$

Now $F(s,S) = F(t,T)$ follows from $s = t$ and the assumption.

Proof of Lemma 13. We show more abstractly for Kleene algebras (see e.g. Möller (1993a)) that

$$a \cdot b \leq 1 \Rightarrow a^* \cdot b^* \leq a^* + b^*\ .$$

The proof is a fixpoint induction on the recursive definition

$$c^* \stackrel{\text{def}}{=} \mu x\,.\,1 + c \cdot x\ ,$$

where μ is the least fixpoint operator, using the continuous predicate

$$PP(x) \stackrel{\text{def}}{=} a^* \cdot x \leq a^* + b^* \wedge x \leq b^*\ .$$

The induction base $PP(0)$ is trivial by strictness of $\cdot$. For the induction step we calculate

$$\begin{array}{ll} & a^* \cdot (1 + b \cdot x) \\ = & \quad \{\!\mid \text{distributivity and neutrality of } 1 \mid\!\} \\ & a^* + a^* \cdot b \cdot x \\ = & \quad \{\!\mid \text{dual fixpoint property of } a^* \mid\!\} \\ & a^* + (1 + a^* \cdot a) \cdot b \cdot x \\ = & \quad \{\!\mid \text{distributivity and neutrality of } 1 \mid\!\} \\ & a^* + b \cdot x + a^* \cdot a \cdot b \cdot x \\ \leq & \quad \{\!\mid \text{by assumption } a \cdot b \leq 1 \text{ monotonicity and neutrality of } 1 \mid\!\} \end{array}$$

$$
\begin{array}{ll}
& a^* + b \cdot x + a^* \cdot x \\
\leq & \{\!\mid \text{by induction hypothesis } PP(x) \text{ and monotonicity} \mid\!\} \\
& a^* + b \cdot b^* + a^* + b^* \\
= & \{\!\mid b \cdot b^* \leq b^* \text{ and idempotence of } + \mid\!\} \\
& a^* + b^*
\end{array}
$$

and

$$
\begin{array}{ll}
& 1 + b \cdot x \\
\leq & \{\!\mid \text{by induction hypothesis } PP(x) \text{ and monotonicity} \mid\!\} \\
& 1 + b \cdot b^* \\
= & \{\!\mid \text{fixpoint property of } b^* \mid\!\} \\
& b^* \ .
\end{array}
$$

Now the claim follows from $(R^*)^{\smile} = (R^{\smile})^*$.

Proof of Lemma 14.

1.
$$
\begin{array}{ll}
& R^{\smile} \cap R^* \\
= & \{\!\mid \text{neutrality} \mid\!\} \\
& R^{\smile}; I \cap R^* \\
\subseteq & \{\!\mid \text{Dedekind's rule, converse} \mid\!\} \\
& (R^{\smile} \cap R^* \,; I^{\smile}) \,; (I \cap R \,; R^*) \\
= & \{\!\mid \text{definition of } \_^+ \mid\!\} \\
& (R^{\smile} \cap R^* \,; I^{\smile}) \,; (I \cap R^+) \\
= & \{\!\mid \text{assumption} \mid\!\} \\
& (R^{\smile} \cap R^* \,; I^{\smile}) \,; \emptyset \\
= & \{\!\mid \text{strictness} \mid\!\} \\
& \emptyset \ .
\end{array}
$$

2.
$$
\begin{array}{ll}
& R^{\smile}; R \cap R^+ \\
\subseteq & \{\!\mid \text{Dedekind's rule, converse} \mid\!\} \\
& (R^{\smile} \cap R^+ \,; R^{\smile}) \,; (R \cap R \,; R^+) \\
= & \{\!\mid \text{definition of } \_^+ \mid\!\} \\
& (R^{\smile} \cap R^* \,; R \,; R^{\smile}) \,; (R \cap R \,; R^+) \\
\subseteq & \{\!\mid \text{assumption, neutrality} \mid\!\} \\
& (R^{\smile} \cap R^*) \,; (R \cap R \,; R^+) \\
= & \{\!\mid \text{by 1.} \mid\!\} \\
& \emptyset \,; (R \cap R \,; R^+) \\
= & \{\!\mid \text{strictness} \mid\!\}
\end{array}
$$

$\emptyset$.

From this we obtain

$$
\begin{array}{ll}
 & R^{\smile}; R \cap (R^{+})^{\smile} \\
= & \quad \{\!\![\text{ converse }]\!\!\} \\
 & (R^{\smile}; R)^{\smile} \cap (R^{+})^{\smile} \\
= & \quad \{\!\![\text{ distributivity }]\!\!\} \\
 & (R^{\smile}; R \cap R^{+})^{\smile} \\
= & \quad \{\!\![\text{ by above }]\!\!\} \\
 & \emptyset^{\smile} \\
= & \quad \{\!\![\text{ strictness }]\!\!\} \\
 & \emptyset \,.
\end{array}
$$

3.

$$
\begin{array}{ll}
 & \overline{I} \cap R^{*} \\
\subseteq & \quad \{\!\![\text{ definition of } \_^{+}]\!\!\} \\
 & \overline{I} \cap (I \cup R^{+}) \\
= & \quad \{\!\![\text{ distributivity }]\!\!\} \\
 & (\overline{I} \cap I) \cup (\overline{I} \cap R^{+}) \\
= & \quad \{\!\![\text{ Boolean algebra, assumption }]\!\!\} \\
 & \emptyset \cup R^{+} \\
= & \quad \{\!\![\text{ neutrality }]\!\!\} \\
 & R^{+} \,.
\end{array}
$$

4.

$$
\begin{array}{ll}
 & R^{\smile}; R \cap \overline{I} \cap R^{*} ; (R^{*})^{\smile} \\
\subseteq & \quad \{\!\![\text{ by Lemma 13 }]\!\!\} \\
 & R^{\smile}; R \cap \overline{I} \cap (R^{*} \cup (R^{*})^{\smile}) \\
= & \quad \{\!\![\text{ distributivity }]\!\!\} \\
 & (R^{\smile}; R \cap \overline{I} \cap R^{*}) \cup (R^{\smile}; R \cap \overline{I} \cap (R^{*})^{\smile}) \\
= & \quad \{\!\![\text{ by 3., converse }]\!\!\} \\
 & (R^{\smile}; R \cap R^{+}) \cup (R^{\smile}; R \cap (R^{+})^{\smile}) \\
= & \quad \{\!\![\text{ by 2. }]\!\!\} \\
 & \emptyset \,.
\end{array}
$$

Proof of Lemma 16.

1. This is immediate from Corollary 12.
2. The assumption $\mathsf{ran}R \cap \mathsf{dom}S = \emptyset$ is equivalent to $R;S = \emptyset$. Now easy regular algebra shows $(R \cup S)^{*} = S^{*};R^{*}$ and hence $(R \cup S)^{+} = S^{+} \cup S^{+};R^{+} \cup R^{+}$. It thus remains to show $S^{+} ; R^{+} \cap I = \emptyset$. For this we first note that $R ; S = \emptyset \Rightarrow S ; R \cap I = \emptyset$, since

$R\,;S \subseteq \emptyset$

$\Leftrightarrow$ {[Schröder equivalences]}

$R^{\smile};\overline{\emptyset} \subseteq \overline{S}$

$\Rightarrow$ {[monotonicity]}

$R^{\smile};I \subseteq \overline{S}$

$\Leftrightarrow$ {[neutrality]}

$I\,;R^{\smile} \subseteq \overline{S}$

$\Leftrightarrow$ {[Schröder equivalences]}

$S\,;R \subseteq \overline{I}$.

Now the claim follows from $R^+\,;S^+ = R^*\,;R\,;S\,;S^* = \emptyset$ by $R\,;S = \emptyset$ and strictness of composition.

3. By distributivity, $(R \cup S)\,;(R \cup S)^{\smile} = R\,;R^{\smile} \cup R\,;S^{\smile} \cup S\,;R^{\smile} \cup S\,;S^{\smile}$. Now the claim is immediate from $S\,;R^{\smile} = (R\,;S^{\smile})^{\smile}$.

Proof of Lemma 22. We show the premise of Lemma 4 by fixpoint induction on the recursive definition of *tree* and the continuous predicate

$$PP(h) \overset{\text{def}}{\Leftrightarrow} \forall\, n, S, T : reach(n,S) \bowtie S = reach(n,S) \bowtie T \Rightarrow h(n,S) = h(n,T)\ .$$

The induction basis $PP(\Omega)$ is trivial. Assume now $PP(h)$. The functional τ associated with the recursive definition of *tree* is

$$\tau(h)(q) = \text{if } ptr(q) = \Diamond \text{ then } \varepsilon \text{ else } \langle h(q.l), q.v, h(q.r)\rangle\ .$$

First we observe that $n \in reach(n,S)$ and $reach(n,S) \bowtie S = reach(n,S) \bowtie T$ imply

$$\begin{aligned} &\{n\} \bowtie S = \{n\} \bowtie T \wedge \\ &reach(l,S) \bowtie S = reach(l,S) \bowtie T \wedge \qquad (*) \\ &reach(r,S) \bowtie S = reach(r,S) \bowtie T\ , \end{aligned}$$

where $l = S_l(n) = T_l(n)$ and $r = S_r(n) = T_r(n)$. Now we calculate

$\tau[h](n,S)$

$=$ {[definition]}

if $n = \Diamond$ then ε
 else $\langle h((n,S).l), (n,S).v, h((n,S).r)\rangle$ fi

$=$ {[by $(*)$ and $PP(h)$]}

if $n = \Diamond$ then ε
 else $\langle h((n,T).l), (n,T).v, h((n,T).r)\rangle$ fi

$=$ {[definition]}

$\tau(h)(n,T)$.

REFERENCES

U. Berger, W. Meixner, B. Möller: Calculating a garbage collector. In: M. Broy, M. Wirsing (eds.): Methods of programming. Lecture Notes in Computer Science **544**. Berlin: Springer 1991, 137–192

R. Bird: Functional algorithm design. Science of Computer Programming **26**, 15–31 (1996)

R.S. Bird, O. de Moor: Algebra of programming. Prentice-Hall 1996

W. Dosch, B. Möller: Calculating a functional module for binary search trees. In: W. Kluge (ed.): Proceedings of the 8th International Workshop on Implementation of Functional Languages, Bonn, Sept. 16–18, 1996. Lecture Notes in Computer Science . Berlin: Springer (to appear). Preliminary version accessible through `http://www.math.uni-augsburg.de/~moeller`

E.C.R. Hehner: A practical theory of programming. Berlin: Springer 1993

C.A.R. Hoare: Proofs of correctness of data representations. Acta Informatica **1**, 271–281 (1972)

E.Meijer, M.Fokkinga, R. Paterson: Functional programming with bananas, lenses, envelopes and barbed wire. In: J. Hughes (ed.): Functional programming and computer architecture. Lecture Notes in Computer Science **523**. Berlin: Springer 1991, 124–144

B. Möller: Formal derivation of pointer algorithms. In: M. Broy (Hrsg.): Informatik und Mathematik. Berlin: Springer1991, 419–440

B. Möller: Development of graph and pointer algorithms. In: B. Möller, H.A. Partsch, S.A. Schuman (eds.): Formal program development. Lecture Notes in Computer Science **755**. Berlin: Springer 1993, 123–160

B. Möller: Towards pointer algebra. Science of Computer Programming **21**, 57–90 (1993)

B. Möller: Linked lists calculated. Submitted for publication (1997)

P. Pepper, B. Möller: Programming with (finite) mappings. In: M. Broy (ed.): Informatik und Mathematik. Berlin: Springer 1991, 381–405

G. Schmidt, T. Ströhlein: Relations and graphs. Discrete Mathematics for Computer Scientists. EATCS Monographs on Theoretical Computer Science. Berlin: Springer 1993

J.M. Spivey: The Z notation, 2nd edition. New York: Prentice-Hall 1994

BIOGRAPHY

Bernhard Möller studied informatics and mathematics at TU Munich and Cornell, with an M.Sc. from Cornell and doctorate and habilitation at TU Munich. Within the project CIP at TU Munich he worked on the design of the wide-spectrum language CIP-L and of the transformation system CIP-S, as well as on the methodology of deductive design. Since 1990 he has been Professor of Informatics at the University of Augsburg. He is a member of IFIP WG 2.1 *Algorithmic Languages and Calculi* and the coordinator of Esprit WG 8533 *NADA - New Hardware Design Methods.*

Deriving a systolic regular language recognizer

*Matteo Vaccari**
Department of Computing Science, Università degli Studi di Milano via Comelico 39, 20135 Milano, Italy. E-mail: `vaccari@dsi.unimi.it`

*Roland Backhouse**
Department of Mathematics and Computing Science, Eindhoven University of Technology
PO Box 513, 5600 MB Eindhoven, The Netherlands. E-mail: `rolandb@win.tue.nl`

Abstract

We present a derivation of a regular language recognizing circuit originally developed by Foster and Kung. We make use of point-free relation algebra, in a style combining elements from earlier work in the Eindhoven Mathematics of Program Construction group, and from Sheeran and Jones' work on Ruby. First we derive non-systolic recognizers, much in the same way as functional programs are derived. Then we make use of standard circuit transformation techniques, recast in the relation algebra framework, to obtain circuits that are very close to the ones presented by Foster and Kung.

Keywords

Regular languages, circuit derivation, program calculation, systolic circuits, relation algebra, relation calculus, retiming, slowdown, silicon compilation

0 INTRODUCTION

In 1982, Foster and Kung presented a specialised silicon compiler that constructs recognizers for regular languages. The compiler was presented without formal justification; indeed, they did not present a formal specification of the functionality of the compiler. Their informal description of the functioning left much room for alternative interpretations.

Subsequently, Backhouse (1983) verified the correctness of Foster and Kung's compiler. His task amounted primarily to reverse engineering — trying to discover the specification satisfied by the compiler. This resulted in the

*Our thanks to Professor Giovanni Degli Antoni and SGS-Thomson for supporting mutual visits which have made this collaboration possible.

discovery of an error in Foster and Kung's construction — acknowledged by Foster in his Ph.D. thesis (1984). Otherwise the formal calculations in Backhouse's report were disappointingly complicated and not judged by its author to be worthy of widespread publication.

In this paper we present a formal *derivation* of Foster and Kung's compiler. The complexities of the earlier *verification* have been overcome in two ways: by exploiting (point-free) relation algebra rather than elementary predicate calculus, and by a judicious decomposition of the design task. Our design consists of first deriving a non-systolic implementation, followed by a transformation of this design to a systolic version using standard techniques ("slowing" and "retiming", Jones and Sheeran 1990).

A precise definition of "systolic" can be found in Leiserson's thesis (1983). For our purposes, a circuit is systolic when it can be seen as a network of processing elements interconnected by wires, these wires being interrupted by delays (registers). The presence of the delays on the wires has an important effect on the minimum clock period that can be assigned to a circuit. In fact, the presence of long wires uninterrupted by delays forces the designer to assign a larger clock period* to the circuit, and that in turn may have a negative effect on the overall performance.

Foster presents a formal verification of the compiler in his Ph.D. thesis (1984). Both the specification and the implementation have been adapted in order to overcome the error in (Foster and Kung 1982). We, ourselves, have as yet been unable to understand Foster's arguments, possibly because we do not understand how to describe the non-standard components he uses as stream transducers. In this paper we take the easy way out and avoid the problem rather than overcome it.

A formal derivation of a similar compiler has also been given by Kaldewaij and Zwaan (1990), but their implementation is not systolic, in the sense that the minimum clock period that can be assigned to their circuits is a function of the length of the regular expression to be matched. In contrast, the circuits that we generate can be assigned a clock period that is independent of the number of sequence operators in the regular expression, although it does depend on the number of star and choice operators.

The paper is organized as follows: in the next two sections, we introduce the reader to relation algebra, and our definition of "circuit". In section 3 we show how to specify the problem with relation algebra. Then in section 4 we derive a first, non-systolic version of the recognizers. In section 5 standard circuit transformations are applied to obtain a systolic version. Finally, in section 6 some conclusions are drawn.

*The clock period is the time between two clock ticks.

1 ABOUT RELATION ALGEBRA

We will write our specifications and our circuits in point-free relation algebra. A brief introduction to our style of relation algebra follows; for a more complete treatment see (Aarts et al. 1992).

A (binary) relation over a set $\mathcal{U}$ is a set of pairs of elements of $\mathcal{U}$. For x,y in $\mathcal{U}$ and R a relation over $\mathcal{U}$, we write $x\langle R\rangle y$ instead of (x, y) in R. When a relation R satisfies $x\langle R\rangle y \wedge z\langle R\rangle y \Rightarrow x{=}z$ we say that the relation is *deterministic*. In that case it may be considered as a function with domain on the right side and target on the left side; we denote by $R.y$ the unique x such that $x\langle R\rangle y$ holds, if such an x exists. The reason for this name is that we usually interpret relations as programs taking input from the right and producing output on the left. In this way a deterministic relation is interpreted as a deterministic program. We usually use the letters f, g, h to stand for deterministic relations. We use the convention that "." associates to the right so that $f.g.x$ should be parsed as $f.(g.x)$. (This is contrary to the convention used in the lambda calculus.)

Relations are ordered by the usual set inclusion ordering. Hence the set of relations forms a complete lattice. The relation corresponding to the empty set is denoted by $\perp\!\!\!\perp$, and the relation that contains all pairs of elements of $\mathcal{U}$ is denoted by $\top\!\!\!\top$. The *identity relation*, I, is defined by $x\langle I\rangle y \;\equiv\; x{=}y$. The composition of two relations R,S is denoted by $R{\circ}S$ and defined by $x\langle R{\circ}S\rangle y \;\equiv\; \exists(z :: \; x\langle R\rangle z \wedge z\langle S\rangle y)$. Composition is associative and has unit element I. The converse of a relation R is written $R^{\cup}$ and is defined by $x\langle R^{\cup}\rangle y \;\equiv\; y\langle R\rangle x$.

A *monotype* is a relation A such that $A \subseteq I$. An example of a monotype is $\mathbf{N}$, defined by $n\langle\mathbf{N}\rangle m \;\equiv\; n{=}m \wedge (n$ is a natural number$)$. There is a clear one-to-one correspondence between the subsets of $\mathcal{U}$ and the monotypes; and this makes it possible to embed set calculus in relation calculus. The *left domain* of relation R, denoted $R{<}$, is the least monotype A such that $A{\circ}R = R$. As its name suggests, $R{<}$ represents the set of all x such that x is related by R to some y.

A *left condition* is a relation R such that $R = R{\circ}\top\!\!\!\top$. Clearly, if R is a left condition, then for all x, $\exists(y :: \; x\langle R\rangle y) \;\equiv\; \forall(z :: \; x\langle R\rangle z)$. This suggests that a left condition may also be interpreted as a set, as we may take it to represent the set of values x such that $\exists(y :: \; x\langle R\rangle y)$. We usually abuse notation by writing $x \in R$ in place of $\exists(y :: \; x\langle R\rangle y)$ when R is a left condition. A *right condition* is defined analogously, but we will not need to use right conditions in this paper.

There is obviously a 1–1 correspondence between monotypes and left conditions given by the functions $R \mapsto R{<}$ and $R \mapsto R{\circ}\top\!\!\!\top$. Making the right choice of which to use can simplify calculations a great deal. We use both in this paper.

The relation $R{\vartriangle}S$ (pronounced *R split S*) is defined as the least relation X such that for all x, y and z, $(x, y)\langle X\rangle z \;\equiv\; x\langle R\rangle z \wedge y\langle S\rangle z$. Note that the requirement that $R \vartriangle S$ be the *least* relation satisfying the above equation in X implies that there is no y such that $x\langle R \vartriangle S\rangle y$ when x is not a pair. That is, the left domain of $R \vartriangle S$ is a set of pairs.

Common mathematical practice is not to make explicit that what is being defined is the least solution of a certain equation. "We define the relation $R \vartriangle S$ by $(x,y)\langle R \vartriangle S\rangle z \;\equiv\; x\langle R\rangle z \wedge y\langle S\rangle z$" is the more usual way to express the above definition. For brevity we adopt this practice from now on.

Split enjoys the property

$$R \vartriangle S \circ f = (R \circ f) \vartriangle (S \circ f) \tag{0}$$

if f is a deterministic relation.

We define $R \times S$ (pronounced R *times* S) by $(x,y)\langle R \times S\rangle(z,v) \;\equiv\; x\langle R\rangle z \wedge y\langle S\rangle v$. The *projection* relations $\ll$ and $\gg$ are defined by $x\langle\ll\rangle(y,z) \;\equiv\; x{=}y$ and $x\langle\gg\rangle(y,z) \;\equiv\; x{=}z$. The following properties are easily proved:

$$\begin{array}{rcl} R \times S \circ T \times U & = & (R \circ T) \times (S \circ U) \\ R \times S \circ T \vartriangle U & = & (R \circ T) \vartriangle (S \circ U). \end{array} \tag{1}$$

To complete this brief survey of relation algebra we must introduce the reflexive, transitive closure of a relation (see e.g. Doornbos, Backhouse and van der Woude 1997), which may be defined for relation R as the least fixed point of the function $X \mapsto I \cup R \circ X$:

$$R^* = \mu(X \mapsto I \cup R \circ X).$$

In (Doornbos et al. 1997) it is proved that the so-called "unique extension property" (uep) of the reflexive, transitive closure:

$$R = S^* \circ T \;\equiv\; R = T \cup S \circ R \tag{2}$$

holds if S is *well-founded* and, furthermore, S is well-founded if it enjoys the property $X = S \circ X \Rightarrow X = \perp\!\!\!\perp$ for all relations X.

The large number of binary operators that we use may make it difficult to parse our expressions; but the precedences were carefully chosen in order to minimise the need for parentheses, and the spacing around operators hints at the way to read a formula. See table 0 for a complete list of precedences.

2 ABOUT CIRCUITS

Following established practice (see Cohn and Gordon 1990, Jones and Sheeran 1990, Rietman 1995) we model a circuit as a relation between arbitrary collections of *streams*, a stream being a total function with domain the integer

$\cup < > {}^* {}^\sigma$	all unary operators
.	function application
$\times + \vartriangle$	product, sum, split
$\circ$	relational composition
$\cup \cap$	union, intersection
$= \subseteq$	equality, inclusion
$\wedge \vee$	conjunction, disjunction
$\Rightarrow \Leftarrow$	implication, consequence
$\equiv$	boolean equivalence

Table 0 Precedence of operators, from highest to lowest

numbers. Abusing language somewhat, we will use the word "circuit" to mean an actual circuit, or a relation between streams as described above. Context should make clear which one is meant. We usually denote streams by the letters a through e.

As an alternative to our definition, it is possible to define streams as functions on the natural numbers (rather than the integers); but this leads to a more complicated theory, where many equalities no longer hold (for details see Jones and Sheeran 1990). Our definition corresponds in a sense to ignoring initialisation problems. One may see here an analogy with traditional derivation of programs where one can factor a proof of correctness into a proof of partial correctness together with a proof of termination. What we have instead is a derivation of a circuit that is correct provided that the circuit can be initialized. This leaves us with the obligation of proving that our circuits can be correctly initialized. We will not devote much space to this latter problem. We trust that the reader will see that our circuits can be initialized provided that there is a way to set the contents of all boolean delays to *false* and all character delays to some value different from the encoding of all symbols in $\mathcal{T}$. We assume that some "reset" wire exists in the implementation that performs this function, and we will not give further mention to this issue.

Given a relation R, a relation between streams can be constructed by "lifting": $a\langle\dot{R}\rangle b \;\equiv\; \forall(n :: \;\; a.n\,\langle R\rangle\, b.n)$. Hence for any R, relation $\dot{R}$ is a circuit. Note that, for deterministic relation f, stream a and integer m, $\dot{f}.a.m = (\dot{f}.a).m$. We refer to this property in our calculations by the hint "lifting". Circuits can be built by relational composition, and product: given R and S, two circuits, the relations $R{\circ}S$ and $R{\times}S$ are also circuits.

A particular relation on streams is the *primitive delay*, denoted by ∂ and defined by

$$a\langle\partial\rangle b \;\equiv\; \forall(n :: \;\; a.(n+1) = b.n).$$

The *delay* relation, written $\lhd$, is a generalisation of primitive delay to arbitrary pairings of streams. It is defined as the least fixed point of function $X \mapsto \partial \cup X{\times}X$:

$$\lhd = \mu(X \mapsto \partial \cup X{\times}X).$$

Delay can be thought of informally as the union of an infinite list of terms $\lhd \;=\; \partial \cup \partial{\times}\partial \cup \partial{\times}(\partial{\times}\partial) \cup (\partial{\times}\partial){\times}\partial \cup (\partial{\times}\partial){\times}(\partial{\times}\partial) \cup \ldots$. The *antidelay* $\rhd$ is defined to be the converse of delay. In the interpretation as circuits, a delay is a memory element that, at every clock tick, outputs the contents of memory on the left side and replaces the contents of memory with the input on its right side. The interpretation of antidelays is the same, with the role of "left" and "right" reversed. Note that both $\lhd$ and $\rhd$ are deterministic.

We define the identity relation for streams in a way that is similar to how we defined delay. The *primitive stream identity* is defined by

$$a\langle\bar{\iota}\rangle b \;\equiv\; \forall(n :: \; a.n = b.n).$$

The identity on arbitrary pairings of streams, denoted by ι, is then defined by

$$\iota = \mu(X \mapsto \bar{\iota} \cup X{\times}X).$$

The delay relations are polytypic in the sense that they apply the primitive delay ∂ to a collection of wires, independently of the shape of the collection. Formally,

$$\lhd\!< \;=\; \lhd\!> \;=\; \iota \;=\; \rhd\!< \;=\; \rhd\!> \tag{3}$$

(Note that this and other properties of delays are proved in a longer version of this paper published as a technical report. Vaccari and Backhouse 1996)

A similar domain property that we use frequently is: for $\Diamond \in \{\lhd, \rhd\}$,

$$\Diamond \circ \iota{\times}\iota \;=\; \Diamond{\times}\Diamond \;=\; \iota{\times}\iota \circ \Diamond. \tag{4}$$

These equations express the fact that applying delay or antidelay to a pair of (collections of) wires ($\Diamond \circ \iota{\times}\iota$) is the same as applying it to each component of the pair ($\Diamond{\times}\Diamond$). From this property, one immediately obtains the following useful distributivity properties: for $\Diamond \in \{\lhd, \rhd\}$,

$$\begin{aligned} \Diamond \circ R{\times}S &= (\Diamond \circ R){\times}(\Diamond \circ S) \\ R{\times}S \circ \Diamond &= (R \circ \Diamond){\times}(S \circ \Diamond) \\ \Diamond \circ R{\vartriangle}S &= (\Diamond \circ R){\vartriangle}(\Diamond \circ S) \end{aligned} \tag{5}$$

and from (0) and the fact that delays are deterministic, one obtains

$$R \vartriangle S \circ \Diamond = (R \circ \Diamond) \vartriangle (S \circ \Diamond).$$

A particular wiring relation is *term* (for "terminator"), defined by

$$term = \iota \vartriangle \iota \circ \top\!\!\top.$$

It is easy to calculate that *term* satisfies, for all a, b and c,

$$(a,b)\langle term\rangle c \equiv a{=}b.$$

Finally, the *feedback* of a circuit R, written R^σ, is defined by $a\langle R^\sigma\rangle b \equiv a\langle R\rangle(b,a)$.

We may now summarize our means of constructing circuits:

0. If R is a relation then $\dot{R}$ is a circuit.
1. The projections $\ll$ and $\gg$ are circuits.
2. *term* is a circuit.
3. If R,S are circuits, then $R \circ S$, $R \times S$, $R \vartriangle S$, and $R^\cup$ are circuits.
4. Delays and antidelays are circuits.
5. If R is a circuit, then R^σ is a circuit.

A circuit R is said to be *combinational* if it is defined exclusively by means of the first four items in the above list; i.e., if delay, antidelay and feedback do not appear in its definition.

A circuit term has an interpretation as a picture that is often useful as an aid to understanding how a circuit term is interpreted as a real circuit. Figure 0 shows the correspondence between pictures and circuit terms. A picture shows which "parts" of a circuit are connected; and interconnections are important in order to evaluate the circuit's performance. In fact, the picture interpretation shows the presence of *combinational paths* in the circuit. A picture may be seen as a graph, where combinational elements and delays are nodes, and wires are edges. A combinational path is a path in the picture that does not contain delays. One important parameter for the efficiency of a circuit implementation is the clock speed. Roughly speaking, the shortest clock period that can be assigned to a circuit implementation grows with the length of the longest combinational path in the circuit. For this reason it is preferable to design circuits with short combinational paths. A circuit is said to be *systolic* when it is built out of small modules, interconnected by wires interrupted by delays (Leiserson 1983).

There are many optimisation techniques that can be used to improve the performance of circuits. Here we will make use of *retiming* and *slowdown*.

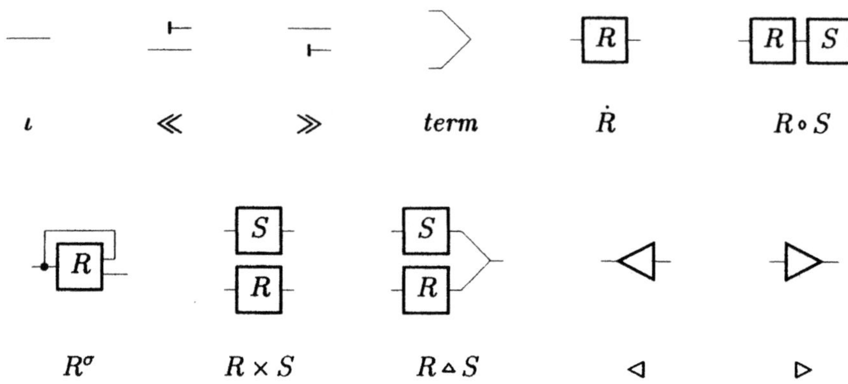

Figure 0 Circuits and their pictures

Retiming (Leiserson and Saxe 1991) is a transformation that is essentially based on the following laws: given that R is a circuit as defined above,

$$\lhd \circ R = R \circ \lhd \quad \text{and} \quad \rhd \circ R = R \circ \rhd. \tag{6}$$

These laws can be proved by structural induction (see the longer version of this paper, Vaccari and Backhouse 1996). Combining (6) with the property that

$$\rhd \circ \lhd = \iota = \lhd \circ \rhd \tag{7}$$

we obtain the properties

$$R = \rhd \circ R \circ \lhd \quad \text{and} \quad R = \lhd \circ R \circ \rhd \tag{8}$$

for all circuits R.

(Note that the retiming law (8) breaks down when the domain of streams is taken to be the natural numbers rather than the integers. Instead of equalities one obtains isomorphisms up to retiming, making calculations more cumbersome.)

A useful property of *term* is that, for all circuits R and $\diamond \in \{\lhd, \rhd\}$,

$$\diamond \circ R \circ \mathit{term} = R \circ \mathit{term}. \tag{9}$$

This is a straightforward consequence of the retiming equations (6) and the domain equations (3). An intuitive understanding of why this law is true can be gained by comparing the picture interpretation of (9), for $R = \iota$, with the

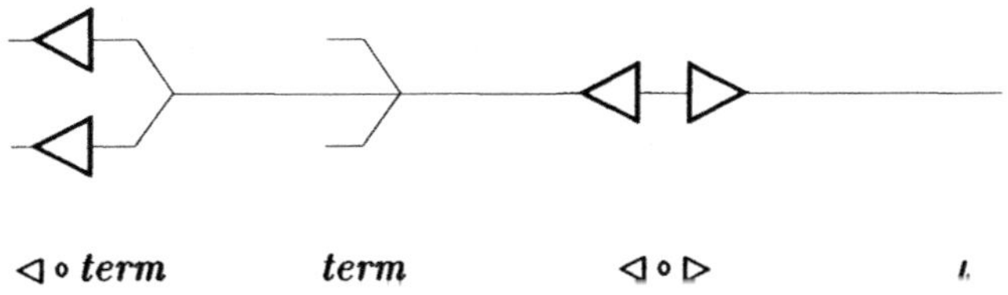

Figure 1 Comparing instances of (9) and (8)

picture interpretation (8), also for $R = \iota$ (see figure 1): the pictures are the same, modulo the orientation of the wires.

Another optimisation technique is slowdown (Jones and Sheeran 1992). Given a circuit R, the circuit $slow.R$ is defined by

$$slow.R \;=\; \mathcal{B} \circ R{\times}R \circ \mathcal{B}^{\cup},$$

where $\mathcal{B}$, pronounced "bundle", is defined by

$$a\langle\mathcal{B}\rangle(b,c) \;\equiv\; \forall(n :: \; b.n = a.(2n) \;\wedge\; c.n = a.(2n+1)).$$

It can be shown by structural induction that, for any circuit R, the circuit $slow.R$ is equal to the one obtained by replacing every occurrence of $\rhd$ and $\lhd$ in R by $\rhd{\circ}\rhd$ and $\lhd{\circ}\lhd$, respectively. The slowed circuit is not equivalent to the original one; it has different timing properties. The reason for implementing a slowed version of a circuit is that the extra delays that are introduced can be shifted around by means of the retiming laws, with the general goal of making the circuit more systolic.

To illustrate the use of slowing and retiming, suppose we are implementing circuit

$$(\iota{\times}\lhd \circ R)^n \circ term \tag{10}$$

for some $n > 0$. The picture interpretation (for $n = 3$) shows a long combinational path:

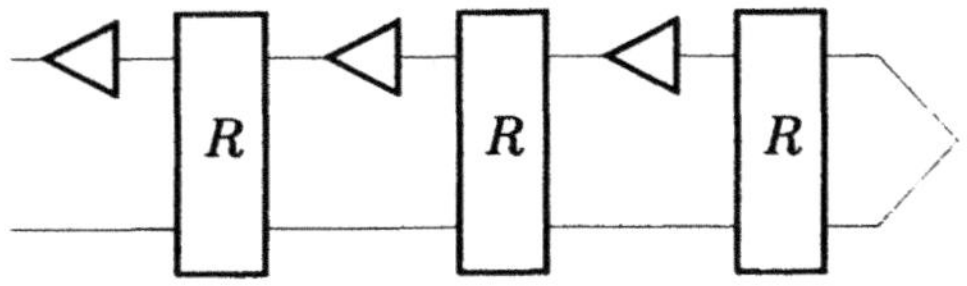

By retiming, one obtains:

$$
\begin{array}{ll}
= & \{ \quad \text{retiming (8)} \quad \} \\
 & (\rhd \circ \iota \times \lhd \circ R \circ \lhd)^n \circ \mathit{term} \\
= & \{ \quad \text{delays, (5) and (7)} \quad \} \\
 & (\rhd \times \iota \circ R \circ \lhd)^n \circ \mathit{term} \\
= & \{ \quad \text{retiming (6)} \quad \} \\
 & (\rhd \times \iota \circ R)^n \circ \lhd^n \circ \mathit{term} \\
= & \{ \quad \text{equation (9)} \quad \} \\
 & (\rhd \times \iota \circ R)^n \circ \mathit{term}.
\end{array}
$$

This transformation does not buy us anything, since the resulting circuit still has a long combinational delay:

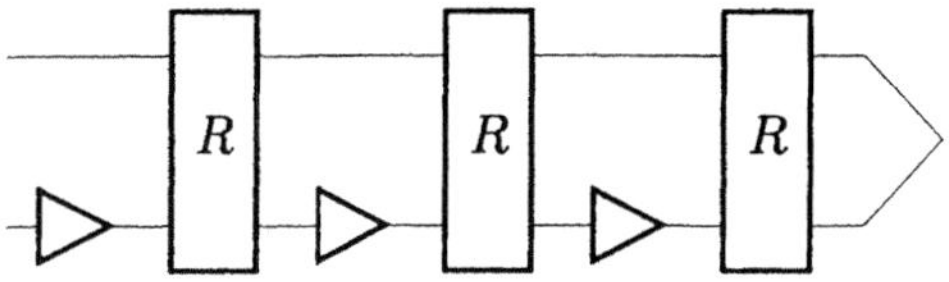

But, if we choose to implement a slowed version of (10) instead, we have:

$$
\begin{array}{ll}
 & \mathit{slow}.((\iota \times \lhd \circ R)^n \circ \mathit{term}) \\
= & \{ \quad \text{slowing is the same as doubling the delays;} \\
 & \quad\quad \text{assume } R \text{ is combinational} \quad \} \\
 & (\iota \times (\lhd \circ \lhd) \circ R)^n \circ \mathit{term} \\
= & \{ \quad \text{fusion (1)} \quad \} \\
 & (\iota \times \lhd \circ \iota \times \lhd \circ R)^n \circ \mathit{term} \\
= & \{ \quad \text{the above derivation,} \\
 & \quad\quad \text{taking } R := \iota \times \lhd \circ R \quad \} \\
 & (\rhd \times \iota \circ \iota \times \lhd \circ R)^n \circ \mathit{term} \\
= & \{ \quad \text{fusion (1)} \quad \} \\
 & (\rhd \times \lhd \circ R)^n \circ \mathit{term}.
\end{array}
$$

The last line is a circuit whose interpretation has no long combinational paths:

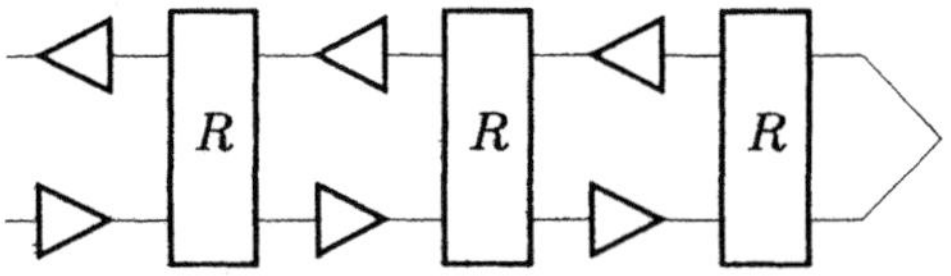

In fact, the length of the longest combinational path is no longer dependent on n. Note that the placement of delays and antidelays implies that the flow of data through the circuit is both from left to right and from right to left; this is called "contra-flow".

We conclude this section with a remark on the realizability of the circuits we derive. In the algebra of relations there is no notion of "input" or "output". When one wishes to implement a relation algebra term as an actual circuit, input and output directions must be assigned to each wire. But not all choices yield an implementable circuit. For instance, if *add* is a relation such that $a\langle add\rangle(b,c) \;\equiv\; a = b+c$, then choosing a as input and b, c as output would yield a non-deterministic circuit. One must pay particular attention to delays and antidelays, since they can be implemented in just one way: every delay must have input on the right side, and output on the left side; and the other way around for antidelays. If there is no way to choose inputs and outputs such that every delay and antidelay is driven in the correct direction, then the circuit is not implementable. A more formal and thorough discussion of implementability is given in Graham Hutton's thesis (1993).

3 THE SPECIFICATION

The problem we want to consider is that of formulating a syntax-directed construction of a systolic circuit that (repeatedly) recognizes strings in the language denoted by a regular expression. The syntax of a regular expression is given by the BNF grammar

$$\mathcal{E} \;::=\; t \mid \mathcal{E}+\mathcal{E} \mid \mathcal{E}\,;\mathcal{E} \mid \mathcal{E}^*,$$

where t stands for all elements of a given finite alphabet $\mathcal{T}$.

To begin with, we define a mapping from $\mathcal{E}$ to the set of stream transducers $\mathcal{F}$, where

$$\mathcal{F} \;=\; Stream(\mathbf{B}) \leftarrow Stream(\mathcal{T})\times Stream(\mathbf{B}).$$

Thus, given a regular expression E, the recognizer for E maps a pair consisting of a stream of characters (elements of $\mathcal{T}$) and a stream of booleans into another stream of booleans. The boolean input is a so-called "enable" signal. A value of *true* for the enable input indicates the start of a new input sequence of characters. For instance, if the expression to be recognized is $t\,;t$, and the set of symbols is $\mathcal{T}=\{t, u\}$, we expect the following behaviour:

output	character (a)	enable bit (e)
0	t	0
0	t	1
0	t	0
1	t	0
0	t	1
0	u	0
0	t	0

As we shall see, a value of *true* for the enable input does not terminate any foregoing sequence of characters. The following is another example of required behaviour:

output	character (a)	enable bit (e)
0	t	0
0	t	1
0	t	1
1	t	0
1	t	0
0	t	0

Usually we use a to range over a stream of input characters and e (for *e*nable bit) to range over a stream of input booleans.

In order to avoid the error in (Foster and Kung 1982) we shall restrict the regular expressions to those expressions not including a subexpression E^* such that the empty word is a member of E. It is well known that this does not reduce the expressive power of regular expressions and that every regular expression can be easily transformed to one of this form.

We denote the isomorphism between strings of booleans and left conditions by *tt* (standing for "times true") and define it by, for all integers m and n and all streams of booleans e,

$$m\langle tt.e\rangle n \;\equiv\; e.m.$$

For instance, if the stream e is defined for all n by $e.n \;\equiv\; n > 0 \wedge (n \text{ is odd})$, then $tt.e = \{1, 3, 5, \ldots\}$. We also introduce a relation, $mem.(E, a)$, on integers for each expression E and each stream of letters a, defined by

$$m\langle mem.(E,a)\rangle n \;\equiv\; a[n,m) \in E,$$

where $a[n, m)$ denotes the string $a.n \;;\; a.(n{+}1) \;;\; \ldots \;;\; a.(m{-}1)$. Note the switch in the order of m and n. Returning to the example where $E = t\,;t$, we have that if the stream a is defined by $a.n = t$ for all n, then $m\langle mem.(t;t,a)\rangle n \equiv m = n+2$. Another way to look at *mem* is as a set transformer. If we compose $mem.(E,a)$ after a left condition, we obtain another left condition:

$$mem.(E,a) \circ (R \circ \top\!\!\top) = (mem.(E,a) \circ R) \circ \top\!\!\top.$$

So if $R \circ \top\!\!\top$ can be interpreted as the set $\{0, 1, 5\}$, then, given a defined as above, $mem.(t\,;t, a) \circ R \circ \top\!\!\top$ could be interpreted as $\{2, 3, 7\}$.

The following properties of *mem* are easily verified (see Vaccari and Backhouse 1996):

$$\begin{array}{rcll} m\langle mem.(t,a)\rangle n & \equiv & m = n{+}1 \;\wedge\; a.n = t & \text{for all } t \in \mathcal{T} \\ mem.(E{+}F, a) & = & mem.(E,a) \cup mem.(F,a) & \\ mem.(E\,;F, a) & = & mem.(F,a) \circ mem.(E,a) & \\ mem.(E^*, a) & = & (mem.(E,a))^*. & \end{array} \qquad (11)$$

These properties provide ample justification for choosing to use relation algebra in the formal specification of the recognizer: the function $E \mapsto mem.(E,a)$ is a homomorphism from the algebra of expressions to the algebra of relations.

We say that a circuit f (formally a stream transducer, i.e., an element of $\mathcal{F}$) *recognizes* regular expression E when the following holds, for all $a \in Stream(\mathcal{T})$ and $e \in Stream(\mathbf{B})$:

$$tt.f.(a,e) \;=\; mem.(E,a) \circ tt.e.$$

A way to read this is: the set of times at which e is *true*, that is $tt.e$, is transformed by *mem* into a set that must be exactly the same as the set of times at which $f.(a,e)$ is true.

4 A NON-SYSTOLIC RECOGNIZER

Once the specification is made clear, deriving a (non-systolic) recognizer is easy. We begin by deriving the recognizer for a single character. We have:

$$m \;\in\; mem.(t,a) \circ tt.e$$

$$
\begin{array}{ll}
\equiv & \{ \text{ composition } \} \\
& \exists(n :: m\langle mem.(t,a)\rangle n \ \wedge \ n \in tt.e) \\
\equiv & \{ \ mem \ \} \\
& \exists(n :: n = m-1 \ \wedge \ a.n = t \ \wedge \ n \in tt.e) \\
\equiv & \{ \text{ one-point rule } \} \\
& a.(m-1) = t \ \wedge \ m-1 \in tt.e \\
\equiv & \{ \text{ lifting, } tt \ \} \\
& ((\dot{=}\, t).a).(m-1) \ \wedge \ e.(m-1) \\
\equiv & \{ \text{ lifting } \} \\
& (e \mathbin{\dot{\wedge}} (\dot{=}\, t).a).(m-1) \\
\equiv & \{ \text{ delay } \} \\
& (\lhd.(e \mathbin{\dot{\wedge}} (\dot{=}\, t).a)).m \\
\equiv & \{ \ tt \ \} \\
& m \in tt.(\lhd.(e \mathbin{\dot{\wedge}} (\dot{=}\, t).a)).
\end{array}
$$

From this we obtain:

$$
\begin{array}{ll}
& f \text{ recognizes letter } t \\
\equiv & \{ \text{ definition } \} \\
& \forall(a,e :: tt.f.(a,e) = mem.(t,a) \circ tt.e) \\
\equiv & \{ \text{ sets } \} \\
& \forall(m,a,e :: m \in tt.f.(a,e) \ \equiv \ m \in mem.(t,a) \circ tt.e) \\
\equiv & \{ \text{ above } \} \\
& \forall(m,a,e :: m \in tt.f.(a,e) \ \equiv \ m \in tt.(\lhd.(e \mathbin{\dot{\wedge}} (\dot{=}\, t).a))) \\
\equiv & \{ \text{ calculus } \} \\
& f = \lhd \circ \dot{\wedge} \circ (\dot{=}\, t) \times \iota .
\end{array}
$$

Next we consider that the expression has the form $E+F$ for some expressions E and F. Suppose that f, g recognize E, F respectively. Then,

$$
\begin{array}{ll}
& h \text{ recognizes } E+F \\
\equiv & \{ \text{ definition } \} \\
& \forall(a,e :: tt.h.(a,e) = mem.(E+F,a) \circ tt.e) \\
\equiv & \{ \ mem\text{, distributivity } \} \\
& \forall(a,e :: tt.h.(a,e) = mem.(E,a) \circ tt.e \cup mem.(F,a) \circ tt.e) \\
\equiv & \{ \text{ hypothesis } \} \\
& \forall(a,e :: tt.h.(a,e) = tt.f.(a,e) \cup tt.g.(a,e)) \\
\equiv & \{ \ tt \text{ and } \cup\text{; } tt \text{ is an isomorphism } \}
\end{array}
$$

$$
\begin{array}{ll}
 & \forall(a,e :: \ h.(a,e) \ = \ f.(a,e) \ \dot{\vee} \ g.(a,e)) \\
\equiv & \qquad \{ \qquad \text{calculus} \qquad \} \\
 & h \ = \ \dot{\vee} \circ f \vartriangle g.
\end{array}
$$

The next case is an expression of the form $E\,;F$ for some expressions E and F. Suppose again that f, g recognize E, F respectively. Then,

$$
\begin{array}{ll}
 & h \text{ recognizes } E\,;F \\
\equiv & \qquad \{ \qquad \text{definition} \qquad \} \\
 & \forall(a,e :: \ tt.h.(a,e) \ = \ mem.(E\,;F,a) \circ tt.e) \\
\equiv & \qquad \{ \qquad mem \qquad \} \\
 & \forall(a,e :: \ tt.h.(a,e) \ = \ mem.(F,a) \circ mem.(E,a) \circ tt.e) \\
\equiv & \qquad \{ \qquad \text{hypothesis} \qquad \} \\
 & \forall(a,e :: \ tt.h.(a,e) \ = \ mem.(F,a) \circ tt.f.(a,e)) \\
\equiv & \qquad \{ \qquad \text{hypothesis} \qquad \} \\
 & \forall(a,e :: \ tt.h.(a,e) = tt.g.(a, f.(a,e))) \\
\equiv & \qquad \{ \qquad tt \text{ is an isomorphism; calculus} \qquad \} \\
 & h \ = \ g \circ \ll \vartriangle f.
\end{array}
$$

The final, and most interesting case, is when the given expression has the form E^* for some E. A circuit containing feedback is clearly needed. This is the case where Foster and Kung's original design contained an error.

The problem occurs because the defining equation of R^*, for any given relation R, does not necessarily have a unique solution. It does have a unique solution if R is well-founded. Anticipating the forthcoming calculation somewhat, we determine a condition for the relation $mem.(E,a)$ to be well-founded. For all E and a, we have:

$$
\begin{array}{ll}
 & X = mem.(E,a) \circ X \\
\Rightarrow & \qquad \{ \qquad \text{Leibniz} \qquad \} \\
 & X \circ \top\!\!\top = mem.(E,a) \circ X \circ \top\!\!\top \\
\equiv & \qquad \{ \qquad \text{pointwise interpretation; define } S = X \circ \top\!\!\top, \\
 & \qquad \qquad \ \ \text{a left condition which we regard as a set} \qquad \} \\
 & \forall(m :: \ m \in S \ \equiv \ \exists(n :: \ m\langle mem.(E,a)\rangle n \ \wedge \ n \in S)) \\
\equiv & \qquad \{ \qquad \bullet \quad \text{assume } mem.(E,a)\!> \subseteq \mathbb{N} \qquad \} \\
 & \forall(m :: \ m \in S \ \equiv \ \exists(n : \ n \in \mathbb{N} : \ m\langle mem.(E,a)\rangle n \ \wedge \ n \in S)) \\
\equiv & \qquad \{ \qquad \text{definition of } mem \qquad \} \\
 & \forall(m :: \ m \in S \ \equiv \ \exists(n : \ n \in \mathbb{N} : \ a[n,m) \in E \ \wedge \ n \in S)) \\
\Rightarrow & \qquad \{ \qquad \bullet \quad \text{assume } \varepsilon \notin E \qquad \}
\end{array}
$$

$$
\begin{array}{ll}
 & \forall(m :: m \in S \equiv \exists(n : n \in \mathbf{N} : n < m \wedge n \in S)) \\
\Rightarrow & \quad \{ \quad \text{predicate calculus} \quad \} \\
 & \quad \forall(m : m \in \mathbf{N} : m \in S \equiv \exists(n : n \in \mathbf{N} : n < m \wedge n \in S)) \\
 & \wedge\ S \subseteq \mathbf{N} \\
\equiv & \quad \{ \quad \text{the natural numbers are well-founded} \quad \} \\
 & S = \perp\!\!\perp \\
\equiv & \quad \{ \quad \text{calculus, } S = X \circ \top\!\!\top \quad \} \\
 & X = \perp\!\!\perp .
\end{array}
$$

We have thus found that the assumptions $\varepsilon \notin E$ and $mem.(E,a)> \subseteq \mathbf{N}$ together imply that $mem.(E,a)$ is well-founded. The second of these assumptions is equivalent to postulating that the stream a is such that if a segment of a is a word in E, then this segment is wholly contained in the non-negative "half". Actually, it simplifies matters if we make an even stronger postulate, namely that for all $n < 0$, the value of $a.n$ is some character not appearing in E. This corresponds to asserting that the circuit is fed invalid input until time 0. One may think of time 0 as the moment after the circuit is reset. Given this assumption, we may henceforth just say that $mem.(E,a)$ is well-founded if $\varepsilon \notin E$.

We are now ready to tackle the derivation of the circuit that recognizes E^*. Assume f recognizes E. Assume also that $\varepsilon \notin E$. Then

$$
\begin{array}{ll}
 & g \text{ recognizes } E^* \\
\equiv & \quad \{ \quad \text{definition} \quad . \} \\
 & \forall(a, e, b :: \ b\langle g\rangle(a,e) \ \equiv \ tt.b = mem.(E^*, a) \circ tt.e).
\end{array}
$$

Now,

$$
\begin{array}{ll}
 & tt.b = mem.(E^*, a) \circ tt.e \\
\equiv & \quad \{ \quad mem\ (11) \quad \} \\
 & tt.b = (mem.(E,a))^* \circ tt.e \\
\equiv & \quad \{ \quad \varepsilon \notin E, \text{ so } mem.(E,a) \text{ is well-founded.} \\
 & \qquad\quad \text{Unique extension property (2).} \quad \} \\
 & tt.b = tt.e \cup mem.(E,a) \circ tt.b \\
\equiv & \quad \{ \quad f \text{ recognizes } E \quad \} \\
 & tt.b = tt.e \cup tt.f.(a,b) \\
\equiv & \quad \{ \quad tt \quad \} \\
 & tt.b = tt.(e \dot{\vee} f.(a,b)) \\
\equiv & \quad \{ \quad tt \text{ is an isomorphism} \quad \} \\
 & b = e \dot{\vee} f.(a,b)
\end{array}
$$

$$\equiv \quad \{ \text{ calculus; define } reorg.((x,y),z) = (y,(x,z)) \ \}$$
$$b = (\dot{\vee} \circ \iota \times f \circ reorg).((a,e),b).$$

Thus

$$g \text{ recognizes } E^*$$
$$\equiv \quad \{ \text{ above } \}$$
$$\forall(a,e,b :: \ b\langle g\rangle(a,e) \ \equiv \ b = (\dot{\vee} \circ \iota \times f \circ reorg).((a,e),b))$$
$$\equiv \quad \{ \text{ feedback } \}$$
$$g = (\dot{\vee} \circ \iota \times f \circ reorg)^\sigma .$$

Summarising the results so far, we have derived a syntax directed translation from $\mathcal{E}$ to $\mathcal{F}$, which we may call τ, defined as follows:

$$\begin{array}{rcll} \tau.t & = & \lhd \circ \dot{\wedge} \circ (\dot{=} t) \times \iota & \text{for all } t \in \mathcal{T} \\ \tau.(E{+}F) & = & \dot{\vee} \circ \tau.E \vartriangle \tau.F & \\ \tau.(E\,;F) & = & \tau.F \circ \ll \vartriangle \tau.E & \\ \tau.E^* & = & (\dot{\vee} \circ \iota \times \tau.E \circ reorg)^\sigma & \end{array} \tag{12}$$

and such that, for all regular expressions E, $\tau.E$ recognizes E.

5 MAKING THE DESIGN SYSTOLIC

The circuits we have derived so far are not systolic; for instance, if one were to build a recognizer for the string "$t\,;u\,;v$", with t, u and v all elements of $\mathcal{T}$, the resulting circuit would be

$$(\lhd \circ \dot{\wedge} \circ (\dot{=} v) \times \iota) \circ \ll \vartriangle (\lhd \circ \dot{\wedge} \circ (\dot{=} u) \times \iota) \circ \ll \vartriangle (\lhd \circ \dot{\wedge} \circ (\dot{=} t) \times \iota).$$

It is apparent from the picture interpretation of the above circuit

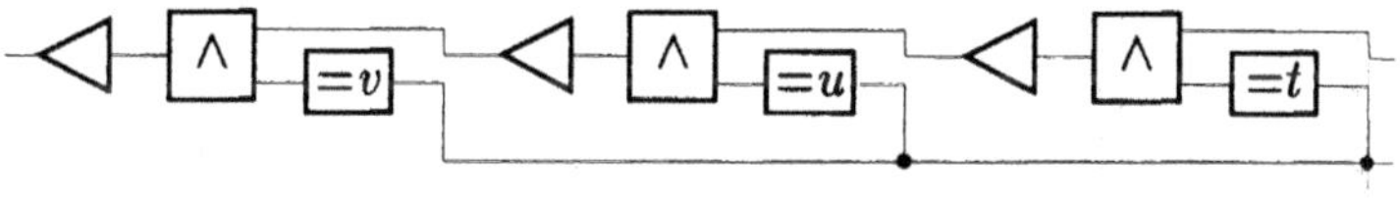

that there is a combinational path from one side to the other of the circuit. Even worse is the fact that for every string recognizer, this path grows in length with the length of the string.

Our strategy for making the design systolic is in three steps. First we rearrange the wires, in order to introduce contra-flow in the circuits (see section 2). Then we make the design modular, by designing a separate cell for each operator (except for sequence, which we regard as the "basic" oper-

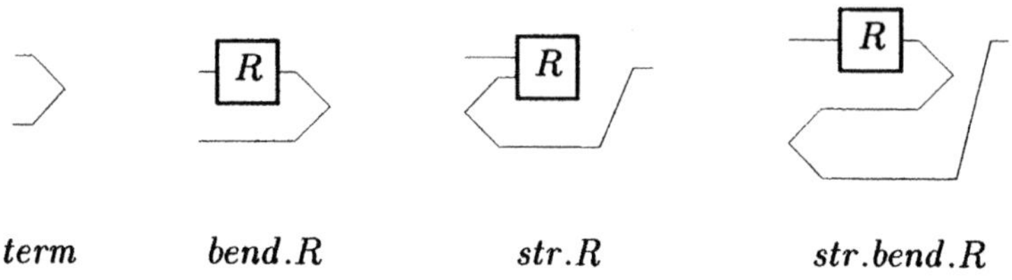

Figure 2 Picture interpretations

ator). Finally we apply retiming and slowdown, in order to make the design as systolic as possible.

As we saw in the example at the end of section 2, a standard way to make a circuit systolic is to apply slowdown and retiming. However, the transformation shown in that example only works when the circuit has contra-flow; that is, when there are two parallel wires where data travel in opposite directions. Given a circuit R, a simple way to introduce contra-flow in it is to implement $bend.R$ instead of R, defined by

$$bend.R = \iota \times R \circ term.$$

It is easy to calculate that, for all a, b and c,

$$(a, b)\langle bend.R\rangle c \equiv b\langle R\rangle a$$

(Note the inversion of a and b, and that c does not appear on the right side.) We may define a transformation str (from "straighten") by

$$b\langle str.R\rangle a \equiv \exists(c :: (a, b)\langle R\rangle c),$$

so that

$$str.bend.R = R \tag{13}$$

(see figure 2). Since $bend$ is defined without mentioning delays, we have that for all R,

$$slow.bend.R = bend.slow.R. \tag{14}$$

Given the above discussion, we propose to change the specification so that instead of implementing $\tau.E$ we decide to implement $\rho.E$ instead, defined by

$$\rho.E = slow.bend.\tau.E.$$

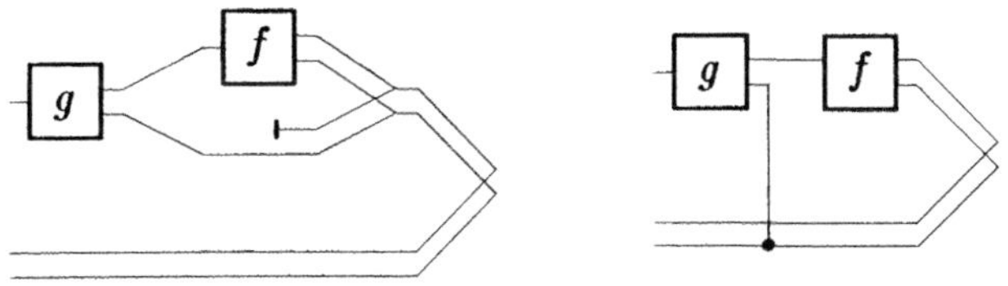

$\iota\times g \circ \iota\times(\ll\triangle f) \circ term$ $\qquad$ $\iota\times g \circ plumb \circ \iota\times f \circ term$

Figure 3 A simplification

Note that in the definition of ρ we foresee the need to apply slowdown; hence the occurrence of *slow*. So much for the introduction of contra-flow.

Another strategy for systolic design is to break the design down into small modules or "cells" of the same "shape", connected in some regular way. Taking inspiration from Foster and Kung, we concentrate on sequence. Consider the expression $\rho.(E\,;F)$. Its picture interpretation suggests a simplification: see figure 3. Let *plumb* be a wiring relation defined by

$$plumb.((x,y),z) = ((x,y),(x,z)).$$

It holds that

$$\iota\times(g \circ \ll\triangle f) \circ term \;=\; \iota\times g \circ plumb \circ \iota\times f \circ term \tag{15}$$

(The proof is omitted. A simple pointwise calculation establishes the property.) By defining a new function $\upsilon.E = \iota \times slow.\tau.E$, equation (15) may be rewritten as

$$\rho.(E\,;F) \;=\; \upsilon.F \circ plumb \circ \rho.E. \tag{16}$$

This result provides the insight for our next step in the process of making the design systolic, i.e. the breaking down of the design into cells. We choose sequence as the "privileged" operator in our design, and implement it by means of equation (16). Every regular expression E other than a sequence will be implemented by a "cell" equal to $\upsilon.E$. For instance, the interconnection of the cells of the recognizer for the expression $t^*\;;\;v\;;\;(t+(u\,;u))$ would have the shape shown in figure 4.

What we are left to do is to come up with designs for the cells $\upsilon.(E+F)$, $\upsilon.E^*$ and $\upsilon.t$, for all $t\in\mathcal{T}$. Let E, F be regular expressions; we calculate for choice:

$$\upsilon.(E+F)$$

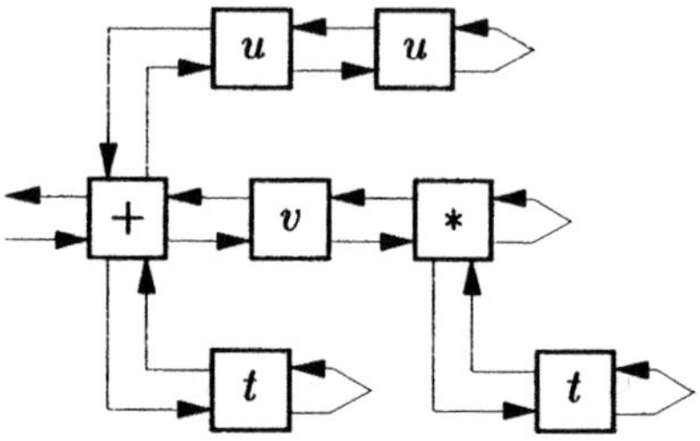

Figure 4 Cells layout for the recognizer of t^* ; v ; $(t+(u;u))$

$$
\begin{aligned}
= &\quad \{ \quad \text{definition of } v \quad \} \\
& \iota \times slow.\tau.(E+F) \\
= &\quad \{ \quad \text{definition of } \tau \quad \} \\
& \iota \times slow.(\dot{\vee} \circ \tau.E \vartriangle \tau.F) \\
= &\quad \{ \quad \text{slowing is the same as doubling delays} \quad \} \\
& \iota \times (\dot{\vee} \circ slow.\tau.E \vartriangle slow.\tau.F) \\
= &\quad \{ \quad \text{equation (13)} \quad \} \\
& \iota \times (\dot{\vee} \circ str.bend.slow.\tau.E \vartriangle str.bend.slow.\tau.F) \\
= &\quad \{ \quad \text{slow commutes with bend (14)} \quad \} \\
& \iota \times (\dot{\vee} \circ str.slow.bend.\tau.E \vartriangle str.slow.bend.\tau.F) \\
= &\quad \{ \quad \text{definition of } \rho \quad \} \\
& \iota \times (\dot{\vee} \circ str.\rho.E \vartriangle str.\rho.F)
\end{aligned}
$$

Note that in the above derivation we have exploited the property $slow.\tau.E = str.\rho.E$ in order to have ρ reappear. By doing so we ensure that the systolic optimizations can be applied recursively.

We have a similar derivation for *star*:

$$
\begin{aligned}
& v.E^* \\
= &\quad \{ \quad \text{definitions of } v,\ \tau \text{ and } slow \quad \} \\
& \iota \times (\dot{\vee} \circ \iota \times slow.\tau.E \circ reorg)^\sigma \\
= &\quad \{ \quad slow.\tau.E = str.\rho.E \quad \} \\
& \iota \times (\dot{\vee} \circ \iota \times str.\rho.E \circ reorg)^\sigma .
\end{aligned}
$$

Finally, for any $t \in \mathcal{T}$, we have

$$
\begin{aligned}
& v.t \\
= &\quad \{ \quad \text{definitions of } \rho,\ \tau \text{ and } slow \quad \}
\end{aligned}
$$

$$
\begin{array}{ll}
& \iota\times(\lhd\circ\lhd\circ\dot{\wedge}\circ(\dot{=}t)\times\iota) \\
= & \{\quad \text{retiming (6) and delays (7), (5)} \quad\} \\
& \rhd\times(\lhd\circ\dot{\wedge}\circ(\dot{=}t)\times\iota)\circ\lhd.
\end{array}
$$

Here we'd like to get rid of the rightmost $\lhd$, but with the current definition of υ we can't. However, the circuits we generate are always of the shape $\upsilon.E \circ \ldots \circ \rho.F$, and by the definition of ρ and equation (9) we have $\lhd \circ \rho.F = \rho.F$. So it's easy to see that dropping the delay is harmless. Formally, all we have to do is to weaken the defining property of υ to

$$\forall(R :: \ \upsilon.E \circ R \circ \pi \ = \ \iota \times \mathit{slow}.\tau.E \ \circ \ R \ \circ \ \pi).$$

By this definition, the expressions for $\upsilon.(E+F)$ and $\upsilon.E^*$ that we previously derived are still valid, as well as equation (16); and the derivation of $\upsilon.t$ becomes:

$$
\begin{array}{ll}
& \upsilon.t\circ R\circ \pi \\
= & \{\quad \text{above} \quad\} \\
& \rhd\times(\lhd\circ\dot{\wedge}\circ(\dot{=}t)\times\iota)\circ\lhd\circ R\circ\pi \\
= & \{\quad \text{equation (9)} \quad\} \\
& \rhd\times(\lhd\circ\dot{\wedge}\circ(\dot{=}t)\times\iota)\circ R\circ\pi.
\end{array}
$$

Summarizing our results, we have

$$
\begin{array}{rcll}
\rho.(E\,;F) & = & \upsilon.E\circ \mathit{plumb}\circ\rho.E & \\
\rho.E & = & \upsilon.E\circ \mathit{term} & \\
\upsilon.(E+F) & = & \iota\times(\dot{\vee}\ \circ\ \mathit{str}.\rho.E \vartriangle \mathit{str}.\rho.F) & \\
\upsilon.E^* & = & \iota\times(\dot{\vee}\ \circ\ \iota\times \mathit{str}.\rho.E\ \circ\ \mathit{reorg})^\sigma & \\
\upsilon.t & = & \rhd\times(\lhd\circ\dot{\wedge}\circ(\dot{=}t)\times\iota) & \text{for all } t\in\mathcal{T}.
\end{array}
$$

These equations can be interpreted as a functional program that translates regular expressions to systolic recognizers.

6 CONCLUSIONS

The transformation ρ that we derived in the last section generates circuits that are very similar to the ones presented by Foster and Kung. If the regular expression to be recognized does not contain choice or star, i.e. it is just a string of characters, then ρ generates a fully systolic string recognizer. The picture interpretation of the recognizer for the string $t\,;u\,;v$ can be seen in figure 5.

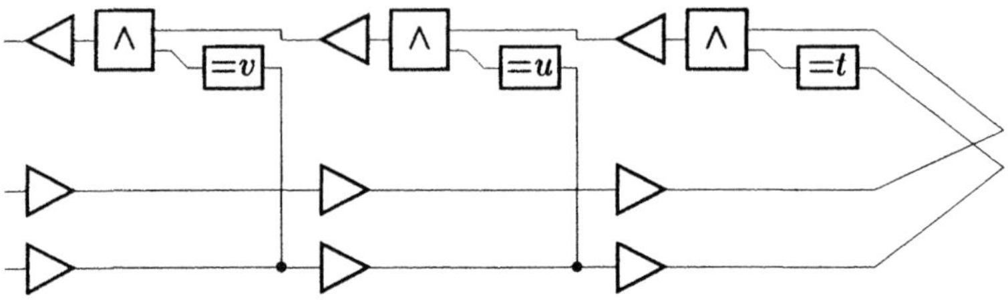

Figure 5 A systolic recognizer for the expression $t\,;u\,;v$

If the regular expression does not have this very special shape the benefit is diminished. Consider for instance expressions of the form

$$E_1 + E_2 + E_3 + \ldots$$

The translation of such expressions has the form

$$\dot{\vee} \circ \tau.E_1 \vartriangle (\dot{\vee} \circ \tau.E_2 \vartriangle (\dot{\vee} \circ \tau.E_3 \vartriangle \ldots)).$$

and here we have combinational paths whose length depends on the number of occurrences of "+" in the expression:

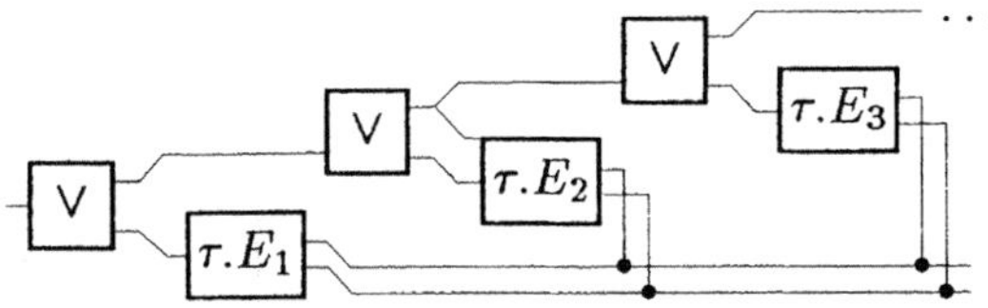

The design presented here is well-optimized for expressions that contain many more ";" operators than "+". (This problem is also present in Foster and Kung's work; they simply fail to observe it.) The first author is currently investigating using a different transformation technique called "pipelining" to overcome this problem.

In the usual squiggol style, one works with syntactic terms that can be interpreted as both mathematical functions, and computer programs. What one does then is to take a term and transform it according to rules that do not change the functional interpretation, but may — and should — change the efficiency of the term interpreted as a program. What we did in the last section is very similar, except that instead of working with a simple term, we had to improve the efficiency of a term-valued function, τ. This is how functions like ρ come into being. Its characterisation as a function from relations to relations is simple; but it is not as easy to specify formally what we expect ρ to do as a function from syntactical terms to syntactical terms. What we had in mind as we worked is "apply the useful transformations as thoroughly as possible." It could prove fruitful to apply further work to develop notations for cleanly specifying term transformation functions of this kind.

An interesting element of our derivation is its use of the unique extension property (uep) for regular languages in the case of a starred expression. The fact that the subexpression should not include the empty word is a necessary and sufficient condition for application of the uep. This is where the error occurred in Foster and Kung's original paper. The non-uniqueness of solutions to certain equations in relation calculus corresponds to indeterminate behaviour in the corresponding circuits.

REFERENCES

Aarts, C., Backhouse, R., Hoogendijk, P., Voermans, E. and van der Woude, J.: 1992, A relational theory of datatypes. Available at URL `ftp://ftp.win.tue.nl/pub/math.prog.construction/book.dvi`.

Backhouse, R. C.: 1983, Specification and proof of a regular language recognizer in synchronous CCS, *Technical Report CSM-53*, University of Essex.

Cohn, A. and Gordon, M.: 1990, A mechanized proof of correctness of a simple counter, *in* K. McEvoy and J. Tucker (eds), *Theoretical Foundations of VLSI Design*, Cambridge Tracts in Theoretical Computer Science, Cambridge University Press.

Doornbos, H., Backhouse, R. and van der Woude, J.: 1997, A calculational approach to mathematical induction. To appear in Theoretical Computer Science.

Foster, M. J.: 1984, *Specialized Silicon Compilers for Language Recognition*, PhD thesis, Computer Science Department, Carnegie Mellon University.

Foster, M. and Kung, H.: 1982, Recognize regular languages with programmable building blocks, *Journal of Digital Systems* **4**(6), 323–332.

Hutton, G.: 1993, *Between Functions and Relations in Calculating Programs*, PhD thesis, Dept. of Computer Science, University of Glasgow.

Jones, G. and Sheeran, M.: 1990, Circuit design in Ruby, *in* J. Staunstrup (ed.), *Formal Methods for VLSI Design. IFIP WG 10.5 Lecture Notes*, North-Holland.

Jones, G. and Sheeran, M.: 1992, Deriving bit-serial circuits in Ruby, *in* A. Halaas and P. B. Denyer (eds), *IFIP Transactions A-1, VLSI 91*, North-Holland. Available at `http://www.comlab.ox.ac.uk/oucl/users/geraint.jones/publications/PRG-TR-3-91.ps.Z`.

Kaldewaij, A. and Zwaan, G.: 1990, A systolic design for acceptors of regular languages, *Science of Computer Programming* **15**(2), 171–183.

Leiserson, C. E.: 1983, *Area-Efficient VLSI Computation*, MIT Press.

Leiserson, C. E. and Saxe, J. B.: 1991, Retiming synchronous circuitry, *Algorithmica* **6**, 5–35.

Rietman, F.: 1995, *A Relational Calculus for the Design of Distributed Algorithms*, PhD thesis, University of Utrecht.

Vaccari, M. and Backhouse, R.: 1996, Deriving a systolic regular language recognizer, *Technical report*, Eindhoven University of Technology. Available at `ftp://ftp.win.tue.nl/pub/math.prog.construction/regpaper.dvi.Z`.

7 BIOGRAPHIES

Matteo Vaccari is a Ph.D. student at the University of Milano. He has written statistics software for medical research, and was involved in the development of a model checker for CSP. He did work on the application of automated reasoning to hardware verification. His main research interests are in the practical application of circuit and program derivation techniques.

Roland Backhouse is Professor in Computing Science at Eindhoven University of Technology. His research area is the mathematics of program construction, in particular the calculational derivation of programs. Since 1990 his main interest has been the development of a generic theory of datatypes based on the point-free relational calculus.

Discussion Session
Monday morning

Lambert Meertens: The question is often asked after the presentation of a calculational technique: Did you find something new this way? Almost always the answer is: No, that was not our aim. I am starting to wonder why it is so rare to find something new using such techniques.

Roland Backhouse: In the case of the systolic regular language recognizer, something new was discovered, though not when the present design was done. The design that Foster and Kung presented was not correct for all regular expressions because of an indeterminacy in the functioning of the circuit for expressions of the form E^{**}. The current derivation makes it very clear where the error was. That is one example where one can actually discover something by algebraic calculation.

Dave Wile: Surely, the whole point of a calculus is to coalesce what is not new. Then you can go on and build something that couldn't have been considered before. For example, without the differential and integral calculus, one would never have considered something like boundary-value problems.

Jim Boyle: But then, why don't we see examples that correspond to boundary value problems?

Michel Sintzoff: A number of people do claim that they have found new algorithms using calculational methods. The problem is that these inventions seem not to be repeatable by others: calculational technology is not transferable. For example, I am still looking for people other than Doug Smith to use his algorithmic schemes to derive new algorithms.

Doug Smith: Eleven years or so ago, we recapitulated a lot of known backtrack algorithms and developed the Kids system to codify them. Five years ago we repeated the exercise for scheduling algorithms, which required elaboration of constraint propagation and backtrack augmentation techniques. Now we have derived dozens of schedulers for a variety of different problems. Are these new algorithms? In a sense they are not, because they can be regarded as a codification and abstraction of existing techniques using state-of-the-art technology. But, as a consequence, the technology has led to algorithms that people hadn't written down before. The real question is, at what point do such abstractions become economical? I think that mechanization is necessary before the economics show up. We are under contract to provide the next generation of schedulers for a couple of government sites. The agencies do not care whether or not the code has been synthesized by machines using a calculational approach, they are interested only in whether they are getting competitive software.

Peter Pepper: There is no clear definition of what 'new' means. For instance, Mercedes, Volkswagen, and so on, build new cars all the time, but these manufacturers never re-invent the principles of cars and engines. Are they doing something new or just applying car-building principles? What we are doing, so to speak, is providing better engineering techniques for building the next car. I once read about a PhD student in Physics who spent four years parallelizing a single algorithm. Surely, we should be providing techniques to help prevent such situations arising?

Wolf Zimmermann: I disagree that we don't have a precise notion of what a new algorithm is. For me, a new algorithm is something that has a better time or space complexity, or a simpler implementation than any previous algorithm.

Tom Maibaum: There is a general hypothesis in Literature that there is something like seven basic stories or themes, and that all literary work is a reiteration and combination of these themes. Algorithmics is similar in that algorithms are generally quite basic, but their combination, programming in the large, is a much more difficult story that is more akin to literary efforts. How can one combine these basic algorithmic themes to get something new? We know next to nothing about how to do this systematically.

Bob Paige: I have used my transformational methodology to invent new algorithms. I cannot answer Sintzoff's observation that I am the only one who can do that – I am not sure that anyone else has tried. And it is not just Doug Smith and I who have been doing this sort of thing. Johan Jeuring has invented a new palindrome algorithm, though I don't know whether the new algorithm was only expressed using the Bird–Meertens formalism, or whether it actually helped the invention. Meertens has also invented some algorithms that he presented to this group at previous meetings. But the question is not that important, if you can demonstrate that a refinement calculus can help, then that is sufficient. Part of the reason that I try to invent new algorithms is that it makes my papers easier to publish. It is a defensive manoeuvre, because anyone trying to argue that my methodology is not viable has a harder task if I can invent five or six of the fastest algorithms around.

Michel Sintzoff: I think we should distinguish between new algorithms and new problems. New problems should be solved using known algorithmic schemes and the paradigms of reuse and scaling-up. To do this work we still have one challenge: to elaborate a common shared calculus. What we have now is as many calculi as researchers.

Jim Boyle: In some sense, the more we abstract the more we defeat the ability to find something new because people then say, oh yes, this is just an instance of that abstraction. The tragedy of Pepper's four year PhD example, I guess, is that none of the result was captured in a form that could be applied to another program.

Alberto Pettorossi: I think we should continue to seek out new languages, new formalisms and new calculi, provided that they are adapted to different needs. There are many formalisms and calculi in mathematics. Calculi constantly improve; for instance, 20 years ago we used Hoare triples to prove correctness, now we use relational calculus. The problem for the future is to go from small-scale verification to large-scale verification, where we have problems of concurrency, distributivity, real-time constraints, and so on.

Peter Pepper: One of the big issues is that we encounter problems that are amalgamations of other problems, and the hard thing to do is to figure out what the subproblems are and how they are interrelated. This is where systems like Kids can help. The other issue is that of languages. There is a desperate need, not for more universal languages, but for application-oriented and domain-specific languages. We should apply our knowledge about calculi and languages to specific problem domains.

Tom Maibaum: I want to make a comment about inventing more and more calculi versus a universal language. In science and engineering one could say, a bit simplistically, that the ubiquitous tool is the differential equation. For me, the analogous tool in computing is not a theory within a single logic, but different logics or, what is the same thing, consequence relations. Such relations characterize the problem domain more accurately than a theory within some fixed universal logic. If you take the view that consequence relations are the equivalent of differential equations in science and engineering, then inventing new calculi is exactly what we should be doing to characterize different problem domains more completely.

Armando Haeberer: I agree with Sintzoff that for the same fundamental relational calculus we have seen about 50 versions, or something like that. I think we need to do some work on standardization.

Jim Boyle: I think we have not adequately conveyed outside our group the fact that our techniques can address the possibility of creating and implementing domain specific languages much more economically. We can write transformations to calculate the implementation of such languages quite easily, and that is something we should convey.

4

A Calculational Fusion System HYLO

Y. Onoue[†], *Z. Hu*[†], *H. Iwasaki*[‡], *and M. Takeichi*[†]
†*Department of Information Engineering, University of Tokyo*
Email: {onoue,hu,takeichi}@ipl.t.u-tokyo.ac.jp
‡*Department of Computer Science*
Tokyo University of Agriculture and Technology
Email: iwasaki@ipl.ei.tuat.ac.jp

Abstract

Fusion, one of the most useful transformation tactics for deriving efficient programs, is the process whereby separate pieces of programs are fused into a single one, leading to an efficient program without intermediate data structures produced. In this paper, we report our on-going investigation on the design and implementation of an automatic transformation system HYLO which performs fusion transformation in a more systematic and more general way than any other systems. The distinguished point of our system is its *calculational* feature based on simple application of transformation laws rather than traditional search-based transformations.

Keywords

Program Calculation, Fusion, Bird-Meertens Formalisms

1 INTRODUCTION

Program transformation has been advocated as the linchpin of a programming paradigm in which the derivation of efficient programs from naive specification of problems is a formal and mechanically supported process (Pettorossi & Proietti 1993). It does not attempt to directly produce a program that is correct, understandable and efficient. Instead, it starts with a program (specification) which is as clear and understandable as possible ignoring any question of efficiency, and successively transforms it to more and more efficient versions based on a set of transformation *tactics*.

Fusion Transformation (or *Fusion* for short), one of such most useful transformation tactics for deriving efficient programs, is the process whereby separate pieces of programs are fused into a single one, typically transforming a multi-pass program into a single pass and thus leading to an efficient program without intermediate data structures. Recently, it has been gaining more and more interest in the functional programming community (Wadler 1988, Chin

1992, Gill, Launchbury & Jones 1993, Takano & Meijer 1995, Hu, Iwasaki & Takeichi 1996*b*).

The purpose of this paper is to report our on-going investigation on the design and implementation of an automatic system HYLO which implements fusion transformation in a more systematic and general way than any other transformation systems. To explain our idea, consider the following example program (Wadler 1988): computing the sum of the squares of the integers from 1 to n.

$$ssf\ n = (sum \circ map\, square \circ upto)\,(1, n)$$

It is defined as a composition of three recursive functions: *upto* generates a list of numbers from 1 to n, *map square* forms the second list by squaring each number in the first list, and *sum* calculates the sum of the numbers in the second list.

This program has the advantage of clarity and higher level of modularity. It constructs the program ssf by gluing three components: "generate the numbers," "square the numbers," and "calculate the sum," which are relatively simple, easy to write, and potentially reusable. However, it relies on the use of intermediate lists to communicate between these components: $upto\,(1, n)$ passes the list $[1, 2, \cdots, n]$ to *map square*, which passes the list $[1, 4, \cdots, n^2]$ to *sum*. Unfortunately, all these intermediate lists need to be produced, traversed, and discarded (even by lazy evaluation), degrading execution time and space dreadfully. To obtain an efficient program, it is our hope that three component functions can be merged into a single one eliminating intermediate data structures. This is exactly what fusion aims to do.

There are mainly two kinds of approaches to fusion transformation: *search-based fusion* and *calculational fusion*. The traditional search-based fusion (Wadler 1988, Chin 1992) turns the composition of recursive functions into a simple function by *fold-unfold* transformations (Burstall & Darlington 1977). For our example, it unfolds recursive definitions of functions *upto*, *map square* and *sum* to some extent, manipulates the expression, and identifies suitable places where subexpressions are to be folded into corresponding function applications. It is called "search-based" because it basically has to keep track of all occurring function calls and introduce function definitions to be searched in the folding step. The process of keeping track of function calls and controlling the steps cleverly to avoid infinite unfolding introduces substantial cost and complexity, which prevents fusion from being practically implemented (Gill et al. 1993).

Our interest is in the calculational fusion (Sheard & Fegaras 1993, Gill et al. 1993, Takano & Meijer 1995, Launchbury & Sheard 1995, Hu et al. 1996*b*, Hu, Iwasaki & Takeichi 1996*c*), which is rather new and has been attracting more and more attention. Different from the search-based fusion whose emphasis is on the transformation process, its emphasis is on the exploration of recursive constructs in each component function so that fusion can be performed directly by applying a simple transformation law: the *Acid Rain Theorem* (Gill et al. 1993, Takano & Meijer 1995). Returning to our example program ssf, let us explain briefly how to fuse the composition part, $sum \circ map\,square \circ upto$, with this approach while leaving the detailed discussions for later.

1. *Deriving Hylomorphisms from Recursive Definitions*
   First of all, we need to rewrite every component recursive function in terms of a specific recursive form called *hylomorphism* (Section 2) represented by a triplet ϕ, η and ψ grouped with special brackets as $[\![\phi, \eta, \psi]\!]$. In fact, almost all recursive functions of interest can be captured by hylomorphisms (Bird & de Moor 1994), and we have proposed an algorithm for deriving hylomorphisms from recursive definitions of functions (Hu et al. 1996*b*). After deriving hylomorphisms for *sum*, *map square* and *upto*, we have the following compositional expression in which each hylomorphism corresponds to the component function:

   $$[\![\phi_1, \eta_1, \psi_1]\!] \circ [\![\phi_2, \eta_2, \psi_2]\!] \circ [\![\phi_3, \eta_3, \psi_3]\!].$$

2. *Capturing Data Production and Consumption Schemes*
   For a composition of two hylomorphisms, there is a useful law called *Acid Rain Theorem* (see Section 2) which says that a composition of two hylomorphisms can be fused into a single one under certain conditions. The theorem expects ϕ and ψ in $[\![\phi, \eta, \psi]\!]$ to be specified as $\tau\, in$ and $\sigma\, out$ respectively. Here, in denotes data constructors and out data destructors. Functions τ and σ are polymorphic and used to capture the scheme of production and consumption of data structures. For the application of the Acid Rain Theorem, we have to derive τ_i and σ_i for some ϕ_i and ψ_i respectively, giving the following expression:

   $$[\![\phi_1, \eta_1, \sigma_1\, out]\!] \circ [\![\tau_2\, in, \eta_2, \sigma_2\, out']\!] \circ [\![\tau_3\, in', \eta_3, \psi_3]\!]$$

3. *Applying Acid Rain Theorem*
   After the preparation by Steps 1 and 2, we can apply the Acid Rain Theorem for fusion. By fusing the latter composition of our example, the program becomes:

   $$[\![\phi_1, \eta_1, \sigma_1\, out]\!] \circ [\![\phi_2', \eta_2', \psi_2']\!].$$

   Repeating Step 2 and 3 to the above composition could yield a single hylomorphism

   $$[\![\phi_1', \eta_1', \psi_1']\!].$$

4. ***Inlining Resulting Hylomorphism***
   Finally, we can inline the resulting hylomorphism into our familiar recursive definition as shown below, removing inefficiency due to hylomorphic structure.

$$\begin{array}{lll} ssf\ n & = & ssf'\ (1,n) \\ & & \text{where} \\ & & ssf'\ (m,n) = \text{case}\ (m > n)\ \text{of} \\ & & \qquad\qquad\qquad True \to 0 \\ & & \qquad\qquad\qquad False \to plus\ (square\ m, ssf'\ (m+1,n)) \end{array}$$

   It is obviously more efficient than the original because all intermediate lists have been successfully eliminated.

The calculational approach has been argued to be more practical (Gill et al. 1993, Takano & Meijer 1995), but to the best of our knowledge, there are no practical fusion systems based on this approach. The difficulties in the design and implementation of a real fusion system lie in two aspects:

- *Development of Constructive Algorithms for Implementing Transformation Laws.* Program calculation, i.e., calculation with programs, is a kind of program transformation which proceeds by means of program manipulation based on a rich collection of transformation laws. These laws, however, are basically developed as a guidance to calculate with programs by hands (not by machine) and most of them are not constructive. Therefore, to implement an automatic calculational fusion system, we must develop *constructive algorithms* for implementing those non-constructive transformation laws (see Section 4.3).
- *Implementation Issues for Practical Use.* In the design and implementation of a practical fusion system, we have to take account of a lot of practical issues. In particular, we should focus on specification *language design*, which should not only be convenient to specify problems but also be general and sufficiently powerful, and *algorithm design*, which should be as much applicable as possible to of a considerable scale programs rather than just some toy examples.

In this paper, we report our on-going investigation on the design and implementation of an automatic system HYLO which performs fusion transformation based on calculational method. Our main contributions are summarized as follows. First, we made the first attempt to apply the idea of a calculational approach to the implementation of a transformation system, not just being limited to theoretical interest, which is in sharp contrast to previous search-based approaches. This work extends our previous work on developing algorithms for implementation of transformation laws. Second, we develop a set of effective algorithms implementing the constructive fusion laws. Third, our HYLO system is a general system which can be applied to a wide class of programs; particularly, it is expected to be used in compilers of functional languages such as Haskell.

The organization of this paper is as follows. After introducing some notations and theoretical results on hylomorphisms in Section 2, we give an overview of the HYLO system in Section 3. Implementation algorithms are presented in Section 4 with transformation examples, and experimental results are given in Section 5. Section 6 gives remarks on the HYLO system and related work.

2 PRELIMINARIES

Recursion plays an important role in function definitions but it does not impose much structure on the form of the definition that may be expressed. Recently, many studies (Meijer, Fokkinga & Paterson 1991, Sheard & Fegaras 1993) have shown that recursion should be structured with some specific forms. The hylomorphism is one such specific recursive form which can describe almost all recursive functions of interest (Meijer et al. 1991, Bird & de Moor 1994, Hu et al. 1996*b*). Informally, by hylomorphism, a function should be defined in the following recursive way:

$$f = \phi \circ (\eta \circ F\, f) \circ \psi.$$

We can read the right hand side in this way: generating some F-structure from the input by ψ; applying f to all recursive components in the F-structure by $F\, f$; manipulating the F-structure into some G-structure by η; and finaly folding the G-structure by ϕ to give the result. Since f can be uniquely determined whenever ϕ, η, ψ, G and F are determined, we usually denote f by $f = [\![\phi, \eta, \psi]\!]_{G,F}$.

Hylomorphisms enjoy many useful calculational laws (see Section 2.3), facilitating program transformation. To be more precise, we shall review previous works on program calculation (Meijer et al. 1991, Fokkinga 1992, Takano & Meijer 1995).

2.1 Functors

Endofunctors can capture both data structure and control structure in a type definition. In this paper, we assume that all data types are defined by endofunctors which are only built up by the following four basic functors. Such endofunctors are known as ***polynomial functors***.

- The **identity** functor I on type X and its operation on functions are defined as follows.

  $I\ X = X, \quad I\ f = f$

- The **constant** functor $!A$ on type X and its operation on functions are defined as follows.

  $!A\ X = A, \quad !A\ f = id$

  where id stands for the identity function.

- The **product** $X \times Y$ of two types X and Y and its operation to functions are defined as follows.

$$
\begin{array}{lcl}
X \times Y & = & \{(x, y) \mid x \in X,\ y \in Y\} \\
(f \times g)\ (x, y) & = & (f\,x,\ g\,y) \\
\pi_1\ (a, b) & = & a \\
\pi_2\ (a, b) & = & b \\
(f \vartriangle g)\ a & = & (f\,a,\ g\,a)
\end{array}
$$

- The **separated sum** $X + Y$ of two types X and Y and its operation to functions are defined as follows.

$$
\begin{array}{lcl}
X + Y & = & \{1\} \times X \cup \{2\} \times Y \\
(f + g)\ (1, x) & = & (1,\ f\,x) \\
(f + g)\ (2, y) & = & (2,\ g\,y) \\
(f \triangledown g)\ (1, x) & = & f\,x \\
(f \triangledown g)\ (2, y) & = & g\,y.
\end{array}
$$

Although the product and the separated sum are defined over two parameters, they can be naturally extended for n parameters. For example, the separated sum over n parameters can be defined by $\Sigma_{i=1}^{n} X_i = \cup_{i=1}^{n}(\{\mathrm{i}\} \times X_i)$ and $(\Sigma_{i=1}^{n} f_i)\ (\mathrm{j}, x) = (\mathrm{j},\ f_j\,x)$ for $1 \leq \mathrm{j} \leq n$.

2.2 Data Types as Initial Fixed Points of Functors

A data type is a collection of data constructors specifying how each element of the data type can be constructed in a finite way. The definition of a data type can be captured by an endofunctor (Fokkinga 1992). Let's look at a concrete example. Consider the data type of ***cons lists*** with elements of type A, which is usually defined by

$$List\ A = Nil\ \mid Cons\,(A,\ List\ A).$$

In our framework, we shall use the following polynomial functor to capture the recursive structure of the data type:

$$F_{L_A} = \ !\mathbf{1}\ +\ !A \times I$$

where **1** denotes the final object, corresponding to (). Strictly speaking, *Nil* should be written as the 0-ary constructor *Nil* (). In this paper, the form of *t* () will be simply denoted as *t*.

In fact, the definition of F_{L_A} can be automatically derived from the original definition of *List A* (Sheard & Fegaras 1993). Besides, we define $in_{F_{L_A}}$, the *data constructor* of *List A*, by

$$in_{F_{L_A}} = Nil \triangledown Cons.$$

It follows that $List\ A = in_{F_{L_A}}\ (F_{L_A}\ (List\ A))$. The inverse of $in_{F_{L_A}}$ is denoted by $out_{F_{L_A}}$, the *data destructor* of *List A*, i.e.,

$$\begin{array}{lcl} out_{F_{L_A}}\ Nil & = & (1, ()) \\ out_{F_{L_A}}\ (Cons\,(a, as)) & = & (2, (a, as)). \end{array}$$

As another example, the data type of the binary trees declared by

$$Tree\ a \ = \ Leaf \mid Node\ (a, Tree\ a, Tree\ a),$$

is captured by the following endofunctor:

$$F_T \ = \ !\mathbf{1} \ + \ !a \times I \times I.$$

In general, functor F determines a data type as its least fixed point, so we denote μF as the data type determined by F.

2.3 Hylomorphisms

The hylomorphism, a general recursive form covering the well-known *catamorphism* and *anamorphism* as its special cases, is defined in triplet form (Takano & Meijer 1995) as follows.

Definition 1 (Hylomorphism in triplet form)
Let F and G be two functors. Given $\phi : G\,A \to A$, $\psi : B \to F\,B$ and natural transformation $\eta : F \dot{\to} G$, the hylomorphism $[\![\phi, \eta, \psi]\!]_{G,F} : B \to A$ is defined as the least fixed point of the following equation.

$$f = \phi \circ \eta \circ F\,f \circ \psi$$ □

Hylomorphisms (Hylo for short) are powerful in description in that practically every recursion of interest (e.g., primitive recursions) can be specified by them (Hu et al. 1996*b*). They are considered to be an ideal recursive form for calculating efficient functional programs. Note that we sometimes omit the subscripts G and F when they are clear from the context.

Hylomorphisms are quite general in that many useful forms are their special cases.

Definition 2 (Catamorphism $(\![-]\!)$, Anamorphism $[\!(-)\!]$)

$$\begin{array}{lcl} (\![\phi]\!)_F & = & [\![\phi, id, out_F]\!]_{F,F} \\ [\!(\psi)\!]_F & = & [\![in_F, id, \psi]\!]_{F,F} \end{array}$$ □

Hylomorphisms enjoy many useful transformation laws. One is called *Hylo Shift Law*:

$$[\![\phi,\eta,\psi]\!]_{G,F} = [\![\phi \circ \eta, id, \psi]\!]_{F,F} = [\![\phi, id, \eta \circ \psi]\!]_{G,G}$$

showing the very useful property that a natural transformation can be shifted around inside a hylomorphism. Another useful law is the *Acid Rain Theorem* (Takano & Meijer 1995), showing how to fuse a composition of two hylomorphisms into a single one.

Theorem 1 (Acid Rain)

$$(a)\quad \frac{\tau : \forall A.\ (F\,A \to A) \to F'\,A \to A}{[\![\phi,\eta_1,out_F]\!]_{G,F} \circ [\![\tau in_F,\eta_2,\psi]\!]_{F',L} = [\![\tau(\phi \circ \eta_1),\eta_2,\psi]\!]_{F',L}}$$

$$(b)\quad \frac{\sigma : \forall A.\ (A \to F\,A) \to A \to F'\,A}{[\![\phi,\eta_1,\sigma out_F]\!]_{G,F'} \circ [\![in_F,\eta_2,\psi]\!]_{F,L} = [\![\phi,\eta_1,\sigma(\eta_2 \circ \psi)]\!]_{G,F'}}$$ □

3 OVERVIEW OF HYLO SYSTEM

Figure 1 shows a schematic overview of our HYLO transformation system. This system is written in a functional language Gofer (Jones 1994), and can easily be ported to other systems such as Haskell. The HYLO system receives a program written in Gofer and returns an improved one as its result where the production of intermediate data structures has been removed by means of fusion transformation.

The front-end of the system does several standard preprocesses such as parsing, renaming, type checking and de-sugaring before producing a program in the core language that will be used hereafter in the transformation steps.

The core language is shown in Figure 2. It is similar to that used by the GHC (Team 1996) system. The main difference between these two languages

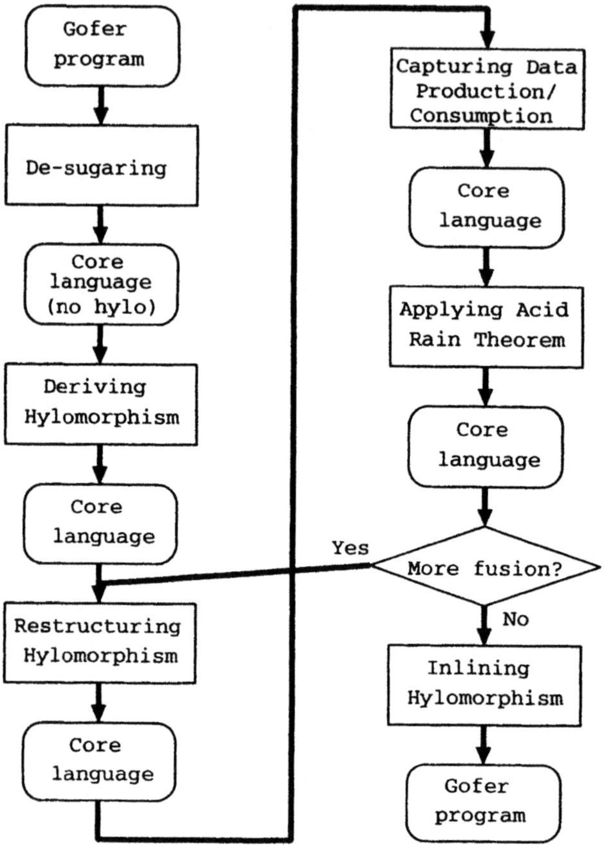

Figure 1 Overview of HYLO System

is that ours has an extra kind of expression for hylomorphism, which plays an important role in fusion transformation. In order to simplify our presentation, we restrict ourselves to single-recursive data types and functions without mutual recursions, since the standard tupling technique can transform mutual recursive definitions to non-mutual ones. Furthermore, we do not allow nested case expressions because they can easily be flattened.

The next step of our transformation process is to receive a program written in the core language and derive hylomorphisms from all the recursive function definitions. As we explained in Section 2.3, a hylomorphism is a representation of a specific form of recursive structure and is manipulable by applying the Acid Rain Theorem. In Section 4.1, we describe the algorithm for deriving hylomorphisms in detail.

We then restructure hylomorphisms to obtain proper hylo-structures suitable for fusion. As the Hylo Shift Law shows, we are allowed to shift some parts of the components of $[\![\phi, \eta, \psi]\!]$ among each other. Our algorithm extracts computations from ϕ and ψ and moves them to the η component. This

$Prog$	::=	$Def; Prog \mid Def$	Program
Def	::=	$v = t$	Definition (non-mutual)
t	::=	v	Variable
	$\mid$	l	Literal (Int,Float,Char,...)
	$\mid$	$(t_1, \cdots, t_n)$	Term tuple
	$\mid$	$\lambda v_s . t$	Lambda expression
	$\mid$	let $v = t_1$ in t_0	Let expression (non-recursive)
	$\mid$	case t_0 of $p_1 \rightarrow t_1; \cdots; p_n \rightarrow t_n$	Case expression
	$\mid$	$v\, t_1 \cdots t_n$	Function application (saturated)
	$\mid$	$C\, t_1 \cdots t_n$	Constructor application (saturated)
	$\mid$	$t_0\, t_1$	Application (general)
	$\mid$	$[\![t_\phi, t_\eta, t_\psi]\!]$	Hylo representation
	$\mid$	(n, t)	Expression with tag
v_s	::=	$v \mid (v_1, \cdots, v_n)$	Argument bounded by λ
p	::=	v	Variable
	$\mid$	$(p_1, \cdots, p_n)$	Tuple
	$\mid$	$C\, p_1 \cdots p_n$	Constructor pattern

Figure 2 HYLO Core Language

process simplifies the ϕ and ψ components to make the next step of transformation easier. In Section 4.2, we fully explain the algorithm for restructuring hylomorphisms.

What we should do next is to prepare for applying the Acid Rain Theorem in order to proceed fusion transformation. We may consider that ϕ and ψ express data production and consumption respectively. For our goal, ϕ and ψ should be converted to the specific forms of τin_F and σout_F for the Acid Rain Theorem to be applicable. The algorithms are presented in Section 4.3.

Now we are ready to apply the Acid Rain Theorem to the result, fusing two hylomorphisms into a single one. This process terminates even if we apply the theorem repeatedly. If there are no fusible hylomorphisms left in the program, we proceed to the next step for inlining. Otherwise, we go back to the restructuring step. In Section 4.4, we describe how the fusion is put into action.

Finally, the hylomorphism representation is inlined into our familiar recursive definitions to get a Gofer program. This inlining process plays the role of the back-end of the system. If we replace the front-end and back-end with those of the practical compiler system, we have a compiler with hylo-fusion optimization.

4 IMPLEMENTATION ALGORITHMS

In this section, we propose several important algorithms for the implementation of the HYLO system. Particularly we shall focus on the algorithms for deriving polymorphic functions for capturing data consumption and construction. The algorithms for deriving and restructuring hylomorphisms are some extensions of those already discussed in (Hu et al. 1996*b*).

4.1 Deriving Hylomorphisms

We extend the algorithm in (Hu et al. 1996*b*) to derive hylomorphisms from recursive definitions, enabling it to be applied to programs in the core language, more general than the previous one with several new expression constructs. Our algorithm, as summarized in Figure 3, basically follows the same thought as in (Hu et al. 1996*b*). We shall omit any detailed description here, but give an informal explanation for understanding the derivation process. The calculation below shows how we can turn the typical recursive definition of function f in pattern matching style:

$$f = \lambda v_s.\ \text{case}\ t_0\ \text{of}\ p_1 \rightarrow t_1; \cdots; p_n \rightarrow t_n$$

into a hylomorphism.

$$
\begin{array}{ll}
f = & \quad \{\text{Definition of } f\} \\
 & \lambda v_s.\ \text{case}\ t_0\ \text{of}\ p_1 \rightarrow t_1; \cdots; p_n \rightarrow t_n \\
= & \quad \{\text{Trick 1: Replacing } t_i \text{ with } g_i\ t_i'\} \\
 & \lambda v_s.\ \text{case}\ t_0\ \text{of}\ p_1 \rightarrow g_1\ t_1'; \cdots; p_n \rightarrow g_n\ t_n' \\
= & \quad \{\text{Using separated sum}\} \\
 & (g_1 \triangledown \cdots \triangledown g_n) \circ (\lambda v_s.\ \text{case}\ t_0\ \text{of}\ p_1 \rightarrow (1,\ t_1'); \cdots; p_n \rightarrow (\mathsf{n},\ t_n')) \\
= & \quad \{\text{Trick 2: Replacing } g_i \text{ with } \phi_i \circ F_i\ f\} \\
 & (\phi_1 \triangledown \cdots \triangledown \phi_n) \circ ((F_1 + \cdots + F_n)\ f) \circ \\
 & \quad (\lambda v_s.\ \text{case}\ t_0\ \text{of}\ p_1 \rightarrow (1,\ t_1'); \cdots; p_n \rightarrow (\mathsf{n},\ t_n')) \\
= & \quad \{\text{Auxiliary definitions } \phi, F, \text{and } \psi\} \\
 & \phi \circ F\ f \circ \psi \\
= & \quad \{\text{Definition of hylomorphism}\} \\
 & [\![\phi, id, \psi]\!]_{F,F} \\
 & \text{where } F = F_1 + \cdots + F_n \\
 & \qquad \phi = \phi_1 \triangledown \cdots \triangledown \phi_n \\
 & \qquad \psi = \lambda v_s.\ \text{case}\ t_0\ \text{of}\ p_1 \rightarrow (1,\ t_1'); \cdots; p_n \rightarrow (\mathsf{n},\ t_n')
\end{array}
$$

Tricks 1 and 2 suggest that if we can find ϕ_i, F_i, t_i' satisfying $t_i = (\phi_i \circ F_i\ f)\ t_i'$ for each t_i, a hylomorphism can be derived from the definition. This derivation heavily depends on Algorithm $\mathcal{D}$ which processes on each term t_i and returns a triple: a set of free variables in t_i but not in any recursive call to f, a set of pairs of a fresh variable and an argument of f in t_i, and a term from t_i

$$
\begin{aligned}
&\mathcal{A}[\![\lambda v_{s_1} \cdots \lambda v_{s_m} .\ \text{case } t_0 \text{ of } p_1 \to t_1; \cdots; p_n \to t_n]\!]\, f \\
&\quad = \lambda v_{s_1} \cdots \lambda v_{s_{m-1}} . [\![\phi_1 \triangledown \cdots \triangledown \phi_n, id, \psi]\!]_{F,F} \\
&\quad \textbf{where } (\{v_{i_1}, \ldots, v_{i_{k_i}}\}, \{(v'_{i_1}, t_{i_1}), \cdots, (v'_{i_{l_i}}, t_{i_{l_i}})\}, t'_i) = \mathcal{D}[\![t_i]\!]\, \{\}\, f\ (i = 1, \ldots, n) \\
&\qquad \phi_i = \lambda(v_{i_1}, \ldots, v_{i_{k_i}}, v'_{i_1}, \ldots, v'_{i_{l_i}}).\ t'_i \\
&\qquad t''_i = (v_{i_1}, \ldots, v_{i_{k_i}}, t_{i_1}, \ldots, t_{i_{l_i}}) \\
&\qquad \psi = \lambda v_{s_m}.\text{case } t_0 \text{ of } p_1 \to (1, t''_1); \cdots; p_n \to (\mathsf{n}, t''_n) \\
&\qquad F_i = !1, \text{ if } k_i = l_i = 0 \\
&\qquad\quad\ = !\Gamma(v_{i_1}) \times \cdots \times !\Gamma(v_{i_{k_i}}) \times I_1 \times \cdots \times I_{l_i}\ \ (I_1 = \cdots = I_{l_i} = I), \text{ otherwise} \\
&\qquad F = F_1 + \cdots + F_n \\
&\qquad \Gamma(v) = \text{return } v\text{'s type}
\end{aligned}
$$

$$
\begin{aligned}
\mathcal{D}[\![v]\!]\, s_l\, f &= \text{if } v \in \mathit{global\_vars} \cup s_l \text{ then } (\{\}, \{\}, v) \text{ else } (\{v\}, \{\}, v) \\
\mathcal{D}[\![l]\!]\, s_l\, f &= (\{\}, \{\}, l) \\
\mathcal{D}[\![(t_1, \ldots, t_n)]\!]\, s_l\, f &= (s_1 \cup \cdots \cup s_n, c_1 \cup \cdots \cup c_n, (t'_1, \ldots, t'_n)) \\
&\quad\ \text{where } (s_i, c_i, t'_i) = \mathcal{D}[\![t_i]\!]\, s_l\, f\ (i = 1, \ldots, n) \\
\mathcal{D}[\![\lambda v_s . t]\!]\, s_l\, f &= (s, c, \lambda v_s . t') \\
&\quad\ \text{where } (s, c, t') = \mathcal{D}[\![t]\!]\, (s_l \cup Var(v_s))\, f \\
\mathcal{D}[\![\text{let } v = t_1 \text{ in } t_0]\!]\, s_l\, f &= (s_0 \cup s_1, c_0 \cup c_1, \text{let } v = t'_1 \text{ in } t'_0) \\
&\quad\ \text{where } (s_1, c_1, t'_1) = \mathcal{D}[\![t_1]\!]\, s_l\, f, (s_0, c_0, t'_0) = \mathcal{D}[\![t_0]\!]\, (s_l \cup \{v\})\, f \\
\mathcal{D}[\![\text{case } t_0 \text{ of } p_1 \to t_1 &= (s_0 \cup \cdots \cup s_n, c_0 \cup \cdots \cup c_n, \text{case } t'_0 \text{ of } p_1 \to t'_1; \cdots; p_n \to t'_n) \\
; \cdots ; p_n \to t_n]\!]\, s_l\, f &\quad\ \text{where } (s_i, c_i, t'_i) = \mathcal{D}[\![t_i]\!] (s_l \cup Var(p_i)) f\ (i = 0, \ldots, n), p_0 = () \\
\mathcal{D}[\![v\ t_1 \cdots t_n]\!]\, s_l\, f &= \text{if } v = f \text{ then} \\
&\qquad \text{if } n = m\ \wedge\ t_i = v_{s_i}\ (1 \le \forall i \le m-1) \\
&\qquad \text{then } (\{\}, \{(u, t_m)\}, u) \\
&\qquad \text{else } \mathit{error}\ (f \text{ should have saturated args and induct on last}) \\
&\quad\ \text{else } (s_0 \cup \cdots \cup s_n, c_0 \cup \cdots \cup c_n, t'_0\ t'_1 \cdots t'_n) \\
&\quad\ \text{where } (s_0, c_0, t'_0) = \mathcal{D}[\![v]\!]\, s_l\, f \\
&\qquad\qquad (s_i, c_i, t'_i) = \mathcal{D}[\![t_i]\!]\, s_l\, f, (i = 1, \ldots, n) \\
&\qquad\qquad u \text{ is a fresh variable} \\
\mathcal{D}[\![C\ t_1 \cdots t_n]\!]\, s_l\, f &= (s_1 \cup \cdots \cup s_n, c_1 \cup \cdots \cup c_n, C\ t'_1 \cdots t'_n) \\
&\quad\ \text{where } (s_i, c_i, t'_i) = \mathcal{D}[\![t_i]\!]\, s_l\, f\ (i = 1, \ldots, n) \\
\mathcal{D}[\![t_0\ t_1]\!]\, s_l\, f &= (s_0 \cup s_1, c_0 \cup c_1, t'_0\ t'_1)) \\
&\quad\ \text{where } (s_i, c_i, t'_i) = \mathcal{D}[\![t_i]\!]\, s_l\, f\ (i = 1, 2) \\
Var(x) &= \text{set of variables in } x
\end{aligned}
$$

Figure 3 Deriving Hylomorphism

with recursive calls to f being replaced by the corresponding fresh variables. It is worth noting that we require, without loss of generality, that function f inducts over its last argument, while the other arguments remain unchanged in every recursive call to f. Note also that Algorithm $\mathcal{A}$ is applied to programs after the renaming process has been done, so all bound variables have been assigned unique names.

We demonstrate how this algorithm works on the example program ssf in Section 1. ssf uses functions sum, map, and $upto$ which are defined in pattern matching way as:

$$\begin{array}{lcl} sum & = & \lambda xs.\ \text{case } xs \text{ of } Nil \rightarrow 0 \\ & & \qquad\qquad\qquad Cons\ (a, as) \rightarrow plus\ (a, sum\ as) \\ map & = & \lambda g.\ \lambda xs.\text{case } xs \text{ of } Nil \rightarrow Nil \\ & & \qquad\qquad\qquad Cons\ (a, as) \rightarrow Cons\ (g\ a,\ map\ g\ as) \\ upto & = & \lambda(m, n).\ \text{case } (m > n) \text{ of } True \rightarrow Nil \\ & & \qquad\qquad\qquad False \rightarrow Cons\ (m, upto\ (m+1, n)). \end{array}$$

We pick up sum from these definitions, and apply Algorithm $\mathcal{A}$ which in turn calls Algorithm $\mathcal{D}$. We have

$$\begin{array}{rcl} \mathcal{D}[\![0]\!]\ \{\}\ sum & = & (\{\}, \{\}, 0) \\ \mathcal{D}[\![plus\ (a, sum\ as)]\!]\ \{\}\ sum & = & (\{a\}, \{(v'_1, sum\ as)\}, plus\ (a, v'_1)) \end{array}$$

with

$$\begin{array}{ll} t'_1 = (), & \phi_1 = \lambda().\ 0 = 0 \\ t'_2 = (a, as), & \phi_2 = \lambda(a, v'_1).\ plus\ (a, v'_1) = plus \end{array}$$

and

$$\begin{array}{lcl} \psi & = & \lambda xs.\ \text{case } xs \text{ of } Nil \rightarrow (1, ()) \\ & & \qquad\qquad Cons\ (a, as) \rightarrow (2, (a, as)) \\ & = & out_F \\ F & = & !1 + !Int \times I. \end{array}$$

So we have derived the following hylomorphism for sum:

$$sum \quad = \quad [\![0 \triangledown plus, id, out_F]\!]_{F,F}.$$

Similarly we can derive hylomorphisms for map and $upto$ as follows.

$$\begin{array}{lcl} map & = & \lambda g.\ [\![\phi, id, out_F]\!]_{F,F} \\ & & \text{where } \phi = \lambda().\ Nil \triangledown \lambda(v, v').\ Cons\ (g\ v, v') \\ upto & = & [\![in_F, id, \psi]\!]_{F,F} \\ & & \text{where } \psi = \lambda(m, n).\ \text{case } (m > n) \text{ of} \\ & & \qquad\qquad True \rightarrow (1, ()) \\ & & \qquad\qquad False \rightarrow (2, (m, (m+1, n))) \end{array}$$

where

$$\begin{array}{lcl} F & = & !1 + !Int \times I \ (= F_{L_{Int}}) \\ in_F & = & Nil \triangledown Cons \\ out_F & = & \lambda xs.\ \text{case } xs \text{ of } Nil \to (1, ()) \\ & & \qquad\qquad Cons\,(a, as) \to (2, (a, as)) \end{array}$$

4.2 Restructuring Hylomorphisms

Generally, the behavior of a hylomorphism $[\![\phi, \eta, \psi]\!]_{G,F}$ could be understood as follows: ψ generates a recursive structure, η transforms one structure into another, and ϕ manipulates on the resulting recursive structure. It is possible that the ϕ and ψ contains the computation which η can do. The aim of restructuring is to extract as much computation as possible from ϕ and ψ and move it to η. This simplifies ϕ and ψ and makes the derivation of the data production and consumption schemes τ and σ easier in the next stage. A basic restructuring algorithm for the ϕ component is given in (Hu et al. 1996*b*) and an extended version of the algorithm is shown in Figure 4. The restructuring algorithm for the ψ component is shown in Figure 5, which was omitted in (Hu et al. 1996*b*).

Algorithm $\mathcal{S}_\phi$ to restructure $\phi = \phi_1 \triangledown \cdots \triangledown \phi_n$ applies an auxiliary algorithm $\mathcal{E}$ to the bodies t_i of lambda expressions ϕ_i. Algorithm $\mathcal{E}$ detects maximal subterms in each t_i without recursive variables and generates a new term t'_i with these subterms substituted by new variables, and $\mathcal{S}_\phi$ makes it as a body of a new lambda expression ϕ'_i. In more detail, the algorithm $\mathcal{E}$ accepts as input a term t_i and a set of *recursive* variables and returns as result a pair: a set of maximal subterms containing no recursive variables with corresponding fresh variables, and a new term from t_i with these subterms substituted by corresponding fresh variables. The computations related to these subterms are then moved to the η component.

As an example, we will restructure the following hylomorphism obtained in the previous section.

$$map\ g = [\![Nil \triangledown \lambda(a, v'_1).\ Cons\,(g\,a, v'_1), id, out]\!]$$

In this case, $\phi_1 = \lambda().\ Nil$ and $\phi_2 = \lambda(a, v'_1).\ Cons\,(\underline{g\,a}, v'_1)$. Here v'_1 is a recursive variable and there is only one maximal non-recursive subterm as underlined. Our algorithm will move $g\,a$ out of ϕ_2 as

$$\begin{array}{l} \phi_2 = \phi'_2 \circ \eta_{\phi_2} \\ \quad \text{where } \phi'_2 = \lambda(u_{2_1}, v'_1).\ Cons(u_{2_1}, v'_1) \\ \qquad\qquad \eta_{\phi_2} = \lambda(a, v'_1).\ (g\,a, v'_1) \end{array}$$

$$\mathcal{S}_\phi[\![[\![\phi_1 \triangledown \cdots \triangledown \phi_n, \eta, \psi]\!]_{G,F}]\!] = [\![\phi'_1 \triangledown \cdots \triangledown \phi'_n, (\eta_{\phi_1} + \cdots + \eta_{\phi_n}) \circ \eta, \psi]\!]_{G',F}$$

where

$$\begin{array}{l}
G_1 + \cdots + G_n = G \\
!\Gamma(v_{i_1}) \times \cdots \times !\Gamma(v_{i_{k_i}}) \times I_1 \times \cdots \times I_{l_i} = G_i \\
\lambda(v_{i_1}, \ldots, v_{i_{k_i}}, v'_{i_1}, \ldots, v'_{i_{l_i}}).\ t_i = \phi_i \ (\text{assume} v'_{i_1}, \ldots, v'_{i_{l_i}} \text{ are recursive variables}) \\
(\{(u_{i_1}, t_{i_1}), \ldots, (u_{i_{m_i}}, t_{i_{m_i}})\}, t'_i) = \mathcal{E}[\![t_i]\!]\{v'_{i_1}, \ldots, v'_{i_{l_i}}\} \\
\eta_{\phi_i} = \lambda(v_{i_1}, \ldots, v_{i_{k_i}}, v'_{i_1}, \ldots, v'_{i_{l_i}}).(t_{i_1}, \ldots, t_{i_{m_i}}, v'_{i_1}, \ldots, v'_{i_{l_i}}) \\
G'_i = !\Gamma(u_{i_1}) \times \cdots \times !\Gamma(u_{i_{m_i}}) \times I_1 \times \cdots \times I_{l_i} \\
G' = G'_1 + \cdots + G'_n \\
\phi'_i = \lambda\,(u_{i_1}, \ldots, u_{i_{m_i}}, v'_{i_1}, \ldots, v'_{i_{l_i}}).\ t'_i
\end{array}$$

Assume that u is a fresh variable in the following:

$$\begin{array}{rcl}
\mathcal{E}[\![v]\!]\, s_r & = & \text{if } Var_{s_r}(v) \text{ then } (\{(u, v)\}, u) \text{ else } (\{\}, v) \\
\mathcal{E}[\![l]\!]\, s_r & = & (\{(u, l)\}, u) \\
\mathcal{E}[\![(t_1, \ldots, t_n)]\!]\, s_r & = & \text{if } \forall i. Var_{s_r}(t'_i) \text{ then } (\{(u, (t_1, \ldots, t_n))\}, u) \\
& & \quad \text{else } (w_1 \cup \cdots \cup w_n, (t'_1, \ldots, t'_n)) \\
& & \text{where } (w_i, t'_i) = \mathcal{E}[\![t_i]\!]\, s_r \ (i = 1, \ldots, n), \\
\mathcal{E}[\![\lambda v.t]\!]\, s_r & = & \text{if } Var_{s_r}(t') \text{ then } (\{(u,\ \lambda v.t)\}, u) \text{ else } (w, \lambda v.t') \\
& & \text{where } (w, t') = \mathcal{E}[\![t]\!]\, s_r \\
\mathcal{E}[\![\text{let } v = t_1 \text{ in } t_0]\!]\, s_r & = & \text{if } Var_{s_r}(t'_0) \wedge Var_{s_r}(t'_1) \text{ then } (\{(u, \text{let } v = t_1 \text{ in } t_0)\}, u) \\
& & \qquad\qquad\qquad \text{else } (w_0 \cup w_1, \text{let } v = t'_1 \text{ in } t'_0) \\
& & \text{where } (w_1, t'_1) = \mathcal{E}[\![t_1]\!]\, s_r,\ \ (w_0, t'_0) = \mathcal{E}[\![t_0]\!]\, s_r \\
\mathcal{E}[\![\text{case } t_0 \text{ of } p_1 \to t_1 & = & \text{if } \forall i. Var_{s_r}(t'_i) \text{ then } (\{(u, \text{case } t_0 \text{ of } p_1 \to t_1; \cdots; p_n \to t_n)\}, u) \\
;\cdots; p_n \to t_n]\!]\, s_r & & \quad \text{else } (w_0 \cup \cdots \cup w_n, \text{case } t'_0 \text{ of } p_1 \to t'_1; \cdots; p_n \to t'_n) \\
& & \text{where } (w_i, t'_i) = \mathcal{E}[\![t_i]\!]\, s_r \ (i = 0, \ldots, n), \\
\mathcal{E}[\![v\ t_1 \cdots t_n]\!]\, s_r & = & \text{if } \forall i. Var_{s_r}(t'_i) \text{ then } (\{(u, v\ t_1 \cdots t_n)\}, u) \\
& & \qquad\qquad \text{else } (w_0 \cup \cdots \cup w_n, t'_0\ t'_1 \cdots, t'_n) \\
& & \text{where } (w_0, t'_0) = \mathcal{E}[\![v]\!]\, s_r,\ \ (w_i, t'_i) = \mathcal{E}[\![t_i]\!]\, s_r \ (i = 1, \ldots, n), \\
\mathcal{E}[\![C\ t_1 \cdots t_n]\!]\, s_r & = & \text{if } \forall i. Var_{s_r}(t'_i) \text{ then } (\{(u, C\ t_1 \cdots t_n)\}, u) \\
& & \qquad\qquad \text{else } (w_1 \cup \cdots \cup w_n, C\ t'_1 \cdots t'_n) \\
& & \text{where } (w_i, t'_i) = \mathcal{E}[\![t_i]\!]\, s_r \ (i = 1, \ldots, n), \\
\mathcal{E}[\![t_0\ t_1]\!]\, s_r & = & \text{if } Var_{s_r}(t'_0) \wedge Var_{s_r}(t'_1) \text{ then } (\{(u, t_0\ t_1)\}, u) \\
& & \qquad\qquad\qquad \text{else } (w_0 \cup w_1, t'_0\ t'_1)) \\
& & \text{where } (w_0, t'_0) = \mathcal{E}[\![t_0]\!]\, s_r,\ \ (w_1, t'_1) = \mathcal{E}[\![t_1]\!]\, s_r \\
\mathcal{E}[\![[\![t_0, t_1, t_2]\!]_{F_0,F_1}]\!]\, s_r & = & \text{if } \forall i. Var_{s_r}(t'_i) \text{ then } (\{(u, [\![t_0, t_1, t_2]\!]_{F_0,F_1})\}, u) \\
& & \qquad\qquad \text{else } (w_0 \cup w_1 \cup w_2, [\![t'_0, t'_1, t'_2]\!]_{F_0,F_1})) \\
& & \text{where } (w_i, t'_i) = \mathcal{E}[\![t_i]\!]\, s_r \ (i = 0, 1, 2), \\
\mathcal{E}[\![(\mathsf{n}, t)]\!]\, s_r & = & \text{if } Var_{s_r}(t') \text{ then } (\{(u, (\mathsf{n}, t))\}, u) \text{ else } (w, (\mathsf{n}, t')) \\
& & \text{where } (w, t') = \mathcal{E}[\![t]\!]\, s_r
\end{array}$$

$$Var_{s_r}(t) = t \text{ is a variable } \wedge\ t \notin s_r$$

Figure 4 Restructuring Hylomorphisms — ϕ part

$$\mathcal{S}_\psi[\![\,[\![\phi,\eta,\psi]\!]_{G,F}\,]\!] = [\![\phi,\eta\circ(\eta_{\psi_1}+\cdots+\eta_{\psi_n}),\psi']\!]_{G,F'}$$

where

$$\begin{aligned}
&\lambda\, v_s.\text{case } t_0 \text{ of } p_1 \to (1,t_1);\cdots;p_n \to (\mathsf{n},t_n) = \psi\\
&F_1+\cdots+F_n = F\\
&!\Gamma(t_{i_1})\times\cdots\times !\Gamma(t_{i_{k_i}})\times I_1\times\cdots\times I_{l_i} = F_i\\
&(t_{i_1},\ldots,t_{i_{k_i}},tt_{i_1},\ldots,tt_{i_{l_i}}) = t_i\\
&\{v_{i_1},\ldots,v_{i_{m_i}}\} = \mathcal{FV}[\![(t_{i_1},\ldots,t_{i_{k_i}})]\!]\,\mathit{global_vars}\\
&\eta_{\psi_i} = \lambda(v_{i_1},\ldots,v_{i_{m_i}},v'_{i_1},\ldots,v'_{i_{l_i}}).(t_{i_1},\ldots,t_{i_{k_i}},v'_{i_1},\ldots,v'_{i_{l_i}})\\
&t'_i = (v_{i_1},\ldots,v_{i_{m_i}},tt_{i_1},\ldots,tt_{i_{l_i}})\\
&F'_i = !\Gamma(v_{i_1})\times\cdots\times !\Gamma(v_{i_{m_i}})\times I_1\times\cdots\times I_{l_i}\\
&F' = F'_1+\cdots+F'_n\\
&\psi' = \lambda\, v_s.\text{case } t_0 \text{ of } p_1 \to (1,t'_1);\cdots;p_n \to (\mathsf{n},t'_n)
\end{aligned}$$

$$\begin{aligned}
\mathcal{FV}[\![v]\!]\,s_g &= \text{if } v\in s_g \text{ then } \{\} \text{ else } \{v\}\\
\mathcal{FV}[\![l]\!]\,s_g &= \{\}\\
\mathcal{FV}[\![(t_1,\ldots,t_n)]\!]\,s_g &= s_1\cup\cdots\cup s_n\\
&\quad \text{where } s_i = \mathcal{FV}[\![t_i]\!]\,s_g\ (i=1,\ldots,n)\\
\mathcal{FV}[\![\lambda v.t]\!]\,s_g &= \mathcal{FV}[\![t]\!]\,(s_g\cup\{v\})\\
\mathcal{FV}[\![\text{let } v=t_1 \text{ in } t_0]\!]\,s_g &= s_0\cup s_1\\
&\quad \text{where } s_1 = \mathcal{FV}[\![t_1]\!]\,s_g,\ \ s_t = \mathcal{FV}[\![t_0]\!]\,(s_g\cup\{v\})\\
\mathcal{FV}[\![\text{case } t_0 \text{ of } p_1\to t_1 &= s_0\cup\cdots\cup s_n\\
;\cdots;p_n\to t_n]\!]\,s_g &\quad \text{where } s_i = \mathcal{FV}[\![t_i]\!]\,(s_g\cup Pat(p_i))\ (i=0,\ldots,n),\ \ p_0=()\\
\mathcal{FV}[\![v\ t_1\cdots t_n]\!]\,s_g &= s_0\cup\cdots\cup s_n\\
&\quad \text{where } s_0 = \mathcal{FV}[\![v]\!]\,s_g,\ \ s_i = \mathcal{FV}[\![t_i]\!]\,s_g\ (i=1,\ldots,n)\\
\mathcal{FV}[\![C\ t_1\cdots t_n]\!]\,s_g &= s_1\cup\cdots\cup s_n\\
&\quad \text{where } s_i = \mathcal{FV}[\![t_i]\!]\,s_g\ (i=1,\ldots,n)\\
\mathcal{FV}[\![t_0\ t_1]\!]\,s_g &= s_0\cup s_1\\
&\quad \text{where } s_0 = \mathcal{FV}[\![t_0]\!]\,s_g,\ \ s_1 = \mathcal{FV}[\![t_1]\!]\,s_g\\
\mathcal{FV}[\![\,[\![t_0,t_1,t_2]\!]_{F_0,F_1}]\!]\,s_g &= s_0\cup s_1\cup s_2\\
&\quad \text{where } s_0 = \mathcal{FV}[\![t_0]\!]\,s_g,\ \ s_1 = \mathcal{FV}[\![t_1]\!]\,s_g,\ \ s_2 = \mathcal{FV}[\![t_2]\!]\,s_g\\
\mathcal{FV}[\![(\mathsf{n},t)]\!]\,s_g &= \mathcal{FV}[\![t]\!]\,s_g
\end{aligned}$$

Figure 5 Restructuring Hylomorphisms — ψ part

and finally give the following structural hylomorphism:

$$map\ g = [\![Nil \triangledown \lambda(u_{2_1},v'_1).\ Cons(u_{2_1},v'_1), id + \lambda(a,v'_1).(g\,a,v'_1), out]\!]$$

This transformation simplifies ϕ of $(map\ g)$ into $Nil \triangledown \lambda(u_{2_1},v'_1).\ Cons(u_{2_1},v'_1)$ (i.e., in) making it easier to apply the Acid Rain Theorem.

Dually, Algorithm $\mathcal{S}_\psi$ restructures ψ in a typical general form:

$$\psi = \lambda v_s.\ \text{case } t_0 \text{ of } p_1 \to (1,t_1);\cdots;p_n \to (\mathsf{n},t_n).$$

It extracts free variables from $t_{i_1},\cdots,t_{i_{k_i}}$, constituents of t_i's, which are not related to recursive parts (corresponding to the identity functor I). New terms t'_i work only as suppliers of free variables, and actual computation is performed by the generated η_{ψ_i}. Shifting η_{ψ_i} to the η component removes many computations from ψ.

4.3 Capturing Schemes of Data Production and Consumption

In order to apply the Acid Rain Theorem for fusion, it is expected that ϕ and ψ in a given hylomorphism $[\![\phi, \eta, \psi]\!]_{G,F} : A \to B$ are described as $\tau\, in_{F_B}$ and $\sigma\, out_{F_A}$ respectively. Here, τ and σ are polymorphic functions and F_A and F_B are functors defining types A and B respectively. Our laws for deriving such τ and σ are as follows, whose proof can be found in (Hu et al. 1996*b*).

Theorem 2 (Deriving Polymorphic Functions)
Under the above conditions, τ and σ are defined by the following two laws.

$$\frac{\forall\alpha.\ (\![\alpha]\!)_{F_B} \circ \phi = \phi' \circ G\, (\![\alpha]\!)_{F_B}}{\tau = \lambda\alpha.\ \phi'}, \qquad \frac{\forall\beta.\ \psi \circ [\!(\beta)\!]_{F_A} = F\, [\!(\beta)\!]_{F_A} \circ \psi'}{\sigma = \lambda\beta.\ \psi'} \qquad \Box$$

This theorem, though being general, does not show clearly how to find ϕ' or ψ' in a constructive way (i.e., by an algorithm). Therefore, to implement an automatic calculational fusion system, we must develop *constructive algorithms* for implementing those non-constructive transformation laws. In this section, we shall propose such basic algorithms; discussing in detail the derivation of τ and making brief remarks on the dual derivation of σ.

(a) Algorithm for Deriving τ

When a composition of two hylomorphisms $[\![\_, \_, out_F]\!]_{\_,F} \circ [\![\phi, \_, \_]\!]_{F',\_}$ is to be fused by the Acid Rain Theorem, Theorem 1 (a), ϕ must be described by a polymorphic function τ, a function abstracting over data constructors, satisfying $\tau\, in_F = \phi$. By typing, we know that ϕ should be $F'\mu F \to \mu F$, meaning that ϕ receives a F'-structure data whose recursive components are of type μF, and then assembles some data of type μF. Our idea of deriving τ from ϕ is thus to detect the data constructors of μF and abstract them.

To be precise, let $C_1, \cdots, C_n$ be the data constructors of μF, namely $in_F = C_1\ \triangledown\ \cdots\ \triangledown\ C_n$, and let $c_1, \cdots, c_n$ be lambda variables used in abstracting $C_1, \cdots, C_n$. We shall derive τ by lambda abstraction of $C_1, \cdots, C_n$ in ϕ and then rewrite ϕ by τ applied to in_F, i.e., $\phi = \tau\, in_F$, where $\tau = \lambda(c_1\ \triangledown\ \cdots\ \triangledown\ c_n).\ \phi'$ meeting Theorem 2.

For the sake of simple presentation, we shall assume without loss of generality that ϕ for which we are going to derive τ is in the following specific form:

$$\phi_1 \triangledown \cdots \triangledown \phi_k : (F'_1 + \cdots + F'_k)\mu F \to \mu F,$$

and each $\phi_i : F'_i \mu F \to \mu F$ is a lambda abstraction:

$$\phi_i = \lambda(v_{i_1}, \cdots, v_{i_{m_i}}\ v'_{i_1}, \cdots, v'_{i_{l_i}}).\ t_i \qquad (1)$$

in which $F'_i = !\Gamma(v_{i_1}) \times \cdots \times !\Gamma(v_{i_{m_i}}) \times I_1 \times \cdots \times I_{l_i}$, i.e., identity functors after constant functors. Here, the lambda variables corresponding to the identity functor I are usually called ***recursive variables*** and are explicitly attached with a prime ($'$). Clearly, if we can derive τ_i for each ϕ_i, it soon follows the τ for ϕ will be $\tau = \lambda cs.\ (\tau_1\ cs\ \ \triangledown \cdots \triangledown\ \ \tau_k\ cs)$. Therefore, our attention turns to the derivation of τ_i from ϕ_i defined by Equation (1). As we know that not every ϕ guarantees existence of τ, some restriction on ϕ becomes necessary. We have two requirements for choosing proper restriction: one is that it should be automatically checkable whether a given ϕ meets the restriction; another is that it should not seriously limit the descriptive power. We borrow a similar idea of *Canonical Terms* in (Sheard & Fegaras 1993) and impose this restriction on ϕ_i in which the term t_i has one of the following forms:

1. ***a variable***: v, bounded in the lambda abstraction;
2. ***a constructor application***: $C\ t'_1\ \cdots\ t'_n$, where C is a data constructor and each t'_i is a term;
3. ***a hylo application***: $[\![\phi'_1 \triangledown \cdots \triangledown \phi'_{n'}, \eta, out]\!]\ v'$, where ϕ'_i is in our restrictive form and v' is a recursive variable;
4. ***a function application***: $f\ t_1\ \cdots\ t_n$, where f is a global function and each term t_i has no reference to any recursive variable.

It is worth noting that our ϕ_i, though looking rather restrictive, is the "core" to which a more general ϕ_i can be transformed. First, the restructuring algorithm in Section 4.2 is a great help, because we simplifies ϕ a lot by moving out many computations not relating to the construction of the resultant data of type μF. In fact, after restructuring, our restrictive term should not include the last form (a function application) because the terms of this form will be extracted and moved to the η component. Second, some constructs like *let*, *case* and application of non-recursive functions need not to be considered because they are removable by preprocessing; local declarations can be lifted to be global, *case* structures can be embedded in hylomorphisms, and application of non-recursive functions can be removed by unfolding. Third, not surprising but convincing, all potentially normalization programs, which have reasonable descriptive power, can be automatically turned into this form (Sheard & Fegaras 1993).

Assume: $F = F_1 + \cdots + F_n$, $in_F = C_1 \triangledown \cdots \triangledown C_n$ and $c_1, \cdots, c_n$ are fresh variables.

$$\begin{array}{lll} \phi & : & F'\mu F \to \mu F \\ \phi & \Rightarrow & \tau in_F \quad \text{where } \tau = \mathcal{F}[\phi] \end{array}$$

where

$$\begin{array}{rl} \mathcal{F}[\phi_1 \triangledown \cdots \triangledown \phi_k] &= \lambda cs.\ (\mathcal{F}[\phi_1]\ cs \triangledown \cdots \triangledown \mathcal{F}[\phi_k]\ cs) \\ \mathcal{F}[\lambda(v_{i_1}, \cdots, v_{i_{m_i}}, v'_{i_1}, \cdots, v'_{i_{l_i}}).\ t_i] & \\ &= \lambda(c_1 \triangledown \cdots \triangledown c_n).\lambda(v_{i_1}, \cdots, v_{i_{m_i}}, v'_{i_1}, \cdots, v'_{i_{l_i}}).\mathcal{F}'[t_i] \end{array}$$

$$\begin{array}{rll} \mathcal{F}'[v] &= (\!|c_1 \triangledown \cdots \triangledown c_n|\!)_F\ v & (*\ v \text{ is not a recursive variable } *) \\ \mathcal{F}'[v'] &= v' & (*\ v' \text{ is a recursive variable } *) \\ \mathcal{F}'[C_i\ t'_1\ \cdots\ t'_{n'}] &= c_i(F_i\ \mathcal{F}'\ (t'_1, \cdots, t'_{n'})) & \\ \mathcal{F}'[[\![\phi', \eta, out_F]\!]_{F',F}\ v'] &= [\![\mathcal{F}[\phi']\ (c_1 \triangledown \cdots \triangledown c_n), \eta, out_F]\!]_{F',F}\ v' & \\ \mathcal{F}'[f\ t'_1\ \cdots\ t'_{n'}] &= (\!|c_1 \triangledown \cdots \triangledown c_n|\!)\ (f\ t'_1\ \cdots\ t'_{n'}) & \end{array}$$

Figure 6 Deriving τ

With the help of these restrictions, our algorithm becomes simpler and the proof of the correctness of the algorithm becomes easier. Now we propose our algorithm $\mathcal{F}'$ to derive τ_i from ϕ_i:

$$\phi_i = \tau_i\, in_F, \quad \text{where } \tau_i = \lambda(c_1 \triangledown \cdots \triangledown c_n).\ \lambda(v_{i_1}, \cdots, v_{i_{m_i}}\ v'_{i_1}, \cdots, v'_{i_{l_i}}).\ \mathcal{F}'[t_i]$$

This lambda abstraction substitutes appropriate occurrences of each constructor of μF in t_i by its corresponding lambda variable. The algorithm $\mathcal{F}'$ is given in Figure 6, performing one of the following processes corresponding to the kind of t_i. Notice that all expressions which $\mathcal{F}'$ are applied to must have the type of μF.

1. When t_i is a variable, do nothing if it is a recursive variable. Otherwise, as it may be bound to an expression that includes μF constructors, we must proceed by applying the catamorphism $(\!|c_1 \triangledown \cdots \triangledown c_n|\!)_F$ to the expression to replace each constructor of μF by the lambda variable c_i.
2. When t_i is a constructor application $C_i\ t'_1 \cdots t'_{n'}$, C_i has to be substituted by the corresponding lambda variable c_i. And the algorithm $\mathcal{F}'$ is recursively applied to its arguments.
3. When t_i is a hylo application $[\![\phi', \eta, out_F]\!]_{F',F}$, our main algorithm $\mathcal{F}$ (not $\mathcal{F}'$) is applied recursively to ϕ'.
4. When t_i is a function application $f\ t_1\ \cdots\ t_n$, we apply $(\!|c_1 \triangledown \cdots \triangledown c_n|\!)$.

(b) Correctness of Algorithm $\mathcal{F}$

When abstracting constructors in ϕ, one might wonder why not just simply substitute in ϕ all occurrences of the constructors of μF with corresponding lambda variables. In fact, special care should be taken here. First, there are two kinds of constructors of μF in ϕ, one is to be substituted and the other is not. To see the difference between them, let us consider an example

$$\phi = \lambda().\ Nil \triangledown \lambda(v, v').\ Cons\ (Cons\ (v, Nil), v').$$

We can derive a correct τ for ϕ as

$$\tau = \lambda(c_1 \triangledown c_2).\ (\lambda().\ c_1 \triangledown \lambda(v, v').\ c_2\ (\underline{Cons\ (v, Nil)}, v')).$$

This tells us that we must not substitute the constructors inside an element of the list (as underlined). In the rule for constructor application in Figure 6, this fact is taken into consideration in applying $\mathcal{F}'$ recursively only to suitable arguments directed by functor F_i. The second point to note is that we have to consider the construction of non-recursive arguments of ϕ which are actually used for producing the final result. In this case we have to substitute them in this phase by applying a catamorphism.

Theorem 3 (Correctness of Algorithm $\mathcal{F}$) For the algorithm in Figure 6, we have that

(i) $\phi = \mathcal{F}[\![\phi]\!]\ in_F$
(ii) $\mathcal{F}[\![\phi]\!] : \forall A.(FA \to A) \to (F'A \to A)$

Proof Sketch. The proof of (i) is straightforward. We can obtain ϕ from $\mathcal{F}[\![\phi]\!]\ in_F$ by recovering $c_1, \cdots, c_n$ with $C_1, \cdots, C_n$ respectively and using the fact that $(\![C_1 \triangledown \cdots \triangledown C_n]\!)_F$ is the identity function over type μF.

As to (ii), it will be true according to Theorem 2 if we can prove that, for any $\phi : F'(\mu F) \to \mu F$, we have

$$\forall \alpha.\ (\![\alpha]\!) \circ \phi = (\mathcal{F}[\![\phi]\!]\ \alpha) \circ F'\ (\![\alpha]\!).$$

This can be done by induction over the structure of ϕ. □

To make the point clear, we demonstrate an example concerning the abstraction of production of a tree instead of a list. Consider the function foo which takes a list and generates a balanced tree:

$$\begin{array}{lll} foo & = & \lambda xs.\ \text{case}\ xs\ \text{of} \\ & & \quad Nil \to Leaf \\ & & \quad Cons\ (a, as) \to Node\ (double\ a, squareNodes\ (foo\ as), foo\ as) \end{array}$$

where *squareNodes* is a hylomorphism:

$$[\![\lambda().Leaf \triangledown \\ \lambda(v,v_1',v_2').\,Node(v,v_1',v_2'), id + \lambda(v,v_1',v_2').(square\ v,v_1',v_2'), out_{F_T}]\!]_{F_T,F_T}$$

and F_T is the functor defining the tree type in Section 2.2. By applying the algorithm for hylomorphism derivation, we have

$$foo = [\![\phi, id, out_{F_{L_A}}]\!]_{F_{L_A},F_{L_A}} \\ \quad \text{where } \phi = \lambda().\ Leaf \triangledown \lambda(v,v').\ Node\ (double\ v, squareNodes\ v', v')$$

which can be restructured into

$$foo = [\![\phi, id + \lambda(v,v').(double\ v, v'), out_{F_{L_A}}]\!]_{F_{L_A},F_{L_A}} \\ \quad \text{where } \phi = \lambda().\ Leaf \triangledown \lambda(v,v').\ Node\ (v, squareNodes\ v', v').$$

Now applying Algorithm $\mathcal{F}$ to derive τ for $\phi : F_L(\mu F_T) \to \mu F_T$ in the above hylo gives our result.

$$\begin{array}{rcl} foo & = & [\![\tau\ in_{F_T}, id + \lambda(v,v').(double\ v, v'), out_{F_{L_A}}]\!]_{F_{L_A},F_{L_A}} \\ & & \text{where } \tau = \lambda(c_1 \triangledown c_2).\ (\lambda().\ c_1 \triangledown \\ & & \qquad \lambda(v,v').\ c_2\ (v, [\![\lambda().c_1\ \triangledown\ \lambda(v,v_1',v_2').c_2\ (v,v_1',v_2'), \\ & & \qquad id + \lambda(v,v_1',v_2').(square\ v,v_1',v_2'), out_{F_T}]\!]_{F_T,F_T}\ v', v')) \end{array}$$

(c) Algorithm for Deriving σ

Another case of applying the Acid Rain Theorem is to fuse the composition of two hylomorphisms like $[\![\_,\_,\psi]\!]_{\_,F'} \circ [\![in_F,\_,\_]\!]_{F,\_}$, where σ must be deribed from ψ such that $\sigma out_F = \psi$. Deriving σ is the ***dual*** process of deriving τ, but from technical point of view, there are some important points worth noting.

Our algorithm is shown in Figure 7, deriving σ from $\psi : \mu F \to F'\mu F$ in the following restrictive form e:

$$\psi = \lambda v_s.\ \text{case } v_s \text{ of } p_1 \to t_1; \cdots; p_n \to t_n$$

in which the expression after the keyword case has been simplified to a variable. The key point of our algorithm is to transform the "implicit" decomposition of input by pattern matching into an "explicit" one by using out_F which decomposes μF into $F\mu F$. To this end, we define $d_1, \ldots, d_n$, which decomposes (unfolds) data of type μF successively by out_F as follows.

$$\begin{array}{rcl} d_1 & = & out_F\ v_s \\ d_2 & = & F\ out_F\ d_1 \\ & \vdots & \\ d_m & = & F^{m-1}\ out_F\ d_{m-1} \end{array}$$

$$
\begin{array}{l}
\psi \;:\; \mu F \to F'\mu F \\
\psi = \sigma\, out_F, \quad \text{where } \sigma = \lambda\beta.\mathcal{G}[\![\psi]\!] \\
\textbf{where} \\
\quad \mathcal{G}[\![\lambda v_s.\text{case } v_s \text{ of } p_1 \to t_1; \cdots; p_n \to t_n]\!] = \\
\qquad \lambda v_s.\text{let } d_1 = \beta\, t_0 \\
\qquad\qquad\quad d_2 = F\,\beta\, d_1 \\
\qquad\qquad\qquad \vdots \\
\qquad\qquad\quad d_m = F^{m-1}\,\beta\, d_{m-1} \\
\qquad\quad \text{in} \\
\qquad\quad \text{case } (d_1, \ldots, d_m) \text{ of} \\
\qquad\qquad p'_1 \to t_1 \\
\qquad\qquad\quad \vdots \\
\qquad\qquad p'_n \to t_n \\
\qquad\quad \text{where } (v_i, q_i) = \mathcal{G}'[\![p_i]\!] \quad (i = 1, \ldots, n) \\
\qquad\qquad\quad [q_{i_1}, \ldots, q_{i_{l_i}}] = q_i \\
\qquad\qquad\quad m = max\{|q_1|, \ldots, |q_n|\} \\
\qquad\qquad\quad p'_i = (q_{i_1}, \ldots, q_{i_{l_i}}, \_, \ldots, \_) \quad \text{(m-tuple)}
\end{array}
$$

$$
\begin{array}{rcl}
\mathcal{G}'[\![v]\!] & = & (v,\ [\,]) \\
\mathcal{G}'[\![C_j\ p_1 \cdots p_n]\!] & = & (\_,\ q) \\
& & \quad \text{where } (v_i, q_i) = \mathcal{G}'[\![p_i]\!] \quad (i = 1, \ldots, n) \\
& & \qquad\qquad q = (\mathrm{j},\ (v_1, \ldots, v_n)) : map\ (\lambda x.(\mathrm{j}, x))\ (zip_n\ q_1 \cdots q_n) \\
\mathcal{G}'[\![(p_1, \ldots, p_n)]\!] & = & (\_,\ q) \\
& & \quad \text{where } (v_i, q_i) = \mathcal{G}'[\![p_i]\!] \quad (i = 1, \ldots, n) \\
& & \qquad\qquad q = zip_n\ q_1 \cdots q_n
\end{array}
$$

/* This zip_n is different from the standard in regard to */
/* supplying wildcard _ at the tail for shorter lists */

Figure 7 Deriving σ

Here F^m is defined inductively by $F^m = F^{m-1} \circ F$. Now, we can substitute $(d_1, \ldots, d_m) : F\mu F \times F^2\mu F \times \cdots \times F^m\mu F$ for $v_s : \mu F$ in ψ, and accordingly, as shown in Figure 7, we apply the algorithm $\mathcal{G}'$ to turn the case patterns of $p_1, \ldots, p_n$ corresponding to the original v_s into $p'_1, \ldots, p'_n$ corresponding to $(d_1, \ldots, d_m)$. Finally, we lambda abstract all out_F's in all d_i's and obtain the result σ.

We omit the explanation and proof of the correctness of the algorithms for deriving σ from ψ. Instead, we give an example. A function calculating the maximum of a nonempty list of integers is defined and transformed into a hylomorphism as:

$$
\begin{array}{lcl}
maximum & = & \lambda xs.\ \text{case } xs \text{ of } Nil \to error \\
& & \qquad\qquad\qquad\quad Cons\ (a, Nil) \to a
\end{array}
$$

$$
\begin{aligned}
& \qquad\qquad\qquad\qquad Cons\ (a, as) \rightarrow max(a, maximum\ as) \\
= \;& [\![\phi, id, \psi]\!]_{F',F'} \\
& \text{where } \phi = error \triangledown id \triangledown max \\
& \qquad \psi = \lambda xs.\ \text{case } xs \text{ of } Nil \rightarrow (1, ()) \\
& \qquad\qquad\qquad\qquad\qquad Cons\ (a, Nil) \rightarrow (2, (a)) \\
& \qquad\qquad\qquad\qquad\qquad Cons\ (a, as) \rightarrow (3, (a, as)) \\
& \qquad F' = !\mathbf{1} + !Int + !Int \times I.
\end{aligned}
$$

We apply Algorithm $\mathcal{G}'$ to the pattern part of the case expression in ψ:

$$
\begin{aligned}
\mathcal{G}'[\![Nil]\!] &= (\_, [(1, ())]) \\
\mathcal{G}'[\![Cons\,(a,\ Nil)]\!] &= (\_, q) \\
&\quad \text{where } (a,\ []) = \mathcal{G}'[\![a]\!] \quad (\_, [(1, ())]) = \mathcal{G}'[\![Nil]\!] \\
&\qquad\quad q = (2,\ (a, \_)) : map\ (\lambda x.\ (2, x))\ (zip\ []\ [(1, ())]) \\
&\qquad\qquad = [(2,\ (a, \_)), (2, (\_, (1, ())))] \\
\mathcal{G}'[\![Cons\,(a,\ as)]\!] &= (\_, q) \\
&\quad \text{where } (a,\ []) = \mathcal{G}'[\![a]\!] \quad (as,\ []) = \mathcal{G}'[\![as]\!] \\
&\qquad\quad q = (2,\ (a, as)) : [] \\
&\qquad\qquad = [(2,\ (a, as))]
\end{aligned}
$$

The longest list produced by $\mathcal{G}'$ is for the second alternative and its length is two. So we apply out_F twice to generate the case expression for switching alternatives. The σ function with a let expression which binds decomposed xs to d_1 and d_2 is given by

$$
\begin{aligned}
\sigma \;=\;& \lambda\beta.\ \mathcal{G}[\![\lambda xs.\ \text{case } xs \text{ of } Nil \rightarrow (1, ()) \\
& \qquad\qquad\qquad\qquad Cons\ (a, Nil) \rightarrow (2, (a)) \\
& \qquad\qquad\qquad\qquad Cons\ (a, as) \rightarrow (3, (a, as))]\!] \\
=\;& \lambda\beta.\ \lambda xs.\ \text{let } d_1 = \beta\ xs \\
& \qquad\qquad\qquad d_2 = F'\ \beta\ d_1 \text{ in} \\
& \qquad\quad \text{case } (d_1, d_2) \text{ of } ((1, ()), \_) \rightarrow (1, ()) \\
& \qquad\qquad\qquad ((2, (a, \_)), (2, (\_, (1, ())))) \rightarrow (2, (a)) \\
& \qquad\qquad\qquad ((2, (a, as)), \_) \rightarrow (3, (a, as)).
\end{aligned}
$$

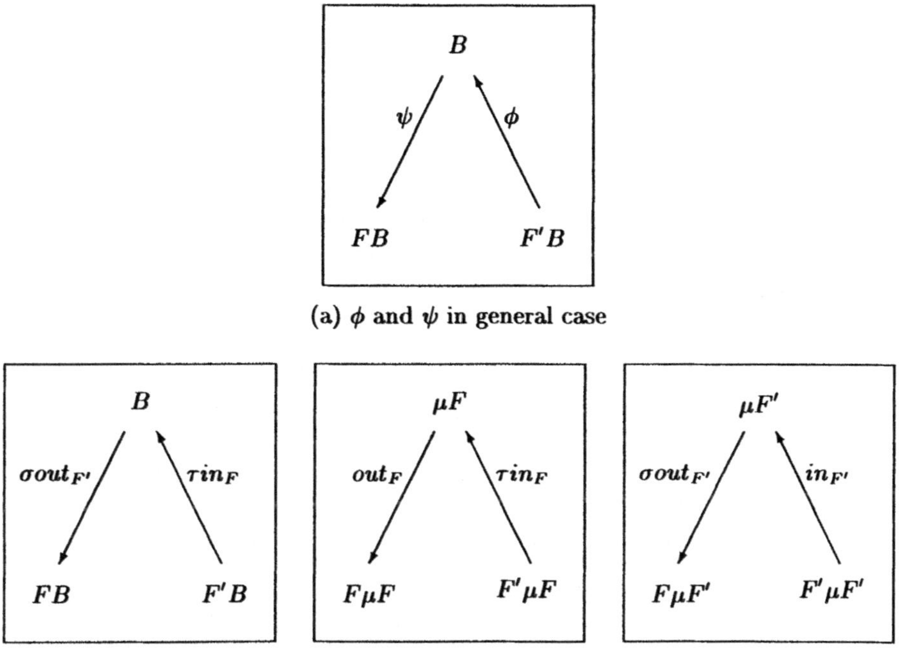

(a) ϕ and ψ in general case

(b) Fusion Impossible (c) $B = \mu F$ (d) $B = \mu F'$

Figure 8 Relation between two hylomorphisms

4.4 Applying Acid Rain Theorem

In this section, we describe how to apply the Acid Rain Theorem for fusion. Theorem 1 indicates that it must have special forms $[\![\_, \_, \tau in_F]\!] \circ [\![out_F, \_, \_]\!]$ or $[\![\_, \_, in_F]\!] \circ [\![\sigma out_F, \_, \_]\!]$ to apply this theorem. Now we are confronted with some technical problems. For example, how to find a potential fusible composition in a program? And how to check automatically if the composition can really be fused by the Acid Rain Theorem?

We define our potential fusible compositions as follows, where there really exist intermediate data structures (rather than the data supported directly by machines such as data of types *float* and *Int*).

Definition 3 (Potential Fusible Composition) A term is called a *potential fusible composition* if (i) it is either in the form of $t_1 \circ t_2$ or in the form of $(t_1\ (t_2\ t))$; and (ii) the domain of t_1 is a data structure defined by an endofunctor. □

We start with the main function to which we apply fusion transformation. We then select a potential fusible composition in the definition body, say $t_1 \circ t_2$, and try to fuse it with the Acid Rain Theorem by obtaining suitable hylomorphisms for both t_1 and t_2. Now consider a fusion of two hylomorphism $h_1 \circ h_2$:

$$\begin{array}{ll} h_1 : B \to C & h_2 : A \to B \\ h_1 = [\![\_,\_,\psi]\!]_{\_,F} & h_2 = [\![\phi,\_,\_]\!]_{F',\_} \end{array}$$

Figure 8 (a) shows the relation between ψ and ϕ, and the data types delivered by them. To apply the theorem, the following procedure is taken. The terms in parentheses indicate the dual condition to be checked at the same time.

1. *Check whether B is μF ($\mu F'$).* Obviously, if B is neither μF nor $\mu F'$ as shown in Figure 8 (b), we cannot obtain the form to which the Acid Rain Theorem is applicable.
2. *Check whether ψ (ϕ) is out_F ($in_{F'}$), in case B is μF ($\mu F'$).* Generally, it is impossible to tell whether two functions are equal or not. But we can judge whether ϕ is in_F by applying ϕ and in_F to all (finite) cases of data type μF and comparing the result values.
3. *Check whether ϕ (ψ) in one hylomorphism can be transformed to τin_F ($\sigma out_{F'}$), if ψ (ϕ) in another is out_F ($in_{F'}$).* By using the algorithms in Figures 6 and 7, we arrive at the state as shown in Figures 8 (c) and (d).

It is the compositions passing these tests that the Acid Rain Theorem can be applied to.

Returning to our running example ssf, we can fuse the derived hylomorphisms successfully. Changing function applications to function composition and noting that

$$[\![\phi_1, \eta_1, out_F]\!]_{F,F} \circ [\![in_F, \eta_2, \psi_2]\!]_{F,F} \Rightarrow [\![\phi_1, \eta_1 \circ \eta_2, \psi_2]\!]_{F,F}$$

lead from the original function ssf to the following.

$$\begin{array}{lll} ssf & = & sum \circ map\ square \circ upto \\ & = & [\![0 \triangledown (+), id, out_F]\!]_{F,F} \circ [\![in_F, id + \lambda(v,v').\ (square\ v, v'), out_F]\!]_{F,F} \circ \\ & & \quad [\![in_F, id, \psi]\!]_{F,F} \\ & = & [\![0 \triangledown (+), id + \lambda(v,v').\ (square\ v, v'), out_F]\!]_{F,F} \circ [\![in_F, id, \psi]\!]_{F,F} \\ & = & [\![0 \triangledown (+), id + \lambda(v,v').\ (square\ v, v'), \psi]\!]_{F,F} \\ & = & \lambda(m,n).\ \text{case}\ (m > n)\ \text{of}\ True \to 0 \\ & & \qquad\qquad\qquad\qquad False \to square\ m + ssf\ (m+1, n) \end{array}$$

4.5 Fusing inside Hylomorphisms

So far we have shown how to fuse between two hylomorphisms. We have not, however, mentioned fusion inside hylomorphisms. At a first glance, it seems that this fusion is very simple; performing fusion transformation for each component in a hylomorphism. But this simple strategy cannot effectively remove intermediate data structures among three components. As a simple example, consider the following hylomorphism (derived from $concat \circ map\ f$):

$$[\![\lambda().() \ \triangledown\ \lambda(u,v).u +\!\!+ v,\ id \triangledown \lambda(a,b).(f\ a,b),\ out]\!]$$

in which each component cannot be fused any more. But if we shift the η part to the ψ part as:

$$[\![\lambda().() \ \triangledown\ \lambda(u,v).f\,u +\!\!+ v,\ id,\ out]\!]$$

then the data structures produced by f become eliminatable as they are consumed by $(+\!\!+\ v)$.

Our idea is to perform fusion for a hylomorphism, say $[\![\phi,\eta,\psi]\!]$, in the following way:

(1) Fuse each component of the hylomorphism $[\![\phi \circ \eta, id, \psi]\!]$;
(2) Restructure the hylomorphism obtained in Step 1 and get $[\![\phi',\eta',\psi']\!]$;
(3) Fuse each component of the hylomorphism $[\![\phi', id, \eta' \circ \psi']\!]$;
(4) Restructure the hylomorphsims obtained in Step 3.

4.6 Inlining Hylomorphisms

Inlining hylomorphisms is the inverse process of hylomorphism derivation. All the hylomorphisms left in a program are transformed back to recursive definitions.

5 PERFORMANCE EVALUATION

All algorithms reported in this paper have been implemented. To evaluate the effectiveness of the HYLO system and get an idea of how much improvement could be gained by our approach, we have investigated the performance of three programs, namely *ssf*, *unlines*, and *queens*, both before and after our fusion transformation. *ssf* is our running example. *unlines*, a program from the Gofer prelude, accepts a list of strings and returns a new string by concatenating all strings separated by the CR character. *queens* is the well-known queens program, placing n queens on an $n \times n$ chess board.

Table 1 Experimental results using Gofer († applies to a text with 100 words)

Program	**Reduction Steps**			**Heap Cells**		
	before fusion	after fusion	ratio	before fusion	after fusion	ratio
$ssf(1000)$	11,015	6,005	0.54	17,030	10,019	0.59
unlines†	4,151	1,759	0.42	8,079	4,393	0.54
$queens(10)$	33,776,593	26,419,252	0.89	65,428,706	50,839,988	0.78

Table 2 Experimental results of *queens* using GHC

	Total Time (secs)		**Heap Cells (mbytes)**	
	before fusion	after fusion	before fusion	after fusion
by cheap fusion	9.41	5.13	61.27	15.55
by hylo fusion	9.41	4.10	61.27	9.38

We proceed our experiments using Gofer interpreter (Version 2.30a) and Glasgow Haskell compiler (GHC for short, Version 0.29). First, these programs were evaluated using Gofer. The experimental results are given in Table 1, showing improvement both in time (reduction steps) and in space (heap-cells). For example, it indicates that our HYLO system can save about half of both reduction steps and heap cells for ssf and *unlines*. To be more concrete, we give both the initial and transformed programs for the queens problem in Figure 9. Its non-triviality shows the power of our HYLO system.

Second, we compiled both the original and transformed queens programs, in order to compare our fusion with the cheap fusion (Gill et al. 1993) which has been already implemented in GHC. We enable and disable the cheap deforestion in GHC by two compile options `-O` and `-fno-foldr-build` respectively. Table 2 gives the experimental results indicating that our fusion gets better results than the cheap fusion; about 20% faster with 60% heap cells. It is also interesting to see that the improvement using GHC is exciting (comparing with that using Gofer); reducing time from 9.41 sec to 4.10 sec and heap cells from 61.27 mbytes to 9.38 mbytes.

6 DISCUSSION AND CONCLUDING REMARKS

Programming with the use of generic control structures which capture patterns of recursions in a uniform way is very significant in program transformation and optimization (Gill et al. 1993, Meijer et al. 1991, Sheard & Fegaras 1993, Launchbury & Sheard 1995, Takano & Meijer 1995). Our work is closely related to these studies. In particular, our work was greatly motivated by the work in (Sheard & Fegaras 1993) and (Takano & Meijer 1995). Sheard and

```
nqueen = 10

queens_initial = (print . sum . concat . queens) nqueen
  where
    queens 0 = [[]]
    queens m = [ p ++ [n] | p <- queens (m-1),
                            n <- [1..nqueen], safe p n ]
    safe p n = all not [ check m n (i,j) | (i,j) <- zip [1..] p]
               where m = length p + 1
    check m n (i,j) = j==n || i+j==m+n || i-j==m-n

queens_transformed = print (
  let
    x681 [] = 0
    x681 ((:) x342 x343)
     = let
        x680 [] = x681 x343
        x680 ((:) x351 x352) = (+) x351 (x680 x352)
       in x680 x342
  in x681
      (let
        x687 x354
         = case ((==) x354 0) of
            True -> (:) [] []
            False ->
             let
              x686 [] = []
              x686 ((:) x375 x376)
               = let
                  x685 x528
                   = case ((<=) x528 nqueen) of
                      True ->
                       case (let
                              x404 = (+) 1 (length x375)
                             in let
                                 x682 ((:) x446 x447,(:) x448 x449)
                                  = (&&) (not ((||) ((==) x448 x528)
                                           ((||) ((==) ((+) x446 x448)
                                                       ((+) x404 x528))
                                                 ((==) ((-) x446 x448)
                                                       ((-) x404 x528)))))
                                         (x682 (x447,x449))
                                 x682 x450 = True
                                in x682 (let
                                          x683 x458
                                           = (:) x458 (x683 ((+) 1 x458))
                                         in x683 1,x375)) of
                        True -> (:) (let
                                      x684 [] = (:) x528 []
                                      x684 ((:) x508 x509)
                                              = (:) x508 (x684 x509)
                                     in x684 x375) (x685 ((+) 1 x528))
                        False -> x685 ((+) 1 x528)
                      False -> x686 x376
                 in x685 1
             in x686 (x687 ((-) x354 1))
       in x687 nqueen))
```

Figure 9 Initial and Transformed *queens* Programs

Fegaras implemented a fusion algorithm called the *normalization algorithm* which can work on the language containing *folds*, a special case of hylomorphisms, as basic recursive form. Because of the restriction of descriptive power of folds, the power of the fusion system is rather limited. On the other hand, Takano and Meijer adopted hylomorphisms as the basic recursive forms rather than folds. Their work was motivated by Gill, Launchbury and Peyton Jones's one-step fusion algorithm (Gill et al. 1993) relying on functions being written in a highly-stylized *build-cata* forms (i.e., folds with data constructors being parameterized), and implemented another one-step fusion algorithm based on the Acid Rain Theorem. However, it is impractical to force programmers to define their recursive definitions only in terms of the specific hylomorphisms so that the Acid Rain Theorem could be applied directly (Launchbury & Sheard 1995).

This work extends our previous work (Hu et al. 1996*b*) in which the automatic algorithms for the derivation of structural hylomorphisms are proposed. The main extensions are as follows. First, we add new language constructs to the original core language for practical reasons, and modify the original algorithms for deriving and restructuring hylomorphisms. Second, we develop our new algorithms for the derivation of polymorphic functions τ and σ implementing the transformation laws given in (Hu et al. 1996*b*). Third, also the most important, we are implementing HYLO, stepping towards a practically-useful fusion system.

Functional programs that HYLO manipulates can be accepted by the Haskell (core) language. The merit is that the verification of the improvement of functional programs after transformation can be done easily by running them on Haskell system. It is hoped that the HYLO system will be embedded in the practical Haskell system.

All transformation algorithms introduced in this paper have been implemented. It is completely mechanical and does not rely on heuristics about how or when transformation is taken. Although we have to wait for the detailed experimental results to say that this system is effective for practical programs, we are absolutely convinced that our calculational approach to fusion transformation makes a good progress in code optimization of functional programs.

Besides evaluating general performance of HYLO, we are currently working on the extension of our algorithms to deal with recursions traversing over multiple data structures (Hu et al. 1996*c*), mutual recursions etc. in order to enable more fusion. In the near future, we are going to extend HYLO to be a general automatic program calculation system, which can optimize functional programs not only by fusion but also by tupling (Hu, Iwasaki, Takeichi & Takano 1997), and accumulating (Hu, Iwasaki & Takeichi 1996*a*), as well as other optimization tactics.

ACKNOWLEDGEMENTS

This paper owes much to the thoughtful and helpful discussions with Akihiko Takano, Fer-Jan de Vries and other CACA members. Thanks are also due to Oege de Moor and Arne John Glenstrup for reading an earlier draft and making a number of helpful suggestions, and to the referees who provided detailed and helpful comments.

REFERENCES

Bird, R. & de Moor, O. (1994), Relational program derivation and context-free language recognition, *in* A. Roscoe, ed., 'A Classical Mind', Prentice Hall, pp. 17–35.

Burstall, R. & Darlington, J. (1977), 'A transformation system for developing recursive programs', *Journal of the ACM* **24**(1), 44–67.

Chin, W. (1992), Safe fusion of functional expressions, *in* 'Proc. Conference on Lisp and Functional Programming', San Francisco, California.

Fokkinga, M. (1992), Law and Order in Algorithmics, Ph.D thesis, Dept. INF, University of Twente, The Netherlands.

Gill, A., Launchbury, J. & Jones, S. P. (1993), A short cut to deforestation, *in* 'Proc. Conference on Functional Programming Languages and Computer Architecture', Copenhagen, pp. 223–232.

Hu, Z., Iwasaki, H. & Takeichi, M. (1996*a*), Caculating accumulations, Technical Report METR 96–03, Faculty of Engineering, University of Tokyo.

Hu, Z., Iwasaki, H. & Takeichi, M. (1996*b*), Deriving structural hylomorphisms from recursive definitions, *in* 'ACM SIGPLAN International Conference on Functional Programming', ACM Press, Philadelphia, PA, pp. 73–82.

Hu, Z., Iwasaki, H. & Takeichi, M. (1996*c*), An extension of the Acid Rain Theorem, *in* '2nd Fuji International Workshop on Functional and Logic Programming', World Scientific, Shonan, Japan.

Hu, Z., Iwasaki, H., Takeichi, M. & Takano, A. (1997), Tupling calculation eliminates multiple data traversals, *in* 'ACM SIGPLAN International Conference on Functional Programming', ACM Press, Amsterdam, The Netherlands. to appear.

Jones, M. P. (1994), Gofer 2.30a release notes.

Launchbury, J. & Sheard, T. (1995), Warm fusion: Deriving build-catas from recursive definitions, *in* 'Proc. Conference on Functional Programming Languages and Computer Architecture', La Jolla, California, pp. 314–323.

Meijer, E., Fokkinga, M. & Paterson, R. (1991), Functional programming with bananas, lenses, envelopes and barbed wire, *in* 'Proc. Conference on Functional Programming Languages and Computer Architecture (LNCS 523)', Cambridge, Massachuetts, pp. 124–144.

Pettorossi, A. & Proietti, M. (1993), Rules and strategies for program transformation, *in* 'IFIP TC2/WG2.1 State-of-the-Art Report', LNCS 755, pp. 263–303.

Sheard, T. & Fegaras, L. (1993), A fold for all seasons, *in* 'Proc. Conference on Functional Programming Languages and Computer Architecture', Copenhagen, pp. 233–242.

Takano, A. & Meijer, E. (1995), Shortcut deforestation in calculational form, *in* 'Proc. Conference on Functional Programming Languages and Computer Architecture', La Jolla, California, pp. 306–313.

Team, T. A. (1996), *Glasgow Haskell Compiler User's Guide ver0.29.*

Wadler, P. (1988), Deforestation: Transforming programs to eliminate trees, *in* 'Proc. ESOP (LNCS 300)', pp. 344–358.

7 BIOGRAPHY

Yoshiyuki Onoue is a Ph.D. student at the University of Tokyo. His research area is the transformation of functional programs, in particular the algorithm and implementation for partial evaluation and fusion transformation.

Zhenjiang Hu is a research associate at the University of Tokyo. He received his BS and MS in computer science from Shanghai Jiao Tong University in 1988 and 1990 respectively, and his Ph.D in information engineering from the University of Tokyo in 1996. His current research concerns functional programming, calculational program transformation systems and program evolution.

Hideya Iwasaki is an associate professor of Faculty of Technology, Tokyo University of Agriculture and Technology. He received the M.E. degree in 1985, the Dr. Eng. Degree in 1988 from the University of Tokyo. His research interests are list processing languages, functional languages, parallel processing, and constructive algorithmics.

Masato Takeichi is a professor in Mathematical Engineering and Information Engineering at the University of Tokyo since 1993. After graduation from the University of Tokyo, he joined the faculty at the University of Electro-Communications in Tokyo before he went back to work at the Univesity of Tokyo in 1987. His research concerns the design and implementation of functional programming languages, and calculational program transfomation systems.

5

Refinement of data parallel programs in PEI

E. Violard, S. Genaud and G.-R. Perrin
ICPS - University Louis Pasteur, Strasbourg
Pôle API - Bd S. Brant, F-67400 Illkirch
{violard,genaud,perrin}@icps.u-strasbg.fr

Abstract

Parallel programs mainly differ from sequential ones in that they include geometrical aspects involved by the hardware architecture. We present in this paper the PEI formalism, which enables to take into account both the geometrical and functional aspects of programs. It provides a refinement calculus mainly used to transform the geometrical characteristics of parallel programs, and we show how it may apply on data parallel programs, in particular for data alignments.

Keywords

Data fields, Data-parallelism, Program transformation, Refinement.

1 INTRODUCTION

Parallel programming is a major challenge for handling efficient computations. It involves two technological issues: a *program* expressed in some dedicated language which supports a parallel programming model, and a *computer* and the parallel execution model it implements. Ideally the programming language should be architecture independent whereas the computations efficiency requires a strong-related architecture implementation.

The relationship between these issues is a matter of compiling techniques as well as programming capabilities: in scientific applications for example, on the one hand parallelizing compilers are able to automatically transform the iteration space, assuming conditions such as the affinity of dependencies and of loop bounds; on the other hand the programmer may help the compiler by using *directives* to indicate a "good" data alignment —that is a data placement that minimizes interprocessor communications. All these techniques are based on *geometrical* transformations either of the iteration space or of the index domains of arrays. Especially, they are of particular interest in the *data parallel programming* model, implemented by programming languages such as High Performance Fortran (HPF 1993) or C*(Thi 1990).

In some sense it shows that, beside a classical functional point of view on programs, geometrical issues in parallel programming or parallelizing compilation have to be considered of main importance for the mastery of efficient computations. The geometrical approach entails an abstract manipulation of array indices, to define and transform:

- the data dependencies in programs,
- the way the data are, or are not, locally accessible,
- their expansion in a multidimensional space of virtual processors,
- *etc.*

The solution might be the use of some methodology for parallel program development, in the same spirit as what is done with the Bird-Meertens Formalism (Bird 1987, Skillicorn 1993). In addition, given the previous considerations on geometry, a specialised methodology might well be needed.

The PEI formalism (in some sense similar to ALPHA (Mauras 1989) or CRYSTAL (Chen, il Choo & Li 1991)) was originally defined (Violard & Perrin 1992, Violard & Perrin 1993) to describe and reason on parallel programs and their implementation. It includes a refinement calculus that makes possible to transform statements by associating algebraic laws and symbolic evaluation of functions with the classical geometrical foundations in this area. Using PEI, the programming activity may refer to a very small set of primitives to design programs. They are:

- the placement of value items in some discrete reference domain, which relates to data dependencies that possibly induce interprocessor communications,
- the definition or the change of the reference domain itself, which enables to change the program structure,
- the application of functions on the value items, which defines the operations carried out by a program.

The relationship between a PEI statement and a data parallel program is quite obvious since PEI expresses, in an abstract way, parallel variables, global operations and communications, and data alignment. Therefore PEI provides a good framework to design and transform data parallel programs (Genaud, Violard & Perrin 1995), and we illustrate how its refinement calculus may be used to deal with the crucial aspect of data alignments.

The paper is organized as follows: section 2 explains the PEI concepts and notations. Section 3 is concerned with the semantic definitions associated with PEI constructs, and section 4 presents how refinement is defined in the formalism. Finally, we illustrate most of the formalism issues, including design and refinement considerations on the *Gaxpy* example drawn from the numerical computation field.

2 DEFINITION OF THE FORMALISM PEI

2.1 PEI data fields

Generally speaking, we can consider a problem as a relation between input and output *multisets* of values. Of course, programming may imply to put these values in a convenient organized directory, depending on the problem terms. In scientific computations for example, items such as arrays are functions on indices: the index set, that is the reference domain, is a part of some $\mathbb{Z}^n$. In PEI such a multiset of value items mapped on a discrete reference domain is called a *data field*.

Let us consider the multiset $\{1, 2, -3, 1\}$. A possible way to map this multiset is to choose indices, for instance $\{0, 1, 2, 3\}$ of $\mathbb{Z}$, to refer to each of the values. This mapping is shown on figure 1(a) and defines the data-field called `V`. Obviously, this multiset might be mapped in a different manner, for example onto points whose indices (i, j) in $\mathbb{Z}^2$, are such that $(0 \leq i, j \leq 1)$ (figure 1(b)). Such a mapping thus defines another data field, let us say `M`. Although their mappings are different, the two data fields represent the same multiset of values and therefore we say they are *equivalent*.

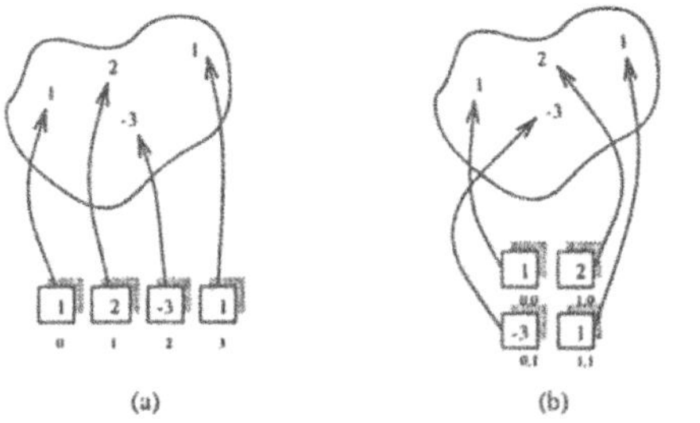

Figure 1 Two different mappings of a multiset of values

Formally, there exists a bijection from the first arrangement to the second one, namely $\sigma(i) = (i \ mod \ 2, i \ div \ 2)$. This relation is expressed in PEI through the equation:

$$\texttt{M} = \texttt{align} :: \texttt{V}$$
$$\text{where} \quad \texttt{align} = \lambda(\texttt{i})|(0 \leq \texttt{i} \leq 3).(\texttt{i mod 2,i div 2})$$

Any PEI program is composed of unoriented equations, each of them connecting two data field expressions. On the example, `M` and `align :: V` have the same set of value items, placed in the same fashion in the same reference domain.

2.2 PEI operations

Expressions are defined by applying operations on data fields. The operations are second-order functions, and fall into three categories:

– the operation used in the expression `align :: V` modifies the reference domain onto which values are mapped. It is called *change of basis* and is denoted by ::

– another operation "moves" values in the reference domain. It is called *geometrical operation* (or routing), and is denoted by $\triangleleft$. Figure 2(a) shows the mapping of values of the data field `W` defined as `W` $=$ `V` $\triangleleft$ `shift`. The function `shift` shifts values one place cyclically to the right and is written in PEI as `shift` = `λ(i)|(0<=i<4).((i-1) mod 4)`. If the function is not injective the operation expresses a broadcast. For instance `W` = `V` ◁ `spread`, where `spread` = `λ(i)|(0<=i<4).(0)` means the value mapped at index point 0 in `V` is broadcasted to index points 0 to 3, to form the data field `W` as shown on figure 2(b).

– the third operation computes the values of a data field, and is called *functional* operation. It is denoted by ▷ and performs an element-wise computation on the data field. For example, `W` = `inc` ▷ `V`, where `inc` = `λ(a).(a+3)`, defines a data field whose values are computed from the `V` values having the same indices (figure 3).

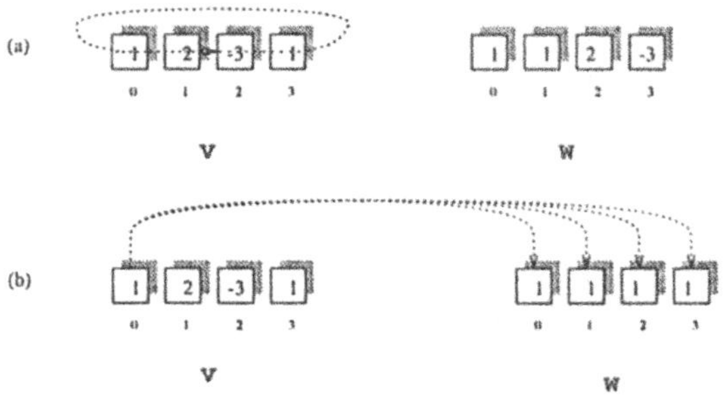

Figure 2 Geometrical operations: (a) one-to-one relation (b) broadcast

The geometrical operation has an inverse in PEI. It defines the *geometrical reduction*, denoted by ;▷ . It may be used for example, to gather all the values of `V` at a particular index point. For instance, the data field `W` verifying `W` = `merge` ;▷ `V`, where `merge` = `λ(i)|(0<=i<4).(0)` has all its values mapped at index point 0, listed in a sequence of arbitrary order. Figure 4 shows a possible solution for `W`.

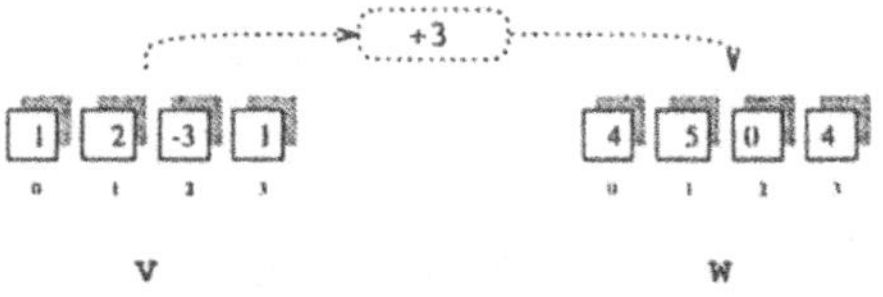

Figure 3 `W` defined by a functional operation applied on `V`

The geometrical reduction is defined as the inverse of the geometrical operation since if it applies on a bijective function it is equal to the geometrical operation applied on the inverse function.

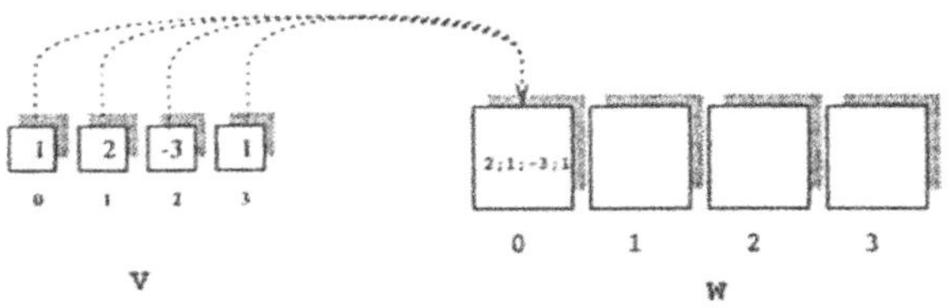

Figure 4 W is defined by a reduction operation applied on V

Last, an internal operation is defined on data fields. It is called ***superimposition*** and denoted by `/&/`. The superimposition of several data fields results in a new data field whose values are sequences. Each sequence is the concatenation of values mapped at the same indices. Figure 5 shows the result of superimposing X and Y.

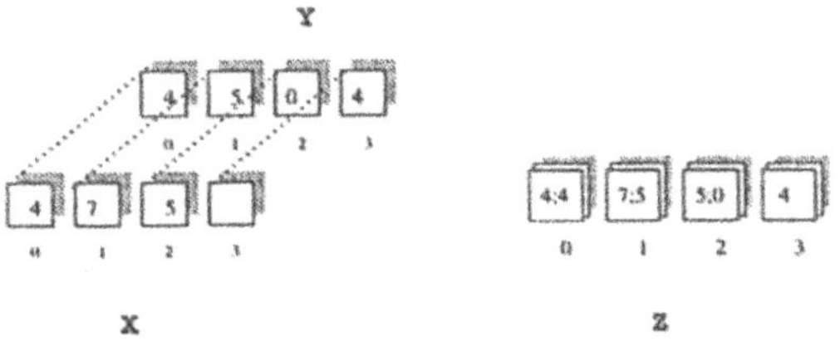

Figure 5 Z is defined by Z = X/&/ Y

2.3 PEI programs and Syntactic issues

A PEI ***statement*** is a set of equations which expresses the relation between input and output data fields. It is a system of equations with the input data fields being the parameters and the output data fields being the unknowns.

A solution is a set of output data fields verifying the system. In the PEI theory, only some statements are programs.

Definition 1 *A* PEI *statement is a* program, *if for any given input data fields set, there exists at most one solution.*

The definition implies that we do not consider statements having non-deterministic solutions as programs.

Let us now make precise some of the syntactic features of the formalism. As typographic conventions, we will use A, B, X, *etc.* for data fields, whereas f, g, *etc.* denote functions. The general form of a PEI statement includes a header composed of the tuples D and R of input and output data fields, and an equation set S:

$$\mathtt{P} : \mathtt{D} \mapsto \mathtt{R}$$
$$\{ \; S$$

We will also use the shorthand $\mathtt{P}\{S\}$ when D and R do not matter.

To improve the readability, only function names appear in the equations, their definition being reported outside the system. Functions are written using a notation derived from the lambda-calculus: a function $\mathtt{f}$ of domain $dom(\mathtt{f}) = \{x \mid P(x)\}$ and image $img(\mathtt{f}) = \{\mathtt{f}(x) \mid P(x)\}$ is denoted as $\lambda(x) \mid P(x).\mathtt{f}(x)$.

We write $\mathtt{f}|_{dom(\mathtt{g})}$ for the part of $\mathtt{f}$ defined on the domain of $\mathtt{g}$, so that $\mathtt{f}|_{dom(\mathtt{g})} = \mathtt{g}$ implies that $\mathtt{f}$ and $\mathtt{g}$ are equal on $dom(\mathtt{g})$. A function $\mathtt{f}$ defined on disjunctive sub-domains is denoted as $\mathtt{f1} \# \mathtt{f2}$, and the domain of a composed function $\mathtt{f} \circ \mathtt{g}$ is $\{x \in dom(\mathtt{g}) \mid \mathtt{g}(x) \in dom(\mathtt{f})\}$.

We will also use the built-in function id, which only matches one-element sequences. The application of id on one element returns this element. It is frequently used to define recursive computations, like in the recursive summation of a sequence of numbers:

$$\mathtt{sum} = \mathtt{id} \; \# \; \lambda(\mathtt{a;b}).(\mathtt{a+sum(b)})$$

The function sum returns the element for one-element sequences and for sequences made of several elements, it returns the first element plus the sum of the rest of the sequence.

2.4 Examples

Let us illustrate through a few examples what PEI programs look like:

Example 1 Addition of a matrix and its transpose

```
MatSum : A ↦ C
 ⎧ A = matrix::A
 ⎨ T = A ◁ transp
 ⎩ C = add ▷ (A /&/T)
 matrix  =  λ(i,j)|(0<=i,j<n).(i,j)
 transp  =  λ(i,j)|(0<=i,j<n).(j,i)
 add     =  λ(a;b).(a+b)
```

– The first equation expresses a pre-condition on the input data field A. It means that A is invariant by applying the change of basis defined by matrix. The change of basis is the identity on the square domain $\{(i,j), 0 \leq i,j < n\}$ of $\mathbb{Z}^2$: as we will see, it means that the discrete domain onto which the values of A are placed is bounded to the square.

– The second equation defines T from A by applying a geometrical operation. It means that the values of T mapped on points (i,j) are those of A mapped on (j,i).

– The third equation defines the output data field C. The right side defines the superimposition of A and T, *i.e.* the set of pairs (a;b), where a ∈ A and b ∈ T. The functional operation above applies the function add to each value of T.
◇

Example 2 Palindromes detection

A vector A of size n is a palindrome if $A_i = A_{n-1-i}$, $\forall i \in [0 \ldots n-1]$. The program below pairs the symmetric values respectively to the middle of the input vector A, and then compares equality of values in each of the pairs, resulting in data field B. To determine whether A is a palindrome or not, all comparison results defined by B must eventually be gathered. This is done through the definition of R. If all results are true then A is a palindrome. The way B values are put together can be written in at least two ways. Here is a first version:

```
Palind1 : A ↦ R
  { A = vector :: A
  { B = equ ▷ (A /&/ A ◁ opp)
  { R = and ▷ (red ;▷ B)

equ     =  λ(a;b).(a=b)
vector  =  λ(i)|(0≤i<n).(i)
opp     =  λ(i)|(0≤i<n).(n-1-i)
red     =  λ(i)|(0≤i<n).(0)
and     =  id # λ(a;b).(a & (and b))
```

In this version, we use a reduction operation that builds a sequence of all the boolean values of B and put it at index point 0 in R. All sequence elements are then logically ANDed. Reduction is thus a straightforward means to gather values, but it is sometimes necessary to indicate an explicit path for the values to be moved.

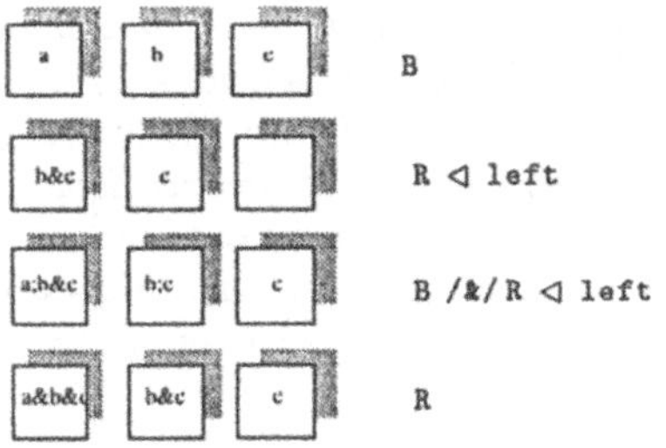

Figure 6 Given B, R is a solution of Palind2 last equation

```
Palind2 : A ↦ R
⎧ A = vector :: A
⎨ B = equ ▷ (A /&/ A ◁ opp)
⎩ R = band ▷ (B /&/ R ◁ left)
equ     =  λ(a;b).(a=b)
vector  =  λ(i)|(0≤i<n).(i)
opp     =  λ(i)|(0≤i<n).(n-1-i)
left    =  λ(i)|(0≤i<n-1).(i+1)
band    =  id # λ(a;b).(a&b)
```

Here, R is recursively defined as the application of a logical AND on the superimposition of B and R shifted one position left. As we can see on figure 6, the data field R is a solution of the last equation because it maps at index point 0 the sequence of all elements of B, the sequence minus one element at index point 1, *etc.* We thus have a data field R very similar to the one in Palind1, in that the evaluation of all B values is in both cases mapped at point 0 (though the order of evaluation might be different). ◇

3 SEMANTICS

PEI semantics is founded on the notion of discrete domain associated with a multiset. As seen earlier, a data field maps the values of a multiset V onto a domain, such that each value can be indexed by a point of the domain. The mapping is therefore a function $v : \mathbb{Z}^n \mapsto V$.

In the previous section we pointed out that V, whose values $\{1, 2, -3, 1\}$ were mapped on the interval [0..3] of $\mathbb{Z}$, can be deduced from M using the σ bijection. Generally speaking, given a multiset V of values, and the mappings $v : \mathbb{Z}^n \mapsto V$ and $v' : \mathbb{Z}^p \mapsto V$, we have the relation $v = v' \circ \sigma$, where σ is a bijection which maps $dom(v)$ to $dom(v')$.

It means that any mapping of a given multiset is arbitrary and always can be deduced from a *reference mapping* (a given processor grid for example) by applying a bijection. By integrating this bijection into the definition of data fields, we express the relation between two mappings of a same multiset. Hence, a data field is a pair of functions $(v : \sigma)$. Moreover, we impose the following constraint: $dom(v)$, called *value domain* must be included in the domain of the bijection σ, called the *reference domain*, so that any transformation of a mapping apply to all the values of the data field. For instance, considering M on figure 7 as a reference mapping representing a processor grid, the value 2 mapped at index point 1 by $V = (v_V : \sigma_V)$ would be computed by processor $\sigma_V(1) = (1,0)$.

Definition 2 *Let V be a multiset of values. Let v be a mapping $\mathbb{Z}^n \mapsto V$ and σ a bijection $\mathbb{Z}^n \mapsto \mathbb{Z}^p$, then $(v : \sigma)$ defines a* data field *if $dom(v) \subseteq dom(\sigma)$.*

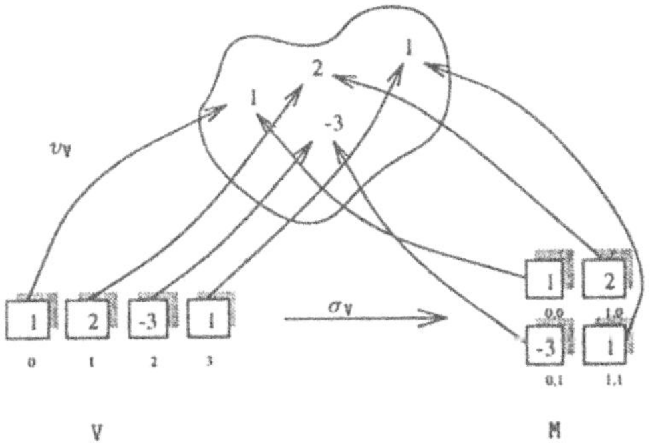

Figure 7 Relation between two equivalent mappings

3.1 Operation semantics

The data field definition enables us to formally describe the operations in PEI. Let us first consider the superimposition internal operation, denoted as /&/ . Let $X_1 = (v_1 : \sigma_1)$ and $X_2 = (v_2 : \sigma_2)$ be two data fields. If $\sigma_1|_{dom(\sigma_2)} = \sigma_2$ or $\sigma_2|_{dom(\sigma_1)} = \sigma_1$, the superimposition defines X_1/&/X_2 as:

$$\begin{cases} (v_1 : \sigma) & \text{on} \quad dom(v_1)\backslash dom(v_2) \\ (w : \sigma) & \text{on} \quad dom(v_1) \cap dom(v_2) \\ (v_2 : \sigma) & \text{on} \quad dom(v_2)\backslash dom(v_1) \end{cases}$$

where $w(z) = v_1(z);v_2(z)$ and $\sigma = \begin{cases} \sigma_1 \text{ if } dom(\sigma_2) \subseteq dom(\sigma_1) \\ \sigma_2 \text{ if } dom(\sigma_1) \subseteq dom(\sigma_2). \end{cases}$

The other operations in PEI are second-order functions. In the following, f, g, *etc.* are functions and X denotes a data field $(v : \sigma)$.

– **Functional operation.** Let f be a function. When applied on a X such that $img(v) \subseteq dom(\mathtt{f})$, the functional operation on f, denoted as f $\triangleright$, defines the element-wise application of f on X. It means that f $\triangleright$ X is $(\mathtt{f} \circ v : \sigma)$.

– **Geometrical operation.** Let g be a function. When applied on a X such that $dom(\mathtt{g}) \subseteq dom(\sigma)$ and $img(\mathtt{g}) \subseteq dom(v)$, the geometrical operation on g, denoted as $\triangleleft$ g, defines the data field X $\triangleleft$ g as $(v \circ \mathtt{g} : \sigma)$.

Conversely, let g be a function. When applied on a X such that $dom(\mathtt{g}) \subseteq dom(v)$ and $img(\mathtt{g}) \subseteq dom(\sigma)$, the **geometrical reduction** on g, denoted as g;$\triangleright$, defines the data field g ;$\triangleright$ X as some data field $(w : \sigma)$ such that $dom(w) = \mathtt{g}(dom(v))$ and $w(z)$ is a sequence of the values $v(y)$, y such that $\mathtt{g}(y) = z$. As a consequence, the next property links reductions and geometrical operations:

Property 1 *The operation* $\texttt{g};\triangleright$ *is equal to the operation* $\triangleleft\ \texttt{g}^{-1}$ *if and only if* $\texttt{g}$ *is bijective.*

– **Change of basis operation.** Let $\texttt{h}$ be a bijection. When applied on a $\texttt{X}$ such that $dom(v) \subseteq dom(\texttt{h})$, the change of basis on $\texttt{h}$, denoted as $\texttt{h::}$, defines the data field $\texttt{h::X}$ as $(v \circ \texttt{h}^{-1} : \sigma \circ \texttt{h}^{-1})$.

Remark – The operations are very similar to the classical Bird-Meertens functions on lists, such as *map* or *reduce*. They differ in that PEI operations include some geometrical aspects in order to meet the data parallel paradigm.

3.2 Equation semantics

Let E denote a data field expression equal to $(v : \sigma)$ and E' denote a data field expression equal to $(v' : \sigma')$. Equation $E = E'$ semantics, denoted as $[\![E = E']\!]$, is the boolean expression $(v = v') \wedge (\sigma = \sigma') \wedge C$, where C is the conjunction of all the conditions involved by the operations appearing in the equation. If the expression equals true, we will say that data fields appearing in the equation *verify* the equation.

For example, given data fields $\texttt{A} = (v_\texttt{A} : \sigma_\texttt{A})$ and $\texttt{B} = (v_\texttt{B} : \sigma_\texttt{B})$, the semantics of the equation $\texttt{A} = \text{add} \triangleright (\texttt{size::B})$ is the boolean expression:

$$\begin{array}{ll} & v_\texttt{A} = \text{add} \circ v_\texttt{B} \circ \texttt{size}^{-1} \wedge \sigma_\texttt{A} = \sigma_\texttt{B} \circ \texttt{size}^{-1} \\ \wedge & dom(v_\texttt{B}) \subseteq dom(\texttt{size}) \wedge img(v_\texttt{B}) \subseteq dom(\text{add}) \end{array}$$

The definition can be extended to an equation set, since data fields must verify all the equations. The semantics of an equation set is therefore the conjunction of the semantics of each equation.

3.3 Data field equivalence

As mentioned in section 2.1, two data fields may be intuitively considered as *equivalent* if they represent the same multiset of values. In this case, according to semantics we will say that these data fields are *weakly equivalent* since only their value domains are considered. Moreover if the data fields have the same reference mapping, we will say that they are *strongly equivalent*.

Definition 3 *Let* $\texttt{X}$ *and* $\texttt{Y}$ *be two data fields. We say that* $\texttt{X}$ *and* $\texttt{Y}$ *are* strongly equivalent *if and only if there exists a bijection* $\texttt{h}$ *such that* $\texttt{Y} = \texttt{h::X}$ *and* $dom(\sigma_\texttt{X}) \subseteq dom(\texttt{h})$.

The change of basis operation gives an intuitive idea about strong equivalence of data fields, because it modifies the mapping of the same multiset of values but maintains the same reference mapping. For example, consider h as the permutation λ`(i)|(0<=i<4).((i-1) mod 4))` and the data field $W = h :: V$, V being the data field presented on figure 7. We observe on figure 8 that the value 2 in W is associated with the same point in the reference mapping as for V: $v_W(0) = v_V \circ h^{-1}(0) = v_V(1) = 2$ and $\sigma_W(0) = \sigma_V \circ h^{-1}(0) = \sigma_V(1) = (1,0)$.

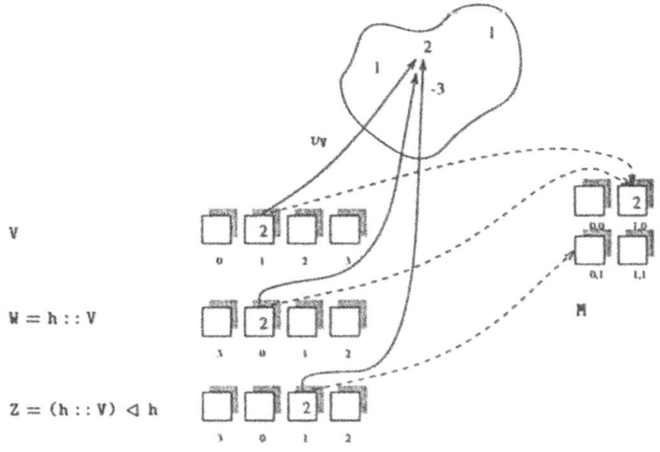

Figure 8 Weak and strong equivalence between data fields

Now, consider the definition $Z = (h :: V) \triangleleft h$ in which Z and V are not strongly equivalent since $\sigma_Z \neq \sigma_V$ ($\sigma_Z = \sigma_V \circ h^{-1}$) though $v_Z = v_V$: they thus are weakly equivalent. By contrast to the previous case, the value 2 in Z ($v_Z(1) = v_V \circ h^{-1} \circ h\ (1) = v_V(1) = 2$) is associated with $\sigma_Z(1) = \sigma_V \circ h^{-1}(1) = \sigma_V(2) = (0,1)$.

Definition 4 *Let* X *and* Y *be two data fields. We say that* X *and* Y *are* weakly equivalent *if and only if they represent the same multiset of values.*

Weak equivalence of data fields can be characterized in PEI expressions, by the following property:

Property 2 *Let* X *be a data field and* Y *a data field expression depending on* X. X *and* Y *are* weakly equivalent *if and only if there exist three bijections* h, h' *and* g, *such that:*

- *either* $(h :: X) \triangleleft g = h' :: Y$ *and* $h(dom(v_X)) = img(g)$,
- *or* $h :: (X \triangleleft g) = h' :: Y$ *and* $dom(v_X) = img(g)$.

4 REFINEMENT AND ABSTRACTION

4.1 General definition

Refinement is a classical process for designing or transforming programs (Back 1988, Morgan 1990). It enables to build a program which satisfies any specification that an initial program satisfies. Refinement is usually defined in the following way, given a satisfaction property, denoted as sat :

Definition 5 *Let P and P′ be two programs, we say that P is refined by P′, and we note $P \sqsubseteq P'$, if and only if for any specification S*

$$P\mathsf{sat}\ S \Rightarrow P'\mathsf{sat}\ S$$

In imperative programming, the satisfaction property may be safety and termination for example. The *weakest pre-conditions* of Dijkstra, denoted $wp(P, post)$, where P is a statement and *post* a predicate can then be used: $wp(P, post)$ is the weakest predicate for which carrying out of P ends in a state which satisfies *post*. It allows to rewrite the previous definition as follows:

$$P \sqsubseteq P' \text{ if and only if } \forall r \cdot wp(P,r) \Rightarrow wp(P',r)$$

Refinement is a continuous process which allows successive statements to be built, from a specification until a program. It defines a partial order between statements, called *refinement relation*. Refinement is usually extended to specifications (Morgan 1990). Using pre- and post-specifications noted as [*pre*,*post*], two particular cases often arise:

$$[p,q] \sqsubseteq [p',q] \text{ if } p \Rightarrow p' \text{ (pre-conditions weakening)}$$
$$[p,q] \sqsubseteq [p,q'] \text{ if } q' \Rightarrow q \text{ (post-conditions strengthening)}$$

Knapp (Knapp 1990) defines refinement in a different manner in order to apply it to UNITY programs (Chandy & Misra 1988). The definition is equivalent, but changes in its formulation because it adapts to specifications expressed in a modal logic. Let s and s' be two states, where $s(p)$ and $s'(q)$ mean that s and s' satisfies p and q respectively. Intuitively, a specification S has the following form:

$$S : \forall s(p) \cdot \exists s'(q) \cdot s \leadsto s' \qquad (1)$$

where the notation $s \leadsto s'$ means that s' is a reachable state from the initial state s. The definition of refinement becomes:

Definition 6 *Let S and S′ be two specifications of the form* (1)*:*

$$S \sqsubseteq S' \textit{ if and only if } S' \Rightarrow S$$

4.2 Refinement of PEI statements

Refinement relation.
The refinement in PEI is close to Knapp's definition, but reasoning is based on first order logic. Let us consider a statement P{S}. The equations of S can be parsed into two exclusive types: the equations which only bind input data fields of P (they form a subset S_1 of S), and the equations which have intermediate or output data fields (these equations form the complementary subset S_2 of S). We call the equations of S_1 the *pre-equations* of P, and the equations of S_2 the *post-equations* of P.

According to the previous semantics definition we can state a property which is satisfied by a statement PEI. Let us call *sat*(P) the property satisfied by statement P: it means that for all input data fields verifying S_1, the solution is a set of output data fields which verify S_2. Alternatively, we can write:

$$sat(\mathtt{P}) : \; [\![S_1]\!] \Rightarrow [\![S_2]\!]$$

For example, we associate with the following statement .

$$\mathtt{P1} \;:\; \mathtt{A} \mapsto \mathtt{B}$$
$$\begin{cases} \mathtt{A} = \mathtt{matrix} :: \mathtt{A} \\ \mathtt{B} = \mathtt{A} \lhd \mathtt{transp} \end{cases}$$
$$\begin{aligned} \mathtt{matrix} &= \lambda(\mathtt{i,j})|(\mathtt{0<=i,j<n}).(\mathtt{i,j}) \\ \mathtt{transp} &= \lambda(\mathtt{i,j})|(\mathtt{0<=i,j<n}).(\mathtt{j,i}) \end{aligned}$$

the property $sat(\mathtt{P1}) : \; [\![(\mathtt{A} = \mathtt{matrix} :: \mathtt{A})]\!] \Rightarrow [\![(\mathtt{B} = \mathtt{A} \lhd \mathtt{transp})]\!]$
which means:

$$\begin{aligned} sat(\mathtt{P1}) : \quad & (v_{\mathtt{A}} = v_{\mathtt{A}} \circ \mathtt{matrix}^{-1}) \wedge (\sigma_{\mathtt{A}} = \sigma_{\mathtt{A}} \circ \mathtt{matrix}^{-1}) \\ & \wedge (dom(v_{\mathtt{A}}) \subseteq dom(\mathtt{matrix})) \\ \Rightarrow \quad & (v_{\mathtt{B}} = v_{\mathtt{A}} \circ \mathtt{transp}) \wedge (\sigma_{\mathtt{B}} = \sigma_{\mathtt{A}}) \\ & \wedge (dom(\mathtt{transp}) \subseteq dom(\sigma_{\mathtt{A}})) \wedge (img(\mathtt{transp}) \subseteq dom(v_{\mathtt{A}})) \end{aligned}$$

The constraints on domains arise from the operations definition : for example $\mathtt{h} :: \mathtt{X}$ is correctly defined only if $dom(v_{\mathtt{X}}) \subseteq dom(\mathtt{h})$.

Definition 7 *Let* P *and* P' *be two statements in* PEI. P *is said* refined by P' *—or* P abstracts P'*— denoted as* $\mathtt{P} \sqsubseteq \mathtt{P'}$, *if* $sat(\mathtt{P'}) \Rightarrow sat(\mathtt{P})$.

Here is some classical examples of refinements in programming languages, such as the weakening of pre-conditions or the strengthening of post-conditions. In PEI, such transformations are expressed through the following property:

Property 3 *Let* P{S_1, S_2} *and* P'{S_1', S_2'} *be two statements, where* S_1, S_1' *are sets of pre-equations, and* S_2, S_2' *are sets of post-equations:*

$$\mathtt{P} \sqsubseteq \mathtt{P'} \quad \begin{array}{ll} \textit{if} & [\![S_2 = S_2']\!] \;\; \textit{and} \;\; [\![S_1]\!] \Rightarrow [\![S_1']\!] \\ \textit{or} & [\![S_1 = S_1']\!] \;\; \textit{and} \;\; [\![S_2']\!] \Rightarrow [\![S_2]\!] \end{array}$$

Proof. Let us assume $[\![S_1]\!] \Rightarrow [\![S'_1]\!]$, then $([\![S'_1]\!] \Rightarrow [\![S_2]\!]) \Rightarrow ([\![S_1]\!] \Rightarrow [\![S_2]\!])$. Similarly, $[\![S'_2]\!] \Rightarrow [\![S_2]\!]$ implies $([\![S_1]\!] \Rightarrow [\![S'_2]\!]) \Rightarrow ([\![S_1]\!] \Rightarrow [\![S_2]\!])$. □

Example 3 Weakening pre-equations

$$\mathtt{P2} : \mathtt{X} \mapsto \mathtt{Y} \quad \begin{cases} \mathtt{X} = \mathtt{vector} :: \mathtt{X} \\ \mathtt{Y} = \mathtt{X} \end{cases}$$

specified by $sat(\mathtt{P2})$:
$[\![\mathtt{X} = \mathtt{vector} :: \mathtt{X}]\!] \Rightarrow [\![\mathtt{Y} = \mathtt{X}]\!]$

$$\mathtt{P3} : \mathtt{X} \mapsto \mathtt{Y} \quad \{ \mathtt{Y} = \mathtt{X}$$

specified by $sat(\mathtt{P3})$:
true $\Rightarrow [\![\mathtt{Y} = \mathtt{X}]\!]$

Let us demonstrate $sat(\mathtt{P3}) \Rightarrow sat(\mathtt{P2})$: $sat(\mathtt{P3})$ can be simplified to $(\mathtt{Y} = \mathtt{X})$ and the property $[\![\mathtt{Y} = \mathtt{X}]\!] \Rightarrow ([\![\mathtt{X} = \mathtt{vector} :: \mathtt{X}]\!] \Rightarrow [\![\mathtt{Y} = \mathtt{X}]\!])$ is true.
◇

Example 4 Strengthening post-equations

$$\mathtt{P4} : \mathtt{X} \mapsto \mathtt{Y} \quad \begin{cases} \mathtt{vector} :: \mathtt{Z} = \mathtt{X} \\ \mathtt{Y} = \mathtt{vector} :: \mathtt{Z} \end{cases}$$

specified by $sat(\mathtt{P4})$: true $\Rightarrow [\![\mathtt{vector} :: \mathtt{Z} = \mathtt{X}]\!] \wedge [\![\mathtt{Y} = \mathtt{vector} :: \mathtt{Z}]\!]$

We have $\mathtt{P3} \sqsubseteq \mathtt{P4}$ since $([\![\mathtt{vector} :: \mathtt{Z} = \mathtt{X}]\!] \wedge [\![\mathtt{Y} = \mathtt{vector} :: \mathtt{Z}]\!]) \Rightarrow [\![\mathtt{Y} = \mathtt{X}]\!]$.
◇

Refinement calculus.
In a more operational way, we define a *refinement calculus* allowing to build a refined statement from a given one. In PEI, the calculus consists in replacing one equation in the initial statement with another one. This can be done

- either by replacing *equal by equal* data fields expressions (cf. *Algebraic laws* hereunder),
- or by changing the reference domain of the equation (cf. *Change of reference domain*),
- or by substituting an equivalent data field for a given one. This requires the definition of a more general refinement relation including data fields equivalence (cf. *Refinement within the equivalence*).

Algebraic laws.
Some algebraic laws on operations can be proved. Assuming some hypotheses, they allow to replace a data field expression by another one in equations. In table 1, we note as $E \longrightarrow E'$ the rewriting of equation E in equation E' by applying such a law. The laws are the basis for the refinement calculus, as stated in the following property. We note as $S[\mathtt{E} \backslash \mathtt{E}']$ the equation set S in which an equation $\mathtt{E}$ has been rewritten as $\mathtt{E}'$, according to the laws.

(1a)	$Y = f1 \triangleright (f2 :: X) \longrightarrow Y = f2 :: (f1 \triangleright X)$
(1b)	$Y = f2 :: (f1 \triangleright X) \longrightarrow Y = f1 \triangleright (f2 :: X)$
(2a)	$Y = (f1 \triangleright X) \triangleleft f2 \longrightarrow Y = f1 \triangleright (X \triangleleft f2)$
(2b)	$Y = f1 \triangleright (X \triangleleft f2) \longrightarrow Y = (f1 \triangleright X) \triangleleft f2$
(3a)	$Y = (f2 :: X) \triangleleft f1 \longrightarrow Y = f2 :: (X \triangleleft f2^{-1} \circ f1 \circ f2)$ with $dom(f1) \cup img(f1) \subseteq img(f2) \wedge dom(v_X) \subseteq dom(f2)$
(3b)	$Y = f2 :: (X \triangleleft f1) \longrightarrow Y = (f2 :: X) \triangleleft f2 \circ f1 \circ f2^{-1}$ with $dom(f1) \cup img(f1) \subseteq dom(f2)$
(3c)	$Y = f1 \ ;\triangleright (f2 :: X) \longrightarrow Y = f2 :: (f2^{-1} \circ f1 \circ f2 \ ;\triangleright X)$ with $dom(f1) \cup img(f1) \subseteq img(f2) \wedge dom(v_X) \subseteq dom(f2)$
(3d)	$Y = f2 :: (f1 \ ;\triangleright X) \longrightarrow Y = f2 \circ f1 \circ f2^{-1} \ ;\triangleright (f2 :: X)$ with $dom(f1) \cup img(f1) \subseteq dom(f2)$
(4a)	$Y = (f1 \circ f2) \triangleright X \longrightarrow Y = f1 \triangleright (f2 \triangleright X)$
(4b)	$Y = f1 \triangleright (f2 \triangleright X) \longrightarrow Y = (f1 \circ f2) \triangleright X$
(5a)	$Y = X \triangleleft (f1 \circ f2) \longrightarrow Y = (X \triangleleft f1) \triangleleft f2$
(5b)	$Y = (X \triangleleft f1) \triangleleft f2 \longrightarrow Y = X \triangleleft (f1 \circ f2)$ with $img(f2) \subseteq dom(f1) \subseteq dom(\sigma_X)$
(6)	$Y = (f1 \circ f2) \ ;\triangleright X \longrightarrow Y = f1 \ ;\triangleright (f2 \ ;\triangleright X)$
(7a)	$Y = (f1 \circ f2) :: X \longrightarrow Y = f1 :: (f2 :: X)$
(7b)	$Y = f1 :: (f2 :: X) \longrightarrow Y = (f1 \circ f2) :: X$ with f1 and f2 two bijections
(8a)	$Y = (X1 \ /\&/ \ X2) \triangleleft f \longrightarrow Y = (X1 \triangleleft f) \ /\&/ \ (X2 \triangleleft f)$
(8b)	$Y = (X1 \triangleleft f) \ /\&/ \ (X2 \triangleleft f) \longrightarrow Y = (X1 \ /\&/ \ X2) \triangleleft f$ with $dom(f) \subseteq dom(\sigma_{X1}) \cap dom(\sigma_{X2})$ $\wedge img(f) \subseteq dom(v_{X1}) \cap dom(v_{X2})$
(9a)	$Y = X \triangleleft (f1 \# f2) \longrightarrow Y = (X \triangleleft f1) \ /\&/ \ (X \triangleleft f2)$
(9b)	$Y = (X \triangleleft f1) \ /\&/ \ (X \triangleleft f2) \longrightarrow Y = X \triangleleft (f1 \# f2)$ with $dom(f1) \cap dom(f2) = \emptyset$
(10)	$Y = (f1 \# f2) \ ;\triangleright X \longrightarrow Y = (f1 \ ;\triangleright X) \ /\&/ \ (f2 \ ;\triangleright X)$
(11a)	$Y = (f :: X1) \ /\&/ \ (f :: X2) \longrightarrow Y = f :: (X1 \ /\&/ \ X2)$
(11b)	$Y = f :: (X1 \ /\&/ \ X2) \longrightarrow Y = (f :: X1) \ /\&/ \ (f :: X2)$

Table 1 Rewriting of equations

Property 4 *Let E and E' be two equations in a* PEI *statement* $\mathtt{P}\{S\}$*:*
- if $E \longrightarrow E'$ *and* E, E' *are pre-equations, then* $\mathtt{P}\{S[E\backslash E']\} \sqsubseteq \mathtt{P}$
- if $E \longrightarrow E'$ *and* E, E' *are post-equations, then* $\mathtt{P} \sqsubseteq \mathtt{P}\{S[E\backslash E']\}$

Proof. We only report the proof for two rules in this paper, assuming they apply in a post-equation.

- Let us consider rule (5a) and prove $p' \Rightarrow p$, where:

$$\begin{aligned} p \;=\; & (v_\mathtt{Y} = v_\mathtt{X} \circ \mathtt{f1} \circ \mathtt{f2}) \wedge (\sigma_\mathtt{Y} = \sigma_\mathtt{X}) \\ & \wedge (dom(\mathtt{f1} \circ \mathtt{f2}) \subseteq dom(\sigma_\mathtt{X})) \wedge (img(\mathtt{f1} \circ \mathtt{f2}) \subseteq dom(v_\mathtt{X})) \\ p' \;=\; & (v_\mathtt{Y} = v_\mathtt{X} \circ \mathtt{f1} \circ \mathtt{f2}) \wedge (\sigma_\mathtt{Y} = \sigma_\mathtt{X}) \\ & \wedge (dom(\mathtt{f1}) \subseteq dom(\sigma_\mathtt{X})) \wedge (dom(\mathtt{f2}) \subseteq dom(\sigma_\mathtt{X})) \\ & \wedge (img(\mathtt{f1}) \subseteq dom(v_\mathtt{X})) \wedge (img(\mathtt{f2}) \subseteq dom(v_\mathtt{X} \circ \mathtt{f1})) \end{aligned}$$

The proposition reduces to:

$$(2) \left\{ \begin{array}{l} v_\mathtt{Y} = v_\mathtt{X} \circ \mathtt{f1} \circ \mathtt{f2} \\ \sigma_\mathtt{Y} = \sigma_\mathtt{X} \\ img(\mathtt{f1}) \subseteq dom(v_\mathtt{X}) \\ img(\mathtt{f2}) \subseteq dom(v_\mathtt{X} \circ \mathtt{f1}) \end{array} \right. \Rightarrow (1) \left\{ \begin{array}{l} img(\mathtt{f1} \circ \mathtt{f2}) \subseteq dom(v_\mathtt{X}) \\ dom(\mathtt{f1} \circ \mathtt{f2}) \subseteq dom(\sigma_\mathtt{X}) \end{array} \right.$$

Let us assume (2) holds. Since $dom(v_\mathtt{X} \circ \mathtt{f1}) \subseteq dom(\mathtt{f1})$, we have $img(\mathtt{f2}) \subseteq dom(\mathtt{f1})$ and from function composition, $img(\mathtt{f1} \circ \mathtt{f2}) = img(\mathtt{f1})$. So $img(\mathtt{f1}) \subseteq dom(v_\mathtt{X})$ can be rewritten $img(\mathtt{f1} \circ \mathtt{f2}) \subseteq dom(v_\mathtt{X})$. Moreover, it implies $dom(\mathtt{f1} \circ \mathtt{f2}) = dom(v_\mathtt{X} \circ \mathtt{f1} \circ \mathtt{f2})$ which equals $dom(v_\mathtt{Y})$. From data field definition we have $dom(v_\mathtt{Y}) \subseteq dom(\sigma_\mathtt{Y})$ and, since $\sigma_\mathtt{Y} = \sigma_\mathtt{X}$, $dom(\mathtt{f1} \circ \mathtt{f2}) \subseteq dom(\sigma_\mathtt{X})$.

- Concerning rule (7a), let us prove $p' \Rightarrow p$, where:

$$\begin{aligned} p \;=\; & (v_\mathtt{Y} = v_\mathtt{X} \circ \mathtt{f2}^{-1} \circ \mathtt{f1}^{-1}) \wedge (\sigma_\mathtt{Y} = \sigma_\mathtt{X} \circ \mathtt{f2}^{-1} \circ \mathtt{f1}^{-1}) \\ & \wedge (dom(v_\mathtt{X}) \subseteq dom(\mathtt{f1} \circ \mathtt{f2})) \\ p' \;=\; & (v_\mathtt{Y} = v_\mathtt{X} \circ \mathtt{f2}^{-1} \circ \mathtt{f1}^{-1}) \wedge (\sigma_\mathtt{Y} = \sigma_\mathtt{X} \circ \mathtt{f2}^{-1} \circ \mathtt{f1}^{-1}) \\ & \wedge (dom(v_\mathtt{X}) \subseteq dom(\mathtt{f2})) \wedge (dom(v_\mathtt{X} \circ \mathtt{f2}^{-1}) \subseteq dom(\mathtt{f1})) \end{aligned}$$

The proposition reduces to:

$$(2) \left\{ \begin{array}{l} dom(v_\mathtt{X}) \subseteq dom(\mathtt{f2}) \\ dom(v_\mathtt{X} \circ \mathtt{f2}^{-1}) \subseteq dom(\mathtt{f1}) \end{array} \right. \Rightarrow (1) \; \{dom(v_\mathtt{X}) \subseteq dom(\mathtt{f1} \circ \mathtt{f2})$$

Let us assume (2) holds. Since $dom(v_\mathtt{X}) \subseteq dom(\mathtt{f2})$ we have:

$$\begin{aligned} dom(v_\mathtt{X} \circ \mathtt{f2}^{-1}) \subseteq dom(\mathtt{f1}) & \Rightarrow \mathtt{f2}(dom(v_\mathtt{X})) \subseteq dom(\mathtt{f1}) \\ & \Rightarrow \mathtt{f2}^{-1}(\mathtt{f2}(dom(v_\mathtt{X}))) \subseteq \mathtt{f2}^{-1}(dom(\mathtt{f1})) \\ & \Rightarrow dom(v_\mathtt{X}) \subseteq dom(\mathtt{f1} \circ \mathtt{f2}) \end{aligned}$$

□

Change of reference domain.
An other way to refine a PEI statement is to change the reference domain of an equation by applying a change of basis on both sides. This fact is expressed by the following rules on which property 4 also applies:

$$\mathtt{Y} = \mathtt{X} \longrightarrow \mathtt{h} :: \mathtt{Y} = \mathtt{h} :: \mathtt{X}$$
$$\text{with } dom(\sigma_\mathtt{X}) \subseteq dom(\mathtt{h}) \wedge dom(\sigma_\mathtt{Y}) \subseteq dom(\mathtt{h})$$

$$\texttt{h::Y} = \texttt{h::X} \quad \longrightarrow \quad \texttt{Y} = \texttt{X} \text{ with } dom(v_{\texttt{X}}) \subseteq dom(\texttt{h})$$

Proof. Let us prove the first rule. Let p be the property deduced from the equation Y = X (the left part of the rule) and let p' be the one deduced from the right part. We have:

$$\begin{array}{rcl} p & = & (v_{\texttt{Y}} = v_{\texttt{X}}) \wedge (\sigma_{\texttt{Y}} = \sigma_{\texttt{X}}) \\ p' & = & (v_{\texttt{Y}} \circ \texttt{h}^{-1} = v_{\texttt{X}} \circ \texttt{h}^{-1}) \wedge (\sigma_{\texttt{Y}} \circ \texttt{h}^{-1} = \sigma_{\texttt{X}} \circ \texttt{h}^{-1}) \\ & & \wedge\ (dom(v_{\texttt{X}}) \subseteq dom(\texttt{h})) \wedge (dom(v_{\texttt{Y}}) \subseteq dom(\texttt{h})) \\ & & \wedge\ (dom(\sigma_{\texttt{X}}) \subseteq dom(\texttt{h})) \wedge (dom(\sigma_{\texttt{Y}}) \subseteq dom(\texttt{h})) \end{array}$$

Let us show that $p' \Rightarrow p$: from $v_{\texttt{Y}} \circ \texttt{h}^{-1} = v_{\texttt{X}} \circ \texttt{h}^{-1}$ and $\sigma_{\texttt{Y}} \circ \texttt{h}^{-1} = \sigma_{\texttt{X}} \circ \texttt{h}^{-1}$, we deduce $v_{\texttt{X}}|_{dom(\texttt{h})} = v_{\texttt{Y}}|_{dom(\texttt{h})}$ and $\sigma_{\texttt{X}}|_{dom(\texttt{h})} = \sigma_{\texttt{Y}}|_{dom(\texttt{h})}$ respectively, and since $dom(v_{\texttt{X}})$, $dom(v_{\texttt{Y}})$, $dom(\sigma_{\texttt{X}})$ and $dom(\sigma_{\texttt{Y}})$ are subsets of $dom(\texttt{h})$, it follows $v_{\texttt{X}} = v_{\texttt{Y}}$ and $\sigma_{\texttt{X}} = \sigma_{\texttt{Y}}$.

The proof of the second rule is quite similar. □

Refinement within the equivalence.
A more general way to refine a PEI statement consists in substituting an equivalent data field for a given one, according to the weak or strong equivalences which were introduced in section 3.3. This can be done by generalizing the previous definition of refinement (definition 7), in order to take equivalence into account.

In the following, we note $S[\texttt{X}\backslash\texttt{X}']$ the equation set S in which one occurrence X has been replaced with another expression X′ of the same data field, and $S[\texttt{X}\backslash\texttt{X}']^*$ when all occurrences of X have been replaced by X′.

Definition 8 *Let* P *and* P' *be two statements, and S be the equation set of* P. *We say that* sat(P') implies sat(P) within data field equivalence, *denoted as* $sat(\texttt{P'}) \overset{\equiv}{\Rightarrow} sat(\texttt{P})$ *if and only if* $sat(\texttt{P'}) \Rightarrow sat(\widehat{\texttt{P}})$ *with:*

- *either* $\widehat{\texttt{P}} = \texttt{P}\{S[\texttt{X}\backslash e(\texttt{X})]^*\}$, *where* e(X) *is an expression depending on* X *and satisfies: for any data field denoted as this* X, *there exists a strongly equivalent data field, say* X′, *such that* e(X′) *and* X *denote the same data field,*
- *or* $\widehat{\texttt{P}} = \texttt{P}\{S[\texttt{E}\backslash e(\texttt{E})]\}$, *where* e(E) *is an expression depending on* E *and satisfies: for any data field denoted as this expression* E, *there exists a weakly equivalent data field expression, say* E′, *such that* e(E′) *and* E *denote the same data field.*

It allows to generalize the previous definition 7 of refinement in PEI as follows:

Definition 9 *Let* P *and* P' *be two statements.* P *is said* refined *by* P' *if and only if* $sat(\texttt{P'}) \overset{\equiv}{\Rightarrow} sat(\texttt{P})$.

Example 5 Refinement within the equivalence

Let us consider the two programs P5 and P6, and show that P5 $\sqsubseteq$ P6 using data fields equivalence.

$$\texttt{P5 : X} \mapsto \texttt{Y} \quad \begin{cases} \texttt{X} = \texttt{square::X} \\ \texttt{Y} = \texttt{X} \end{cases} \qquad \texttt{P6 : X} \mapsto \texttt{Y} \quad \begin{cases} \texttt{X} = \texttt{square::X} \\ \texttt{Z} = \texttt{X} \\ \texttt{transp::Y} = \texttt{Z} \end{cases}$$

$$\texttt{square} = \lambda\texttt{(i,j)|(0<=i,j<n).(i,j)}$$
$$\texttt{transp} = \lambda\texttt{(i,j)|(0<=i,j<n).(j,i)}$$

Let us consider $\widehat{\texttt{P5}}$ obtained from P5 by replacing Y with (transp::Y') and then by renaming Y' as Y (since Y and Y' are strongly equivalent). The properties we consider are then:

$$sat(\widehat{\texttt{P5}}) : [\![\texttt{X} = \texttt{square::X}]\!] \Rightarrow [\![\texttt{transp::Y} = \texttt{X}]\!]$$
$$sat(\texttt{P6}) : [\![\texttt{X} = \texttt{square::X}]\!] \Rightarrow ([\![\texttt{Z} = \texttt{X}]\!] \wedge [\![\texttt{transp::Y} = \texttt{Z}]\!])$$

It is straightforward that $sat(\texttt{P6}) \Rightarrow sat(\widehat{\texttt{P5}})$ because the equality on data fields is transitive. Then $sat(\texttt{P6}) \stackrel{\equiv}{\Rightarrow} sat(\texttt{P5})$ and P5 $\sqsubseteq$ P6.
◇

5 CASE STUDY: *GAXPY*

The example studied in this section is a variant of the *Gaxpy* operation (Golub & Loan 1989), which is merely a computation of the form: $c = Ax + y$, $A \in \mathbb{R}^{m \times n}$, $x \in \mathbb{R}^n$, $y \in \mathbb{R}^m$. We only consider in this article the particular case where $y = x$, which operation is often iterated to compute $A(\ldots(A(Ax+x)+x)\ldots)+x$, for example in the conjugate gradient method.

Due to its extensive usage in numerical computations, many implementations of the operation have been proposed for parallel computers. We show two data parallel versions of the algorithm: the first version takes into account hardware restrictions that are sometimes encountered (for instance, diagonal values cannot be broadcasted along a dimension on *CM-200* and *CM-5* computers (Petiton & Emad 1996)), whereas the second version does not consider this restriction. Thus the two algorithms differ in their data placement, and we show that one algorithm can be deduced from the other.

The initial algorithm is described on figure 9(a) and is transcribed by the program Gaxpx1: it consists in aligning x (represented by data field X) on the first row of the matrix (B0). Then, x is replicated on all the matrix rows to form the data field B. Such an alignment enables to compute all the products at one time (P). All P values have then to be added row-wise to obtain Ax, the result being arbitrarily placed on last column (C0). The addition of Ax with x requires C0 to be transposed (C1); eventually the result $Ax + x$ lies on first row of the matrix (C).

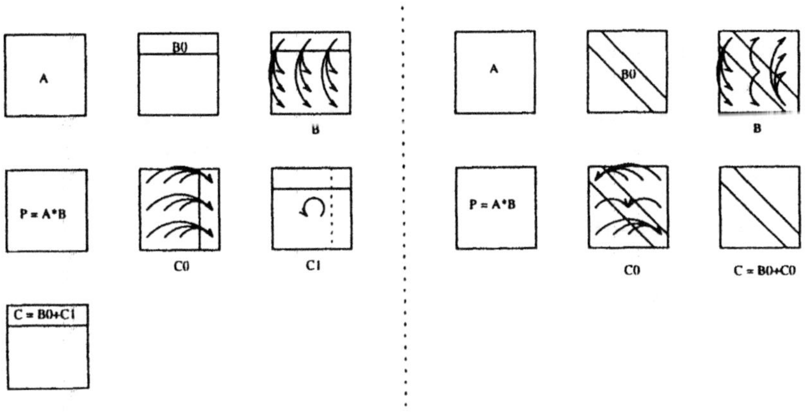

(a) (b)

Figure 9 (a) Initial algorithm (b) Improved algorithm

```
Gaxpx1 : (A,X) ↦ C
  ⎧ A = matrix :: A
  ⎪ X = align :: B0
  ⎪ B = B0 ◁ spread
  ⎨ P = prod ▷ (A /&/ B)
  ⎪ C0 = sum ▷ (red ;▷ P)
  ⎪ C1 = C0 ◁ col2row
  ⎩ C = add ▷ (B0 /&/ C1)
  matrix   =  λ(i,j)|(0≤i,j<n).(i,j)
  align    =  λ(i,j)|(i=0 & 0≤j<n).(j)
  spread   =  λ(i,j)|(0≤i,j<n).(0,j)
  red      =  λ(i,j)|(0≤i,j<n).(i,n-1)
  col2row  =  λ(i,j)|(i=0 & 0≤j<n).(j,n-1)
  add      =  λ(a;b).(a+b)
  prod     =  λ(a;b).(a*b)
  sum      =  id # λ(a;b).(a+sum b)
```

If the hardware requirements support broadcast of diagonal values, then we can design a more efficient program, as sketched on figure 9(b). Hence, the alignments of x and Ax on the diagonal makes the transposition phase useless. On parallel computers, such an operation involves a costly interprocessor communication so that removing this phase results in an important performance gain.

We show that the new program can be obtained from Gaxpx1 using the refinement calculus. The idea is to realign B0 and C0 by mapping them onto the diagonal.

5.1 Vector realignments

First, we change the definition of B0 relatively to X (we change X alignment) by applying the following change of basis (equal to its inverse), that swaps diagonal and first row points:

$$\texttt{row2diag} = \begin{array}{l} \lambda(\texttt{i},\texttt{j})|(\texttt{i}=0\,\&\,0\le \texttt{j}<\texttt{n}).(\texttt{j},\texttt{j})\ \# \\ \lambda(\texttt{i},\texttt{j})|(\texttt{i}\neq 0\,\&\,\texttt{i}=\texttt{j}\,\&\,0\le \texttt{j}<\texttt{n}).(0,\texttt{j})\ \# \\ \lambda(\texttt{i},\texttt{j})|(\texttt{i}\neq 0\,\&\,\texttt{i}\neq \texttt{j}\,\&\,0\le \texttt{i},\texttt{j}<\texttt{n}).(\texttt{i},\texttt{j}) \end{array}$$

From definitions 8 and 9, a refined program is obtained by replacing all occurrences of B0 by (row2diag :: B0):

$$\texttt{Gaxpx1'} : (\texttt{A},\texttt{X}) \mapsto \texttt{C}$$
$$\left\{ \begin{array}{lr} \texttt{A} = \texttt{matrix} :: \texttt{A} & \\ \texttt{X} = \texttt{align} :: (\texttt{row2diag} :: \texttt{B0}) & (i) \\ \texttt{B} = (\texttt{row2diag} :: \texttt{B0}) \lhd \texttt{spread} & (ii) \\ \texttt{P} = \texttt{prod} \rhd (\texttt{A} \ /\&/\ \texttt{B}) & \\ \texttt{C0} = \texttt{sum} \rhd (\texttt{red}\ ;\!\rhd\ \texttt{P}) & \\ \texttt{C1} = \texttt{C0} \lhd \texttt{col2row} & \\ \texttt{C} = \texttt{add} \rhd (\texttt{row2diag} :: \texttt{B0}\ /\&/\ \texttt{C1}) & \end{array} \right.$$

We obtain a new alignment from the previous statement, by applying some algebraic rules:

$$\begin{array}{lll} (i) & \longrightarrow & \textit{"rewriting rule (7b)"} \\ & & \texttt{X} = \texttt{align} \circ \texttt{row2diag} :: \texttt{B0} \\ & \longrightarrow & \textit{"function renaming"}, \\ & & \text{let } \texttt{align2} = \texttt{align} \circ \texttt{row2diag} = \lambda(\texttt{i},\texttt{j})|(\texttt{i}=\texttt{j}\,\&\,0\le \texttt{j}<\texttt{n}).(\texttt{j}) \\ & & \texttt{X} = \texttt{align2} :: \texttt{B0} \end{array}$$

Intuitively, the data field B has the same values in both versions, but their origins are different; it is a typical case of weak equivalence. From definition 8 and 9, (ii) may be replaced by

$$\texttt{B} = (\texttt{row2diag} :: ((\texttt{row2diag} :: \texttt{B0}) \lhd \texttt{spread})) \lhd \texttt{row2diag}$$

The expression can be successively transformed into the following equations where i denotes the identity on $\mathbb{Z}^2$:

$\texttt{B} = (\texttt{row2diag}::((\texttt{row2diag}::\texttt{B0}) \lhd \texttt{spread})) \lhd \texttt{row2diag}$

$\longrightarrow$ "*rewriting rule (3a)*",
as $img(\texttt{spread}) \subseteq img(\texttt{row2diag})$
and $dom(v_{\texttt{B0}}) \subseteq dom(\texttt{row2diag})$ from (i),
and "*function renaming*",

$$
\begin{aligned}
\text{let } \texttt{spread2} &= \texttt{row2diag} \circ \texttt{spread} \circ \texttt{row2diag} \\
&= \lambda(\texttt{i},\texttt{j})|(0 \le \texttt{i},\texttt{j} < \texttt{n}).(\texttt{j},\texttt{j})
\end{aligned}
$$

$\texttt{B} = (\texttt{row2diag}::(\texttt{row2diag}::(\texttt{B0} \lhd \texttt{spread2}))) \lhd \texttt{row2diag}$

$\longrightarrow$ "*rewriting rule (7b)*"
$\texttt{B} = (\texttt{i}|_{dom(\texttt{row2diag})}::(\texttt{B0} \lhd \texttt{spread2})) \lhd \texttt{row2diag}$

$\longrightarrow$ "*simplification*", since $dom(\texttt{spread2}) \subseteq dom(\texttt{row2diag})$
$\texttt{B} = (\texttt{B0} \lhd \texttt{spread2}) \lhd \texttt{row2diag}$

$\longrightarrow$ "*rewriting rule (5b)*", since $dom(\texttt{spread2}) \subseteq dom(\sigma_{\texttt{B0}})$
$\texttt{B} = \texttt{B0} \lhd \texttt{spread2} \circ \texttt{row2diag}$

$\longrightarrow$ "*definition of* spread2", $\texttt{spread2} = \texttt{spread2} \circ \texttt{row2diag}$
$\texttt{B} = \texttt{B0} \lhd \texttt{spread2}$

The following refined program summarizes the previous refinements:

$$
\texttt{Gaxpx2} : (\texttt{A},\texttt{X}) \mapsto \texttt{C}
\left\{
\begin{array}{l}
\texttt{A} = \texttt{matrix}::\texttt{A} \\
\texttt{X} = \texttt{align2}::\texttt{B0} \\
\texttt{B} = \texttt{B0} \lhd \texttt{spread2} \\
\texttt{P} = \texttt{prod} \rhd (\texttt{A} \ /\&/\ \texttt{B}) \\
\texttt{C0} = \texttt{sum} \rhd (\texttt{red}\ ;\!\rhd\ \texttt{P}) \\
\texttt{C1} = \texttt{C0} \lhd \texttt{col2row} \\
\texttt{C} = \texttt{add} \rhd (\texttt{row2diag}::\texttt{B0}\ /\&/\ \texttt{C1})
\end{array}
\right.
$$

Similarly, we change the alignment of Ax (C0) using the change of basis:

$$
\begin{aligned}
\texttt{col2diag} = \ & \lambda(\texttt{i},\texttt{j})|(\texttt{j}=\texttt{n}-1\ \&\ 0 \le \texttt{i} < \texttt{n}).(\texttt{i},\texttt{i})\ \# \\
& \lambda(\texttt{i},\texttt{j})|(\texttt{j} \ne \texttt{n}-1\ \&\ \texttt{i}=\texttt{j}\ \&\ 0 \le \texttt{i} < \texttt{n}).(\texttt{i},\texttt{n}-1)\ \# \\
& \lambda(\texttt{i},\texttt{j})|(\texttt{j} \ne \texttt{n}-1\ \&\ \texttt{i} \ne \texttt{j}\ \&\ 0 \le \texttt{i},\texttt{j} < \texttt{n}).(\texttt{i},\texttt{j})
\end{aligned}
$$

From definitions 8 and 9, we can refine Gaxpx2 in:

$$
\texttt{Gaxpx2'} : (\texttt{A},\texttt{X}) \mapsto \texttt{C}
\left\{
\begin{array}{ll}
\texttt{A} = \texttt{matrix}::\texttt{A} & \\
\texttt{X} = \texttt{align2}::\texttt{B0} & \\
\texttt{B} = \texttt{B0} \lhd \texttt{spread2} & \\
\texttt{P} = \texttt{prod} \rhd (\texttt{A} \ /\&/\ \texttt{B}) & \\
\texttt{col2diag}::\texttt{C0} = \texttt{sum} \rhd (\texttt{red}\ ;\!\rhd\ \texttt{P}) & (iii) \\
\texttt{C1} = (\texttt{col2diag}::\texttt{C0}) \lhd \texttt{col2row} & (iv) \\
\texttt{C} = \texttt{add} \rhd (\texttt{row2diag}::\texttt{B0}\ /\&/\ \texttt{C1}) &
\end{array}
\right.
$$

As shown on figure 9(b), P values are gathered on the diagonal to form C0. The data field P and (col2diag : : P) ◁ col2diag are weakly equivalent. We obtain a new reduction by applying some rewriting rules on the following expression:

col2diag :: C0 = sum ▷ (red ;▷ ((col2diag :: P) ◁ col2diag))

⟶ "*rewriting rule (3a)*", since $dom(v_P) \subseteq dom(\text{cold2diag})$
col2diag :: C0 = sum ▷ (red ;▷ (col2diag :: (P ◁ col2diag)))

⟶ "*rewriting rule (3c) and function renaming*",
let red2 = col2diag ∘ red ∘ col2diag = λ(i,j)|(0≤i,j<n).(i,i)
col2diag :: C0 = sum ▷ (col2diag :: (red2 ;▷ (P ◁ col2diag)))

⟶ "*rewriting rule (1a)*"
col2diag :: C0 = col2diag :: (sum ▷ (red2 ;▷ (P ◁ col2diag)))

⟶ "*change of reference domain*"
as $dom(v_{C0}) \subseteq dom(\text{col2diag})$ from equation (*iv*)
C0 = sum ▷ (red2 ;▷ (P ◁ col2diag))

The following steps allows the routing col2diag to be removed in the last expression:

⟶ "*definition of* red2", red2 = red2 ∘ col2diag
C0 = sum ▷ (red2 ∘ col2diag ;▷ (P ◁ col2diag))

⟶ "*rewriting rule (6) and property 1*", col2diag equals to its inverse
C0 = sum ▷ (red2 ;▷ ((P ◁ col2diag) ◁ col2diag))

⟶ "*rewriting rule (5b)*", since $dom(\text{col2diag}) \subseteq dom(\sigma_P)$
C0 = sum ▷ (red2 ;▷ (P ◁ $\text{i}|_{dom(\text{col2diag})}$))

⟶ "*simplification*", since $dom(\text{col2diag}) \subseteq dom(v_P)$
C0 = sum ▷ (red2 ;▷ P)

We thus have:

Gaxpx3 : (A,X) ↦ C
{
A = matrix :: A
X = align2 :: B0
B = B0 ◁ spread2
P = prod ▷ (A /&/ B)
C0 = sum ▷ (red2 ;▷ P)
C1 = (col2diag :: C0) ◁ col2row (*vi*)
C = add ▷ (row2diag :: B0 /&/ C1)

5.2 Transposition removing

Intuitively, C0 and B0 are both aligned on the diagonal, making the transposition defined by C1 useless. As B0 is aligned using row2diag, we have to introduce row2diag in the expression of C0. The idea is to decompose col2diag using row2diag. Since col2diag realigns B0 onto the last column, we have to complete row2diag by a change of basis that swaps the last column and the first row. Let `row2col` be this change of basis:

$$\texttt{row2col} = \begin{array}{l} \lambda(i,j)|(j=n-1 \,\&\, 0 \le i < n).(0,i) \ \# \\ \lambda(i,j)|(j \ne n-1 \,\&\, i=0 \,\&\, 0 \le j < n).(j,n-1) \ \# \\ \lambda(i,j)|(j \ne n-1 \,\&\, i \ne 0 \,\&\, 0 \le i,j < n).(i,j) \end{array}$$

Since `col2diag` and `row2col` ∘ `row2diag` are equal on the value domain of `C0`, the data fields `col2diag :: C0` and `row2col ∘ row2diag :: C0` are weakly equivalent. Moreover, `row2col ∘ row2diag :: C0` can be rewritten as `row2col :: (row2diag :: C0)` from rewriting rule (7a), and `col2row` is equal to `row2col` on the first row (*i.e.* the value domain of `row2diag :: C0`). Therefore we can conclude that data fields `C1` and `row2diag :: C0` are weakly equivalent. This allows the new statement `Gaxpx3` to be obtained by substituting `row2diag :: C0` for `C1` definition, using weak equivalence implication (definition 8):

$$\texttt{Gaxpx3'} : (\texttt{A},\texttt{X}) \mapsto \texttt{C}$$
$$\left\{ \begin{array}{l} \texttt{A} = \texttt{matrix :: A} \\ \texttt{X} = \texttt{align2 :: B0} \\ \texttt{B} = \texttt{B0} \lhd \texttt{spread2} \\ \texttt{P} = \texttt{prod} \rhd (\texttt{A /\&/ B}) \\ \texttt{C0} = \texttt{sum} \rhd (\texttt{red2} \ ;\!\rhd \ \texttt{P}) \\ \texttt{C} = \texttt{add} \rhd (\texttt{row2diag :: B0 /\&/ row2diag :: C0}) \end{array} \right.$$

We obtain the final statement from the previous one by applying the change of basis defined by `row2diag` on `C` and by using rules (11a), (1a) and the change of reference domain in the last equation.

$$\texttt{Gaxpx4} : (\texttt{A},\texttt{X}) \mapsto \texttt{C}$$
$$\left\{ \begin{array}{l} \texttt{A} = \texttt{matrix :: A} \\ \texttt{X} = \texttt{align2 :: B0} \\ \texttt{B} = \texttt{B0} \lhd \texttt{spread2} \\ \texttt{P} = \texttt{prod} \rhd (\texttt{A /\&/ B}) \\ \texttt{C0} = \texttt{sum} \rhd (\texttt{red2} \ ;\!\rhd \ \texttt{P}) \\ \texttt{C} = \texttt{add} \rhd (\texttt{B0 /\&/ C0}) \end{array} \right.$$

6 CONCLUSION

We have presented in this paper a formalism designed for the construction and derivation of parallel programs. In particular, it has shown to be well suited to data parallel programs specifications, and the case study in last section showed a specific but nonetheless crucial kind of transformation for that model, which mainly concerns data alignments. In addition to the PEI theory, some tools have been developed to ease the use of PEI:

- a type-checker that infers the domains of the data fields in a statement, and therefore controls the data fields consistency. Furthermore, the inference of domain information allows conditions required by refinement rules to be easily checked,
- the refinement calculus can be done through a dedicated tool. It browses a statement, in which any data field expression may be selected and refined, the appropriate rewriting rule being automatically applied,
- some other prototype tools, such as a PEI-CAML and PEI-HPF compiler, should also enlarge the potential use of PEI.

REFERENCES

Back, R. J. (1988), 'A calculus of refinements for program derivations', *Acta Informatica* **25**, 593–624.

Bird, R. S. (1987), Introduction to the theory of lists, *in* M. Broy, ed., 'Logic of Programming and Calculi of Discrete Design', Springer-Verlag, pp. 3–42.

Chandy, K. M. & Misra, J. (1988), *Parallel Program Design :* A foundation, Addison Wesley.

Chen, M., il Choo, Y. & Li, J. (1991), *Parallel Functional Languages and Compilers*, ACM Press.

Genaud, S., Violard, E. & Perrin, G.-R. (1995), Transformations techniques in PEI, *in* P. Magnusson, S. Haridi & A. Khayri, eds, 'LNCS', EURO-PAR95 Parallel Processing, Springer-Verlag, Stockholm, Sweden, pp. 131–142.

Golub, G. H. & Loan, C. F. V. (1989), *Matrix Computations*, 2nd edn, The John Hopkins University Press.

HPF (1993), *High Performance Fortran Language Specification*, 1.0 edn.

Knapp, E. (1990), 'An exercise in the formal derivation of parallel programs: Maximum flows in graphs', *ACM Transactions on Programming Languages and Systems* **12**, 203–223.

Mauras, C. (1989), ALPHA : un langage équationnel pour la conception et la programmation d'architectures parallèles synchrones, PhD thesis, Université de Rennes I.

Morgan, C. (1990), *Programming from specifications*, C.A.R. Hoare, Prentice Hall Ed., Endlewood Cliffs, N.J.

Petiton, S. & Emad, N. (1996), *A data parallel scientific computation introduction*, Vol. LNCS 1132, Springer Verlag, pp. 45–62.

Skillicorn, D. B. (1993), The Bird-Meertens formalism as a parallel model, *in* J. Kowalik & L. Grandinetti, eds, 'NATO ARW "Software for Parallel Computation"', Springer-Verlag.

Thi (1990), *C* Programming Guide*.

Violard, E. & Perrin, G.-R. (1992), 'PEI : a language and its refinement calculus for parallel programming', *Parallel Computing* **18**, 1167–1184.

Violard, E. & Perrin, G.-R. (1993), PEI : a single unifying model to design parallel programs, *in* A. Bode, M. Reeve & G. Wolf, eds, 'PARLE 93, LNCS', Springer-Verlag, pp. 500–516.

7 BIOGRAPHIES

ERIC VIOLARD has been an assistant professor at the University of Besancon (France) since 1993 where he submitted a doctorate in 1992. He is currently working at the ICPS laboratory in Strasbourg. His research work is concerned with design of parallel programs by transformation techniques. His current works concern the foundations of PEI.

STÉPHANE GENAUD received a PhD in computer science from Louis Pasteur University of Strasbourg (France) in 1997. He is currently a lecturer at IUT d'informatique de Strasbourg. His research interests are in languages and methods for parallel programming.

GUY-RENÉ PERRIN received his PhD in 1976 and his higher doctorate in 1985. Since this date he has been a professor in Computer Science at the University of Besançon (France) where he was head of the Computer Science Department and of the Postgraduate Research Courses. Since 1994 he is a professor at the University Louis Pasteur at Strasbourg, where he is head of the ICPS research team. He is currently engaged in research on automatic parallelization techniques and data parallel programming.

6

Solving Large Systems of Differential Equations in Parallel Using Covers and Skeletons

M. Südholt[†], *C. Piepenbrock*[‡], *K. Obermayer*[‡] *and P. Pepper*[‡]

[†]*Projet Lande, INRIA/IRISA-Rennes, France,* sudholt@irisa.fr
[‡]*Fachbereich Informatik, Institut für Kommunikations- und Softwaretechnik, TU Berlin, Germany,* {piep, oby, pepper}@cs.tu-berlin.de

Abstract

The design and implementation of parallel algorithms for distributed memory architectures is much harder than the development of sequential algorithms. This is mainly due to the communication and synchronization that is necessary to manage distributed data correctly. This paper applies a methodology for the transformational derivation of parallel programs using data distribution algebras that enable an abstract description of data distribution issues. Algorithms are formulated using skeletons, that is, specialized higher-order functions with particular parallel implementations. The methodology is applied to a the solution of a system of ordinary differential equations where convolutions can be computed using the Fast Fourier transformation. The example illustrates the practical optimization problems for a development model of the visual system that involves large scale neural network simulations. Finally, this algorithm is compared to an implementation of the same system of equations in the programming language C* on a CM-5.

Keywords

Functional programming, parallel programming, numerical algorithm, program transformation, skeleton, data distribution algebra

1 INTRODUCTION

The numerical solution of large systems of differential equations is one of the most challenging problems in the field of scientific computing. For many problems such systems are so large that only parallel computers possess the computational power necessary to solve the equations. Unfortunately, efficient parallel algorithms cannot simply be developed as extensions of their sequential counterparts. The spatial aspect of parallel algorithms—that is, the distribution of processes and data across the processing units of the parallel computer—constitutes a salient characteristic that is not encountered in the design of sequential algorithms.

Parallel algorithms that operate on distributed data have to communicate data at suitable synchronization points, which means that the temporal aspects of parallel algorithms are also much more complex than in the sequential case. Parallel programming in general is therefore much more error-prone, and it is considerably more difficult to verify and validate parallel than sequential algorithms. Moreover, the (commercial) availability of a multitude of parallel architectures complicates the development of portable parallel methodologies. Automatic program derivation by program transformation promises to yield a solution: transform high-level abstract specifications manually/automatically via less abstract intermediate specifications to efficient executable programs.

We see our approach as a step towards a compiler that performs an automatic transformational development of parallel algorithms in a functional setting. The essential ideas can be characterized as follows. We emphasize the distribution aspect from the very beginning of the design. The basic catchwords for this part of our approach are **data distribution algebras** describing so-called **covers**. Both the spatial distribution and the temporal evaluation are specified by abstract, high-level, functional language concepts, and the pertinent catchword here is **skeletons**. Finally, there is an underlying concept of program deduction that leads from high-level specifications to lower-level implementations. Instead of interactive program synthesis systems, however, we see powerful compilation techniques that can take over at a very early stage of the deduction process.

In contrast to imperative approaches, equational reasoning can be applied in a functional setting (semi-)automatically—a procedure that ensures the correctness of an implementation by the use of correctness-preserving transformations. Moreover, it supports portability across different target architectures by architecture-dependent transformations.

Our approach is based on a number of design decisions. Before dwelling on the technical details, we briefly discuss the considerations that motivate them.

The programmer must be in control of the distribution of the data over the local memories. The predominant parallel architectures on the market nowadays are MIMD machines with distributed memory (such as the CRAY T3E or the IBM SP2). There are strong indications that they will remain the forerunners in the future. In these architectures the distribution of the data over the local memories is the main factor that determines the communication amount. Experience has shown that in most cases the really "good" distributions rely on the properties of the application at hand—which a compiler cannot detect.

The programmer's control over the data distribution must be expressible in abstract mathematical terms, (ideally) without any explicit reference to communication features. As a consequence, we develop a description technique for data structures that amalgamates two viewpoints:

- In one view, data structures are standard mathematical objects that are amenable to standard functional treatment.
- But at the same time, data structures induce another view, which reflects a distribution over processors and the corresponding communication.

This requirement leads us to the introduction of so-called "covers", which are treated in detail in Section 3.2.

The programming model has to reflect the homogeneous nature of the underlying processors. Parallel (MIMD) computers are homogeneous in the sense that they consist of processors of the same kind, which, moreover, are connected in a regular way. Even though the technicalities of the processors and their connections should not concern the programmer, but be left to the compiler, the distinction of a homogeneous environment (as opposed to a network of heterogeneous machines) should be reflected in the programming model. As a consequence, our "covers" have to be described in terms of regular data structures, thus leading to the notion of "data distribution algebras" (discussed in Section 3.3) which are used to define skeletons implementing a SPMD programming model. In particular, this regular design explicitly supports the scalability of algorithms defined on such data structures.

1.1 Notation

Constructive calculi for program development in a functional setting feature quantifier- and index-free notations that rely on suitable concrete representations of data structures. For instance, the geometric representation of matrices used throughout this paper is defined as follows (cf. Pepper & Möller 1991, Bird 1989).

DEFINITION 1
The geometric representation of two-dimensional matrices is defined as

```
STRUCTURE Matrix[α]
   SORT α
   SORT matrix
   FUN □ : matrix                                     -- empty matrix
   FUN ⊡ _ : α → matrix                               -- one-element matrix
   FUN _ ◫ _ : matrix × matrix → matrix               -- horizontal composition
   FUN _ ⊟ _ : matrix × matrix → matrix               -- vertical composition
   FUN _ _ ⊞ _ _ : matrix × matrix × matrix × matrix → matrix
   AXM (a ⊟ b) ◫ (c ⊟ d) = a c ⊞ b d = (a ◫ c) ⊟ (b ◫ d)
   ...
   GENERATE matrix BY □ ⊡ ◫ ⊟
   GENERATE matrix BY □ ⊡ ⊞
```

The notation is based on concepts from the functional language OPAL. It should be essentially self-explanatory.

The above structure introduces a module for matrices over elements of a (parameter) sort α (to argue about the height, width and dimension of matrices, we use the functions `height`, `width` and `dim`, respectively.) Functionalities are introduced by the keyword FUN. Notations such as _ ◫ _ introduce infix operators, where the placeholders '_' indicate the parameter positions. The corresponding function definitions marked by DEF are given in this article using only standard constructs that are customary in functional programming, such as function composition (denoted by the composition operator '$\circ$') and the like. We will also state some derivable equivalences, which are introduced by the keyword THM.(Free) type definitions that are introduced by TYPE are used to define product types and to define constructor und selector functions on the free type.

The structures used in our approach are defined by (parametrized) algebraic specifications because this formalism is best suited for transformations based on equational reasoning. The above definition enables the formulation of laws in a much simpler and comprehensive way than with other formulations:

THM **Monoid**[**matrix**, $\square$, $\boxminus$]

THM **height**(**a** $\boxminus$ **b**) = **height**(**a**) + **height**(**b**)

The specification function `cost` is used to express properties about the communication costs of parallel algorithms.

Our remaining notations are standard: functions are specified using first-order predicate formulae. Function application — curried and/or uncurried — is bracketed, and standard operations on lists and related data types (e.g. vectors) are used: '#' denotes the length of lists or vectors, '::' prepends an element, 'ft' yields the first element, 'rt' the rest, and 'front' all elements except the last one.

2 MODELLING RECEPTIVE FIELD DEVELOPMENT IN THE VISUAL CORTEX

2.1 Visual Cortex

We now introduce a problem that involves solving large systems of differential equations. It is a massively parallel neural network simulation for the development of simple cell receptive fields in the visual cortex. Models and simulations in the neurosciences often involve large networks of neurons that require powerful tools for parallel computation. In the following sections we will demonstrate our approach of data distribution algebras using the mathematical model underlying this example.

In this section we briefly describe (*i*) how the brain can extract simple features from visual images; (*ii*) how the neurons involved in this process may have initally developed proper connections between each other; and (*iii*) how this development process of a large number of neurons may be modelled mathematically. The resulting model (see equation 1) is the basis for our implementations.

Images in the visual field are picked up by photoreceptor cells in the retina. Neurons transmit the image information to the cortex where it is interpreted. In a first step, the cortex extracts simple features from the images such as the position and orientation of edges and the eye from which a stimulus originates. Such feature detector cells can be found in layer IVc of the visual cortex V1. Hubel & Wiesel (1962) characterized them as simple cells and proposed a model for the neuronal connections in the primary visual pathways leading from the eyes via the lateral geniculate nucleus (LGN) to the visual cortex (see figure 1, left). They hypothesize that a cortical neuron becomes **orientation selective** if it receives input from alternating patches of light contrast (ON) and dark contrast (OFF) sensitive cells. In consequence, the neuron would respond maximally to an oriented light bar pattern that matches these receptive field patches (see Figure 1 left). At the same time each cortical neuron receives input signals mostly from only one of the two eyes and thus exhibits **ocular dominance**.

It is remarkable that for light bar stimuli at all angles that are flashed anywhere in one of the two eyes, a neuron can be found in V1 that responds optimally to this stimulus. Furthermore, neighbouring simple cells specialize on similar stimuli and form ordered feature maps (e.g. an ocular dominance map and an orientation selectivity map). Such **cortical maps** are a fundamental principle of cortical organization and can be found in many parts of the brain.

The complex neuronal wiring patterns from figure 1 are not completely genetically determined. Instead, their development depends on cell activity—they are "learned from experience". Based on a simple Hebbian learning mechanism a number of models have been put forward to explain the emergence of orientation selectivity and ocular dominance in simple cells and cortical map formation (Linsker 1986, Miller 1994, Obermayer et al. 1992, Erwin et al. 1995). The Hebbian rule simple states that a synaptic connection between two neurons becomes stronger if they are concurrently active. Here, we introduce a successful **correlation based learning model**.

2.2 Mathematical Model

The model uses simple connectionist-type neuron models: their activity is represented by a value that corresponds to the mean firing rate, i.e. a short time average over its cell membrane potential. This cell output depends on the activity of all the connected input neurons weighted by their connection strength. Neurons connect via synapses, and the connection strength is a value that includes the number of synapses between two neurons as well as their efficiency.

In our model (see figure 1, right), a neuron of LGN population i at location α connects to a cortical neuron at location x with synaptic strength $S^i_{\alpha,x}$. Activity patterns from the retinas (V^i_α) are projected to the LGN (activities P^i_α) and from there on to the cortex (O_x). All locations α, x are measured in retinal coordinates because all the projections are at least roughly topographic.

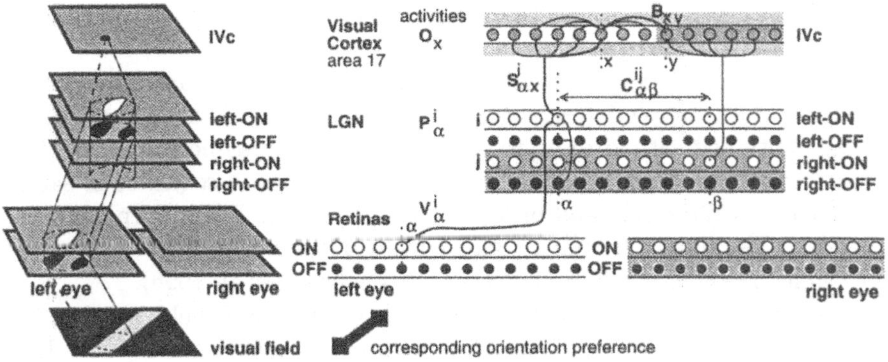

Figure 1 Left: Schematic drawing of the primary visual pathways and the Hubel and Wiesel model for simple cells. The synaptic connections for one cortical cell are shown as black and white patches. The neuron has left-eye ocular dominance and responds best to a light bar stimulus of the shown orientation. **Right:** The correlation-based learning model for simple cells (as on the left, the one-dimensional layers of neurons have to be implemented as two-dimensional sheets).

The correlation-based learning model assumes that orientation selectivity and ocular dominance of cortical simple cells are properties of the LGN-to-cortex connection strengths $S^i_{\alpha,x}$ (Linsker 1986, Miller 1994). Learning starts after the retina, the LGN and the cortex have developed their layered structure and after the formation of topographic but otherwise unspecific connections $S^i_{\alpha,x}$. Then the connection strengths $S^i_{\alpha,x}$ change from the stimuli in the retina by a Hebbian learning rule and orientation selectivity and ocular dominance emerges. The Hebbian principle yields the (linearized) correlation-based learning model (Miller 1994, Piepenbrock et al. 1996, Erwin & Miller 1995).

$$\frac{d}{dt}S^i x_{\alpha,x}(t) = \eta A_{\alpha,x} \sum_{j,\beta,y} I_{x,y} C^{ij}_{\alpha,\beta} S^j_{\beta,y}(t) - \gamma S^i_{\alpha,x}(t), \quad 0 \leq S^i_{\alpha,x}(t) \geq 1 \qquad (1)$$

$$\text{where} \quad C^{ij}_{\alpha,\beta} = \langle P^i_\alpha P^j_\beta \rangle \qquad I_{x,y} = \sum_{n=0}^{\infty} (B^n)_{x,y} \qquad (2)$$

The parameter η is the **learning rate**. The synaptic arbor function $A_{\alpha,x}$ conserves the **topographic mapping** and represents the maximum number of synapses between an LGN neuron at α and a cortical neuron at x (it is localized and thus zero for large distances $|\alpha - x|$). The intra-cortical interaction function I includes the effects of all connections among the cortex cells and ensures the emergence of the **cortical maps** (the cortical cells excite each other at short and inhibit each other at larger distances $|x - y|$). The two-point correlation functions C incorporates the driving force of the learning process: the **activity patterns** in the LGN that originate in the retinas. The term $-\gamma S^i_{\alpha,x}(t)$ constrains synaptic growth and keeps the $S^i_{\alpha,x}$ non-negative and the total synaptic connection strength for each cortical neuron constant (a nonlinear operation).

To implement this model, we choose constant functions A and I and initialize the synaptic connection strengths $S^i_{\alpha,x}$ unspecifically. (This means random values multiplied with A to establish the initial topographic mapping.) Then we compute the correlation functions C by generating a sequence of sample stimuli V^i_α on the retina and propagating them to the LGN (Piepenbrock et al. 1996). The retinal stimuli V^i_α may consist of spontaneous noise-like activity (Miller 1994) or wave-like patterns (Piepenbrock et al. 1996).

To simulate the development of the simple-cell receptive field, we only have to integrate Equation 1 numerically, in the simplest case using the Euler method. Note, however, that the location indexes α and x each denote two-dimensional position vectors, i.e. $S^i_{\alpha,x}$ is a five-dimensional data object.

The problem of numerically integrating a system of differential equations like Equation 1 is a very common problem in neural network modelling as well as in engineering in general. It is the size of the system that makes the problem difficult in practice. To simulate a large number of cortical neurons (e.g. 128 by 128), we need a parallel computer to make the computations feasible.

Equation 1 has been implemented in C* on a CM-5 parallel computer. In Section 4.4 we discuss this implementation and show that the most difficult part of a traditional imperative solution consists of the management of distributed data and algorithms. These data distribution issues are the motivation for this paper and an efficient solution may be derived using our methodology. This is the main reason for employing the methodology presented in this paper.

2.3 Fast Fourier Transformations and Data Distribution

To simulate the neuronal development, we numerically integrate a difference version of Equation 1 step by step. This can be quite straightforwardly implemented using Fast Fourier transformations because the summation at the core of Equation 1 simply represents a high-dimensional convolution (over the indexes β, y, and j). Here, we use the convolution theorem which states that a convolution of two functions is equal to the inverse Fourier transform of the product of their Fourier transforms. This reduces the number of necessary operations from $O(n^2)$ for a convolution by simple summation to $O(n \log n)$ for an implementation using the Fast Fourier Transform (FFT) (where n is the number of cortical or LGN neurons). Using Fourier transformations (denoted by subscription) and a data-parallel multiplication operation (denoted by '$\cdot$'), this sum can therefore be implemented in a functional setting as a matrix expression

$$(I_x \cdot ((C_\alpha \cdot S_\alpha)_{\alpha^{-1}})_x)_{x^{-1}} \qquad (3)$$

where the subscripts denote the axes along which the annotated matrix expressions are transformed — i.e. C_α ($C_{\alpha^{-1}}$) denotes the (inverse) Fourier transformation of C along (the dimension represented by the) axis α. In the remainder of this paper we consider expressions of this kind as functional programs.

In this paper we are not interested in the functional algorithm for the parallel computation of Fourier transformations. Instead, we assume that a suitable parallel algorithm (called FFT below) for Fourier transformations is part of a library of basic skeletons, which in turn is a part of the so-called skeleton hierarchy (cf. Darlington et al. 1993, Pepper & Südholt 1997). What we are interested in, however, is the interplay between the distribution of the matrix data and the computation of convolutions using Fourier transformations.

Typical implementations of Fast Fourier transformations on MIMD architectures expose several characteristics that interact with data distribution issues. As a paradigmatic example for our methodology, we use the characteristics of the Fast Fourier sub-routines of the library of Thinking Machine's CM-5 (TMC 1993). Some aspects of these characteristics depend on the underlying machine architecture. A skeleton-based approach is quite suitable in this case because it enables the portable implementation of machine-dependent features using architecture-specific transformations.

The efficiency of the computation of convolutions using Fourier transformations on the CM-5 critically depends on two properties that interact with the underlying data distribution (Here we only consider the parameters of the Fourier transformation that are necessary for the derivation of the communication statements. A complete implementation of the FFT library function would obviously necessitate taking into account scaling, multiple instances along different axes, etc.):

1. The matrix elements belonging to an axis along which the matrix is transformed should be local to a processor because the Fourier transformation can then be performed as a purely local operation. The composition of transformations of different matrices and along different axes can therefore be sped up by suitable data redistribution operations that ensure that all transformations can operate locally.
2. The elements of the input and output matrix of a Fourier transformation may be ordered using two different address orderings. A Fourier transformation is executed more efficiently if the address orderings of elements of an axis along which the transformation takes place are different. The address orderings of elements of an axis that is not transformed, however, must be equal.

We account for the first condition by specifying the distribution of matrices using covers and deriving low-level skeletons that implement cover transformations used to "localize" data elements. This issue is the subject of Sections 3.4 and 4.3, respectively.

For referring in implementations to the axes along which Fourier transformations take place, we introduce three auxiliary types:

```
TYPE control  == control(op: operation, inOr: adrOrd, outOr: adrOrd)
TYPE operation  == nop forward inverse
TYPE adrOrd  == normal bitreversed
```

The types **control**, **operation** and **adrOrd** represent the parameters that define the transformation along an axis, i.e. which kind of Fourier transformation has to be performed along an axis and the address ordering of the input and output data elements. Control parameters are thus the programming means used to "implement" the axis annotations $\_\alpha, \_{\mathtt{x}}$ in Equation 3.

The second condition can be formalized algebraically using a function **fft** which embeds the library function FFT and conceals the details of its low-level implementation.

DEFINITION 2 (FOURIER TRANSFORMATION)
The Fourier transformation is specified by

```
1  FUN fft : matrix[α] × seq[control] → matrix[α]
2  SPC fft(M, c)  ==  M'                    --  FFT (M , c )  ==  M '
3      PRE (dim(M) = #(c) ⇒
4          (fft(M, c')  ==  M'  ∧  c ≠ c'  ⇒
5           ∀0 ≤ i ≤ #(c) :   (op(c!i) ≠ nop ⇒
6                               inOr(c!i) ≠ outOr(c!i) ∨ inOr(c'!i) = outOr(c'!i))
7                           ∧ (op(c!i) = nop ⇒
8                               inOr(c!i) = outOr(c!i) ∨ inOr(c'!i) ≠ outOr(c'!i))
9          ))  ⟹  cost(fft(M, c)) ≪ cost(fft(M, c'))
10     POST M' = FFT(M, c)
```

The first antecedent of the precondition (Line 3) states that there has to be a control parameter in c for each dimension of the matrix M. The second antecedent (Lines 4–8) formalizes the restriction imposed above on address orderings: the Fourier transformation **fft**(M, c) is computed more efficiently than a different transformation **fft**(M, c′) (computing the same result matrix) if the input and output orders of all axes along which a tranformation takes place are different (Lines 5–6). All elements that belong to dimensions whose axes are not transformed have to use the same input and output ordering (Lines 7–8). Note that the relation between the different costs of the evaluation of **fft**(M, c) and **fft**(M, c′) can be quantified — we only use the relation '≪' here for simplicity — based on the implementation of FFT. The postcondition (Line 10), finally, states that **fft**(M, c) actually computes a Fourier transformation using (a specification of) the library function FFT.

3 DATA DISTRIBUTION

As outlined in the introduction, it is mandatory that our programming model takes distribution issues into consideration. This is already the case today to some extent in certain extensions of FORTRAN (such as HPF, HPF Forum

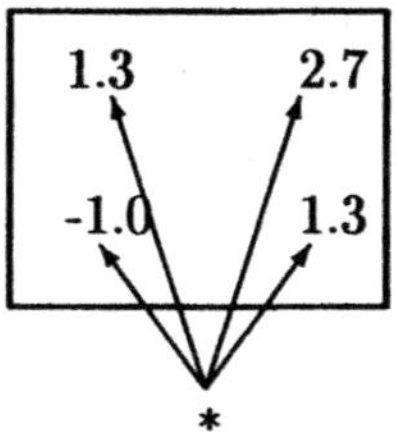

Figure 2 A matrix as a bundle of arrows

1993) and C/C++ (such as Split-C, Culler et al. 1993) and C* (Tichy et al. 1992). But we feel that most of these additions are not very systematic and that they are frequently introduced at much too low a level (see C* example in Section 4.4). The goal of our approach is to provide a programming model whereby distribution issues can be described at a high and abstract level geared towards the needs of application domains as opposed to low-level hardware features. In accordance with the prevailing paradigm for the design of parallel software, we restrict ourselves (in this paper at least) to regular communication structures and do not consider arbitrarily communicating processing systems.

3.1 Representing Data Structures

As a first problem, we encounter the necessity for an abstract notion of what we mean by "data structures". Intuitively, we may characterize this idea by pointing to typical examples such as sequences, trees, matrices, vectors and graphs. On the basis of a given programming language, such as Pascal or FORTRAN, we may characterize the available data structures by considering all type constructors of the language. But in generic settings, such as algebraic specifications, it is less clear how data structures like lists can be distinguished from atomic data like floating-point numbers.

In mathematical terms, we sketch our viewpoint as follows:

DEFINITION 3 (DATA STRUCTURE)
***A data structure** (such as a matrix or a tree) over a set S of elements is a bundle of arrows from a one-element set into S (see Figure 2).*

This slightly clumsy use of arrows (The terminology we employ here is borrowed from category theory. The word "bundle" is used as a synonym for set. At first sight this looks very much like we are talking about pointers, but — as will be seen in a moment — this is only one possible implementation of the abstract concept.) is necessitated by the well-known difficulty of distinguishing multiple occurrences of the same value in a data structure. Using this abstraction, we can extract representation issues. For example, in the matrix in Figure 2 the arrow $* \to 2.7$ would be represented classically by the index pair (1,2). But in a more geometric setting, it might be represented by a selector north-east, or in a recursive definition (similar to the specification `Matrix` in Section 1.1) by the composition of selectors `top` $\circ$ `right`.

3.2 Covers

In connection with data distributions, the concept of **substructures** is obviously fundamental. In our setting, its definition is trivial.

DEFINITION 4 (SUBOBJECT)
*A **subobject** B of a structure A is a subset of the bundle of arrows. We denote the corresponding inclusion morphism by $B \hookrightarrow A$.*

Our goal is, of course, to split a given data structure into subobjects and to distribute these subobjects over the available processors. We therefore have to provide the means for expressing such splittings. Traditionally, one uses partitionings (that is, all subobjects are disjoint) for this purpose. However, we came to the conclusion that this restriction is inadequate. Indeed, allowing the subobjects to overlap is — as will be seen later on — the clue to a much more comprehensible programming style. This motivates the introduction of structures of overlapping substructures, the so-called covers.

DEFINITION 5 (COVER)
*Semantically, a **cover** C of a structure A is a set $C = \{B_i \mid i \in I\}$ of subobjects $B_i \hookrightarrow A$ of A such that their union yields A again, that is, $\bigcup C = \bigcup_{i \in I} B_i = A$. (Recall that structures are sets of arrows.) Moreover, the following requirements have to be met:*

- *Every subobject $B_i \in C$ is partitioned into an own part and a foreign part.*
- *The own parts of the B_i form a partitioning of A.*

Forming the union of two subobjects is often called gluing, thus emphasizing the fact that their overlapping parts are identified. Gluing will be denoted here as $A \boxminus B$.

A partitioning, therefore, is a special case of a cover where the subobjects $B_i \in C$ are pairwise disjoint; in other words, the foreign parts are all empty.

These definitions also entail that the foreign part of each B_i is contained in the own part of some (possibly several) B_j.

Before we proceed with the presentation of our basic concepts, we will briefly review the motivation behind the approach: if we have to compute some function f on a data structure A, that is, $B = f(A)$, then we want to find covers C_A and C_B such that the corresponding subobjects B_i and A_i

can be computed by $B_i = f'(A_i)$ for some suitable function f'. (Actually, the situation is slightly more complex, because there are variations of this simplistic paradigm. But this is exactly what skeletons will be used for later on.)

The purpose of this design is evident: we expect to have B_i and the own part of A_i on the same processor. But for calculating B_i we also need the foreign part of A_i — which determines the communication overhead. So the concept of covers enables an abstract specification of communication requirements.

Note the restriction we apply here: write access can only be applied to the own data of a processor, i.e. remote accesses are only read commands. (If concurrent write accesses were allowed, the consistency of independent computations performed on overlapping covers could be ensured — regardless of any restrictions — by a sheaf-theoretic semantics (Pepper & Südholt 1997).)

But — as mentioned earlier — this restriction is fulfilled in many applications. Moreover, it is weakened to a large extent by the flexibility of the underlying transformational approach to program development: during different stages of the derivation of a parallel program different covers (and domains of possible write access with them) can be considered.

Semantical Framework. Although a complete definition of the formal semantics of data structures, covers and cover operators is beyond the scope of this paper, a short sketch should be helpful for the reader.

The methodology is based on three concepts that are specified algebraically: data structures, covers and skeletons. The algebraic specifications are given a loose semantics.The constituent properties of covers thus cannot be ensured by construction, but are treated as proof obligations. Because loose specifications are often unwieldy, we use the abstract representation introduced in Section 3.1 to distinguish particular models of the specifications. Besides, this model can be naturally used to define other notions that are important in constructive program development, such as the shape and contents of a data structure or the equivalence of different concrete representations of the same data structure (see Pepper & Südholt 1997).

3.3 Cover Operators and Data Distribution Algebras

Covers do not necessarily support homogeneous computations. Arbitrary collections of arbitrarily shaped subobjects may form a cover, but clearly we can only work decently with well-structured covers that exhibit some homogeneity.

Example: A typical situation is illustrated in Figure 3. A matrix is to be distributed over (in this example) $q = 3$ processors. In the light of the properties of the application, we opt for an overlapping row-block cover consisting of $q - 2$ (hence, in our illustration, only 1) inner row blocks plus a top and a bottom borderline block. Each of the inner row blocks consists of

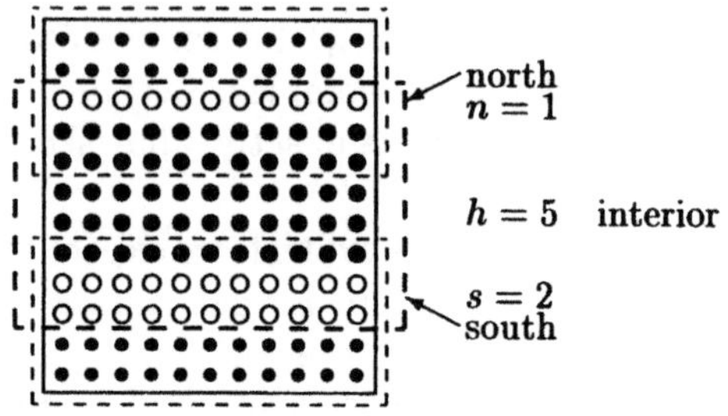

Figure 3 An overlapping row-block cover with 3 blocks

- the own part, that is, of h interior rows, and
- the foreign part, that is, of n "northern" and s "southern" rows. (Such situations, where there are foreign parts both to the north and the south, only work deadlock-free, when certain computational patterns hold for the detailed algorithm.)

For the top and the bottom block, the northern and southern rows, respectively, are missing.

As mentioned earlier, the idea behind this design is that the own part will be assigned to the processor's local memory, whereas the foreign parts provide the compiler with the information necessary to derive the appropriate communication patterns. (In the situation shown in Figure 3, where we assume $n = 1, s = 2$ and $h = 5$, two rows need to be communicated from the bottom processor to the middle processor, and one row from the top processor to the middle processor.) The actual computation of the middle processor is described as if it were working on a matrix with $n+h+s = 8$ rows — without any mention of communication. (End of example)

This example clearly illustrates the basic ingredients needed for defining covers. We are dealing with three kinds of data structure:

- the original structure: `matrix`[`real`];
- the structure of the substructures: **`block`** $\stackrel{\text{def}}{=}$ `matrix`[`real`]
- the covering structure: `vector`[`block`] = `vector`[`matrix`[`real`]]

In addition, we have to specify the way in which the original matrix is viewed as a vector of matrices, defining in particular the size of the vector and the overlapping parts. But before we tackle this in detail, we want to settle the question of the overall framework.

Recall that a data structure is a bundle of arrows into some base type; hence, all our data structures are generic which we denote, for example, by `matrix`[α] or `vector`[β], or simply by `matrix`[_] when the name of the parameter sort is not needed. As explained above, the definition of a cover involves three generic structures: the original sort `obj`[_], the subobject sort `sub`[_] and the cover sort cover[_]. (Remember that the different occurrences of the placeholder '_' may refer to different expressions.)

Moreover, we employ a pair of functions split and glue for defining the relationship of the cover to the original object. Semantically speaking,

- split defines how the original bundle of arrows is mapped onto a set of (not necessarily disjoint) bundles which cover the original bundle, and how this set is made into a data structure itself.
- glue defines how the original object can be recovered from its parts.

DEFINITION 6 (COVER SPECIFICATION)
A cover is a refinement of the following specification

```
COVER Cover
  SORT obj[_]                                   -- the original object
  SORT sub[_]                                   -- the subobjects in the cover
  SORT cover[_]                                 -- the structure of the cover
  FUN split : obj[_] → cover[sub[_]]
  FUN glue : cover[sub[_]] → obj[_]
  AXM glue ∘ split = id
```

The row-block cover, for example, can be defined by two functions
FUN split : matrix[α] → vector[matrix[α]]
FUN glue : vector[matrix[α]] → matrix[α]

The geometric representation of matrices defined in Section 1.1 enables us to specify distributions in a very concise manner, as illustrated by the following definition (cf. Figure 3):

DEFINITION 7 (ROW-BLOCK COVER)
The (overlapping) row-block cover is defined by

```
COVER RowBlock[q, n, s]
  FUN q, n, s : nat
  REFINES Cover USING obj[_]     == matrix[_]
                      sub[_]     == matrix[_]
                      cover[_]   == vector[_]
  AXM split(Mat) = Vec  ⇒  #(Vec) = q
                           ∧ height(Vec.i) = height(Vec.j) ± 1
                           ∧ top(Vec) COVERED BY IS[s]
                           ∧ (B ∈ inner(Vec) ⇒ B COVERED BY NIS[n, s])
                           ∧ bottom(Vec) COVERED BY NI[n]
  AXM glue(Vec) = ⧉/Vec
  FUN _⧉_ : matrix[α] × matrix[α] → matrix[α]
  AXM height(N) = n ∧ height(S) = s
      ⇒ (A ⊟ N ⊟ S) ⧉ (N ⊟ S ⊟ B) = (A ⊟ N ⊟ S ⊟ B)
```

where '/' denotes the skeleton "reduce" introduced in Section 4.

Because this definition should be mostly self-explanatory, we only mention the following details: the row-block cover covers matrices with vectors of matrices (Lines 3–5) and has as many components as there are processors (Line 6). Consequently, the size of the components is not fixed, but the components are approximately the same size (Line 7). The inner blocks are partitioned as specified by NIS[n, s] (see below).

This specification characterizes all relevant aspects of the concept of row-block covers. Together with the axiom glue ∘ split = id, we can follow, for instance, that two adjacent blocks of the cover consist of contiguous parts of the original matrix. But, for the sake of readability, we have refrained from excluding all pathological border cases. Assume, for instance, that the size n of the northern part is larger than the inner size h (see Figure 3). In this case the communication of the elements of a northern foreign part would involve more than the southern neighbouring component.

For the sake of completeness, we also show the cover specification of NIS (the other two are defined analogously).

```
COVER NIS[n, s]
  FUN n, s : nat
  REFINES Cover USING obj[_]    == matrix[_]
                      sub[_]    == matrix[_]
                      cover[_]  == triple[_]
  TYPE triple[_] == (FOREIGN north : matrix[_],
                     OWN     inner : matrix[_],
                     FOREIGN south : matrix[_])
  AXM split(Mat) = triple(N, I, S) ⇒ height(N) = n ∧ height(S) = s
  AXM glue(triple(N, I, S)) = N ⊟ I ⊟ S
```

The covers of a given data structure (such as matrices in this paper) form an algebra, which we call the **data distribution algebra**. Such an algebra introduces further operations on covers, such as "mapping" covers over covers. (This definition only makes sense if the covers, i.e. the splitting and gluing functions, have suitable types. This condition can be met by defining covers using partially defined subobjects. With this technique, all covers of a data type $D[\alpha]$ can be defined to be of type $D[D[\alpha]]$ (cf. Pepper & Südholt 1997).)

Definition 8 (Cover composition)
Let C_1, C_2 be covers, such that $obj_2[\_] = sub_1[\_]$. Then the ***composed cover*** *$C_2 * C_1$ is defined by (where '∗' below denotes the map skeleton introduced in Section 4.2)*

$\mathtt{split} = (\mathtt{split}_2\ *) \circ \mathtt{split}_1$

$\mathtt{glue} = \mathtt{glue}_2 \circ (\mathtt{glue}_1\ *)$

The foreign parts of the composed cover are determined by

$\mathtt{foreign}(C_2 * C_1) = \mathtt{foreign}(C_1) \cup \mathtt{foreign}(C_2)$

Here, the set of arrows belonging to the foreign part of a cover is defined by $\mathtt{foreign}(C) = \bigcup_{s \in C} \mathtt{foreign}(s)$. The condition on the foreign part implicitly also determines the own part of the composed cover.

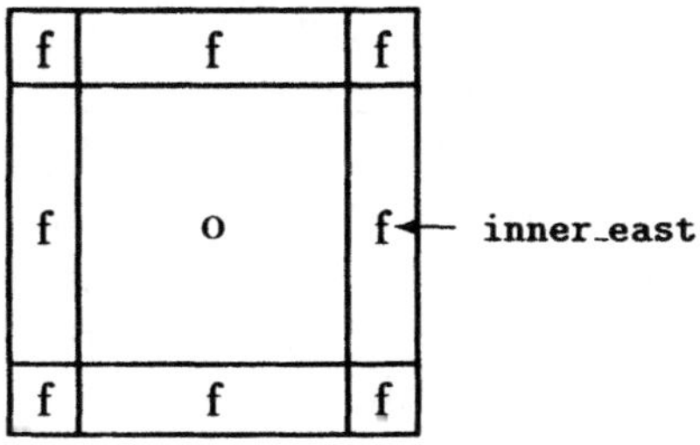

Figure 4 Own and foreign parts of a tile

3.4 Higher-Dimensional Matrix Covers

The cortex equation (Equation 1 on page 6) uses four-dimensional coefficient matrices, because only the position vectors denoted by α and x are relevant here. In Section 2.3 we indicated that we capture some of the characteristics concerning the efficiency of the Fourier transformations using suitable covers, i.e. we examine the following functional algorithm

$$dS = \mathsf{norm} * (I_x^{\mathcal{I}} \cdot \ (C_\alpha^{\mathcal{C}} \cdot \ S_\alpha^{\mathcal{S}})_{\alpha^{-1}})_x)_{x^{-1}} \qquad (4)$$

where the calligraphic letters $\mathcal{I}$, $\mathcal{C}$ and $\mathcal{S}$ denote the covers of the corresponding matrices. norm is the functional implementation corresponding to the term γS in Equation 1 which normalizes the matrix elements as described in Section 2.2.

An important observation, motivated by the deliberations in Section 2.3, is that the Fourier transformations are only performed along two dimensions, instead of along four dimensions. Consequently, we do not define genuine four-dimensional covers, but "lift" suitable two-dimensional covers to four dimensions. This is also the reason why we do not need constructors for higher-dimensional matrices here. All relevant aspects can be specified using the constructors for the two-dimensional case defined in Section 1.1 and the lifting operator defined below.

For simplicity, we choose tiling covers as the basic two-dimensional covers. Instead of defining the tiling cover in an ad hoc manner, we "superimpose" a row-block cover on a column-block cover. The column-block cover is structurally equivalent to a row-block cover and can be defined algebraically using a specification isomorphism:

```
1  COVER ColBlock[p, w, e]  ==  im(RowBlock[q, n, s])
2        WHERE im(p) == q,            im(n) == w,         im(s) == e,
3              im(height) == width,   im(⊟) == ◫,
4              im(north) == west,     im(south) == east
```

In Lines 2–3, the specification isomorphism `im` maps the parameters and operations of the cover `RowBlock` onto those of `ColBlock` (note that the objects, subobjects and cover sort remain the same). In Line 4, the selectors of the local covers are renamed so as to better fit identifiers.

From the axiom $(\mathbf{a\ b} \boxplus \mathbf{c\ d}) = (\mathbf{a} \,\square\!\square\, \mathbf{b}) \boxminus (\mathbf{c} \,\square\!\square\, \mathbf{d})$ that holds for the geometric representation of matrices, the theorem

```
THM RowBlock[r,n,s] *∪ ColBlock[c,w,e] = ColBlock[c,w,e] *∪ RowBlock[r,n,s]
```

follows. From the definition of the composition operator $*_\cup$ (Definition 8) we can derive that each subobject here consists of a matrix (its own part) surrounded by matrices forming the foreign part (see Figure 4). We use the previous theorem to define the tiling cover.

DEFINITION 9 (TILING COVER)

```
1 COVER Tile[r · c,n,s,w,e] == RowBlock[r,n,s] *∪ ColBlock[c,w,e]
2   FUN inner _ east: matrix[α] → matrix[α]
3   DEF inner _ east == inner ∘ east
4     ...
```

On Lines 2–3, **inner _ east** defines a selector used to access the tile forming the middle-eastern edge of the foreign part. (The selectors **inner** and **east** are defined as part of the covers **RowBlock** and **ColBlock**, respectively; the analogous definitions for the north-eastern foreign part etc. are missing.) The selectors are used in functions that are defined on the cover, such as the Fourier transformation.

A suitable four-dimensional cover can be defined by lifting the tiling cover to four dimensions using the (product) cover operator $\times$. This operator can easily be defined algebraically using projections on two dimensions:

> Let C_1, C_2 be two-dimensional matrix covers. Then the **product cover** $C_1 \times C_2$ is defined by the requirement
>
> AXM $(C_1 \times C_2)|_{\mathtt{dim}(1,2)} = C_1 \ \wedge\ (C_1 \times C_2)|_{\mathtt{dim}(3,4)} = C_2$

We are now ready to define the covers used in Equation 4. Assuming that the identifier x there refers to the plane determined by the first and second, and α to the third and fourth dimension, the four-dimensional covers are defined as the product,

DEFINITION 10
Let $\mathtt{id}_C$ *be the identity cover defined by* **split = glue = id**.[1]

```
DEF 𝒳 == id × Tile[t₁,n₁,s₁,w₁,e₁]
DEF 𝒴 == Tile[t₂,n₂,s₂,w₂,e₂] × id
```

where **id** denotes the identity cover, $t_1 \cdot t_2$ processors are available and the parameters $n_1, \ldots, e_2$ denote the overlap that depends on the underlying algorithm computing the Fast Fourier transformation. (We come back to this issue in Section 4.3.) The choice of identity cover $\mathtt{id}_C$ is motivated by the observation made in Section 2.3 that (the parallel implementation of the) Fourier transformations are computed most efficiently if the elements along the axes to be transformed are stored locally at a processor. Data distribution (indicated by the tiling covers) should therefore only be specified for the dimensions that are not transformed.

The basic covers used in Equation 4 can then be defined by

DEFINITION 11 (BASIC COVERS)
Let $\mathcal{X}, \mathcal{Y}$ be the covers defined in the last definition.

DEF $\mathcal{S} = \mathcal{C}$	$==$	$\mathcal{X}$
DEF $\mathcal{I}$	$==$	$\mathcal{Y}$

4 SKELETONS

As mentioned earlier, skeletons are certain higher-order functions that are amenable to "good" parallel implementations. Such skeletons exist for all kinds of data structures, but to give a first intuitive flavour we present some of the simplest ones for the case of lists:

- The most basic skeleton is "map", which applies a function to all elements of a list. This function is usually written in infix notation using the symbol '*'.
  FUN $* : (\alpha \to \beta) \to \mathbf{seq}[\alpha] \to \mathbf{seq}[\beta]$
  DEF $\mathtt{f} * \langle a_1, \ldots, a_n \rangle = \langle \mathtt{f}(a_1), \ldots, \mathtt{f}(a_n) \rangle$
  Its parallel implementation is trivial: the sequence elements are distributed across the processing units and the function is applied separately at each processor. Note that the number of processors can be smaller than the number of sequence elements without additional complications. This parallel computation thus induces no communication (except for the initial distribution) at all.
- A close relative of "map" is "zip", which combines two argument lists into a result list by applying an operation to each pair of corresponding elements:
  FUN $\curlyvee : (\alpha \times \beta \to \gamma) \to \mathbf{seq}[\alpha] \times \mathbf{seq}[\beta] \to \mathbf{seq}[\gamma]$
  DEF $\langle a_1, \ldots a_n \rangle \curlyvee_{\oplus} \langle b_1, \ldots b_n \rangle = \langle a_1 \oplus b_1, \ldots, a_n \oplus b_n \rangle$
  This skeleton also requires no communication if the elements of the two sequences have been distributed accordingly beforehand.
- Another basic skeleton is the "reduce" skeleton (denoted by the infix symbol '/'), which reduces a non-empty list to a single value:
  FUN $/ : (\alpha \times \alpha \to \alpha) \to \mathbf{seq}[\alpha] \to \alpha$
  DEF $\oplus/\langle a_1, \ldots, a_n \rangle = a_1 \oplus \ldots \oplus a_n$
  This skeleton can be implemented efficiently (on suitable architectures) in parallel by distributing the data logically in a tree-like fashion and computing the reduction bottom-up from the leaves to the root. Note that $\oplus$ has to be associative.

Besides these general skeletons, more specific ones have been derived from algorithm design tactics (e.g. skeletons for divide-and-conquer or approximation algorithms) or lower-level characteristics such as near-neighbour communication.

Our approach to the transformational development of parallel programs is in line with most other modern skeleton-based approaches in that it should provide a universal set of skeletons that can be used (in principle) to express all other skeletons. This is in contrast to the first approaches to programming by skeletons (Cole 1989), where each skeleton was intended to be some sort of indivisible entity not expressible by a combination of other skeletons — if skeleton composition was not forbidden altogether.

4.1 Implementing the Cortex Equation Functionally

We are now ready to present the functional algorithm that solves the cortex equation (Equation 1). The algorithm shown in Equation 4 introduces appropriate covers for the element matrices. The efficient computation of Fourier transformations, however, necessitates data redistributions as discussed in Section 2.3. We take this into account by inserting cover transformations (denoted by expressions of the form $\mathcal{C}_2 \leftarrow \mathcal{C}_1$) into the final algorithm (remember that $\mathcal{X}$, $\mathcal{Y}$ denote the basic covers developed in Section 3.4).

$$dS = \mathsf{norm} * ((\mathcal{X} \leftarrow \mathcal{Y}) \circ (I_x^{\mathcal{Y}} \cdot \; ((\mathcal{Y} \leftarrow \mathcal{X}) \circ (C_\alpha^{\mathcal{X}} \cdot \; S_\alpha^{\mathcal{X}})_{\alpha^{-1}}))_x)_{x^{-1}} \tag{5}$$

To complete this functional program, we have three things to do: define the cover-parallel multiplication '$\cdot$', define the map-skeleton '$*$' on (overlapping) covers and implement the cover transformations $\mathcal{X} \leftarrow \mathcal{Y}$ and $\mathcal{Y} \leftarrow \mathcal{X}$.

The cover-parallel multiplication can be defined using the zip-skeleton as

```
FUN · : matrix[real] × matrix[real] → matrix[real]
DEF · == Υ(·real)
```

where '$\cdot_{\mathtt{real}}$' denotes the multiplication function on reals. In the next two sections, we address the remaining issues.

4.2 The Generalized Map Skeleton

The algorithm shown as Equation 5 contains functions that are mapped onto covered matrices. The function `norm`, for instance, is used to normalize all elements of matrices that are covered by a tiling cover. In Section 2.2, it is mentioned that the function `norm` has to constrain the total synaptic strength of the elements belonging to the dimension x. This operation is local to the dimension α: using the cover transformation $\mathcal{X} \leftarrow \mathcal{Y}$ in Equation 5, this becomes a localized operation.

In addition to constraining the dS, it is also necessary to clip the values of the S at every integration step, i.e. restrict them such that they fit in the interval $[0 \ldots 1]$. (This task is denoted by norm′ below.) This is obviously quite a simple case, because this computation can be done using a disjoint cover (although we have not introduced a partitioning in Equation 5 explicitly), given that no communication is necessary.

The definition of the tiling cover as defined in Section 3.4 consists (in our case) of matrices, of matrices of real values. The function norm should obviously normalize the "inner" real values, i.e. we have the following implementation in mind:

```
FUN norm′ : matrix[real] → matrix[real]
DEF norm′(M)  ==  normReal * M
```

where the function normReal is applied to the components of the covered matrix, that is, matrices parameterized by basic types and the operator * is the map-skeleton on matrices.

The map-skeleton can be defined as generalizing this pattern:

DEFINITION 12 (MAP SKELETON)
Realizing a function f *based on the* **map skeleton** *is defined as:*

```
SKELETON Map[f, g] OVER  Cover
   FUN f :  obj[α] → obj[β]
   FUN g :  sub[α] → sub[β]
   ENRICH Cover BY
   DEF f(A)   ==   glue(g * split(A))
```

As a prerequisite, the cover cover[_] *must possess a map operator '*'.*

Skeletons implicitly specify communication through the access (of g in Definition 12, for instance) to the foreign parts of substructures of the underlying cover. Thus, parameterizing skeletons with covers allows the derivation of cost information based on the cover (and skeleton) definitions (although it does not provide a solution to the monotonicity problem of transformational program derivation (cf. Skillicorn 1993)). This information can be used to characterize communication free computations as illustrated in the next section, apply replication of foreign parts in order to avoid communication or directing equations such that they become cost reducing transformations (cf. Pepper & Südholt 1997).

The above example norm′ also illustrates a nice property that holds when the overall object and the subobjects have the same type, and when f is already defined using the map operator:

```
THM ∀A : obj[α] . g * A  =  glue(g * split(A))
```

This theorem states that a function g is mapped over an object A by first splitting the original object, mapping g over the resulting cover and gluing the resulting subobjects together to form the result object.

Coming back to our overall algorithm, the main program in Equation 5 can be augmented by the following instantiation of the map-skeleton, which introduces the function norm′

```
IMPORT Map[norm′, normReal] OVER  Tile[p, 0, 0, 0, 0]
```

The zip-skeleton used in the definition of the function '·' above can easily be defined in terms of a map over pairs of covers.

4.3 Deriving Low-Level Communication Code

The last gap that has to be filled in order to implement Equation 5 is the definition of the cover transformations between the different convolution computations.

(Non-)Local Fast Fourier Transformations. In Section 2.3, an important property of Fast Fourier transformations (on the CM-5) was mentioned: they are computed most efficiently (which means without communication in this case) if the elements belonging to the dimensions that are transformed can be accessed locally. This can be expressed as a property of the underlying data distribution using a transposition function '$\_^{\mathtt{T}}$':

THEOREM 1 (LOCAL FFT)
Let M *be a matrix and* c *a control specification. Then we have*

$$\begin{array}{l} \text{THM} \quad \mathtt{M}\ \text{COVERED BY}\ \mathtt{C} \Rightarrow \\ \quad (\mathtt{cost}(\mathtt{fft}(\mathtt{M},\mathtt{c})) = 0 \iff \\ \quad\quad \forall 0 \le \mathtt{i} \le \#(\mathtt{c}) :\ \mathtt{op}(\mathtt{c}) \ne \mathtt{nop} \Rightarrow \exists \mathtt{s} \in \mathtt{C} :\ \mathtt{M}|_{\mathtt{dim}(\mathtt{i})} \subseteq \mathtt{own}(\mathtt{s})) \end{array}$$

where the specification function own *yields the own part of a subobject.*

Performing a Fast Fourier transformation along a non-local axis is equivalent on the CM-5 to transposing the matrix such that the axis is local, computing the transformation and transposing the result. This gives rise to the equivalence

THEOREM 2 (TRANSPOSED FFT)
Let M *be a matrix and* c *a control specification. Then we have*

$$\mathtt{fft}(\mathtt{M},\mathtt{c}) \ = \ (\mathtt{fft}(\mathtt{M}^{\mathtt{T}},\mathtt{c}))^{\mathtt{T}}$$

The communication costs of the transpositions are obviously not negligible. While we illustrate below how algorithms defined as skeletons that operate on covers provide hints how to calculate these costs, let us only assume for the moment that cost(_^T) $\gg$ 0.

Deriving the Cover Transformations. Because convolutions are calculated using Fast Fourier transformations (cf. Equation 5), the previous two theorems can be used to derive properties of the implementation of convolutions. Theorem 2 yields an alternative method for computing convolutions:

THEOREM 3 (TRANSPOSED CONVOLUTION)
Let M, N *be matrices and* c *a control specification. Then we have*

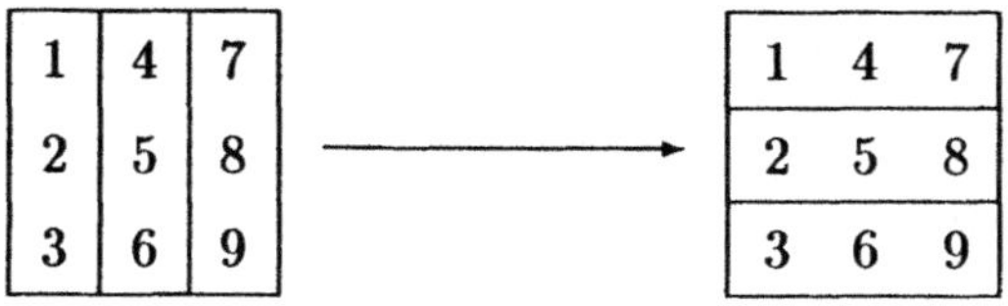

Figure 5 Two-dimensional transposition operation

THM	$(\mathtt{M}_c\ \mathtt{N}_c)_{c^{-1}} = (((\mathtt{M}^T)_c\ (\mathtt{N}^T)_c)^T)_{c^{-1}}$

Furthermore, Theorem 1 and the fact that transposition involves communication
(`cost(_^T)` $\gg$ 0) allow us to assign different costs to the lhs and rhs of Theorem 3. This is, however, only possible if the compiler knows how the input matrices are distributed. Since in our framework the covers defined in Definitions 10 and 11 yield exactly the necessary information, the compiler can choose between the two possible implementations. We can conclude that the transformations have to be implemented as

FUN $\mathcal{Y} \leftarrow \mathcal{X}, \mathcal{Y} \leftarrow \mathcal{X}$: `matrix` $\rightarrow$ `matrix`
DEF $\mathcal{Y} \leftarrow \mathcal{X}$ == `transpose`(α)
DEF $\mathcal{X} \leftarrow \mathcal{Y}$ == `transpose(x)`

where the function `transpose`: `control` $\rightarrow$ `matrix` $\rightarrow$ `matrix` transposes its argument matrix such that the axes that are to be transformed (as given in the control parameter) become local.

The definition of the low-level skeleton `transpose` shows how covers can be used to abstractly specify communication. Consider the two-dimensional transposition operation shown in Figure 5. This transposition can be implemented, for instance in a master-slave environment, by first collecting all elements at the master and then redistributing them in a second phase. The collection phase can be implemented by covering the argument matrix by the tiling cover and using an access to the right overlapping part to accumulate the elements that form a row:

```
trans * M WHERE M COVERED BY Tile(t,0,0,0,1)
FUN trans : matrix → matrix
DEF trans(t) == ...inner _ east(t)...
```

The function `trans` is defined on a tiling cover that overlaps one column to the east. It accesses the middle part of the overlap (the element to the right) using a call to the selector function `inner _ east`. If this operation is synchronized such that `trans` is applied to a tile `t` after it has been applied to the left neighbour of `t`, all elements of a row are accumulated on a processor. As shown in Pepper & Südholt (1997) covers allow the concise specification of this and similar classes of synchronized behaviour by recursive equations on covers.

Because the other operations of the implementation shown in Equation 5 (except the cover transformations) are localized operations, we can further derive that the basic tiling covers can be defined as partitionings, i.e. that we can define

```
DEF n1 = s1 = w1 = e1 = n2 = s2 = w2 = e2    ==    0
```

in Definition 10.

4.4 Comparison with C*

We implemented Equation 1 on Thinking Machine's CM-5 and the core code fragments are shown in table 1. The Connection Machine 5 is a massively parallel distributed-memory computer and the data-parallel programming language is C*, a dialect of C. Operations in C* are automatically performed in parallel if they use special parallel data objects—the **shapes**. The number of parallel processors, however, is not known until runtime when the data is distributed according to rules that should minimize the communication overhead.

This implementation is particularly well suited for a comparison with our approach because C* is an imperative programming language designed to provide some of the features that we suggest in our functional programming methodology such as parallel code, automatic data distribution, and implicit data communication between processing nodes.

The program uses four-dimensional shapes (Line 2) (and an array of such shapes for the fifth dimension). The CM Scientific Software Library provides a Fourier transformation that can be used to transform high dimensional data. We define controls (Lines 6–8) for the FFT for forward and backward transformation (*i*) along the two LGN dimensions and (*ii*) along the cortical dimensions.

First, we allocate the shape (Line 10–13), i.e. we tell the system how much data the parallel variables will hold ($32 \times 32 \times 32 \times 32$ elements) and how to distribute the data across the system. The default rule for data distribution assumes an equal amount of communication along each of the shape dimensions. This default distribution would be optimal for an FFT along all four dimensions. For our particular problem, however, it proved to be more efficient to keep the two data axes local to a processor along which most operations take place, and then transpose the data when necessary (just as we discussed in the previous sections). Thus, to increase the performance we request a data distribution where the the first two dimensions are evenly distributed according to the default rule and the third and fourth dimension are arranged in serial order (i.e. local to a processor). Once a shape is declared it can be used to generate data objects (Lines 3, 4, 14).

The main loop of the program (Lines 18–49) then consists of Fourier transforming the data along the α axes (Lines 20-24), then multiplying it with the FFT of C (Lines 27-34) and transforming it back (Line 35). Then we redistribute the data to make the x axes local (Line 38), convolve with I (Lines 39-42) and transpose back. Finally, the constraint normalizes the synaptic

```
/* declare parallel variable shape and pointers to parallel variables */
shape [][][][]ModelMap;
double:ModelMap *S[4], *dS[4], *C_fft[4], *I_fft, *A;
CMSSL_double_complex_t:ModelMap *S_fft[4], SUM_fft;

CMSSL_fft_control_t
  forward_lgn_ctrl[4] = {no_fft, no_fft, fwd_fft, fwd_fft},
  inverse_lgn_ctrl[4] = {no_fft, no_fft, inv_fft, inv_fft};

/* allocate parallel variable shape with serial LGN axes */
ModelMap = allocate_detailed_shape (&ModelMap, 4, {32, 32, 32, 32}, NULL,
  {CMC_news_order, CMC_news_order, CMC_serial_order, CMC_serial_order},
  NULL, NULL, NULL);
/* allocate all parallel variables; setup FFT */
/* compute A; randomly initialize S; compute I and C and FFT them */
... code missing ...

for (iter = 0; iter < no_iterations; iter++) {
  /* FFT S along LGN dimensions: S --FFT--> S_fft */
  for (i = 0; i < 4; i++) {
    re (*S_fft[i]) = *S[i];
    im (*S_fft[i]) = 0.0;
    CMSSL_fft_detailed (S_fft[i],CMSSL_cmpx_to_cmpx,forward_lgn_ctrl,id)
  }

  for (i = 0; i < 4; i++) {
    re (*SUM_fft) = 0.0;
    im (*SUM_fft) = 0.0;
    for (j = 0; j < 4; j++) {
      /* convolve S with C means multiply S_fft with C_fft */
      cind = ((i/2==j/2) ? 0 : 2) + (i+j)%2; /* choose 1 of the 4 C's */
      re (*SUM_fft) += re (*S_fft[j]) * C_fft[cind];
      im (*SUM_fft) += im (*S_fft[j]) * C_fft[cind];
    }
    CMSSL_fft_detailed (SUM_fft,CMSSL_cmpx_to_cmpx,inverse_lgn_ctrl,id);

    /* transpose data; FFT; multiply w. I_fft; FFT back; transp. back */
    [pcoord(2)][pcoord(3)][pcoord(0)][pcoord(1)]re(SUM_fft)= re(SUM_fft);
    CMSSL_fft_detailed (SUM_fft,CMSSL_cmpx_to_cmpx,forward_lgn_ctrl,id);
    re (*SUM_fft) *= I_fft;
    im (*SUM_fft) *= I_fft;
    CMSSL_fft_detailed (SUM_fft,CMSSL_cmpx_to_cmpx,inverse_lgn_ctrl,id);
    [pcoord(2)][pcoord(3)][pcoord(0)][pcoord(1)]*d_S[i] = re(*SUM_fft);
    *d_S[i] *= learn_step_size * *A;
  }

  /* compute constraint term (gamma) and update the weights */
  ... code missing ...
}
```

Table 1 C* program for the computation of Equation 1

weights for each cortical cell (Line 47/48; code not shown) which is local to the α axes.

C* tries to conceal as much of the parallel architecture from the programmer as possible. Data objects can be declared and used without knowing about the hardware which makes C* a portable language. However, the default shapes are designed for "average" communication needs, no mechanism for (semi-automatic) data rearrangement depending on the communication costs assessment is provided. Shapes have to be "hand made" (like in our example, Line 11) when the default data distribution is not optimal for the parallel problem at hand. Shape declaration, and by that means, data distribution is an a-priori decision that is independent of the rest of the C* program. Therefore it is not elegantly possible to redistribute data when appropriate (see e.g. the shape transposition in lines 38 and 43 that is easily possible only because all four shape dimensions have the same size. Alternatively, we can redistribute a data object in memory by declaring a second shape of the same size but with a different layout in memory and then casting the data.)

From this discussion it should be clear that the data-parallel constructs of C* support only a very restricted programming model in comparison to the methodology presented in this paper. Shapes, for instance, are a very restricted subset of partitioned covers. Hence, the communication and synchronization requirements have to be implemented explicitly and cannot be derived as with our methodology. Furthermore, C* does not provide any means to specify the constraints on address orderings as is done in Section 2.3 (These requirements are (rather informally) described in the library description (TMC 1993)).

5 CONCLUSION

In this paper we have presented an extension of the skeleton methodology by covers. This abstraction enables us to declaratively treat two important aspects of parallel programming that are commonly dealt with in an ad hoc manner. First, data distribution algebras enable a high-level and precise specification method for data distribution issues. They have been shown to be useful for providing the information necessary to derive communication statements for data redistribution. This feature has been shown to largely simplify the formulation of parallel algorithms in comparison to data-parallel imperative methodologies.

Second, the methodology enables the concise definition of architecture-specific features. This information can then be used for deriving the low-level communication code.

5.1 Related Work

The derivation of sequential programs by program transformation has long been a topic of research (Feather 1987, Bauer et al. 1985). More recently, this research has focused on the application of constructive calculi for the derivation of parallel programs. While Cole (1989) introduced **skeletons** in an imperative framework, most work — starting with the work of Darlington et al. (1993) — has concentrated on applicative calculi (Pelagatti 1993, Geerling 1996, Bratvold 1993), because the integration of skeletons into applicative programming languages is very smooth and leads to descriptions that are quite close to mathematical specifications. Considerable attention in the field of the transformational derivation of parallel programs has also been given to the so-called **Bird-Meertens Formalism** (Meertens 1986, Bird 1989). Skillicorn (1992) works on categorial data types that provide a set of polymorphic types together with a restricted class of functions, called catamorphisms, which are relatively easy to parallelize. Skeletons can, however, also be integrated into other calculi besides the Bird-Meertens Formalism. Geerling (1996), for instance, uses skeletons in an assertion-based calculus formulated in a Dijkstra-style logic framework. Most of this work — with the exception (to a certain degree) of Bratvold (1993) and Skillicorn (1993) — does not explain how to break down transformations for automatic compilation guided by appropriately chosen cost functions. However, the research did yield a proliferation of transformational derivations useful for practical problems (Pepper 1993, Pepper et al. 1993).

There are some approaches to the transformational development of parallel programs that rely on the concept of **shapes** (Jay & Cockett 1994). Shapes represent containers for data elements and can be manipulated using their polymorphic properties. While this approach requires analysis methods that are quite similar to ours, all the other approaches put forward up to now only deal with disjoint shapes. Shapes have also been applied to non-transformational imperative frameworks for parallel programming (see, for example, work concerning the object-oriented language Sather (Schmidt 1992)). Similar data distribution techniques are also diffusing (to a small extent) into conventional imperative programming languages. One such example are the distribution directives of High Performance Fortran (HPF Forum 1993).

REFERENCES

Bauer, F. et al. (1985), *The Munich Project CIP. Vol. I: The Wide Spectrum Language CIP-L*, number 183 *in* 'LNCS', Springer Verlag, Berlin.

Bird, R. S. (1989), Lectures on constructive functional programming, *in* M. Broy, ed., 'Constructive Methods in Computing Science', Vol. 55 of *NATO ASI, F*, Springer, pp. 151–216.

Bratvold, T. A. (1993), A skeleton-based parallelising compiler for ML, *in* R. Plasmeijer & M. van Eekelen, eds, 'Implementation of Functional Languages', U. Nijmegen. TR 93-21.

Cole, M. (1989), *Algorithmic Skeletons: Structured Management of Parallel Computation*, MIT Press.

Culler, D. E. et al. (1993), Parallel programming in Split-C, *in* 'Supercomputing'.

Darlington, J. et al. (1993), Parallel programming using skeleton functions, *in* A. Bode, M. Reeve & G. Wolf, eds, 'PARLE '93', pp. 146–160.

Erwin, E. & Miller, K. (1995), 'Modeling joint development of ocular dominance and orientation in primary visual cortex', *Proc. of the CNS.*

Erwin, E., Obermayer, K. & Schulten, K. (1995), 'Models of orientation and ocular dominance columns in the visual cortex: A critical comparison', *Neur. Comp.* **7**, 425–468.

Feather, M. S. (1987), A survey and classification of some program transformation approaches and techniques, *in* L. Meertens, ed., 'Program Specification & Transformation', North-Holland.

Geerling, M. (1996), Transformational Development of Data-Parallel Algorithms, PhD thesis, Katholieke Universiteit Nijmegen.

HPF Forum (1993), 'High Performance Fortran', *Scientific Programming.*

Hubel, D. H. & Wiesel, T. N. (1962), 'Receptive fields, binocular interaction and functional architecture in the cat's visual cortex', *Journal of Physiology London* **160**, 106–154.

Jay, C. & Cockett, J. (1994), Shapely types and shape polymorphism, *in* D. Sannella, ed., 'Programming Languages and Systems - ESOP '94', LNCS, Springer Verlag, pp. 302–316.

Linsker, R. (1986), 'From basic network principles to neural architecture: Emergence of orientation selective cells', *Proceedings of the National Academy of Science USA* **83**, 8390–8394.

Meertens, L. (1986), Algorithmics — towards programming as a mathematical activity, *in* 'CWI Symposium on Mathematics and Computer Science', North-Holland, pp. 289–334.

Miller, K. (1994), 'A model for the development of simple cell receptive fields and the ordered arrangements of orientation columns through activity-dependent competition between ON- and OFF-center inputs', *Journal of Neuroscience* **14**, 409–441.

Obermayer, K., Blasdel, G. G. & Schulten, K. (1992), 'A statistical mechanical analysis of self-organization and patte rn formation during the development of visual maps', *Phys. Rev. A* **45**, 7568–7589.

Pelagatti, S. (1993), A Methodology for the Development and the Support of Massively Parallel Programs, PhD thesis, Universita di Pisa-Genova-Udine.

Pepper, P. (1993), Deductive derivation of parallel programs, *in* R. Paige, J. Reif & R. Wachter, eds, 'Parallel Algorithm Derivation and Program Transformation', Kluwer Academic, chapter 1, pp. 1–53. Also as TR 92-23, TU Berlin.

Pepper, P. & Möller, B. (1991), Programming with (finite) mappings, *in* M. Broy, ed., 'Informatik und Mathematik', Springer Verlag, pp. 381–405.

Pepper, P. & Südholt, M. (1997), Deriving parallel numerical algorithms using data distribution algebras: Wang's algorithm, *in* 'Proc. of the 30rd Hawaii International Conference on System Sciences'.

Pepper, P., Exner, J. & Südholt, M. (1993), Functional development of massively parallel programs, *in* D. Bjorner et al., eds, 'Formal Methods in Programming and Their Applications. LNCS 735', Springer Verlag, pp. 217–238.

Piepenbrock, C., Ritter, H. & Obermayer, K. (1996), 'Linear correlation-based learning models require a two-stage process for the development of orientation and ocular dominance', *Neural Processing Letters* **3**, 31–37.

Schmidt, H. W. (1992), Data-parallel object-oriented programming, *in* 'Fifth Australian Supercomputer Conference, Melbourne', 263–272.

Skillicorn, D. B. (1992), The Bird-Meertens Formalism as a parallel model, *in* 'NATO ARW "Software for Parallel Computation"'.

Skillicorn, D. B. (1993), 'Deriving parallel programs from specifications using cost information', *Science of Computer Programming.*

Tichy, W. F., Philippsen, M. & Hatcher, P. (1992), 'A critique of the programming language C*', *Communications of the ACM* **35**(6), 21–24.

TMC (1993), *CMSSL for C**, Thinking Machines Corp.

6 BIOGRAPHY

Mario Südholt is a member of the declarative language group at the research institute in computer science Irisa/Inria-Rennes, France. He received his Masters degree in computer science from the University of Coblence in 1992 and will complete his PhD at the Technical University of Berlin, Germany, in June 1997. His research interests cover the formal derivation of sequential and parallel algorithms, (declarative) programming languages and formal models for the description of software architectures.

Christian Piepenbrock is a member of the Neural Information Processing Group at the Department of Computer Science at the Technical University of Berlin. He received his Masters degree in the interdisciplinary program in Computer Science and Biology from the University of Bielefeld in 1995. His research interests are models for the structure and development of neuronal networks in the visual system and the simulation of such parallel networks.

Dr. Klaus Obermayer is Professor for Neural Information Processing at the Department of Computer Science at the Technical University of Berlin. He received his Masters degree in physics in 1987 from the University of Stuttgart and his PhD in 1992 from the Technical University in Munich, Germany. His research interests cover the areas "computational neuroscience", statistical physics of neural networks and the application of artificial neural networks in signal processing and data analysis.

Peter Pepper received a Masters Degree in Mathematics and a PhD in Computer Science from the Technical University Munich. Since 1985 he has been Professor for Computer Science at the Technical University of Berlin, where he holds a chair in Compiler Construction and Programming Languages. He is a member of GI, ACM, EATCS, IFIP working groups WG 2.1 and WG 14.3, and an affiliate of IEEE. His research interests cover functional programming, algebraic specification, transformational program development, formal derivation of parallel algorithms and software engineering for safety-critical systems.

Discussion Session
Monday afternoon

Jim Boyle: I would like to ask the last speaker, do you think that, assuming you had the manpower to complete the derivation to C^* code, would the result be more or less efficient than the hand-written program that you showed?

Mario Südholt: The efficiency of the final algorithm depends on the level at which you let the user interact with the system. Another question is what can we do with the transformation that accompanies the basic covers and the skeletons relating them. We have several case studies where we get almost optimal algorithms, but this depends on the specific communication behaviour assigned to skeletons, which is different than that used in our paper. The communication says, when access to a foreign part is required, does the owner have to perform the computations before or after the access? With explicit control over synchronization, you get optimal algorithms in many cases.

Peter Pepper: Parallel algorithms in the literature are usually presented by some high-level informal description, followed by a program in which each variable had probably two or three indices, followed by an efficiency analysis. It is clear to me, since many of these indices contain mistakes, that in most cases the efficiency analysis was based on the informal description, not on the algorithm as presented. Numerical analysts think in terms of matrices, and there is a huge gap between this level and the C^* or HP Fortran code. Our work is concerned to lift the level of the programming. At least in that area, I don't think we have new algorithms, just an easier way to describe good algorithms. At the moment I would be happy if we can come up with the best algorithms that peoples have invented already, but with a shorter description, and one that enables variations of the algorithms to be programmed more easily.

Jim Boyle: I want to direct the same question to Perrin, do you have any indication of how the derived implementation in PEI would compare with a hand-crafted one?

Guy-René Perrin: I would give the same answer as Peter Pepper. We are only able to abstract what practitioners do, and to understand how they do what they do, and how we can find variations on algorithms and data distributions.

Wolf Zimmermann: This is to both speakers on data parallelism. You all start from an initial data distribution. Why don't you assume initially that you have to share the memory, then you don't need to worry about data distribution? So, for example, people who consider implementation of parallel algorithms as a scheduling problem, first more or less schedule the computations and then derive from that the appropriate data distributions.

Mario Südholt: One answer to this question is that there are models for shared memory programming that can be embedded into distributed architectures so that the algorithms are equally efficient. However, there are algorithms that are not of this form. At present I have not seen a programming methodology restricted to these pro-shared memory architectures that can be applied in a generality that is sufficient for practical programming.

Guy-René Perrin: When you program a shared-memory machine, practitioners say that what you measure is the efficiency of the machine, not the algorithm. I think it is not useful to draw a strict difference between these two points because if you have a shared-memory machine, you have a real problem of locality if it is a non-uniform memory access machine. So its better to say that the real work is about the locality of data in order to achieve either a shared-memory machine with cache memory, or distributed-memory machines.

Wolf Zimmermann: I agree with your answers, but somehow you misunderstood my question. I asked about the starting point, and I would say that starting with a shared-memory program would be cheaper. What people in scheduling theory do is to look at the operations being performed and model them as a directed acyclic graph, and then schedule the operations so that the execution time is minimized. In several cost models, they can even give performance guarantees.

Peter Pepper: The initial specification shouldn't talk about machines at all. When you are talking about parallelism, it is already a first step toward implementation. Then you can make your mind up whether you first model it as a shared or distributed-memory problem. My experience is that once you start going towards the shared-memory model, its very hard to find the way back to the distributed-memory model later on. The point is that data locality is the decisive issue in distributed-memory machines. These are the predominant machines in the market and I am pretty sure that they will continue to be predominant in the future. I believe that one day we will just see networks of workstations linked together. So, knowledge about locality is application dependent. If you pretend that there is shared memory, the compiler or runtime system is unable in most cases to figure out where the data should be kept. My conclusion is that we should allow the user to express his knowledge about locality as soon as possible and on as high a level as possible. The trick, of course, is not to let this complicate the algorithmic thinking, but to keep the solutions simple enough while still being able to express locality issues.

Helmut Partsch: To change the topic, in previous working conferences we had the benefit of having people outside the environment of WG2.1 because they sometimes raised provocative questions. One of the referee's reports on a (non-accepted) paper for this conference was that it was a very nice calculation, but so what? If I interpret this right, there was a general kind of doubt about the things we are doing here. Any comments on that?

Richard Bird: It seems desperately important to me that we do not rehearse exactly the same worries and anxieties that we had 11 years ago at the Bad Tölz meeting. What we should be doing is looking at progress. Have we made any progress in 11 years? I think we have; there is a maturity about the presentations today that just wasn't there 11 years ago. New young people are coming into the field because the subject of program calculation is one that excites and interests them. As long as the topic remains stimulating and not stagnating for you, I don't think you should worry about relevance to industry or technology transfer. We shouldn't ignore it, though. If there is a knock on the door, then fling it open quickly. Interaction is extremely fruitful, but soul-searching is not.

Peter Pepper: I would like to agree. There has been progress, and there is clearer understanding of the things that remain to be done. It takes a while for this progress to get into the industrial community. We have to wait 10 or 15 years before industry knocks at our doors.

Doug Smith: Industry is not going to knock on our doors in 10 or 15 years, since most funding is for doing applied research now. No one is going to make the stuff work for us, we have to bite the bullet and do it ourselves. It is worthwhile conducting more elaborate experiments to provide evidence that there is going to be some payoff. I am not saying that everyone should do that, but we need more groups who can invest the effort in implementation. The downside is that it is very expensive from the research point of view to get immersed is a domain deeply enough to do something significant.

Tom Maibaum: I don't know how many of you remember Tapsoft '85 when David Parnas stood up and said that you theoreticians have not told us which languages and which methods to use to improve our software engineering. Sometime later in the conference, Maurice Nivat stood up and said, of course not, that's not what scientists do. There is a lot of evidence that over a suitable time scale theoretical ideas do become everyday technology used in industry. For example, consider relational database theory in the late 60s and early 70s; nowadays nobody needs to know about the mathematics, they just use it in management information systems. The same story is true of parsing. When I was an undergraduate all the theory courses were about parsing and automata theory. Nobody studies it any more because they can use the technology without having to know the mathematics behind it. One day others will use systems such as Kids not because they know the mathematics but because enough knowledge will be encapsulated in the system. This is where I think the algebraic specification people are going wrong. They won't affect industry now because industry is not going to invest an enormous amount of money in time and education with ignorant people to use these kinds of languages.

It is only slowly over time that people will have the tools, both conceptual – because of their education – and technical, to make it work.

Alberto Pettorossi: One reason we have made progress is that we have concentrated on the simple but significant idea of equational reasoning. What is lacking is the meta-level reasoning to drive such calculations. A challenge for the future is to expose useful kinds of meta-level reasoning.

Peter Pepper: Just to add one more example to what Tom Maibaum has said about ideas moving into areas where people just use the technology. Just recently, Bruce Shriver during the HICSS conference addressed key technologies for the future. I was surprised to see that number 2 on his list was optimizing compilers. His argument was that many speed-ups were due simply to better compiler technology. If I look at compilers I see many techniques developed by this community being moved into compilers. This is an example where people do not sit down and use our methods to calculate programs, but just write higher-level programs than before and use the compiler to do the work for them.

7

Refinement of Parameterized Algebraic Specifications

Yellamraju V. Srinivas
Kestrel Institute
3260 Hillview Avenue, Palo Alto, CA 94304, USA
Email: srinivas@kestrel.edu, Tel: (415)493-6871, Fax: (415)424-1807

Abstract
A refinement relation for parameterized algebraic specifications is introduced in which the body specification is refined covariantly (i.e., specialized) while the parameter specification is refined contravariantly (i.e., generalized). This refinement is similar to the subtyping relation between function types. Assuming a few relatively weak axioms about parameterized specifications, refinement is shown to satisfy the expected properties for software development in-the-large: independent refinement of body and parameter, and closure under sequential composition, instantiation and a suitable form of 'horizontal' composition.

Keywords
Parameterized specifications, mixed-variance refinement, compositionality

1 INTRODUCTION

The primary subject of this paper is a general notion of refinement for parameterized specifications. Many notions of refinement have been previously proposed in the literature (Ehrig & Kreowski 1982, Ganzinger 1983, Goguen & Meseguer 1982, Sannella & Tarlecki 1988, Sannella & Wirsing 1982, Ehrig & Mahr 1990, Ehrig & Große-Rhode 1994). In many of these, the parameter is not refined; in some, the parameter is refined, either in the same direction as the body (covariant refinement) or in the opposite direction (mixed-variance refinement). We investigate the properties of a somewhat more flexible mixed-variance refinement relation.

Consider, for example, a specification for sorting, which is parameterized on a total order. After refinement, we will have a program, say mergesort. Such a program is typically parameterized, not on a total order, but the ***signature*** of a total order, i.e., a type and a binary relation; this is because most programming languages cannot express the requirement that the relation satisfy the axioms of a total order. Indeed, 'merge' and 'mergesort' may be defined as operations on sequences given any binary relation; although these functions will always produce a result, the results may not be meaningful. However, when 'merge' is given sorted sequences and a total order as arguments, it will produce a sorted sequence. To show the correctness of such a refinement, we need a refinement relation between parameterized specifications in which the parameter can be changed.

The refinement relation that is described in this paper is similar to the subtyping relation between function types: the body is specialized while the parameter is generalized. In our example above, mergesort is a valid refinement of the sorting specification, if after instantiation by a total order, mergesort is a refinement of sorting.

Our notion of refinement is mostly independent of the semantics of parameterized specifications. We show that, assuming a few relatively weak axioms about parameterized specifications, refinement satisfies the expected properties for software development in-the-large: independent refinement of body and parameter, and closure under sequential composition, instantiation and a suitable form of horizontal composition. The existence of such a refinement calculus is especially pleasing, given that several semantics have been proposed for parameterized specifications (Ehrig *et al.* 1981, Bidoit 1987, Wirsing 1986).

2 SPECIFICATIONS, MORPHISMS, INTERPRETATIONS

We will assume a category of specifications and morphisms in which finite colimits exist. The constructions and calculations in this paper are based on this category and sub-categories consisting of morphisms with special properties. We only discuss models briefly; for this purpose, we assume a (contravariant) functor *Mod* which assigns to each specification a category of models and to each morphism $\sigma: A \to B$ a functor $\_|_\sigma: \mathit{Mod}(B) \to \mathit{Mod}(A)$ called *reduct* functor.

Example specifications use a specific logic, namely the logic of SPECWARE, a formal software development system currently being developed at Kestrel (Srinivas & Jüllig 1995). A specification in SPECWARE is a finite presentation of a theory in higher-order logic, i.e., a finite collection of sorts, operations, and axioms (Lambek & Scott 1986). A specification morphism in SPECWARE is a finite map from sorts to sorts and operations to operations such that the ranks of operations are preserved and axioms translate to theorems.

2.1 Refinement by Interpretations

The general notion of refinement is that a specification B refines a specification A if there is a construction which produces models of A from models of B (Sannella & Tarlecki 1988). Specification morphisms serve this purpose because associated with every morphism $\sigma: A \to B$ there is a reduct functor $\_|_\sigma$ which produces models of A from models of B. Morphisms, however, are too weak to represent refinements which normally occur during software development. So, we use a more general notion, ***interpretations***, which are specification morphisms from the source specification to a definitional extension (see below) of the target specification. Methodologically, we believe that two different kinds of arrows are useful in software developement: a simple arrow (morphism) for structuring specifications, and a more flexible arrow (interpretation) for refining specifications.

2.2 Definitional Extensions

Definitional extensions are a subclass of morphisms, those which extend a specification with only defined sorts and operations, while otherwise leaving the specification unchanged. Model theoretically, the reduct functor corresponding to a definitional extension is an isomorphism.

Different logics may have different notions of definability. For example, in SPECWARE, to define an operation $f: A \to B$ in a specification S, we must exhibit a formula φ of S which denotes the graph of f. The formula φ must contain exactly two free variables $x: A$, $y: B$ and must be provably functional in S:

$$S \vdash \forall x: A \cdot \exists! y: B \cdot \varphi(x, y).$$

S can then be extended with the operation f and its defining axiom

$$\forall x: A,\ y: B \cdot f(x) = y \iff \varphi(x, y).$$

2.3 Axioms for definitional extensions

Rather than formally defining definitional extensions, we will assume the following axioms which will be sufficient for our constructions and calculations:

1. An identity morphism is a definitional extension.
2. A definitional extension is an epimorphism.
3. Definitional extensions are closed under composition.
4. Pushouts preserve definitional extensions.

Figure 1 renders these axioms pictorially. Definitional extensions are indicated in diagrams* by $\xrightarrow{\;d\;}$ and pushouts by  .

---

*All diagrams are assumed to be commutative unless stated otherwise. Labels on arrow shafts (e.g., $\xrightarrow{\;d\;}$, $\xrightarrow{\;p\;}$) are properties of arrows, whereas labels above or below (e.g., $\xrightarrow{x}$) are names of arrows.

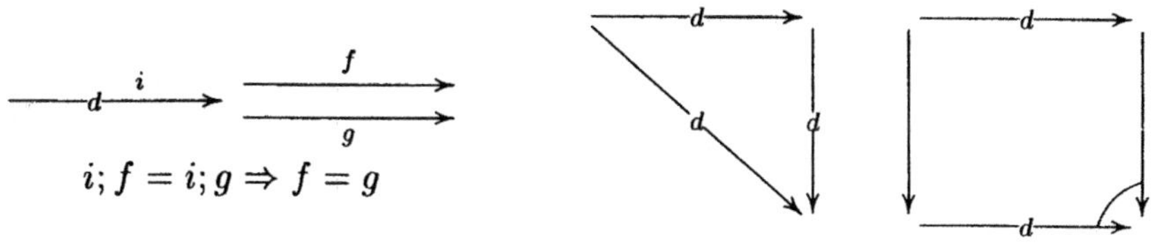

Figure 1 Axioms for definitional extensions.

Alternatively, these axioms will be theorems if we assume that the model functor *Mod* maps pushouts to pullbacks and if we define a definitional extension to be a morphism whose image via *Mod* is an isomorphism.

2.4 Interpretations

DEFINITION 2.1: *Interpretation.* An ***interpretation*** $\rho: A \Rightarrow B$ from a specification A (called ***domain*** or ***source***) to a specification B (called ***codomain*** or ***target***) is a pair of morphisms $A \longrightarrow B_+ \xleftarrow{d} B$ with common codomain B_+ (called ***mediating*** specification or simply ***mediator***), such that the target-to-mediator morphism is a definitional extension. □

Interpretations are a suitable notion of refinement because models of the source specification can be constructed from models of the target specification by first expanding them along the definitional extension and then taking reducts.

Specifications and interpretations form a category with composition defined as in Figure 2. We use the facts that definitional extensions are closed under composition and are preserved by pushouts. Equality of interpretations is defined by reducing it to equality of morphisms using the construction in Figure 3. In other words, the mediator specification may contain extra defined sorts and operations which are not in the image of the source-to-mediator morphism.

The category of specifications and interpretations is finitely cocomplete if the category of specifications and morphisms is. Both categories have the same initial object. Pushouts of interpretations are constructed as shown in Figure 4 (note that a morphism may be construed as an interpretation, by pairing it with an identity definitional extension). A proof of universality is given in the appendix.

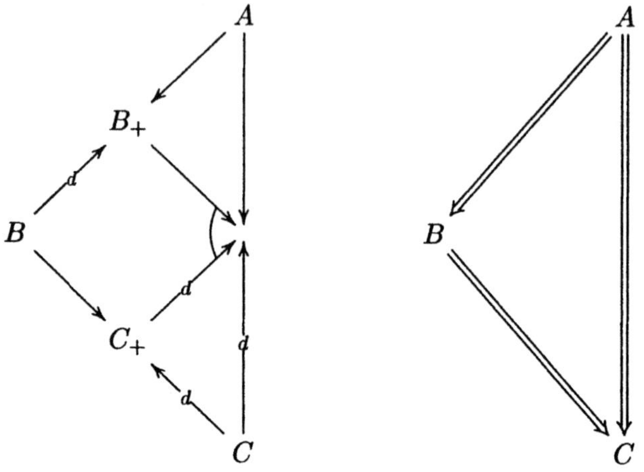

Figure 2 Composition of interpretations.

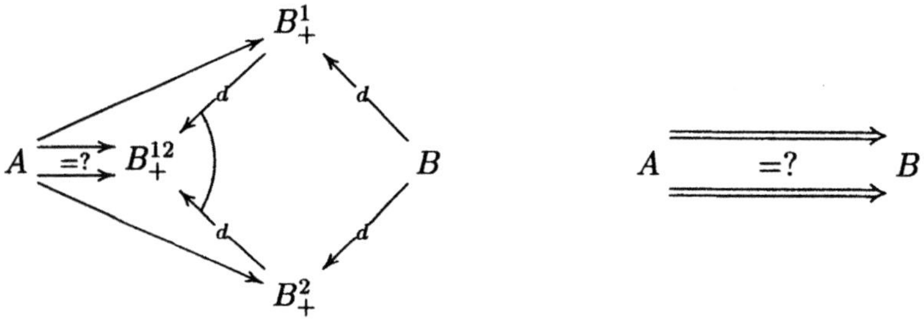

Figure 3 Equality of interpretations.

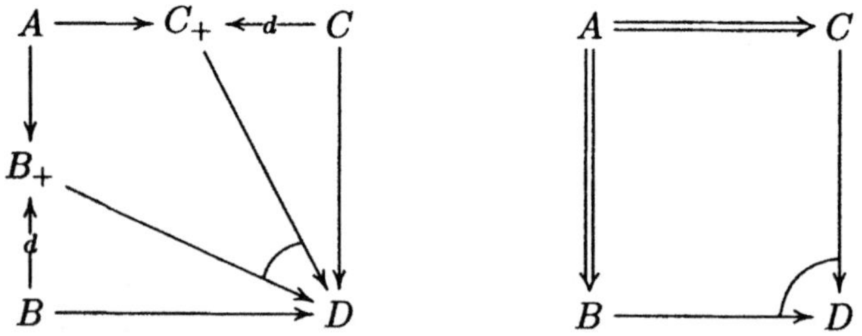

Figure 4 Pushout of interpretations.

Note. Diagrams on the left are in the category of specifications and morphisms; those on the right are in the category of specifications and interpretations.

3 PARAMETERIZED SPECIFICATIONS

A parameterized specification is a specification morphism with special properties. The domain is called the ***parameter*** and the codomain the ***body*** of the parameterized specification. The morphism shows how the parameter is a part-of (or fits into) the body.

The parameter represents the variable part and may be ***instantiated*** by providing a morphism into an ***instantiating*** (or ***actual***) specification. The result of this instantiation is obtained by computing the pushout of the parameterizing morphism and the instantiating morphism. Since the parameter is a specification, it can contain axioms which will impose semantic constraints on any specification that is used to replace the parameter.

This approach to parameterization is similar to that adopted in CLEAR (Burstall & Goguen 1977). Semantically, a parameterized specification represents some flavor of function mapping models of the parameter to models of the body. For example, with intial semantics for specifications, a parameterized specification can denote a free functor (Ehrig *et al.* 1981). Or with loose semantics, it may denote a class of functors (Bidoit 1987, Ehrig & Große-Rhode 1994).

Rather than assume a particular semantics, we will assume some axioms about parameterized specifications, and use these axioms in defining and reasoning about refinement. In the rest of the paper, the phrase 'parameterized specification' will be abbreviated by 'pspec'.

3.1 Axioms for pspecs

1. An identity morphism is a pspec.
2. Pspecs are closed under composition.
3. A definitional extension is a pspec.
4. Pushouts preserve pspecs.

Pspecs are indicated in diagrams by $\xrightarrow{p}$.

3.2 Instantiation with interpretations

While reasoning with refinements of pspecs, it is convenient to be able to instantiate a pspec with an interpretation rather than a morphism, as shown in Figure 5. Syntactically, this means that some of the vocabulary in the parameter is not already present in the instantiating specification, so it needs to be extended before the parameter can be mapped via a morphism. Semantically, an interpretation represents a restriction of the model class, so instantiation with an interpretation is similar to that by a morphism.

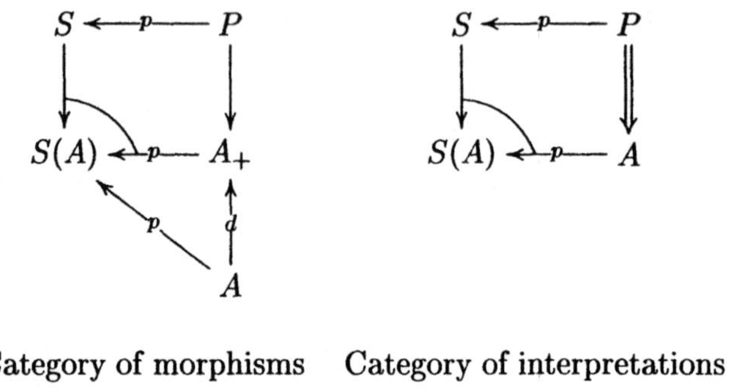

Figure 5 Instantiation of pspecs with interpretations.

Notation. The instantiation of a pspec s: $P \longrightarrow S$ with an interpretation $a: P \Rightarrow A$ will be written as $s(a)$ and will ambiguously denote either the pushout specification $S(A)$ or the resulting pspec $A \longrightarrow S(A)$. The notation $S(A)$, with S and A being specifications rather than morphisms, will sometimes be used to denote the pushout specification when the parameterization and instantiation morphisms are clear from the context.

Instantiation with interpretations emphasizes the asymmetry between the parameterization and instantiation morphisms: the former is like a 'part-of' relation while the latter is like an 'is-a' relation. Yet instantiations behave like pushouts; indeed, they *are* pushouts in the category of specifications and interpretations. We record below a well known property of pushouts that we will subsequently use in our constructions.

LEMMA 3.1: *Cascaded instantiations.* In the commuting diagram below,

1. if both the squares are instantiations, then the outer rectangle is also one, and
2. if the left square and the outer rectangle are instantiations, then the right square is also one.

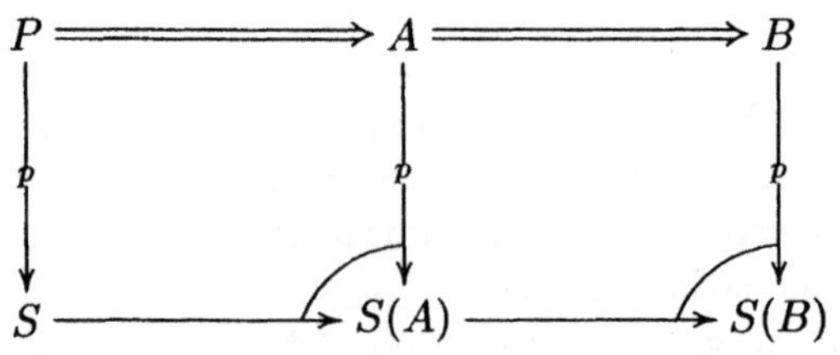

□

spec ELEM
sort ELEM
end-spec

spec SEQ
sorts ELEM, SEQ
op $[\,]$: SEQ
op $\_ : \_$: ELEM, SEQ $\to$ SEQ
axiom $a: S \neq [\,]$
axiom $a: S = b: T \Rightarrow S = T$
axiom $\{\,[\,], \_ : \_\,\}$ *construct* SEQ
op $[\_]$: ELEM $\to$ SEQ
axiom $[a] = a: [\,]$
end-spec

spec TOT
sort ELEM
op $\_ \leq \_$: ELEM, ELEM $\to$ BOOL
axiom $x \leq x$
axiom $x \leq y \wedge y \leq x \Rightarrow x = y$
axiom $x \leq y \wedge y \leq z \Rightarrow x \leq z$
axiom $x \leq y \vee y \leq x$ —*totality*
end-spec

spec SORTING
import SEQ(TOT)
op ordered?: SEQ $\to$ BOOL
definition of ordered? *is*
ordered?$([\,])$
ordered?$([a])$
ordered?$(a: b: S)$
iff $a \leq b \wedge$ ordered?(S)
end-definition
op perm?: SEQ, SEQ $\to$ BOOL
—*definition omitted*
op sort: SEQ $\to$ SEQ
axiom sort$(S) = T$
iff perm?$(S, T) \wedge$ ordered(T)
end-spec

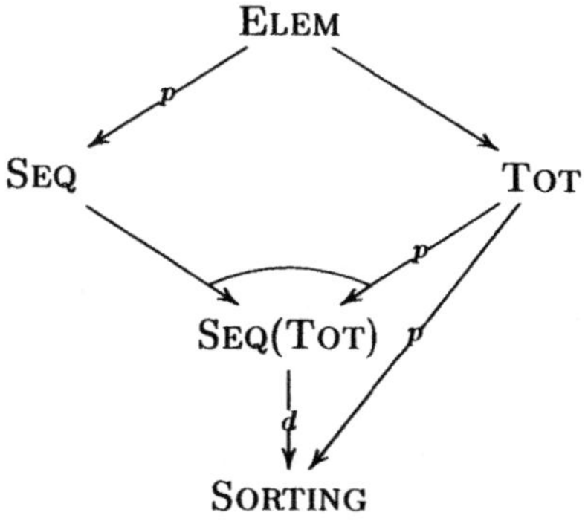

Figure 6 A parameterized specification for sorting.

EXAMPLE 3.1: ***Parameterized specifications.*** Figure 6 shows two parameterized specifications, one for sequences and one for sorting.

The specification for sequences, SEQ, is parameterized on the type of the elements. The parameter specification ELEM postulates a sort for the elements but leaves the sort unconstrained. The specification SEQ contains two operations for constructing sequences, two axioms which characterize equality of sequences, and an induction axiom.

To specify sorting, we need sequences in which the elements have a total order. Such sequences are obtained by instantiating SEQ with the specification for a total order, TOT. The specification SORTING extends this instantiation with predicates used to define sorting. SORTING is itself parameterized with TOT. □

4 REFINEMENT OF PARAMETERIZED SPECIFICATIONS

As noted in the introduction, we will consider refinements in which the body is refined covariantly while the parameter is refined contravariantly. Semantically, a pspec behaves like a function from models of the parameter to models of the body. Such a function can be refined to, or realized by, another function which has a larger domain. Hence, in a pspec refinement, the parameter is relaxed or refined contravariantly. Since the target pspec has a less constrained parameter, it must first be instantiated with the source parameter. With the parameters matched, the bodies may then be related by an interpretation.

DEFINITION 4.1: ***Pspec interpretation.*** A ***pspec interpretation*** $s \overset{p}{\Longrightarrow} s'$ from a pspec s: $P \overset{p}{\longrightarrow} S$ to a pspec s': $P' \overset{p}{\longrightarrow} S'$ is a pair of interpretations, $\langle \pi : P' \Rightarrow P, \beta : S \Rightarrow s'(\pi) \rangle$, where π refines the parameter contravariantly and β refines the body of the source pspec into the instantiation of the target pspec with π, such that $s; \beta = s'(\pi)$. □

Figure 7 renders this definition pictorially, and also shows two special cases of pspec interpretations in which either the body or the parameter is refined via the identity. Every pspec interpretation can be decomposed into a pair consisting of a body refinement followed by a parameter refinement. This decomposition will be used subsequently to build up other constructions with pspec interpretations.

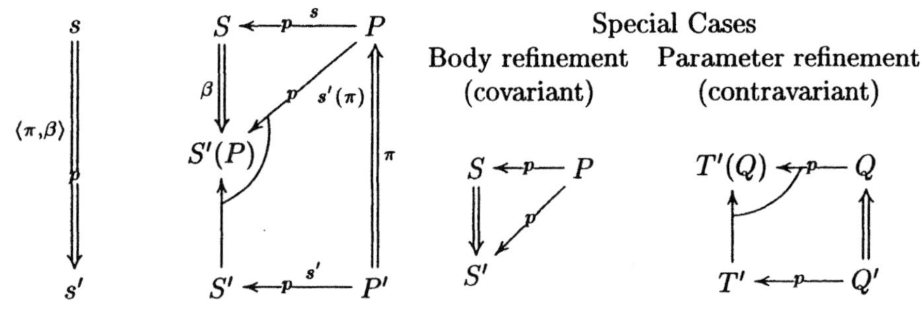

Figure 7 Refinement of pspecs.

```
spec TOT-SIG
 sort ELEM
 op _ ≤ _: ELEM, ELEM → BOOL
end-spec

spec MSORT
 import SEQ(TOT-SIG)
 op merge: SEQ, SEQ → SEQ
 definition of merge is
   merge([], T) = T
   merge(S, []) = S
   merge(a: S, b: T) =
   if a ≤ b then a: merge(S, b: T)
    else b: merge(a: S, T)
 end-definition
 op split: SEQ → SEQ, SEQ
        —definition omitted
 op msort: SEQ → SEQ
 definition of msort is
   msort([]) = []
   msort([a]) = [a]
   msort(a: b: S) =
   let ⟨S1, S2⟩ = split(a: b: S) in
    merge(msort(S1), msort(S2))
 end-definition
end-spec
```

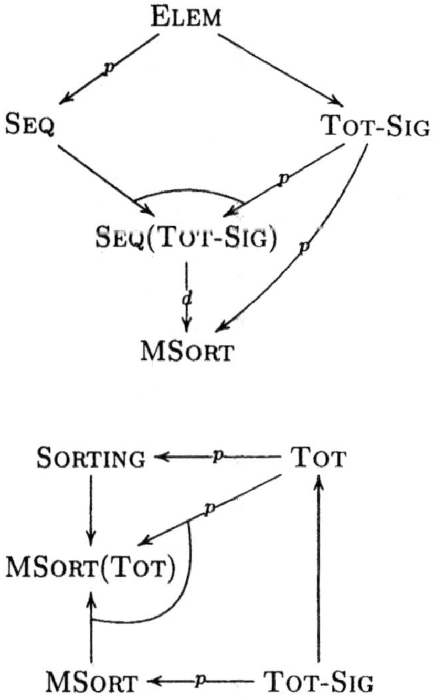

Figure 8 Pspec interpretation for sorting.

EXAMPLE 4.2: ***Pspec interpretation.*** Figure 8 shows a pspec interpretation from the pspec for sorting to a mergesort specification parameterized on the signature of a total order, i.e., a sort together with a binary relation.

The top right part of the figure shows the construction of the target pspec MSORT: SEQ is instantiated with the signature of a total order, TOT-SIG, and then extended with definitions of split, merge and mergesort. Note that this mergesort operation, although a total function, is not guaranteed to produce a sequence which is ordered, because the $\leq$ operation may not be a total order. Yet, this is the mergesort operation that is implemented in most programming languages.

The bottom right part of the figure shows a pspec interpretation. The target parameter TOT-SIG is refined into the source parameter TOT via an inclusion morphism. Once the two parameters are connected, the sorting specification can be refined into the instantiation of the target pspec, MSORT(TOT). The latter specification has enough axioms about $\leq$ to show the correctness of the refinement. □

5 INSTANTIATION OF PSPEC INTERPRETATIONS

Instantiating a pspec yields another pspec. This process can be lifted to pspec interpretations: any interpretation of the original pspec yields an interpretation of the instantiated pspec.

Figure 9 shows the effect of instantiation on a pspec interpretation. In the left half of the figure, we only consider a body refinement. Universality of instantiation yields a unique interpretation from the instantiation of the source pspec, $S(A)$, to the instantiation of the target pspec, $S'(A)$. In the right half of the figure, this is combined with parameter refinement. Using lemma 3.1, composing the parameter refinement with the instantiation yields another parameter refinement.

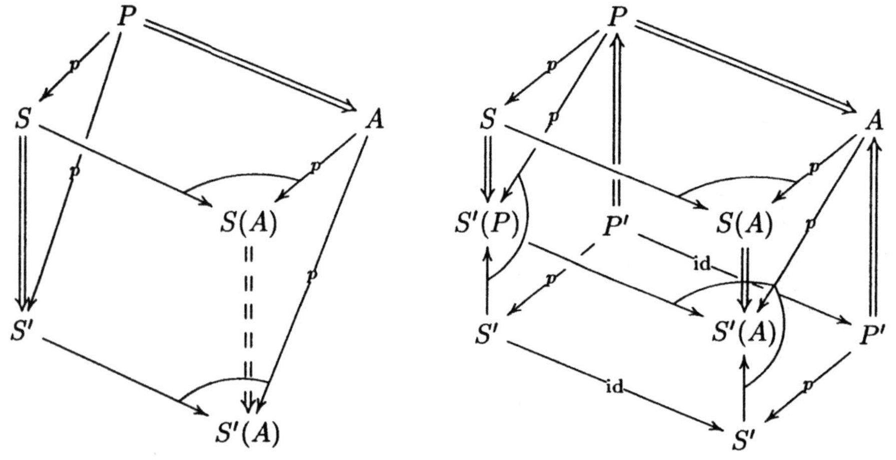

Figure 9 Instantiation of pspec interpretations.

5.1 Independent refinement of pspec and actual

The main reason for parameterizing a specification is the possibility of independently refining the parameterized specification and the instantiating (or actual) specification, and later combining the two refinements, with the parameter capturing the interface between the two. In Figure 10, we show how to parallely compose a pspec interpretation and an interpretation of the actual to obtain an interpretation of the instantiation. The body interpretation is first transferred along the instantiation (as in Figure 9). The resulting pspec, $A \xrightarrow{p} S'(A)$, is then instantiated using the interpretation of the actual. The result, as shown in the right half of the figure, is an interpretation from

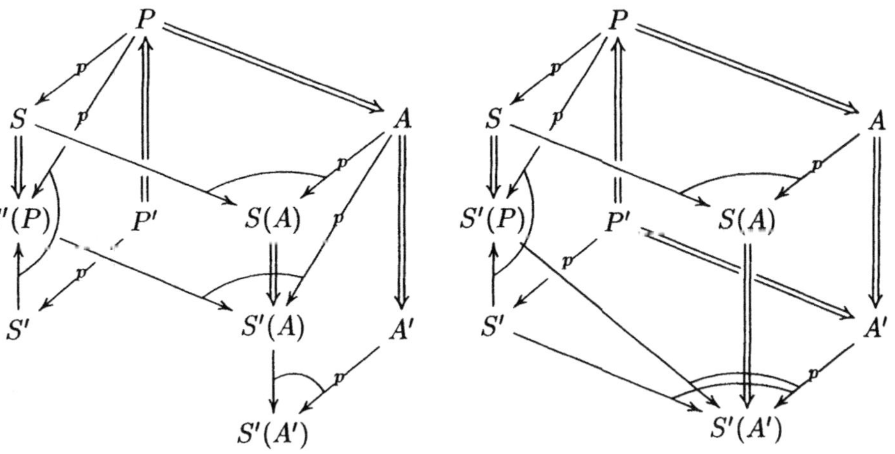

Figure 10 Parallel composition of pspec and actual interpretations.

the instantiation of the source pspec with the actual to the instantiation of the target pspec with the refinement of the actual.

The information in the parallel composition of a pspec interpretation and an actual interpretation is completely contained in the body interpretation of the pspec and the interpretation of the actual. In the right half of Figure 10, just as $S(A)$ is covered by the pushout morphisms $S \rightarrow S(A) \leftarrow A$ and $S'(A')$ is covered by the pushout morphisms $S' \rightarrow S'(A') \leftarrow A'$, so is the parallely composed interpretation $S(A) \Rightarrow S'(A')$ covered by the morphism pair from $S \Rightarrow S'(P)$ and the morphism pair from $A \Rightarrow A'$.

5.2 Instantiation with sharing

In the instantiations we have considered until now, the only part shared by the body and the actual is the parameter. Sometimes, the body and actual share more: e.g., both may import a standard specification such as that of integers. In this case, a simple instantiation will create two copies of the integer specification in the instantiated specification. We can avoid this by explicitly indicating the extra sharing, via morphisms, and taking the colimit of the larger diagram. In the top part of Figure 11, we explicitly indicate extra sharing via two morphisms from the shared specification C. The effect of this sharing is a (coequalizing) morphism from the unshared instantiation $S(A)$ to $S(A)_C$ in which the two copies of C are collapsed.

Now, to parallely compose the pspec and actual refinements, we have to ensure that the shared part is refined similarly in both the body and the actual. This compatibility requirement is satisfied by exhibiting morphisms*

*A morphism of interpretations is a pair of specification morphisms, one between the do-

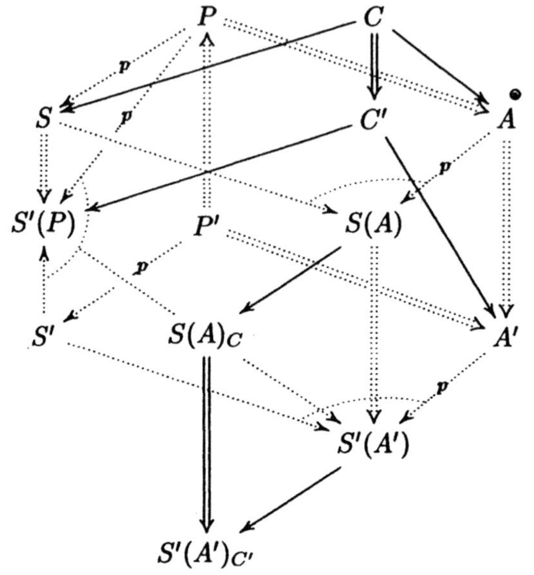

Figure 11 Refinement of shared instantiation.

from the interpretation of the shared part to the interpretations of the body and actual. Then, the target also becomes a shared instantiation, $S'(A')_{C'}$, and we get an interpretation from $S(A)_C$ by universality. The construction is similar to the parallel composition of a diagram refinement, as described in (Srinivas & Jüllig 1995).

6 A CATEGORY OF PSPEC INTERPRETATIONS

It is easy to see that body interpretations and parameter interpretations are each closed under sequential composition. Figure 12 shows the sequential, or vertical, composition of (general) pspec interpretations. The main part of the construction is conversion of a parameter interpretation followed by a body interpretation into a body interpretation followed by a parameter interpretation. This is done by instantiating the second body interpretation with the first parameter interpretation (as in Figure 9). Thus pspecs and pspec interpretations form a category, with the obvious identity arrows, and associativity following from the associativity property for interpretations and pushouts.

To define equality of pspec interpretations, we have to handle isomorphisms between instantiations of the target pspec. Given two pspecs, $s\colon P \xrightarrow{p} S$

mains and one between the codomains, such that the resulting square commutes in the category of specifications and interpretations.

and s': $P' \xrightarrow{p} S'$, two pspecs interpretations, $\langle \pi: P' \Rightarrow P, \beta: S \Rightarrow s'(\pi) \rangle$ and $\langle \pi': P' \Rightarrow P, \beta': S \Rightarrow s'(\pi') \rangle$, are equal if $\pi = \pi'$ and $\beta = \beta'; i$ where i: $s'(\pi') \xrightarrow{\sim} s'(\pi)$ is the isomorphism between the instantiations of the target pspec with the two (equal) parameter interpretations.

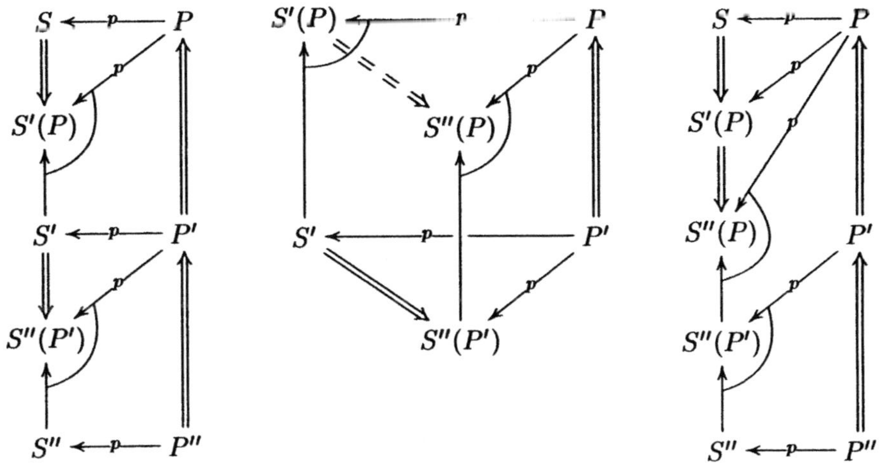

Figure 12 Sequential (vertical) composition of pspec interpretations.

7 HORIZONTAL COMPOSITION OF PSPEC INTERPRETATIONS

Consider an instantiation of a pspec by the body of another pspec. The result is another pspec parameterized on the parameter of the second pspec. A typical example is Set(Seq(X)). Any instantiation of such a 'iterated' pspec satisfies an associativity law, e.g., Set(Seq(Nat)) = (Set(Seq))(Nat); the former is cascaded instantiation while the latter is an instantiation of an iterated pspec. This associativity law is depicted in Figure 13 and follows from the properties of pspecs and instantiations.

We now consider the construction of an interpretation for an iterated pspec from interpretations of the component pspecs. This construction is always possible for body refinements, as shown in the top half of Figure 14. The source iterated pspec $Q \xrightarrow{p} T \xrightarrow{p} S(T)$ is obtained by instantiating the outer pspec $P \xrightarrow{p} S$ with the body of the inner pspec $Q \xrightarrow{p} T$. The specification $S'(T')$ is obtained by instantiating the target of the outer pspec refinement, $P \xrightarrow{p} S'$, with the inner pspec refinement, $P \Rightarrow T \Rightarrow T'$. Universality of $S(T)$ yields a unique interpretation from $S(T)$ to $S'(T')$, and

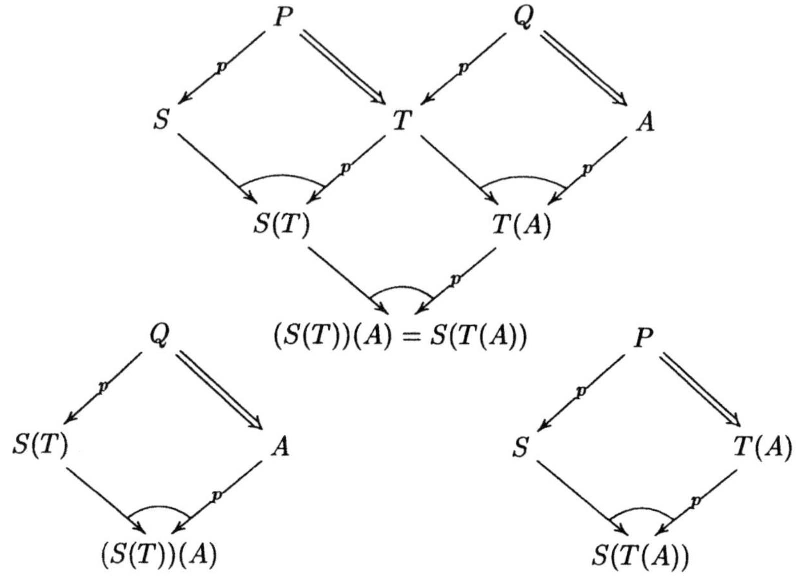

Figure 13 Associativity of instantiation.

hence a body refinement from the source iterated pspec $Q \xrightarrow{p} S(T)$ to the target iterated pspec $Q \xrightarrow{p} S'(T')$.

If parameter refinements are included, then the parameter refinement of the outer pspec must factor through the body refinement of the inner pspec. In this case, the two target pspecs can be connected to form an iterated pspec and the two pspec interpretations can be combined horizontally, as shown in the bottom half of Figure 14. First, the outer body refinement is transferred to the iterated pspec using the construction in the top half of the figure. Then, a target iterated pspec is constructed by connecting the two target pspecs, $P' \xrightarrow{p} S'$ and $Q' \xrightarrow{p} T'$, with an interpretation $P' \Rightarrow T'$; this interpretation is obtained by factoring the composition $P' \Rightarrow P \Rightarrow T \Rightarrow T'(Q)$ through the morphism $T' \to T'(Q)$.* The outer target pspec $P' \xrightarrow{p} S'$ is then instantiated to obtain the specification $S'(T')$. Universality of $S'(T')$ yields a unique morphism to $S'(T'(Q))$ and also makes the square from T' to $S'(T'(Q))$ a pushout, hence producing a pspec refinement from the source iterated pspec $Q \xrightarrow{p} S(T)$ to the target iterated pspec $Q' \xrightarrow{p} S'(T')$.

*If this factoring is not possible, then the two pspec interpretations cannot be horizontally composed.

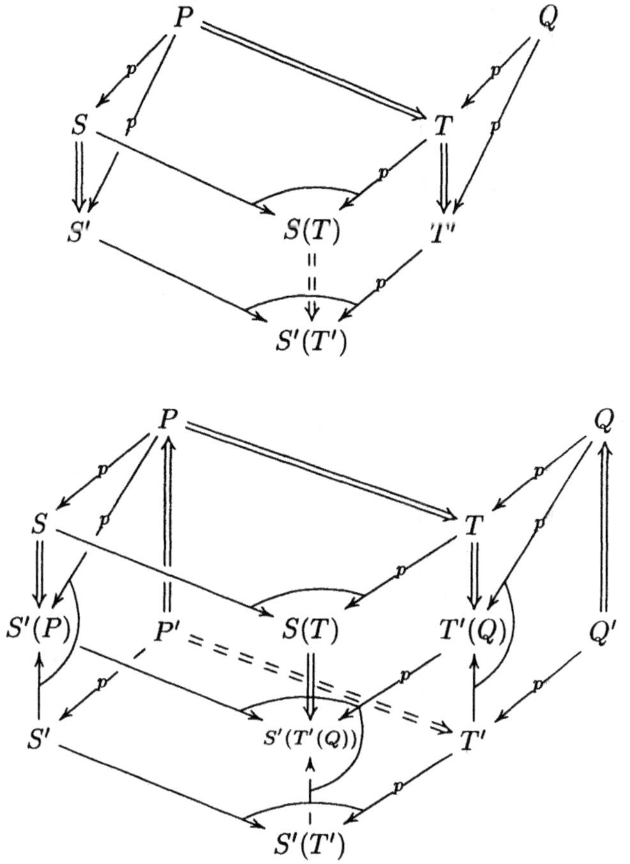

Figure 14 Construction of interpretations for iterated pspecs.

7.1 Commutativity of horizontal composition and instantiation

Given an associative instantiation such as Set(Seq(Nat)) = (Set(Seq))(Nat), we can obtain an interpretation of the resulting specification into two ways: by first refining the inner instantiation and then the outer, or by first composing the two pspec refinements and then refining the instantiation of the iterated pspec. We now show that both paths yield the same interpretation; in other words, associativity of instantiation lifts to pspec interpretations, or horizontal composition of pspec interpretations commutes with instantiation.

In Figure 15, we extend the horizontal composition shown in Figure 14 with instantiations. The top plane shows the associative construction of the instantiation $S(T(A))$ (cf. Figure 13). Similarly, the bottom plane shows the decomposition of $S'(T'(A'))$.

The top right cube shows the construction of the refinement from $T(A)$ to

$T'(A')$ by parallely composing the refinements of $Q \xrightarrow{p} T$ and A (cf. Figure 10). The top left and middle cubes together refine $S(T(A))$ by composing the refinements of $P \xrightarrow{p} S$ and $T(A)$.

Now consider the decomposition $(S(T))(A)$. By omitting the middle and top right cubes, we have a refinement of an iterated pspec (cf. Figure 14). The middle and top right cubes together parallely compose the resulting pspec refinement with the refinement of A.

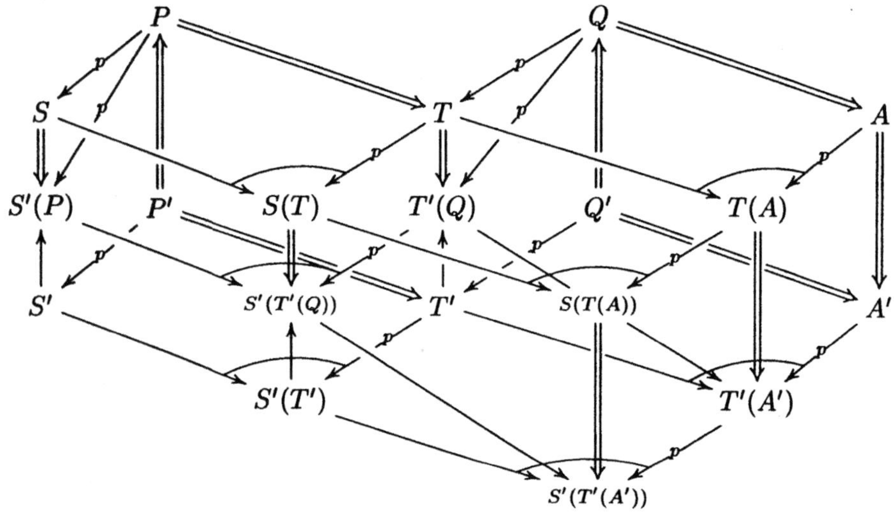

Figure 15 Associative instantiation of iterated pspec interpretations.

8 CONCLUDING REMARKS

We have introduced a refinement arrow of mixed variance for parameterized specifications and demonstrated several key properties of this arrow. These properties are evidence that covariant refinement of the body and contravariant refinement of the parameter yields a natural refinement relation for parameter specifications. This naturalness is further reinforced by the commonly used mixed variance subtyping relation between function types. Indeed, parameterized specifications are semantically functions which map models of the parameter to models of the body.

The constructions in this paper are based on relatively weak assumptions about parameterized specifications. The most important assumption is that of being preserved by pushouts. Closure under composition is a kind of transitivity property that seems to be basic. Closure under definitional extensions states that the distinction between theories and presentations is not critical.

However, more investigation may reveal the need for stronger assumptions about parameterized specifications. For example, conservative extensions satisfy the axioms (in logics with an interpolation property), but it is not clear if it is useful to construe them as parameterized specifications.

Finally, we would like to contrast the morphisms and diagrams approach adopted here with the lambda-abstraction approach to parameterization that is used by some authors. Diagram chasing is sometimes more involved than manipulating expressions; consider, for example, refinement of iterated pspecs. However, it appears that the flexibility given by explicit morphisms is almost always required in practice. Real software is incredibly detailed and demands powerful bookkeeping tools.

8.1 Related Work

A refinement arrow of mixed variance was described by Ehrig & Mahr (1990) and by Sannella & Wirsing (1982). Using the notation of this paper, their refinement arrow is a pair of interpretations such that the square in the left half of Figure 16 commutes.. Such a square can be decomposed into a body refinement followed by a parameter refinement, as shown in the right half of Figure 16. Thus, this refinement arrow is somewhat less general than ours: in ours, the body interpretation need not factor through the target instantiation. We believe that, in most cases, it is not possible to find an interpretation directly between the source and target bodies. Indeed, the purpose of connecting the two parameters and instantiating the target pspec is to provide a sufficiently strong base for refining the body of the source pspec (cf. Figure 8).

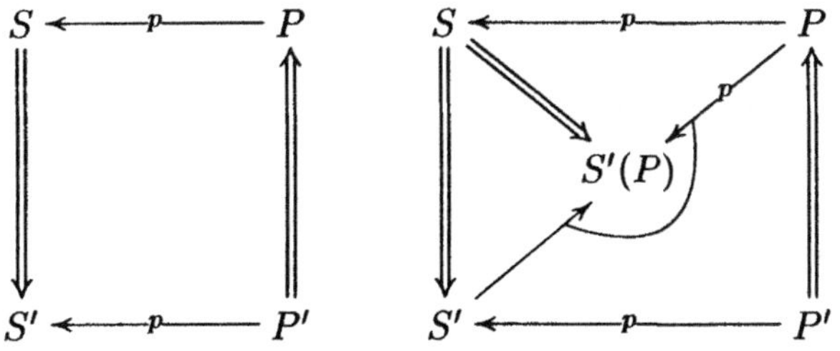

Figure 16 Another refinement arrow for pspecs.

Ehrig & Große-Rhode (1994) adopt an axiomatic approach to parameterized specifications to abstract away from the various semantics: a pspec denotes a class of functors closed under composition and amalgamated extension. This is similar to our axioms about pspecs, provided they are transferred to the semantic level via a model functor *Mod* which transforms pushouts to pullbacks. They consider covariant refinement in this framework. Covariant refinement can be treated as instantiation followed by body refinement, and its properties follows from this decomposition. On the other hand, mixed-variance refinement seems to be fundamental, in the sense that it cannot be built up from other primitive notions.

Acknowledgements

Discussions with Richard Jüllig clarified and simplified some of the concepts in this paper; in particular, the use of interpretations to instantiate parameterized specifications was proposed by him. This work was supported by the Office of Naval Research contract N00014-93-C-0274.

9 APPENDIX: PUSHOUT OF INTERPRETATIONS

LEMMA 9.1: *Epimorphism pushout.* In any category, if an arrow factors via an epimorphism as in the diagram on the left below, the factoring is also a pushout, as in the diagram on the right below.

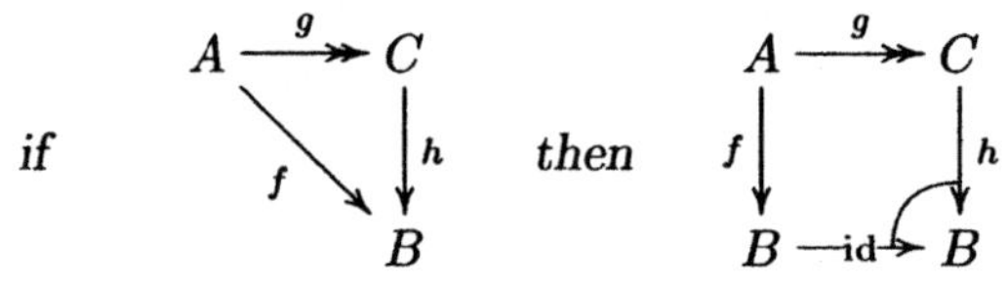

PROOF. Given any cocone $B \xrightarrow{j} E \xleftarrow{k} C$, we must find a unique arrow $B \xrightarrow{w} E$ such that $j = \mathrm{id}_B; w$ and $k = h; w$ (see diagram below). The former equation uniquely determines w to be equal to j. The latter equation follows from the following calculation:

	$f; j = g; k$	—cocone into E
$\Longleftrightarrow$	$(g; h); j = g; k$	—hypothesis about f
$\Longleftrightarrow$	$h; j = k$	—since g is epi
$\Longleftrightarrow$	$h; w = k$	—since $j = w$

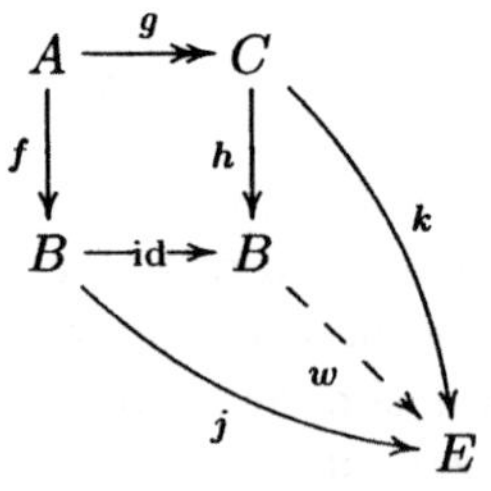

□

COROLLARY 9.2: ***Factoring a definitional extension.***

if 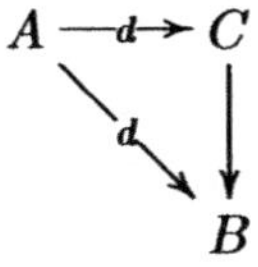

then 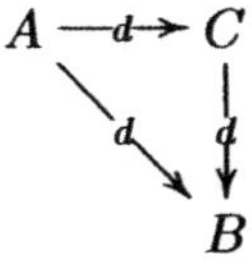

PROOF A definitional extension is an epimorphism, so the triangle on the left is a pushout, and pushouts preserve definitional extensions. □

COROLLARY 9.3: ***Extra definitions in interpretation mediator.***

if 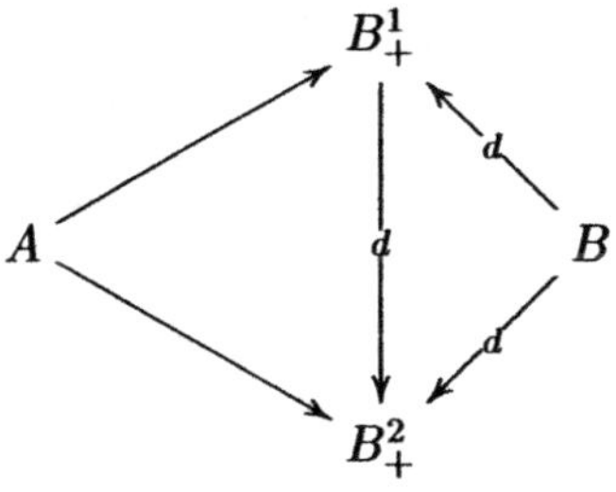

then 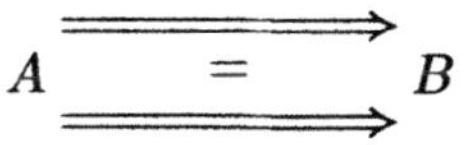

□

COROLLARY 9.4: ***Factoring via a definitional extension.*** The commuting diagram of morphisms on the left below may be construed as the commuting diagram of interpretations on the right below.

if 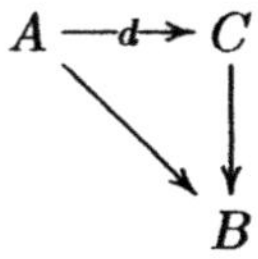

then 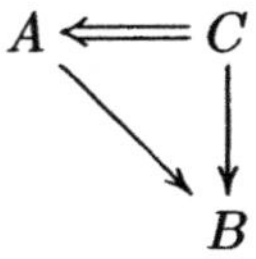

□

LEMMA 9.5: ***Universality of interpretation pushout.*** The pushout of two interpretations, constructed as shown in Figure 4, is universal.
PROOF.
Existence of witness. In the diagram on the left below, $B \overset{f}{\Longleftarrow} A \overset{g}{\Longrightarrow} C$ are the two given interpretations, and the morphisms $B \overset{g'}{\longrightarrow} D \overset{f'}{\longleftarrow} C$ form the pushout cocone (in the category of interpretations). Given any other cocone $B \overset{j}{\Longrightarrow} A \overset{k}{\Longleftarrow} C$, we must find an interpretation $w: D \Rightarrow E$ which factors this cocone through the pushout cocone.

In the diagram on the right below, the pushout and the given cocone are expanded out to show the effect of the equation $f; j = g; k$. From the definitions of composition and equality for interpretations, we get the (pushout) specifications E_3, E_4 and E_5 and the equation $(A \rightarrow B_+ \rightarrow E_3 \rightarrow E_5) =$

$(A \to C_+ \to E_4 \to E_5)$. Universality of D (in the category of morphisms) yields the witness morphism $D \to E_5$.

We thus get the witness interpretation $w: (D \to E_5 \leftarrow E)$ (in the category of interpretations). It is a straightforward diagram chase and application of Corollary 9.3 to check that this witness satisfies the required properties of $g'; w = j$ and $f'; w = k$.

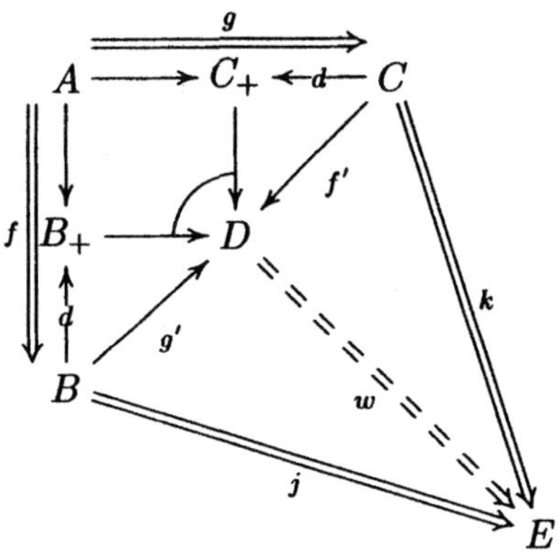

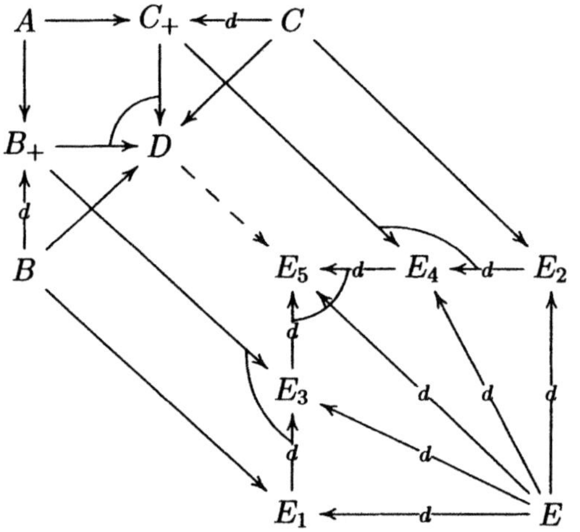

Uniqueness of witness. Suppose there are two interpretations $v, w: D \Rightarrow E$ which factor the cocone $\langle j, k\rangle$ through the pushout cocone $\langle g', f'\rangle$, as shown in the diagram below. We will show that these two interpretations are equal, thus making the witness unique.

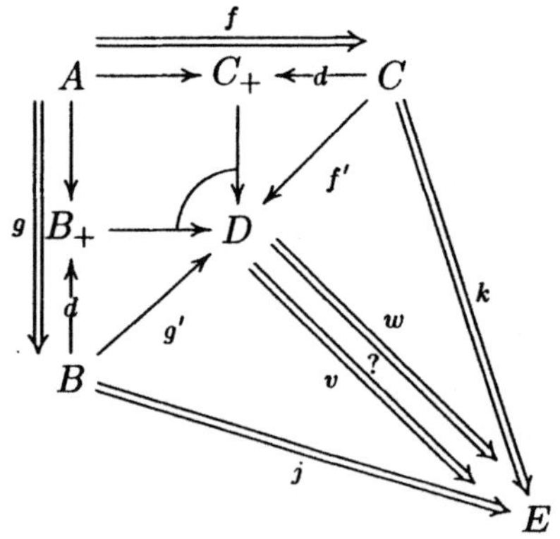

Using Corollary 9.4, we can construct from the given cocone $\langle j, k\rangle$ another cocone $\langle j', k'\rangle$ from the morphism pair $B_+ \leftarrow A \to C_+$ to E, such that the two interpretations v and w factor this cocone through the pushout cocone $B_+ \to D \leftarrow C_+$. This construction is shown in the diagram on the left below.

In the diagram on the right below, the interpretations are expanded and forced to have a common mediator, E_8. Universality of the pushout D (in the category of morphisms) implies that the two morphisms $D \to E_6 \to E_8$ and $D \to E_7 \to E_8$ are equal, because they both factor the cocone $\langle (B_+ \to E_3 \to E_8), (C_+ \to E_4 \to E_8) \rangle$. Thus the two interpretations $v\colon (D \to E_6 \leftarrow E)$ and $w\colon (D \to E_7 \leftarrow E)$ are equal.

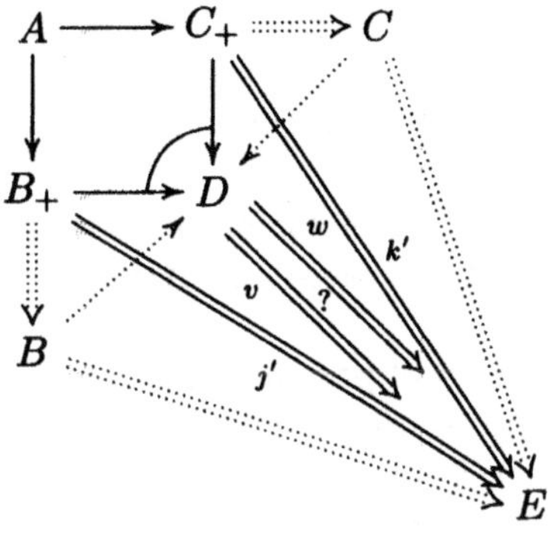

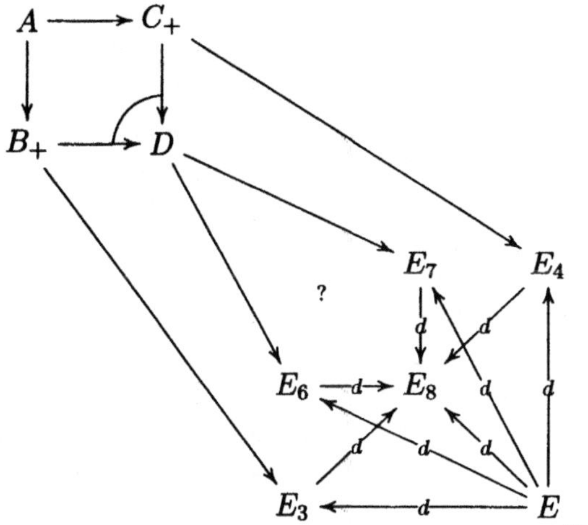

□

REFERENCES

Bidoit, M. (1987), The stratified loose approach: A generalization of initial and loose semantics, *in* 'Recent Trends in Data Type Specification', Vol. 332 of *Lecture Notes in Computer Science*, Springer-Verlag, Gullane, Scotland, pp. 1–22.

Burstall, R. M. & Goguen, J. A. (1977), Putting theories together to make specifications, *in* 'Proc. 5th Int. Joint Conf. on Artificial Intelligence', pp. 1045–1058.

Ehrig, H. & Große-Rhode, M. (1994), 'Functorial theory of parameterized specifications in a general specification framework', *Theoretical Computer Science* **135**, 221–266.

Ehrig, H. & Kreowski, H. J. (1982), Parameter passing commutes with implementation of parameterized data types, *in* '9^{th}ICALP', Vol. 140 of *Lecture Notes in Computer Science*, Springer-Verlag, Aarhus, Denmark, pp. 197–211.

Ehrig, H., Kreowski, H. J., Thatcher, J., Wagner, E. & Wright, J. (1981), Parameter passing in algebraic specification languages, *in* 'Proceedings, Workshop on Program Specification', Vol. 134 of *Lecture Notes in Computer Science*, Springer-Verlag, Aarhus, Denmark, pp. 322–369.

Ehrig, H. & Mahr, B. (1990), *Fundamentals of Algebraic Specification 2: Module Specifications and Constraints*, Vol. 21 of *EATCS Monographs on Theoretical Computer Science*, Springer-Verlag, Berlin.

Ganzinger, H. (1983), 'Parameterized specifications: Parameter passing and implementation with respect to observability', *ACM Transactions on Programming Languages and Systems* **5**(3), 318–354.

Goguen, J. A. & Meseguer, J. (1982), Universal realization, persistent interconnection and implementation of abstract modules, *in* '9^{th}ICALP', Vol. 140 of *Lecture Notes in Computer Science*, Springer-Verlag, Aarhus, Denmark, pp. 265–281.

Lambek, J. & Scott, P. J. (1986), *Introduction to Higher Order Categorical Logic*, Cambridge University Press, Cambridge.

Sannella, D. & Tarlecki, A. (1988), 'Towards formal development of programs from algebraic specifications: Implementations revisited', *Acta Informatica* **25**, 233–281.

Sannella, D. & Wirsing, M. (1982), Implementation of parameterized specifications, *in* '9^{th}ICALP', Vol. 140 of *Lecture Notes in Computer Science*, Springer-Verlag, Aarhus, Denmark, pp. 473–488. Extended abstract.

Srinivas, Y. V. & Jüllig, R. (1995), Specware:^{tm} formal support for composing software, *in* B. Moeller, ed., 'Proceedings of the Conference on Mathematics of Program Construction', Springer-Verlag, Berlin, pp. 399–422. Lecture Notes in Computer Science, Vol. 947.

Wirsing, M. (1986), 'Structured algebraic specifications: A kernel language', *Theoretical Computer Science* **42**, 123–249.

BIOGRAPHY

Dr. Y. V. Srinivas received an M.Tech. in Computer Science from the Indian Institute of Technology, Kanpur, in 1985, and a Ph.D. in Computer Science from the University of California, Irvine, in 1991. He has been with Kestrel Institute since then. His research interests include formal specification (especially algebraic specification), the use of abstract mathematics in software specification and design (topology, category theory, sheaf theory), domain analysis, and formalization of design information.

8

Towards a Compositional Interpretation of Object Diagrams

J.C. Bicarregui, K.C. Lano and T.S.E. Maibaum*
Department of Computing, Imperial College of Science, Technology and Medicine,
180 Queens Gate, London SW7 2BZ.
jcb1@doc.ic.ac.uk

Abstract

We develop a compositional interpretation of object model and statechart diagrams as used in the "Syntropy" method of Object-Oriented Analysis and Design. Separate theories are constructed for object instances, class managers and associations which are then combined with categorical constructions to yield a formal interpretation of the complete system.

We compare the use of state attributes to abstractly interpret history with temporal axioms governing behaviours and contrast the logical notion of locality with object-oriented data encapsulation. We consider the interpretation of statecharts partitioning the overall statespace and defining transitions between partitions and give a formal interpretation to event parameters, filters, preconditions and postconditions. We observe that some features of Syntropy are not amenable to this systematic modular interpretation.

Keywords

Formal methods, modular specification object-oriented, OO, Syntropy, object calculus, action logic, temporal logic, encapsulation.

---

*J.C. Bicarregui is on secondment from the Rutherford Appleton Laboratory.

1 INTRODUCTION

Syntropy [Cook and Daniels (1994)] is an Object-Oriented methodology that includes a range of techniques for a wide spectrum of software engineering tasks from domain modelling to implementation. It is a second generation OO method and includes some degree of formal specification based on Z-like [Spivey (1989)] annotations and Statecharts [Harel (1987)]. However, some other notations and techniques employed in Syntropy are explained only through example in the source material.

In this paper we define a compositional approach to the interpretation of Syntropy Type View diagrams and Statecharts. We interpret diagrams as logical theories in the Object Calculus [Fiadeiro and Maibaum (1991)]. As far as possible separate diagram elements are interpreted as separate theories which are then combined via the categorical constructors of the Object Calculus. This incremental approach makes the interpretation suitable as a basis for a support system which would provide a formal basis for the validation and verification of system specifications.

1.1 Syntropy

Syntropy [Cook and Daniels (1994)] is a methodology for object-oriented analysis and design similar to OMT [Rumbaugh, J. et al.(1991)] with additional formal specification elements derived from Z [Spivey (1989)].

Three separate levels of modelling are used in Syntropy:

- *essential models*, which model the problem domain of the application;
- *specification models*, which abstractly model the requirements of the application; and
- *implementation models*, which model the required software in detail.

At each of these three levels, type view diagrams depict the structure of object classes. Objects have attributes of non-object types. Associations between classes are depicted by connecting lines. A diagrammatic notation for behaviours similar to Statecharts [Harel (1987)] is also used at each of the three levels. Additionally, object interaction graphs (termed *mechanisms* in Syntropy) are used at the implementation level.

Syntropy adopts a number of mathematical notations, however, a semantics is only indicated for data models. In addition, there is no formal definition of refinement between models.

Unlike the use in Syntropy, but in keeping with other OO formalisms, we will use the term "Class" rather than "Object Type" for the collection of possible similar object instances. We reserve the word "type" for values without object identifiers. We use the word "sort" for the types of the logical theories.

1.2 The Object Calculus

The Object Calculus [Fiadeiro and Maibaum (1991)] is a formalism based on structured first order theories composed by morphisms between them.

An object calculus theory models a component of a system. It consists of a set $\mathcal{S}$ of constant symbols, a set $\mathcal{A}$ of ***attribute symbols*** (denoting time-varying data) and a set $\mathcal{G}$ of ***action symbols*** (denoting atomic operations). Axioms describe the types of the attributes and dynamic properties of the actions.

A global, discrete linear model of time is adopted (eg. Lamport (1991)) and axioms are specified using temporal logic operators including: $\bigcirc$ (in the next state), $\bullet$ (in the previous state), $\mathcal{U}$ (strong until), $\mathcal{S}$ (strong since), $\Box$ (always in the future), $\blacksquare$ (always in the past), $\diamond$ (sometime in the future) and $\blacklozenge$ (sometime in the past). The predicate **BEG** is true exactly at the first moment.

The temporal operators are also expression constructors. If e is an expression, $\bigcirc$e denotes the value of e in the next time interval, etc.

In the style of Institutions [Goguen and Burstall (1984)], theories are composed by morphisms to yield a modular definition of a whole system. The Object Calculus defines a notion of locality which ensures that only actions local to a particular theory can effect the value of the local attributes. For each theory we have a logical axiom

$$\bigvee_{g_i \in \mathcal{G}} g_i \vee \bigwedge_{a \in \mathcal{A}} a = \bigcirc a$$

1.3 Overview

In the next section we discuss the interpretation of object types. We define the theory of a class in terms of theories of a generic instance and a class manager. Then, in Section 3, we discuss how class theories are combined to model associations between classes via a generic theory for association managers which is extended to model any cardinality and lifetime dependencies of the particular association. We observe that subtyping associations are equivalent to a particular combination of lifetime and cardinality constraints. In Section 4, we interpret Statecharts, distinguishing the concept of a state transition, which can be interpreted in the instance theory, from the corresponding system event, which is required to be interpreted in the theory of the relevant subsystem. We formalise preconditions and postconditions, filters, and non-interfering concurrency which can be specified via orthogonal statecharts. In Section 5, we apply the formalisation described to a simple example taken from Cook and Daniels (1994) and, in Section 6, we conclude with a discussion of further areas of the Syntropy method which have yet to be formalised. The Appendix gives details of the theories of the example.

2 INTERPRETING OBJECT TYPES

Figure 1 depicts a fragment of a Syntropy type view diagram. A single class, **A**, is defined with two attributes, **f** and **g**, of (non-object) types $\mathbf{T}_1$ and $\mathbf{T}_2$ respectively. (Note that object-typed attributes are given via associations, see Section 3.)

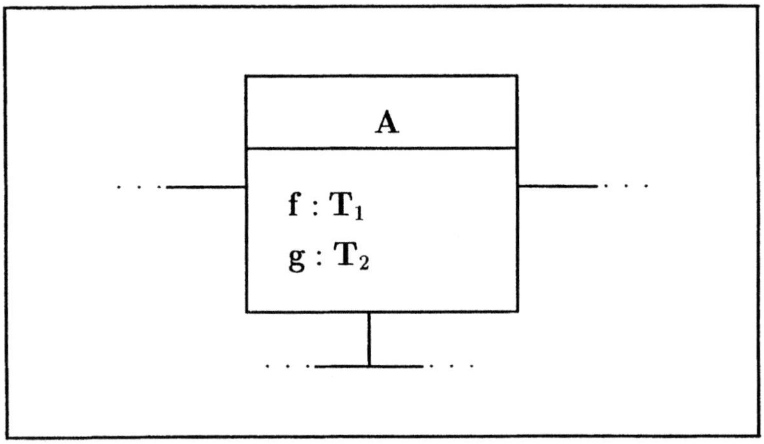

Figure 1 Part of a type view diagram.

Such a diagram can be seen as a view of a typical object of the class, or it can be interpreted as depicting the entire class of such objects. To interpret this diagram, we define two Object Calculus theories. The first gives the theory of a single instance of the class, the second manages the collection of currently existing instances. A number of the former are then be combined with the latter to form the theory of the class.

2.1 The signature of a generic instance

We define a theory, $\mathbf{A_i}$, for a typical object of this class. In the first instance, we treat the object as a "white box" with read and write access to each attribute. Later, in Section 4, we will use information in the statechart to refine the actions available.

The theory of the instance introduces a sort for the type of each attribute, there are no constant (or function) symbols and, for each attribute, there is an attribute symbol for the observer operation and an action symbol for the updater operation. The arrows decorating the action symbols are intended to suggest the writing of the attribute.

$\mathcal{S} = \{\mathbf{T}_1, \mathbf{T}_2\}$
$\mathcal{A} = \{\mathbf{f} : \mathbf{T}_1, \mathbf{g} : \mathbf{T}_2\}$
$\mathcal{G} = \{\mathbf{init} : \mathbf{T}_1 \times \mathbf{T}_2, \overleftarrow{\mathbf{f}} : \mathbf{T}_1, \overleftarrow{\mathbf{g}} : \mathbf{T}_2\}$

Writing to an attribute sets its value in the next state and initialising it sets the value of both attributes

$\overleftarrow{\mathbf{f}}\ (\mathbf{t}_1) \Rightarrow \bigcirc\mathbf{f} = \mathbf{t}_1$
$\overleftarrow{\mathbf{g}}\ (\mathbf{t}_2) \Rightarrow \bigcirc\mathbf{g} = \mathbf{t}_2$
$\mathbf{init}(\mathbf{t}_1, \mathbf{t}_2) \Rightarrow \overleftarrow{\mathbf{f}}\ (\mathbf{t}_1) \wedge \overleftarrow{\mathbf{g}}\ (\mathbf{t}_2)$

The "locality" requirement of the Object Calculus ensures that only local actions can change the local attributes, but we require a stronger condition that only the appropriate updater actions can affect each attribute, eg.

$\neg\ \overleftarrow{\mathbf{f}} \Rightarrow \mathbf{f} = \bigcirc\mathbf{f}$

self A key technique used in OO notations is that an individual object can refer to itself as **self** whilst it's external identity (its object identifier) is given by the class. As in Fiadeiro and Maibaum (1991), we interpret **self** using **A**-morphisms which add the extra parameter to the attributes and actions (see Section 2.3).

2.2 The signature of the class

The creation and deletion of instances is accomplished through a class manager. Class manager and class instances are then combined to form the theory of the class. The definition of the class manager is independent of the structure of **A** and so is defined in terms of a general class type **X**.

The class manager theory, **M**, introduces a sort for identifiers of objects, **@X** and no constant symbols. It is convenient to define an attribute, $\overline{\mathbf{X}}$, to record the finite set of currently existing instances. There are actions to create and kill objects.

$\mathcal{S} = \{\ \mathbf{@X}\ \}$
$\mathcal{A} = \{\ \overline{\mathbf{X}} : \mathbb{F}\mathbf{@X}\ \}$
$\mathcal{G} = \{\ \mathbf{create} : \mathbf{@X};\ \mathbf{kill} : \mathbf{@X}\ \}$

Note that creating an instance does not initialise it. Creation and initialisation are brought together in the action **new** defined below.

We cannot create an existing object nor delete a non-existent one (*pre-create* and *pre-kill*):

$\mathbf{create}(\mathbf{x}) \Rightarrow \mathbf{x} \notin \overline{\mathbf{X}}$
$\mathbf{kill}(\mathbf{x}) \Rightarrow \mathbf{x} \in \overline{\mathbf{X}}$

Creation adds an object to the set of existing objects and deletion removes it (*post-create* and *post-kill*)

$\mathbf{create}(\mathbf{x}) \Rightarrow \mathbf{x} \in \bigcirc\overline{\mathbf{X}}$
$\mathbf{kill}(\mathbf{x}) \Rightarrow \mathbf{x} \notin \bigcirc\overline{\mathbf{X}}$

Note that we prefer this implicit form of axiomatisation to an assignment-like definition of "postconditions" such as: $\mathbf{create(x)} \Rightarrow (\bigcirc\overline{\mathbf{X}}) = \overline{\mathbf{X}} \cup \{ \mathbf{x} \}$ as this would preclude the possibility of two creations or deletions occurring simultaneously.

We require that objects are only added or removed from the set of existing objects by creation and deletion

$\neg\, \mathbf{create(x)} \wedge \neg\, \mathbf{kill(x)} \Rightarrow (\mathbf{x} \in \overline{\mathbf{X}} \Leftrightarrow \mathbf{x} \in \bigcirc\overline{\mathbf{X}})$

Note that this too is a form of intra-theory locality stronger than the default locality condition. It is the converse of consequence of the four pre/post axioms and can be broken down to

$\mathbf{x} \notin \overline{\mathbf{X}} \wedge \mathbf{x} \in \bigcirc\overline{\mathbf{X}} \Rightarrow \mathbf{create(x)}$

$\mathbf{x} \in \overline{\mathbf{X}} \wedge \mathbf{x} \notin \bigcirc\overline{\mathbf{X}} \Rightarrow \mathbf{kill(x)}$

Hence the six conditions can be condensed to

$\mathbf{create(x)} \Leftrightarrow \mathbf{x} \notin \overline{\mathbf{X}} \wedge \mathbf{x} \in \bigcirc\overline{\mathbf{X}}$

$\mathbf{kill(x)} \Leftrightarrow \mathbf{x} \in \overline{\mathbf{X}} \wedge \mathbf{x} \notin \bigcirc\overline{\mathbf{X}}$

which concisely characterise the two actions.

We may wish to give an initialisation stating, for example, that the set of existing objects is initially empty (*initialisation*)

$\mathrm{BEG} \Rightarrow \overline{\mathbf{X}} = \varnothing$

2.3 Embedding instances in the class

At any point in time, there are a finite number of living instances. The theories of these are combined with the theory of the class manager via morphisms which name each instance according to the identifier given when it is created (Figure 2).

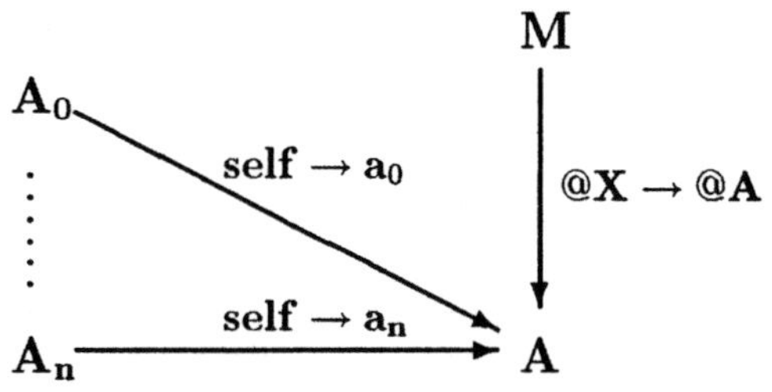

Figure 2 Instance and class manager theories are embedded in the theory of the class.

We combine the theory of each instance with the theory of the class via an **@A**-morphism which adds an extra parameter of type **@A** to each attribute and action symbol [Fiadeiro and Maibaum (1992)]. This is equivalent to defining **self** as a constant in the instance theory which acts as a (dummy) place-holder for later identification with the object identifiers in the class theory†.

The resultant theory, **A**, has an attribute **att(a)** for each attribute **att** of each existing instance **a**. For example, for instance $\mathbf{a_i}$ and attribute **f**, there is an attribute $\sigma_{\mathbf{i}}(\mathbf{f})$ in the class theory. In effect **f** is a (finite) partial function from @**A** to $\mathbf{T}_1$. We define a syntactic sugar which names the $\sigma_{\mathbf{i}}(\mathbf{f})$ conveniently

$\mathbf{f} : @\mathbf{A} \rightarrow \mathbf{T}_1$

$\mathbf{a_i}.\mathbf{f} = \sigma_{\mathbf{i}}(\mathbf{f})$

So, in **A**, **f** is a partial function from @**A** to $\mathbf{T}_1$ which is written in the right. A similar approach is taken to the naming of instance actions.

new A **new** action is defined in the theory of the class. **new** has a parameter for an object identifier from @**A** and a parameter for each attribute instance

$\mathbf{new} : @\mathbf{A} \times \mathbf{T}_1 \times \mathbf{T}_2$

new "exposes" the new identifier which can be understood as being passed from or being returned to the environment. **new** sets the instance identifier and attribute values by calling the **create** and **init** actions of the imported theories

$\mathbf{a_i}.\mathbf{new}(\mathbf{t}_1, \mathbf{t}_2) \Leftrightarrow \mathbf{a_i}.\mathbf{create} \wedge \mathbf{a_i}.\mathbf{init}(\mathbf{t}_1, \mathbf{t}_2)$

Note that creation and initialisation happen simultaneously: as the axioms for initialisation only constrain the values of the attribute in the next state, creation ensures that the new object then exists. **new** can be thought of as a defined (action) symbol.

---

†A morphism, σ, of object signatures from $\theta_1 = (\Sigma_1, \mathbf{A}_1, \Gamma_1)$ to $\theta_2 = (\Sigma_2, \mathbf{A}_2, \Gamma_2)$ is a triple comprising: a morphism of algebraic signatures $\sigma_\nu : \Sigma_1 \rightarrow \Sigma_2$; for each $\mathbf{f} : \mathbf{s}_1, \ldots, \mathbf{s_n} \rightarrow \mathbf{s}$ in $\mathbf{A}_1$, an attribute symbol $\sigma_\alpha(\mathbf{f}) : \sigma_\nu(\mathbf{s}_1), \ldots, \sigma_\nu(\mathbf{s_n}) \rightarrow \sigma_\nu(\mathbf{s})$ in $\mathbf{A}_2$; and, for each $\mathbf{g} : \mathbf{s}_1, \ldots, \mathbf{s_n}$ in Γ_1, an action symbol $\sigma_\gamma(\mathbf{g}) : \sigma_\nu(\mathbf{s}_1), \ldots, \sigma_\nu(\mathbf{s_n})$ in Γ_2.
Given a signature morphism, the translation of formulae is defined according to their structure in the usual way, and given two object descriptions, (θ_1, Φ_1) and (θ_2, Φ_2), a morphism, $(\theta_1, \Phi_1) \rightarrow (\theta_2, \Phi_2)$, is a signature morphism which preserves validity and locality, ie. for which we have: $\Phi_2 \Rightarrow_{\theta_2} \sigma(\mathbf{p})$ is valid for each valid $\mathbf{p} \in \theta_1$; and $\Phi_2 \Rightarrow_{\theta_2} (\theta_1 \rightarrow_\sigma \theta_2)$, where $\Rightarrow_{\theta_2}$ is entailment in θ_2, and $(\theta_1 \rightarrow_\sigma \theta_2)$ is the θ_2 formula which is the translation of the locality axiom of θ_1.
Given a sort **A**, and a morphism of object signatures, σ, the **A**-morphism, $\sigma_\mathbf{A}$, is the same as σ except that it adds an extra parameter of sort **A** to each attribute and action symbol. Thus for example, for given $\mathbf{a} : \mathbf{A}$, for each attribute symbol **f** and $\mathbf{e_i} : \mathbf{s_i}$, $\sigma_\mathbf{A}(\mathbf{f}(\mathbf{e}_1, \ldots, \mathbf{e_n})) = \sigma_\mathbf{A}(\mathbf{f})(\mathbf{a}, \sigma_\mathbf{A}(\mathbf{e}_1), \ldots, \sigma_\mathbf{A}(\mathbf{e_n}))$.

2.4 History and the state

Note that we have, up to this point, avoided the use of any temporal operator other than "next". This is because all behaviour determining history has been explicitly stored in the attributes. However, for example, we may wish to require that it is not possible for an object to be "reborn"

$$\mathbf{create(x)} \Rightarrow \neg \Diamond \mathbf{create(x)}$$

The use of the indefinite temporal operator indicates that more history would be required to be stored in the state in order to implement such behaviour. In general, there is a tension between putting history in the attributes and using more sophisticated temporal descriptions in the axioms which can be understood if the state is seen as an abstract interpretation of the history of past actions. This is discussed further in Section 3.5.

A state-based presentation without rebirth can be given by augmenting the state with a "memory" of past objects. $\overline{\mathbf{X}}$ now distinguishes between objects that have lived and those which have not.

$$\overline{\mathbf{X}} : @\mathbf{X} \rightarrow \{ \mathbf{unborn}, \mathbf{alive}, \mathbf{dead} \}$$

Axioms chart the evolution of objects from **unborn**, through **alive**, to **dead**.

$$\text{BEG} \Rightarrow \forall \mathbf{x} : @\mathbf{X} \bullet \overline{\mathbf{X}}(\mathbf{x}) = \mathbf{unborn}$$
$$\mathbf{create(x)} \Leftrightarrow \overline{\mathbf{X}}(\mathbf{x}) = \mathbf{unborn} \wedge \bigcirc\overline{\mathbf{X}}(\mathbf{x}) = \mathbf{alive}$$
$$\mathbf{kill(x)} \Leftrightarrow \overline{\mathbf{X}}(\mathbf{x}) = \mathbf{alive} \wedge \bigcirc\overline{\mathbf{X}}(\mathbf{x}) = \mathbf{dead}$$

On the other hand, a purely temporal axiomatisation of the class manager can be given without use of $\overline{\mathbf{X}}$

$$\mathbf{create(x)} \Rightarrow \neg \Diamond \mathbf{create(x)}$$
$$\mathbf{kill(x)} \Rightarrow \neg \Diamond \mathbf{kill(x)}$$
$$\mathbf{kill(x)} \Rightarrow \blacklozenge \mathbf{create(x)}$$

Note that the two-valued $\overline{\mathbf{X}}$ can now be recovered as the set of instances which have been created but not killed

$$\overline{\mathbf{X}} = \{ \mathbf{x} : @\mathbf{X} \mid \bullet((\neg \mathbf{kill(x)})\ \mathcal{S}\ \mathbf{create(x)}) \}$$

which forms the basis of the equivalence of the two presentations.

3 INTERPRETING ASSOCIATIONS

We now formalise the notion of an association as depicted in Figure 3. We will interpret the association without any knowledge of the structure of the objects it associates (although we do assume each class theory has been constructed from instance theories and class manager theory as defined above). Thus we have a generic theory of associations. We then use a renamed copy of this theory for each particular association in the model.

We begin with the most general case, a many-many association depicted by the black "blobs" at each end of the connecting line. The same approach will also work for other cardinalities of association by requiring further axioms

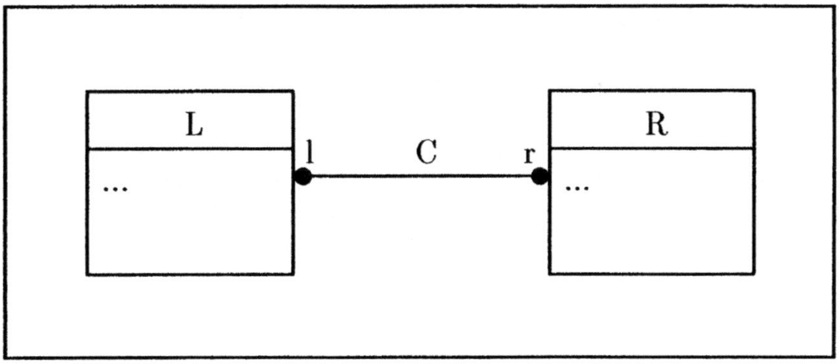

Figure 3 A simple association.

for the constrained cases. For this section we consider only how to interpret associations at the level of the classes. In some circumstances, such as when the association has attributes of its own, it may be desirable to make a two level construction as was done for object classes.

The association is interpreted as a many-many relation **rl** between object identifiers for the class on the left, **@L** and the class on the right, **@R**. (Note that this turns out to be considerably more convenient $\mathbf{r} : \mathbf{@L} \rightarrow \mathbb{F}\mathbf{@R}$ and $\mathbf{l} : \mathbf{@R} \rightarrow \mathbb{F}\mathbf{@L}$, such functions can be defined from the relation if required.) **rl** plays the same role as $\overline{\mathbf{X}}$, it is the set of existing links in the association. The theory signature is:

$\mathcal{S} = \{\ \mathbf{@L}, \mathbf{@R}\ \}$
$\mathcal{A} = \{\ \mathbf{lr} : \mathbb{F}(\mathbf{@L} \times \mathbf{@R})\ \}$
$\mathcal{G} = \{\ \mathbf{link} : \mathbf{@L} \times \mathbf{@R}, \mathbf{unlink} : \mathbf{@L} \times \mathbf{@R}\ \}$

As for object classes, we require axioms for adding and removing pairs from the relation and again have an "instance-by-instance" locality requirement which yields a characterisation of the two actions

$\mathbf{link(l, r)} \Leftrightarrow \mathbf{(l, r)} \notin \mathbf{lr} \wedge \mathbf{(l, r)} \in \bigcirc\mathbf{lr}$
$\mathbf{unlink(l, r)} \Leftrightarrow \mathbf{(l, r)} \in \mathbf{lr} \wedge \mathbf{(l, r)} \notin \bigcirc\mathbf{lr}$

In this case, as there are no identifiers for links, we do not require no-rebirth.

Again, it may be appropriate to add an axiom concerning the initialisation such as

$\mathrm{BEG} \Rightarrow \mathbf{lr} = \varnothing$

There is no axiomatic constraint between **link** for the association and **create** for the object classes here. Such constraints are given when the theories of objects and association are brought together. In keeping with encapsulation, there are no actions to update or inspect the associated object instances directly.

3.1 Bringing association and Objects together

Now assume that **A** and **B** are associated by **C** in a diagram **D**. **D** is interpreted as the co-limit of the theories for **A**, **B** and **C**. The class manager theories for **A** and **B** provide the "glue" which brings theories of objects and associations together. **C** is "glued" to each of **A** and **B** by identifying **@L** and **@R** with **@A** and **@B** respectively. Where names would otherwise clash, they are subscripted by the name of the theory from which they originate. Purely for convenience, **lr** is renamed to **ab** in **D**.

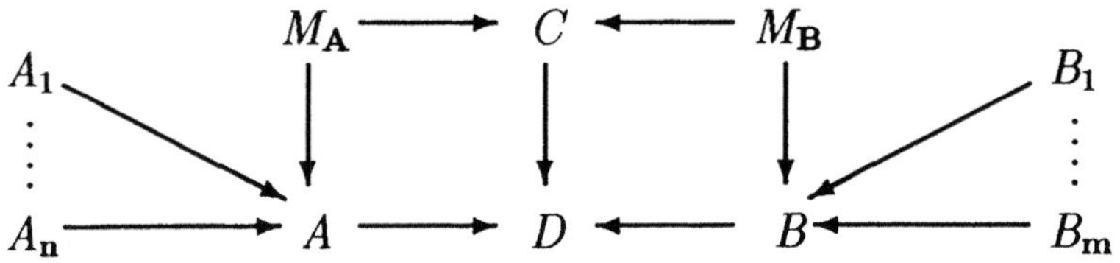

Figure 4 The type view diagram is interpreted as the colimit of the object and association theories.

We now add axioms to **D** which interpret the particular kind of association required.

3.2 One-many, many-one and one-one associations

Firstly, whatever kind of association is required, it can only link existing objects

$\mathbf{ab} \subseteq \overline{\mathbf{A}} \times \overline{\mathbf{B}}$

This is ensured by axioms which synchronise creation actions in the association and class manager theories

$\mathbf{link(a,b)} \Rightarrow \mathbf{a} \in \overline{\mathbf{A}} \vee \mathbf{a.create_A}$

$\mathbf{link(a,b)} \Rightarrow \mathbf{b} \in \overline{\mathbf{B}} \vee \mathbf{b.create_B}$

This can be written as an extra, trans-theory, postcondition for **link**

$\mathbf{link(a,b)} \Rightarrow \mathbf{a} \in \bigcirc\overline{\mathbf{A}} \wedge \mathbf{b} \in \bigcirc\overline{\mathbf{B}}$

which, due to locality, yields the above synchronisation between **link** and **create**.

Optional unary associations (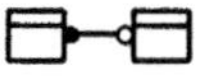)

If the "blob" on the right is white, that is each $\overline{\mathbf{A}}$ is associated with at most one $\overline{\mathbf{B}}$, then the relation is a (partial) map from **@A** to **@B**. This can be interpreted purely in the theory of the association

$$\mathbf{ab} : @\mathbf{A} \twoheadrightarrow @\mathbf{B}$$

ie.

$$(\mathbf{a}, \mathbf{b}) \in \mathbf{ab} \land (\mathbf{a}, \mathbf{b}') \in \mathbf{ab} \rightarrow \mathbf{b} = \mathbf{b}'$$

This is ensured within the association theory by strengthening the constraints on **link**

$$\mathbf{link}(\mathbf{a}, \mathbf{b}) \Rightarrow \mathbf{a} \notin \operatorname{dom} \mathbf{ab}$$
$$\mathbf{link}(\mathbf{a}, \mathbf{b}) \land \mathbf{link}(\mathbf{a}, \mathbf{b}') \Rightarrow \mathbf{b} = \mathbf{b}'$$

Compulsory unary associations (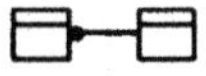)

If the blob on the right is missing altogether, that is each $\overline{\mathbf{A}}$ is associated with exactly one $\overline{\mathbf{B}}$, then the map is total on $\overline{\mathbf{A}}$. This is a constraint between association and class manager theories

$$\operatorname{dom} \mathbf{ab} = \overline{\mathbf{A}}$$

Note that we do not require the map to be surjective since an **@B** can be associated with an empty set of **@A**s.

Again this can be ensured by trans-theory conditions

$$\mathbf{a}.\mathbf{create}_{\mathbf{A}} \Leftrightarrow \mathbf{a} \notin \operatorname{dom} \mathbf{ab} \land \mathbf{a} \in \operatorname{dom} \bigcirc \mathbf{ab}$$
$$\mathbf{a}.\mathbf{kill}_{\mathbf{A}} \Leftrightarrow \mathbf{a} \in \operatorname{dom} \mathbf{ab} \land \mathbf{a} \notin \operatorname{dom} \bigcirc \mathbf{ab}$$

Conversely, for the one-many case, we have conditions on $\mathbf{ab}^{-1}$.

One-one associations (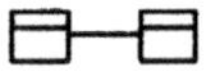)

In the one-one case, we simply have both of these sets of axioms and so we can conclude that **A**s and **B**s must be created and deleted in lock-step and therefore that there are always the same number of $\overline{\mathbf{A}}$s as $\overline{\mathbf{B}}$s.

3.3 Dealing in Diamonds ()

A "diamond" on the association is a constraint concerning the lifetimes of the associated objects. Diamonds can be interpreted independently of multiplicities.

A diamond at the right hand end of the association, indicates that **A**s can only exist if linked with some (set of) **B**s and that this set must be constant throughout the **A**s lifetime. Therefore, while an **A** exists, each state transition preserves the set of links involving it

$$\mathbf{a} \in \overline{\mathbf{A}} \land \mathbf{a} \in \bigcirc\overline{\mathbf{A}} \Rightarrow \{\ \mathbf{a}\ \} \lhd \mathbf{ab} = \{\ \mathbf{a}\ \} \lhd \bigcirc \mathbf{ab}$$

This is ensured if **A**s can be linked to **B**s only when they are created, and unlinked only when deleted

$$\mathbf{link}(\mathbf{a}, \mathbf{b}) \Rightarrow \mathbf{a} \notin \overline{\mathbf{A}} \land \mathbf{a} \in \bigcirc\overline{\mathbf{A}}$$
$$\mathbf{unlink}(\mathbf{a}, \mathbf{b}) \Rightarrow \mathbf{a} \in \overline{\mathbf{A}} \land \mathbf{a} \notin \bigcirc\overline{\mathbf{A}}$$

There are similar rules for a diamond on the left of an association.

3.4 Subtypes ( )

We can view subtyping as a particular form of association where, the object identifiers are drawn from the same set of tokens

$\mathbf{@B = @A}$

and the association function is the identity on $\overline{\mathbf{B}}$

$\mathbf{ab} = \{\ (\mathbf{b}, \mathbf{b}) \mid \mathbf{b} \in \overline{\mathbf{B}}\ \}$

This is derived from

$\mathbf{link(a, b)} \Leftrightarrow \mathbf{a = b} \wedge \mathbf{b} \notin \overline{\mathbf{B}} \wedge \mathbf{b} \in \bigcirc\overline{\mathbf{B}}$

$\mathbf{unlink(a, b)} \Leftrightarrow \mathbf{a = b} \wedge \mathbf{b} \in \overline{\mathbf{B}} \wedge \mathbf{b} \notin \bigcirc\overline{\mathbf{B}}$

Since $\mathbf{ab} \subseteq \overline{\mathbf{A}} \times \overline{\mathbf{B}}$ we have that all **B**s are **A**s

$\overline{\mathbf{B}} \subseteq \overline{\mathbf{A}}$

If the supertype is abstract, as is assumed when a number of dynamic subtypes are defined for a supertype, then the subtype instances partition the supertype instances

$\overline{\mathbf{A}} = \bigcup \overline{\mathbf{B_i}}$

$\mathbf{i \neq j} \Rightarrow \overline{\mathbf{B_i}} \cap \overline{\mathbf{B_j}} = \varnothing$

If **B** is a subtype of **A**, then each **B** is associated with exactly one **A**, and each **A** with zero or one **B**. Furthermore, the lifetime of the **B** is subsumed within the lifetime of its associated **A**. So a triangle pointing to the left is equivalent to a diamond on the left and a white blob on the right (Figure 5).

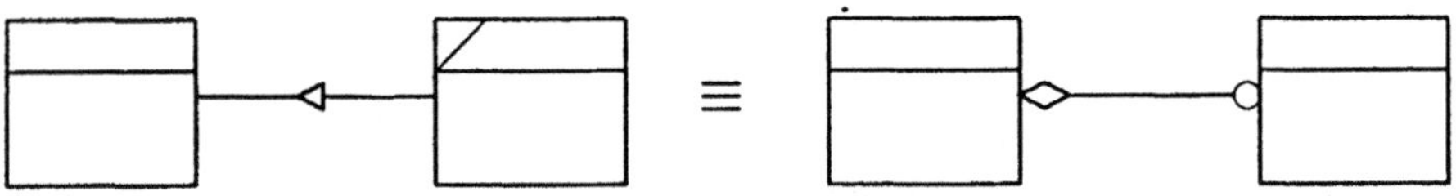

Figure 5 Equivalent diagrams for dynamic subtyping.

If the subtype is static (ie. there is no subtype migration), indicated by the lack of a diagonal line on the subtype, then additionally the lifetime of the **A** is exactly the same as the lifetime of the **B** and so there is a diamond at the other end also (Figure 6).

Figure 6 Equivalent diagrams for static subtyping.

In either case we can derive the following

$\mathbf{a.create_B} \Rightarrow \mathbf{a} \in \bigcirc\overline{\mathbf{A}}$
$\mathbf{a.kill_A} \Rightarrow \mathbf{a} \notin \bigcirc\overline{\mathbf{B}}$
which therefore ensures
$\mathbf{a.create_B} \wedge \mathbf{a} \notin \overline{\mathbf{A}} \Rightarrow \mathbf{a.create_A}$
$\mathbf{a.kill_A} \wedge \mathbf{a} \in \overline{\mathbf{B}} \Rightarrow \mathbf{a.kill_B}$

3.5 A note on Encapsulation and locality

We have seen some alternative presentations of theories where axioms focus on changes to the state or on permitted sequences of actions. Recall the Object Calculus definition of locality which can be paraphrased as:

> "The values of local attributes are determined by local actions"

There is a converse side to encapsulation which concerns how the state influences the actions. The behaviour of an object should depend only on it's own state, ie.

> "The effect of local actions is determined by the local attributes"

That is, the local state transition resulting from a particular local action should be determined by the values of the local attributes. This can be formalised as follows. For any set of local actions $\mathbf{S} \subseteq \mathcal{G}$, define

$$\mathbf{just(S)} \mathrel{\hat{=}} \bigwedge_{g_i \in S} g_i \wedge \bigwedge_{g_i \in \mathcal{G} \setminus S} \neg g_i$$

Then, for any $\mathbf{S} \subseteq \mathcal{G}$, we require

$$\bigwedge_{a_i \in \mathcal{A}} a_i = v_i \wedge \mathbf{just(S)} \wedge \bigcirc\phi \quad \Rightarrow \quad \Box(\bigwedge_{a_i \in \mathcal{A}} a_i = v_i \wedge \mathbf{just(S)} \Rightarrow \bigcirc\phi)$$

Which can be read as:

> "If from some state, doing exactly some set of actions results in a state where some property holds, then whenever in the first state, the same set of actions will result in the same state."

Here the formula ϕ should concern the attributes only and not contain any temporal operators. This could be considered to be part of the object-oriented notion of encapsulation and may therefore be appropriate in its formalisation.

4 INTERPRETING STATECHARTS

Statecharts are the most complex and semantically rich notation employed by Syntropy. Based on Harel's Statecharts, they depict the state space of an object, partitioned according to "those states which distinguish the possible orderings of events" [Cook and Daniels (1994) p. 91]. Statecharts have distinct interpretations at the essential, specification and implementation modelling levels. We focus on the essential level, but many of the semantic interpretations also apply to the specification and implementation levels.

State classes, depicted by boxes with a diagonal line in their top left hand corner, represent varying subsets of the objects of the superclass where an individual instance can move between the subtypes. Statecharts define the transitions which take instances from one state class to another.

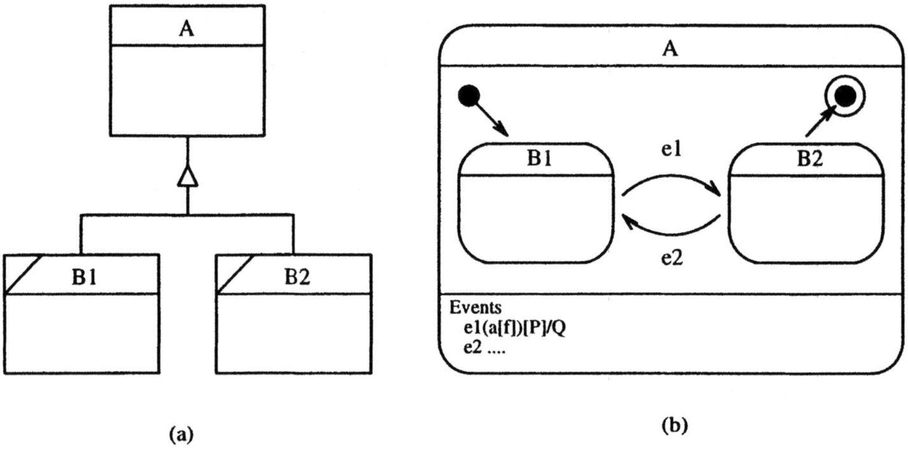

Figure 7 State types and statechart for class **A**.

For example, Figure 7 depicts a class with two state subtypes, $\mathbf{B}_1$ and $\mathbf{B}_2$. The subtypes in Figure 7(a) correspond to the states in Figure 7(b). The arrow from the solid blob indicates that the object is created in state $\mathbf{B}_1$ and the arrow to the ringed blob represents object deletion from state $\mathbf{B}_2$. The other arrows indicate state transitions $\mathbf{e}_1$ and $\mathbf{e}_2$ which take the object from state $\mathbf{B}_1$ to state $\mathbf{B}_2$ and back respectively. In the essential model, the lack of further arrows indicates that, for example, $\mathbf{e}_1$ "cannot happen" when the object is in state $\mathbf{B}_2$.

In Syntropy, the effect of transitions is specified by preconditions and postconditions similar to those used in Z or VDM. For example, $\mathbf{e}_1[\mathbf{P}]/\mathbf{Q}$, indicates that transition $\mathbf{e}_1$ can only occur if the predicate **P** holds and that the two-state predicate **Q** must hold between the before and after states when $\mathbf{e}_1$ occurs.

Further semantics is given by **Events** listed in the textual part at the bottom of the statechart. Events are system-wide, but can be targeted at particular objects by the use of parameters and filters. Typically, events effect a state transition in a single object of the class and have the same name as a state transition in the diagrammatic part of the statechart. Unlike the use in

Syntropy, we make a syntactic distinction between the event and its associated transitions by capitalising the event name and indexing the transition names.

In Syntropy, the instance targeted by the event is generally passed as a parameter, **a**, of the object type (c.f. the extra parameter introduced in the **A**-morphism). In this case, the default filter, $\mathbf{a} = \mathbf{self}$, is assumed to indicate that only the object passed as parameter responds to the event. More complex situations can be modelled using this mechanism where the filter, **f**, is a predicate identifying which events the **self** object should react to.

The same event can correspond to more than one transition in the diagrammatic part of the statechart. Where the sources of the arrows are different states, the state gives the precondition for the transition. Where the same event name labels two arrows from the same state, the choice between them is indicated by separate explicit preconditions which are annotated directly on the arrows.

4.1 Interpreting state types and events

The information in the class diagram is interpreted as in Sections 2 and 3. The statechart defines the actions of the classes which replace the white box actions described in Section 2.1. Each arrow in the statechart represents a class of possible state transitions and is interpreted as an action of the instance theory. Several arrows can be used to describe different cases of a particular system event. The event is interpreted as an action in the theory of the subtype/supertype subsystem and is synchronised with the instance actions that correspond to the required state changes. For example, in the above diagram, if $\mathbf{e}_1$ and $\mathbf{e}_2$ are different cases of the same event $\mathbf{E}(\mathbf{a})$ then $\mathbf{e}_1$ and $\mathbf{e}_2$ are interpreted as separate actions in the instance theory of **A** whereas $\mathbf{E}(\mathbf{a})$ is interpreted in the theory of the $\{\ \mathbf{A}, \mathbf{B}_1, \mathbf{B}_2\ \}$ subsystem and then synchronised with $\mathbf{e}_1$ and $\mathbf{e}_2$ via an axiom of the form

$$\mathbf{E}(\mathbf{a}) \Rightarrow \mathbf{a}.\mathbf{e}_1 \vee \mathbf{a}.\mathbf{e}_2$$

Filters More generally, events are of the form $\mathbf{E}(\mathbf{p}[\mathbf{F}])$, where the parameter **p** is a list of object or value parameters and the filter **F** is a predicate involving the parameters, **self** and the class constants. Object instances that satisfy the filter will undergo the corresponding transition (depending on their state and precondition), whereas objects for which a filter fails to hold ignore the associated event

$$\mathbf{E}(\mathbf{p}[\mathbf{F}]) \Rightarrow (\forall\, \mathbf{a} \in @\mathbf{A} \bullet \mathbf{a}.\mathbf{F} \Rightarrow \mathbf{a}.\mathbf{e}_1 \vee \mathbf{a}.\mathbf{e}_2)$$

Here $\mathbf{a}.\mathbf{F}$ is **F** with **a** substituted for **self**. For example, in the default case, where **F** is $\mathbf{p} = \mathbf{self}$, then $\mathbf{a}.\mathbf{F}$ is $\mathbf{p} = \mathbf{a}$ and we regain the simpler condition above.

Note that when an event is not listed for a statechart, we require the event to go undetected by the object (rather than be blocked). In order to ensure this, we interpret unlisted events as having a filter of **false**.

Interpreting preconditions Preconditions in the essential model are intended to specify that certain transitions "cannot occur" in given circumstances. Thus we interpret preconditions as (blocking) guards which prevent execution of the transition they annotate. Consider the transition $\mathbf{e_1[P]/Q}$ from state $\mathbf{B_1}$ to state $\mathbf{B_2}$. We define a *permission axiom* in the instance theory

$$\mathbf{e_1 \Rightarrow P}$$

which expresses that $\mathbf{e_1}$ can only occur when $\mathbf{P}$ holds.

Note, that this interpretation prevents preconditions from being weakened in refinement, that is, such transformations do not yield theory extensions. Thus subtyping form 5 of Chapter 8 of Cook and Daniels (1994) (weakening preconditions) is not valid in essential models. (In specification models, on the other hand, preconditions are to be interpreted as assumptions: any behaviour is valid if a transition is executed when its precondition is false. So preconditions *can* be weakened in specification models.)

At the class level, each transition is also guarded by the state from which it occurs, for example, we have

$$\mathbf{a.e_1 \Rightarrow a \in \overline{B_1}}$$

Postconditions Postconditions are expressed in terms of the change between attribute values of the current state and those after the transition. Modifications to associations which result from postconditions defining a change to one end only are assumed to be made explicit in the postcondition.

For the above transition with postcondition, $\mathbf{Q}$, we have the *state-transition* axiom

$$\mathbf{e_1 \Rightarrow Q}$$

where $\mathbf{Q}$ is a predicate in attribute symbols $\mathbf{f_i}$ and $\mathbf{f_i'}$ and we replace $\mathbf{f_i'}$ with $\bigcirc\mathbf{f_i}$ in $\mathbf{Q}$.

At the class level, the event additionally moves the targeted instances to state $\mathbf{B_2}$

$$\mathbf{a.e_1 \Rightarrow a \in \bigcirc\overline{B_2}}$$

Synchronous time and single threading for instances Syntropy assumes that external events are totally ordered and that the system responds instantaneously to them corresponding approximately to supersteps in Statecharts under the synchronous model of time. The condition that no two external events cannot co-occur is rather awkward to formalise requiring the assertion of pairswise exclusivity between all external events. This can, of course, only be given at the level of the entire specification, once a closed system is assumed.

As there are no generated events in essential models, it is possible to assert that distinct transitions cannot occur for the same object in a single time interval (*disjointness axioms for transitions*)

$$\mathbf{\neg\,(a.e_1 \wedge a.e_2)}$$

where $\mathbf{e_1}$ and $\mathbf{e_2}$ are distinct transitions. (In specification models on the other hand, generated events can lead to race conditions. Unlike Statecharts, where this possibility is allowed and leads to non-determinism, Syntropy stipulates that such specifications are incorrect.)

4.2 Orthogonal state machines

Syntropy allows non-interfering concurrency to be specificed via orthogonal statecharts as in Figure 8. The state space is now the cartesian product of the spaces indicated by the two statechart components. For example, there are four states defined in the example: $(\mathbf{B}_1, \mathbf{C}_1), (\mathbf{B}_1, \mathbf{C}_2), (\mathbf{B}_2, \mathbf{C}_1), (\mathbf{B}_2, \mathbf{C}_2)$. Several possibilities for synchronisation arise: the separate event lists act as another form of filter. When an event which appears in both event lists occurs, both state components must undergo a corresponding state transition as permitted by the filters and preconditions in the corresponding component diagram. If the event appears in one list only, the other component ignores the event as if it were filtered out.

To interpret the orthogonal statechart components, we simply consider each component separately. The treatment of unlisted events ensures that the correct behaviour is specified when events are listed in only some components (see Section 5.1).

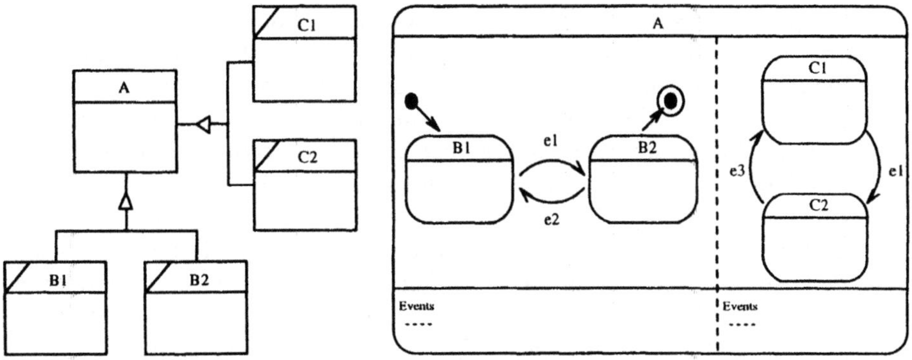

Figure 8 Orthogonal Statechart components.

5 EXAMPLE

We now illustrate the approach described above by applying it to a simple example taken from Cook and Daniels (1994). A type view diagram and statechart for a bottling plant are depicted in Figure 9. The class **Bottle** has two attributes giving its capacity and contents. Two dynamic subtypes are defined. A bottle is **Empty** when its capacity is greater than its contents and **Full** when its contents exceed its capacity. (These conditions can easily be formalised by giving invariants on the subtypes. The preservation of the invariant by each local action then becomes a useful validation proof for the specification.)

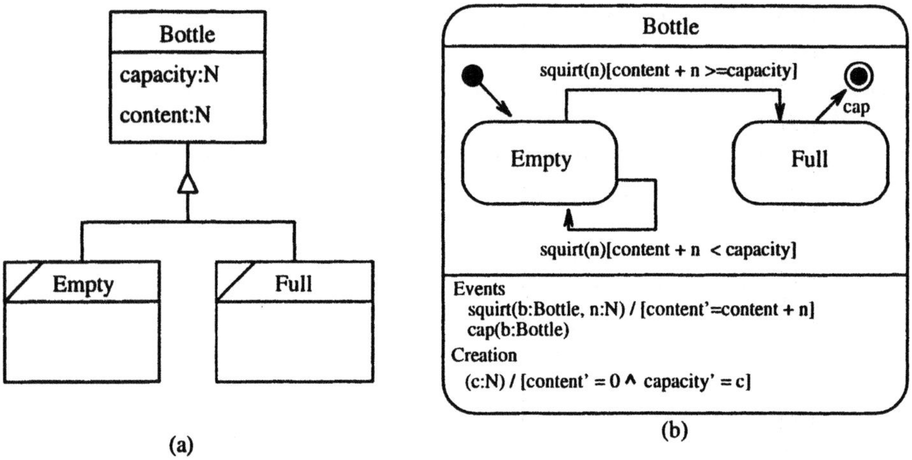

Figure 9 State types and statechart for Bottle example.

The type view diagram is interpreted via three instance theories, one for the **Bottle** class and one each for the subtypes **Empty** and **Full**, although in this case the instance theories for the subtypes are trivial. A class manager theory is defined for each of these classes and a theory for each of the two subtyping associations. These are brought together via the constructions described in Sections 2 and 3. Details can be found in the appendix.

Actions are defined in the instance theory for bottles for each transition in the statechart. Events are interpreted in the theory of the system and synchronised with the instance actions. For example, **squirt** is interpreted as two actions $\mathbf{squirt_1(n)}$ and $\mathbf{squirt_2(n)}$ in the instance theory of bottle and an event $\mathbf{Squirt(b, n)}$ in the theory for the entire bottle subsystem.

We obtain the following axioms in the Bottle Instance theory, **BI**

$$\mathbf{squirt_1(n) \Rightarrow cont + n \geq capy}$$
$$\mathbf{squirt_2(n) \Rightarrow cont + n < capy}$$
$$\mathbf{squirt_1(n) \Rightarrow \bigcirc cont = cont + n}$$
$$\mathbf{squirt_2(n) \Rightarrow \bigcirc cont = cont + n}$$

In the theory of the Bottle-Empty subsystem we obtain

$$\mathbf{b.squirt_1(n) \Rightarrow b \in \overline{Empty}}$$
$$\mathbf{b.squirt_1(n) \Rightarrow b \notin \bigcirc\overline{Empty}}$$
$$\mathbf{b.squirt_2(n) \Rightarrow b \in \overline{Empty}}$$
$$\mathbf{b.squirt_2(n) \Rightarrow b \in \bigcirc\overline{Empty}}$$

and in the theory of the Bottle-Full subsystem we obtain, for example,

$$\mathbf{b.squirt_1(n) \Rightarrow b \in \bigcirc\overline{Full}}$$

The action for the system event **Squirt(b, n)** is defined in the theory of the whole Bottle subsystem and synchronised with the instance actions via

$$\mathbf{Squirt(b,n)} \Rightarrow \mathbf{b.squirt_1(n)} \vee \mathbf{b.squirt_2(n)}$$

Note that the preconditions for the squirt transitions ensure that exactly one of these occurs.

One can now derive properties involving other system actions, for example, it is straightforward to prove that

$$\mathbf{Squirt(b,n)} \wedge \mathbf{b.cont} + \mathbf{n} \geq \mathbf{b.capy} \Rightarrow \mathbf{kill_{Empty}(b)} \wedge \mathbf{create_{Full}(b)}$$

5.1 Orthogonal Statecharts

The Bottling Plant statechart is now extended by an orthogonal component which describes the motion of the bottles (Figure 10.)

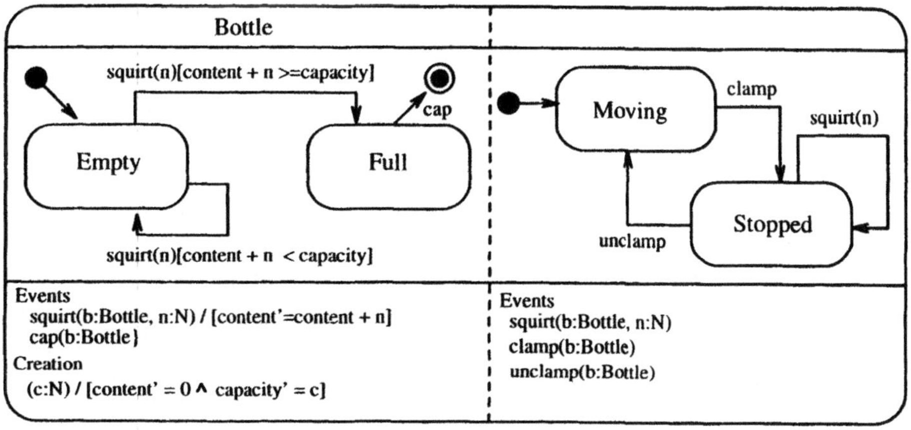

Figure 10 Orthogonal concurrency in bottling plant example.

The new events represent the motion of the bottles. Bottles are either moving or stopped and clamping and unclamping actions mark the change between these states. A bottle can only be filled (via squirt events) when it is stopped.

The synchronisation between the two halves of the statechart is through the squirt operation. The appearance of squirt on the right hand side of the statechart is interpreted as a third transition, $\mathbf{squirt_3}$, in the instance theory, and signifies that squirt can only occur when the bottle is stopped. (The fact that cap does not appear on the right hand side means that, rather unrealistically, a bottle can be capped whether moving or stopped.)

The concurrent composition of statecharts is modelled by the disjoint sum of theories. The default treatment of filters, where a single parameter of class Bottle is presented in the textual part and indicates the instance to which the event is directed, ensures the correct synchronisation. **Squirt(b, n)** can only occur if precondition for one of $\mathbf{squirt_1}$ or $\mathbf{squirt_2}$ and the precondition of

$\mathbf{squirt_3}$ hold. When more complex filters are used the axiomatisation is less straightforward and has to be undertaken in the class theory.

6 CONCLUSIONS AND FURTHER WORK

We have formalised some aspects of class diagrams and statecharts as used in the "Syntropy" method of Object Oriented Analysis and Design. We have shown that a formal and modular semantics can be given to Syntropy essential models and developed an orthogonal interpretation of various types of association. We found that subtyping reduces to a particular combination of cardinality and lifetime constraints.

We explored the relationship between the presentation of theories of objects using temporal conditions on actions and their presentation using constraints on states and state transitions. In particular, the availability of temporal operators yields a choice between axioms that define the required traces of actions and axioms that define the relationship between actions and attributes. The style adopted here has been to define axioms describing the preconditions and postconditions of actions in terms of the attributes. This gives a style of specification very similar to that of model-oriented formalisms such as VDM and Z.

In interpreting Statecharts, we distinguished between local actions for instance state transitions and system actions for events. We adopted a style of axiomatisation where the local effect of actions is interpreted directly in terms of the local attributes and synchronisation between actions in different theories is given implicitly by trans-theory constraints on attributes. Were theories to be executable, these implicit constraints would require implementation to ensure the synchronisations between actions of different classes.

There remain many constructs in Syntropy that have not been addressed. Significantly, we have only interpreted essential models, some aspects of specification and implementation models are similar, others would require further work. Within essential models, we have not attempted to formalise nested statecharts nor associations with attributes. Demonstrating the correctness of refinements between levels of model is not even addressed informally in Syntropy.

On the whole, the syntax for "navigation expressions" used in Syntropy Statecharts corresponds to the expression language available as the theories are built up. However, Syntropy allows expressions in the diagrammatic part of statecharts which mention associations and hence could not be interpreted in the instance theory of the object class. Such expressions make the specification non compositional and would therefore have to be interpreted at the level of the appropriate subsystem.

There are also some examples which cannot be systematically interpreted using the combination of instance and system theories described above. In particular, we have only treated the case where the events in the textual part of the statechart take precisely one more parameter than the corresponding transitions in the diagrammatic part. The Syntropy source material also gives examples where this is not the case. For example, the events "TransferContents" (p. 114), which switches the contents of two bottles, and "RadioButton" (p. 117), which switches off all other buttons when one is pressed, cannot be modelled in this way.

In several examples, filters are used which depend on associated objects (rather than the class in question) and so would have to be interpreted at the system level. The usefulness of such "clever tricks" which make specifications concise but opaque is debatable. Such specifications would require a complex synchronisation of actions from the instance, class and association theories. It is hard to imagine how they could be interpreted systematically.

The above two examples of the non-standard use of filters are both difficult to understand informally and hard to formalise. the present authors suggest that they are best avoided.

The use of **new** in postconditions also requires special treatment as it introduces side-effects into the expression language. It is well known that such features complicate semantics considerably.

The treatment of unborn and dead instances requires infinite colimit diagrams. It is believed that these infinite colimits are well behaved because the morphisms are almost everywhere trivial, however, the underlying mathematics for this does need to be rehearsed.

The formalisation of diagrammatic notations as presented here is of benefit both as a means of making precise the meaning to the constructs involved and also to enable reasoning about specifications constructed. In practice, not only may one wish to give justifications of design decisions in terms of particular validation and verification criteria but also there may be some general purpose healthiness conditions which can be checked for any specification. A number of "rules" about correct specifications are given informally for Syntropy, it would be interesting to formalise these and to consider which can be checked automatically and which should be considered to be "proof obligations" requiring more sophisticated reasoning to discharge them.

APPENDIX: THEORIES FOR THE BOTTLING PLANT EXAMPLE

Theory	*BI (BottleInstance)*
Extends	ϕ with
Sig	
Atts	$\mathbf{capy} : \mathbb{N}$
	$\mathbf{cont} : \mathbb{N}$
Acts	$\mathbf{create} : \mathbb{N}$
	$\mathbf{squirt_1} : \mathbb{N}$
	$\mathbf{squirt_2} : \mathbb{N}$
	$\mathbf{cap}$
Axs	$\mathbf{create(n)} \Rightarrow \bigcirc\mathbf{cont} = 0 \wedge \bigcirc\mathbf{capy} = \mathbf{n}$
	$\mathbf{squirt_1(n)} \Rightarrow \mathbf{cont} + \mathbf{n} \geq \mathbf{capy}$
	$\mathbf{squirt_2(n)} \Rightarrow \mathbf{cont} + \mathbf{n} < \mathbf{capy}$
	$\mathbf{squirt_1(n)} \Rightarrow \bigcirc\mathbf{cont} = \mathbf{cont} + \mathbf{n} \wedge \bigcirc\mathbf{capy} = \mathbf{capy}$
	$\mathbf{squirt_2(n)} \Rightarrow \bigcirc\mathbf{cont} = \mathbf{cont} + \mathbf{n} \wedge \bigcirc\mathbf{capy} = \mathbf{capy}$

The theories *FullInstance* and *EmptyInstance* are empty.

Theory	*(BM) BottleManager*
Extends	ϕ with
Sig	$\mathbf{@B} : \mathbb{F}\mathbf{@B}$
Atts	$\overline{\mathbf{B}}$
Acts	$\mathbf{create} : \mathbf{@B}$
	$\mathbf{kill} : \mathbf{@B}$
Axs	$\mathbf{create(b)} \Leftrightarrow \mathbf{b} \notin \overline{\mathbf{B}} \wedge \mathbf{b} \in \bigcirc\overline{\mathbf{B}}$
	$\mathbf{kill(b)} \Leftrightarrow \mathbf{b} \in \overline{\mathbf{B}} \wedge \mathbf{b} \notin \bigcirc\overline{\mathbf{B}}$

We have chosen not to require no-rebirth. **EmptyManager** and **FullManager** are similar.

Theory	*(BC) Bottle Class*
Extends	**BI**, **BM** with
Sig Atts Acts	 $\mathbf{new} : \mathbf{@B}, \mathbb{N}$
Axs	$\mathbf{b.new(n)} \Leftrightarrow \mathbf{create_{BM}(b)} \wedge \mathbf{b.create_{B}(n)}$ $\mathbf{kill(b)} \Leftrightarrow \mathbf{b.cap}$

Theory	*BE (Bottle-Empty Association)*
Extends	**BM**, **EM** with
Sig Atts Acts 	$\mathbf{@B}, \mathbf{@E}$ $\mathbf{be} : \mathbb{F}(\mathbf{@B}, \mathbf{@E})$ $\mathbf{link} : \mathbf{@B}, \mathbf{@E}$ $\mathbf{unlink} : \mathbf{@B}, \mathbf{@E}$
Axs	$\mathbf{link(b,e)} \Leftrightarrow \mathbf{(b,e)} \notin \mathbf{be} \wedge \mathbf{(b,e)} \in \bigcirc\mathbf{be}$ $\mathbf{unlink(b,e)} \Leftrightarrow \mathbf{(b,e)} \in \mathbf{be} \wedge \mathbf{(b,e)} \notin \bigcirc\mathbf{be}$ $\mathbf{link(b,e)} \Rightarrow \mathbf{b} \notin \mathrm{dom}\,\mathbf{be}$ $\mathbf{link(b,e)} \wedge \mathbf{link(b,e')} \Rightarrow \mathbf{e} \neq \mathbf{e'}$ $\mathbf{link_C(b,e)} \Rightarrow \mathbf{e} \notin \mathrm{ran}\,\mathbf{be}$ $\mathbf{link(b,e)} \wedge \mathbf{link(b',e)} \Rightarrow \mathbf{b} \neq \mathbf{b'}$

Theory	*BES (Bottle-Empty System)*
Extends	**BC**, **EC**, **BE** with
Sig Atts Acts	
Axs	$\mathbf{link(b,e)} \Rightarrow \mathbf{b} \in \bigcirc\overline{\mathbf{B}} \wedge \mathbf{e} \in \bigcirc\overline{\mathbf{E}}$ $\mathbf{e.create_{EM}} \Leftrightarrow \mathbf{e} \notin \mathrm{ran}\,\mathbf{be} \wedge \mathbf{e} \in \mathrm{ran}\bigcirc\mathbf{be}$ $\mathbf{e.kill_{EM}} \Leftrightarrow \mathbf{e} \in \mathrm{ran}\,\mathbf{be} \wedge \mathbf{e} \notin \mathrm{ran}\bigcirc\mathbf{be}$ $\mathbf{link(b,e)} \Rightarrow \mathbf{e} \notin \overline{\mathbf{E}} \wedge \mathbf{e} \in \bigcirc\overline{\mathbf{E}}$ $\mathbf{unlink(b,e)} \Rightarrow \mathbf{e} \in \overline{\mathbf{E}} \wedge \mathbf{e} \notin \bigcirc\overline{\mathbf{E}}$ $\mathbf{link(b,e)} \Leftrightarrow \mathbf{b} = \mathbf{e} \wedge \mathbf{e} \notin \overline{\mathbf{E}} \wedge \mathbf{e} \in \bigcirc\overline{\mathbf{E}}$ $\mathbf{unlink(b,e)} \Leftrightarrow \mathbf{b} = \mathbf{e} \wedge \mathbf{e} \in \overline{\mathbf{E}} \wedge \mathbf{e} \notin \bigcirc\overline{\mathbf{E}}$ $\mathbf{b.squirt_1(n)} \Rightarrow \mathbf{b} \in \overline{\mathbf{Empty}}$ $\mathbf{b.squirt_2(n)} \Rightarrow \mathbf{b} \in \overline{\mathbf{Empty}}$ $\mathbf{b.squirt_2(n)} \Rightarrow \mathbf{b} \in \bigcirc\overline{\mathbf{Empty}}$ $\mathbf{b.squirt_1(n)} \Rightarrow \mathbf{b} \notin \bigcirc\overline{\mathbf{Empty}}$

Similar theories are defined for Bottle-Full Association (BF) and Bottle-Full System (BFS). The Bottle-Empty System and Bottle-Full System are brought together into Bottle-Empty-Full System (BEFS)

Theory	*(BEFS) Bottle-Empty-Full System*
Extends	**BES**, **BFS** with
Sig Atts Acts	
Axs	$\overline{\mathbf{B}} = \overline{\mathbf{E}} \cup \overline{\mathbf{F}}$ $\overline{\mathbf{E}} \cap \overline{\mathbf{F}} = \phi$ $\mathbf{Squirt(b, n)} \Rightarrow \mathbf{b.squirt_1(n)} \vee \mathbf{b.squirt_2(n)}$

The composition of the whole system is depicted in Figure 11.
Notes:

- The base theory ϕ is assumed to define the primitive sorts and constants of the specification language such as $\mathbb{N}$ and $\mathbb{B}$.
- The **extends** component names any theory which embeds into this and gives any renamings (not shown) established by the morphism
- When a symbol is embedded into a theory by more than one route with different renamings a separate copy is required for each embedding. (If the renamings are equal then only one copy is produced.)

REFERENCES

Cook, S. and Daniels, J. (1994) *Designing Object Systems with Syntropy*. Prentice Hall.

Fiadeiro, J. and Maibaum, T. (1992) Temporal Theories and Modularisation Units for Concurrent System Specification. *Formal Aspects of Computing*, Vol.4, No. 3, pp. 239-272. Springer Verlag.

Fiadeiro, J. and Maibaum, T. (1991) Describing, Structuring and Implementing Objects, in de Bakker *et al.*, *Foundations of Object Oriented languages*, LNCS 489, Springer-Verlag, 1991.

Goguen, J. and Burstall, R. (1984) Introducing Institutions, In Clarke and Kozen, eds. *Logics of Programs*, pp. 221-256, Springer-Verlag.

Harel, D. (1987) Statecharts: A Visual Formalism for Complex Systems, *Sci. Comput. Prog.* **8** pp. 231-274 .

Lamport, L. (1991) *The Temporal Logic of Actions*, Digital Technical Report 79, Systems Research Center, 130 Lytton Avenue, Palo Alto, Califiornia 94301. December 25th.

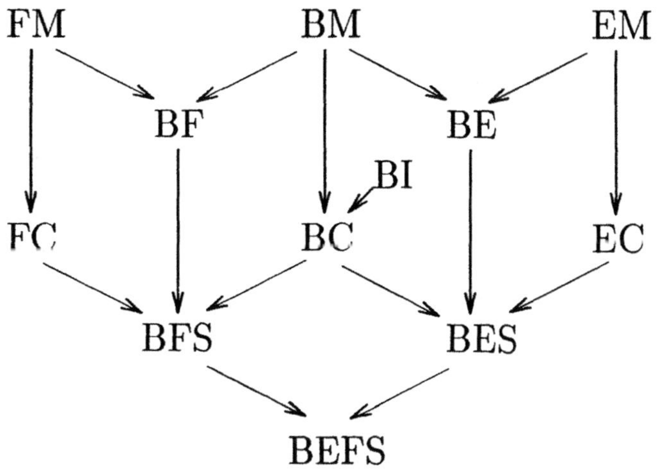

Figure 11 Colimit Diagram for Bottle System.

Rumbaugh, J. *et al* (1991) *Object-Oriented Modelling and Design*, Prentice-Hall, Englewoods Cliffs, New Jersey.

Spivey, M.(1989) *The Z Notation: a Reference Manual*, Prentice-Hall.

7 BIOGRAPHY

Juan Bicarregui is a Research Fellow in the Department of Computing, Imperial College of Science, Technology and Medicine, London. He has a BSc and MSc in Mathematics a PhD in Computer Science. His research interests lie in the development and application of Formal Methods.

He is currently investigating the formal underpinnings of Object Oriented methods. Previous research has included the provision of support for the formal development through the Mural proof assistant; case studies and comparisons in the use VDM, Z and B; and development of a proof theory for VDM.

He is currently on secondment from the Rutherford Appleton Laboratory.

His web pages can be found at: http://theory.doc.ic.ac.uk/ jcb1 and http://www.cis.rl.ac.uk/people/jcb/contact.html.

Defining and Detecting Feature Interactions

Marc Frappier
Université de Sherbrooke
Département de mathématiques et d'informatique, Sherbrooke, Québec, Canada, J1K 2R1, Marc.Frappier@dmi.usherb.ca

Ali Mili
University of Ottawa
Department of Computer Science, Ottawa, Ontario, Canada, K1N 6N5, amili@csi.uottawa.ca

Jules Desharnais
Université Laval
Département d'informatique, Ste-Foy, Québec, Canada, G1K 7P4, Jules.Desharnais@ift.ulaval.ca

Abstract

We describe a relational method for specifying features and detecting feature interactions. The method allows for an independent specification of system features, and for a detection of interaction between features. The method is based on the lattice of relational specifications: the system specification is given as the conjunction (lattice operator meet) of the features; a feature interaction is detected when the meet of the features does not exist. Examples of detection are given using logic programming.*

Keywords

Feature interactions, relational specifications, logic programming

1 INTRODUCTION

Over the past years, the problem of feature interaction has drawn considerable interest in the research community (Bowen *et al.* 1989, Bouma *et al.* 1994, Cheng *et al.* 1995). A feature is a collection of functionalities that are added incrementally in a software system. A feature interaction occurs whenever their specifications contradict each other by producing conditions that no behavior can satisfy.

---

*This research is supported by the Natural Sciences and Engineering Research Council of Canada.

This problem is especially acute in telecommunication systems (Bowen *et al.* 1989), where the number of features is impressive: some systems offer up to 800 features, both for technical reasons (e.g., heterogeneity of the telephone network) and for providing users with complex services (e.g., features like call waiting, credit-card calling, voice mail, etc.). Other domains like banking, medical and management information systems are also subject to this problem. It is an important issue in software engineering, because it occurs at various phases of the software life cycle. In this paper, we focus on the specification phase. More specifically, we will discuss the specification generation step and the specification validation step of this phase.

To deal with feature interactions at the specification phase, a method must allow for the independent definition of features. At the validation step, a method must allow for the detection of interactions between features. To tackle these two aspects, we base our approach on the refinement lattice of specifications (Boudriga *et al.* 1992). In this framework, the specification of a feature is given by a relation between the inputs and the outputs of the system. The combination of the features is given by taking the greatest lower bound of all features. This framework allows us to propose a formal definition of a feature interaction: we say that two (or more) features interact if they do not have a greatest lower bound in the refinement lattice. Finally, detecting an interaction consists in proving that the greatest lower bound does not exist.

We write inductive definitions of relations using axioms in the predicate calculus. For the sake of readability, we favor the use of a tabular format for writing specifications. We have identified three general classes of tabular specifications which are pervasive in inductive specifications: base cases, reduction and swapping (equivalence classes). We detect interactions mainly using resolution as a rule of inference.

We illustrate our approach with a simple telephone system, the plain old telephone system (POTS), to which we add features like call waiting (CW) and three-way calling (TWC). We construct a relational specification for each object (POTS, CW and TWC) in a stepwise manner, and then we discuss the detection of interactions.

This paper is structured as follows. In Sect. 2, we describe our approach to writing inductive relational specifications. In Sect. 3, we provide the specifications of the POTS and of features TWC and CW. We introduce our formal definition of feature interaction in Sect. 4. We discuss its generality in light of some classifications proposed in the literature. We also illustrate how interactions can be proved. Finally, we conclude with some remarks in Sect. 5.

2 INDUCTIVE RELATIONAL SPECIFICATIONS

In this section, we describe our method for constructing relational specifications, and we provide a formal semantics for the specification language.

2.1 Relational Specifications

One may describe the input-output behavior of a system using a heterogeneous binary relation between the history of inputs and the outputs. Formally, let I be the set of possible system inputs, let I^+ be the set of all possible non empty finite sequences of elements of I, and let O be the set of possible system outputs; a specification (binary relation) R is a subset of $I^+ \times O$.

As a simple example of a relational specification, we may consider a counter object. The initial value of the counter is zero; it is incremented by 1 after submitting input inc; it is decremented by 1 after submitting input dec; the value of the counter is displayed by submitting input val. The input set of the counter object is given by:

$$I \triangleq \{\mathsf{inc}, \mathsf{dec}, \mathsf{val}\} \ .$$

The output set of the counter object is given by:

$$O \triangleq \mathbf{Integer} \cup \{\tau\} \ .$$

The symbol τ denotes the case where the counter produces no visible output for a given sequence of inputs. We now provide some examples of elements (pairs) of a relation R specifying the counter object. We use a dot (".") for the concatenation of input sequences; we use $s \lhd R \rhd s'$ to denote that the pair (s, s') is an element of relation R.

$\mathsf{val} \lhd R \rhd 0$
$\mathsf{inc} \lhd R \rhd \tau$
$\mathsf{inc.val} \lhd R \rhd 1$
$\mathsf{val.inc.dec} \lhd R \rhd \tau$
$\mathsf{val.inc.dec.val} \lhd R \rhd 0$
$\mathsf{val.inc.dec.inc.val} \lhd R \rhd 1$

The first pair indicates that the counter produces an output value of zero after receiving input element val; it satisfies the requirement that the initial value of the counter is zero. The second pair indicates that the counter produces no output after receiving input element inc. The third pair illustrates why we need a relation on input sequences, instead of just considering input elements, to specify the behavior of the counter. For input val, the output of the counter depends on the number of dec and inc that were previously submitted to the counter. For instance, after starting the system, if the user submits input inc, and then submits input val, the output of the counter is 1, according to the third pair. Hence, in an input sequence $s_1. \ldots .s_n$, we interpret s_1 as the first input submitted since the start of the system, s_2 as the second, and s_n as the last input submitted.

When the image set of an input sequence is not a singleton, we say that the specification is nondeterministic. When implementing a nondeterministic specification, the designer may choose any output from the image set. There are other forms of relational specifications which are slightly more powerful for expressing nondeterminacy. For instance, some authors (e.g., (Broy 1995, Deck *et al.* 1992, Wang *et al.* 1994)) use relations on the history of inputs and the history of outputs (i.e., $I^+ \times O^+$), usually including timing requirements. We have chosen to restrict to a less expressive class of specifications (i.e., relations on $I^+ \times O$), since it is sufficiently general to cover a large class of applications, and its specifications are easier to read and write.

2.2 Inductive Relational Definitions

The complete specification of the counter cannot be given by simply enumerating its input-output pairs; it is impractical, and unfeasible since there is an infinite number of pairs. One could construct a specification using the set builder notation $\{(s, s') \in I^+ \times O | p(s, s')\}$, but it is not always easy. Instead, we propose to define our relations inductively.

We consider the language of first order logic with the usual connectives in the following binding order from highest to lowest: $\neg$, $\wedge$, $\vee$, $\{\Leftarrow, \Rightarrow\}$, $\Leftrightarrow$, $\{\forall, \exists, \bigwedge_j, \bigvee_j\}$. Binding order is modified by means of parentheses. We also use $(, \ldots ,)$ to denote a tuple, and $\{ , \ldots , \}$ to denote a set. Other function symbols and relation symbols may be used in the context of a particular specification. We use x, y, z, possibly subscripted, for individual variables and a, b, c for constants. Relational constants (i.e., constant symbols whose denotations are binary relations) are written using capital letters (usually R, or a meaningful name like $POTS$).

Using this language, an inductive definition of a relation is given by a set of axioms of the form $(\bigwedge_{i=1}^{n} A_i) \Rightarrow B$, where n is a natural number (possibly equal to 0), and A_i and B are metavariables for predicates. However, for readability, we usually write our axioms in the form:

$$\frac{A_1 \wedge \ldots \wedge A_n}{B} \quad ,$$

in order to clearly delineate the boundary between premises and the conclusion of $\Rightarrow$. This notation is particularly handy for complex axioms. There is no risk of confusing axioms with inference rules: we do not introduce any new inference rule in this paper; the only inference rule we use is resolution in Sect. 4.

To give the reader a quick understanding of how we write inductive definitions of relations, we will use the factorial function as an example. The reader is certainly familiar with the inductive (or recursive) definition of the factorial function. Let f denote the factorial function.

$$f(0) = 1 \ , \quad f(n) = n * f(n-1) \text{ if } n > 0$$

The inductive definition of a relational constant R corresponding to the factorial function, i.e., the relation $\{(s, s') | s' = f(s)\}$, may be defined as follows.

$$\text{(fact-1): } \frac{}{0 \triangleleft R \triangleright 1} \qquad \text{(fact-2): } \frac{x \triangleleft R \triangleright y}{x+1 \triangleleft R \triangleright (x+1) * y}$$

To further illustrate the concept, we now provide a specification for the counter object, which we denote again by relational constant R. The following is its first axiom.

$$\text{(cnt-1): } \frac{}{\{(\mathsf{val}, 0), (x.\mathsf{inc}, \tau), (x.\mathsf{dec}, \tau)\} \subseteq R}$$

Symbol x in axiom cnt-1 is a variable ranging over I^*. This axiom provides that the initial value of the counter object is zero, and that there is no output for input sequences ending with inc and dec. We now provide axioms defining the output of the system for input sequences ending with val.

$$\text{(cnt-2): } \frac{x.\mathsf{val} \triangleleft R \triangleright y}{x.\mathsf{inc}.\mathsf{val} \triangleleft R \triangleright y + 1}$$

$$\text{(cnt-3): } \frac{x.\mathsf{val} \triangleleft R \triangleright y}{x.\mathsf{dec}.\mathsf{val} \triangleleft R \triangleright y - 1}$$

$$\text{(cnt-4): } \frac{x.x' \triangleleft R \triangleright y \wedge x' \neq \varepsilon}{x.\mathsf{val}.x' \triangleleft R \triangleright y}$$

Axiom cnt-2 provides that an input symbol inc increments the value of the counter by one. Similarly, axiom cnt-3 provides that an input symbol dec decrements the value of the counter by one. Axiom cnt-4 indicates that symbol val does not modify the value of the counter. We may use these axioms to prove that a pair (s, s') is in relation R. For instance, we give a proof of the following statement:

$\mathsf{inc}.\mathsf{val}.\mathsf{dec}.\mathsf{val} \triangleleft R \triangleright 0$

Proof.

$\mathsf{inc}.\mathsf{val}.\mathsf{dec}.\mathsf{val} \triangleleft R \triangleright 0$

$\Leftarrow \quad \langle$ cnt-3 $\rangle$
$\mathsf{inc.val.val} \triangleleft R \triangleright 1$
$\Leftarrow \quad \langle$ cnt-4 $\rangle$
$\mathsf{inc.val} \triangleleft R \triangleright 1$
$\Leftarrow \quad \langle$ cnt-2 $\rangle$
$\mathsf{val} \triangleleft R \triangleright 0$
$\Leftarrow \quad \langle$ axiom cnt-1 $\rangle$
true □

2.3 A Least Fixpoint Semantics

In this section, we provide a semantics for our inductive definitions. We focus on the interpretation of the relational constants used in a set of axioms, and we assume the usual interpretations for other symbols like pairing, concatenation, equality and set extension. So far, our examples used only one relational constant, but several relational constants (e.g., POTS, TWC and CW in Sect. 2) may be defined in a specification, for modularity and readability reasons.

Traditionally, the semantics of an inductive definition is given as the least fixpoint of a function extracted from the set of axioms (Apt 1990, Gunter *et al.* 1990, Mosses 1990). We will proceed in a similar fashion to provide a semantics of an inductive definition of relations. In the following prototypical example of an axiom,

$$\frac{p \wedge \bigwedge_{j=1}^{n} e_j \triangleleft R_j \triangleright f_j}{g \triangleleft R \triangleright h} \; ,$$

e_j, f_j, g and h are terms, R_j and R are relational constants, and p is a formula in which R and R_j do not occur. The free variables of an axiom are implicitly universally quantified. Let $\vec{x}$ be the free variables. We associate with such an axiom a function on the space $\mathbb{P}(\{R_1, \ldots, R_n, R\} \times I^+ \times O)$ given by:

$$\mathcal{F}(X) \triangleq \{(R, t, t') | \exists \vec{x} : p \wedge (\bigwedge_j (R_j, e_j, f_j) \in X) \wedge (t, t') = (g, h)\} \; .$$

Hence, function $\mathcal{F}$ takes as input a set of triples and returns a set of triples. Informally, a triple (R, s, s') means that the pair (s, s') is in relation R. To illustrate how functions are associated with axioms, consider axiom cnt-1. For the sake of brevity, its conclusion is expressed using $\subseteq$ instead of $\_\triangleleft\_\triangleright\_$. We may replace this axiom by the following three axioms.

(cnt-5): $\dfrac{}{\mathsf{val} \triangleleft R \triangleright 0}$

(cnt-6): $\dfrac{}{x.\mathsf{inc} \triangleleft R \triangleright \tau}$

(cnt-7): $\overline{x.\mathsf{dec} \lhd R \rhd \tau}$

The corresponding functions are:

$$\mathcal{F}_{\text{cnt-5}}(X) \triangleq \{(R,t,t')|(t,t') = (\mathsf{val},0)\}$$

$$\mathcal{F}_{\text{cnt-6}}(X) \triangleq \{(R,t,t')|\exists x : (t,t') = (x.\mathsf{inc},\tau)\}$$

$$\mathcal{F}_{\text{cnt-7}}(X) \triangleq \{(R,t,t')|\exists x : (t,t') = (x.\mathsf{dec},\tau)\} \ .$$

The function corresponding to axiom cnt-2 is:

$$\mathcal{F}_{\text{cnt-2}}(X) \triangleq \{(R,t,t')|\exists x,y : (R,x.\mathsf{val},y) \in X \wedge (t,t') = (x.\mathsf{inc.val},y+1)\}$$

The function associated with a set of axioms is simply given by the pointwise union of the functions associated with the axioms. Let $\mathcal{R}_1,...,\mathcal{R}_n$ be the axioms of an inductive definition of relations, and let $\mathcal{F}_1,...,\mathcal{F}_n$ be the functions associated with these axioms. Then the function corresponding to the set of axioms is given by:

$$\mathcal{F}(X) \triangleq \bigcup_{i=1}^{n} \mathcal{F}_i(X) \ .$$

Each $\mathcal{F}_i$ is continuous wrt to $\subseteq$ (see proof in appendix A). Hence, function $\mathcal{F}$ is continuous wrt $\subseteq$. Theorem 4.5 in (Davey *et al.* 1990) provides that a continuous function over a CPO has a least fixpoint, which we denote by $\mu\mathcal{F}$. Since sets form a CPO under $\subseteq$, it follows that function $\mathcal{F}$ has a least fixpoint wrt $\subseteq$.

We define the interpretation of a relational constant R using the least fixpoint of function $\mathcal{F}$. This least fixpoint is given by $\bigcup_{n\geq 0} \mathcal{F}^n(\emptyset)$ (see theorem 4.5 in (Davey *et al.* 1990)), where $\mathcal{F}^0$ is the identity function and $\mathcal{F}^n(X) = \mathcal{F}(\mathcal{F}^{n-1}(X))$. The interpretation of a relational constant R is given by $\{(s,s')|(R,s,s') \in \mu\mathcal{F}\}$. It follows easily from the definition of $\mathcal{F}$ that this interpretation of the relational constants is a model for the set of axioms considered.

3 SPECIFICATION OF A TELEPHONE SYSTEM

The traditional case study for feature interaction detection is a telephone system augmented with a certain number of features. In this section, we provide a relational specification of the basic services offered by a telephone system. Our objective here is more to provide a basis for illustrating the detection of feature interactions than to provide a complete specification or to check its consistency.

The system boundary comprises the communication switches and the communication network. The inputs to the system are sent by telephone units, and the outputs are received by telephone units. We impose no limit on the number of users and the number of connections. We assume that the system produces an output immediately after receiving an input, and before receiving the next input.

3.1 The Space of the Specification

We consider the following input space for our telephone specification.

$$\begin{aligned} I \triangleq\ & \{\mathsf{PkUp}\} \times \mathbf{PhoneId} \cup \\ & \{\mathsf{HgUp}\} \times \mathbf{PhoneId} \cup \\ & \{\mathsf{Dial}\} \times \mathbf{PhoneId} \times \mathbf{PhoneId} \end{aligned}$$

An input (PkUp, n), where n represents the identification number of the calling party's phone, is sent to the telephone system when a user picks up the handset. For simplicity, we will assume that the identification number, which uniquely identifies a telephone, is the same as the telephone number. Input (HgUp, n) is sent when user n hangs up the telephone, typically to terminate a call. Input $(\mathsf{Dial}, n_1, n_2)$ is sent when user n_1 dials the phone number of user n_2.

The output space of the telephone system is defined as follows.

$$\begin{aligned} O \triangleq\ & \mathbb{P}(\{\mathsf{DiTo}\} \times \mathbf{PhoneId} \cup \\ & \{\mathsf{Ring}\} \times \mathbf{PhoneId} \times \mathbf{PhoneId} \cup \\ & \{\mathsf{BuTo}\} \times \mathbf{PhoneId} \cup \\ & \{\mathsf{Conn}\} \times \mathbf{PhoneId} \times \mathbf{PhoneId} \cup \\ & \{\mathsf{Disc}\} \times \mathbf{PhoneId} \times \mathbf{PhoneId}) \end{aligned}$$

Hence, an output is a set of commands. For the POTS, visible outputs are singletons, but for TWC and CW, outputs may be sets of several elements. The empty set $(\emptyset)$ indicates that the system produces no visible output. Output element (DiTo, n) corresponds to the dial tone that user n hears after picking up the handset to place a call. Output $(\mathsf{Ring}, n_1, n_2)$ causes the telephone of user n_2 to produce an audible ring, typically indicating that there is an incoming call while the telephone of user n_1 receives a ring tone. Dually, output (BuTo, n) indicates to caller n that the dialed unit is busy.

Output $(\mathsf{Conn}, n_1, n_2)$ corresponds to the establishment of a connection between users n_1 and n_2, after which these two users can start a conversation. Output $(\mathsf{Disc}, n_1, n_2)$ terminates a connection between n_1 and n_2, typically after an input (HgUp, n_i) has been sent by one of the parties.

3.2 POTS Specification

In writing the specification of the POTS, we have found that axioms could be divided in three classes: base case axioms, reduction axioms and swap axioms. Moreover, each class can be written using a tabular format which is a lot more readable than the usual plain mathematical notation of premises over conclusion. Hence, in the next sections, we provide our POTS specification under a tabular format whose meaning shall be made precise.

(a) Base Case Axioms

We provide two tables for the base cases. Table 1 provides the axioms when a successful connection is established between two users. Table 2 describes the cases where no connection is made.

Table 1 Cumulative Table for a Successful Connection

No	Premise	Input	Output
B-1		(PkUp, n_1)	$\{(\mathsf{DiTo}, n_1)\}$
B-2	$n_1 \neq n_2$	$(\mathsf{Dial}, n_1, n_2)$	$\{(\mathsf{Ring}, n_1, n_2)\}$
B-3		(PkUp, n_2)	$\{(\mathsf{Conn}, n_1, n_2)\}$
B-4	$n \in \{n_1, n_2\}$	(HgUp, n)	$\{(\mathsf{Disc}, n_1, n_2)\}$
B-5	$n' \in \{n_1, n_2\} \setminus \{n\}$	(HgUp, n')	$\emptyset$

Each table has a different interpretation in terms of axioms. We say that Table 1 is cumulative. Each line in the table represents one axiom. Let p_n, s_n and s'_n be respectively the premise, the input and the output of line n. Then the axiom associated with line n is:

$$\frac{p_1 \wedge \ldots \wedge p_n}{s_1 . \ldots . s_n \triangleleft POTS \triangleright s'_n} \, .$$

For instance, the axioms associated with lines B-2 and B-4 are, respectively:

$$\text{(B-2):}\ \frac{n_1 \neq n_2}{(\mathsf{PkUp}, n_1).(\mathsf{Dial}, n_1, n_2) \triangleleft POTS \triangleright \{(\mathsf{Ring}, n_1, n_2)\}} ,$$

$$\text{(B-4):}\ \frac{n_1 \neq n_2 \ \wedge\ n \in \{n_1, n_2\}}{\begin{array}{c}(\mathsf{PkUp}, n_1).(\mathsf{Dial}, n_1, n_2).(\mathsf{PkUp}, n_2).(\mathsf{HgUp}, n) \\ \triangleleft POTS \triangleright \\ \{(\mathsf{Disc}, n_1, n_2)\}\end{array}} .$$

Our tabular format avoids the unnecessary repetition of premises and input sequences from one axiom to another. Also, it provides a quick and clear visualization of the behavior for prototypical input sequences, e.g., the establishment of a successful connection.

To illustrate the meaning of axioms in Table 1, let us consider the following scenario. The telephone system is just started. The first input it receives is a PkUp from user a_1. Axiom B-1 states that the telephone system must produce output $\{(\mathsf{DiTo}, a_1)\}$. After receiving this dial tone, user a_1 dials user a_2. User a_2 cannot be busy, since the telephone system has just been started, and the only preceding input is (PkUp, a_1). The telephone system produces a ring tone to user a_1 and rings the phone of user a_2 (axiom B-2). User a_2 picks up his phone, and the system establishes a connection between a_1 and a_2 (axiom B-3). To end the conversation, either of the two users may hang up its phone, and the telephone system disconnects the two users (axiom B-4). When the other user hangs up, the system produces no visible output (axiom B-5).

Table 2 is not cumulative. The axiom associated with line n is simply given by:

$$\frac{p_n}{s_n \triangleleft POTS \triangleright s'_n} .$$

For instance, the axiom associated with line B-6 is:

$$\text{(B-6):}\ \frac{}{(\mathsf{PkUp}, n_1).(\mathsf{PkUp}, n_2).(\mathsf{Dial}, n_1, n_2) \triangleleft POTS \triangleright \{(\mathsf{BuTo}, n_1)\}} .$$

It may seem that we should add axioms in Table 2 to deal with symmetric cases. For instance, axiom B-6 does not cover input sequence

$$(\mathsf{PkUp}, n_2).(\mathsf{PkUp}, n_1).(\mathsf{Dial}, n_1, n_2) .$$

There is also a similar case for axiom B-8. However, we do not need to, because these cases are handled by swap axioms, which we discuss in Sect. (c).

It is important to note that in our base cases we do not deal with input

Table 2 Unsuccessful Connection Attempts

No	Input	Output
B-6	$(\mathsf{PkUp}, n_1).(\mathsf{PkUp}, n_2).(\mathsf{Dial}, n_1, n_2)$	$\{(\mathsf{BuTo}, n_1)\}$
B-7	$(\mathsf{PkUp}, n_1).(\mathsf{Dial}, n_1, n_1)$	$\{(\mathsf{BuTo}, n_1)\}$
B-8	$(\mathsf{PkUp}, n_1).(\mathsf{PkUp}, n_2).(\mathsf{Dial}, n_1, n_3).(\mathsf{Dial}, n_2, n_3)$	$\{(\mathsf{BuTo}, n_2)\}$
B-9	$(\mathsf{PkUp}, n_1).(\mathsf{HgUp}, n_1)$	$\emptyset$
B-10	$(\mathsf{PkUp}, n_1).(\mathsf{Dial}, n_1, n_2).(\mathsf{Dial}, n_1, n_3)$	$\emptyset$

sequences starting with Dial or HgUp. We do so because we assume that a telephone cannot send a Dial or a HgUp before first sending a PkUp. According to our definition of correctness, which we present in Sect. 4.1, a correct implementation of our telephone specification could abort or produce any output for an input sequence which is not in the domain of the specification. In an industrial environment, it would be important to consider robustness in the specification, and to determine what to do for "invalid" input sequences. Such analysis is outside the scope of this paper. A simple strategy would be to produce no visible output for any input sequence which is not in the domain of *POTS*. Hence, we could define a robust POTS specification by stating that:

$$ROBUST\_POTS = POTS \cup \{(s, \emptyset) | s \in I^+ \wedge s \notin dom(POTS)\} \ .$$

This axiom produces a total relation.

(b) Reduction Axioms

The base cases provide the output for basic input sequences. For more complex input sequences, we use reduction axioms that eliminate symbols from the input sequence. By recursively applying reduction axioms, a complex input sequence is reduced to a base case input sequence, and then the corresponding output may be derived.

We provide two reduction tables: Table 3 illustrates how completed calls are removed from the input sequence, while Table 4 deals with the removal of calls in progress.

These two tables are interpreted in terms of axioms in the same manner. Let p, *pre*, *discard*, *post* be respectively the condition, the prefix, the discard and the postfix of line n, and let y be a fresh variable with respect to line n. Then the associated axiom is:

$$\frac{p \ \wedge \ pre.post \lhd POTS \rhd y}{pre.discard.post \lhd POTS \rhd y} \ .$$

Table 3 Reduction Axioms - Complete Connection Cycle

No	Condition	Prefix	Discard	Postfix
R-11	$x' \neq \varepsilon$	x	$(\mathsf{PkUp}, n_1).(\mathsf{HgUp}, n_1)$	x'
R-12	$x' \neq \varepsilon$	x	$(\mathsf{PkUp}, n_1).(\mathsf{Dial}, n_1, n_2).$ (HgUp, n_1)	x'
R-13	$x' \neq \varepsilon$	$x.(\mathsf{Dial}, n_1, n_2)$	$(\mathsf{Dial}, n_1, n_3)$	x'
R-14	$x' \neq \varepsilon$	$x.(\mathsf{Dial}, n_1, n_2)$	$(\mathsf{Dial}, n_3, n_2)$	x'

Table 4 Reduction Axioms - Connection in Progress

No	Condition	Prefix	Discard	Postfix
R-15		x	(PkUp, n_2)	(PkUp, n_1)
R-16	$n_2 \neq n_3$	x	$(\mathsf{Dial}, n_1, n_2)$	(PkUp, n_3)
R-17	$n_1 \neq n_2 \wedge n_1 \neq n_3$	x	(PkUp, n_1)	$(\mathsf{Dial}, n_2, n_3)$
R-18	$n_1 \neq n_3 \wedge n_2 \neq n_4$	x	$(\mathsf{Dial}, n_1, n_2)$	$(\mathsf{Dial}, n_3, n_4)$
R-19	$n_1 \neq n_2$	x	(PkUp, n_1)	(HgUp, n_2)
R-20		x	$(\mathsf{Dial}, n_1, n_2)$	(HgUp, n_3)

For instance, the axiom associated with line R-16 is:

$$\text{(R-16)}: \frac{n_2 \neq n_3 \;\wedge\; x.(\mathsf{PkUp}, n_3) \lhd POTS \rhd y}{x.(\mathsf{Dial}, n_1, n_2).(\mathsf{PkUp}, n_3) \lhd POTS \rhd y} \;.$$

This axiom provides that the behavior of the POTS, when input element (PkUp, n_3) is received, does not depend on input element $(\mathsf{Dial}, n_1, n_2)$ if the latter is the immediate predecessor of the former, and if $n_2 \neq n_3$. To illustrate the application of reduction axioms, assume we want to prove that:

$$(\mathsf{PkUp}, a_1).(\mathsf{PkUp}, a_2).(\mathsf{Dial}, a_2, a_3).(\mathsf{Dial}, a_1, a_4) \lhd POTS \rhd (\mathsf{Ring}, a_1, a_4) \;,$$

where the a_i are distinct constants.

Proof.

$$(\mathsf{PkUp}, a_1).(\mathsf{PkUp}, a_2).(\mathsf{Dial}, a_2, a_3).(\mathsf{Dial}, a_1, a_4) \lhd POTS \rhd \{(\mathsf{Ring}, a_1, a_4)\}$$

$\Leftarrow$ $\langle$ R-18 $\rangle$

$(\mathsf{PkUp}, a_1).(\mathsf{PkUp}, a_2).(\mathsf{Dial}, a_1, a_4) \triangleleft POTS \triangleright \{(\mathsf{Ring}, a_1, a_4)\}$

$\Leftarrow$ $\langle$ R-17 $\rangle$

$(\mathsf{PkUp}, a_1).(\mathsf{Dial}, a_1, a_4) \triangleleft POTS \triangleright \{(\mathsf{Ring}, a_1, a_4)\}$

$\Leftarrow$ $\langle$ B-2 $\rangle$

true □

(c) Swap Axioms

There are some complex input sequences to which our reduction axioms do not apply. Hence, we propose swap axioms to transform an input sequence, by swapping input elements, into another input sequence which has the same behavior. Swap axioms are applied until a reduction axiom may be applied. Table 5 provides the list of swap axioms for the POTS.

Table 5 Swap Axioms

No	Condition	Input 1	Input 2
S-21		(PkUp, n_1)	(PkUp, n_2)
S-22	$n_1 \neq n_3 \wedge n_2 \neq n_4$	$(\mathsf{Dial}, n_1, n_2)$	$(\mathsf{Dial}, n_3, n_4)$
S-23		(HgUp, n_1)	(HgUp, n_2)
S-24	$n_1 \neq n_2 \wedge n_1 \neq n_3$	(PkUp, n_1)	$(\mathsf{Dial}, n_2, n_3)$
S-25	$n_1 \neq n_2$	(PkUp, n_1)	(HgUp, n_2)
S-26	$n_1 \neq n_2 \wedge n_1 \neq n_3$	(HgUp, n_1)	$(\mathsf{Dial}, n_2, n_3)$

Two axioms are associated with a line n in a swap table in the following manner: let p, s_1, s_2 be respectively the condition, input element 1, and input element 2 of line n, and let x, x', y be three variables; then the associated axioms are:

$$\frac{p \wedge x' \neq \varepsilon \wedge x.s_1.s_2.x' \triangleleft POTS \triangleright y}{x.s_2.s_1.x' \triangleleft POTS \triangleright y},$$

$$\frac{p \wedge x' \neq \varepsilon \wedge x.s_2.s_1.x' \triangleleft POTS \triangleright y}{x.s_1.s_2.x' \triangleleft POTS \triangleright y}.$$

Obviously, when s_1 is the same as s_2 modulo variable renaming, then only one axiom is generated. For instance, the axiom associated with line S-26 is:

$$\text{(S-26)-1:}\quad \frac{\begin{array}{c} n_1 \neq n_2 \,\wedge\, n_1 \neq n_3 \,\wedge\, x' \neq \varepsilon \,\wedge \\ x.(\mathsf{HgUp}, n_1).(\mathsf{Dial}, n_2, n_3).x' \triangleleft POTS \triangleright y \end{array}}{x.(\mathsf{Dial}, n_2, n_3).(\mathsf{HgUp}, n_1).x' \triangleleft POTS \triangleright y}\ .$$

$$\text{(S-26)-2:}\quad \frac{\begin{array}{c} n_1 \neq n_2 \,\wedge\, n_1 \neq n_3 \,\wedge\, x' \neq \varepsilon \,\wedge \\ x.(\mathsf{Dial}, n_2, n_3).(\mathsf{HgUp}, n_1).x' \triangleleft POTS \triangleright y \end{array}}{x.(\mathsf{HgUp}, n_1).(\mathsf{Dial}, n_2, n_3).x' \triangleleft POTS \triangleright y}\ .$$

These axioms provide that HgUp and Dial may be swapped as long as they do not occur at the end of the input sequence and that they have distinct origins and destinations. The following proof illustrates the combined action of reduction and swap axioms.

$$\begin{array}{ll}
 & (\mathsf{PkUp}, a_1).(\mathsf{PkUp}, a_3).(\mathsf{Dial}, a_1, a_2).(\mathsf{HgUp}, a_1).(\mathsf{Dial}, a_3, a_2) \triangleleft POTS \triangleright \\
 & \{(\mathsf{Ring}, a_3, a_2)\} \\
\Leftarrow & \qquad\qquad \langle\ \text{S-24}\ \rangle \\
 & (\mathsf{PkUp}, a_1).(\mathsf{Dial}, a_1, a_2).(\mathsf{PkUp}, a_3).(\mathsf{HgUp}, a_1).(\mathsf{Dial}, a_3, a_2) \triangleleft POTS \triangleright \\
 & \{(\mathsf{Ring}, a_3, a_2)\} \\
\Leftarrow & \qquad\qquad \langle\ \text{S-25}\ \rangle \\
 & (\mathsf{PkUp}, a_1).(\mathsf{Dial}, a_1, a_2).(\mathsf{HgUp}, a_1).(\mathsf{PkUp}, a_3).(\mathsf{Dial}, a_3, a_2) \triangleleft POTS \triangleright \\
 & \{(\mathsf{Ring}, a_3, a_2)\} \\
\Leftarrow & \qquad\qquad \langle\ \text{R-12}\ \rangle \\
 & (\mathsf{PkUp}, a_3).(\mathsf{Dial}, a_3, a_2) \triangleleft POTS \triangleright \{(\mathsf{Ring}, a_3, a_2)\} \\
\Leftarrow & \qquad\qquad \langle\ \text{B-2}\ \rangle \\
 & \mathbf{true}
\end{array}$$

3.3 Three-Way Calling Specification

The feature three-way calling (TWC) allows a phone to establish a connection with a third party. Its specification may be given under the same tabular format as for the POTS specification. The input space is $I' \triangleq I \cup \{\mathsf{TWCAdd}\} \times \mathbf{PhoneId} \cup \{\mathsf{TWCDel}\} \times \mathbf{PhoneId} \cup \{\mathsf{FlHk}\} \times \mathbf{PhoneId}$.

Feature TWC is activated and deactivated for a user n_1 by sending inputs (TWCAdd, n_1) and (TWCDel, n_1) respectively. Feature TWC is triggered by input (FlHk, n_1) (flash hook), which allows user n_1, while talking to n_2, to initiate a connection with a third party n_3. The output space is the same as for the POTS specification.

Specification TWC is built on top of POTS. For the purpose of illustrating the detection of feature interactions, the specification of the base cases for a successful TWC connection (Table 6) and the reduction table for calls in progress (Table 7) are sufficient. For the sake of concision, we use the following abbreviation:

$$\mathsf{c1} \triangleq (\mathsf{PkUp}, n_1).(\mathsf{Dial}, n_1, n_2).(\mathsf{PkUp}, n_2)$$

In the sequel, any occurrence of an abbreviation may be replaced by its defining expression.

Table 6 Cumulative Table for a Successful TWC Connection

No	Premise	Input	Output
B-27		(TWCAdd, n_1)	$\emptyset$
B-28	$n_1 \neq n_2$	$\mathsf{c1}.(\mathsf{FlHk}, n_1)$	$\{(\mathsf{DiTo}, n_1), (\mathsf{Disc}, n_1, n_2)\}$
B-29	$n_1 \neq n_2 \wedge$ $n_1 \neq n_3 \wedge$ $n_2 \neq n_3$	$(\mathsf{Dial}, n_1, n_3)$	$\{(\mathsf{Ring}, n_1, n_3)\}$
B-30		(PkUp, n_3)	$\{(\mathsf{Conn}, n_1, n_3)\}$
B-31		(FlHk, n_1)	$\{(\mathsf{Conn}, n_1, n_2), (\mathsf{Conn}, n_2, n_3)\}$
B-32	$\{n_1', n_2', n_3'\} =$ $\{n_1, n_2, n_3\}$	(HgUp, n_3')	$\{(\mathsf{Disc}, n_1', n_3'), (\mathsf{Disc}, n_2', n_3')\}$
B-33	$\{n_1'', n_2''\} =$ $\{n_1', n_2'\}$	(HgUp, n_2'')	$\{(\mathsf{Disc}, n_1', n_2')\}$
B-34		(HgUp, n_1'')	$\emptyset$

Table 7 Reduction Axioms - Connection in Progress for TWC

No	Condition	Prefix	Discard	Postfix
R-35	$n_1 \neq n_2$	x	(PkUp, n_1)	(FlHk, n_2)
R-36	$n_1 \neq n_3$	x	$(\mathsf{Dial}, n_1, n_2)$	(FlHk, n_3)
R-37	$n_1 \neq n_2$	x	(FlHk, n_1)	(FlHk, n_2)

Note that Table 6 does not provide the behavior for prefixes of input sequence $(\mathsf{TWCAdd}, n_1).\mathsf{c1}$. This choice stems from the fact that the behavior of the TWC feature is the same as the POTS for input sequences that do not contain a FlHk. Hence, we may add the following axiom to express this fact.

$$\text{(R-38)}: \frac{x' \neq \varepsilon \wedge x'' \in \{(\mathsf{TWCAdd}, n_1), (\mathsf{TWCDel}, n_1)\} \wedge x.x' \triangleleft POTS \triangleright y}{x.x''.x' \triangleleft TWC \triangleright y}$$

3.4 Call Waiting

When user n_1 is connected with user n_2, and user n_3 calls n_1, a BuTo is sent to n_3 according to the POTS specification. The feature call waiting (CW) modifies this behavior by notifying n_1, through a WaitTone, that someone else is calling him, and by sending a RingTone to n_3. User n_1 may establish a connection with n_3 by doing a FlHk, which also puts user n_2 on hold. By doing a FlHk again, user n_1 terminates his connection with n_3 and resumes his connection with n_2. If user n_1 hangs up instead of getting back to n_2, the system rings him to let him know that n_2, the held party, is still waiting. Feature CW is activated and deactivated for a user n_1 by sending inputs (CWAdd, n_1) and (CWDel, n_1) respectively.

The specification of CW must cover some very peculiar cases, and is not straightforward to define (see, e.g., (Cameron *et al.* 1994)). For the purpose of illustrating feature interaction detection, we will concentrate on most typical basic cases, which is enough to illustrate interactions with the TWC feature.

Specification CW is also built on top of POTS. Cumulative Table 8 describes the base cases for a successful CW connection. We use the following abbreviation:

$$\mathsf{c2} \triangleq (\mathsf{PkUp}, n_3).(\mathsf{Dial}, n_3, n_1)$$

Finally, feature CW should not be affected by input elements indicating that feature TWC is activated or deactivated for some user, and vice-versa. We may state this fact using the following reduction axioms.

$$\text{(R-44)}: \frac{x' \neq \varepsilon \wedge x'' \in \{(\mathsf{TWCAdd}, n_1), (\mathsf{TWCDel}, n_1)\} \wedge x.x' \triangleleft CW \triangleright y}{x.x''.x' \triangleleft CW \triangleright y}$$

$$\text{(R-45)}: \frac{x' \neq \varepsilon \wedge x'' \in \{(\mathsf{CWAdd}, n_1), (\mathsf{CWDel}, n_1)\} \wedge x.x' \triangleleft TWC \triangleright y}{x.x''.x' \triangleleft TWC \triangleright y}$$

4 FEATURE INTERACTIONS

In this section, we describe how interactions between features are detected. For this purpose, we need to introduce the lattice of specifications.

Table 8 Cumulative Table for a Successful CW Connection

No	Premise	Input	Output
B-39		(AddCW, n_1)	$\emptyset$
B-40	$n_1 \neq n_2 \wedge$ $n_1 \neq n_3 \wedge$ $n_2 \neq n_3$	c1.c2	$\{(\mathsf{RingTone}, n_3), (\mathsf{WaitTone}, n_1)\}$
B-41		(FlHk, n_1)	$\{(\mathsf{Disc}, n_1, n_2), (\mathsf{Conn}, n_1, n_3)\}$
B-42		(FlHk, n_1)	$\{(\mathsf{Conn}, n_1, n_2), (\mathsf{Disc}, n_1, n_3)\}$
B-43		(HgUp, n_3)	$\emptyset$

4.1 The Lattice of Specifications

The lattice of specification is based on the refinement ordering. We say that a relation P refines a relation Q (written $P \sqsubseteq Q$) iff $dom(Q) \subseteq dom(P)$ and, for all s in the domain of Q, $s.P \subseteq s.Q$ (Mili *et al.* 1987), where $s.R$ denotes the image set of element s by relation R. Relation $\sqsubseteq$ is an ordering (reflexive, transitive and antisymmetric).

To solve the feature interaction problem, it is not necessary, in this paper, to deal with the notion of correctness of a program with respect to a specification, since we are only interested at this point in writing and validating specifications. However, we will briefly discuss this notion to justify our choice of the refinement ordering.

We say that a program p is totally correct with respect to (or satisfies) a specification R if, for any input sequence $s \in dom(R)$, program p terminates and produces an output s' such that $(s, s') \in R$; for any input sequence not in the domain of R, program p may deliver any output, or it may fail to terminate. This notion of total correctness is captured by the refinement relation. Let P be the relation corresponding to the input-output behavior of program p (i.e., $(s, s') \in P$ if and only if p always terminates for input sequence s, and may produce output s'). Then, p is totally correct with respect to R if and only if $P \sqsubseteq R$.

Under the refinement ordering, relations form a complete join-semilattice (Desharnais *et al.* 1995), i.e., a least upper bound exists for any non empty set of relations. In programming terms, the least upper bound, which we denote by $\sqcup$, offers a choice between two specifications: a program satisfying either P or Q satisfies $P \sqcup Q$.

The greatest lower bound of two relations P and Q exists iff the following condition is satisfied:

$$\forall s : s \in dom(P) \land s \in dom(Q) \Rightarrow \exists s' : (s, s') \in P \land (s, s') \in Q . \qquad (1)$$

We refer to this condition as the consistency condition, and we denote it by $cs(P, Q)$. The following formula (Desharnais *et al.* 1995) generalizes this definition:

$$cs(\{R_j : j \in J\}) \triangleq L \subseteq (\bigcap_{j \in J} R_j \cup \overline{R_j \circ L}) \circ L ,$$

where J is an arbitrary non empty index set, L is the universal relation and $\circ$ is the relational product. In programming terms, the greatest lower bound, which we denote by $\sqcap$, represents the conjunction of specifications: a program satisfying $P \sqcap Q$ must satisfy P and Q.

4.2 Definition of Feature Interaction

For the feature interaction problem, we need the ability to define each feature independently, and to define the combination of all features. In our relational framework, each feature is given by a relation, and the combination of the features is given by the greatest lower bound of the features. To see the adequacy of this choice, observe that a program p that satisfies the combination of all features must satisfy them individually. Hence, we have $P \sqsubseteq R_i$ for each feature R_i. It follows that P is a lower bound, in the refinement ordering, of the set of features $\{R_1, \ldots, R_n\}$. A sound representation of the combination of all features is the greatest lower bound, since a program refines the greatest lower bound if and only if it refines each feature individually — by definition. Stated formally, we have:

$$(\bigwedge_{i=1}^{n} P \sqsubseteq R_i) \Leftrightarrow P \sqsubseteq \bigsqcap_{i=1}^{n} R_i .$$

When describing a collection of features independently, a specifier must verify that the features are consistent, which ensures that there exists a greatest lower bound. On this basis, we are led to the following definition.

Definition 1 *Given a set* $\{R_1, \ldots, R_n\}$ *of relational specifications of features, we say that there is an interaction between these features if and only if*

$\neg cs(R_1, \ldots, R_n)$. *We say that these features interact for input sequence s if and only if*

$$(\bigwedge_{i=1}^{n} s \in dom(R_i)) \wedge \neg\exists s' : \bigwedge_{i=1}^{n} (s, s') \in R_i \ . \tag{2}$$

A collection of features interact for some input sequence s if they are all defined for s, and if they cannot agree on one common output. We have found that several examples of feature interactions listed in (Cameron *et al.* 1994), which contains a classification of feature interactions, satisfy Def. 1. For instance, feature Call Waiting is known to interact with feature Three-Way Calling for the following input sequence, which we denote by s_1:

$$(\mathsf{TWCAdd}, a_1).(\mathsf{CWAdd}, a_1).(\mathsf{PkUp}, a_1).(\mathsf{Dial}, a_1, a_2).$$
$$(\mathsf{PkUp}, a_2).(\mathsf{PkUp}, a_3).(\mathsf{Dial}, a_3, a_1).(\mathsf{FlHk}, a_1)$$

In feature Three-Way Calling, the only output (since this feature is deterministic) corresponding to s_1 is:

$$\{(\mathsf{DiTo}, a_1), (\mathsf{Disc}, a_1, a_2)\} \ .$$

In feature Call Waiting, the only output (CW is also deterministic) corresponding to s_1 is:

$$\{(\mathsf{Conn}, a_1, a_3), (\mathsf{Disc}, a_1, a_2)\} \ .$$

The consistency condition (Eq. 1) between TWC and CW is not satisfied for input sequence s_1. Hence, there does not exist a greatest lower bound for these two features, nor does there exist a program that satisfies both features simultaneously. There are other sequences causing an interaction between CW and TWC. For instance, input elements (TWCAdd, a_1) and (CWAdd, a_1) can be swapped, and the outputs are the same for each feature respectively. Several other swaps are possible. The input sequence consisting of the first 7 symbols of s_1 also causes an interaction, since the output of TWC for that sequence is $\{(\mathsf{BuTo}, a_3)\}$, whereas the output is $\{(\mathsf{Ring}, a_3), (\mathsf{WaitTone}, a1)\}$ for CW.

Our definition is strong enough to cover cases of interaction between n features even if none can be detected for any subset of $n-1$ features. For instance, assume that we have 3 features R_1, R_2, R_3 with the following behavior:

$$\begin{array}{ll} s \lhd R_1 \rhd s_a & s \lhd R_1 \rhd s_b \\ s \lhd R_2 \rhd s_b & s \lhd R_2 \rhd s_c \\ s \lhd R_3 \rhd s_a & s \lhd R_3 \rhd s_c \end{array}$$

Considered by pairs, these features are consistent. However, when taken altogether, they do not satisfy the consistency condition, since for input s there is no output common to all of them.

There are several other examples of feature interactions listed in (Cameron *et al.* 1994) which satisfy Def. 1. Without providing a specification of these features, we briefly illustrate how some of these interactions satisfy our definition.

1. **Call Waiting and Answer Call**
   Feature answer call (AC) allows to redirect a call to a busy line to an answering service (like a Voice Mail, or an operator). The following input sequence causes a feature interaction.

   $$(\mathsf{ACAdd}, a_1).(\mathsf{CWAdd}, a_1).(\mathsf{PkUp}, a_1).(\mathsf{Dial}, a_1, a_2).$$
   $$(\mathsf{PkUp}, a_2).(\mathsf{PkUp}, a_3).(\mathsf{Dial}, a_3, a_1)$$

   For this sequence, the output of feature CW is

   $$\{(\mathsf{RingTone}, a_3), (\mathsf{WaitTone}, a_1)\} \ ,$$

   whereas the output for feature AC is something like

   $$\{(\mathsf{VoiceMail}, a_3, a_1)\} \ .$$

2. **Call Forward on Busy and Originating Call Screening**
   The call forward on busy (CFB) feature is similar to the answer call feature, except that it redirects calls to a third number instead of an answering service. The originating call screening (OCS) feature allows a user to prevent connections from his phone to some other phone (especially useful for parents to prevent their kids to call some expensive pay lines). A feature interaction occurs for the following input sequence.

   $$(\mathsf{CFBAdd}, a_1, a_2).(\mathsf{OCSadd}, a_1, a_2).(\mathsf{PkUp}, a_1).(\mathsf{Dial}, a_1, a_1).(\mathsf{PkUp}, a_2)$$

   In this sequence, feature CFB redirects calls destined to a_1, when a_1 is busy, to a_2; feature OCS prevents calls from a_1 to a_2. The interaction occurs when a_1 calls itself. The only output for CFB is $\{(\mathsf{Conn}, a_1, a_2)\}$. The output for

OCS is best described by showing the axiom in OCS's specification which applies in this case.

$$\text{(OCS-46):}\quad \frac{\begin{array}{l} x = x_1.(\mathsf{OCSadd}, n_1, n_2).x_2 \;\wedge \\ (\mathsf{OCSDel}, n_1, n_2) \not\preceq x_2 \;\wedge\; x_2 \neq \varepsilon \\ \Rightarrow \\ (\mathsf{Conn}, n_1, n_2) \notin y \end{array}}{x \triangleleft OCS \triangleright y}$$

Predicate $x \preceq y$ indicates that x is a segment of y. A program satisfying axiom OCS-46 cannot produce an output $\{(\mathsf{Conn}, n_1, n_2)\}$ if the OCS feature is active between n_1 and n_2. Hence, features CFB and OCS have no common output, and they are inconsistent. Note that axiom OCS-46 allows any other (undesired) output (e.g., $(\mathsf{Conn}, a_1, a_3)$, or (Ring, a_3)) for the input sequence above causing the interaction. However, feature OCS is never used alone as a specification, but always in combination with other features (e.g., POTS). The greatest lower bound of these features constrains the behavior, and eliminates undesired outputs. Axiom OCS-46 also illustrates why we need nondeterminacy (i.e., relations) in specifications.

3. **Originating Call Screening and Abbreviated Dialing**
Feature Abbreviated Dialing (ABD) allows to define an alias for a phone number. A feature interaction between ABD and OCS occurs for the following input sequence:

$$(\mathsf{ABDSet}, a_1, a_2, a_3).(\mathsf{OCSadd}, a_1, a_3).(\mathsf{PkUp}, a_1).(\mathsf{Dial}, a_1, a_2).(\mathsf{PkUp}, a_3)$$

In this sequence, a_2 is an alias for a_3, and OCS prevents calls from a_1 to a_3. The interaction occurs when a_1 dials a_2. Feature ABD will redirect this call to a_3, but feature OCS prevents that. In ABD, the output for the sequence above is $\{(\mathsf{Conn}, a_1, a_3)\}$. Feature OCS allows other outputs but not this one. Hence, the two features are inconsistent.
Note that our specification of OCS may seem to catch the inconsistency one input element "too late". For instance, in the example above, OCS allows phone a_3 to ring, but it does not allow making a connection when a_3 is picked up. However, it does not really matter at what point the interaction is picked up, as long as it is at some point. After an interaction is detected, the specifier should review the entire input sequence causing it, not only the last symbol. Moreover, because features should be independent as much as possible, it is inappropriate in OCS to deal with all the different ways of making a connection (like ABD, CFB or other call forwarding features).

Other feature interactions listed in (Cameron *et al.* 1994) are not covered by our definition. Some of them are related to implementation issues. For instance, feature Call Forwarding Unconditional interacts with a PBX (Private

Branch Exchange) implementation of Terminating Call Screening, because the PBX drops one of the three phone numbers carried in a typical implementation of CFU. Other examples which are listed as feature interactions in (Kimbler *et al.* 1995) appear to us to be more a question of defining the behavior of a feature for complex input cases, rather than an interference between several features. For instance, they mention an interaction between Call Waiting and itself, for the following input sequence, which represents the case where two Call-Waiting subscribers put each other on hold.

$$\begin{array}{l}(\mathsf{CWAdd}, a_1).\mathsf{CWAdd}, a_2).(\mathsf{PkUp}, a_1).\\(\mathsf{Dial}, a_1, a_2).(\mathsf{PkUp}, a_2).(\mathsf{PkUp}, a_3).\\(\mathsf{Dial}, a_3, a_1).(\mathsf{FlHk}, a_1).(\mathsf{PkUp}, a_4).\\(\mathsf{Dial}, a_4, a_2).(\mathsf{FlHk}, a_2).(\mathsf{HgUp}, a_2)\end{array}$$

The question raised in (Kimbler *et al.* 1995) for this input sequence is what should be the output? According to one interpretation of the informal, general description of feature CW (see Sect. 3.4), a_2 should be rung back, because a_1 is on hold from the viewpoint of the connection between a_2 and a_4. Another interpretation is that a_2 is the held party between a_1 and a_3. Hence, when a_2 hangs up, a_1 is left in a normal connection with a_3, and a_2 is idle (detached from his connection to a_1, and ready to answer a call or place a call).

In our framework, we would not consider this as a feature interaction, unless one could find a way of specifying CW as a combination of sub-features. Rather, this particular issue could be resolved in two ways. It could be specified nondeterministically, that is, the specification would allow two possible outputs: $\emptyset$, for the case where a_2 is left idle, and $\{(\mathsf{Ring}, a_2)\}$, for the case where a_2 is rung back. This nondeterminacy leaves more freedom at the design stage for selecting the easiest solution to implement. A more restrictive alternative is to make the specification deterministic by selecting one of the two possible outputs.

Although our definition of feature interaction covers several typical examples cited in the literature (e.g., (Cameron *et al.* 1994)), it is quite specific. The expression "feature interaction" is sometimes understood in a very general sense. The reader may have in mind other legitimate cases of feature interactions, like violation of assumptions or unexpected behavior after adding features, which may not satisfy our definition. The mathematical characterization of the notion of feature interaction is not an easy task, and our definition will certainly evolve as more cases of interactions are identified and studied.

4.3 Detection of Feature Interactions

According to our definition of feature interaction (Def. 1), one could detect interactions between feature CW and TWC by proving that the following formula holds:

$$\begin{array}{l} \exists s : s \in dom(CW) \ \wedge \ s \in dom(TWC) \ \wedge \\ \neg \exists s' : (s, s') \in CW \ \wedge \ (s, s') \in TWC \ . \end{array} \tag{3}$$

We will prove this formula using logic programming and SLD-resolution (Apt 1990). This formula and the axioms of specifications TWC and CW translate easily into a logic program: axioms are already in the form of clauses (i.e., universally quantified formulas of the form $A \Leftarrow B$), and the formula to prove is a goal (i.e., an existentially quantified formula).

(a) The Prolog Connection

For simplicity, we use lists to represent sequences, sets and tuples, and we use the predicate append to manipulate lists. Although there are several details involved, the reader may get a good idea of the translation by looking at two examples. For instance, the base case axiom B-28 in Table 6 translates into the following Prolog clause in Edinburgh syntax:

```
twc([[twcadd,N1],[pickup,N1],[dial,N1,N2],
     [pickup,N2],[flashhook,N1]],
    [[dialtone,N1],[disc,N1,N2]])
  :- N1\==N2.
```

In the clause above, relation TWC is represented by binary predicate `twc`. Its first argument is the input sequence, which is given as a list of lists. The inner lists represent tuples of I. The second argument of `twc` is the output, given again by a list of lists, since the outputs of our telephone system are sets. The following clause represents the translation of reduction axiom R-36 in Table 7.

```
twc(X,Y) :- Post=[[FlashHook,N3]],
            append(X1,Post,X),
            append(Pre,[[dial,N1,N2]],X1),
            N1\==N3,
            append(Pre,Post,X2),twc(X2,Y).
```

Base case, reduction and swap axioms can all be translated into Prolog clauses following this pattern, in a quite straightforward manner. Eq. 3 is translated in the following conjunction of goals:

```
cw(X,_),twc(X,_),not((cw(X,Y),twc(X,Y))).
```

The metapredicate `not` succeeds if the proof of the conjunction of its goal arguments fails.

(b) Proving the interaction

The search tree generated by SLD-resolution using the linear search strategy of Prolog would be too long to illustrate. Rather, we content ourselves with listing the clauses (axioms) involved in a successful proof of the conjunction of goals.

The literal `cw(X,_)` is successfully proved by application of axioms R-44 and B-41, which results in the following substitution for `X` (given using sequences and concatenation instead of lists, for brevity and simplicity).

$$(\mathsf{TWCAdd}, n_1).(\mathsf{CWAdd}, n_1).(\mathsf{PkUp}, n_1).(\mathsf{Dial}, n_1, n_2).$$
$$(\mathsf{PkUp}, n_2).(\mathsf{PkUp}, n_3).(\mathsf{Dial}, n_3, n_1).(\mathsf{FlHk}, n_1)$$

The next goal, `twc(X,_)`, succeeds, by application of axioms R-45, R-36, R-35 and B-28. It remains to prove the goal given by the metapredicate `not`. The two goals given as its argument fail, since there is no axiom that allows TWC and CW to produce a common output for the current substitution of `X`. Thus, the goal `not(...)` succeeds, and a feature interaction has been detected.

So far, for the purpose of illustration we have deliberately dodged several issues in the detection of a feature interaction. As the reader probably suspects, the search strategy in the application of axioms is crucial for finding a proof. An infinite tree may be generated without ever reaching a successful branch of the tree. For instance, had we inverted the order of the goals `cw(X,_)` and `twc(X,_)`, the interpreter would have entered an infinite loop in trying to find a common input sequence for TWC and CW, because the linear search strategy of Prolog implies looping over the first recursive axiom (e.g., R-38, where TWC appears on both sides of `:-`). To implement a more robust search strategy, Prolog may not be an excellent candidate. Moreover, the treatment of `not` and clauses likes $n_1 \neq n_2$ deserves special care. We are currently in the process of defining a good search strategy, taking into account these issues.

5 CONCLUSION

In this paper, we have proposed a definition of feature interaction which is general enough to cover most of the typical examples cited in the literature. The relational calculus and the refinement lattice form the foundations of this definition. Because these foundations have been studied for systems development (Boudriga *et al.* 1992, Broy 1995, Desharnais *et al.* 1995, Mills *et al.* 1986, Möller 1991), our definition lays on a solid theoretical basis, and it is well integrated into systems development.

Our inductive style for writing specifications and its tabular representation make our specifications quite readable, and quite concise compared to other formalisms. Our specification of the POTS fits on one page; other comparable specifications (e.g., (Blom *et al.* 1994, Butler 1994, Faci *et al.* 1994, Gammelgaard *et al.* 1994)) are of the same length, or extend on several pages. The readability stems from the self-containment of axioms: an axiom can be understood individually, without having to consider other axioms; it corresponds to a set of input-output pairs. Specifications may also be incomplete and, still, be meaningful and allow for the detection of interactions.

This inductive style seems appropriate for proving the existence of interactions. We have illustrated how interactions could be detected using Prolog. Although it is not the best candidate for theorem proving, the simple translation between our axioms and Prolog clauses provides good indications that our definition is amenable to automated proof, provided that we define a more intelligent search strategy to deal with swap axioms, reduction axioms, equality and negation by failure. This is an interesting problem that we will investigate in future work.

Several authors have proposed definitions of feature interactions and methods for detecting them (see (Bouma *et al.* 1994, Cheng *et al.* 1995)). The approach of (Gammelgaard *et al.* 1994) is the closest one to ours: the authors consider axiomatic specifications of deterministic labeled transition systems; two features interact if their joint specification cannot be satisfied by a labeled transition system. A similar approach is used in (Blom *et al.* 1994), where specifications are given in temporal logic, and interactions correspond to inconsistencies. In (Faci *et al.* 1994), features are specified in LOTOS, and interactions are detected by defining goals and by showing that they are unreachable. Object-Z is used in (Butler 1994) for specifying features; interactions are detected through violations of invariants and pre-conditions.

Acknowledgments The authors would like to thank Jalel Kamoun for introducing them to the feature interaction problem, Serge Colle and Elias Rafoul for helpful discussions, and the anonymous referees for pointing several unclarities.

6 APPENDIX A - PROOF

Theorem 1 *Let $\mathcal{F}$ be a function associated with an axiom and defined as follows.*

$$\mathcal{F}(X) \triangleq \{(R,t,t') | \exists \vec{x} : p \wedge (t,t') = (g,h) \wedge \bigwedge_j (R_j, e_j, f_j) \in X\}$$

Then, function $\mathcal{F}$ is continuous with respect to the inclusion ordering on sets.

Proof. Let D be a directed set of triples. We have to show that

$$\mathcal{F}(\bigcup D) = \bigcup \mathcal{F}(D) \ .$$

$$\begin{array}{ll}
 & (R,t,t') \in \mathcal{F}(\bigcup D) \\
\Leftrightarrow & \qquad \langle \text{ definition of } \mathcal{F} \ \rangle \\
 & \exists \vec{x} : (t,t') = (g,h) \ \wedge \ p \ \wedge \ \bigwedge_j \exists d : d \in D \wedge (R_j, e_j, f_j) \in d \\
\Leftrightarrow & \qquad \langle \text{ distribute } \bigwedge_j \text{ over } \exists d\text{, since } D \text{ is directed } \rangle \\
 & \exists \vec{x} : (t,t') = (g,h) \ \wedge \ p \ \wedge \ \exists d : d \in D \wedge \bigwedge_j (R_j, e_j, f_j) \in d \\
\Leftrightarrow & \qquad \langle \text{ push } \exists d \text{ outside } \rangle \\
 & \exists d : d \in D \ \wedge \ \exists \vec{x} : (t,t') = (g,h) \ \wedge \ p \ \wedge \ \bigwedge_j (R_j, e_j, f_j) \in d \\
\Leftrightarrow & \qquad \langle \text{ definition of } \mathcal{F} \ \rangle \\
 & \exists d : d \in D \ \wedge \ (R,t,t') \in \mathcal{F}(d) \\
\Leftrightarrow & \qquad \langle \ \rangle \\
 & (R,t,t') \in \bigcup \mathcal{F}(D)
\end{array}$$

□

REFERENCES

Apt, K.R. (1990) Logic Programming, in *Handbook of Theoretical Computer Science, Vol. B*, J. van Leeuwen, ed., North-Holland, 493–574.

Blom, J., B. Jonsson, L. Kempe (1994) Using Temporal Logic for Modular Specification of Telephone Services, in *Feature Interactions in Telecommunications Software Systems*, W. Bouma and H. Velthuijsen, eds, IOS Press, 197–216.

Boudriga, N., F. Elloumi, A. Mili (1992) On The Lattice of Specifications: Applications to a Specification Methodology, *Formal Aspects of Computing* **4** 544–571.

Bouma, W., H. Velthuijsen (1994) *Feature Interactions in Telecommunications Software Systems.* IOS Press.

Bowen, T.F., F.S. Dworak, C.H. Chow, N. Griffeth, G.E. Herman, Y-J. Lin (1989) The Feature Interaction Problem in Telecommunications Systems, in *Proc. 7th Int. Conf. on Software Engineering for Telecommunication Switching Systems*, 59–62.

Broy, M. (1995) Mathematics of Software Engineering, in *Mathematics of Program Construction, 3rd Int. Conf.*, B. Möller, ed., Springer-Verlag, Lecture Notes in Computer Science 947, 18–48.

Butler, M.J. (1994) Feature Interaction Analysis Using Z, in *Report on Methods and Tools for Service Creation (First Version) Part II: Methods and Tools for Service Interaction Analysis*, CEC RACE project 2017 SCORE, R2017/SCO/WP2/DS/L/018/b2. `ftp://ftp.abo.fi/pub/cs/papers/michael/fiz.ps.Z`.

Cameron, E.J., N. Griffeth, Y.-J. Linand, M.E. Nilson, W.K. Schnure, H. Velthuijsen (1994) A Feature Interaction Benchmark for IN and Beyond, in *Feature Interactions in Telecommunications Software Systems*, W. Bouma and H. Velthuijsen, eds, IOS Press, 1–23. `ftp://thumper.bellcore.com/pub/nancyg/benchmark.ps`

Cheng, K.E., T. Ohta (1995) *Feature Interactions in Telecommunications III.* IOS Press.

Davey, B.A., H.A. Priestley (1990) *Introduction to Lattices and Order.* Cambridge University Press.

Deck, M.D., M.G. Plaszkoch, R.C. Linger and H.D. Mills (1992) Extended Semantics for Box Structures. *Proceedings, 25th Hawaii International Conference on Systems Sciences.* Kauwai, Hawaii, 382–393.

Desharnais, J., N. Belkhiter, S. Ben Mohamed Sghaier, F. Tchier, A. Jaoua, A. Mili, and N. Zaguia (1995) Embedding a Demonic Semilattice in a Relation Algebra. *Theoretical Computer Science* **149** 333–360.

Faci, M., L. Logrippo (1994) Specifying Features and Analysing their Interactions in a LOTOS Environment, in *Feature Interactions in Telecommunications Software Systems*, W. Bouma and H. Velthuijsen, eds, IOS Press, 136–151.

Gammelgaard, A., J.E. Kristensen (1994) Interaction Detection, a Logical Approach, in *Feature Interactions in Telecommunications Software Systems*, W. Bouma and H. Velthuijsen, eds, IOS Press, 178–196.

Gunter, C.A., D.S. Scott (1990) Semantic Domains, in *Handbook of Theoretical Computer Science, Vol. B*, J. van Leeuwen, ed., North-Holland, 635–674.

Kimbler, K.H. Velthuijsen (1995) Feature Interaction Benchmark, KPN Research, PO Box 421, 2260 AK Leidschendam, The Netherlands, 1–13. `http://www.docs.uu.se/docs/fi/benchmark.ps.gz`

Mills, H.D., R.C. Linger, A.R. Hevner (1986) *Principles of Information Systems Analysis and Design*, Academic Press.

Möller, B. (1991) Relations as a Program Development Language. In *Constructing Programs from Specifications*, B. Möller, ed., Proc. IFIP TC 2/WG 2.1 Pacific Grove, CA, USA, May 13–16, North-Holland, 373–397.

Mili, A., J. Desharnais, F. Mili (1987) Relational Heuristics for the Design of Deterministic Programs. *Acta Informatica* **24**(3) 239–276.

Mosses, P.D. (1990) Denotational Semantics, in *Handbook of Theoretical Computer Science, Vol. B*, J. van Leeuwen, ed., North-Holland, 575–631.

Wang, Y., Parnas, D.L. (1994) Simulating the Behavior of Software Modules by Trace Rewriting. *IEEE Transactions on Software Engineering*, **20**(10) 750–759.

7 BIOGRAPHY

Marc Frappier is a professor of computer science at the University of Sherbrooke. He earned a Ph.D. in computer Science from the University of Ottawa in 1995. His research interests include the mathematics of software specification and design.

Ali Mili earned the Ph.D. from the University of Illinois and the Doctorat ès Sciences d'État from the University of Grenoble. His research interests are in software engineering, ranging from managerial aspects to technical aspects.

Jules Desharnais is a professor of computer science at Université Laval. He completed a B.Sc. in 1982 and a M.Sc. in 1985, both in computer science at Université Laval. He received a Ph.D. in computer Science from McGill University in 1989. His research interests include formal specification methods, the mathematics of program construction and relation algebras.

Synthesising Interconnections

J.L.Fiadeiro and A.Lopes
Department of Informatics,
Faculty of Sciences,University of Lisbon
Campo Grande, 1700 Lisboa, PORTUGAL
telephone: 351-1-7500087, fax: 351-1-7500084
{llf,mal}@di.fc.ul.pt

T.S.E.Maibaum
Department of Computing,
Imperial College of Science, Technology and Medicine
180 Queen's Gate, London SW7 2BZ, UNITED KINGDOM
telephone: 44-171-5948281, fax: 44-171-5948282
tsem@doc.ic.ac.uk

Abstract

In the context of the modular and incremental development of complex systems, viewed as interconnections of interacting components, new dimensions and new problems arise in the calculation of programs from specifications. A particularly important aspect for extending existing methods to address composite systems is the ability, given programs that realise component specifications, to synthesise the interconnections between them in such a way that the system specification is realised. Taking our cue from earlier work on General Systems Theory (Goguen, 1973) and more recent work on parallel program design (Fiadeiro and Maibaum, 1996), we discuss, characterise and provide solutions for the synthesis of interconnections using a categorical framework in which components are modelled as objects (either specifications or programs) and morphisms are used to express interconnections between components.

Keywords

Synthesis, interconnection, incremental development, complex systems.

1 INTRODUCTION

Given a class *SPEC* of specifications, a class *PROG* of programs and a relation *sat* in *PROG*×*SPEC*, methods for the calculation of programs from specifications aim at supporting the development, for every specification S, of a program P such that P *sat* S. A subclass of such techniques are synthesis methods which produce, in a systematic, algorithmic way, a program *Syn*(S) for every specification S in such a way that *Syn*(S) *sat* S. Well known examples are the synthesis of communicating processes and synchronisation skeletons from temporal logic specifications (Emerson and Clarke, 1982, Manna and Wolper, 1984).

To have serious impact in today's software development environment, the methods addressing the calculation/synthesis of individual program units must be extended or supplemented to encompass multicomponent (and even hybrid) systems. Our aim in this paper is to investigate the requirements that the calculation of systems of interconnected components, rather than single, isolated programs, imposes on specifications, programs and the relationship between them.

The calculation of composite systems, viewed as interconnections of simpler, interacting components, raises new and challenging questions, namely in support of reuse and incrementality. In an incremental software development discipline, it should not be necessary to recalculate the whole system each time the specification of a new component is added. It should be possible to calculate only a program that realises the specification of the new component and its interconnections to the old system. We should be able to support situations where some components are automatically synthesised from their specifications, other components are developed from scratch, e.g. using transformational techniques, and yet other components are reused from previous developments.

The fact that, in composite systems, some of the components may correspond to human or physical agents, provides further evidence for the need to integrate program calculation methods into a modular development discipline, namely in conjunction with methods and techniques that exist for the development of various (possibly different kinds of) components (e.g. synthesis methods for hardware components or control systems).

The ability to calculate interconnections between given realisations of component specifications from the interconnections that have been provided at the specification level, seems to be the key ingredient for extending existing methods for calculating programs from specifications to address composite systems and, hence, support incremental development. Ideally, we should be able to *synthesise* interconnections, by which we mean a systematic, hopefully automatable, way of generating interconnections. The question which we propose to address in this paper is the nature of the programming and specification formalisms, and of the relationship between them, which the necessity of synthesising interconnections imposes.

Concerns about the systematic development of composite systems can be found in the literature. The work reported in (Feather, 1987, 1989, Fickas and Helm,

1992) in particular should be noted. However, these approaches are mostly concerned with the problem of *decomposing* a system specification into components, and assume a *closed system* point of view. In this paper, we take the dual point of view, i.e. we address *composition* in an *open systems* context, which we think is more appropriate for the concerns that we have expressed above, namely incrementality and reuse. Our view is also consistent with recent work on *architectural design* (e.g. Shaw and Garlan, 1995), which emphasises the importance of establishing the overall architecture of the system early on in the design process.

In order to analyse the impact that the systems view and incremental development disciplines have on calculation methods, we need a framework in which specifications, programs and the relationships between them can be formally described. The simple-minded view of classes and relations recalled in the first paragraph is clearly not appropriate for capturing systems of interconnected components. Instead, we shall adopt the categorical approach proposed by J.Goguen for General Systems Theory (e.g., Goguen, 1973, Goguen and Ginali, 1978). Capitalising on our recent work on reactive system specification (Fiadeiro and Maibaum, 1992) and parallel program design (Fiadeiro and Maibaum, 1996), we shall view both $\mathcal{PROG}$ and $\mathcal{SPEC}$ as categories in which systems of interconnected components are modelled through diagrams (in the categorical sense).

In this setting, we shall formally characterise synthesis of interconnections and formulate general conditions that guarantee the ability to synthesise interconnections. These conditions are related to the existence of adjunctions between $\mathcal{PROG}$ and $\mathcal{SPEC}$. Because the existence of adjunctions is a very strong property, we explore situations where weaker conditions apply, making synthesis of interconnections more practicable. These weaker conditions rely on stronger structural properties of the formalisms involved and can be related to properties exhibited by so called coordination languages and models (Ciancarini and Hankin, 1996). Examples will be given using propositional linear temporal logic and the parallel program design language COMMUNITY.

2 THE CATEGORICAL VIEW OF SYSTEMS

In the early 70's, J. Goguen proposed the use of categorical techniques in *General Systems Theory* for unifying a variety of notions of system behaviour and their composition techniques (Goguen, 1973, Goguen and Ginali, 1978). His approach has been summarised in a very simple but far reaching principle: "given a category of widgets, the operation of putting a system of widgets together to form a super-widget corresponds to taking a colimit of the diagram of widgets that shows how to interconnect them". In this section, we illustrate the application of these principles to reactive system specification and parallel program design.

2.1 Interconnecting specifications

The application of the categorical approach to reactive system specification builds on the theory of institutions developed in (Goguen and Burstall, 1992), namely on the use of theories (or theory presentations) of a logic (institution) as building blocks in the construction of structured specifications.

We shall now illustrate the approach using propositional linear temporal logic. See (Fiadeiro and Maibaum, 1992) for a similar account using first-order temporal logic.

Definition/Proposition 2.1: The linear temporal logic institution LTL is defined as follows:

- its category of signatures is *SET*.
- the grammar functor defines, for every signature Σ, the set of *linear temporal propositions* LTL(Σ) as follows:

  ϕ ::= a | $(\neg\phi)$ | $(\phi\supset\psi)$ | **beg** | $(\phi\mathbf{U}\psi)$

  for $a\in\Sigma$. A signature morphism $f{:}\Sigma\rightarrow\Sigma'$ induces the translation $\underline{f}$: LTL(Σ)$\rightarrow$LTL(Σ') defined as follows:

  $\underline{f}(\phi)$ ::= f(a) | $\neg\underline{f}(\phi)$ | $\underline{f}(\phi)\supset\underline{f}(\psi)$ | **beg** | $\underline{f}(\phi)\mathbf{U}\underline{f}(\psi)$.
- the model functor is defined as follows: for every signature Σ, a Σ-model consists of a mapping M: $\Sigma\rightarrow 2^{\omega}$. We denote by Mod($\Sigma$) the set of all Σ-models. Given a signature morphism $f{:}\Sigma\rightarrow\Sigma'$, for every M$\in$Mod($\Sigma'$) we define $M|_f\in$Mod(Σ) by $M|_f(a)$=M(f(a)).
- the satisfaction relation is defined as follows: a Σ-proposition ϕ is said to be true in a Σ-model M at instant $i\in\omega$ (which we write $(M,i)\models_\Sigma\phi$) iff:
  - for all $a\in\Sigma$, $(M,i)\models_\Sigma a$ iff $i\in M(a)$;
  - $(M,i)\models_\Sigma\neg\phi$ iff $(M,i)\not\models_\Sigma\phi$;
  - $(M,i)\models_\Sigma\phi\supset\psi$ iff $(M,i)\models_\Sigma\phi$ implies $(M,i)\models_\Sigma\psi$;
  - $(M,i)\models_\Sigma$**beg** iff i=0;
  - $(M,i)\models_\Sigma\phi\mathbf{U}\psi$ iff there exists j>i such that $(M,j)\models_\Sigma\psi$ and, for all k such that $i<k\leq j$, $(M,k)\models_\Sigma\phi$.

  A Σ-proposition ϕ is said to be true in M, which we denote by $M\models_\Sigma\phi$, iff $(M,i)\models_\Sigma\phi$ for every $i\in\omega$. Given $\Phi\subseteq$LTL(Σ) and $\phi\in$LTL(Σ), $\Phi\models_\Sigma\phi$ iff, for every Σ-model M, $M\models_\Sigma\phi$ whenever $M\models_\Sigma\psi$ for every $\psi\in\Phi$. ∎

Some remarks seem to be in order:

- each signature provides a set of propositional symbols (to be interpreted as the set of actions that a given component can perform);
- every signature has an associated language generated from the propositional symbols, the usual propositional connectives, the propositional constant **beg** (denoting the initial instant of time) and the temporal operator **U** ("until");
- propositions are interpreted over the natural numbers; that is, a linear, discrete temporal structure is chosen;
- the interpretation of the temporal operator **U** ("until") is different from other uses that can be found in the literature, e.g. (Goldblatt, 1987): it is "strict",

i.e. it does not include the present, and $\phi U \psi$ requires ϕ to be satisfied when ψ becomes satisfied;

- the following operators can be defined as abbreviations:
  - $\mathbf{F}^+\phi \sim$ (true $\mathbf{U}$ ϕ), "sometime in the future ϕ, being neutral wrt ϕ now"
  - $\mathbf{F}\phi \sim (\mathbf{F}^+\phi \vee \phi)$, "sometime in the future ϕ, possibly now"
  - $\mathbf{G}^+\phi \sim (\neg \mathbf{F}^+(\neg\phi))$, "always in the future ϕ but not necessarily now"
  - $\mathbf{G}\phi \sim (\neg \mathbf{F}(\neg\phi))$, "always in the future ϕ, including now"
  - $\phi \mathbf{W} \psi \sim (\phi \mathbf{U} \psi) \vee \mathbf{G}^+(\phi \wedge \neg\psi)$, "$\phi$ until ψ but, possibly, never ψ"

Specifications are taken as theories in this institution:

Definition 2.2: The objects of the category *SPEC* of specifications are the pairs (Σ,Φ), where Σ is a signature and $\Phi \subseteq LTL(\Sigma)$ is closed under consequence (i.e. $\Phi \models_\Sigma \phi$ implies $\phi \in \Phi$). A morphism $f:(\Sigma_1,\Phi_1) \rightarrow (\Sigma_2,\Phi_2)$ is a signature morphism $f:\Sigma_1 \rightarrow \Sigma_2$ such that $\underline{f}(\Phi_1) \subseteq \Phi_2$. ∎

A specification is usually given through a finite set of axioms (a presentation). The specification thus presented consists of all the consequences of the axioms, i.e. of the closure of the set of axioms. We denote by $\Phi^\bullet$ the closure of Φ, i.e. $\Phi^\bullet = \{\phi \in LTL(\Sigma) \mid \Phi \models_\Sigma \phi\}$.

In a specification, the signature indicates what is the language of the component being specified and the axioms correspond to the properties that the component is required to satisfy. Specification morphisms are translations between the languages of the two theory presentations such that the theorems of the first specification are translated to theorems of the second. Notice that the axioms are propositions that are required to be satisfied at every instant of time.

As an example, consider the following specification of a vending machine:

specification vending machine is
sign coin, cake, cigar, reset
axioms beg ⊃ (¬cake∧¬cigar∧¬reset) ∧ (coin ∨ (¬cake∧¬cigar∧¬reset)Wcoin)
coin ⊃ (¬coin ∧ ¬reset)W(cake ∨ cigar)
(cake ∨ cigar) ⊃ (¬cake ∧ ¬cigar ∧ ¬coin)Wreset
reset ⊃ (¬cake ∧ ¬cigar ∧ ¬reset)Wcoin
cake ⊃ (¬cigar)

That is to say, the machine is initialised so as to accept only coins. Once it accepts a coin it can deliver either a cake or a cigar (but not both). After delivering a cake or a cigar it can only be reset, after which it is ready to accept more coins.

In order to illustrate the categorical approach to composition, assume that it becomes necessary to interconnect a regulator to the vending machine in order to prevent it from selling cigars. The specification of a regulator is quite simple:

specification regulator **is**
sign trigger, action
axioms trigger ⊃ G¬action

That is to say, a regulator can perform two actions, *trigger* and *action*. After performing *trigger*, *action* can no longer occur.

It remains to show how to connect the regulator to the vending machine. Intuitively, we want *action* to be synchronised with *cigar* and *trigger* with *coin* so that the action of accepting a coin triggers the cigar option to be blocked.

In the categorical approach, interconnections are established through diagrams. For the purpose at hand, we need a communication channel between *vending machine* and *regulator*. This channel is specified as having two ports with no required properties:

specification channel **is**
sign a, b
axioms

The configuration of the required system can be given by the following diagram:

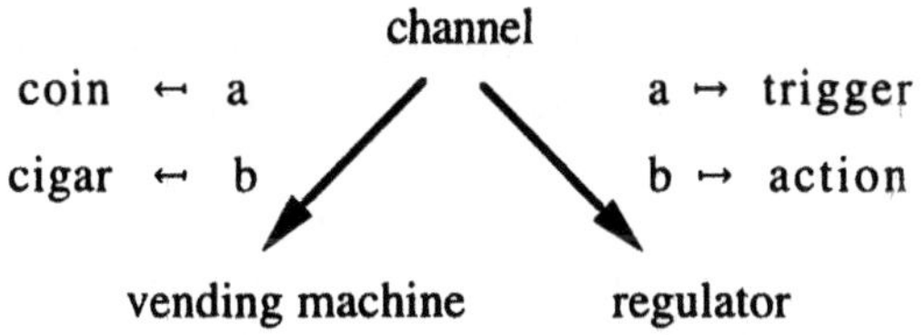

The properties of the resulting system can be obtained by the colimit of its configuration diagram:

Proposition 2.3: The category *SPEC* is finitely cocomplete. Its initial object is $(\emptyset,\emptyset)$ and the pushout of $f_1:(\Sigma,\Phi)\to(\Sigma_1,\Phi_1)$ and $f_2:(\Sigma,\Phi)\to(\Sigma_2,\Phi_2)$ is given by $g_1:(\Sigma_1,\Phi_1)\to(\Sigma',\Phi')$ and $g_2:(\Sigma_2,\Phi_2)\to(\Sigma',\Phi')$, where g_1 and g_2 result from the pushout of f_1 and f_2 as signature morphisms (the resulting signature Σ' is the amalgamated sum of Σ_1 and Σ_2 relative to f_1 and f_2) and $\Phi'=(\underline{f}_1(\Phi_1)\cup\underline{f}_2(\Phi_2))^{\bullet}$. ∎

This is a property of any institution (Goguen and Burstall, 1992). It tells us that the set of axioms of the resulting specification consists of the union of the translations of the axioms of the components. Because the union of sets of formulae has the same logical value as their conjunction, the categorical approach complies with the "composition as conjunction" idea recently put forward in (Abadi and Lamport, 1993) for parallel composition of reactive systems.

The specification of the system that results from interconnecting the vending machine and the regulator as above is given below, assuming that the morphisms that connect *vending machine* and *regulator* to the new specification are the identity and (trigger ↦ coin, action ↦ cigar), respectively:

specification regulated vending machine **is**
sign coin, cake, cigar, reset
axioms **beg** $\supset$ (¬cake∧¬cigar∧¬reset) ∧ (coin ∨ (¬cake∧¬cigar∧¬reset)**W**coin)
coin $\supset$ (¬coin ∧ ¬reset)**W**(cake ∨ cigar)
(cake ∨ cigar) $\supset$ (¬cake ∧ ¬cigar ∧ ¬coin)**W**reset
reset $\supset$ (¬cake ∧ ¬cigar ∧ ¬reset)**W**coin
cake $\supset$ (¬cigar)
coin $\supset$ **G**¬cigar

2.2 Parallel program design in a categorical framework

In (Fiadeiro and Maibaum, 1996), we further showed how parallel program design in the language COMMUNITY (similar to UNITY (Chandy and Misra, 1988) and IP – Interacting Processes (Francez and Forman, 1996)) can be formalised using the same categorical techniques. The underlying computational model is also similar to Action Systems (Back ad Kurki-Suonio, 1988), but we should point out that the Action Systems approach, at least in relation to transformational development, is oriented to *decomposition* of systems into components. As explained in the introduction, our focus is on *composition*, which may explain some differences wrt Action Systems.

From a categorical point of view, objects are programs and morphisms capture superpositions. The colimit construction corresponds to a generalised parallel composition operator with synchronisation constraints (i.e. to superimposition in the sense of (Francez and Forman, 1996)).

We shall now illustrate these points by using a subset of COMMUNITY. The simplification consists in omitting data type declarations and external attributes. More precisely, we shall assume a fixed signature (S,Ω) in the usual algebraic sense (Ehrig and Mahr, 1985), i.e. S is a set (of sort symbols) and Ω is an $S^*{\times}S$-indexed family (of function symbols), together with a set DT of (first-order) axioms over (S,Ω) defining the properties of the operations.

A COMMUNITY program P in this simplified version has the following structure:

$$P \equiv \quad \textit{var} \;\; V \quad \textit{init} \;\; I \quad \textit{do} \;\; \mathop{[\!]}_{g\in\Gamma} \; g{:}\,[B(g) \rightarrow \mathop{\|}_{a\in D(g)} a{:=}F(g,a)]$$

where

- V is the set of attributes used by the program (i.e. the program "variables"); each attribute is typed by a data sort in S;
- Γ is the set of *action names*; each action name has an associated statement (see below) and can act as a *rendez-vous* point for program synchronisation;
- I is a condition on the attributes – the initialisation condition;
- for every action g∈Γ, B(g) is a condition on the attributes – the *guard* of the action;
- for every action g∈Γ, D(g)⊆V is the set of attributes that action *g* can change; we also denote by D(a), where a∈V, the set of actions that can change *a*;
- for every action g∈Γ and attribute a∈D(g), F(g,a) is a term of the same sort as a.

As an example, consider the following program corresponding to the vending machine specified in the previous section (the correspondence will be formalised later on):

```
program vending machine is
var    ready, served_cake, served_cigar : bool
init   ready ∧ (served_cake ∨ served_cigar)
do     coin : [ready ∧ (served_cake ∨ served_cigar)
                  → ready:=false || served_cake:=false || served_cigar:=false]
       [] cake : [¬ready ∧ ¬(served_cake ∨ served_cigar)
                  → served_cake:=true || served_cigar:=false]
       [] cigar: [¬ready ∧ ¬(served_cake ∨ served_cigar)
                  → served_cigar:=true || served_cake:=false]
       [] reset: [¬ready ∧ (served_cake ∨ served_cigar)
                  → ready:=true]
```

Formally,

Definition 2.4: A *program signature* is a tuple (V,Γ) where

- V is an S-indexed family of sets where S is the set of sorts. In the sequel, V is also taken as the union of all these sets (assumed disjoint).
- Γ is a 2^V-indexed family of sets. We denote by D(g) the type of each g in Γ (the set of attributes that action *g* can change). We also denote by D(a), where $a \in V$, the set of actions that can change *a*, i.e., $D(a)=\{g \in \Gamma : a \in D(g)\}$. In the sequel, Γ is also taken as the union of all these sets (assumed disjoint).

All these sets of symbols are assumed to be finite and mutually disjoint. ∎

Definition 2.5: Given a signature $\theta=(V,\Gamma)$, the language of terms is defined as follows, for every sort $s \in S$:

$$t_s ::= a \mid c \mid f(t_{s_1},\ldots,t_{s_n})$$

for $a \in V_s$, $c \in \Omega_{<>,s}$ and $f \in \Omega_{<s_1,\ldots,s_n>,s}$.

The language of propositions is defined as follows:

$$\phi ::= (t_{1s} =_s t_{2s}) \mid (\phi_1 \supset \phi_2) \mid (\phi_1 \vee \phi_2) \mid (\phi_1 \wedge \phi_2) \mid (\neg\phi) \quad ∎$$

For simplicity, whenever *t* is a Boolean term, we will abbreviate the proposition (t=true) to *t*. This simplification was used already in the example above.

Definition 2.6: A *program* is a pair (θ,Δ) where θ is a signature (V,Γ) and Δ, the *body* of the program, is a triple (I,F,B) where

- I is a θ-proposition (constraining the initial values of the attributes);
- F assigns to every action $g \in \Gamma$ a map that, to every $a \in D(g)$, assigns a term of the same sort as a; if D(g) is empty, we denote F(g) by *skip*;
- B assigns to every action $g \in \Gamma$ a proposition (its guard). ∎

It is easy to recognise in this definition the basic features of parallel programs, namely guarded simultaneous assignments. Model-theoretic semantics for this language can be found in (Fiadeiro and Maibaum, 1995, 1996). A proof-theoretic semantics will be given in section 2.3 below.

A categorical formalisation of program interconnection and composition can also be given based on a notion of morphism that captures what in the literature is known as superposition or superimposition (e.g. Chandy and Misra, 1988, Francez and Forman, 1996).

Definition/Proposition 2.7: Given program signatures $\theta_1=(V_1,\Gamma_1)$ and $\theta_2=(V_2,\Gamma_2)$, a ***signature morphism*** σ from θ_1 to θ_2 consists of a pair $(\sigma_\alpha:V_1\rightarrow V_2,\sigma_\gamma:\Gamma_1\rightarrow\Gamma_2)$ of functions such that (1) for every $s\in S$ and for every $a\in V_{1_s}$, $\sigma_\alpha(a)\in V_{2_s}$, and (2) for every action $g\in\Gamma_1$, $\sigma_\alpha(D_1(g))\subseteq D_2(\sigma_\gamma(g))$. Program signatures and morphisms constitute a category *SIG*. ∎

Signature morphisms define translations between the languages associated with each signature in the obvious way:

Definition 2.8: Given a signature morphism σ: $\theta_1 \rightarrow \theta_2$,

$$\sigma(t) ::= \sigma(a) \mid c \mid f(\sigma(t),\ldots,\sigma(t))$$

$$\sigma(\phi) ::= \sigma(t_1)=\sigma(t_2) \mid \sigma(\phi_1)\supset\sigma(\phi_2) \mid \sigma(\phi_1)\vee\sigma(\phi_2) \mid \sigma(\phi_1)\wedge\sigma(\phi_2) \mid \neg\sigma(\phi)$$ ∎

Definition/Proposition 2.9: A *superposition morphism* $\sigma:(\theta_1,\Delta_1)\rightarrow(\theta_2,\Delta_2)$ is a signature morphism σ: $\theta_1\rightarrow\theta_2$ such that

1. For all $g_1\in\Gamma_1, a_1\in D_1(g_1), \models_{\theta_2} B_2(\sigma(g_1)) \supset \sigma(F_1(g_1,a_1))=F_2(\sigma(g_1),\sigma(a_1))$.
2. $\models_{\theta_2} (I_2 \supset \sigma(I_1))$.
3. For every $g_1\in\Gamma_1$, $\models_{\theta_2} (B_2(\sigma(g_1)) \supset \sigma(B_1(g_1)))$.
4. For every $a_1\in V_1$, $D_2(\sigma(a_1))\subseteq\sigma(D_1(a_1))$.

Programs and superposition morphisms constitute a category *PROG*. ∎

Given a signature θ, we denote by $\models_\theta$ the extension of the consequence relation of the first-order logic over the language of the data types and attributes with the axioms DT of the data types.

Requirements 1 and 2 correspond to the preservation of the functionality of the base program: (1) the effects of the instructions are preserved and (2) so are the initialisation conditions. Requirement 3 allows guards to be strengthened but not to be weakened. Requirement 4 corresponds to a locality condition: new actions cannot be added to the domains of attributes of the source program. That is to say, no new actions can change the old attributes. Together with the fact that signature morphisms preserve the domains of actions, it implies that the domains of the attributes remain the same up to translation, i.e. $D_2(\sigma(a_1))=\sigma(D_1(a_1))$ for every $a_1\in V_1$. (This formalises a key ingredient of program structure and encapsulation. See (Fiadeiro and Maibaum, 1992, 1995, 1996).)

We shall now describe how complex programs can be put together from components in much the same way as we did for specifications:

Proposition 2.10: The category *PROG* is finitely cocomplete. ∎

The proof of this result can be found in (Fiadeiro and Maibaum, 1996). Basically, pushouts work as follows:

- actions are synchronised according to the rendez-vous points established by the actions of the middle program (channel) and morphisms; the resulting joint actions have the following properties:
  - their domain is the union of the domains of the joined actions;
  - they perform the parallel composition of the assignments of the joined actions;

– if the interconnecting morphisms are injective (which is usually the case), they are guarded by the conjunction of the guards of the joined actions; otherwise, see (Fiadeiro and Maibaum, 1996);

- the initialisation condition of the resulting program is given by the conjunction of the initialisation conditions of the component programs.

As an example, consider the program:

```
program costumer is
var    bal:int
init   bal>0
do     pay: [bal>0 → bal:=bal–1] [] eat: [true → skip]
```

This program models the behaviour of a customer. We are going to interconnect it with *vending machine* using the following channel:

```
program channel is
var
init   true
do     a: [true → skip] [] b: [true → skip]
```

The configuration diagram for the required system is as follows:

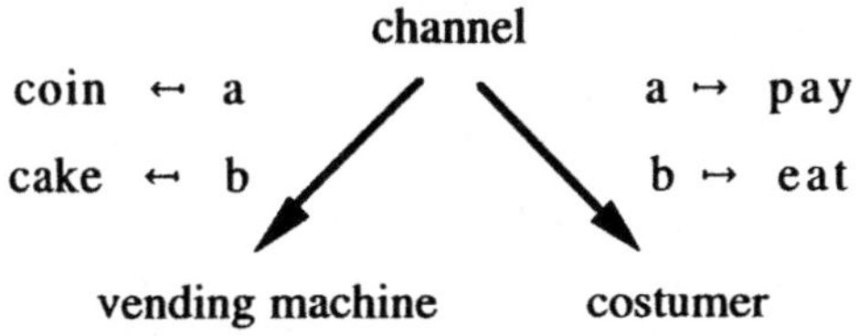

Its pushout is given, up to isomorphism, by

```
program served customer is
var    ready, served_cake, served_cigar:bool, bal:int
init   ready ∧ (served_cake ∨ served_cigar) ∧ bal>0
do     pay_coin : [ready ∧ (served_cake ∨ served_cigar) ∧ bal>0
          → ready:=false || served_cake:=false || served_cigar:=false || bal:=bal-1]
       [] eat_cake : [¬ready ∧ ¬served_cake ∧ ¬served_cigar
                        → served_cake:=true || served_cigar:=false]
       [] cigar: [¬ready ∧ ¬(served_cake ∨ served_cigar)
                        → served_cigar:=true || served_cake:=false]
       [] reset: [¬ready ∧ (served_cake ∨ served_cigar)
                        → ready:=true]
```

together with (coin↦ pay_coin, cake↦ eat_cake, cigar↦ cigar, reset↦ reset, ready↦ ready, served_cake↦ served_cake, served_cigar↦ served_cigar) and (pay↦ pay_coin, eat↦ eat_cake) as morphisms connecting *vending machine* and *costumer* to *served customer*, respectively.

This program is a simple superposition of *vending machine* – it strengthens the guard of the action *coin* with the guard of *pay* – (bal>0) and enriches its assignment with (bal:=bal–1).

2.3 Relating programs to specifications

In (Fiadeiro and Maibaum, 1995) we have further shown how the satisfaction relation between programs and specifications can be formalised in this setting.

Definition/Proposition 2.11: Every program signature (V,Γ) defines the temporal signature $V\cup\Gamma$. Because V and Γ are disjoint, this mapping extends to a functor, i.e. every morphism of program signatures extends to a morphism of temporal signatures. ∎

Consider now the first-order extension FLTX of the linear temporal logic defined in 2.1 which also includes the operator **X** (next). (See (Fiadeiro and Maibaum, 1992) for details.)

Definition/Proposition 2.12: Given a program (θ,Δ) where $\theta=(V,\Gamma)$ and $\Delta=(I,F,B)$, let $Int((\theta,\Delta))$ be the following set of propositions in the language of $FLTX(V\cup\Gamma)$:

- the proposition (**beg** ⊃ I);
- for every action $g\in\Gamma$, the proposition $(g \supset B(g) \wedge (\bigwedge_{a\in D(g)} \mathbf{X}a=F(g,a)))$;
- for every $a\in V$, the proposition $(\bigvee_{g\in D(a)} g) \vee (\mathbf{X}a=a)$

1. We define $Spec((\theta,\Delta))=(\Gamma,LTL(\Gamma)\cap(Int((\theta,\Delta))\cup DT)^{\bullet})$ where DT is the collection of axioms defining the underlying data type.
2. The mapping *Spec*: $\mathcal{PROG}\rightarrow\mathcal{SPEC}$ extends to a functor. ∎

The propositions in *Int*(P) capture the semantics of P: the first axiom establishes that I is an initialisation condition; the second set of axioms formalises the assignment – if *g* is about to occur, the next value of attribute *a* is the current value of F(g,a) – and establishes B(g) as a necessary condition for the occurrence of *g*; the last set of axioms (the locality axioms) capture locality of attributes: every attribute remains invariant if the next state transition is not performed by an action in its domain.

For instance, *Int*(vending machine) consists of

beg ⊃ ready ∧ (served_cake ∨ served_cigar)
coin ⊃ ready ∧ (served_cake ∨ served_cigar) ∧
  X¬ready ∧ **X**¬served_cake ∧ **X**¬served_cigar
cake ⊃ ¬ready ∧ ¬(served_cake ∨ served_cigar) ∧
  Xserved_cake ∧ **X**¬served_cigar
cigar ⊃ ¬ready ∧ ¬(served_cake ∨ served_cigar) ∧
  X¬served_cake ∧ **X**served_cigar
reset ⊃ ¬ready ∧ (served_cake ∨ served_cigar) ∧ **X**ready
coin ∨ reset ∨ **X**ready=ready
coin ∨ cake ∨ cigar ∨ **X**served_cake=served_cake
coin ∨ cake ∨ cigar ∨ **X**served_cigar=served_cigar

and *Spec*(vending machine) contains all the theorems in the language of {coin,cake,cigar,reset} that can be derived from this set, which can easily be shown to include the axioms of the specification of the vending machine.

Definition 2.13: A *realisation* of a specification S is a pair (σ,P) such that P:*PROG* and σ is a specification morphism S→*Spec*(P), i.e. *Int*(P) ⊨ σ(ϕ) for every ϕ∈S.

∎

Realisations generalise the notion of satisfaction by allowing the program and the specification to be over different signatures. More concretely, the program is allowed to have features that are not relevant to the specification (like the attributes). The morphism from S to *Spec*(P) corresponds to the way in which P realises S, i.e., intuitively, it records the *design decisions* (namely the choice of attributes) that lead from S to P (seen as a design exercise carried out in *SPEC*). Notice that the morphism σ in a realisation (σ,P) of a specification S may be the result of a composition of other morphisms, i.e. of a stepwise refinement process that ends in program P.

The notion of realisation can be extended to (configuration) diagrams:

Definition 2.14: Let *S*: *I*→*SPEC* be a specification diagram and *P*: *I*→*PROG* a program diagram with the same shape. Assume that, for every node i:*I*, $\mathcal{P}_i$ is a realisation of $\mathcal{S}_i$ through a morphism η_i. We say that *P* is a realisation of *S* through $(\eta_i)_{i:I}$ when, for every f:i→j in *I*, $\mathcal{S}_f;\eta_j=\eta_i;Spec(\mathcal{P}_f)$. ∎

The conditions $\mathcal{S}_f;\eta_j=\eta_i;Spec(\mathcal{P}_f)$ require that, in addition to the individual components, the interconnections be realised as well.

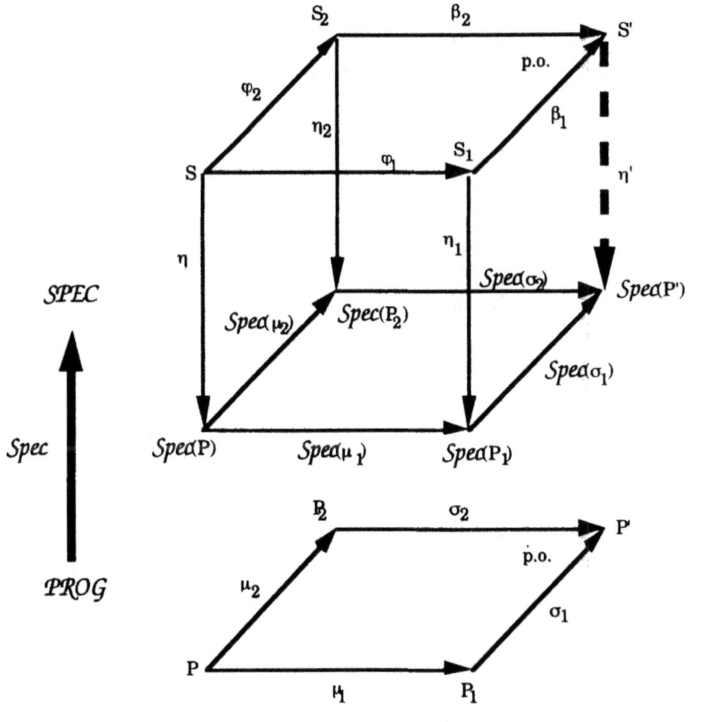

Theorem 2.15: Let $\mathcal{S}: I \to \mathcal{SPEC}$ be a specification diagram and $\mathcal{P}: I \to \mathcal{PROG}$ a program diagram such that $\mathcal{P}$ is a realisation of $\mathcal{S}$ through $(\eta_i)_{i:I}$. Then, the colimit of $\mathcal{P}$ is a realisation of the colimit of $\mathcal{S}$ in an essentially unique way. ∎

The picture in the previous page illustrates this theorem for a simple interconnection diagram. The existence and unicity of the morphism η' is guaranteed by the universal properties of colimits.

We should point out that this theorem holds for any functor *Spec* between categories of programs and of specifications. That is to say, it does not depend on the nature of the program design language (as long as it can be defined as a category) or of the specification logic (as long as it can be defined as an institution).

3 SYNTHESIS IN A CATEGORICAL FRAMEWORK

3.1 Motivation

Consider given a category $\mathcal{PROG}$ of programs and a category $\mathcal{SPEC}$ of specifications together with a functor *Spec*: $\mathcal{PROG} \to \mathcal{SPEC}$ as above. The intended support for the synthesis of interconnections can be explained as follows.

Given realisations of component specifications (either obtained through traditional transformational methods, or synthesised directly from the specifications, or reused from previous developments), we would like to be able to synthesise the interconnections between the programs in such a way that the program diagram realises the specification diagram. That is to say, given specifications S_1 and S_2 (newly) interconnected via morphisms $\varphi_1: S \to S_1$ and $\varphi_2: S \to S_2$, and realisations (σ_1, P_1), (σ_2, P_2) of S_1 and S_2, respectively, one would like to be able to synthesise a realisation (σ, P) of S and morphisms $\mu_1: P \to P_1$ and $\mu_2: P \to P_2$ such that $\sigma; \mathit{Spec}(\mu_i) = \varphi_i; \sigma_i$ $(i=1,2)$.

As mentioned in the introduction, synthesis of interconnections appears to be a straightforward way of extending existing methods for calculating programs from specifications, and synthesis methods in particular, to composite systems. The idea is that the individual components are calculated/synthesised using traditional methods, after which the interconnections between them are synthesised.

Another motivation is the ability to support incremental development in the sense that the addition of a component to a system should not require the recalculation (or the resynthesis) of the whole system but only of the new component and its interconnections to the previous system.

In order to illustrate these points, consider the system consisting of the vending machine and the regulator as specified in section 2.1. In section 2.2, we provided a realisation of the specification of the vending machine. We would now like to use the synthesis method of (Manna and Wolper, 1984) to realise the specification of the regulator and, then, synthesise the interconnections between the two programs in order to obtain a realisation of the specification diagram.

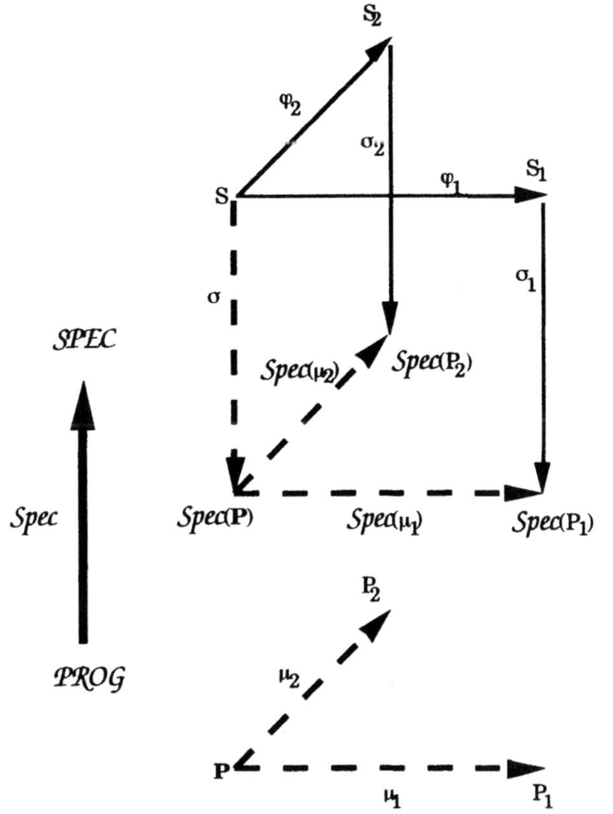

The application of the synthesis method to the formula **G**(trigger ⊃ **G**¬action)* returns the following automaton where the state on the left corresponds to the satisfiability of {**G**(trigger ⊃ **G**¬action)} and the state on the right to the satisfiability of {**G**¬action}:

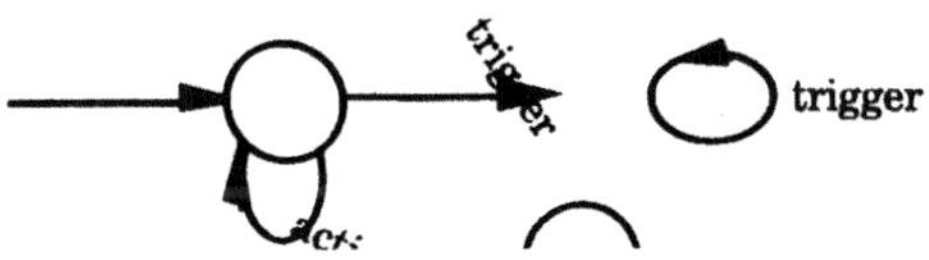

This automaton is easily formalised as a COMMUNITY program: the two states are modelled through the values of an attribute *state*; the guards and assignments are translated directly from the automaton.

* The formula is prefixed with **G** because the procedure used in (Manna and Wolper, 1984) is based on an anchored version of temporal logic whereas the axioms of a specification express requirements that have to hold in every state of the component.

program regulator **is**
var state:[1,2]
init state=1
do trigger: [true → state:=2] [] action: [state=1 → *skip*]

It remains to synthesise the interconnections between this program and the vending machine program. This is the problem that we are going to address in the rest of the paper.

3.2 Synthesising morphisms

The general statement of what it means to synthesise interconnections makes it clear that it is both necessary to synthesise the middle program (the "channel") and the morphisms** that are required to interconnect the given programs. Because, in the general case, any object can be used in an interconnection, this suggests, rather obviously, that a functor $\mathcal{Syn}: \mathcal{SPEC} \rightarrow \mathcal{PROG}$ is required. The properties that a functor is required to satisfy on identities and composition of morphisms make enough sense to be accepted without any discussion.

The fact that we now have a functor implies that we have a way of associating a program with every specification. That is to say, we now have an implicit way of synthesising programs from specifications. In particular, given a specification diagram $\mathcal{S}: I \rightarrow \mathcal{SPEC}$, the functor $\mathcal{Syn}$ generates (synthesises), by composition, a program diagram $\mathcal{P}=\mathcal{S};\mathcal{Syn}: I \rightarrow \mathcal{PROG}$. Because nothing can be assumed about the algorithmic nature of this association, $\mathcal{Syn}$ can also be interpreted as the result of some choices made among the possible transformations that a particular method provides for calculating programs from specifications.

More than programs, synthesis must return realisations. That is to say, $\mathcal{Syn}(S)$ must be provided together with a morphism $\eta_S: S \rightarrow \mathcal{Spec}(\mathcal{Syn}(S))$. The existence of η_S also expresses the correctness criterion for $\mathcal{Syn}$. Moreover, $\mathcal{Syn}$ must respect the interconnections in the following sense: given a specification diagram $\mathcal{S}: I \rightarrow \mathcal{SPEC}$, it is necessary that the program diagram $\mathcal{P}=\mathcal{S};\mathcal{Syn}$ be a realisation of $\mathcal{S}$ through $(\eta_{\mathcal{S}_i})_{i:I}$ as defined in 2.14, i.e. we must have, for every arrow f:i→j in I, $\mathcal{S}_f;\eta_{\mathcal{S}_j}=\eta_{\mathcal{S}_i};\mathcal{Spec}(\mathcal{P}_f)$.

But these are the ingredients that define a natural transformation. Hence, $\mathcal{Syn}$ must be provided together with a natural transformation $\eta: 1_{\mathcal{SPEC}} \rightarrow \mathcal{Syn};\mathcal{Spec}$.

As motivated in the case of the vending machine and the regulator, the ability to reuse an existing system when adding a component to it should also be supported, i.e. synthesis should be able to be integrated into an incremental development process. That is to say, given a configuration diagram

** Note that synthesising morphisms has already attracted some attention in the literature in the context of the KIDS system where the focus is on transforming (first-order) specifications into efficient algorithms (Smith, 1990, 1993). See also (Dimitrakos, 1996) for further development of these ideas.

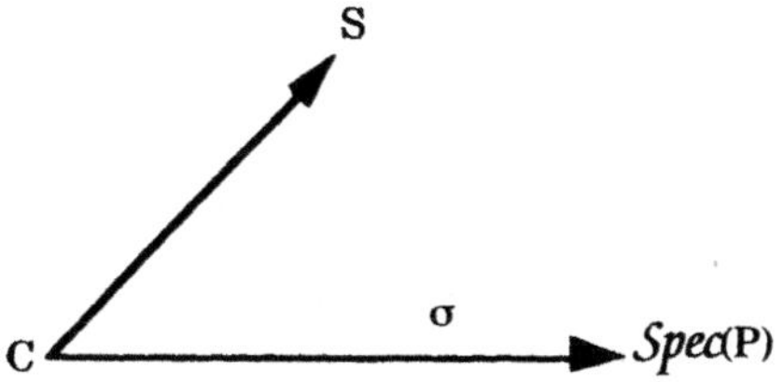

where P represents the existing system (e.g. the program *vending machine*) and S the specification of the component that is to be added (e.g. the regulator), we should be able to synthesise an interconnection between P and any program that realises S. This means that, given $\sigma{:}C \rightarrow \mathit{Spec}(P)$ we should be able to synthesise $\sigma'{:}\mathit{Syn}(C) \rightarrow P$ in such a way that the interconnection is respected, i.e. $\sigma = \eta_C;\mathit{Spec}(\sigma')$. This is equivalent to defining a (natural) bijection between the morphisms $C \rightarrow \mathit{Spec}(P)$ and the morphisms $\mathit{Syn}(C) \rightarrow P$. But this is, precisely, the property that characterises the existence of an adjunction from $\mathcal{SPEC}$ to $\mathcal{PROG}$ (MacLane, 1971). Hence:

Thesis 3.1: Given a category $\mathcal{PROG}$ of programs and a category $\mathcal{SPEC}$ of specifications together with a functor $\mathit{Spec}{:}\ \mathcal{PROG} \rightarrow \mathcal{SPEC}$, synthesis of interconnections is characterised by the existence of a left adjoint of *Spec* (which we call *Syn*). ∎

Notice that the counit of the adjunction $\varepsilon_P{:}\mathit{Syn}(\mathit{Spec}(P)) \rightarrow P$ is not necessarily an isomorphism because *Spec*(P) may not be powerful enough to fully characterise P (we cannot guarantee that the specification domain is expressive enough to capture the semantics of P in full). The direction of the morphism reflects the fact that if we synthesise from the strongest specification of a program P, we obtain a program that cannot be stronger than P. Hence, the morphism ε_P provides a sort of "universal adaptor" between the program synthesised from *Spec*(P) and P itself.

The existence of a left adjoint to the functor $\mathit{Spec}{:}\ \mathcal{PROG} \rightarrow \mathcal{SPEC}$ is quite a strong property, which is not surprising because the ability to synthesise any specification is itself, in intuitive terms, a very strong property. In the literature, examples of synthesis from temporal logic specifications can be found, both from propositional linear temporal logic as above (Manna and Wolper, 1984) and from branching time logic (Emerson and Clarke, 1982). These approaches synthesise finite state automata, which are easily implemented as COMMUNITY programs as illustrated in section 3.1.

Difficulties are certain to arise in attempting to generalise these methods to the systems view. On the one hand, the functor *Spec* as defined in section 2.3 does not handle liveness properties. In order to extend this mapping to include liveness, we know that the functorial property is lost (more specifically, program morphisms do not necessarily map to specification morphisms). There are methods for dealing with this situation (Fiadeiro, 1996) but it is not yet clear how they can be combined with synthesis. On the other hand, it is not clear that the way synthesis methods generate states is compatible with the minimality requirements of adjunctions. This is an area of current research.

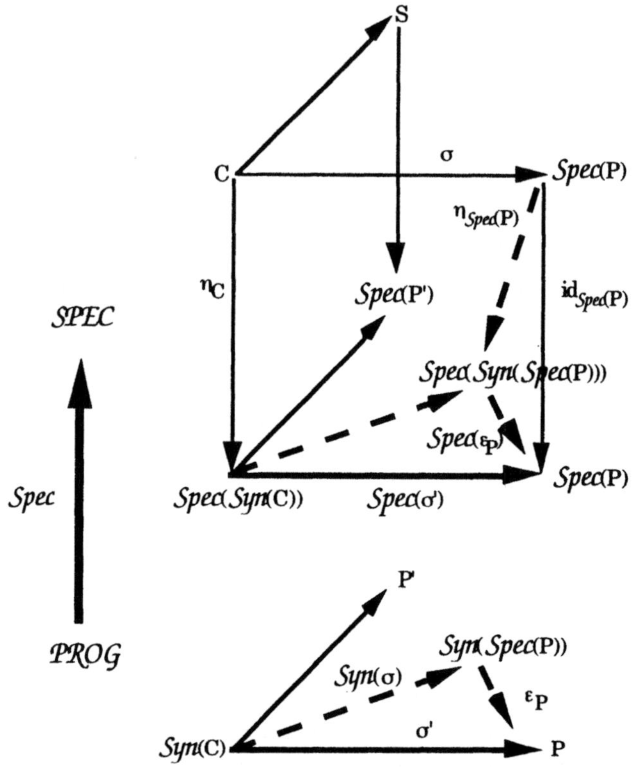

In any case, the limited expressive power of the specification formalisms for which program synthesis has been shown to be possible (for instance, the results on synthesis mentioned above are only valid for propositional logics) means that synthesis of interconnections based on the existence of an adjunction will have little impact on program development. We shall see in the next section that a wide class of specification formalisms allow for a much weaker characterisation of synthesis of interconnections.

3.3 Synthesising channels

The conclusion, suggested by section 3.2, that the ability to synthesise interconnections is difficult to achieve, results from the fact that interconnections were taken to be expressed through arbitrary diagrams. In such cases, because any object can be used as a "channel" in an interconnection, synthesis of arbitrary interconnections requires the ability to synthesise programs from arbitrary specifications and, thus, arbitrary morphisms, which necessitates an adjunction.

However, the very examples used in section 2 suggest that we may explore the notion of interconnection a little further.

We start by recalling that finite cocompleteness – the ability to compute the colimit of every finite diagram – derives from the existence of initial objects and pushouts. We can, therefore, concentrate on pushouts as elementary interconnections.

On the other hand, the example that we used in section 2.1 for illustrating interconnection at the specification level used for channel an empty theory presentation, i.e. just a signature. This makes sense because the axioms of the middle specification (channel) play no role in the computation of the pushout. Indeed, recalling proposition 2.3, the theorems of the resulting specification are computed directly from the axioms of the components. Only the signature of the middle specification has a non redundant role in computing the pushout, namely in establishing the required interconnections.

Hence, it seems that, in circumstances that we have to determine, "channels" constitute just a subclass of the objects, which implies that the synthesis of interconnections only requires that a subclass of the specifications be synthesisable, as well as only the morphisms that have their origin in this subclass, i.e. channels. This is the direction that we are going to explore in the rest of the paper.

The relationship between theories and channels as empty theory presentations is also characterised by the existence of a faithful functor that "forgets" the theorems. In fact, this functor is a right adjoint of the (full) inclusion functor, i.e. channels define a coreflective subcategory. This property allows us to prove that the pushout of any two morphisms σ_1:C→C_1 and σ_2:C→C_2 can be made through a diagram in which the middle object is a channel, i.e. results from an empty theory presentation. Indeed, consider the morphisms $\sigma'_i=\varepsilon_C;\sigma_i$ where ε_C is the counit of the coreflection. Let μ_i:C_i→C' be a pushout of the σ_i. We prove that μ_i:C_i→C' are also a pushout of the σ'_i.

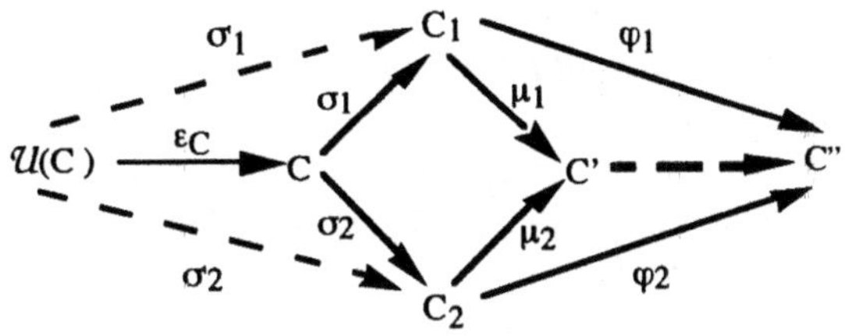

For this purpose, let φ_i:C_i→C" be s.t. $\sigma'_1;\varphi_1=\sigma'_2;\varphi_2$, i.e. $\varepsilon_C;\sigma_1;\varphi_1=\varepsilon_C;\sigma_2;\varphi_2$. Because, when the right adjoint is faithful, each counit is an epi (MacLane, 1971), we obtain $\sigma_1;\varphi_1=\sigma_2;\varphi_2$. The result then follows from the fact that the μ_i:C_i→C' are a pushout of the σ_i.

The straightforward generalisation of the case in which channels are a coreflective subcategory of the category of components is the existence of a full embedding $\mathcal{F}$: $\mathcal{X}\to\mathcal{C}$ from a category $\mathcal{X}$ of channels to a category $\mathcal{C}$ of components that admits a right adjoint $\mathcal{U}$. This is what happens if we take channels to be signatures instead of empty theory presentations. This also corresponds to the notion of coreflection used in (Sassone et al, 1993) for models of concurrency.

Definition 3.2: A category $\mathcal{C}$ is said to be *coordinated over* a category $\mathcal{X}$ iff it admits a faithful coreflector $\mathcal{U}:\mathcal{C}\rightarrow\mathcal{X}$, i.e. a faithful, right adjoint functor $\mathcal{U}$ for which the units are identities. ▮

Notice that, in those conditions, the left adjoint is a full embedding (MacLane, 1971).

Theorem 3.3: Let $\mathcal{C}$ be a category coordinated over $\mathcal{X}$ and $\mathcal{F}$ be the left adjoint. Then, any interconnection between objects of $\mathcal{C}$ can be made through a diagram of the form

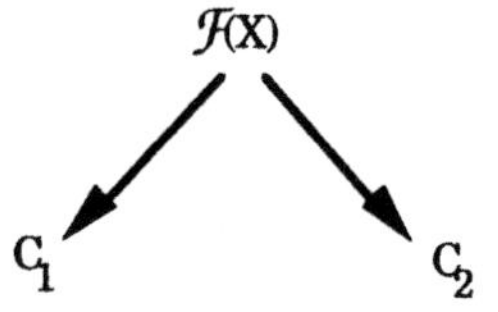

where X is an object of $\mathcal{X}$. ▮

This theorem means that the category $\mathcal{X}$ provides the *channels* through which any interconnection between objects of $\mathcal{C}$ can be established.

The ability to provide such a clean separation between individual components and their interaction is typical of coordination models and languages (Ciancarini and Hankin, 1996). Hence, the use of the adjective *coordinated* to characterise such situations.

Hence, it seems that, for the purpose of synthesising interconnections in coordinated specification formalisms, all that we are required is to synthesise from objects of the form $\mathcal{F}(X)$ and morphisms of the form $\mathcal{F}(X)\rightarrow S$. The following theorem proves it:

Theorem 3.4: Let $\mathcal{PROG}$ and $\mathcal{SPEC}$ be two categories together with a functor *Spec*: $\mathcal{PROG}\rightarrow\mathcal{SPEC}$ such that

1. $\mathcal{SPEC}$ is coordinated over a category $\mathcal{X}$ with coreflector $\mathcal{U}$ and embedding $\mathcal{F}$;
2. $\mathcal{PROG}$ admits a right adjoint $\mathcal{V}:\mathcal{PROG}\rightarrow\mathcal{X}$ with left adjoint $\mathcal{G}$;
3. *Spec*;$\mathcal{U}=\mathcal{V}$ and $\mathcal{G}$;*Spec*$=\mathcal{F}$.

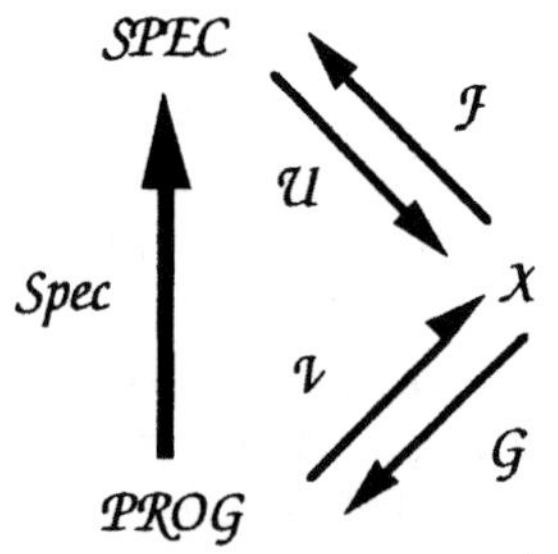

Then, given objects S_1 and S_2 of $\mathcal{SPEC}$ interconnected via morphisms $\varphi_1:\mathcal{F}(X)\rightarrow S_1$ and $\varphi_2:\mathcal{F}(X)\rightarrow S_2$, and realisations (σ_1,P_1), (σ_2,P_2) of S_1 and S_2, respectively, we can synthesise an interconnection $\mu_1:Y\rightarrow P_1$ and $\mu_2:Y\rightarrow P_2$ that realises (φ_1,φ_2) as follows:

– Y is $\mathcal{G}(X)$, which realises $\mathcal{F}(X)$ through the identity morphism;

– $\mu_i = \mathcal{G}(\mathcal{U}(\varphi_i;\sigma_i));\varepsilon_{P_i}$ where ε is the counit of the adjunction between $\mathcal{G}$ and $\mathcal{V}$.

proof:

- from 3, $Spec(\mathcal{G}(X))=\mathcal{F}(X)$, hence $\mathcal{G}(X)$ does realise $\mathcal{F}(X)$ through the identity;
- $\varphi_i;\sigma_i: \mathcal{F}(X)\rightarrow Spec(P_i)$, so $\mathcal{U}(\varphi_i;\sigma_i)$: $\mathcal{U}(\mathcal{F}(X))\rightarrow \mathcal{U}(Spec(P_i))$;
  but $\mathcal{U}(\mathcal{F}(X))=X$ and $\mathcal{U}(Spec(P_i))=\mathcal{V}(P_i)$, so $\mathcal{U}(\varphi_i;\sigma_i)$): $X\rightarrow\mathcal{V}(P_i)$ which implies

  $\mathcal{G}(\mathcal{U}(\varphi_i;\sigma_i));\varepsilon_{P_i}$: $\mathcal{G}(X)\rightarrow P_i$
- it remains to prove that the interconnections are respected, i.e. $Spec(\mu_i)=\varphi_i;\sigma_i$;
  but $Spec(\mu_i) = Spec(\mathcal{G}(\mathcal{U}(\varphi_i;\sigma_i)));Spec(\varepsilon_{P_i}) = \mathcal{F}(\mathcal{U}(\varphi_i;\sigma_i));Spec(\varepsilon_{P_i})$;
  this implies $\mathcal{U}(Spec(\mu_i)) = \mathcal{U}(\mathcal{F}(\mathcal{U}(\varphi_i;\sigma_i)));\mathcal{U}(Spec(\varepsilon_{P_i})) = \mathcal{U}(\varphi_i;\sigma_i);\mathcal{V}(\varepsilon_{P_i})$;
  the equations in 3 imply that the units of the adjunction between $\mathcal{G}$ and $\mathcal{V}$ are also identities, which in turn implies that $\mathcal{V}(\varepsilon_{P_i})$=id;
  hence, $\mathcal{U}(Spec(\mu_i))=\mathcal{U}(\varphi_i;\sigma_i)$;

because $\mathcal{U}$ is faithful, we obtain $Spec(\mu_i)=\varphi_i;\sigma_i$. ∎

Notice that, in the conditions of this theorem, *Spec* does not need to be right adjoint and, hence, this theorem covers more situations than thesis 3.1. In order to get a clearer view of the relationship between theorem 3.4 and the characterisation given in 3.1, consider the following corollary:

Corollary 3.5: Let $\mathcal{PROG}$ and $\mathcal{SPEC}$ be two coordinated categories with coreflectors $\mathcal{U}$:$\mathcal{SPEC}\rightarrow\mathcal{X}$ (with embedding $\mathcal{F}$) and $\mathcal{V}$:$\mathcal{PROG}\rightarrow\mathcal{Y}$ (with embedding $\mathcal{G}$). Let *Spec*: $\mathcal{PROG}\rightarrow\mathcal{SPEC}$ and *Chan*: $\mathcal{Y}\rightarrow\mathcal{X}$ be functors such that $Spec;\mathcal{U}=\mathcal{V};Chan$. Then, if *Chan* admits a left adjoint $\mathcal{H}$ such that $\mathcal{H};\mathcal{G};Spec=\mathcal{F}$, we can synthesise interconnections in the sense of theorem 3.4. ∎

This corollary simply means that, in order to be able to synthesise interconnections between coordinated formalisms, it is sufficient to have an adjunction between the two categories of channels involved. Naturally, this case covers thesis 3.1 in the trivial case when both $\mathcal{PROG}$ and $\mathcal{SPEC}$ are taken to be coordinated over themselves. Notice that theorem 3.4 is also recovered from 3.5 in the trivial case in which $\mathcal{PROG}$ is taken to be coordinated over itself. However, we should stress that, in theorem 3.4, $\mathcal{PROG}$ is not necessarily coordinated over $\mathcal{X}$: although the equations make $\mathcal{V}$ a coreflector, it does not have to be faithful, meaning that $\mathcal{X}$ does not have to cover all possible interconnections in $\mathcal{PROG}$.

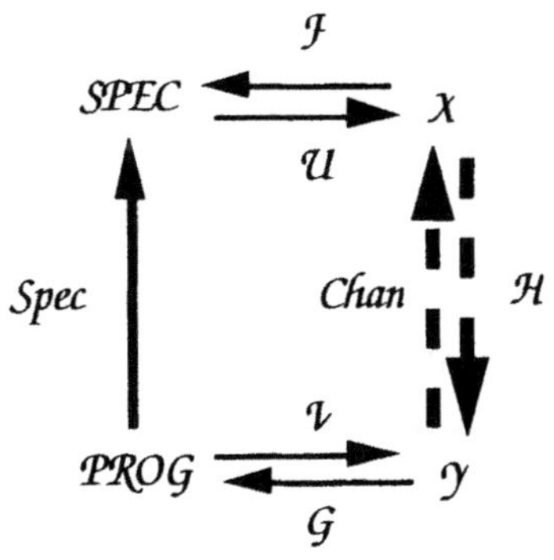

It remains to discuss the applicability of these results.

Proposition 3.6: Let $\mathcal{SPEC}$ be the category of theories of an institution. Then, $\mathcal{SPEC}$ is coordinated over the underlying category $\mathcal{SIGN}$ of signatures. ∎

That is to say, any specification formalism that results from an institution satisfies the requirements of theorem 3.4.

Concerning the conditions on the "programming" category, general results cannot be given in the sense that there is not a notion which, like institutions, abstracts away from program design languages. Hence, we have to analyse each case individually, which we will illustrate using the category of COMMUNITY programs defined in section 2.2.

Proposition 3.7: The category $\mathcal{PROG}$ of COMMUNITY programs admits a right adjoint $\mathcal{V}:\mathcal{PROG}\rightarrow\mathcal{SET}$ that maps every program to the set of its actions.
proof: consider the mapping $\mathcal{G}$ that, to every set Γ, assigns the empty program over the
signature $(\emptyset,\Gamma)$, i.e. $\mathcal{G}(\Gamma)$ ≡ *var* $\emptyset$
init true
do $\|_{g\in\Gamma}$ g: [true → *skip*]

It is easy to see that $\mathcal{G}$ extends to a functor. We are going to prove that $\mathcal{G}$ is a left adjoint of $\mathcal{V}$. Let Γ be any set. Because $\mathcal{V}(\mathcal{G}(\Gamma))=\Gamma$, we can take identities for units. Hence, it remains to prove that, for any program P, if $\sigma:\Gamma\rightarrow\mathcal{V}(P)$ is a total function, then σ defines a morphism $\mathcal{G}(\Gamma)\rightarrow P$. It is clear that σ defines a signature morphism between the two programs because the signature of $\mathcal{G}(\Gamma)$ contains no attributes. On the other hand, all the conditions for a signature morphism to be a program morphism are met: the initialisation and the guards are universal, and the fact that there are no attributes implies that there is nothing else to prove. ∎

Proposition 3.8: Linear temporal logic and COMMUNITY support synthesis of interconnections.
proof: in order to apply theorem 3.4, and using 3.6 and 3.7, it remains to prove conditions 3. But these are easily checked once we notice that $\mathcal{S}pec$ projects every program signature to the corresponding set of actions. On the other hand, at the semantic level, it is easy to see that $\mathcal{G}(\Gamma)$ only generates tautologies. ∎

Notice that linear temporal logic and COMMUNITY do not illustrate corollary 3.5: the functor $\mathcal{V}$ defined in 3.7 is not faithful and, hence, $\mathcal{PROG}$ is not coordinated over temporal signatures. Indeed, it is simple to see that actions alone cannot be used as channels for programs – attributes are needed as well. We can extend COMMUNITY to a formalism coordinated over program signatures, for which it is trivial to obtain an adjunction wrt temporal signatures. This extension is, however, outside the scope of this paper.

We can now use theorem 3.4 to synthesise the interconnections between the program *vending machine* and the program *regulator* synthesised using Manna and Wolper's methods from the specification given in section 2.1.

According to 3.4, the program synthesised from the specification

specification channel **is**
sign a, b
axioms

is

program channel **is**
var
init true
do a: [true → *skip*] [] b: [true → *skip*]

and the synthesised morphisms are

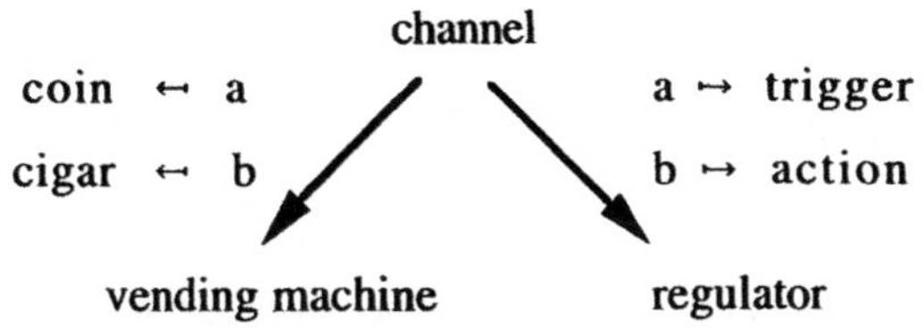

Notice that the pushout of this diagram returns the program:

program regulated vending machine **is**
var ready, served_cake, served_cigar:bool; state:[1,2]
init ready ∧ (served_cake ∨ served_cigar) ∧ state=1
do coin : [ready ∧ (served_cake ∨ served_cigar)
→ ready:=false || served_cake:=false || served_cigar:=false || state:=2]
[] cake : [¬ready ∧ ¬(served_cake ∨ served_cigar)
→ served_cake:=true || served_cigar:=false]
[] cigar: [state=1 ∧ ¬ready ∧ ¬(served_cake ∨ served_cigar)
→ served_cigar:=true || served_cake:=false]
[] reset: [¬ready ∧ (served_cake ∨ served_cigar)
→ ready:=true]

which strengthens the guard of the action *cigar* with the guard of *action* – (state=1). Hence, this action will never be undertaken after *coin* occurs.

4 CONCLUDING REMARKS

We addressed the problem of synthesising interconnections in the development of systems of interacting components. The main motivation for this study has been the integration of calculation methods in general, and synthesis in particular, within an incremental and reuse-based approach to system development. In the context of such development disciplines, it is essential to be able to synthesise the interconnections that are required for extending an existing system with new components from the interconnections provided at the specification level, so that the system does not need to be recalculated or resynthesised each time it needs to be extended.

In order to address the problem independently of specific specification and program design languages, we chose to work within a categorical framework in the spirit of Goguen's approach to General Systems Theory. In the adopted framework, components are modelled as objects, and complex systems are modelled as diagrams that depict the way in which the components of the system are interconnected. The morphisms of the different categories are used to express interconnections.

We showed that the ability to synthesise interconnections in such a general framework depends on the existence of a left adjoint to the functor that maps every program to its "strongest" specification. Because the existence of an adjunction is quite a restrictive condition, certainly for more expressive specification formalisms, we searched for weaker conditions based on stronger structural properties of the individual formalisms.

We showed that if the specification formalism is coordinated over a category of channels, a concept that we introduced for the first time in this paper and which reflects the properties of an emerging class of languages and models (Ciancarini and Hankin, 1996), then any interconnection can be synthesised provided that an adjunction can be found between the categories of programs and of channels. In the case where the two formalisms involved are coordinated over corresponding categories of channels, this amounts to the existence of an adjunction between the two categories of channels (specification and program channels), which is a much weaker requirement than the existence of an adjunction between the formalisms themselves.

Because every specification formalism that results from an institution is coordinated over the category of signatures, this result seems to have a wide application. On the program side, we showed that although the category of COMMUNITY programs is not coordinated, it admits an adjunction wrt the category of temporal signatures and, hence, supports the synthesis of interconnections. COMMUNITY is a language for parallel program design similar to UNITY (Chandy and Misra, 1988) and IP (Francez and Forman, 1996), which shows that our result is at least applicable to reactive system development in this class of languages. In this respect, we also discussed how existing methods for the calculation of programs from specifications, such as the synthesis methods proposed in (Emerson and Clarke, 1982, Manna and Wolper, 1984), can be combined with the proposed techniques for synthesising interconnections.

An obvious question to consider is the extent to which these ideas can be realised in practical software development environments. We are aware of several strands of work which are based on similar principles or which could be extended to realise these techniques. The work at Kestrel Institute on the Specware™ environment (Srinivas and Jüllig, 1995) (an extension of the earlier KIDS ideas (Smith, 1990)) is based on the use of category theory as a framework for representing and analysing specification and program structure. We are also aware of a project at the Laboratório de Métodos Formais at PUC in Rio de Janeiro, where Armando Haeberer is building a software development environment to support object-oriented design using ideas related to those outlined above as the semantic basis for formalising object-oriented methods.

Acknowledgements

We would like to thank the anonymous referees for many enlightening comments which, we are sure, have helped to clarify the messages in the paper.

This work was partially supported by the Esprit WG 8319 (MODELAGE), JNICT through contract PRAXIS XXI 2/2.1/MAT/46/94 (ESCOLA) and PCSH/OGE/1038/95 (MAGO), and the EPSRC through contracts GR/K67331 and GR/K68783.

5 REFERENCES

Abadi, M. and Lamport, L. (1993) Composing Specifications. *ACM Transactions on Programming Languages and Systems* **15**(1), 73-132.

Back, R. and Kurki-Suonio, R. (1988) Distributed Cooperation with Action Systems. *ACM Transactions on Programming Languages and Systems* **10**(4), 513-554.

Ciancarini, P. and Hankin, C. (1996), *Coordination Languages and Models*, in LNCS 1061, Springer-Verlag.

Chandy, K. and Misra, J. (1988), *Parallel Program Design - A Foundation*. Addison-Wesley.

Dimitrakos, T. (1996), *The Implementation of **PO**-specifications*, Research Report, Imperial College.

Ehrig, H. and Mahr, B. (1985), *Fundamentals of Algebraic Specification 1: Equations and Initial Semantics*. Springer-Verlag.

Emerson, E. and Clarke, E. (1982), Using Branching Time Logic to Synthesize Synchronisation Skeletons. *Science of Computer Programming* **2**, 241-266.

Feather, M. (1987), Language Support for the Specification and Development of Composite Systems. *ACM Transactions on Programming Languages and Systems* **9**(2), 198-234.

Feather, M. (1989) Constructing Specifications by Combining Parallel Elaborations. *IEEE Transactions on Software Engineering***15**(2), 198-208.

Fiadeiro, J. (1996) On the Emergence of Properties in Component-Based Systems, in M.Wirsing and M.Nivat (eds) *AMAST'96*, LNCS 1101, Springer-Verlag, 421-443.

Fiadeiro, J. and Maibaum, T. (1992) Temporal Theories as Modularisation Units for Concurrent System Specification. *Formal Aspects of Computing* **4**(3), 1992, 239-272.

Fiadeiro, J. and Maibaum, T. (1995) Interrconnecting Formalisms: supporting modularity, reuse and incrementality, in G.E.Kaiser (ed) *Proc. 3rd Symp. on Foundations of Software Engineering*, ACM Press, 72-80.

Fiadeiro, J. and Maibaum, T. (1996) Categorical Semantics of Parallel Program Design. *Science of Computer Programming*, in print.

Fickas, S. and Helm, B. (1992), Knowledge Representation and Reasoning in the Design of Composite Systems. *IEEE Transactions on Software Engineering* **18**(6), 470-482.

Francez, N. and Forman, I. (1996), *Interacting Processes*. Addison-Wesley.

Goguen, J. (1973), Categorical Foundations for General Systems Theory, in F.Pichler and R.Trappl (eds) *Advances in Cybernetics and Systems Research*, Transcripta Books, 121-130.

Goguen, J. and Burstall, R. (1992), Institutions: Abstract Model Theory for Specification and Programming. *Journal of the ACM* **39**(1), 95-146.

Goguen, J. and Ginali, S. (1978) A Categorical Approach to General Systems Theory, in G.Klir (ed) *Applied General Systems Research*, Plenum, 257-270.

Goldblatt, R. (1987) *Logics of Time and Computation*. CSLI.

MacLane, S. (1971) *Category Theory for the Working Mathematician*. Springer-Verlag.

Manna, Z. and Wolper, P. (1984) Synthesis of Communicating Processes from Temporal Logic Specifications. *ACM Transactions on Programming Languages and Systems* **6**(1), 68-93.

Sassone, V., Nielsen, M. and Winskel, G. (1993), A Classification of Models for Concurrency, in E.Best (ed) *CONCUR'93*, LNCS 715, Springer-Verlag, 82-96.

Shaw, M. and Garlan, D. (1995), Formulations and Formalisms in Software Architectures, in J.Leeuwen (ed) *Computer Science Today*, LNCS 1000, Springer-Verlag, 307-323.

Smith, D. (1990), KIDS – a Semi-Automatic Program Development System. *IEEE Transactions on Software Engineering* **16** (9), 1024-1043.

Smith, D. (1993) Constructing Specification Morphisms. *Journal of Symbolic Computation* **15** (5-6), 571-606.

Srinivas, Y. and Jüllig, R. (1995), Specware™ : Formal Support for Composing Software, in B.Möller (ed) *Mathematics of Program Construction*, LNCS 947, Springer-Verlag.

BIOGRAPHY

José Luiz Fiadeiro is Associate Professor in Computing Science at the University of Lisbon. His research interests include software specification formalisms and methods, especially as applied to component-based, reactive systems, and their integration in the wider area of General Systems Theory.

Antónia Lopes is Assistant Lecturer at the University of Lisbon. She received an MSc degree in Applied Mathematics from the Technical University of Lisbon (1993) and she is now working towards a PhD on compositionality in the modular specification of reactive systems.

Tom Maibaum is Professor and Head of the Computing Department of Imperial College. His research interests are in formal methods for software engineering, including theories of specification and implementation, object-oriented systems, and non-classical logics in Computing.

A Powerful Transformation Rule, its Applications and Variants

Klaus Achatz and Helmuth Partsch
Department of Computer Science, University of Ulm,
89069 Ulm, Germany
E-mail: {achatz,partsch}@informatik.uni-ulm.de,
Tel: +49 731 502-4161, Fax: -4162

Abstract
This paper introduces, discusses and proves a transformation rule to convert specifications of set-valued functions defined by set comprehension into functional implementations. The power of the rule is illustrated by several examples, among them a Prolog interpreter. Also, variants of the rule for specifications involving existential quantification and arbitrary choice are presented and illustrated by representative examples.

Keywords
Transformational programming, backtracking, set comprehension, functional implemention

1 INTRODUCTION

Transformational programming is short for a methodology of constructing programs from formal problem specifications by stepwise application of formal, semantics-preserving transformation rules. In the following the reader is assumed to be basically familiar with the idea of transformational programming and its basic principles. A brief introduction and an overview can be found, e.g., in (Bauer et al., 1989) or (Boiten et al., 1992). For a comprehensive treatment of the subject, cf. (Partsch, 1990).

In this paper we mainly introduce a powerful transformation rule to convert specifications of set-valued functions defined by set comprehension into executable functional implementations.

The general form of such a specification reads

$f(X)$ **where**
  f: **m** $\rightarrow$ **set of n**
  $f(x) =_{def} \{y\text{: } \mathbf{n} \mid Q(x, y)\}$.

It asks for computing the value of a function f for some initial argument value X of type **m**, where f computes the set of all y of type **n** such that the argument of f and y are related by some predicate Q.

Example:
A typical instance of such a specification is provided by the N-Queens problem which asks for finding all ways to place N mutually non-attacking queens on an $N \times N$ chessboard:

$$\begin{array}{l} \mathit{queens}(N)\ \textbf{where} \\ \quad \mathit{queens}\text{: } \textbf{nat} \rightarrow \textbf{set of nsequ} \\ \quad \mathit{queens}(n) =_{\text{def}} \{\mathit{sp}\text{: } \textbf{nsequ} \mid \#\mathit{sp} = n \wedge \mathit{isposseq u}(\mathit{sp}, n) \wedge \mathit{nconf}(\mathit{sp})\}. \end{array}$$

Here

$$\textbf{nsequ} =_{\text{def}} \textbf{sequ of nat}$$

is the type of sequences of natural numbers used to represent positions of queens in the different columns of the chessboard;

$$\#sp = n$$

checks whether the length of sequence sp is equal to n;

$$\begin{array}{l} \mathit{isposseq u}\text{: } \textbf{nsequ} \times \textbf{nat} \rightarrow \textbf{bool} \\ \mathit{isposseq u}(s, n) =_{\text{def}} \forall\ i\text{: } \textbf{nat} \mid 1 \le i \le \#s \ \Delta\ s[i] \le n \end{array}$$

restricts the elements of **nsequ** to those less or equal to n, and

$$\begin{array}{l} \mathit{nconf}\text{: } \textbf{nsequ} \rightarrow \textbf{bool} \\ \mathit{nconf}(s) =_{\text{def}} \forall\ (i, j\text{: } \textbf{nat} \mid 1 \le i, j \le \#s \wedge i \ne j) \mid \\ \qquad\qquad s[i] \ne s[j] \wedge \textbf{abs}(s[i] - s[j]) \ne \textbf{abs}(i - j) \end{array}$$

guarantees that all positions in the different columns are "nonattacking", i.e., do not mutually occupy the same row or the same diagonal.

The rule we will present deals with the above kind of specifications and can be profitably used for all kinds of problems that ask for a set of complex objects that may somehow be built up incrementally, possibly involving backtracking. The rule emerged when dealing with a formal derivation of a Prolog interpreter from a descriptive specification. It turned out that most transformation steps in this concrete exercise were independent of the particular problem and that the remaining ones could be abstracted appropriately. Meanwhile, the rule has been successfully applied to numerous non-trivial examples, some of which are presented in this paper. More examples and a detailed treatment of those presented here can be found in (Achatz, Partsch, 1996).

1.1 Notational conventions

Within our rules and examples, we use the following notational conventions.

1.1.1 Fonts

Italic is used for all bound variables. Scheme parameters (for expressions in rules) are denoted by upright-uppercase letters (augmented with "arguments" to indicate potential dependencies). And for types (and type variables) we employ boldface-lowercase symbols.

1.1.2 Data types

Type variables (in program schemes) are denoted by single boldface letters (such as **m** or **n**). As basic types, we assume to have available natural numbers (with type **nat** and the usual operations) as well as booleans.

Based on basic types, more complex ones may be built by forming supertypes (e.g., **m** | **n** comprising all elements of types **m** and **n**) and record types (e.g., (*a*: **m**, *b*: **n**) denoting pairs of elements of types **m** and **n** respectively, where *a* and *b* are selectors for the first (second) argument).

More complex types we will use are sets, sequences, and maps. For respective formal definitions in terms of algebraic types we refer to (Partsch, 1990). The intuition of the basic operations of these types (appearing in the examples) is as follows:

sets (typ **set of**) with operations

- $\emptyset$ the empty set
- $\cup$ set union
- $\subseteq$ subset relation
- $\in$ element relation

sequences (type **sequ of**) with operations

- [] the empty sequence
- **hd** (**lst**) first (last) element of a (non-empty) sequence
- **tl** (**fst**) (non-empty) sequence without first (last) element
- ++ concatenation of sequences (also used to append single elements)
- $s[i]$ i-th element of a (non-empty) sequence s
- $\#s$ length of sequence s
- $\in$ element relation

maps (correspondences defined by an algebraic type EMAP, cf. [Partsch 90]) with operations

- $\emptyset$ the empty map
- $\circ$ composition of maps

- *m*[*i*] the "value" of map *m* for "argument" *i*
- *dom* the domain of the map
- *ran* the range of the map
- *m*[*i*] ←*a* map *m* with "value" of *i*-th "argument" updated to *a*.

1.1.3 Programs and program schemes

For programs and program schemes a mainly self-explanatory Pascal-like notation is used with a strict, call-by-value semantics. For a complete definition of the language used, we refer to (Bauer et al., 1985). Some of the less conventional notations (and their meaning) are:

- {*a*: **m** | P(*a*)} set comprehension, denoting the set of all elements *a* (of type **m**) for which P(*a*) holds
- **some** *a*: **m** | P(*a*) (non-deterministic) choice, denoting some element *a* (of type **m**) which satisfies P(*a*)
- (**m** | P(*a*)) subtype of **m**, comprising all elements *a* (of type **m**) which fulfil P(*a*); also used for assertions in the domain of functions
- #{...} cardinality of a set
- Δ (∇) sequential conjunction (disjunction)

As an abbreviation, we omit the type **m** where it is obvious.

1.1.4 Transformation rules

Transformation rules are denoted as $\begin{array}{c} I \\ \Updownarrow \\ O \end{array} [C$ resp. $\begin{array}{c} I \\ \Downarrow \\ O \end{array} [C$.

I is the input scheme of the rule, *O* its output scheme. The double arrow means semantic equivalence, the single arrow descendance. *C* is a set of applicability conditions, all of which are (implicitly) universally quantified clauses (consisting of a premise, ⊢ as an implicational symbol, and a semantic relation over program schemes – equivalence or descendance – as a consequence). Within applicability conditions, ≡ is used to denote semantic equivalence, and ⊆ to denote descendance. If there is no premise, also ⊢ will be left out. The syntactic constraints (following a rule) give sufficient (but not neccessarily minimal) information to infer complete typing of all expressions and functions involved. For details on the logical background of transformation rules, cf. (Partsch, 1990).

To shorten the presentation of the rules we furthermore use the following

General convention

In all transformation rules definedness and determinacy are assumed for all expression symbols and auxiliary functions. Also, all program schemes are supposed to be syntactically valid and context-correct.

1.2 Outline of the following sections

In Sect. 2 we formally develop our central transformation rule, give some intuition on how to use it, and illustrate the essential steps by means of our running example, the N-Queens problem. Section 3 deals with some applications of the rule. In this context, the treatment of the N-Queens problem will be completed by giving all proof obligations that result from instantiating the applicability conditions of our rule and by sketching how to satisfy them. As another example, the problem of a Prolog interpreter is treated in a condensed form. In Sect. 4 some variants of the rule from Sect. 2 are discussed. These variants deal with other specification constructs (such as existential quantification or non-deterministic choice) and are also illustrated by examples (from the area of parsing). As a particular variant we will also show in Sect. 4 that, under additional constraints, our rule from Sect. 2 indeed simplifies to a form one would intuitively expect. Section 5, finally, deals with related work and draws some conclusions.

2 A POWERFUL TRANSFORMATION RULE

In this section, we give a stepwise formal derivation which is based on certain assumptions (called **postulate** below). At the end, the starting point of this formal derivation, the final result, and all assumptions used in the derivation will be compiled into a corresponding transformation rule.

2.1 Derivation of the transformation rule

Our derivation is split up into several phases each of which is given in a calculational style. The single steps of the respective calculations are labelled for later reference. For the details of the basic transformations used in reasoning, we refer the reader to (Partsch, 1990).

The starting point of our derivation is the program scheme

$$
\begin{array}{l}
f(X) \ \textbf{where} \\
\quad f\colon \mathbf{m} \rightarrow \mathbf{set\ of\ n} \\
\quad f(x) =_{\text{def}} \{y\colon \mathbf{n} \mid \mathrm{Q}(x,y)\}.
\end{array}
$$

Obviously, the definition of *queens* as given in Sect. 1 matches this scheme and yields the instantiations

f, X, x, y	**by** *queens, N, n, sp*
$\mathrm{Q}(x, y)$	**by** $\mathrm{Q}(n,sp) \mathrel{\hat=} \#sp = n \wedge ispossequ(sp, n) \wedge nconf(sp)$.

To be able to compute f we require

postulate (0) $(\#\{y\colon \mathbf{n} \mid \mathrm{Q}(x, y)\} < \infty) \equiv \mathbf{true}$

which guarantees the finiteness of the set to be computed.

(a) As a first step, we transform $f(X)$ into $g(X)$ for a suitably defined function g. To this end we define

g: **m** → **set of n**
$g(u) =_{def} g'(u, \mathrm{E}, \emptyset)$

and

g': (u: **m** × v: **r** × s: **set of n** | P(X, u, v)) → **set of n**
$g'(u, v, s) =_{def} s \cup \{y\text{: } \mathbf{n} \mid \mathrm{Q}'(u, v, y)\}$.

The intuition behind this step is the idea of "embedding", that is the introduction of a suitably initialized function with additional parameters. The purpose of the additional parameters in g' is as follows:

- The parameter v of type **r** basically serves to incrementally construct elements of the set aimed at with E being kind of a neutral element to start with. Type **r** is supposed to be a "supertype" of **n** – in most applications identical with **n** or a product type with a component of type **n**.
- The parameter s of type **set of n** is used as an accumulator for the set to be constructed, and, obviously, initialized with Ø.

P is an invariant (for g') to couple the additional parameter of type **r** to the original one (of type **m**) for which

postulate (1) $\mathrm{P}(X, X, \mathrm{E}) \equiv$ **true**

is required; that is P holds for the initial values.

Predicate Q' is a "weaker" form of the original predicate Q that takes the incremental construction of elements of type **r** into account. In most applications, Q' will simply be of the form

$$\mathrm{Q}'(u, v, y) \equiv \exists y' \mid c(v, y') = y \,\Delta\, \mathrm{Q}(u, y')$$

with c being a "constructor" for elements of type **r**.

To establish the relationship between Q and Q' we require

postulate (2) $\mathrm{Q}(x, y) \equiv \mathrm{Q}'(x, \mathrm{E}, y)$

To establish the equivalence of $f(X)$ with $g(X)$ we calculate as follows:

$g(X)$
  ≡ [(a1) unfold g; **postulate** (1)]
$g'(X, \mathrm{E}, \emptyset)$
  ≡ [(a2) unfold g' ; neutrality of Ø w.r.t. ∪]
$\{y \mid \mathrm{Q}'(X, \mathrm{E}, y)\}$
  ≡ [(a3) **postulate** (2)]
$\{y \mid \mathrm{Q}(X, y)\}$

≡ [(a4) fold f]

$f(X)$.

Since f has a defined value due to the general convention and **postulate** (0), so do g and g' according to the above reasoning.

Example (cont.):
If we further instantiate

g, g', u, v **by** qu, qu', n, p

and choose to instantiate

$P(X, u, v)$	**by**	$P(u, n, p) \mathrel{\widehat{=}} \#p \leq n \wedge isposssequ(p, n) \wedge nconf(p)$
E	**by**	[] (* the empty sequence of columns to start with *)
$Q'(u, v, y)$	**by**	$Q'(n, p, sp) \mathrel{\widehat{=}} \exists\, s'$: **nsequ** $\mid sp = p{+}{+}s' \wedge Q(n, p)$ (* the existence of a possible extension of p to obtain a complete sequence of positions with the requested properties *)

we obtain (as an intermediate form) for our running example:

$qu(N)$ **where**
qu: **nat** → **set of nsequ**
$qu(n) =_{def} q'(n, [], \emptyset)$

q': **nat** × **nsequ** × **set of nsequ** → **set of nsequ**
$q'(n, p, s) =_{def} s \cup \{sp \mid \exists\, s'$: **nsequ** $\mid sp = p{+}{+}s' \wedge Q(n, p)\}$

(b) Next, we aim at transforming g' as defined above. To this end, we calculate as follows:

$g'(u, v, s)$
≡ [(b1) unfold g']
$s \cup \{y \mid Q'(u, v, y)\}$
≡ [(b2) case-introduction; distributivity of ∪ over conditional]
if $T(u, v)$ **then** $s \cup \{y \mid Q'(u, v, y)\}$ **else** $s \cup \{ y \mid Q'(u, v, y)\}$ **fi**

T is a termination condition that serves a two-fold purpose: for the very first call of g' it has to cover the "trivial case" (i.e., the case when E is already a solution for the initial input value X); for all other recursive calls of g' it has to "signal" that the incremental construction of an element of type **r** has been completed.

To be able to continue our derivation we need addditional information. To this end we require

postulate (3) $\mathrm{P}(X, u, v) \land \mathrm{T}(u, v) \equiv$ **true** $\vdash \mathrm{H}(u, v) \equiv \{y \mid \mathrm{Q}'(u, v, y)\}$
postulate (4) $\mathrm{P}(X, u, v) \land \neg\mathrm{T}(u, v) \equiv$ **true** $\vdash$
$\{y \mid \mathrm{Q}'(u, v, y)\} \equiv$
$\bigcup_{i = 1..n(u, v)} \{y \mid \mathrm{B}(i, u, v) \land \mathrm{Q}'(\mathrm{K}(i, u, v), \mathrm{R}(i, u, v), y)\}]$

Postulate (3) gives the information how to construct the solution upon termination using an expression H. In most applications H will be of the simple form $\mathrm{H}(u, v) \equiv \{v\}$, i.e. a singleton set.

Postulate (4) gives the information on how to split up the computation of the desired set into subcomputations the number of which, $n(u,v)$, may (dynamically) depend on the actual parameter values. The expressions K and R characterize the modification of the parameters within subcomputations.

Moreover, in order to be able to deal with the union in **postulate** (4) in an efficient way, we also require

postulate (5) $next(k, u, v) \subseteq$
some k': **nat** $\mid k' \in \{i$: **nat** $\mid k+1 \le i \le n(u, v)+1 \land$
$\forall i'$: **nat** $\mid k < i' < i \Rightarrow \neg\mathrm{B}(i', u, v)\}$

Postulate (5) describes an operation *next* which is characterized non-deterministically on purpose in order to be able to choose a descendant that allows pruning the computation by cutting off unsuccessful branches before they are entered. Obviously, the choice $next(k, u, v) =_{\mathrm{def}} k+1$ is a valid descendant that satisfies this postulate.

Our calculation then proceeds as follows:

$\equiv$ [(b3) modification using **postulate** (3) and **postulate** (4)]
if $\mathrm{T}(u, v)$ **then** $s \cup \mathrm{H}(u, v)$
else $s \cup \bigcup_{i = 1..n(u, v)} \{y \mid \mathrm{B}(i, u, v) \land \mathrm{Q}'(\mathrm{K}(i, u, v), \mathrm{R}(i, u, v), y)\}$ **fi**

$\equiv$ [(b4) simplification using **postulate** (5)]
if $\mathrm{T}(u, v)$ **then** $s \cup \mathrm{H}(u, v)$
else $s \cup \bigcup_{i = next(0, u, v)..n(u, v)} \{ y \mid \mathrm{B}(i, u, v) \land \mathrm{Q}'(\mathrm{K}(i, u, v), \mathrm{R}(i, u, v), y)\}$
fi

$\equiv$ [(b5) abstraction]
if $\mathrm{T}(u, v)$ **then** $s \cup \mathrm{H}(u, v)$ **else** $g''(next(0, u, v), u, v, s)$ **fi**
where
g'': (k: **nat** $\times$ u: **m** $\times$ v: **r** $\times$ s: **set of n** $\mid \mathrm{P}(X, u, v)) \rightarrow$ **set of n**
$g''(k, u, v, s) =_{\mathrm{def}}$
$s \cup \bigcup_{i = k..n(u, v)} \{y \mid \mathrm{B}(i, u, v) \land \mathrm{Q}'(\mathrm{K}(i, u, v), \mathrm{R}(i, u, v), y)\}$.

Example (cont.):
For our running example we choose the instantiations

$\mathrm{T}(u, v)$	**by**	$\mathrm{T}(n, p) \triangleq \#p = n$
$\mathrm{H}(u, v)$	**by**	$\mathrm{H}(n, p) \triangleq \{p\}$
$n(u, v)$	**by**	$n(n, p) \triangleq n$
$\mathrm{B}(i, u, v)$	**by**	$\mathrm{B}(k, n, p) \triangleq nc(p, k)$ **where**

nc: **nsequ** × **nat** → **bool**
$nc(p, k) =_{\mathrm{def}} \forall (i\text{: } \mathbf{nat} \mid 1 \le i \le \#p)\text{:}$
$\quad p[i] \ne k \wedge \mathbf{abs}(p[i] - k) \ne \mathbf{abs}(i - (\#p+1))$
(* checks whether k does not "attack" any of the elements of p *)

$\mathrm{K}(i, u, v)$	**by**	$\mathrm{K}(k, n, p) \triangleq n$
$\mathrm{R}(i, u, v)$	**by**	$\mathrm{R}(k, n, p) \triangleq p{+}{+}k$
$next(k, u, v)$	**by**	$next$: **nat** × **nat** × **nsequ** → **nat**

$next(k, n, p) =_{\mathrm{def}} \mathbf{min}\ \{i\text{: } \mathbf{nat} \mid k+1 \le i \le n + 1\ \Delta$
$\quad \forall i'\text{: } \mathbf{nat} \mid k < i' < i \Rightarrow i' \in p\}$

and obtain as the next intermediate version

q': **nat** × **nsequ** × **set of nsequ** → **set of nsequ**
$q'(n, p, s) =_{\mathrm{def}}$ **if** $\#p = n$ **then** $s \cup \{p\}$ **else** $q''(next(0, n, p), n, p, s)$ **fi**

q'': **nat** × **nat** × **nsequ** × **set of nsequ** → **set of nsequ**
$q''(k, n, p, s) =_{\mathrm{def}} s \cup \bigcup_{i = k..n} \{sp \mid nc(p, i)\ \Delta$
$\quad \exists s'\text{: } \mathbf{nsequ} \mid sp = (p{+}{+}i){+}{+}s' \wedge \#sp = n \wedge isposseq u(sp, n) \wedge nconf(sp)\}$.

(c) Third, we transform g'' as defined in (b). We reason as follows:

$g''(k, u, v, s)$
$\equiv$ [(c1) unfold g'']
$s \cup \bigcup_{i = k..n(u, v)} \{y \mid \mathrm{B}(i, u, v)\ \Delta\ \mathrm{Q}'(\mathrm{K}(i, u, v), \mathrm{R}(i, u, v), y)\}$
$\equiv$ [(c2) case-introduction; simplification of **then**-branch]
if $k > n(u, v)$ **then** s
else $s \cup \bigcup_{i = k..n(u, v)} \{y \mid \mathrm{B}(i, u, v)\ \Delta\ \mathrm{Q}'(\mathrm{K}(i, u, v), \mathrm{R}(i, u, v), y)\}$ **fi**.

For the **else**-branch we reason as follows:

$s \cup \bigcup_{i = k..n(u, v)} \{y \mid \mathrm{B}(i, u, v)\ \Delta\ \mathrm{Q}'(\mathrm{K}(i, u, v), \mathrm{R}(i, u, v), y)\}$
$\equiv$ [(c3) $\cup$-split in **else**-branch]
$s \cup \{y \mid \mathrm{B}(k, u, v)\ \Delta\ \mathrm{Q}'(\mathrm{K}(k, u, v), \mathrm{R}(k, u, v), y)\} \cup$
$\quad \bigcup_{i = k+1..next(k,u,v)-1} \{y \mid \mathrm{B}(i, u, v)\ \Delta\ \mathrm{Q}'(\mathrm{K}(i, u, v), \mathrm{R}(i, u, v), y)\} \cup$

$\bigcup_{i = next(k,u,v)..n(u,v)} \{y \mid B(i, u, v) \,\Delta\, Q'(K(i, u, v), R(i, u, v), y)\}$

$\equiv$ [(c4) simplification: def. *next* $\Rightarrow \bigcup_{i = k+1..next(k,u,v)-1} \{...\} \equiv \emptyset$]

$s \cup \{y \mid B(k, u, v) \,\Delta\, Q'(K(k, u, v), R(k, u, v), y)\} \cup$
$\bigcup_{i = next(k,u,v)..n(u,v)} \{y \mid B(i, u, v) \,\Delta\, Q'(K(i, u, v), R(i, u, v), y)\}$

$\equiv$ [(c5) case introduction; simplification]

if $B(k, u, v)$
then $s \cup \{ y \mid Q'(K(k, u, v), R(k, u, v), y)\} \cup$
$\bigcup_{i = next(k,u,v)..n(u,v)} \{y \mid B(i, u, v) \,\Delta\, Q'(K(i, u, v), R(i, u, v), y)\}$
else $s \cup \bigcup_{i = next(k,u,v)..n(u,v)} \{y \mid B(i, u, v) \,\Delta\, Q'(K(i, u, v), R(i, u, v), y)\}$ **fi**

Our next steps aim at folding g' and g''. Since both functions have the same invariant P, we have to make sure that the invariant is maintained. To this end, we require

postulate (6) $1 \le i \le n(u, v) \,\Delta\, P(X, u, v) \,\Delta\, \neg T(u, v) \,\Delta\, B(i, u, v) \equiv$ **true** $\vdash$ $P(X, K(i, u, v), R(i, u, v)) \equiv$ **true**

Our calculation then continues as follows

$\equiv$ [(c6) fold g' - **postulate** (6) guarantees assertion; termination below]

if $B(k, u, v)$
then $g'(K(k, u, v), R(k, u, v), s) \cup$
$\bigcup_{i = next(k,u,v)..n(u,v)} \{y \mid B(i, u, v) \,\Delta\, Q'(K(i, u, v), R(i, u, v), y)\}$
else $s \cup \bigcup_{i = next(k,u,v)..n(u,v)} \{ y \mid B(i, u, v) \,\Delta\, Q'(K(i, u, v), R(i, u, v), y)\}$ **fi**

$\equiv$ [(c7) fold g'' - assertion remains valid; termination below]

if $B(k, u, v)$ **then** $g''(next(k, u, v), u, v, g'(K(k, u, v), R(k, u, v), s))$
else $g''(next(k, u, v), u, v, s)$ **fi**.

Altogether, we have:

$g''(k, u, v, s) =_{def}$
if $k > n(u, v)$ **then** s
elsf $B(k, u, v)$ **then** $g''(next(k, u, v), u, v, g'(K(k, u, v), R(k, u, v), s))$
else $g''(next(k, u, v), u, v, s)$ **fi**

Example (cont.)
Applying this to our running example we yield

q'': **nat** × **nat** × **nsequ** × **set of nsequ** → **set of nsequ**
$q''(k, n, p, s) =_{\text{def}}$
  if $k > n$ **then** s
  elsf $nc(p, k)$ **then** $q''(next(k, n, p), n, p, q'(n, p{+}{+}k, s))$
  else $q''(next(k, n, p), n, p, s)$ **fi**.

(d) It remains to prove termination of g' and g'' which is required for the correctness of the folding steps. By our general convention, all expressions are defined. In the result obtained so far, g' can be eliminated by unfolding its calls in g and g'':

$g(X)$ **where**
  $g(x) =_{\text{def}}$ **if** $\mathrm{T}(x, \mathrm{E})$ **then** $\emptyset \cup \mathrm{H}(x, \mathrm{E})$
    else $g''(next(0, x, \mathrm{E}), x, \mathrm{E}, \emptyset)$ **fi**

  $g''(k, u, v, s) =_{\text{def}}$
    if $k > n(u, v)$ **then** s
    elsf $\mathrm{B}(k, u, v)$ **then**
      $g''(next(k, u, v), u, v,$
        if $\mathrm{T}(\mathrm{K}(i, u, v), \mathrm{R}(i, u, v))$
        then $s \cup \mathrm{H}(\mathrm{K}(i, u, v), \mathrm{R}(i, u, v))$
        else $g''(next(0, \mathrm{K}(i, u, v), \mathrm{R}(i, u, v)),$
          $\mathrm{K}(i, u, v), \mathrm{R}(i, u, v), s)$ **fi**)
    else $g''(next(k, u, v), u, v, s)$ **fi**

Simplification and distributivity of function call over conditional (in g'') then yields

$g''(k, u, v, s) =_{\text{def}}$
  if $k > n(u, v)$ **then** s
  elsf $\mathrm{B}(k, u, v)$ **then**
    if $\mathrm{T}(\mathrm{K}(i, u, v), \mathrm{R}(i, u, v))$
    then $g''(next(k, u, v), u, v, s \cup \mathrm{H}(\mathrm{K}(i, u, v), \mathrm{R}(i, u, v)))$
    else $g''(next(k, u, v), u, v, g''(next(0, \mathrm{K}(i, u, v), \mathrm{R}(i, u, v)),$
      $\mathrm{K}(i, u, v), \mathrm{R}(i, u, v), s))$ **fi**
  else $g''(next(k, u, v), u, v, s)$ **fi**

Termination of g is obvious provided g'' terminates. To prove termination of g'' we define the following (lexicographic) termination ordering $\angle$ on **nat** × **m** × **r** × **set of n**:

$$(k, u, v, s) \angle (k', u', v', s') \Leftrightarrow \quad v < v' \vee (v = v' \wedge n(u, v) - k < n(u, v) - k')$$
$$\vee \quad u < u' \vee (u = u' \wedge n(u, v) - k < n(u, v) - k')$$

which is well-defined, if we have a well-founded ordering < either on **m** or **r**. Therefore we require

$$\textbf{postulate } (7)\ 1 \le i \le n(u, v) \wedge \mathrm{B}(i, u, v) \equiv \textbf{true} \vdash$$
$$(\mathrm{R}(i, u, v) < v) \equiv \textbf{true} \textbf{ where } \mathrm{WF\text{-}ORD}(\mathbf{r}, <) \textbf{ or}$$
$$(\mathrm{K}(i, u, v) < u) \equiv \textbf{true} \textbf{ where } \mathrm{WF\text{-}ORD}(\mathbf{m}, <)$$

Then, for the recursive calls of g'' we have

$$(next(k, u, v), u, v, s \cup \mathrm{H}(\mathrm{K}(i, u, v), \mathrm{R}(i, u, v))) \angle (k, u, v, s)$$

[by def. of $\angle$ next]

$$(next(0, \mathrm{K}(i, u, v), \mathrm{R}(i, u, v)), \mathrm{K}(i, u, v), \mathrm{R}(i, u, v), s) \angle (k, u, v, s)$$

[by **postulate** (7)]

$$(next(k, u, v), u, v, g''(\,next(0, \mathrm{K}(i, u, v), \mathrm{R}(i, u, v)), \mathrm{K}(i, u, v), \mathrm{R}(i, u, v), s)) \angle (k, u, v, s)$$

[by def. of $\angle$ and *next*]

$$(next(k, u, v), u, v, s) \angle (k, u, v, s)$$

[by def. of $\angle$ and *next*]

Hence, g'' terminates.

Example (cont.):
For the proof of termination, we refer the reader to Sect. 3.1, where the solution of the N-Queens problem is completed.

2.2 The rule

Obviously, the derivation given in Sect. 2.1 is a (constructive) proof of a transformation rule composed of

- the initial specifiction as input scheme
- the result of the derivation as output scheme
- the set of postulates as applicability conditions.

Additionally, the derivation above can be slightly generalized to also cover specifications of the form

$$f(x) =_{\mathrm{def}} \{r(X, y)\text{: } \mathbf{n} \mid \mathrm{Q}(x, y)\}$$

(where ZF set abstraction is used as an abbreviation for $\{q\text{: } \mathbf{n} \mid \exists\, y\text{: } \mathbf{p} \mid q = r(X, y) \wedge \mathrm{Q}(x, y)\}$), since the substitution of y by $r(X, y)$ does not invalidate our derivation.

With this generalization our rule reads:

$f(X)$ **where**
$$f(x) =_{def} \{r(X, y) \colon \mathbf{n} \mid Q(x, y)\}$$

$$
\begin{array}{ll}
(0) & (\#\{r(X, y) \mid Q(x, y)\} < \infty) \equiv \mathbf{true} \\
(1) & P(X, X, E) \equiv \mathbf{true} \\
(2) & Q(x, y) \equiv Q'(x, E, y) \\
(3) & P(X, u, v) \,\Delta\, T(u, v) \equiv \mathbf{true} \vdash H(u, v) \equiv \{r(X, y) \mid Q'(u, v, y)\} \\
(4) & P(X, u, v) \,\Delta\, \neg T(u, v) \equiv \mathbf{true} \vdash \{r(X, y) \mid Q'(u, v, y)\} \equiv \\
 & \quad \bigcup_{i = 1..n(u, v)} \{r(X, y) \mid B(i, u, v) \,\Delta \\
 & \qquad\qquad\qquad Q'(K(i, u, v), R(i, u, v), y)\} \\
(5) & next(k, u, v) \subseteq \mathbf{some}\ k' \colon \mathbf{nat} \mid k' \in \{i \colon \mathbf{nat} \mid k{+}1 \le i \le n(u, v){+}1 \\
 & \qquad\qquad \Delta\ \forall\, i' \colon \mathbf{nat} \mid k < i' < i \Rightarrow \neg B(i', u, v)\} \\
(6) & 1 \le i \le n(u, v) \,\Delta\, P(X, u, v) \,\Delta\, \neg T(u, v) \,\Delta\, B(i, u, v) \equiv \mathbf{true} \vdash \\
 & \quad P(X, K(i, u, v), R(i, u, v)) \equiv \mathbf{true} \\
(7) & 1 \le i \le n(u, v) \,\Delta\, B(i, u, v) \equiv \mathbf{true} \vdash \\
 & \quad (R(i, u, v) < v) \equiv \mathbf{true}\ \ \mathbf{where}\ \text{WF-ORD}(\mathbf{r}, <)\ \mathbf{or} \\
 & \quad (K(i, u, v) < u) \equiv \mathbf{true}\ \ \mathbf{where}\ \text{WF-ORD}(\mathbf{m}, <)
\end{array}
$$

$g(X)$ **where**
$$g(x) =_{def} g'(x, E, \emptyset)$$

$g'(u, v, s) =_{def}$
  if $T(u, v)$ **then** $s \cup H(u, v)$ **else** $g''(next(0, u, v), u, v, s)$ **fi**

$g''(k, u, v, s) =_{def}$
  if $k > n(u, v)$ **then** s
  elsf $B(k, u, v)$ **then** $g''(next(k, u, v), u, v, g'(K(k, u, v), R(k, u, v), s))$
  else $g''(next(k, u, v), u, v, s)$ **fi**

Syntactic constraints

$$
\begin{array}{l}
\text{KIND}[r] = \mathbf{m} \times \mathbf{p} \rightarrow \mathbf{n} \\
\text{KIND}[f, g] = \mathbf{m} \rightarrow \mathbf{set\ of\ n} \\
\text{KIND}[g'] = (u \colon \mathbf{m} \times v \colon \mathbf{r} \times s \colon \mathbf{set\ of\ n} \mid P(X, u, v)) \rightarrow \mathbf{set\ of\ n} \\
\text{KIND}[g''] = (k \colon \mathbf{nat} \times u \colon \mathbf{m} \times v \colon \mathbf{r} \times s \colon \mathbf{set\ of\ n} \mid P(X, u, v)) \rightarrow \mathbf{set\ of\ n} \\
\text{KIND}[next] = (\mathbf{nat} \times \mathbf{m} \times \mathbf{r}) \rightarrow \mathbf{nat}
\end{array}
$$

Admittedly, the whole bunch of applicability conditions looks complicated at a first glance, due to the many expressions to be "invented" and the lot of resulting proof obligations. As to the first, one should keep in mind that in most applications the simple forms as commented above are sufficient - which substantially reduces the amount of work for finding suitable instantiations. As to the latter, it will be examplified with the queens example below, that, whenever suitable instantiations have been found, all proofs of the instantiated applicability conditions are straightforward or even trivial.

3 SOME APPLICATIONS OF THE RULE

In this section we complete the treatment of the queens example and deal with another (non-trivial) problem to illustrate the power of our rule and how to use it.

3.1 The N-Queens Problem completed

In summary, the application of our rule to the queens problem (with r instantiated by the identity on its second argument, and WF-ORD(**r**, <) instantiated by (**nsequ**, $a < b \Leftrightarrow n - \#a < n - \#b$)) results in the following program:

> $qu(N)$ **where**
> qu: **nat** → **set of nsequ**
> $qu(n) =_{\text{def}} q'(n, [], \emptyset)$
>
> q': **nat** × **nsequ** × **set of nsequ** → **set of nsequ**
> $q'(n, p, s) =_{\text{def}}$
>   **if** $\#p = n$ **then** $s \cup \{p\}$ **else** $q''(next(0, n, p), n, p, s)$ **fi**
>
> q'': **nat** × **nat** × **nsequ** × **set of nsequ** → **set of nsequ**
> $q''(k, n, p, s) =_{\text{def}}$
>   **if** $k > n$ **then** s
>   **elsf** $nc(p, k)$ **then** $q''(next(k, n, p), n, p, q'(n, p{+}{+}k, s))$
>   **else** $q''(next(k, n, p), n, p, s)$ **fi**.

It remains to prove the instantiated applicability conditions (which is straightforward or even trivial):

(0) $(\#\{sp: \textbf{nsequ} \mid \#sp = n \wedge isposseq u(sp, n) \wedge nconf(sp)\} < \infty) \equiv \textbf{true}$

Trivial, as already **nsequ** restricted by *isposseq u* has only finitely many elements (for any n).

(1) $(\#[] \le n \wedge isposseq u([], n) \wedge nconf([])) \equiv \textbf{true}$

Obviously, $\#[] = 0 \le n$, $isposseq u([], n)$, and $nconf([])$ are all true.

(2) $\#sp = n \wedge isposseq u(sp, n) \wedge nconf(sp) \equiv$
$\quad\quad \exists\, s'$: $\textbf{nsequ} \mid sp = []{+}{+}s' \wedge \#sp = n \wedge isposseq u(sp, n) \wedge nconf(sp)$

Trivial, as for $s' \equiv sp$ the righthand side expression simplifies to the one on the lefthand side.

(3) $(\#p \le n \wedge isposseq u(p, n) \wedge nconf(p))\ \Delta\ \#p = n \equiv \textbf{true} \vdash$
$\quad\quad \{p\} \equiv \{sp: \textbf{nsequ} \mid \exists\, s': \textbf{nsequ} \mid sp = p{+}{+}s' \wedge \#sp = n \wedge$
$\quad\quad\quad\quad isposseq u(sp, n) \wedge nconf(sp)\}$

From $\#p = n$, $\#sp = n$, and $sp = p{+}{+}s'$, it follows that $\#s' = 0$, and, thus, $s' = []$. Hence, the set on the righthand side of the consequence simplifies to

$$\{sp\text{: }\mathbf{nsequ} \mid sp = p \wedge \#sp = n \wedge isposseq u(sp, n) \wedge nconf(sp)\}.$$

The equality of both sets then follows from the premise on p.

(4) $(\#p \le n \wedge isposseq u(p, n) \wedge nconf(p)) \mathbin{\Delta} \#p < n \equiv \mathbf{true} \mid$

$$\{sp\text{: }\mathbf{nsequ} \mid \exists\, s'\text{: }\mathbf{nsequ} \mid sp = p{+}{+}s' \wedge \#sp = n \wedge isposseq u(sp, n) \wedge nconf(sp)\} \equiv$$

$$\bigcup_{i=1..n} \{sp\text{: }\mathbf{nsequ} \mid nc(p, i) \mathbin{\Delta} \exists\, s'\text{: }\mathbf{nsequ} \mid sp = (p{+}{+}i){+}{+}s' \wedge \#sp = n \wedge isposseq u(sp, n) \wedge nconf(sp)\}$$

Due to the premise $\#p < n$ and associativity of ++, the lefthand side of the consequence can be rewritten into

$$\{sp\text{: }\mathbf{nsequ} \mid \exists\, s'\text{: }\mathbf{nsequ},\, i\text{: }\mathbf{pos}(n) \mid sp = (p{+}{+}i){+}{+}s' \wedge \#sp = n \wedge isposseq u(sp, n) \wedge nconf(sp)\}$$

where i: $\mathbf{pos}(n)$ abbreviates $(i\text{: }\mathbf{nat} \mid 1 \le i \le n)$.

Since $\neg nc(p, i)$ implies $\neg nconf((p{+}{+}i){+}{+}s')$, the existential quantification on i can be restricted to those i that satisfy $nc(p, i)$. The requested equality then follows from the general rule

$$\{x \mid \exists\, y, z \mid \mathrm{P}(z) \wedge \mathrm{Q}(x, y, z)\} \equiv \bigcup_{z \mid \mathrm{P}(z)} \{x \mid \exists\, y \mid \mathrm{Q}(x, y, z)\}.$$

(5) $\mathbf{min}\ \{i\text{: }\mathbf{nat} \mid k{+}1 \le i \le n + 1 \mathbin{\Delta} \forall\, i'\text{: }\mathbf{nat} \mid k < i' < i \Rightarrow i' \in p\} \subseteq$

$$\mathbf{some}\ k'\text{: }\mathbf{nat} \mid k' \in \{i\text{: }\mathbf{nat} \mid k{+}1 \le i \le n{+}1 \mathbin{\Delta} \forall\, i'\text{: }\mathbf{nat} \mid k < i' < i \Rightarrow \neg nc(p, i')\}$$

Obviously, $i' \in p$ implies $\neg nc(p, i')$. $\mathbf{min}\ m$ is always a descendant of $\mathbf{some}\ x \mid x \in m$.

(6) $1 \le i \le n \mathbin{\Delta} (\#p \le n \wedge isposseq u(p, n) \wedge nconf(p)) \mathbin{\Delta} \#p < n \mathbin{\Delta} nc(p, i) \equiv \mathbf{true}$
$\vdash \#(p{+}{+}i) \le n \wedge isposseq u(p{+}{+}i, n) \wedge nconf(p{+}{+}i) \equiv \mathbf{true}$

$\#p < n$ implies $\#(p{+}{+}i) \le n$, $isposseq u(p{+}{+}i, n)$ follows immediately from the premise, and $nconf(p{+}{+}i)$ follows from $nconf(p)$ and $nc(p, i)$.

(7) $1 \le i \le n \mathbin{\Delta} nc(p, i) \equiv \mathbf{true} \vdash n - \#(p{+}{+}i) < n - \#p \equiv \mathbf{true}$

The consequence is even true for arbitrary n, p, and i.

Remarks

- The choice of *next* as defined above (instead of the generally possible choice $next(k) =_{def} k+1$) is a simple optimization (according to the remark on *next* in Sect. 2).
- As a further improvement, we could have added another parameter to keep all possible candidate positions to be added to the current sequence. This would require modified instantiations, viz.

P(X, u, v) **by** $\#p \leq n \wedge isposseq u(p, n) \wedge nconf(p) \wedge$
$\forall (i: \mathbf{pos}(n) \mid i \in c) \mid nc(p, i)$

E **by** $([], \{i: \mathbf{pos}(n)\})$
B(i, u, v) **by** $c \neq \emptyset$
R(i, u, v) **by** $(p{+}{+}i, \{k: \mathbf{pos}(n) \mid nc(p{+}{+}i, k)\})$.

Together with

$$next(k, c) =_{def} \textbf{if } c \neq \emptyset \textbf{ then } \textbf{min } c \textbf{ else } n+1 \textbf{ fi}$$

these modified instantiations then would have resulted in

qu(*N*) **where**
  $qu(n) =_{def} q'(n, [], \{i: \mathbf{pos}(n)\}, \emptyset)$
  $q'(n, p, c, s) =_{def}$
    if $\#p = n$ **then** $s \cup \{p\}$ **else** $q''(next(0, c), n, p, c, s)$ **fi**
  $q''(k, n, p, c, s) =_{def}$
    if $k > n$ **then** s
    elsf $c \neq \emptyset$ **then**
      $q''(next(k, c), n, p, c, q'(n, p{+}{+}k, \{i: \mathbf{pos}(n)\} \mid nc(p{+}{+}k, i)\}, s))$
    else $q''(next(k, c), n, p, c, s)$ **fi**.

As a further improvement – which is left to the interested reader – one could think of applying finite differencing to efficiently compute the new candidate set in the first recursive call of g''.

3.2 A Prolog Interpreter

A Prolog interpreter takes a Prolog program and a query and yields as a result either the set of all substitutions (for the variables in the query) such that the instantiated query is a logical consequence from the program, or it does not terminate. If there is no substitution (such that the instantiated query follows from the program) the result is the empty set.

To formally specify the problem, we first have to define the notions of program, query, and substitution. A program is a sequence of clauses (or rules) each of which consists of a literal as its lefthand side and a (possibly empty) sequence of literals as its righthand side. A literal in turn consists of a predicate symbol and a (possibly empty) sequence of terms (as arguments). And a term is either a constant symbol, a variable symbol, or a function symbol together with a sequence of terms as arguments. All this can straightforwardly be formalized as follows:

$$\mathbf{program} =_{\text{def}} \mathbf{sequ\ of\ clause}$$
$$\mathbf{clause} =_{\text{def}} (lhs\text{: }\mathbf{literal}, rhs\text{: }\mathbf{sequ\ of\ literal})$$
$$\mathbf{literal} =_{\text{def}} (ps\text{: }\mathbf{predsymb}, st\text{: }\mathbf{sequ\ of\ term})$$
$$\mathbf{term} =_{\text{def}} \mathbf{const} \mid \mathbf{var} \mid (\mathbf{functsymb}, \mathbf{sequ\ of\ term}).$$

A query is a sequence of literals, and a substitution is an association of variable symbols with terms. Again, formalization is straightforward:

$$\mathbf{query} =_{\text{def}} \mathbf{sequ\ of\ literal}$$
$$\mathbf{subst} =_{\text{def}} \mathbf{EMAP(var, term, =)}.$$

To construct a substitution and simultaneously to prove that the instantiated query gl follows from the program p, a prolog interpreter uses sld-resolution which is captured by the following derivability relation:

$$\underset{p}{\rightarrow} : \mathbf{query} \times \mathbf{subst} \times \mathbf{query} \times \mathbf{subst} \rightarrow \mathbf{bool}$$
$$(gl, \Theta) \underset{p}{\rightarrow} (gl', \Theta \circ \Theta') =_{\text{def}}$$
$$\exists\, c \in p \mid gl' = (rhs(c') \mathbin{++} \mathbf{tl}gl)\Theta' \wedge$$
$$c' = rn(c, gl) \wedge unify(\mathbf{hd}gl, lhs(c')) \neq \mathbf{fail}\ \Delta$$
$$\Theta' = unify(\mathbf{hd}gl, lhs(c'))$$

where

$\Theta \circ \Theta'$ denotes the composition of the substitutions Θ and Θ',
$a\Theta$ denotes the application of the substitution Θ to a,
rn: **clause** × **query** → **clause**
$rn(c, gl) =_{\text{def}}$
« clause c with all variables renamed such that they do not occur in gl »

and (with c_i and v_i denoting constant and variable symbols, respectively, f, g denoting function symbols, and r_i, s_i denoting terms)

$$\mathbf{struct} =_{\text{def}} \mathbf{term} \mid \mathbf{literal}$$

$$unify\text{: }\mathbf{struct} \times \mathbf{struct} \rightarrow \mathbf{subst} \mid \mathbf{fail}$$
$$unify(c_1, c_2) =_{\text{def}} \mathbf{if}\ c_1 = c_2\ \mathbf{then}\ \emptyset\ \mathbf{else\ fail\ fi}$$
$$unify(c_1, v_2) =_{\text{def}} (c_1\ \mathbf{for}\ v_2)$$
$$unify(c_1, g(r_1,\ldots, r_k)) =_{\text{def}} \mathbf{fail}$$
$$unify(v_1, c_2) =_{\text{def}} (c_2\ \mathbf{for}\ v_1)$$
$$unify(v_1, v_2) =_{\text{def}} \mathbf{if}\ v_1 \neq v_2\ \mathbf{then}\ (v_2\ \mathbf{for}\ v_1)\ \mathbf{else}\ \emptyset\ \mathbf{fi}$$

$unify(v_1, g(r_1,..., r_k)) =_{def}$
if $notoccurs(v_1, g(r_1,..., r_k))$ **then** $(g(r_1,..., r_k)$ **for** $v_1)$ **else fail fi**
$unify(f(s_1,..., s_n), c_2) =_{def}$ **fail**
$unify(f(s_1,..., s_n), v_2) =_{def}$
if $notoccurs(v_2, f(s_1,..., s_n))$ **then** $(f(s_1,..., s_n)$ **for** $v_2)$ **else fail fi**
$unify(f(s_1,..., s_n), g(r_1,..., r_k)) =_{def}$
if $f = g \wedge n = k$ **then** $unifylist([s_1,..., s_n], [r_1,..., r_k], \emptyset)$ **else fail fi**

notoccurs: **var** × **struct** → **bool**
$notoccurs(v, s) =_{def}$ « v does not occur in s »

unifylist: **sequ of struct** × **sequ of struct** × **subst** → **subst | fail**
$unifylist([], [], \Theta) =_{def} \Theta$
$unifylist(g{+}{+}gl, h{+}{+}hl, \Theta) =_{def}$
if $\Theta' \neq$ **fail then** $unifylist(gl\Theta', hl\Theta', \Theta \circ \Theta')$ **else fail fi**
where $\Theta' = unify(g, h)$

Equipped with this environment, a formal specification of a prolog interpreter is as follows:

interprete(P, A) **where**
interprete: **program** × **query** → **set of subst**
$interprete(p, gl) =_{def} \{\Theta |_{vars(A)} \mid (gl, \emptyset) \underset{P}{\rightarrow}^{*} ([], \Theta)\}$

where
$\Theta |_{vars(A)}$ denotes Θ restricted to those variable symbols occurring in A
and
$\underset{P}{\rightarrow}^{*}$ denotes the reflexive transitive closure of $\underset{P}{\rightarrow}$.

Correct application of our transformation rule requires to satisfy the applicability condition

$$(\#\{\Theta |_{vars(A)} \mid (gl, \emptyset) \underset{P}{\rightarrow}^{*} ([], \Theta)\} < \infty) \equiv \mathbf{true}.$$

Whereas in the previous example, the corresponding proof obligation was straightforward to be shown, it is less trivial here. Indeed, it only can be proved if both the program and the query satisfy additional constraints the detailed treatment of which is beyond the scope of this paper. A similar remark holds for condition (7) about the existence of a suitable well-founded ordering. Therefore we simply take these applicability conditions for granted and yield as result of rule application (as to the respective instantiations, cf. (Achatz, Partsch, 1996)):

$int(P, A)$ **where**

int: **program** × **query** → **set of subst**

$int(p, gl) =_{\text{def}} int'(p, gl, \emptyset, \emptyset)$

int': **program** × **query** × **subst** × **set of subst** → **set of subst**

$int'(p, gl, \Phi, s) =_{\text{def}}$

if $gl = []$ **then** $s \cup \{\Phi\ |_{vars(A)}\}$

else $int''(next(0, p, gl,), p, gl, \Phi, s)$ **fi**

int'': **nat** × **program** × **query** × **subst** × **set of subst** →
set of subst

$int''(k, p, gl, \Phi, s) =_{\text{def}}$

if $k > \#p$ **then** s

elsf $\Phi' \neq$ **fail**

then $int''(next(k, p, gl), p, gl,$
$int'(p, (rhs(rn(p[k], gl)) +\!\!+ \text{tl}gl)\Phi', \Phi \circ \Phi', s))$

else $int''(next(k, p, gl), p, gl, \Phi, s)$ **fi**

where $\Phi' = unify(\text{hd}gl, lhs(rn(p[k], gl)))$

$next$: **nat** × **program** × **query** → **nat**

$next(k, p, gl) =_{\text{def}}$

min$\{i$: **nat** $\mid (k+1 \le i \le \#p \ \Delta\ ps(lhs(p[i])) = ps(\textbf{hd}\ gl)) \ \nabla\ i = \#p+1\}$

3.3 Further examples

Of course, there are many more problems our rule might be applied to. Apart from the additional ones dealt with in (Achatz, Partsch, 1996) (i.e., all permutations of a sequence, all partitions of a natural number, all subsequences of a sequence, a knapsack-problem, all topological sortings, all maximal, cycle-free paths from a given node), these range, for example, from mathematical problems (e.g, all subsets of a set, all partitions of a set, all subsets of a set up to a fixed size), combinatorial problems (e.g., space-filling puzzles, other known problems on the chessboard), or further graph problems.

4 VARIANTS OF THE GENERAL RULE AND THEIR APPLICATIONS

In the following we discuss a couple of "variants" of our general rule and illustrate them by respective examples. These "variants" look very similar to our general rule, although they deal with different kinds of specifications and require (slightly) different applicability conditions. Using the word "variant" is simply motivated by the fact that the proofs of these rules only marginally deviate from the proof of our general rule.

4.1 Variant 1: Existential quantification

4.1.1 The rule

$f(X)$ **where**
$f(x) =_{def} \exists\, y\colon \mathbf{p} \mid Q(x, y)$

$\updownarrow$
(1), (2), (5), (6), (7) as in general rule
(3) $P(X, u, v) \,\Delta\, T(u, v) \equiv \mathbf{true} \vdash \mathbf{true} \equiv \exists\; y\colon \mathbf{p} \mid Q'(u, v, y)$
(4) $P(X, u, v) \,\Delta\, \neg T(u, v) \equiv \mathbf{true} \vdash$
$\exists\; y\colon \mathbf{p} \mid Q'(u, v, y) \equiv$
$\exists_{i = 1..n(u,v)} \exists\, y\colon \mathbf{p} \mid B(i, u, v) \,\Delta\, Q'(K(i, u, v), R(i, u, v), y)$

$g(X)$ **where**
$g(x) =_{def} g'(x, E, \mathbf{false})$

$g'(u, v, s) =_{def}$ **if** $T(u, v)$ **then true else** $g''(next(0, u, v), u, v, s)$ **fi**

$g''(k, u, v, s) =_{def}$
if $s \vee k > n(u, v)$ **then** s
elsf $B(k, u, v)$ **then** $g''(next(k, u, v), u, v, g'(K(k, u, v), R(k, u, v), s))$
else $g''(next(k, u, v), u, v, s)$ **fi**

Syntactic constraints

$KIND[f, g] = \mathbf{m} \rightarrow \mathbf{bool}$
$KIND[g'] = (u\colon \mathbf{m} \times v\colon \mathbf{r} \times s\colon \mathbf{bool} \mid P(X, u, v)) \rightarrow \mathbf{bool}$
$KIND[g''] = (k\colon \mathbf{nat} \times u\colon \mathbf{m} \times v\colon \mathbf{r} \times s\colon \mathbf{bool} \mid P(X, u, v)) \rightarrow \mathbf{bool}$
$KIND[next] = (\mathbf{nat} \times \mathbf{m} \times \mathbf{r}) \rightarrow \mathbf{nat}$

Proof (changes)

a) (a2'): unfold g' ; neutrality of **false** w.r.t. $\vee$
b) (b2'): case-introduction; distributivity $\vee$ over conditional
c) (c3'): $\vee$-split in **else**-branch

4.1.2 An Application: Top-down recognition (for context-free grammars)
Given a context-free grammar $G = (N, T, Z, P)$ (where N is a non-empty set of nonterminal symbols, T a non-emtpy set of terminal symbols which is disjoint from N, $Z \in N$, and P is a non-empty set of context-free productions consisting of a nonterminal symbol as its lefthand side and a (possibly empty) sequence of (nonterminal or terminal) symbols as its righthand side) and a terminal word w, it is requested to check whether w is derivable from Z using P.

Using

nont $=_{def}$ « nonterminal symbols »
term $=_{def}$ « terminal symbols »
symb $=_{def}$ **nont | term**
prod $=_{def}$ (*lhs*: **nont**, *rhs*: **sequ of symb**)

the problem can be formalized by

recognize(*P*, *W*) **where**
recognize: **sequ of prod** × **sequ of term** → **bool**
recognize(*p*, *w*) $=_{def}$ ∃ *y*: **sequ of term** | $[Z] \xrightarrow[p]{}^{*} y \wedge y = w$

where

$\xrightarrow[p]{}$: **sequ of symb** × **sequ of symb** → **bool**
$x \xrightarrow[p]{} y =_{def} \exists\, l, r$: **sequ of symb**, *i*: **nat** |
$x = l{+}{+}lhs(p[i]){+}{+}r \wedge y = l{+}{+}rhs(p[i]){+}{+}r$

and

$\xrightarrow[p]{}^{*}$ denotes the reflexive transitive closure of $\xrightarrow[p]{}$.

The result of rule application is

rec(*P*, *W*) **where**
rec: **sequ of prod** × **sequ of term** → **bool**
rec(*p*, *w*) $=_{def}$ *rec'*(*p*, *w*, [*Z*], **false**)

rec': **sequ of prod** × **sequ of term** × **sequ of symb** × **bool** →
bool
rec'(*p*, *w*, *v*, *s*) $=_{def}$
if $w = [\,] \wedge v = [\,]$ **then true else** *rec"*(*next*(1, *p*, *v*), *p*, *w*, *v*, *s*) **fi**

rec": **nat** × **sequ of prod** × **sequ of term** × **sequ of symb** × **bool**
→ **bool**
rec"(*k*, *p*, *w*, *v*, *s*) $=_{def}$
if $s \vee k > \#p{+}1$ **then** *s*
elsf ($k \le \#p \wedge v \ne [\,]$ Δ **hd***v* = *lhs*(*p*[*k*])) ∨
($k = \#p{+}1 \wedge w \ne [\,] \wedge v \ne [\,]$ Δ **hd***w* = **hd***v*)
then *rec"*(*next*(*k*, *p*, *v*), *p*, *w*, *v*,
rec'(*p*, **if** $k \le \#p$ **then** *w* **else tl***w* **fi**,
if $k \le \#p$ **then** *rhs*(*p*[*k*])++**tl***v* **else tl***v* **fi**, *s*))
else *rec"*(*next*(*k*, *p*, *v*), *p*, *w*, *v*, *s*) **fi**

next: **nat** × **sequ of prod** × **sequ of symb** → **nat**
next(*k*, *p*, *v*) $=_{def}$
min {*i*: **nat** | ($k{+}1 \le i \le \#p$ Δ *lhs*(*p*[*i*]) = **hd***v*) ∇ $i = \#p{+}1$}

where *rec*" can be further transformed into

$rec''(k, p, w, v, s) =_{def}$
  if $s \vee k > \#p+1$ **then** s
  elsf $k \leq \#p \wedge v \neq [] \,\Delta\,$ **hd**$v = lhs(p[k])$
    then $rec''(next(k, p, v), p, w, v, rec'(p, w, rhs(p[k]){+}{+}$**tl**$v, s))$
  elsf $k = \#p+1 \wedge w \neq [] \wedge v \neq [] \,\Delta\,$ **hd**$w =$ **hd**v
    then $rec''(next(k, p, v), p, w, v, rec'(p,$ **tl**$w,$ **tl**$v, s))$
  else $rec''(next(k, p, v), p, w, v, s)$ **fi**.

Similar to the Prolog interpreter, proving termination is slightly more difficult than in most of the other examples. In fact, as is known, absence of left-recursion in the grammar is necessary for the proof of termination.

Of course, we could have chosen an even "stronger" definition for *next*, viz.

$next(k, p, v) =_{def}$
  min $\{i$: **nat** $\mid (k+1 \leq i \leq \#p \,\Delta\, lhs(p[i]) =$ **hd**$v \,\Delta$
    $\exists\, z$: **symb** $\mid$ **hd**$v \underset{p}{\rightarrow}$ **hd**$w{+}{+}z) \,\nabla\, i = \#p+1\}$

which obviously reflects the idea of LL(1) recognition.

4.2 Variant 2: Non-deterministic choice

4.2.1 The rule

$f(X)$ **where**
  $f(x) =_{def}$
    if $\{y$: **p** $\mid Q(x, y)\} \neq \emptyset$ **then some** y: **p** $\mid Q(x, y)$ **else dummy fi**

  (1), (2), (5), (6), (7) as in general rule
  (3) $P(X, u, v) \,\Delta\, T(u, v) \equiv$ **true** $\vdash H(u, v) \in \{y \mid Q'(u, v, y)\} \equiv$ **true**
  (4) $P(X, u, v) \,\Delta\, \neg T(u, v) \equiv$ **true** $\vdash$
    some y: **p** $\mid Q'(u, v, y) \equiv$ **some** y: **p** $\mid \exists_{i\,=\,1..n(u,v)} (B(i, u, v) \,\Delta$
      $Q'(K(i, u, v), R(i, u, v), y))$

$g(X)$ **where**
  $g(x) =_{def} g'(x, E,$ **dummy**$)$

  $g'(u, v, s) =_{def}$ **if** $T(u, v)$ **then** $H(u, v)$ **else** $g''(next(0, u, v), u, v, s)$ **fi**

  $g''(k, u, v, s) =_{def}$
    if $s \neq$ **dummy** $\vee\, k > n(u, v)$ **then** s
    elsf $B(k, u, v)$ **then** $g''(next(k, u, v), u, v, g'(K(k, u, v), R(k, u, v), s))$
    else $g''(next(k, u, v), u, v, s)$ **fi**

Syntactic constraints
  KIND$[f, g] =$ **m** $\rightarrow$ **n** $\mid$ **dummy**

KIND[g'] = (u: **m** × v: **r** × s: **n** | **dummy** | P(X, u, v)) → **n** | **dummy**
KIND[g''] = (k: **nat** × u: **m** × v: **r** × s: **n** | **dummy** | P(X, u, v)) →
n | **dummy**
KIND[*next*] = (**nat** × **m** × **r**) → **nat**

Proof (changes)

a) Define
a © b $=_{def}$ **if** *def*(a) **then** a [] *def*(b) **then** b **else dummy fi where**
def(**some** y | Q) $=_{def}$ {y | Q} ≠ Ø
def(x) $=_{def}$ x ≠ **dummy**.
(a2'): unfold g'
(a3'): cond. (2); unfold ©
b) (b2'): case-introduction
(b3'): ⊇ for ≡
c) (c2'): ⊇ for ≡
(c3'): ∨-split in **else**-branch
(c5'): case introduction in **else**-branch; simplification using **some** y | (B ∨ C) ≡ (**some** y | B) © (**some** y | C)

4.2.2 An Application: Bottom-up parsing (of context-free grammars)

Given a context-free grammar G (as defined in the previous example) and a terminal word w, it is asked for computing a sequence of shift and reduce actions the application of which allows to reduce w to the axiom Z of G provided such a sequence exists; if not, the result should be **error**.

For a formal specification of this problem we define **nont**, **term**, **symb**, and **prod** as in the previous example. The sequence of shift and reduce actions is defined by

srsequ $=_{def}$ « sequences of S (= *shift*) and R(X, α) (= *reduce with* (X, α)) ».

The application of such a sequence to a terminal word is specified by

apply: **sequ of prod** × **sequ of symb** × **sequ of term** →
sequ of symb × **sequ of term**
apply([], *st*, *w*) $=_{def}$ (*st*, *w*)
apply(S++*srs*, *st*, *t*++*w*) $=_{def}$ *apply*(*srs*, *st*++*t*, *w*)
apply(R(X, α)++*srs*, *st*++α, *w*) $=_{def}$ *apply*(*srs*, *st*++X, *w*).

With these prerequisites, the original problem may be specified as follows:

parse(P, [],W) **where**
parse: **sequ of prod** × **sequ of symb** × **sequ of term** →
srsequ | **error**
parse(p, *st*, *w*) $=_{def}$

if $\{y$: **srsequ** $\mid apply(y, st, w) = ([Z], [])\} \neq \emptyset$
then some y: **srsequ** $\mid apply(y, st, w) = ([Z], [])$ **else error fi**.

The result of rule application is

$par(P, [], W)$ **where**
par: **sequ of prod** × **sequ of symb** × **sequ of term** →
srsequ | **error**
$par(p, st, w) =_{def} par'(p, st, w, [], \textbf{error})$

par': **sequ of prod** × **sequ of symb** × **sequ of term** ×
srsequ × **srsequ** | **error** → **srsequ** | **error**
$par'(p, st, w, sr, s) =_{def}$
if $w = [] \wedge st = [Z]$ **then** sr **else** $par''(1, p, st, w, sr, s)$ **fi**

par'': **nat** × **sequ of prod** × **sequ of symb** × **sequ of term** ×
srsequ × **srsequ** | **error** →**srsequ** | **error**
$par''(k, p, st, w, sr, s) =_{def}$
if $s \neq$ **error** $\vee k > \#p+1$ **then** s
elsf $(k \leq \#p \wedge \exists s' \mid st = s'{+}{+}rhs(p[k])) \vee (k = \#p+1 \wedge w \neq [])$
then $par''(k+1, p, st, w, sr,$
$par'(p,$ **if** $k \leq \#p$ **then** $(s'{+}{+}lhs(p[k]), w)$
else $(st{+}{+}\textbf{hd}w, \textbf{tl}w)$ **fi**,
if $k \leq \#p$ **then** $sr{+}{+}\mathrm{R}(p[k])$ **else** $sr{+}{+}\mathrm{S}$ **fi**, $s))$
else $par''(k+1, p, st, w, sr, s)$ **fi**

where par'' can be further transformed into

$par''(k, p, st, w, sr, s) =_{def}$
if $s \neq$ **error** $\vee k > \#p+1$ **then** s
elsf $k \leq \#p \wedge \exists s' \mid st = s'{+}{+}rhs(p[k])$
then $par''(k+1, p, st, w, sr, par'(p, s'{+}{+}lhs(p[k]), w, sr{+}{+}\mathrm{R}(p[k]), s))$
elsf $k = \#p+1 \wedge w \neq []$
then $par''(k+1, p, st, w, sr, par'(p, st{+}{+}\textbf{hd}w, \textbf{tl}w, sr{+}{+}\mathrm{S}, s))$
else $par''(k+1, p, st, w, sr, s)$ **fi**.

Again, as in the case of top-down recognition, additional constraints on the grammar are necessary for the proof of termination.

4.3 Variant 3: A special instance of the rule

4.3.1 The rule

Differently to the previous variants, we now consider a variant that is obtained by specializing the general rule by

- defining $n(u, v) =_{def} 1$ and $next(k, u, v) =_{def} k+1$

- instantiating these definitions and simplifying the resulting expressions
- skipping the dependencies (on i) of the expressions K, R, and B.

This leads to the following specialization of our general rule:

$f(X)$ **where**

$f(x) =_{\text{def}} \{r(X, y)\text{: } \mathbf{n} \mid Q(x, y)\}$

(0), (1), (2), (3) as in general rule

(4) $P(X, u, v) \Delta \neg T(u, v) \equiv \mathbf{true} \vdash$
$\{r(X, y) \mid Q'(u, v, y)\} \equiv \{r(X, y) \mid B(u, v) \Delta Q'(K(u, v), R(u,v), y)\}$

(6) $P(X, u, v) \Delta \neg T(u, v) \Delta B(u, v) \equiv \mathbf{true} \vdash$
$P(X, K(u, v), R(u, v)) \equiv \mathbf{true}$

(7) $B(u, v) \equiv \mathbf{true} \vdash$ $(R(u, v) < v) \equiv \mathbf{true}$ **where** WF-ORD(**r**, <) **or**
$(K(u, v) < u) \equiv \mathbf{true}$ **where** WF-ORD(**m**, <)

$g(X)$ **where**

$g(x) =_{\text{def}} g'(x, E, \emptyset)$

$g'(u, v, s) =_{\text{def}}$ **if** $T(u, v)$ **then** $s \cup H(u, v)$ **else** $g''(1, u, v, s)$ **fi**

$g''(k, u, v, s) =_{\text{def}}$

if $k > 1$ **then** s
elsf $B(u, v)$ **then** $g''(k+1, u, v, g'(K(u, v), R(u, v), s))$
else $g''(k+1, u, v, s)$ **fi**

Syntactic constraints

as in general rule

Intuitively, under these particular constraints, one would expect a linear recursive output scheme. Indeed, this can be obtained by further transformation:

(a) $g''(2, u, v, s)$

$\equiv$ [instantiation]

s

(b) $g''(1, u, v, s)$

$\equiv$ [unfold g'']

if $1 > 1$ **then** s
elsf $B(u, v)$ **then** $g''(2, u, v, g'(K(u, v), R(u, v), s))$ **else** $g''(2, u, v, s)$ **fi**

$\equiv$ [simplification of conditional]

if $B(u, v)$ **then** $g''(2, u, v, g'(K(u, v), R(u, v), s))$ **else** $g''(2, u, v, s)$ **fi**

$\equiv$ [(a)]

if $B(u, v)$ **then** $g'(K(u, v), R(u, v), s)$ **else** s **fi**

(c) $g'(u, v, s)$

$\equiv$ [unfold g']

if $\mathrm{T}(u, v)$ **then** $s \cup \mathrm{H}(u, v)$ **else** $g''(1, u, v, s)$ **fi**

$\equiv$ [(b)]

if $\mathrm{T}(u, v)$ **then** $s \cup \mathrm{H}(u, v)$
elsf $\mathrm{B}(u, v)$ **then** $g'(\mathrm{K}(u, v), \mathrm{R}(u, v), s)$ **else** s **fi**

(d) Define $g'''(u, v) =_{\mathrm{def}} g'(u, v, \emptyset)$. Then

$g'''(u, v)$

$\equiv$ [unfold g''']

$g'(u, v, \emptyset)$

$\equiv$ [unfold g' as obtained in (b)]

if $\mathrm{T}(u, v)$ **then** $\emptyset \cup \mathrm{H}(u, v)$
elsf $\mathrm{B}(u, v)$ **then** $g'(\mathrm{K}(u, v), \mathrm{R}(u, v), \emptyset)$ **else** $\emptyset$ **fi**

$\equiv$ [simplification; fold g''']

if $\mathrm{T}(u, v)$ **then** $\mathrm{H}(u, v)$ **elsf** $\mathrm{B}(u, v)$ **then** $g'''(\mathrm{K}(u, v), \mathrm{R}(u, v))$ **else** $\emptyset$ **fi**

Altogether, we have derived a new (linear recursive) output scheme:

$g(X)$ **where**
  g: **m** → **set of n**
  $g(x) =_{\mathrm{def}} g'''(x, \mathrm{E})$ **where**
    g''': (u: **m** × v: **r** | $\mathrm{P}(X, u, v)$) → **set of n**
    $g'''(u, v) =_{\mathrm{def}}$
      if $\mathrm{T}(u, v)$ **then** $\mathrm{H}(u, v)$
      elsf $\mathrm{B}(u, v)$ **then** $g'''(\mathrm{K}(u, v), \mathrm{R}(u, v))$ **else** $\emptyset$ **fi**.

4.3.2 An application: Prime factors of a natural number (≥ 2)

Given a natural number n (≥ 2), it is asked to compute the sequence of all prime factors of n in increasing order.

The output type may be formally specified by

psequ $=_{\mathrm{def}}$ (s: **natsequ** | $\forall\ 1 \le i \le \#s\ \Delta\ prime(s[i])$)

where,

prime: **nat** → **bool**
prime(x) $=_{\mathrm{def}}$ « x is a prime number ».

Using, additionally,

prod: **psequ** → **nat**
prod(sp) $=_{\mathrm{def}}$ **if** sp = [] **then** 1 **else** **hd**sp * *prod*(**tl**sp) **fi**

and

$$ordered\text{: } \mathbf{psequ} \rightarrow \mathbf{bool}$$
$$ordered(sp) =_{\text{def}} \text{« } sp \text{ is increasingly ordered »}$$

a complete formal specification of the problem is given by

```
all-primes(N) where
    all-primes: nat → set of psequ
    all-primes(n) =def {sp: psequ | prod(sp) = n ∧ ordered(sp)}.
```

The result of rule application is (where **div** denotes integer division, and *divides*(*c*, *n*) tests divisibility):

```
primes(N) where
    primes: nat → set of psequ
    primes(n) =def prs(n, [], 2)

    prs: (nat × psequ × nat) → set of psequ
    prs(n, s, c) =def
        if n = 1 then {s}
        elsf true then prs(if divides(c, n) then n div c else n fi,
                           if divides(c, n) then (s++c, c)
                           else (s, next(c)) fi)
        else Ø fi

    next: nat → nat
    next(c) =def if c=2 then 3 else c+2 fi
```

where *prs* can be further transformed (using simplification of conditional; distributivity of function call and conditional; simplification) into

```
prs(n, s, c) =def
    if n = 1 then {s}
    elsf divides(c, n) then prs(n div c, s++c, c) else prs(n, s, next(c)) fi.
```

4.4 Further variants

Similar to variants 1 and 2 (where the initial specification asked for some expression over a set rather than the set itself), further variants could be given (and proved in an analogous way) to deal with other set expressions (e.g., **min**, **max**, or the like).

So far, we also have only considered variants where the alternatives resulting from the splitting of the computation according to applicability condition (4) are considered in an ordered way. Of course, we can also give analogous variants where the union

$$\bigcup_{i = 1..n(u,\, v)} \{r(X, y) \mid B(i, u, v) \,\Delta\, Q'(K(i, u, v), R(i, u, v), y)\}$$

in condition (4) is replaced by

$$\bigcup_{x \in m(u,\, v)} \{r(X, y) \mid B(x, u, v) \Delta Q'(K(x, u, v), R(x, u, v), y)\}$$

and by using

$m(u, v) \setminus \{x\}$	**for**	$next(k, u, v)$
$u \setminus \{x\}$	**for**	$K(x, u, v)$
$m(u, v) = \emptyset$	**for**	$k > n(u, v)$.

Since, however, efficient computation requires an ordering of these alternatives anyhow, we have refrained from giving these variants explicitly.

5. RELATED WORK AND CONCLUDING REMARKS

As its main contribution, this paper has presented a powerful transformation rule to convert specifications of set-valued functions defined by set comprehension into executable functional implementations that basically show the behaviour of backtrack algorithms. From this central transformation rule we have furthermore derived several variants to cope with related problems and their solution by backtracking.

5.1 Related work

Early papers that dealt with the problem of backtracking from a methodical point of view are (Gerhart, Yelowitz, 1976) and (Broy, Wirsing, 1980). Both papers give kind of functional program schemes to characterize and discuss the idea of backtracking, but do not investigate the problem of how to transform descriptive specifications into these functional schemes.

A treatment of backtracking as a solution to search problems which is fairly close to our approach can be found in the work of Doug Smith (cf., e.g., (Smith, 1986), (Smith, 1988), or (Smith, 1990) – also for further references). He gives various design strategies which achieve roughly the same effect as the application of our rule. Also the entirety of conditions required to apply these strategies is basically comparable to our applicability conditions. The main difference in the two approaches – apart from having a strategy there and a compact rule here – is in various technical aspects. Also, it is not quite clear how the variants we deal with fit into Smith's approach.

Of course, our rules presented in this paper also show many relationships to the rules presented in (Partsch, 1990). E.g., the rule "∃-elimination by backtracking II" may be considered a specialized form of variant 2 presented here, and the rule "computing qualifiers for a finite set" is but a particular special case of our central rule. Moreover, a difference in methodically looking at the problem is worth mentioned here. Whereas in (Partsch, 1990) we primarily concentrate on solutions for the existence problem and present tactics to extend these solutions to also cover the "some" or the "set-of-all" problem, we started here the other way round which considerably reduces the amount of work for concrete applications.

5.2 Concluding remarks

In some sense, the problems our rule is able to deal with, can be viewed as generate-and-test problems to produce sets the elements of which are characterized by some predicate. Although the only real restriction for the application of the rule is provided by the applicability conditions, best use of the rule can be made for those problems where the elements of the solution are "complex" (i.e., not directly computable from the input) and where the search space is large (maybe infinite) and not easily enumerable. For "simpler" problems (not showing these characteristics) application of the rule is well possible, but usually will require additional effort to simplify the result.

It is obvious, that our rule is primarily aimed at languages with the initially mentioned semantic characteristics. For these, the rule offers a possibility to convert non-operational, descriptive specifications into operational ones – maybe as a first step towards further improving efficiency or switching to an imperative implementation. In the context of a non-strict, lazy functional language (such as Gofer), the value of our rule may be doubted, since in such a language our initial specifications may be directly executed. For all our examples, however, corresponding comparisons (with Gofer implementations of the respective program versions) have shown a substantial increase in efficiency (through application of our rule) also for a non-strict, lazy functional language.

The main problem in using the given transformation rules for concrete applications is in finding the appropriate instantiations required by the applicability conditions. Although some guidance (in finding instantiations) is given by the conditions themselves as well as by the remarks in Sect. 2, three major creative activities remain to be done:

- finding a suitable way of splitting the problem into subproblems (condition (4))
- inventing an appropriate invariant P (conditions (2) and (5)), and
- defining a suitable ordering for the proof of termination (condition (6)).

Once a suitable instantiation has been found, the verification of the resulting proof obligations is straightforward and even gives potential for automation using a theorem prover. Experience (when dealing with all the examples given here and in (Achatz, Partsch, 1996)) has confirmed the assumption that the reverse of this statement also holds: Whenever complicated proof obligations resulted from some instantiation, it turned out that the real problem was with the instantiation rather than the proof obligation.

6 REFERENCES

Achatz, K. and Partsch, H.A. (1996) From Descriptive Specifications to Operational ones: A powerful transformation rule, its applications and variants. Faculty for Informatics, University of Ulm, Nr. 96-13, Ulmer Informatik-Berichte, 1996.

Bauer, F.L. and Berghammer, R. and Broy, M. and Dosch, W. and Geiselbrechtinger, F. and Gnatz, R. and Hangel, E., Hesse, W.and Krieg-Brückner, B. and Laut, A. and Matzner, T. and Möller, B. and Nickl, F. and Partsch, H. and Pepper, P. and Samelson, K. and Wirsing, M. and Wössner, H. (1985) The Munich project CIP. Volume I: The wide spectrum language CIP-L. Lecture Notes in Computer Science **183**, Springer, Berlin.

Bauer, F.L. and Möller and B., Partsch and H., Pepper, P. (1989) Programming by formal reasoning - computer-aided intuition-guided programming. IEEE Transactions on Software Engineering **15**:2, 165-180.

Boiten, E.A. and Partsch, H.A. and Tuijnman, D. and Völker, N. (1992) How to produce correct software - an introduction to formal specification and program development by transformations. The Computer Journal **35**:6, 547-554.

Broy, M. and Wirsing, M. (1980) Program development: from enumeration to backtracking. Information Processing letters **10**:4,5, 193-197.

Gerhart, S.L. and Yelowitz, L. (1976) Control structure abstractions of the backtracking programming technique. Proc. 2nd Int. Conf. on Software Engineering, October 13-15, 1976, San Francisco, Ca., 44-49. Also: IEEE Transactions on Software Engineering **2**:4, 285-292.

Partsch, H.A. (1990) Specification and transformation of programs - a formal approach to software development. Springer, Berlin

Smith, D.R. (1987) On the design of generate-and-test algorithms: subspace generators. Technical Report KES.U.86.6, Kestrel Institute, Palo Alto, Ca., 1986. Also: Meertens, L.G.L.T. (ed.): Program specification and transformation. Amsterdam: North-Holland, 207-220.

Smith, D.R. (1988) The structure and design of global search algorithms.Technical Report KES.U.87.12, Kestrel Institute, Palo Alto, Ca.Smith, D.R. (1990) KIDS: a semiautomatic program development system. IEEE Transactions on Software Engineering **16**:9, 1024-1043.

7 BIOGRAPHY

Prof. Dr. Helmuth Partsch got his degree (Dipl.-Inform.) in informatics (with mathematics as a minor) from the Technical University of Munich. There, he also received his Ph D (Dr. rer. nat.) and his Habilitation degree. From 1986 till 1992 he held a chair for Software Engineering at the University of Nijmegen, the Netherlands. Since 1993 he heads the department *Programming Methodology and Compiler Construction* in the faculty for informatics at the University of Ulm, Germany. Prof. Partsch's research interests are in formal software development, notably in formal specification and program constuction by transformations. A particular focus of his research activities is the integration of formal methods with traditional Software Engineering techniques.

Klaus Achatz got his degree (Dipl.-Math.) in mathematics (with informatics as a minor) from the University of Augsburg. Since 1993, he is a research and teaching assistant in the department *Programming Methodology and Compiler Construction* in the faculty for informatics at the University of Ulm. Klaus Achatz's research interests are in the integration of formal concepts with (object-oriented) Software Engineering methods.

Program Derivation via List Introduction

Alberto Pettorossi * *and Maurizio Proietti* **

Department of Informatics, University of Roma Tor Vergata,
Via della Ricerca Scientifica, 00133 Roma, Italy.
email: adp@iasi.rm.cnr.it
***IASI-CNR, Viale Manzoni 30, 00185 Roma, Italy.*
email: proietti@iasi.rm.cnr.it

Abstract

We present a new program transformation strategy based on the introduction of lists. This strategy overcomes some of the limitations of the tupling strategy, and in particular, it allows us to derive linear recursive programs when the tupling strategy is not successful. The linear recursive programs one may derive using this new strategy, have in most cases very good time and space performance. We present our list introduction strategy in the case of definite logic programs, but it can also be applied in the case of functional programs thereby improving some transformation techniques proposed by Cohen (1983) and by Chin and Hagiya (1995).

Keywords

Program transformation, logic programming, unfolding/folding transformation rules, tupling strategy, generalization strategy, list introduction strategy.

1 INTRODUCTION

There are various methodologies for developing programs from specifications, and in particular, for program modules of small size, one can follow the *transformation methodology*, which has been first advocated by Burstall and Darlington (1977) in the case of functional programs. This methodology is very useful in practice, because among other advantages, it can be applied to the derivation of programs written in different programming languages and it can also simplify the proofs of program correctness. In particular, in the so called 'rules + strategies' approach, correctness proofs are avoided because the rules are guaranteed to preserve program semantics.

The transformation methodology has been first applied to logic programs by Tamaki and Sato (1984), and it has been developed for programs with and without negation in the bodies of the clauses. Different sets of transformation rules have been suggested for the different classes of logic programs under consideration and the different semantics to be preserved. The interested reader may refer to Pettorossi and Proietti (1994) for a survey of recent results in the area of logic program transformation.

In this paper we consider definite logic programs, that is, no negated atoms are allowed in the bodies of the clauses, and we use the following transformation rules described in Tamaki and Sato (1984): (i) *definition introduction*, which allows us to define new predicates, often called eureka predicates in the literature, by the introduction of new clauses, (ii) *unfolding*, which consists of an application of SLD-resolution, (iii) *folding*, which substitutes an instance of the body of a clause by the corresponding instance of the head, and (iv) *goal replacement*, which replaces an old goal by a new goal. In particular, let us consider a clause C of a program P and a goal G_1 in the body of C. We can replace G_1 by the new goal G_2 if $M(P) \models \forall\overline{X}.(\exists\overline{Y}.\ G_1 \leftrightarrow \exists\overline{Z}.\ G_2)$, where $M(P)$ denotes the least Herbrand model of P, $\overline{X}$ is the *tuple* of the variables occurring in the clause obtained from C by removing G_1, $\overline{Y}$ is the tuple of the variables occurring in G_1 and not in $\overline{X}$, and $\overline{Z}$ is the tuple of the variables occurring in G_2 and not in $\overline{X}$.

For the strategies we focus our attention on the tupling and generalization strategies described in Burstall and Darlington (1977), Pettorossi (1977), Darlington (1981), and Pettorossi and Proietti (1994). We first show some of their limitations and we then propose a new strategy, called *list introduction*, to overcome these limitations.

The tupling and generalization strategies

Let us begin by recalling the basic facts about the *tupling strategy*. We are given a clause of the form:

$C.\quad H \leftarrow A_1, \ldots, A_m, B_1, \ldots, B_n$

with $m \geq 1$ and $n \geq 0$. The application of the tupling strategy amounts to the introduction of a new predicate, say t, defined by a clause of the form:

$T.\quad t(X_1, \ldots, X_k) \leftarrow A_1, \ldots, A_m$

where the arguments $X_1, \ldots, X_k$ of t are the distinct variables occurring in at least one of the atoms $A_1, \ldots, A_m$ and also occurring elsewhere in C. We then fold clause C w.r.t. the atoms $A_1, \ldots, A_m$ using clause T, and we finally look for the recursive definition of the predicate t by performing some unfolding and goal replacement steps followed by suitable folding steps using clause T itself.

The tupling strategy can be used for transforming C into a set of linear recursive clauses, that is, a set of clauses such that the body of each of them contains at most one predicate call which depends (possibly via other predicate calls) on the predicate in the corresponding head. In order to achieve this objective via the application of the tupling strategy, the following additional constraint should hold: every folding step using clause T should replace in the body where it is applied, all calls depending on the head predicate by a single call of t. Thus, in particular, the atoms $A_1, \ldots, A_m$ should contain all calls of the head predicate of C.

The application of the tupling strategy may result in an improvement of program performance because in the derived programs we need to evaluate only once the subgoals which are common to the computations evoked by the tupled atoms $A_1, \ldots, A_m$. Moreover, by tupling we can also avoid multiple visits of data structures and the construction of intermediate bindings.

In order to derive a recursive definition of the predicate t introduced by tupling it is often necessary to introduce some extra predicates. This can be done by the *generalization strategy* which we now describe.

Suppose that by performing unfolding and goal replacement steps, from a clause introduced by an application of the tupling strategy, like clause T above, we derive a new clause (possibly, together with other clauses) of the form:

$U.\quad P \leftarrow E_1, \ldots, E_r, F_1, \ldots, F_s$

and from U, by further unfoldings and goal replacements which do not involve $F_1, \ldots, F_s$, we derive:

$V.\quad Q \leftarrow H_1, \ldots, H_r, L_1, \ldots, L_t$

such that, for $i = 1, \ldots, r$, H_i has the same predicate symbol occurring in E_i.

By generalization we may introduce the new predicate g defined by the clause:

$G.\quad g(X_1, \ldots, X_d) \leftarrow J_1, \ldots, J_r$

where (i) the goal $J_1, \ldots, J_r$ is the most specific generalization of both $E_1, \ldots, E_r$ and $H_1, \ldots, H_r$, so that $(J_1, \ldots, J_r)\ \theta_E = (E_1, \ldots, E_r)$ and $(J_1, \ldots, J_r)\ \theta_H = (H_1, \ldots, H_r)$ for some substitutions θ_E and θ_H (as usual, when specifying these substitutions we assume that the clauses U, V, and G have pairwise disjoint sets of variables), and (ii) $X_1, \ldots, X_d$ are (not necessarily all) variables occurring in $J_1, \ldots, J_r$, which allow us to fold both U and V using G (see, for instance, Pettorossi and Proietti (1994)). This last condition amounts to say that a variable, say X, occurring in $J_1, \ldots, J_r$, should be included among the arguments of g iff X/u is a binding in $\theta_E \cup \theta_H$ such that u is *either* (i) a non-variable term, *or* (ii) a variable occurring in one of the atoms $P, F_1, \ldots, F_s, Q, L_1, \ldots, L_t$, *or* (iii) a variable occurring in a term z for some binding Y/z in $\theta_E \cup \theta_H$ with $Y \neq X$.

We then fold clause U using clause G and we look for the recursive definition of predicate g.

We also assume that it is possible to apply the generalization strategy starting from an initial clause which has been introduced not by tupling, but by a previous application of the generalization strategy itself, like clause G above.

A successful application of the tupling strategy

We illustrate this point by looking at the familiar derivation of a linear-time program for computing the Fibonacci numbers starting from the following exponential-time program.

1. $fib(0, s(0)) \leftarrow$
2. $fib(s(0), s(0)) \leftarrow$
3. $fib(s(s(N)), F) \leftarrow fib(s(N), F1),\ fib(N, F2),\ plus(F1, F2, F)$

with the usual clauses for *plus*. This program requires a number of *plus* operations which is exponential w.r.t. the value of N. We are able to derive a linear-time program by transforming clause 3, which is not linear recursive because of the two calls of *fib* in its body, into a set of linear recursive clauses. We start off by applying the tupling strategy, and we introduce the following clause:

4. $t\_fib(N, F1, F2) \leftarrow fib(s(N), F1),\ fib(N, F2)$

in which we tupled together the two atoms $fib(s(N), F1)$ and $fib(N, F2)$ of clause 3.

Now, by folding, we may transform clause 3 into the following clause:

5. $fib(s(s(N)), F) \leftarrow t\_fib(N, F1, F2),\ plus(F1, F2, F)$

which is linear recursive. As suggested by the tupling strategy, we now look for a recursive definition of the newly introduced predicate *t_fib*, as follows. By unfolding clause 4 we get:

6. $t\_fib(0, s(0), s(0)) \leftarrow$
7. $t\_fib(s(N), F1, F2) \leftarrow fib(s(N), F11),\ fib(N, F12),$
   $plus(F11, F12, F1),\ fib(s(N), F2)$

We have that the predicate *fib* is functional, that is,

$\forall N, X, Y.\ fib(N, X),\ fib(N, Y) \leftrightarrow fib(N, X),\ X = Y$

holds in the least Herbrand model of the given Fibonacci program. Thus, we can apply the goal replacement rule and transform clause 7 into the following one:

8. $t\_fib(s(N), F1, F2) \leftarrow fib(s(N), F11),\ fib(N, F12),$
   $plus(F11, F12, F1),\ F11 = F2$

By unfolding clause 8 w.r.t. the atom $F11 = F2$, we get:

9. $t\_fib(s(N), F1, F11) \leftarrow fib(s(N), F11),\ fib(N, F12),$
   $plus(F11, F12, F1)$

Now the two calls of *fib* in clause 9 are an instance of the body of clause 4 and, by folding, we get the following linear recursive clause:

10. $t\_fib(s(N), F1, F2) \leftarrow t\_fib(N, F11, F2),\ plus(F11, F2, F1)$

The final program, made out of clauses 1, 2, 6, and 10, is linear recursive and it requires, as we desired, only a linear number of *plus* operations for evaluating a call of *fib*.

The success of this derivation is due to the fact that by applying the unfolding and goal replacement rules to clause 4, from two calls of the Fibonacci predicate we generate again two calls of that predicate (see clause 9). Thus, by tupling together those two calls as we did in clause 4, we derive, after a folding step, a linear recursive program.

A limitation of the tupling and generalization strategies

In general, for any given initial program it is not the case that by tupling together a *fixed* number of predicate calls, we are able to derive a linear recursive program. Indeed, in the next example, we show that in order to get a linear recursive program we should tuple together an *unbounded* number of predicate calls, that is, a number of calls which depends on the values in the input goal.

Let us consider the following *World Series Odds* problem taken from Aho, Hopcroft, and Ullman (1983), page 312. Two persons, A and B, are playing a sequence of games to see who is the champion, that is, the first to win n games for some given n. We assume that each person has a 0.5 chance of winning any particular game. We use the predicate $p(I, J, K)$ to denote that at the end of the current game, (i) A needs to win I games in the future to be the champion, (ii) B needs to win J games in the future to be the champion, and (iii) K is a rational number between 0 and 1, denoting the probability that A will eventually be the champion. To compute predicate p we may use the following program:

1. $p(0, s(J), 1) \leftarrow$
2. $p(s(I), 0, 0) \leftarrow$
3. $p(s(I), s(J), K) \leftarrow p(I, s(J), K1),\ p(s(I), J, K2),\ ave(K1, K2, K)$

where s denotes the successor function and $ave(K1, K2, K)$ holds iff K is the average of $K1$ and $K2$. To understand clause 3, notice that the probability K of A becoming the champion in the case where A needs to win $s(I)$ games in the future and B needs to win $s(J)$ games in the future, can be computed as follows. Let us consider the case where A wins the next game. In this case $p(I, s(J), K1)$ holds, being $K1$ the probability that A wins the game. In the opposite case where A loses the next game, we have that $p(s(I), J, K2)$ holds. Since the probability that A wins (or loses) the next game is 0.5, then K is the average of $K1$ and $K2$.

In order to derive a linear recursive program we may apply the tupling strategy and introduce the following new predicate:

4. $tp(I, J, K1, K2) \leftarrow p(I, s(J), K1),\ p(s(I), J, K2)$

By unfolding clause 4 w.r.t. the atom $p(I, s(J), K1)$ we get:

5. $tp(0, J, s(0), K2) \leftarrow p(s(0), J, K2)$
6. $tp(s(I), J, K1, K2) \leftarrow p(I, s(J), K3),\ p(s(I), J, K4),$
   $ave(K3, K4, K1),\ p(s(s(I)), J, K2)$

In the body of clause 6 there are three calls of p and we cannot reduce their number to two by exploiting the functionality of p.

Actually, one can prove the following general result: given any sequence S of clauses starting from clause 4 such that any clause is obtained from the previous one by unfolding a p call using clause 3, and applying functionality of p whenever possible, we have that the set of *all* calls of the predicate p in a clause of S is *not* an instance of the set of *all* calls of p in a previous clause of S.

The proof of this result is related to the construction of a dag (see Fig. 1) which has the shape of a Pascal Triangle and it is built as follows: we start from the two initial calls $p(I, s(J), K1)$ and $p(s(I), J, K2)$, and then given any p call, we generate its two son calls by performing an unfolding step using clause 3. Indeed, we have that after any number of unfolding steps starting from clause 4 using clause 3, the set of p calls in the body of every generated clause is (the renaming of) a frontier of that dag. By a *frontier* we mean a set of p calls which is generated from the initial set $\{p(I, s(J), K1),\ p(s(I), J, K2)\}$ after zero or more replacements of a p call by the corresponding two son calls.

By construction the p calls in the dag of Fig. 1 satisfy the following properties: (i) when going from any p call to its left child the first argument is decreased by one and the second argument is unchanged, (ii) when going from any p call to its right child the second argument is decreased by one and the first argument is unchanged, and (iii) the third argument of any p call is the average of the third arguments of its two son calls.

Therefore, by tupling together any fixed number of p calls we will never be able to fold all p atoms and thus, we cannot derive a linear recursive program. Moreover, the generalization strategy does not help because if we replace an atom by a more general one, we do not affect the number of p atoms which are generated during the unfolding process.

The objective of the paper is to show that by suitable generalizations performed according to our *list introduction strategy*, one can indeed obtain a linear recursive program in cases where the tupling strategy does not work such as the ones illustrated by the World Series Odds example we have shown above.

Analogous problems concerning the derivation of linear programs have been considered by other authors for the case of imperative and functional languages in Cohen (1983) and Chin and Hagiya (1995). Cohen's solution is

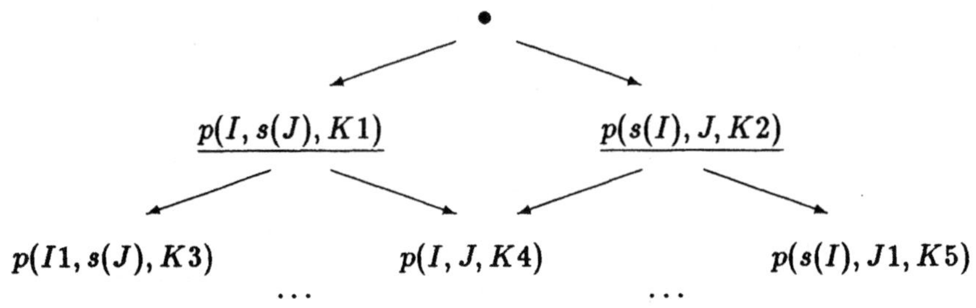

Figure 1 Directed acyclic graph of the p calls generated from the body of clause 4 (see the underlined atoms). This dag has the shape of a Pascal Triangle and the two sons of every p call are generated by unfolding that call using clause 3. We have that $I = s(I1)$ and $J = s(J1)$.

based on some abstract interpretation of the program at hand. By that analysis one determines, given the value of the input, the size of the smallest array needed for storing the results of the different function calls and thus, one avoids all redundant computations. Similarly, in Chin and Hagiya (1995) the proposed solution is based on the use of the memoization technique and a preliminary abstract interpretation of the initial program is necessary for determining the size of the array required.

The approach we describe in this paper is an improvement over those described in Cohen (1983) and in Chin and Hagiya (1995), because it makes use of standard transformational techniques only, and no abstract interpretation of the given program is required. In particular, by using our list introduction strategy together with the tupling and generalization strategies, we are able to derive programs where no repeated computations are performed. As already mentioned, our technique which is based on the introduction of lists of values, works also in the cases when the introduction of arrays of any fixed length is not successful.

Our basic idea can be described as follows. During program transformation we replace a sequence of atoms, say $p(X_1, \ldots), \ldots, p(X_n, \ldots)$, by the single atom $p\_list([X_1, \ldots, X_n], \ldots)$ where we have generalized one of the arguments of the predicate p to a list. The definition of the new predicate p_list is provided in such a way that redundant information is removed. For instance, all redundant occurrences of the variable Y in the sequence $p(X_1, Y), \ldots, p(X_n, Y)$ are eliminated by replacing that sequence by the atom $p\_list([X_1, \ldots, X_n], Y)$ whose recursive definition is as follows:

$$p\_list([\,], Y) \leftarrow$$
$$p\_list([X|Xs], Y) \leftarrow p(X, Y),\ p\_list(Xs, Y)$$

We will show that by combining list introduction with tupling and generalization, we are able to derive a final program with the desired performance.

As already mentioned, our technique is presented here with reference to logic programs, but it can easily be applied also in the case of functional programs.

The list introduction strategy can be considered as an extension of the tupling strategy whereby the sequence of atoms $p(X_1, Y), \ldots, p(X_n, Y)$ is replaced by the atom $t(X_1, \ldots, X_n, Y)$ where t is defined by the clause:

$T1.\quad t(X_1, \ldots, X_n, Y) \leftarrow p(X_1, Y), \ldots,\ p(X_n, Y)$

The main advantage of the list introduction strategy over tupling is that by list introduction we are able to replace a sequence of atoms of the form $p(X_1, Y), \ldots,\ p(X_n, Y)$, with $n \geq 0$, by a single atom $p\_list([X_1, \ldots, X_n], Y)$, whereas by using the tupling strategy, only sequences of n atoms with predicate p, for some fixed value of n, can be replaced by the corresponding t atom of clause $T1$.

An idea related to the list introduction strategy by which sequences of atoms are encoded into list arguments, was also used in the so-called *compiling control* transformation technique described in Bruynooghe, De Schreye, and Krekels (1989). However, compiling control does not follow the 'rules + strategies' approach, and it needs ad hoc correctness proofs which we do not need here because we rely on the correctness of the transformation rules.

The paper is structured as follows. In the next section we present the derivation of a linear recursive program for the familiar N-queens problem. During this derivation we see the list introduction strategy in action. This strategy is formally defined in Section 3. In that section we also show how list introduction can be combined with tupling and generalization. In Section 4 we show that by our combination of tupling, generalization, and list introduction, it is possible to derive a linear recursive program for solving the World Series Odds problem in quadratic time. Finally, in Section 5 we compare our paper with related work in the area of program transformation and we discuss the issue of mechanizing our proposed list introduction strategy.

2 AN EXAMPLE OF PROGRAM TRANSFORMATION BY LIST INTRODUCTION

Let us consider the familiar N-queens problem: we are required to place N queens on an $N \times N$ board so that no two queens lie on the same horizontal, vertical, or diagonal line. A board configuration with this property is said to be *safe*. Below we will present the initial *N-queens* program, which can be viewed as the formal specification of the given problem. This initial program, similar to the one at page 253 in Sterling and Shapiro (1994), computes the solutions by generating board configurations and checking their safeness.

An $N \times N$ board configuration Qs is represented by a list $[\langle 1, C_1\rangle, \ldots, \langle N, C_N\rangle]$, where each pair $\langle i, C_i\rangle$ for $i \in \{1, \ldots, N\}$ and $C_i \in \{1, \ldots, N\}$ denotes a queen-position in row i and column C_i.

Initial N-queens program

1. $queens(N, Qs) \leftarrow firstnumbers(N, Ns), placequeens(1, Ns, Qs),$
   $safeboard(Qs)$
2. $placequeens(R, [\,], [\,]) \leftarrow$
3. $placequeens(R, Ns, [\langle R, C\rangle | Qs]) \leftarrow select(C, Ns, Ns1),\ R1\ is\ R + 1,$
   $placequeens(R1, Ns1, Qs)$
4. $safeboard([\,]) \leftarrow$
5. $safeboard([Q|Qs]) \leftarrow safequeen(Q, Qs),\ safeboard(Qs)$
6. $safequeen(Q, [\,]) \leftarrow$
7. $safequeen(Q1, [Q2|Qs]) \leftarrow notattack(Q1, Q2),\ safequeen(Q1, Qs)$

The definitions of the predicates *firstnumbers*, *select*, and *notattack* are the following ones: $firstnumbers(N, Ns)$ holds iff Ns is the list of the first N positive integers, that is, $Ns = [1, \ldots, N]$; $select(C, Ns, Ns1)$ holds iff the list $Ns1$ is obtained from the list Ns of integers by deleting an occurrence of the integer C; and $notattack(Q1, Q2)$ holds iff the queen-position $Q1$ is not on the same diagonal of the queen-position $Q2$.

Notice that, in each board configuration generated by *placequeens*, only one queen may be placed on a given row or column, and thus, in order to check the safeness property it is only required to verify that no two queens lie on the same diagonal.

Our initial program is a typical application of the *generate-and-test* technique and it is highly inefficient, because many unsafe board configurations are generated. At page 255 of the book by Sterling and Shapiro (1994) the authors propose a more efficient *accumulator* version of the *N-queens* program which uses an accumulator to store partially generated board configurations. This accumulator parameter allows us to check whether or not a queen to be placed on the board, is on the same diagonal of an already placed queen. By doing so, backtracking may occur before an unsafe $N \times N$ board configuration is completely generated.

By applying our proposed transformation technique we will mechanically derive a program which is similar to the accumulator program version. Indeed, the use of list introduction, tupling, and generalization, will allow us to realize the so called *filter promotion* strategy described by Darlington (1978) and Bird (1984), by which the safeness test is 'promoted' into the generation process and the number of generated unsafe board configurations is decreased. A similar effect may also be achieved by the *compiling control* technique described in Bruynooghe, De Schreye, and Krekels (1989), which works by transforming a given initial logic program into a new program whose execution simulates the execution of the initial program under a more sophisticated control strategy.

In this example the filter promotion strategy can be realized by tupling together all calls of the predicates in the body of a clause which act on the same board configuration. This means that we have to apply the tupling strategy in such a way that the following constraint is satisfied: every folding step performed by using a clause introduced by tupling should produce a clause whose body contains at most one occurrence of a variable denoting a board configuration.

The tupling strategy starts off by introducing the definition of the new predicate r through the following clause:

R. $r(Ns, Qs) \leftarrow placequeens(1, Ns, Qs),\ safeboard(Qs)$

whose body is the conjunction of the atoms occurring in the body of clause 1 and sharing the variable Qs which denotes a board configuration. By folding clause 1 using clause R, we get:

$$queens(N, Qs) \leftarrow firstnumbers(N, Ns),\ t1(Ns, Qs)$$

Now we look for the recursive clauses defining the predicate r. By unfolding clause R w.r.t. the atoms *placequeens* and *safeboard*, we get:

$$r([\,],[\,]) \leftarrow$$
$$r(Ns, [\langle 1, C\rangle | Qs]) \leftarrow select(C, Ns, Ns1),\ R1\ is\ 1{+}1,\ placequeens(R1, Ns1, Qs),\ safeboard([\langle 1, C\rangle | Qs])$$

In order to get a clause whose body has only one occurrence of the variable Qs, we would like to fold this last clause we have derived by using clause R. But, unfortunately, this is not possible because '$placequeens(R1, Ns1, Qs)$, $safeboard([\langle 1, C\rangle | Qs])$' is not an instance of the body of that definition. However, to perform that folding step we may apply the generalization strategy, and we may introduce the predicate t by the following clause:

8. $t(N, Ns, Qs) \leftarrow placequeens(N, Ns, Qs),\ safeboard(Qs)$

whose body is the most specific generalization of the goal

$placequeens(R1, Ns1, Qs),\ safeboard([\langle 1, C\rangle | Qs])$

we wanted to fold, and the body of clause R.

Now the predicate *queens* can be expressed in terms of the newly introduced predicate t by folding clause 1 using clause 8 whereby deriving the following clause:

9. $queens(N, Qs) \leftarrow firstnumbers(N, Ns),\ t(1, Ns, Qs)$

whose body contains only one occurrence of Qs as desired. However, the body of clause 8 still has more than one occurrence of the variable Qs denoting a board configuration, and therefore no real gain has been achieved by this folding step. Indeed, in order to get a significant efficiency improvement, we need to avoid multiple occurrences of the variable Qs at each level of recursion. This is why, as prescribed by the tupling strategy, the transformation process now proceeds by looking for a recursive definition of the predicate t, such that the body of each clause contains at most one occurrence of any variable denoting a board configuration. In order to get this recursive definition, we will first unfold clause 8 w.r.t. *placequeens*, and then the resulting clause w.r.t. *safeboard*. By doing so we get:

10. $t(R, [\,], [\,]) \leftarrow$
11. $t(R, Ns, [\langle R, C\rangle | Qs]) \leftarrow select(C, Ns, Ns1),\ R1\ is\ R{+}1,$
$placequeens(R1, Ns1, Qs),\ \underline{safequeen(\langle R, C\rangle, Qs)},$
$safeboard(Qs)$

(In this clause and in clause 13 we have underlined some atoms for a reason which we will explain below.) It is now possible to fold clause 11 using clause 8, and by doing so we get the following recursive clause for the predicate t:

12. $t(R, Ns, [\langle R, C\rangle | Qs]) \leftarrow select(C, Ns, Ns1),\ R1\ is\ R{+}1,$
$t(R1, Ns1, Qs),\ safequeen(\langle R, C\rangle, Qs)$

Unfortunately, clause 12 contains two occurrences of the variable Qs denoting a board configuration and the evaluation of the predicate t still has an inefficient generate-and-test behaviour.

To overcome this difficulty, instead of folding clause 11, we continue the derivation process by unfolding clause 11. Indeed, if we unfold clause 11 w.r.t. the *placequeens* atom and then we unfold the derived clause w.r.t. the *safeboard* atom, we derive the following clause:

13. $t(R, Ns, [\langle R, C\rangle, \langle R1, C1\rangle | Qs]) \leftarrow select(C, Ns, Ns1),\ R1\ is\ R{+}1,$
$select(C1, Ns1, Ns2),\ R2\ is\ R1{+}1,$
$notattack(\langle R, C\rangle, \langle R1, C1\rangle),\ placequeens(R2, Ns2, Qs),$
$\underline{safequeen(\langle R, C\rangle, Qs)},\ \underline{safequeen(\langle R1, C1\rangle, Qs)},$
$safeboard(Qs)$

If we now apply the tupling strategy and we fold the goal

$placequeens(R2, Ns2, Qs),\ safeboard(Qs)$

in clause 13 using clause 8, we get two calls of the predicate *safequeen* and a call of t all sharing the variable Qs which denotes a board configuration, and therefore we will not do this folding step.

We may try to continue the program transformation process by applying the generalization strategy. But, unfortunately, there is no pair of goals, say $E_1, \ldots, E_r$ and $H_1, \ldots, H_r$, such that: (i) they occur in the bodies of the clauses 11 and 13, respectively, (ii) they have a common generalization, and (iii) they contain all atoms sharing the variable Qs which occur in the bodies of clauses 11 and 13, respectively.

Although the tupling and the generalization strategies do not work, we may continue our transformation process as we now indicate, and this will provide an example of the list introduction strategy we want to introduce in this paper. We make the key observation that in clause 11 there is *one* atom with predicate *safequeen* and in clause 13, derived from clause 11 by unfolding, there are *two* atoms with predicate *safequeen* (see the underlined atoms). If we continue the unfolding process, we generate a clause with three *safequeen* atoms, and so on.

All these *safequeen* atoms are variants of each other and they share the second argument Qs. As we will show in more detail in the next section, this allows us to apply the list introduction strategy by defining the following new predicate *safequeen_list* which is the so called *list generalization* of the predicate *safequeen*:

14. $safequeen\_list([\,], Qs) \leftarrow$
15. $safequeen\_list([\langle R, C\rangle|Ps], Qs) \leftarrow safequeen(\langle R, C\rangle, Qs),$
$\qquad safequeen\_list(Ps, Qs)$

By clause 14 an atom of the form $safequeen\_list([\,], Qs)$ can be added to the body of any clause, for any instance of Qs. This step can be viewed as an application of the goal replacement rule. Also, by folding using clause 15, any goal which is an instance of '$safequeen(\langle R, C\rangle, Qs),\ safequeen\_list(Ps, Qs)$' can be replaced by the corresponding instance of $safequeen\_list([\langle R, C\rangle|Ps], Qs)$. Thus, by using clauses 14 and 15, any conjunction of n atoms, with $n \geq 0$, of the form

$$safequeen(\langle R1, C1\rangle, Qs), \ldots,\ safequeen(\langle Rn, Cn\rangle, Qs)$$

occurring in the body of a clause, can be replaced by the atom

$$safequeen\_list([\langle R1, C1\rangle, \ldots, \langle Rn, Cn\rangle], Qs)$$

In particular, clauses 11 and 13 may be transformed into the following clauses 16 and 17, respectively:

16. $t(R, Ns, [\langle R, C\rangle|Qs]) \leftarrow select(C, Ns, Ns1),\ R1\ is\ R{+}1,$
$\qquad placequeens(R1, Ns1, Qs),\ safequeen\_list([\langle R, C\rangle], Qs),$
$\qquad safeboard(Qs)$
17. $t(R, Ns, [\langle R, C\rangle, \langle R1, C1\rangle|Qs]) \leftarrow select(C, Ns, Ns1),\ R1\ is\ R{+}1,$
$\qquad select(C1, Ns1, Ns2),\ R2\ is\ R1{+}1,$
$\qquad notattack(\langle R, C\rangle, \langle R1, C1\rangle),\ placequeens(R2, Ns2, Qs),$
$\qquad safequeen\_list([\langle R, C\rangle, \langle R1, C1\rangle], Qs),$
$\qquad safeboard(Qs)$

We are now able to apply the generalization strategy and we introduce a new predicate *gent* defined by the following clause:

18. $gent(X, Y, Qs, R, C, Ps) \leftarrow placequeens(X, Y, Qs),$
$\qquad \underline{safequeen\_list([\langle R, C\rangle|Ps], Qs)},\ safeboard(Qs)$

whose body is the most specific generalization (see the underlined atoms) of the goal

$placequeens(R1, Ns1, Qs),\ \underline{safequeen\_list([\langle R, C\rangle], Qs)},\ safeboard(Qs)$

in the body of clause 16 and the goal

$placequeens(R2, Ns2, Qs),\ \underline{safequeen\_list([\langle R, C\rangle, \langle R1, C1\rangle], Qs)},\ safeboard(Qs)$

in the body of clause 17. Then, by folding clause 11 we get:

19. $t(R, Ns, [\langle R, C\rangle | Qs]) \leftarrow select(C, Ns, Ns1),\ R1\ is\ R{+}1,$
$gent(R1, Ns1, Qs, R, C, [\,])$

The program derived so far is made out of clauses 9, 10, 19, together with the clauses which are required for the evaluation of the predicate *gent* defined by clause 18. Thus, we are left with the task of deriving a recursive definition of this predicate.

By unfolding clause 18 w.r.t. *placequeens* we get:

20. $gent(R, [\,], [\,], R, C, Ps) \leftarrow safequeen\_list([\langle R, C\rangle | Ps], [\,])$
21. $gent(R1, Ns1, [\langle R1, C1\rangle | Qs], R, C, Ps) \leftarrow$
$select(C1, Ns1, Ns2),\ R2\ is\ R1{+}1,$
$placequeens(R2, Ns2, Qs),$
$safequeen\_list([\langle R, C\rangle | Ps], [\langle R1, C1\rangle | Qs]),$
$safeboard([\langle R1, C1\rangle | Qs])$

Since $safequeen\_list([\langle R, C\rangle | Ps], [\,]) \leftrightarrow true$ in the least Herbrand model of the program at hand (see clauses 14 and 15), by applying goal replacement to clause 20 we get:

20.1 $gent(R, [\,], [\,], R, C, Ps) \leftarrow$

By unfolding clause 21 w.r.t. *safequeen_list* and the resulting clause w.r.t. *safequeen*, we get:

22. $gent(R1, Ns1, [\langle R1, C1\rangle | Qs], R, C, Ps) \leftarrow$
$select(C1, Ns1, Ns2),\ R2\ is\ R1{+}1,$
$placequeens(R2, Ns2, Qs),$
$notattack(\langle R, C\rangle, \langle R1, C1\rangle),\ \underline{safequeen(\langle R, C\rangle, Qs)},$
$safequeen\_list(Ps, [\langle R1, C1\rangle | Qs]),$
$safeboard([\langle R1, C1\rangle | Qs])$

By unfolding clause 22 w.r.t. *safequeen_list* we get:

23. $gent(R1, Ns1, [\langle R1, C1\rangle | Qs], R, C, [\,]) \leftarrow$
$select(C1, Ns1, Ns2),\ R2\ is\ R1{+}1,$
$placequeens(R2, Ns2, Qs),$
$notattack(\langle R, C\rangle, \langle R1, C1\rangle),\ safequeen(\langle R, C\rangle, Qs),$
$safeboard([\langle R1, C1\rangle | Qs])$
24. $gent(R1, Ns1, [\langle R1, C1\rangle | Qs], R, C, [\langle R3, C3\rangle | Ps1]) \leftarrow$
$select(C1, Ns1, Ns2),\ R2\ is\ R1{+}1,$
$placequeens(R2, Ns2, Qs),$
$notattack(\langle R, C\rangle, \langle R1, C1\rangle),\ safequeen(\langle R, C\rangle, Qs),$
$safequeen(\langle R3, C3\rangle, [\langle R1, C1\rangle | Qs]),$
$safequeen\_list(Ps1, [\langle R1, C1\rangle | Qs]),$
$safeboard([\langle R1, C1\rangle | Qs])$

By unfolding clause 24 w.r.t. $safequeen(\langle R3, C3\rangle, [\langle R1, C1\rangle | Qs])$ we have:

25. $gent(R1, Ns1, [\langle R1, C1\rangle|Qs], R, C, [\langle R3, C3\rangle|Ps1]) \leftarrow$
$select(C1, Ns1, Ns2),\ R2\ is\ R1{+}1,$
$placequeens(R2, Ns2, Qs),$
$notattack(\langle R, C\rangle, \langle R1, C1\rangle),\ \underline{safequeen(\langle R, C\rangle, Qs),}$
$notattack(\langle R3, C3\rangle, \langle R1, C1\rangle),\ \underline{safequeen(\langle R3, C3\rangle, Qs),}$
$safequeen\_list(Ps1, [\langle R1, C1\rangle|Qs]),$
$safeboard([\langle R1, C1\rangle|Qs])$

Let us now look at the unfolding process from clause 22 to clause 25. Similarly to the unfolding steps which lead from clause 11 to clause 13, we have that in clause 22 there is one atom with predicate *safequeen* and in clause 25 there are two atoms with predicate *safequeen* (see the underlined atoms). All these *safequeen* atoms are variants of each other and they all share the variable *Qs* denoting a board configuration. Thus, we may apply the list introduction strategy (see Section 3) as follows.

By applying the goal replacement rule we replace the underlined atom of clause 22 by $safequeen\_list([\langle R, C\rangle], Qs)$ and the two underlined atoms of clause 25 by the atom $safequeen\_list([\langle R, C\rangle, \langle R3, C3\rangle], Qs)$. We get the following clauses:

26. $gent(R1, Ns1, [\langle R1, C1\rangle|Qs], R, C, Ps) \leftarrow$
$select(C1, Ns1, Ns2),\ R2\ is\ R1{+}1,$
$placequeens(R2, Ns2, Qs),$
$notattack(\langle R, C\rangle, \langle R1, C1\rangle),\ safequeen\_list([\langle R, C\rangle], Qs),$
$safequeen\_list(Ps, [\langle R1, C1\rangle|Qs]),$
$safeboard([\langle R1, C1\rangle|Qs])$

27. $gent(R1, Ns1, [\langle R1, C1\rangle|Qs], R, C, [\langle R3, C3\rangle|Ps1]) \leftarrow$
$select(C1, Ns1, Ns2),\ R2\ is\ R1{+}1,$
$placequeens(R2, Ns2, Qs),$
$notattack(\langle R, C\rangle, \langle R1, C1\rangle),$
$notattack(\langle R3, C3\rangle, \langle R1, C1\rangle),$
$safequeen\_list([\langle R, C\rangle, \langle R3, C3\rangle], Qs),$
$safequeen\_list(Ps1, [\langle R1, C1\rangle|Qs]),$
$safeboard([\langle R1, C1\rangle|Qs])$

Now we perform a generalization step and we introduce the predicate *ggent* defined by the following clause:

28. $ggent(R2, Ns2, Qs, R, C, Ps1, Ps2, R1, C1) \leftarrow$
$placequeens(R2, Ns2, Qs),$
$safequeen\_list([\langle R, C\rangle|Ps1], Qs),$
$safequeen\_list(Ps2, [\langle R1, C1\rangle|Qs]),$
$safeboard([\langle R1, C1\rangle|Qs])$

The body of this clause is the most specific generalization of the following two goals E and H occurring in the body of clauses 26 and 27, respectively:

E. $placequeens(R2, Ns2, Qs)$, $safequeen\_list([\langle R, C\rangle], Qs)$,
$safequeen\_list(Ps, [\langle R1, C1\rangle | Qs])$, $safeboard([\langle R1, C1\rangle | Qs])$

H. $placequeens(R2, Ns2, Qs)$, $safequeen\_list([\langle R, C\rangle, \langle R3, C3\rangle], Qs)$,
$safequeen\_list(Ps1, [\langle R1, C1\rangle | Qs])$, $safeboard([\langle R1, C1\rangle | Qs])$

Notice that E and H are the sets of atoms in the body of clauses 26 and 27, respectively, depending on the variable Qs.

We can then fold clause 26 using clause 28 and we get:

26.f $gent(R1, Ns1, [\langle R1, C1\rangle | Qs], R, C, Ps) \leftarrow$
$select(C1, Ns1, Ns2)$, $R2$ *is* $R1{+}1$,
$notattack(\langle R, C\rangle, \langle R1, C1\rangle)$,
$ggent(R2, Ns2, Qs, R, C, [\,], Ps, R1, C1)$

The program derived so far is made out of clauses 9, 10, 19, 20.1, 26.f, together with the clauses for the evaluation of the predicate *ggent* defined by clause 28. Thus, we are now left with the task of deriving a recursive definition of this predicate.

This derivation is shown in the Appendix. It is a derivation very similar to the one we have done above for the predicate *gent*. The final program we get is as follows:

N-queens program with accumulators

9. $queens(N, Qs) \leftarrow firstnumbers(N, Ns)$, $t(1, Ns, Qs)$

10. $t(R, [\,], [\,]) \leftarrow$

19. $t(R, Ns, [\langle R, C\rangle | Qs]) \leftarrow select(C, Ns, Ns1)$, $R1$ *is* $R{+}1$,
$gent(R1, Ns1, Qs, R, C, [\,])$

20.1 $gent(R, [\,], [\,], R, C, Ps) \leftarrow$

26.f $gent(R1, Ns1, [\langle R1, C1\rangle | Qs], R, C, Ps) \leftarrow$
$select(C1, Ns1, Ns2)$, $R2$ *is* $R1{+}1$,
$notattack(\langle R, C\rangle, \langle R1, C1\rangle)$,
$ggent(R2, Ns2, Qs, R, C, [\,], Ps, R1, C1)$

29.3 $ggent(R2, Ns2, Qs, R, C, Ps1, [\,], R1, C1) \leftarrow$
$gent(R2, Ns2, Qs, R1, C1, [\langle R, C\rangle | Ps1])$

30.3 $ggent(R2, Ns2, Qs, R, C, Ps1, [\langle R3, C3\rangle | Ps2], R1, C1) \leftarrow$
$notattack(\langle R3, C3\rangle, \langle R1, C1\rangle)$,
$ggent(R2, Ns2, Qs, R3, C3, [\langle R, C\rangle | Ps1], Ps2, R1, C1)$

This program performs much less backtracking than the initial program and its operational behaviour is similar to the *accumulator program* given in Sterling and Shapiro (1994) at page 255. By clause 19 for predicate t, the first queen position $\langle R, C\rangle$ is selected and predicate *gent* is called with its last argument bound to the empty list. This last argument of *gent* stores the board configuration generated so far, except for the first queen position (whose row and column correspond to the fourth and fifth argument of *gent*, respectively). When a new queen is placed at position $\langle R1, C1\rangle$ and it is not attacked by a queen in position $\langle R, C\rangle$, the predicate *ggent* checks whether or not this queen is attacked by any previously placed queen whose position is in *Ps* (see clause 26.f). In case it is not attacked, the configuration is updated (see clause 29.3), otherwise, by backtracking, a different queen-position is considered. If no position for the new queen is safe, then by backtracking, the position of a previously placed queen, if any, is modified.

As a final remark, notice that we can simplify the final program we have derived by unfolding clause 9 w.r.t. the atom $t(1, Ns, Qs)$. We leave this task to the reader.

3 THE LIST INTRODUCTION STRATEGY

In this section we formally present our list introduction strategy which is used to replace a list of goals by a single atom having a list of values as one of its arguments. We have already mentioned that the list introduction strategy extends the tupling strategy so that, for instance, we may replace a list of atoms of the form:

(1) $p(X_1, Y), \ldots, p(X_n, Y)$

by the single atom $p\_list([X_1, \ldots, X_n], Y)$ where the occurrences of Y in the p atoms have been replaced by a single occurrence of Y in the second argument of *p_list*, thereby avoiding the redundant occurrences of the variable Y. We already saw that the predicate *p_list* can be defined as follows:

$$p\_list([\,], Y) \leftarrow$$
$$p\_list([X|Xs], Y) \leftarrow p(X, Y),\ p\_list(Xs, Y)$$

In this case the use of the *p_list* predicate corresponds to the use of the higher-order function *map* in a functional programming language. Indeed, we have that:

$$map\ (\lambda x.p(x, Y))\ [X_1, \ldots, X_n] = [p(X_1, Y), \ldots, p(X_n, Y)]$$

However, it is not always the case that redundant arguments in a list of atoms occur at the same argument position. For instance, let us consider the following list of atoms:

(2) $q(T_0, X_1, T_1), q(T_1, X_2, T_2), q(T_2, X_3, T_3), \ldots, q(T_{n-1}, X_n, T_n)$

where every atom has its third argument equal to the first argument of the atom to its right. In this case we can avoid the intermediate variables $T_1, \ldots, T_{n-1}$ by replacing the given list (2) of atoms by the atom $q\_list(T_0, [X_1, \ldots, X_n], T_n)$, defined as follows:

$$q\_list(T, [\,], T) \leftarrow$$
$$q\_list(T_0, [X|Xs], T_n) \leftarrow q(T_0, X, T_1),\ q\_list(T_1, Xs, T_n)$$

The use of the predicate *q_list* is similar to the use of the higher-order function *foldl* when q is a predicate such that $q(T, X, T')$ holds iff $T \oplus X = T'$ for some function $\oplus$. Indeed, we have that: $q\_list(T_0, [X_1, \ldots, X_n], T_n)$ holds iff $foldl \ \oplus \ T_0 \ [X_1, \ldots, X_n] = T_n$, where as usual, $foldl \ \oplus \ T \ [\ ] = T$ and $foldl \ \oplus \ T_0 \ [X_1, \ldots, X_n] = (\ldots(T_0 \oplus X_1) \ldots \oplus X_n)$.

Now for any given predicate p we provide a general definition of *p_list* which works in particular for lists of atoms of kind (1) and (2) shown above. In this general definition we also consider the case of a list of possibly *non-atomic* goals such that each goal may contain internal variables, that is, variables occurring in that goal only, and not elsewhere in the clause where that goal occurs. In general, a variable X occurring in a goal G in the body of a clause C is said to be an *internal variable of G in C* iff each occurrence of X in C is also an occurrence of X in G.

Recall that by $\overline{X}$ we denote a tuple of variables $\langle X_1, \ldots, X_n \rangle$ for some $n \geq 0$. The empty tuple is denoted by ε. When no confusion arises, we will feel free to identify the variable Z with the singleton tuple $\langle Z \rangle$. Two tuples $\overline{X}$ and $\overline{Y}$ of variables are *disjoint* iff no variable occurs in both of them. In order to denote goals and to refer to the variables occurring in them, we use greek letters with tuple arguments, so that, for instance, $\pi(\overline{V}_1, \ldots, \overline{V}_n)$ denotes a goal such that (i) each of its variables occurs in at least one of the tuples $\overline{V}_1, \ldots, \overline{V}_n$, and (ii) for $i = 1, \ldots, n$, every variable in $\overline{V}_i$ occurs in the goal.

Definition 1. Let $\pi(\overline{I}, \overline{T}, \overline{X}, \overline{T}', \overline{Y})$ be a goal where $\overline{I}, \overline{T}, \overline{X}, \overline{T}'$, and $\overline{Y}$ are pairwise disjoint tuples of variables. A goal R occurring in the body of a clause C is said to be a *goal list of length n based on $\pi(\overline{I}, \overline{T}, \overline{X}, \overline{T}', \overline{Y})$* iff it is of the form:

$$\pi(\overline{I}_1, \overline{T}_0, \overline{X}_1, \overline{T}_1, \overline{Y}),\ \pi(\overline{I}_2, \overline{T}_1, \overline{X}_2, \overline{T}_2, \overline{Y}),\ \ldots,\ \pi(\overline{I}_n, \overline{T}_{n-1}, \overline{X}_n, \overline{T}_n, \overline{Y})$$

where: (i) $n \geq 0$, (ii) $\overline{I}_1, \ldots, \overline{I}_n, \overline{T}_0, \ldots, \overline{T}_n, \overline{X}_1, \ldots, \overline{X}_n$, and $\overline{Y}$ are pairwise disjoint tuples of variables, (iii) for $i = 1, \ldots, n$, $\overline{I}_i$ is a tuple of internal variables of $\pi(\overline{I}_i, \overline{T}_{i-1}, \overline{X}_i, \overline{T}_i, \overline{Y})$ in C, and (iv) $\overline{T}_1, \ldots, \overline{T}_{n-1}$ are tuples of internal variables of R in C.

In this definition of a goal list R the order of the arguments is significant. For example, if we interchange the first and fifth arguments of the n variants of the goal $\pi(\overline{I}, \overline{T}, \overline{X}, \overline{T}', \overline{Y})$ in R (that is, for $i = 1, \ldots, n$, we interchange $\overline{I}_i$ with $\overline{Y}$), then we obtain a goal R' which is not a goal list. Indeed, in R' the first argument of every π goal is the tuple $\overline{Y}$, while the definition of a goal list requires two different π goals to have two disjoint tuples of variables as first argument.

Notice also that in the definition of a goal list we use five tuples of variables. This is not a restriction, because tuples may consist of any number of variables (even zero).

To see an example of a goal list, let us consider the clause:

$$D.\quad h(U_0, V_0, U_3, V_3, X_1, Y) \leftarrow r(U_0, U_1),\ s(V_1, Y, V_0),\ t(I_1, X_1),\ r(U_1, U_2),\ s(V_2, Y, V_1),\ t(I_2, X_2),\ r(U_2, U_3),\ s(V_3, Y, V_2),\ t(I_3, X_3)$$

The body of D is a goal list of length 3 based on the goal $\delta(I, \langle U, V\rangle, X, \langle U', V'\rangle, Y)$ which is $r(U, U')$, $s(V', Y, V)$, $t(I, X)$. (In the arguments of δ we have identified $\langle I\rangle$, $\langle X\rangle$, and $\langle Y\rangle$ with I, X, and Y respectively.)

In the following definition we present the concept of list generalization. Given a goal $\pi(\overline{I}, \overline{T}, \overline{X}, \overline{T}', \overline{Y})$, by list generalization we introduce a new predicate *p_list* whose second argument is a list.

Definition 2. The *list generalization* of the goal $\pi(\overline{I}, \overline{T}, \overline{X}, \overline{T}', \overline{Y})$ is the predicate *p_list* defined by the following two clauses:

$$C1.\quad p\_list(\overline{T}, [\,], \overline{T}, \overline{Y}) \leftarrow$$

$$C2.\quad p\_list(\overline{T}_0, [\overline{X}|Xs], \overline{T}_n, \overline{Y}) \leftarrow \pi(\overline{I}, \overline{T}_0, \overline{X}, \overline{T}_1, \overline{Y}),\ p\_list(\overline{T}_1, Xs, \overline{T}_n, \overline{Y})$$

For instance, the list generalization of the goal $\delta(I, \langle U, V\rangle, X, \langle U', V'\rangle, Y)$ considered above, is the predicate *d_list* defined by the clauses:

$$D1.\quad d\_list(\langle U, V\rangle, [\,], \langle U, V\rangle, Y) \leftarrow$$

$$D2.\quad d\_list(\langle U_0, V_0\rangle, [X|Xs], \langle U_n, V_n\rangle, Y) \leftarrow r(U_0, U_1),\ s(V_1, Y, V_0),\ t(I_1, X_1),\ d\_list(\langle U_1, V_1\rangle, Xs, \langle U_n, V_n\rangle, Y)$$

The clauses for the predicate *p_list* introduced by list generalization can often be simplified by replacing each tuple of k arguments by k distinct arguments and by dropping arguments which are empty tuples.

We will now present some properties of the predicate *p_list* which are used in the derivations presented in this paper.

Property P1. Let P be a program where the predicate *p_list* is defined by clauses $C1$ and $C2$ above. For any goal list R of length n, with $n \geq 0$, based on $\pi(\overline{I}, \overline{T}, \overline{X}, \overline{T}', \overline{Y})$, of the form

$$\pi(\overline{I}_1, \overline{T}_0, \overline{X}_1, \overline{T}_1, \overline{Y}),\ \pi(\overline{I}_2, \overline{T}_1, \overline{X}_2, \overline{T}_2, \overline{Y}),\ \ldots,\ \pi(\overline{I}_n, \overline{T}_{n-1}, \overline{X}_n, \overline{T}_n, \overline{Y})$$

we have that:

$$M(P) \models \forall \overline{T}_0, \overline{X}_1, \ldots, \overline{X}_n, \overline{T}_n, \overline{Y}.\ ((\exists \overline{I}_1, \ldots, \overline{I}_n, \overline{T}_1, \ldots, \overline{T}_{n-1}.\ R) \leftrightarrow p\_list(\overline{T}_0, [\overline{X}_1, \ldots, \overline{X}_n], \overline{T}_n, \overline{Y})) \qquad \square$$

This Property P1 allows us to perform a crucial step when applying the list introduction strategy in the sense that, as specified in the Introduction, we may replace in a clause C the goal list R by the atom $p\_list(\overline{T}_0, [\overline{X}_1, \ldots, \overline{X}_n], \overline{T}_n, \overline{Y})$.

Property P2. Let P be a program where the predicate *p_list* is defined by clauses $C1$ and $C2$ above. We have that:

$$M(P) \models \forall \overline{T}_0, L_1, L_2, \overline{T}_n, \overline{Y}.$$
$$((\exists \overline{T}.\ (p\_list(\overline{T}_0, L_1, \overline{T}, \overline{Y}),\ p\_list(\overline{T}, L_2, \overline{T}_n, \overline{Y}))) \leftrightarrow$$
$$\exists L.\ (append(L_1, L_2, L),\ p\_list(\overline{T}_0, L, \overline{T}_n, \overline{Y})))$$

where *append* is the predicate for list concatenation. □

By this equivalence, we may replace in a clause C a goal of the form '$p\_list(\overline{T}_0, L_1, \overline{T}, \overline{Y}),\ p\_list(\overline{T}, L_2, \overline{T}_n, \overline{Y})$' by the goal '$append(L_1, L_2, L), p\_list(\overline{T}_0, L, \overline{T}_n, \overline{Y})$'.

By Property P2, the predicate *p_list* defines a *homomorphism* w.r.t. the list structure in its second argument, in the sense of Bird and Meertens (1987).

Let us now describe the list introduction strategy. This strategy combined with the tupling strategy is able to deal with the case where an unbounded number of calls should be tupled together to derive efficient programs. The application of the list introduction strategy essentially consists in: (i) matching a given clause, say U, with a previously derived clause, say V, as in the case of the application of the generalization strategy, (ii) performing some goal replacement steps using Property P1, thereby deriving the new clauses *U_list* and *V_list*, and finally (iii) introducing a new predicate defined by a clause whose body is the most specific generalization of goals occurring in the bodies of *U_list* and *V_list*.

We first introduce the following concept.

Definition 3. Let us consider two goals R_1 and R_2 which are goal lists of length n_1 and n_2, respectively, based on the same goal. We say that the goal R_2 is an *extension* of the goal R_1 iff $n_2 > n_1$.

The List Introduction Strategy

Let us consider the clause C defining a new predicate introduced by applying the tupling or generalization strategies as we have described them in the Introduction. Suppose that by performing unfolding and goal replacement steps, from clause C we derive a clause of the form:

$U.\quad P \leftarrow E_1, \ldots, E_r,\ F,\ H_1, \ldots, H_t$

and from U, by further applications of the unfolding and goal replacement rules not involving $H_1, \ldots, H_t$, we derive:

$V.\quad Q \leftarrow I_1, \ldots, I_r,\ L,\ M_1, \ldots, M_d$

where: (i) for $j = 1, \ldots, r$, E_j and I_j are atoms with the same predicate symbol, (ii) F and L are goal lists based on the same goal, say $\pi(\overline{I}, \overline{T}, \overline{X}, \overline{T}', \overline{Y})$, and (iii) L is an extension of F.

Step 1. By list generalization of $\pi(\overline{I}, \overline{T}, \overline{X}, \overline{T}', \overline{Y})$ we introduce the new predicate *p_list* defined by clauses $C1$ and $C2$ as in Definition 2.

Step 2. By applying Property P1 we replace F and L by the atoms $p\_list(\ldots, \ell_F, \ldots)$ and $p\_list(\ldots, \ell_L, \ldots)$, respectively. The values of the list arguments ℓ_F and ℓ_L occurring in the second argument positions in those atoms, are the ones which make Property P1 true. Thus, we derive the following two clauses:

U_list. $P \leftarrow E_1, \ldots, E_r,\ p\_list(\ldots, \ell_F, \ldots),\ H_1, \ldots, H_t$

V_list. $Q \leftarrow I_1, \ldots, I_r,\ p\_list(\ldots, \ell_L, \ldots),\ M_1, \ldots, M_d$

We have that the length of ℓ_L is strictly greater than the length of ℓ_F, because L is an extension of F.

Step 3. By the generalization strategy, we introduce the new predicate:

G. $genp\_list(V_1, \ldots, V_k) \leftarrow N_1, \ldots, N_r,\ p\_list(\ldots, \ell, \ldots)$

whose body is the most specific generalization of the goal

$E_1, \ldots, E_r,\ p\_list(\ldots, \ell_F, \ldots)$

occurring in the body of *U_list* and the goal

$I_1, \ldots, I_r,\ p\_list(\ldots, \ell_L, \ldots)$

occurring in the body of *V_list*. The variables $V_1, \ldots, V_k$ are chosen as already indicated in the generalization strategy described in the Introduction.

Step 4. We fold clause *U_list* using clause *G*.

Step 5. Finally, we look for the recursive definition of the newly introduced predicate *genp_list*. For deriving this recursive definition we may perform unfolding, folding, and goal replacement steps, including goal replacements based on Properties P1 and P2. □

The reader may verify that the derivation of the N-queens program in Section 2 has been performed according to the combination of the tupling, generalization, and list introduction strategies presented in this section. In particular, clauses 11, 13, 16, 17, and 18 of that derivation correspond, respectively, to the clauses U, V, *U_list*, *V_list*, and G we have now mentioned when describing the five steps of the list introduction strategy.

4 THE WORLD SERIES ODDS EXAMPLE

In this section we return to the World Series Odds example considered in Section 1 and we show that we can derive a quadratic time program from the exponential time specification by using our list introduction strategy together with the tupling and generalization strategies.

For the reader's convenience, we recall here the clauses of the initial program.

1. $p(0, s(J), 1) \leftarrow$
2. $p(s(I), 0, 0) \leftarrow$
3. $p(s(I), s(J), K) \leftarrow p(I, s(J), K1),\ p(s(I), J, K2),\ ave(K1, K2, K)$

We also recall that by applying the tupling strategy we have introduced the following predicate:

4. $tp(I, J, K1, K2) \leftarrow p(I, s(J), K1),\ p(s(I), J, K2)$

By unfolding and goal replacement steps using the functionality of p, from clause 4 we derive:

$$7.\quad tp(s(I), s(J), K1, K2) \leftarrow p(I, s(s(J)), K3),\ p(s(I), s(J), K4),\ p(s(s(I)), J, K5),\ ave(K3, K4, K1),\ ave(K4, K5, K2)$$

In the Introduction we have already stated that the application of the tupling strategy cannot be successful in our case, and thus, we may try to apply the list introduction strategy. The application of this new strategy is also suggested by the fact that the number of p atoms is increasing when performing successive unfolding steps.

Notice, however, that the list of p atoms in clause 7 is *not* an extension of the list of p atoms in clause 4 because, in particular, those atoms are not variants of each other. Thus, in order to apply the list introduction strategy we need to derive from clauses 4 and 7 two other clauses which satisfy the conditions for the clauses U and V (see the list introduction strategy in Section 3).

The derivation of these new clauses can be done by using the so called *generalization + equality introduction* rule (see Proietti and Pettorossi (1995)) which is an instance of the goal replacement rule. It consists in replacing a goal, say $A_1, \ldots, A_n$, by the goal $Gen_1, \ldots, Gen_n,\ X_1 = t_1, \ldots, X_r = t_r$, such that $(Gen_1, \ldots, Gen_n)\theta = A_1, \ldots, A_n$, where θ is the substitution $\{X_1/t_1, \ldots, X_r/t_r\}$. Notice that by this rule we promote a term to a variable, and thus, it is always possible to generate a list of p atoms which are variants of each other.

By using the generalization+equality introduction rule we transform clauses 4 and 7 into the following two clauses which satisfy the necessary conditions for applying the list introduction strategy:

$$8.\quad tp(I, J, K1, K2) \leftarrow J1 = s(J),\ p(I, J1, K1),\ I1 = s(I),\ p(I1, J, K2)$$

$$9.\quad tp(s(I), s(J), K1, K2) \leftarrow J2 = s(J1),\ p(I, J2, K3),\ I1 = s(I),\ J1 = s(J),\ p(I1, J1, K4),\ I2 = s(I1),\ p(I2, J, K5),\ ave(K3, K4, K1),\ ave(K4, K5, K2)$$

Indeed, let us consider the goal:

F: $J1 = s(J),\ p(I, J1, K1),\ I1 = s(I)$

in the body of clause 8 and the following goals in the body of clause 9:

L_1: $J2 = s(J1),\ p(I, J2, K3),\ I1 = s(I)$, and

L_2: $J1 = s(J),\ p(I1, J1, K4),\ I2 = s(I1)$

Let $\mu(\varepsilon, \langle J1, I\rangle, K1, \langle J, I1\rangle, \varepsilon)$ be the goal

$J1 = s(J),\ p(I, J1, K1),\ I1 = s(I)$.

The goal F and the goals L_1 and L_2 are all variants of the goal $\mu(\varepsilon, \langle J1, I\rangle, K1, \langle J, I1\rangle, \varepsilon)$. Actually, F and (L_1, L_2) are goal lists based on the same goal $\mu(\varepsilon, \langle J1, I\rangle, K1, \langle J, I1\rangle, \varepsilon)$. Moreover, (L_1, L_2) is an extension of F. Thus, we may apply the list introduction strategy. Here are the corresponding five steps.

Step 1. By list generalization of $\mu(\varepsilon, \langle J1, I\rangle, K1, \langle J, I1\rangle, \varepsilon)$ we define the following predicate:

10. $m\_list(J2, I, [\,], J2, I) \leftarrow$
11. $m\_list(J1, I, [K1|Ks], Jn, In) \leftarrow J1 = s(J),\ p(I, J1, K1),\ I1 = s(I),$
    $m\_list(J, I1, Ks, Jn, In)$

where we have replaced tuples of variables by distinct arguments and we have dropped arguments with empty tuples.

Step 2. By Property P1 clauses 8 and 9 can be transformed into the following two clauses, respectively (they correspond to the clauses *U_list* and *V_list* of the list introduction strategy in Section 3):

12. $tp(I, J, K1, K2) \leftarrow m\_list(J1, I, [K1], J, I1),\ p(I1, J, K2)$
13. $tp(s(I), s(J), K1, K2) \leftarrow m\_list(J2, I, [K3, K4], J, I2),$
    $p(I2, J, K5),$
    $ave(K3, K4, K1),\ ave(K4, K5, K2)$

Step 3. By the generalization strategy we introduce the following new predicate:

14. $genm\_list(J1, I, K1, Ks, J, K2) \leftarrow m\_list(J1, I, [K1|Ks], J, I1),$
    $p(I1, J, K2)$

whose body is the most specific generalization of the goal:

$m\_list(J1, I, [K1], J, I1),\ p(I1, J, K2)$ occurring in the body of clause 12, and the goal

$m\_list(J2, I, [K3, K4], J, I2),\ p(I2, J, K5)$ occurring in the body of clause 13.

Step 4. We fold clause 12 by using the newly introduced predicate *genm_list* and we get:

15. $tp(I, J, K1, K2) \leftarrow genm\_list(J1, I, K1, [\,], J, K2)$

Step 5. We are now left with the task of finding a recursive definition of *genm_list*. This task may be accomplished by applying for a few more times the list introduction and generalization strategies. For lack of space we will not present here the entire derivation. The final program one may derive is as follows:

1. $p(0, s(J), 1) \leftarrow$
2. $p(s(I), 0, 0) \leftarrow$
3. $p(s(I), s(J), K) \leftarrow tp(I, J, K1, K2),\ ave(K1, K2, K)$

15. $tp(I, J, K1, K2) \leftarrow genm\_list(J1, I, K1, [\,], J, K2)$

16. $genm\_list(s(A), 0, 1, B, C, D) \leftarrow new1(A, C, s(0), B, D)$
17. $genm\_list(s(A), s(B), C, D, E, F) \leftarrow$
$new2(A, B, G, [\,], H, E, D, F),\ ave(G, H, C)$

18. $new1(A, A, B, [\,], C) \leftarrow p(B, A, C)$
19. $new1(s(A), B, 0, [1|C], D) \leftarrow new1(A, B, s(0), C, D)$
20. $new1(s(A), B, s(C), [D|E], F) \leftarrow$
$new2(A, C, G, [\,], H, B, E, F),\ ave(G, H, D)$

21. $new2(0, A, B, C, D, 0, [\,], 0) \leftarrow new1(E, 0, A, [B|C], D)$
22. $new2(s(A),B,C,D,E,s(A), [\,], F) \leftarrow append(D, [E], Z),$
$new1(G, A, B, [C|Z], J),\ ave(E, J, F)$
23. $new2(s(A),B,C,D,E,F, [G|H], I) \leftarrow append(D, [E], Z),$
$new2(A, B, C, Z, M, F, H, I),\ ave(E, M, G)$

This derived program is linear recursive and it can be shown that $O(m\times n)$ calls of *ave* are required for evaluating a goal of the form $p(s^m(0), s^n(0), K)$. Our final program could be simplified by unfolding the call of *tp* in clause 3, and also unfolding the calls of *genm_list* in the derived clause. We may then discard the clauses which define *tp* and *genm_list* (that is, clauses 15, 16, and 17) because they will never be used for the evaluation of a call of *p*.

Notice that Property P2 is indeed used in our World Series Odds program for deriving the clauses which define the predicate *new*2, as it is shown by the occurrences of the *append* predicate in those clauses. The use of the *append* predicate could easily be removed in favour of cheaper *cons* operations by applying standard transformation techniques.

To conclude this section we would like to comment on the fact that some preliminary generalization + equality introduction steps were necessary to transform clauses 4 and 7 before applying the list introduction strategy. The problem of when and how to perform the suitable generalization + equality introduction steps is not trivial and we are currently studying techniques to address this problem in a systematic way.

5 RELATED WORK AND FINAL DISCUSSION

The tupling and generalization strategies are well established techniques for program derivation using the 'rules + strategies' approach as indicated in Burstall and Darlington (1977). In the case of logic programming these strategies work by combining together several predicate calls so that their interactions can be exploited, and their collective evaluation is more efficient than the sequence of evaluations of the single calls in isolation. A limitation of the tupling and generalization strategies is that the number of calls which can be combined together is fixed independently of the input. Basically, the tupling and generalization strategies correspond to the introduction of *arrays* of fixed length.

The extension of these strategies we propose in this paper, allows us to combine a number of calls which depends on the input, by introducing *lists* of values which encode sequences of predicate calls.

A related idea of encoding sequences of goals by lists of values was also used in the compiling control transformation technique proposed by Bruynooghe, De Schreye, and Krekels (1989). Compiling control works by first generating a symbolic representation of the computation of a given class of calls and then synthesizing a new program from that symbolic computation. Thus, compiling control does not follow the 'rules + strategies' approach, and as already mentioned, it needs ad hoc correctness proofs which we do not need here because we rely on the correctness of the rules. Moreover, our technique for list introduction allows us to avoid redundant information when a sequence of goals is encoded as a list, thereby avoiding useless intermediate data structures. In this sense, our list introduction strategy is also an extension of the strategy for avoiding unnecessary variables presented in Proietti and Pettorossi (1995).

Our transformational approach also contrasts with other approaches considered in the case of functional languages for solving similar problems such as those described in Cohen (1983) and in Chin and Hagiya (1995), where static analysis techniques are used to precompute the sizes of the arrays required depending on the size of the input.

We have shown through some examples, that list introduction can be used to derive linear recursive programs. Obviously, by encoding sequences of goals using lists, we may encode any stack of suspended predicate calls and by doing so, any program can be transformed into a program where all clauses have at most one call in their body (and therefore they are linear recursive). Thus, our transformation technique is related to the *continuation passing style transformation* proposed by Wand (1980) for functional programs. It is also related to the transformation into binary form proposed for logic programs by Tarau and Boyer (1990), where the stack of suspended computations is encoded as an argument. However, as already mentioned, our list introduction strategy may avoid some redundant computations and, as shown by our examples, it may allow for exponential speedups.

Various issues naturally arise when looking for an efficient mechanization of our technique based on the tupling, generalization, and list introduction strategies. These issues are common to many methods for logic program derivation by transformation and in particular, during the derivation process we have to choose: (i) the atoms to be tupled together when introducing the new eureka definition at the beginning of the transformation process, (ii) the atoms to unfold during program derivation, (iii) the two clauses to be considered for the application of the generalization strategy or the list introduction strategy, and finally, (iv) the sequences of goals to be replaced by a single atom when applying list introduction.

It is not easy to present general and powerful techniques for addressing all these issues in a completely satisfactory way, and we can only offer partial answers for the time being.

For to Point (i) one suitable suggestion is to tuple in the new definition the atoms which have common arguments or have arguments with shared variables. Indeed, if one gets a recursive definition of that newly introduced predicate by folding, it is often the case that the construction of intermediate data structures is avoided and the generate-and-test behaviour of the derived program is improved, similarly to what one can achieve by using the filter promotion technique (see, for instance our N-queens example in Section 2). Another suggestion is to tuple together all calls which occur in the body of a clause and depend on the head predicate of that clause so to derive a linear recursive clause (see, for instance our World Series Odds example in Section 4). More generally, a suitable form of the initial eureka definition may be decided after analyzing the program at hand (see, for instance, the work by Cohen (1983)).

For Point (ii) and Point (iii) much work has been done in the framework of several related techniques, such as *supercompilation* in Turchin (1986), *deforestation* in Wadler (1990), the automation of the tupling strategy in Chin (1993), *partial evaluation* in Jones, Gomard and Sestoft (1993), as well as the already mentioned techniques for compiling control and avoiding unnecessary variables. Since the list introduction strategy is, in principle, independent of the specific way in which we specify the unfolding and the generalization steps, we may use many results presented in the above mentioned papers.

Finally, for Point (iv) we would like to notice that, for a given clause, there may be several ways, possibly conflicting ones, of applying the list introduction strategy and replacing a sequence of goals by a single atom. It is hard to define general policies to choose among these conflicting options. However, in practice, it is often quite simple to make these choices because there are suitable restrictions both on the classes of programs under consideration and the syntactic forms of the programs to be derived by transformation.

APPENDIX

Derivation of the recursive definition of the predicate *ggent* defined by clause 28.

By unfolding clause 28 w.r.t. $safequeen\_list(Ps2, [\langle R1, C1\rangle | Qs])$ we get clauses 29 and 30:

29. $ggent(R2, Ns2, Qs, R, C, Ps1, [\,], R1, C1) \leftarrow$
$\quad placequeens(R2, Ns2, Qs),$
$\quad safequeen\_list([\langle R, C\rangle | Ps1], Qs),$
$\quad safeboard([\langle R1, C1\rangle | Qs])$

30. $ggent(R2, Ns2, Qs, R, C, Ps1, [\langle R3, C3\rangle | Ps2], R1, C1) \leftarrow$
$\quad placequeens(R2, Ns2, Qs),$
$\quad safequeen\_list([\langle R, C\rangle | Ps1], Qs),$
$\quad safequeen(\langle R3, C3\rangle, [\langle R1, C1\rangle | Qs]),$
$\quad safequeen\_list(Ps2, [\langle R1, C1\rangle | Qs]),$
$\quad safeboard([\langle R1, C1\rangle | Qs])$

By unfolding clause 29 w.r.t. $safeboard([\langle R1, C1\rangle | Qs])$ we get:

29.1 $ggent(R2, Ns2, Qs, R, C, Ps1, [\,], R1, C1) \leftarrow$
$\quad placequeens(R2, Ns2, Qs),$
$\quad \underline{safequeen\_list([\langle R, C\rangle | Ps1], Qs)},$
$\quad \underline{safequeen(\langle R1, C1\rangle, Qs)},\ safeboard(Qs)$

By folding the underlined atoms in clause 29.1 using clause 15, we get:

29.2 $ggent(R2, Ns2, Qs, R, C, Ps1, [\,], R1, C1) \leftarrow$
$\quad placequeens(R2, Ns2, Qs),$
$\quad safequeen\_list([\langle R1, C1\rangle, \langle R, C\rangle | Ps1], Qs),$
$\quad safeboard(Qs)$

By folding the whole body of clause 29.2 using clause 18, we get:

29.3 $ggent(R2, Ns2, Qs, R, C, Ps1, [\,], R1, C1) \leftarrow$
$\quad gent(R2, Ns2, Qs, R1, C1, [\langle R, C\rangle | Ps1])$

By unfolding clause 30 w.r.t. $safequeen(\langle R3, C3\rangle, [\langle R1, C1\rangle | Qs])$:

30.1 $ggent(R2, Ns2, Qs, R, C, Ps1, [\langle R3, C3\rangle | Ps2], R1, C1) \leftarrow$
$\quad placequeens(R2, Ns2, Qs),$
$\quad \underline{safequeen\_list([\langle R, C\rangle | Ps1], Qs)},$
$\quad notattack(\langle R3, C3\rangle, \langle R1, C1\rangle),$
$\quad \underline{safequeen(\langle R3, C3\rangle, Qs)},$
$\quad safequeen\_list(Ps2, [\langle R1, C1\rangle | Qs]),$
$\quad safeboard([\langle R1, C1\rangle | Qs])$

By folding the underlined atoms in clause 30.1 using clause 15, we get:

30.2 $ggent(R2, Ns2, Qs, R, C, Ps1, [\langle R3, C3\rangle | Ps2], R1, C1) \leftarrow$
$\quad \underline{placequeens(R2, Ns2, Qs)},$
$\quad notattack(\langle R3, C3\rangle, \langle R1, C1\rangle),$
$\quad \underline{safequeen\_list([\langle R3, C3\rangle, \langle R, C\rangle | Ps1], Qs)},$
$\quad \underline{safequeen\_list(Ps2, [\langle R1, C1\rangle | Qs])},$
$\quad \underline{safeboard([\langle R1, C1\rangle | Qs])}$

By folding the underlined atoms in clause 30.2 using clause 28, we get:

30.3 $ggent(R2, Ns2, Qs, R, C, Ps1, [\langle R3, C3\rangle | Ps2], R1, C1) \leftarrow$
$\quad notattack(\langle R3, C3\rangle, \langle R1, C1\rangle),$
$\quad ggent(R2, Ns2, Qs, R3, C3, [\langle R, C\rangle | Ps1], Ps2, R1, C1).$

ACKNOWLEDGMENTS

We would like to thank D. De Schreye for many fruitful conversations and for comments on the N-queens example presented in this paper. S. Renault implemented an interactive program transformation system which helped us for the development of the examples. This work has been partially supported by the EC under the HCM Project 'Logic Program Synthesis and Transformation', the INTAS Project 93-1702, MURST 40% (Italy), and Progetto Coordinato 'Programmazione Logica' of the CNR (Italy).

REFERENCES

[1] Aho, A., Hopcroft, J.E. and Ullman, J.D. (1983) *Data Structures and Algorithms.* Addison-Wesley.

[2] Bird, R.S. (1984) The Promotion and Accumulation Strategies in Transformational Programming. *ACM Transactions on Programming Languages and Systems,* 6(4):487–504.

[3] Bird, R.S. and Meertens, L.G.L.T. (1987) Two Exercises Found in a Book on Algorithmics. In L.G.L.T. Meertens, editor, *TC2/WG 2.1 Working Conference on Program Specification and Transformation, Bad Tölz, Germany,* 451–457. North-Holland.

[4] Bruynooghe, M., De Schreye, D. and Krekels, B. (1989) Compiling control. *Journal of Logic Programming,* 6:135–162.

[5] Burstall, R.M. and Darlington, J. (1977) A transformation system for developing recursive programs. *Journal of the ACM,* 24(1):44–67.

[6] Chin, W.-N. (1993) Towards an automated tupling strategy. In *Proceedings of ACM SIGPLAN Symposium on Partial Evaluation and Semantics Based Program Manipulation, PEPM '93, Copenhagen, Denmark,* 119–132. ACM Press.

[7] Chin, W.-N. and Hagiya, M. (1995) A transformational method for dynamic-sized tabulation. *Acta Informatica,* 32:93–115.

[8] Cohen, N.H. (1983) Eliminating redundant recursive calls. *ACM Transactions on Programming Languages and Systems,* 5(3):265–299.

[9] Darlington, J. (1978) A synthesis of several sorting algorithms. *Acta Informatica,* 11:1–30.

[10] Darlington, J. (1981) An experimental program transformation system. *Artificial Intelligence,* 16:1–46.

[11] Jones, N.D., Gomard, C.K. and Sestoft, P. (1993) *Partial Evaluation and Automatic Program Generation.* Prentice Hall.

[12] Pettorossi, A. (1977) Transformation of programs and use of tupling strategy. In *Proceedings Informatica 77, Bled, Yugoslavia,* 1–6.

[13] Pettorossi, A. and Proietti, M. (1994) Transformation of logic programs: Foundations and techniques. *Journal of Logic Programming,* 19,20:261–320.

[14] Proietti, M. and Pettorossi, A. (1995) Unfolding-definition-folding, in this order, for avoiding unnecessary variables in logic programs. *Theoretical Computer Science*, 142(1):89–124.

[15] Sterling, L.S. and Shapiro, E. (1994) *The Art of Prolog*. The MIT Press, Cambridge, Massachusetts. Second Edition.

[16] Tamaki, H. and Sato, T. (1984) Unfold/fold transformation of logic programs. In S.-Å. Tärnlund, editor, *Proceedings of the Second International Conference on Logic Programming, Uppsala, Sweden*, 127–138. Uppsala University.

[17] Tarau, P. and Boyer, M. (1990) Elementary logic programs. In P. Deransart and J. Małuszyński, editors, *Proceedings PLILP '90*, 159–173. Springer-Verlag.

[18] Turchin, V.F. (1986) The concept of a supercompiler. *ACM TOPLAS*, 8(3):292–325.

[19] Wadler, P.L. (1990) Deforestation: Transforming programs to eliminate trees. *Theoretical Computer Science*, 73, 231–248.

[20] Wand, M. (1980) Continuation-based program transformation strategies. *Journal of the ACM*, 27(1):164–180.

6 BIOGRAPHIES

Alberto Pettorossi received his laurea degree in Electronic Engineering from La Sapienza University, Rome (Italy), in 1971. From that university he also obtained in 1972 the Specialization degree in Control Systems and Computing. From 1975 until 1988 he was a researcher of the Italian National Research Council at IASI in Rome. In 1979 he obtained the Master degree in Computer Science from Syracuse University, NY, USA. In 1984 he obtained the PhD degree in Computer Science from Edinburgh University, UK. Since 1988 he is an associate professor of Computer Science at the University of Rome Tor Vergata, Italy.

Maurizio Proietti received his laurea degree in Mathematics from La Sapienza University, Rome (Italy), in 1984. He joined the National Research Council of Italy (CNR) in 1988 and he currently works as a researcher at the Institute of Analysis of Systems and Informatics (IASI) in Rome. His research interests include program transformation, specialization, synthesis, and verification in the context of functional and logic programming.

13

Toward a calculus for abstract syntax trees

D. S. Wile
University of Southern California / Information Sciences Institute
4676 Admiralty Way, Marina del Rey, CA USA
(310) 822-1511 (310) 823-6714 (FAX) wile@isi.edu

Abstract

Metaprogramming – writing programs that manipulate programs as data – requires a formal foundation in order that people be able to reason about the effects of their metaprograms. Of equal importance, metaprogramming requires an intuitive foundation that facilitates most frequent, natural manipulations of programs as data. In the past, the program transformation community has characterized well means for expressing pattern-matching and individual transformations. This report concentrates on developing a calculus for characterizing transformation *application* by providing operators on *abstract syntax trees* and studying their relationships. The work builds directly on the *Theory of Lists* developed by Meertens and Bird and an extension to the *Theory of Binary Labeled Trees* developed by Gibbons. Although the foundations for the theory lie in category theory, the presentation should be accessible to a wide audience interested in program manipulation systems.

Keywords

Metaprogramming, programming calculus, transformations, abstract syntax trees

Sponsored by the Defense Advanced Research Projects Agency contracts numbers: F30602-93-C-0240 and F3062-96-2-0224.

1 THE THEORY OF LISTS AND THEORIES IN GENERAL

In 1981 Lambert Meertens challenged the members of IFIP WG2.1 – the Algol group – to develop a theory of "algorithmics."* Over time that vision has crystallized to mean, for sufficiently constrained domains of interest to programming, to develop a set of data abstractions and operators on those abstractions that characterize the domain so well that:

- algorithms for manipulating the abstractions can be readily expressed by people familiar with the domain;
- most reasoning about the algorithms can be *calculational*. The need for induction proofs for reasoning about the algorithms has been subsumed by the design of the abstractions and especially, of the operators.

In the domain of program manipulation itself, *metaprogramming,* the program transformation community has characterized well means for expressing pattern-matching and individual transformations (Heckmann, 1988, Huet, 1978, Paulson, 1983). Moreover, recent efforts with category-theoretic approaches to describing program manipulation (Jeuring, 1995) have provided a sound foundation for transformation application. This report focuses on providing a rich set of operators that correlate well with the intuitive operations used by practitioners in the field of program transformation, operators missing from these latter efforts or inaccessible because of their category-theoretic basis.

Soon after his challenge, Lambert and Richard Bird developed the *Theory of Lists* (Bird, 1987), characterizing regular manipulations of lists. The Theory of Lists is of primary interest for the philosophical and pedagogical reasons just stated. Manipulations of lists are described with operators appropriate for scanning and reducing data contained in lists. Reasoning about their efficient implementation is equational, or transformational, not requiring inductive proofs and finding elusive invariants.

Syntactically, the notation used to express the Theory of Lists is extremely concise, overloading operators and functional composition in a way similar to, but more powerful than APL, often in ways akin to linear algebra, for example, where the space of linear functions over a vector space itself is a vector space. Over time even the developers of the Theory of Lists have come to realize that this conciseness is a two-edged sword. On the one hand, people familiar with the "squiggles" in the notation – the language has even been dubbed "Squigol" – have tremendous facility in what they can express. On the other, convincing newcomers to the notation to use it is difficult because it requires a large investment in learning time.

Hence, subsequent theories developed by members of the group have become less notation-intensive and more focused on the operators necessary for their expression. For some time after the Theory of Lists was developed, developers of theories were enamored of finding "homomorphisms," "catamorphisms, " and "paramorphisms" for data structures under study (Meertens, 1992, Malcolm,

* In Wheeling, West Virginia, 1980.

1990). These functionals (functions with functions as arguments), arising from category theory, characterize the natural structural induction for any structure. Indeed, finding the catamorphism for a data type is important, but it is also straightforward. The difficult part of designing a calculus is in discovering the interesting and *useful* operators that specialize the catamorphism, that is, finding a good set of operators and a sufficient set of transformations for manipulating those operators meaningfully.

This report attempts to lay the foundation of a calculus for abstract syntax trees, similar to that provided by the Theory of Lists. (It will sometimes be referred to as the "metaprogramming calculus," of which the theory of abstract syntax trees is only a part.) It is instructive first to examine the Theory of Lists briefly to establish terminology and conventions for the later development.

Syntax Conventions

In the Theory of Lists, expressions are sequences of operators and operands interpreted within a right-to-left precedence scheme; in addition, typing is used to eliminate parentheses. In the present formulation of the metaprogramming calculus, the conciseness of the Theory of Lists is forgone in order to relate better to notations already well-understood by most readers. An adaptation of Haskell (Hudak,1992) will be used, demonstrated presently with definitions for some of the functions in the Theory of Lists, definitions used later as well.

First, although the Theory of Lists is based on the concatenate constructor, a similar theory can be based on the simple Lisp "cons" constructor (here written ":") that joins an element and a list, producing a new list with the element as it first element and the list as the rest of the list (Malcolm, 1990). Generally, one specifies the type of functions in Haskell, even though the translator can figure them out. *Map_list,* called *map* in Haskell, takes a function and a list as arguments and returns a list:

map_list :: (*a* -> *b*) -> [*a*] -> [*b*]

This is read: "*map_list* takes a function from *a*s to *b*s and a list of *a*s and returns a list of *b*s." Function definition in Haskell uses argument pattern matching. Each pattern in turn is matched with the arguments of the function during invocation. The first definition whose pattern matches* defines the value of the function. The definition of *map_list* tests for the empty list before defining the recursive case:

map_list *f* [] = []
map_list *f* (*x*:*xs*) = (*f x*) : (map_list *f xs*)

In the definition of *map_list* the *map_list* function is applied recursively to the tail of the list, *xs*, after which the application of the function to the first element of the list is consed onto the result. Parentheses could be eliminated from this definition, but for clarity they are being retained throughout this report.

* And whose guard succeeds, as we will see later.

The most fundamental of the list functions is *right_reduce* (what Haskell calls the *foldr* operator).

```
right_reduce            ::  (a -> b -> b) -> b -> [a] -> b

right_reduce f z []     =   z
right _reduce f z (x:xs) =  f x (right_reduce f z xs)
```

This "catamorphism" function can actually be used to define all the other list functions in the Theory of Lists.

It is very common for the function *f* to be an associative binary operator and for that operator to have an identity element, I_f. In this case we can use a functional, *reduce_list*, that applies the operator between all the elements in the structure:

```
reduce_list             ::  (a -> a-> a) -> [a] ->  a

reduce_list ⊗ s         =   right_reduce (⊗) I⊗ s
```

It is useful to have a *concatenation* operator, written "++", in what follows. Naturally, its identity element is the empty sequence. It will never be used in pattern matching (since such matches are often ambiguous). An especially useful list function that uses concatenation and illustrates Haskell's *guards* is the *filter_list* function:

```
filter_list             ::  (a -> Boolean) -> [a] -> [a]

filter_list f s         =   reduce_list (++) (map_list g s)
                  where g a    | f a    = [a]
                        g a             = []
```

Here, the function *g* has a guard, indicated by the "|" symbol, that calls the argument predicate, *f a*; when that predicate is true, the first definition of *g* is used. Otherwise, the second. Hence, each element of the mapped function is either a singleton list or an empty list. The reduction then concatenates all these together, thereby eliminating those for which the predicate, *f*, was false.

Idiosyncratic Conventions

In Haskell, if all the patterns (and their associated guards) fail to match, the failure value *bottom* is returned. When bottom is returned in Haskell, the program fails. In what follows, I am adopting a different convention: a distinguished *failure value* is returned when all defining patterns fail to match. It is passed upwards like an exception until caught by an operaator testing for this value. Two operators are available to test for this value. The *defined* operator returns *true* if its operand has a normal value; *false*, if it has the failure value. The *otherwise* operator, written "?," is defined as follows:

```
(?)                          :: a -> a -> a

(?) x y      | defined x     = x
(?) x y                      = y
```

Defining the *defined* function requires a straight-forward, but wordy, extension to Haskell. Each type in the metaprogram that occurs in an *otherwise* operator must be extended with a failure value. Then the *defined* function must be defined for each of these types. Then the definition of each function, *f,* that returns a value from that type is extended with:

```
f _ ... _          =     failure_value
```

(In Haskell, the "wildcard" symbol, underscore, indicates that the matched argument's value will not be used in the definition.) Finally, every function that uses an argument of the type must be redefined to match only when the failure value is not passed in.

Haskell has several conventions that allow one to produce extremely concise expressions. The use of precedence is one. Another is the use of "sections," which allows one to omit arguments to functions, turning them into lambda expressions implicitly. Here an analogous shorthand is introduced for functions that is more general and slightly less difficult to read. The scope of the lambda expression and the position of variables' occurrences are made explicit; only the names of the variables are implicit ("#" and "##"). (Haskell uses the "\" symbol for *lambda.*)

```
#(... # ...)             =  \ x -> (... x ...)
##(... # ... ## ...)     =  \ x y -> (... x ... y ...)
```

Thus,

```
#(a + #) 3               =  \ x -> (a + x) 3
                         =  a + 3
##(f # (g ## #)) 3 4     =  \ x y -> (f x (g y x)) 3 4
                         =  f 3 (g 4 3)
```

An operator related to *otherwise*, *first to apply*, written "??," is useful for applying one of several possible transformations. It is defined:

```
(??)                     ::  (a -> b) -> (a -> b) -> (a -> b)

(??) f g                 =   #( (f #) ? (g #))
```

Catamorphisms

In order to produce a calculus – a set of transformations used for manipulating a set of operators – it is necessary to characterize *inductive* manipulations by introducing operators that take operators as arguments, i.e. functionals. Two such functionals are *map_list* and *reduce_list*, presented above.

Such functionals are defined inductively on the *construction* functions characterizing the data type; for lists, *cons* and *empty*, [].* In fact, one form of functional characterizes *all* forms of structural inductive functions for lists; this form is called a *catamorphism*. It is beyond the scope of this report to explain why such a function is so characteristic of the data type, but it is worth reemphasizing two important points that will carry over into the definitions of labeled trees:

- Finding the catamorphism for the data type is important, such as *reduce_list* for lists, but it is also straightforward.
- Discovering the interesting and *useful* operators that specialize the catamorphism is where the difficulty lies in producing a good calculus for manipulating the data structures, that is, finding a good set of operators and a sufficient set of transformations for manipulating those operators.

Indeed, some of the transformations come "for free" by relating the specialized operators to the catamorphism, so called promotion theorems, for example. Consider the definitions of *map_list* and *filter_list* above, in terms of the catamorphism:

map_list *f l*	=	right_reduce ##([*f* #] ++ ##) [] *l*
filter_list *f l*	=	right_reduce ##((**if** *f* # **then** [#] **else** []) ++ ##) [] *l*

Mapping and filtering are operations that occur over and over again when manipulating lists. Hence, it is important to identify these patterned applications of reduction.

Moreover, it is quite difficult to see without these definitions that, for example,

map_list *f* (map_list *g l*) = map_list ($f \circ g$) *l*

Or that, if $f \Rightarrow g$:

filter_list *g* (filter_list *l f*) = filter_list *f l*

That is, the patterns for these equivalences in terms of the *reduce_list* formulations are extremely complex and not readily matched by humans. However, these are the kinds of transformations one needs to perform to do various analysis or abstract interpretation tasks.

Similarly, in what follows the catamorphism for labeled trees is readily defined, but the importance of the calculus is in identifying those operators that are interesting on labeled trees to do the tasks required for metaprogramming, i.e. for manipulating programs as data.

* [*a*,*b*,*c*] is then used to abbreviate *a* : *b* : c : [].

2 LABELED TREES

An important intermediate step in the development of a theory for abstract syntax trees is the development of labeled trees. Other theories of labeled trees have been proposed, first by Meertens (1988), whose so-called "rose trees" have labeled tip nodes, but only structures in the nonterminals (no labels). I proposed a precursor to the current proposal not long thereafter (Wile, 1988); the present proposal is considerably more elegant. Runciman (1989) began a development which has an unnatural construction operator that, although quite concise and elegant, is inappropriate for extension into abstract syntax trees. Gibbons (1991, 1993) developed a theory of labeled binary trees in his dissertation. His later work uses the same definition for trees as here (Jones, 1993, Gibbons, 1994), but I am not aware of a full reformulation of the theory for these trees. Nonetheless, it is fair to characterize the theory of labeled trees presented herein as a reformulation (and reinvention) of Gibbons' work. It is hoped that the development herein is accessible to a wider audience than that that readily understands Gibbons' category-theoretical treatment.

Each labeled tree is a node consisting of a datum and a list of children. In Haskell such an abstract data type, *Tree*, is defined:

data Tree *a*	=	Node *a* [Tree *a*]
label (Node *x ts*)	=	*x*
children (Node *x ts*)	=	*ts*

This defines the ADT, *Tree a*, where *a* is a type, the type of the labels of the tree. Instances of such trees are constructed using the *Node* constructor. The *label* and children destructors pick out the respective subcomponents of the *Node*.

Maps

There are several operators that, although they restructure trees, they retain some of the original structure; hence, they are called *maps* to connote the similarity of result. The first map operator, *relabel*, is quite simple. It changes the labels on a tree, potentially based on the entire subtree which it relabeling, while leaving the structure intact. One might want to use such an operator to relabel an abstract syntax tree with the variables used freely within each subtree, for example. The operator is defined:

relabel	::	(Tree *a* -> *b*) -> Tree *a* -> Tree *b*
relabel *r t*@(Node *l s*)	=	Node (*r t*) (map_list #(relabel *r* #) *s*)

(In Haskell, the @ operator binds the variable to its left to the entire structure matching the pattern on its right, here *Node l s*.)

Very simple examples will be used to describe the effects of the operators. They will all be based on the labeled tree:

```
(9 (9 (12 (10 (1)) (15)))
   (6 (1) (1))
   (7 (10 (1)) (4) (15)))
```

where this more concise representation of labeled trees (Lisp, actually) is interpreted as follows: the label of the tree is the first element of the list and the children are the rest of the list. We will call this tree "trivial."

Hence,

relabel #(length (children #) + 3) trivial =

```
(6 (4 (5 (4 (3)) (3)))
      (5 (3) (3))
      (6 (4 (3)) (3) (3)))
```

The *prune* operator is a most useful operator that allows whole branches of the tree to be pruned away or substituted for. Its use in metaprogramming for substitution should be clear.

prune	::	(Tree *a* -> Tree *a*) -> Tree *a* -> Tree *a*
prune *p t* | defined (*p t*)	=	*p t*
prune *p* (Node *l s*)	=	Node *l* (map_list #(prune *p* #) *s*)

Hence, if we wished to substitute for each tree labeled "12" a child labeled with "7" instead, with a sequence which dropped off the first element of the original, we could write:

prune *f* trivial
    where *f* (Node 12 (*x*:*xs*)) = Node 7 *xs*

to produce:

```
(9 (9 (7 (15)))
      (6 (1) (1))
      (7 (10 (1)) (4) (15)))
```

Reduction, Accumulation and Scanning Operators

Analogous to the Theory of List's *reduce_list* operator, the *reduce_tree* operator accumulates information from the leaves to the nodes, using an associative operator. (It will often be necessary to relabel or prune trees before applying this operator.)

reduce_tree	::	(*a* -> *a* -> *a*) -> Tree *a* -> *a*
reduce_tree ⊗ (Node *l s*)	=	(reduce_list (⊗) (map_list #(reduce_tree (⊗)

#) *s*))

⊗ *l*

Notice that the second occurrence of ⊗ in the definition is the argument to *reduce_list*, and the third occurrence is the application of it to the recursive result and *l*.

Because "*reduce_list* ⊗ *[]*" is an identity element for ⊗,

reduce_tree (⊗) (Node *l* []) = *l*

For example, "*reduce_tree trivial* +" is the sum of the labels, *101*. The leaves of a tree are found with the simple reduction:

```
leaves t                  =  reduce_tree (++) (relabel f t)
          where f (Node l [])  = [l]
                f t            = []
```

When applied to trivial, this produces:

(1 15 1 1 1 4 15)

The postfix sequence for a tree is simply

```
postfix t                 =  reduce_tree (++) (relabel f t)
          where f (Node l s) = [l]
```

When applied to *trivial* this would produce:

(1 10 15 12 9 1 1 6 1 10 4 15 7 9)

Notice that to make sense of such a sequence, the arity associated with each label acting as an operator would need to be known.

An operator analogous to the Theory of List's *right_reduce* is the *synthesize* operator. It applies its (nonassociative) operator argument to all the information from below as well as the current node (the tree) to determine its value:

```
synthesize              ::  ([b] -> Tree a-> b) -> Tree a -> b

synthesize f t@(Node l s)  =  f (map_list #(synthesize f #) s) t
```

The prefix sequence for our example can be written:

```
prefix t                  =  synthesize f t
          where f ss (Node l s) = [l]++( reduce_list (++) ss)
```

When applied to *trivial* this produces:

(9 9 12 10 1 15 6 1 1 7 10 1 4 15)

The synthesize operator is the most general of the operators. It is like the catamorphism *reduce_list* above, only technically it is called a *paramorphism*, because it takes the original "element" of the data type – the tree here - as an argument as well as the information accumulated from below. (This is not really more general, for the function below can pass up the original tree; it is just a convenience in that functions are often sensitive to the tree, especially the label.) In fact, all of the operators defined above can be defined using *synthesize*. In particular, the following three equivalences hold:

Synthesis reduction:

reduce_tree ⊗ *t* = synthesize *f t*
where *f ss* (Node *l s*) = (reduce_list (⊗) *ss*) ⊗ *l*

Synthesis relabel:

relabel *r t* = synthesize ##(Node (*r* ##) #) *t*

Synthesis prune:

prune *p t* = synthesize g *t*
where g *ss t* | defined (*p t*) = *p t*
g *ss* (Node *l s*) = Node *l ss*

The operators above take information from below in the tree and synthesize it into the label of a similar tree. However, the final operators, *inherit* and *positional_inherit*, work the other way around; they take information and pass it down the tree by relabeling the subnodes:

inherit :: (*b* -> Tree *a* -> *b*) -> *b* -> Tree *a* -> Tree *b*

inherit *f b t*@(Node *l s*) = Node *n* (map_list #(inherit *f* n #) *s*)
where n = *f b t*

A function that inherits its depth in the tree is:

depth *t* = inherit ##(#+1) 0 *t*

Applying this to *trivial* produces:

(1 (2 (3 (4 (5)) (4)))
(2 (3) (3))
(2 (3 (4)) (3) (3)))

Using inherit, there is no way to pass information down to the children while differentiating which position the child was in. This is often needed when writing analytical functions. For example, when type-checking, one would pass a different target type down to a *conditional*'s *predicate* position than to the *then* and *else* positions. Hence, *positional_inherit* is takes the children into consideration:

```
positional_inherit       :: (b -> Tree a -> [b]) -> b  -> Tree a -> Tree b

positional_inherit f a t :: Node a map_list ##(positional_inherit f # ##)
                                          (map_list first
                                            (zip_list (f t a) (children t)))
                    where first (a,_) = a
```

This rather tricky formulation forces the resulting tree shape to be the same as the original by insisting that the function, *f*, return a list of the same length as the children, by zipping it with them and then projecting out the results.

In the Theory of Lists there are "scanning" versions of the reduction operators, versions that produce sequences with the accumulated values associated at the appropriate positions in the list. Analogous operators for trees are "labeling" versions of reduce and synthesize, named *reduce_label* and *synthesize_label*, respectively:

```
reduce_label f t       =  relabel #(reduce_tree f #) t
synthesize_label f t   =  relabel #(synthesize f #) t
```

Hence,

```
reduce_label (+) trivial  =

(101 (47 (38 (11 (1)) (15)))
       (8 (1) (1))
       (37 (11 (1)) (4) (15)))
```

and

```
synthesize_label ##(prefix ##) trivial
```

labels each tree with its prefix sequence:

```
((9 9 12 10 1 15 6 1 1 7 10 1 4 15)
    ((9 12 10 1 15) ((12 10 1 15) ((10 1) ((1))) ((15))))
    ((6 1 1) ((1)) ((1)))
    ((7 10 1 4 15) ((10 1) ((1))) ((4)) ((15))))
```

The Relabeling Theorem

Relabeling a tree by invoking a function whose value is computed recursively on the tree is apparently exorbitantly expensive! However, it may describe especially well the way one conceptualizes a metaprogramming activity.

Concerns for efficiency within a calculus should be separable; they should only arise if it appears that an efficient version of a function could not be gotten by transformation and other formal manipulations. The following theorem should assuage some of these concerns for this particular operator:

The Relabeling Theorem:

relabel #(synthesize *f* #) *t* ≡ synthesize g *t*
where g *ss t* = Node (*f* (map_list label *ss*) *t*) *ss*

Hence, only a single recursive pass is required to accumulate at the labels, information synthesized from the tree below.

Since the proof of this theorem is typical of proofs on trees, it is included in the text for illustrative purposes. Perhaps the most important (and obvious) need is for an induction proof principle. It is simple: to prove a property of a tree, first prove it for the leaves. It may then be assumed to hold of the subtrees in the proof.

Proof. In this proof, a lemma is useful:

synthesize *f t* = label (synthesize g *t*)

Proof of lemma.
Leaves:

synthesize *f* (Node *l* [])

= *f* (map_list #(synthesize *f* #) []) (Node *l* []) — def of synth
= *f* [] (Node *l* []) — def of map_list

N.B., this equivalence is referred to as the "sublemma" in the remaining proofs.

label (synthesize g (Node *l* []))

= label (g [] (Node *l* [])) — sublemma
= *f* (map_list label []) (Node *l* []) — def of g
= *f* [] (Node *l* []) — def of map_list

QED *leaves.*

label (synthesize g *t*)

= label (g (map_list #(synthesize g #) (children *t*)) *t*) — def of synth.
= let *ss* = map_list #(synthesize g #) (children *t*) — def of g
in label (Node (*f* (map_list label *ss*) *t*) *ss*)

```
= let ss = map_list #(synthesize g #) (children t)              def of label
     in (f (map_list label ss) t)
= f (map_list (map_list #(synthesize g #) (children t)) label) t  subst for ss
= f (map_list #(label (synthesize g #)) (children t)) t         dist map_list
= f (map_list #(synthesize f #) (children t)) t                 inductive hyp
= synthesize f t                                                def of synth
```

QED *lemma*.
Then,
Leaves:

```
relabel #(synthesize f #) (Node l [])

= Node (synthesize f (Node l []))                               def of relabel
        (map_list #(relabel #(synthesize f #) #) [])
= Node (synthesize f (Node l [])) []                            def of map_list
= Node (f [] (Node l [])) []                                    sublemma

synthesize g (Node l [])

= g [] (Node l [])                                              sublemma
= Node (f (map_list label []) (Node l [])) []                   def of g
= Node (f [] (Node l [])) []                                    def of map_list
```

QED leaves.

```
synthesize g t

= g (map_list #(synthesize g #) (children t)) t                 def of synth
= let ss = map_list #(synthesize g #) (children t)
   in Node (f (map_list label ss) t) ss                         def of g
= let ss = map_list  #(synthesize g #) (children t)             subst for ss
   in Node (f (map_list  label (map_list #(synthesize g #) (children t))) t) ss
= let ss = map_list #(synthesize g #) (children t)              dist map_list
   in Node (f (map_list #(label (synthesize g #)) (children t)) t) ss
= let ss = map_list  #(synthesize g #) (children t)             apply lemma
   in Node (f (map_list  #(synthesize f #) (children t)) t) ss
= let ss = map_list  #(synthesize g #) (children t)             def of  synth.
   in Node (synthesize f t) ss
= let ss = map_list #(relabel #(synthesize f #) #) (children t) inductive hyp.
   in Node (synthesize f t) ss
= Node (synthesize f t)                                         subst for ss
        (map_list #(relabel #(synthesize f #) #) (children t))
= relabel #(synthesize f #) t                                   def of relabel
```

QED Theorem

It should be emphasized that the use of induction is **not** the norm in calculus proofs. In fact, it is exactly what a calculus is designed to avoid. However, there are always fundamental promotion theorems, like the relabeling theorem, that require such proofs.* A complete version of the calculus will certainly not require its users to invent and prove such theorems.

Zipping Trees

Another notion from the Theory of Lists is the idea of "zipping" data, putting data from corresponding structures into a single structure with corresponding data. For example, from two sequences we might form a sequence of pairs:

zip_list *s* []	=	[]
zip_list [] *t*	=	[]
zip_list (*a*:*s*) (*b*:*q*)	=	(*a*,*b*): (zip_list *s q*)

We then extend the meaning of *map_list* to apply binary operators and functions of two arguments to the elements of the pairs (Haskell's *zip_with*):

map_list *f* (zip_list (*a*:*s*) (*b*:*q*)) = (*f a b*) : (map_list *f* (zip_list *s q*))

Here we extend the zip notion pairwise to the labels of trees as follows:

zip_tree (Node *l s*) (Node *m q*)
= Node (*l*,*m*) (map_list zip_tree (zip_list *s q*))

This operator is especially useful for accumulating inherited and synthesized attributes of a tree. In some ways the operator is rather ugly, but functional techniques for avoiding its usage are even more obscure. The author's Popart system (Wile, 1991) allows the tree to be decorated with attributes instead.

Examples

A few more examples may illustrate the simple labeled tree operators better. To count the nodes of a tree we merely need to relabel each node with the integer 1 and reduce with the sum:

count *t* = reduce_tree (+) (relabel #(1) *t*)

Similarly, the maximum depth of a tree can be found by taking the *max* subtree size from below, and adding 1:

max_depth *t* = synthesize ##((reduce_list (max) #)+ 1) *t*

---

* In fact, because *synthesize* is a "paramorphism" there is an elegant, inductionless proof of this very theorem using a promotion theorem from category theory. But the approach here is to try to make these operators accessible to a wider audience than that familiar with category theory.

This relies on *0* being the identity element for *maximum*. Notice that in this function, like many, the synthesized function can ignore the original tree when accumulating.
To find the minimal label of a tree:

minimum_label *t* = reduce_tree (min) *t*

Whether *x* is one of the labels of the tree:

contains *t x* = reduce_tree (or) (relabel #(label # == *x*) *t*)

Postfix order:

postfix *t* = reduce_tree (++) (relabel #([label #]) *t*)

A tree labeled with each node's distance from the root:

distance *t* = inherit ##(# + 1) 0 *t*

3 ABSTRACT SYNTAX TREES

The goal of an abstract syntax is to describe the structural essence of a language (Donzeau-Gouge, 1984). Syntax trees are *operators* – describing the important concepts in a language, applied to *typed operands* – describing the important components associated with the concept. Each operand is named with the *role* it plays in the concept. Trees are classified in a tree of types known as *phyla* – describing inheritance relationships between concepts.* Abstract syntax trees terminate in a prespecified set of primitive types, such as *identifier* and *integer*.

For example, an *if-then-else tree* will have a structure that contains three slots, one for each of the *predicate*, the *then branch* and the *else branch*. Labeled trees may be used to model abstract syntax trees; the various slots of the trees will correspond *positionally* to sequence elements. It will not matter which positions correspond, but merely that the correspondence be consistent throughout the tree.

For abstract syntax tree examples, the label type will be the *operators* of the abstract syntax categories plus the lexical categories for the terminal nodes. For example,

data Keywords = IF | BLOCK | LOOP | PLUS | *ID* | ASSIGN | NUM

Node ASSIGN [Node ID$_a$ [], Node PLUS [Node ID$_a$ [],Node NUM$_1$ []]

* Here, the classification aspects of abstract syntax trees are not modeled. The theory must be extended to incorporate that concept.

would then represent a node with the label, *ASSIGN*, with two children: a node with label ID_a, and a node with label *PLUS*, etc., which would represent what is written $a := a+1$ using concrete syntax. Notice again that the leaf nodes are constructed using the empty sequence of children.*

Consider the following example written in concrete syntax.

```
begin
      integer a, b;
      real c;
      a + b - c
end
```

A corresponding abstract syntax representation might be:

```
(Block
 (Declaration_list
  (Declaration (Declaration_Type (Integer))
               (Identifier_list (Identifier (A))
                                (Identifier (B))))
  (Declaration (Declaration_Type (Real ))
               (Identifier_list (Identifier (C)))))
 (Expression_list
  (Operation
   (Operation
     (FunctionCall (Identifier (A))
                   (Expression_list))
     (PlusOp (+))
     (FunctionCall (Identifier (B))
                   (Expression_list)) )
   (PlusOp (+))
   (FunctionCall (Identifier (C ))
                 (Expression_list)))))
```

To map this into the labeled-tree representation, we need only use the abstract syntax class names as labels for internal tree nodes, and the lexical constants and identifiers as labels of terminal nodes of the tree. Notice that lists of elements are translated into labels of the form, *x_list*. This tree will be referred to as "toy" in the examples below.

Some interesting functions can now be defined for these abstract syntax trees. The following function returns the identifier used locally by a node:

* Technically we need a type for *Keywords* that includes the types for the terminal nodes of the tree, of course. That is being finessed here by writing ID_a.

```
uses (Node Identifier [(Node id [])])   = [id]
uses t                                  = []
```

A function the extracts the *identifiers* declared in a block, *declares,* can be specified as:

```
declares (Node Declaration [ignore_type, (Node Identifier_list il)])
                          =  map_list (\ Node Identifier [Node id []]-> id)
il
declares t                =  []
```

Now, to label trees with the sets of identifiers they declare and use, respectively, the following functions can be applied:

```
l_declares t              =  relabel declares t
l_uses t                  =  relabel uses t
```

The application, *l_declares toy,* is:

```
(()
    (() ((A B) (() (())) (() (() (())) (() (())))))
       ((C) (() (())) (() (() (())))))
    (() (() (() (() (() (())) (())))
          (() (()))
          (() (() (())) (())))
       (() (()))
       (() (() (())) (()))))
```

The application, *l_uses toy,* is:

```
(() (() (() (() (())) (() ((A) (())) ((B) (()))))
          (() (() (())) (() ((C) (())))))
       (() (() (() (() ((A) (())) (())))
            (() (()))
            (() ((B) (())) (())))
          (() (()))
          (() ((C) (())) (()))))
```

Notice that the type over which the tree labels are defined is "set of identifiers." Given these labelings, we can label a tree with the identifiers declared above a node as

```
declared_above t       =  inherit ##(# union (label ##)) [] (l_declares t)
```

Similarly, we can label the tree with the variables used *somewhere* below in the tree:

```
used_below t           =  reduce_label (union) (l_uses t)
```

To label the tree with the variables used freely in any given context, we must pass *up* the tree, only those variables used freely below not trapped by the variables declared here:

uses_freely *t* = synthesize_label *f* (zip_tree (*l*_uses *t*) (*l*_declares *t*))
where *f s* (Node (u,d) q) = (list_reduce *s* (union)) union (u -- d)

where, here, "--" is set difference.

The application *uses_freely toy* produces:

```
(() (() (() (() (())) ((A B) ((A) (())) ((B) (())))))
        (() (() (())) ((C) ((C) (()))))))
     ((A B C)
       ((A B)
         ((A) ((A) ((A) (())) (())))
         (() (()))
         ((B) ((B) (())) (())))
       (() (()))
       ((C) ((C) (())) (())))))
```

Operators Specialized for Abstract Syntax Trees

Some specific operators can be defined that greatly enhance the ability to manipulate and transform abstract syntax trees. First, *copy_synthesize* copies those trees where its argument function does not apply, but passes up the application of the function to those that do:

copy_synthesize :: ([Tree *a*] -> Tree *a* -> Tree *a*) -> Tree *a* -> Tree *a*

copy_synthesize *f t* = synthesize ##((*f* # ##) ? (Node (label ##) #)) *t*

The utility of *copy_synthesize* is most evident when used in the *simplify* operator.

simplify :: (Tree *a* -> Tree *a*) -> Tree *a* -> Tree *a*

simplify *f t* = copy_synthesize ##(*f* (Node (label ##) #)) *t*

For example, a transformation function could transform *x* + *x* into *2* * *x*:

double (Node Operation [*x* ,(Node PlusOp [(Node + [])]), *y*])
| *x* == *y* = Node Operation [Node Num [Node 2 []],
(Node MulOp [(Node * [])]), *x*]

Applying this in a *simplify* operation to the following tree:

```
(Operation
     (FunctionCall (Identifier (Q))
                   (Expression_list))
     (PlusOp (+))
     (Operation
       (FunctionCall (Identifier (A))
                     (Expression_list))
       (PlusOp (+))
       (FunctionCall (Identifier (A))
                     (Expression_list))))
```

will yield:

```
(Operation
     (FunctionCall (Identifier (Q))
                   (Expression_list))
     (PlusOp (+))
     (Operation
       (Num (2))
       (MulOp (*))
       (FunctionCall (Identifier (A))
                     (Expression_list))))
```

Notice that it does this by trying to apply *double* to the innermost trees first, including those of *Identifier* and *FunctionCall*. These will return the failure value, which causes synthesize to use the original tree instead. When it reaches the level of the *Operation* with the *PlusOp* it will succeed and use the *MulOP* version of the abstract syntax tree produced by *double*. It will then go to the outermost *Operation* and fail to apply, causing it to return the transformed value of the children with the label of the parent.

Sometimes the *fixed point* operator is needed to insure that all possible ways of applying a transformation have been tried:

```
fp                              :: a -> (a -> a) -> a

fp a f          | a == (f a)    = a
fp a f                          = fp (f a) f
```

It is used often enough with *simplify* that it is worth introducing the *canonicalize* operator:

```
canonicalize                    :: (Tree a -> Tree a) -> Tree a -> Tree a

canonicalize f t                = fp t #(simplify f #)
```

(It is important to try to find simplifying transformations (in the metaprogramming space) to eliminate such calls. A major problem for future research in the calculus is to characterize functions for which "fixed-point fusion" transformations can be applied to eliminate the exponential growth entailed here.)

List Form Operators

The "_list" forms in the abstract syntax tree occur essentially everywhere an iterated form occurs in the concrete syntax. Hence, their occurrence is frequent and, in fact, there are very stylized operations that are applied to such forms. For example, at one stage in a transformation one might want to remove all occurrences of macro definitions from a program represented in an abstract syntax tree. One would like to simply filter those out of every declaration list. That is easily accomplished using the *list form* operators.

The primary list form operator is, *list synthesize*, defined: *

list_synthesize :: ([Tree *a*] -> [Tree *a*] -> [Tree *a*]) -> Tree *a* -> Tree *a*

list_synthesize *f t* = copy_synthesize g *t*
where g *rr* (Node *l s*) | (*L? l*) = Node *l* (*f rr s*)

(Here, *L?* holds when its argument label ends with the "_list" suffix.) Now two versions of functions that filter out particular sequence elements are provided: *bottom up* versions and *top down* versions. The bottom up versions are easier to define.

First, *bottom_up filter* is defined to remove certain elements from the list.

bottom_up_filter :: (Tree *a* -> Boolean) -> Tree *a* -> Tree *a*

bottom_up_filter *f t* = list_synthesize ##(filter_list *f* #) *t*

Such a filter might be used to remove the *macros* from the declaration lists mentioned above.

A function that splices in particular elements is provided:

bottom_up_splice :: (Tree *a* -> [Tree *a*]) -> Tree *a* -> Tree *a*

bottom_up_splice *f t* = list_synthesize ##(reduce (map # *f*) (++)) *t*

Splicing is often used in *unfolding* operations, where, for example, a single declaration may need to turn into several lower level declarations. Such might be the case in a preprocessor for a language that extends the language with the concept of *relation*. Then the splicing function might declare two access functions to provide associative access in the translation.

---

* This may need to be reformulated to pass along the type of the list elements.

Top down versions of the above functions rely on discovering a *zero* of particular functions:

zero :: (*a* -> *a*) -> *a* -> Boolean

zero *f x* = *f x* == *x*

Then an auxiliary function, *tdl_synthesize*, is defined that looks for zeros of the function applied to the lists in the original tree. When it finds one, it uses the recursive result being passed up by the *list_synthesize*. Otherwise, it uses the result of the applied function on the original tree.

tdl_synthesize :: ([Tree *a*] -> [Tree *a*] -> [Tree *a*]) -> Tree *a* -> Tree *a*

```
tdl_synthesize f t        =  list_synthesize g t
                     where g  rr (Node l s) | (zero f s) = rr
                           g  rr (Node l s)              = s
```

Top_down filter, is then defined in terms of this:

top_down_filter :: (Tree *a* -> Boolean) -> Tree *a* -> Tree *a*

top_down_filter *f t* = tdl_synthesize ##(filter_list *f* ##) *t*

Similarly, a top down version of the splice function is defined:

top_down_splice :: (Tree *a* -> [Tree *a*]) -> Tree *a* -> Tree *a*

top_down_splice *f t* = tdl_synthesize ##(reduce_list (++) (map_list *f* ##)) *t*

The choice of whether to use top down or bottom up functions is usually dependent on whether the language being processed is recursive. When it is not, the top down version should be more efficient.

4 LARGE EXAMPLE DEVELOPMENT

A very large example has been programmed in the calculus and using a precursor to the calculus developed here (Wile, 1986). The task is to transform the language used to specify grammars to YACC into a "tastefully designed" abstract syntax definition for the same language in C++. Details and considerable more motivation for this are presented in (Wile, 1996). However, the specialized operators described above are well represented in this metaprogram, so they will be sketched below.

The task is accomplished in three stages. First, the YACC input syntax is mapped into Popart's grammar description syntax (Wile, 1991), called "WBNF" herein. Then the algorithm in Figure 1 massages the grammar into a form that would be considered "good style" as a grammar to be input to Popart. Such grammars take advantage of Popart's ability to specify higher-level concepts, such as iteration, optionality, and precedence. The conventions used in Popart grammars are:

- concatenation: block := declarations statements;
- alternation: declaration := function | procedure;
- constant lexical items: plusop := '+ | '-;
- optionality: int := 'integer identifier { 'in range };
- "Kleene plus": statements := statement + ;
- lists with separators: funcall := identifier '(expr ^ ', ');
- precedence: expr := < ('+ | '-), ('* | '/), '^ > primitive;
- nesting: 'declare ('integer | 'real) variable;
- variable lexical items: LEXEME <| alphanumeric;

A set of heuristics is used to map into this language, sometimes occasioning the introduction of new productions and the elimination of originals.

The final stage of conversion consists of mapping the WBNF language into a suitable abstract syntax representation in C++. Both the conversion into WBNF and the conversion from WBNF into an abstract syntax are quite simple and are omitted here. This and other details of the Common Lisp / Popart implementation are available from the author.

Figure 1 specifies the essence of the major transformation being accomplished.

A brief "walk" through the *normalize* program will illustrate the use of the abstract syntax-specific operators. First, consider an example portion of a YACC grammar:

```
model:           specification
   specification:          definition | definition specification
definition:      type_dcl SEMI | const_dcl SEMI | except_dcl SEMI |
                 interface SEMI | module SEMI
```

The (omitted) program referred to above will have converted this into Popart:

```
model            :=    specification ;
   specification :=    definition | definition specification ;
   definition    :=    type_dcl '; | const_dcl '; | except_dcl '; |
                       interface '; | module '; ;
```

The first thing the normalize algorithm does is to analyze the usage of nonterminal names in the grammar, keeping track of the *top_level_productions* (*TLP*) in a manner similar to the function *uses_freely* defined above.

So the first real transformation of *G* is to apply two transformations,

```
normalize_wbnf G = 9
  let top_level_productions = TLP G
     simplified           = canonicalize (T_distribute ?? T_unnest) G
     iterated             =
                 fp simplified
                       #(bottom_up_splice
                                   (T_introduce_iteration ?? #([#])) #)
     normal_recursion        =
       bottom_up_splice
                    (T_introduce_precedence ??
                                   Ts_normalize_left_recursion #([#]))
                    iterated
      to_unfold            =
       productions (top_down_filter R_unfoldable normal_recursion)
     all_unfolded          =
       canonicalize #(unfold_into # to_unfold) normal_recursion
     pruned               =
        prune
          rename_duplicates
          (prune
             T_add_compaction
              (prune all_unfolded #(was_unfolded # to_unfold)))
     constant_patterns       = reduce_tree (union) (relabel foldable_constants
pruned)
     constant_productions   = map_list define_constant_production
constant_patterns
     constants_added        = prune #(fold_constants # constant_productions)
pruned
     concatenate_constants s@((Node Production l):x) o
                          = s ++ constant_productions
     concatenate_constants s o = s
      productions_added = list_synthesize concatenate_constants
constants_added
      used_somewhere p = reachable p productions_added
top_level_productions

in top_down_filter used_somewhere productions_added
```

Figure 1: WBNF Normalization Example

T_distribute and *T_unnest*, exhaustively until they no longer apply, using the *canonicalize* operator. (These transformations are available from the author in an appendix to this paper.) The distribution transformation takes alternatives and variously groups them or turns them into options. For example,

```
specification    :=    definition | definition specification ;
```

will be turned into

```
specification    :=    definition { specification } ;
```

One stage of the transformation process will turn

```
definition    :=    type_dcl '; | const_dcl '; | except_dcl '; |
                    interface '; | module '; ;
```

into

```
definition    :=    ( type_dcl | const_dcl ) '; | except_dcl '; |
                    interface '; | module '; ;
```

This will then become:

```
definition    :=    (( type_dcl | const_dcl ) | except_dcl ) '; |
                    interface '; | module '; ;
```

Hence, the unnesting transformations are ultimately needed to get the result:

```
definition    :=    ( type_dcl | const_dcl | except_dcl |
                    interface | module ) '; ;
```

which is actually produced.

The repeated application of *simplify* until it converges – the *canonicalize* operator – is necessary here, as far as I can tell. In addition to promotion of operators into a single synthesize pass, it will be even more important to understand under what circumstances the *least-fixed-point* operator can be pushed inside the computation, known as the "fixed-point fusion" problem (Jeuring, 1995). Understanding how to incorporate Kibler'*s* results (Kibler, 1978) will be important here, too.

To go on with the algorithm, the next phase is to introduce Popart'*s* iterative constructs into the grammar. For example,

```
key_list    :=  key |  key COMMA key_list
```

will turn into

```
key_list    :=    key ^ ' , ;
```

This is accomplished by looking for particular recursive definitions by the transformation *Ts_introduce_iteration*. This transformation produces a sequence of productions as its result. This introduction can be done as a simple splice of one or more productions into the existing set of productions. (An extra production is needed when the repeated element is not a simple nonterminal, like *key* was here. Popart only allows the repetition of nonterminals.) Once again, this process needs to be reapplied until all iteration has been extracted, using the *least-fixed-point* operator.

Precedence and the forms of left recursion that Popart permits are then introduced. Since these cannot produce results that can further need reduction, they can be spliced in in a single pass.

Now there are two kinds of productions that normally do not occur in WBNF grammars. It is fairly rare to have a production like *key_list*; rather, its definition is unfolded into its usage context. Similarly, whenever the entire right hand side of a production is optional, it is more common to put the optionality with the situation in which it is optional. Hence,

```
interface_header :=        'INTERFACE identifier opt_inheritance_spec
                           opt_type_property_list ;
opt_inheritance_spec       := { ': inheritance_spec } ;
inheritance_spec :=        scoped_name ^ ', ;
opt_type_property_list :=    { type_property_list } ;
```

should be turned into:

```
interface_header :=        ' INTERFACE identifier { ' : scoped_name ^ ' , }
                           { type_property_list } ;
```

Hence, the algorithm first determines which productions have right hand sides that are simply options or iterations. It then unfolds the definitions, even those that are to be unfolded into themselves, until no more unfolding can occur. For example, the *inheritance_spec* disappeared in the example above, for just this reason. A more efficient version would do a topological sort, based on an analysis of which productions use which others after the precedence and left recursion introduction, and then unfold the definitions. Then the definitions are unfolded into the rest of the grammar using the *prune* operator.

Two more prunings deal with technical details of Popart's WBNF. As was hinted at above, the way Popart produces an abstract syntax from a WBNF specification is to create field names for each of the nonterminals on the right hand side of a production. It is rare for the same nonterminal to occur twice and mean the same thing. Hence, the *rename_duplicates* function generates unique names for each occurrence of a nonterminal name on the right hand side. Some productions, such as alternatives of simple nonterminals, need not have any representation in the abstract syntax. Such productions are said to be represented *compactly* in Popart. "||"at the end of a production indicates that it may not have

* Indeed, there may be productions whose mnemonic value is useful. The actual program allows the user to specify these in the interface.

an abstract syntax representation. Hence, these two prunings get the syntax ready for producing an abstract syntax.

Another detail concerning the relationship between concrete and abstract syntaxes is that alternations of constants in the concrete syntax often correspond to variant record keys in the abstract syntax. Hence, the next pass is concerned with finding the *constant_patterns* that occur within the tree and breaking them out explicitly into their own *constant_productions*. The constant patterns are then folded out of the tree using a prune with *fold_constants*.

Hence, the last three passes would have taken:

```
switch_type_spec        := integer_type | char_type | boolean_type |
                           enum_type | scoped_name ;
inverse_traversal_path  := identifier ' :: identifier ;
key_spec                := ( ' KEY | ' KEYS ) key ^ ' , ;
```

and introduced:

```
switch_type_spec        := integer_type | char_type | boolean_type |
                           enum_type | scoped_name || ;
inverse_traversal_path  := identifier#A ' :: identifier#B ;
key_spec                := con_1 key ^ ' , ;
con_1                   := ' KEY | ' KEYS ;
```

The *concatenate_constants* "pass" would have introduced the definition of *con_1*.

Finally, all that is left to do is to eliminate the productions that are not used any more, using the *reachable* function (which again must do an analysis similar to *uses_freely* above), based on the set of *top_level_productions,* in the filter, *used_somewhere*

5 RELATED WORK

The works of Meertens (1988) and Gibbons (1991, 1993, 1994) are most related to the labeled tree theory developed herein. Since Meertens' trees have no labels on the nonterminal nodes, they really cannot be used effectively to model abstract syntax trees. Tricks like making the first subtree be a leaf node carrying the type, or pairing trees and subsequences, etc., would destroy the beauty of the reduction operators applied to the trees. However, Meertens' development is most like the present, much in the spirit of the Theory of Lists (Bird, 1987). His work has many more theorems and goes on to great depths in categorizing how trees can be evaluated in different orders, etc. The present work must be reexamined page-by-page for insights and cross-over theorems. Similar insights must be sought from Jeuring and Swierstra's recent work (1995), wherein catamorphisms specialized to any particular abstract syntax are produced automatically.

The catamorphism theorem of Meertens (1992) and its generalization by Malcolm (1990) form the stepping-off point for Gibbons' labeled binary trees. His operators are slightly different from those presented here. For example, his *reduce* corresponds to *synthesize*, but only the label is passed with the reducts to the reduce operator rather than the whole tree. This cannot matter, since it is a trivial matter to produce a tree with the entire child sequence as its label in his calculus. Gibbons too has many theorems, especially concerning catamorphisms, that can be brought across to the theory presented herein. The major theorems from his work concern the efficiency of combinations of operators. These will be especially important for the present development if these operators are ever used in production versions of program manipulation systems.

Although these influences are most directly related to the motivation for the study of the abstract syntax tree abstractions, considerable early work in transformation systems and theorem proving systems is consonant with the substance of the operators arrived at for the calculus. Huet and Lang (1978) emphasized the importance of second-order patterns to such a calculus very early on, pointing to the use of structured editor commands as the operational means for expressing transformation application.

Paulson (1983) in the PPLAMBDA language (based on LCF) arrived at several of the same operators for the manipulation of proof trees and other rewriting strategies as are described here. For example his *FIRST_FCONV* is like my *first to apply*. (As with Huet and Lang, he emphasized the matching aspects of what would be a calculus for proof manipulation.) His set of tacticals should be examined in terms of the calculus presented here in the context of general abstract syntax tree manipulation.

Reinhold Heckmann's (1988) language for tree transformations in the PROSPECTRA system is especially relevant to the present work. Although his work also concerns the pattern-matching aspects of a metaprogramming calculus, some of his "functionals" are reminiscent of the operators presented here. For example, his *Extend* operator is a "flat" version of the splicing operator presented here. His mechanism for applying transformations is quite rudimentary, despite the rather well-developed pattern language presented in (Heckmann, 1988).

In fact, neither Heckman, nor Huet and Lang, nor Paulson, focus on the recursive structure of transformation application that is featured in the calculus here. Indeed, the various means for expressing transformations presented in these works could be used in concert with this calculus. (Using Paulson's tactics would *not* be germane, however, for one cannot reason about the calculus if the entirety of recursive function theory is available within the operators!)

Naturally, attribute grammars (Reps, 1982) are also related to these operators, as competitors, in fact. They motivated the naming of the *inherit* and *synthesize* operators. One hopes that the incremental update analysis will have analogs in the metaprogramming calculus.

Many other relationships exist, e.g. with Lieberherr's (1995) adaptive programming methodology, where implicit paths replace the various mapping operators defined here. Code walking techniques are also relevant (Goldman, 1989), especially as targets for compilation of the metaprogramming calculus.

6 CONCLUSIONS

The foundations for a calculus for metaprogramming will include a calculus for pattern matching and primitive transformation as well as a calculus for transformation application. The operators presented above can form the basis for a calculus for transformation application. The operators presented have been found useful in a large, practical transformational development, and seem consonant with other transformation tasks undertaken by the author in the past.

The elegance of the category theoretic foundations for the fundamental operators should provide immediately, so-called "promotion theorems" as rules to be used in the calculus.

As usual, much more remains to be done. First, I would like to find some design principle for understanding exactly which operators to include as fundamental to the calculus. For example, there are two rather obvious functions on labeled trees – suggested by a reviewer of the paper – that I have not found particularly useful when manipulating abstract syntax trees, namely the catamorphism for labeled trees and a map function that relabels based purely on the current label. Moreover, I only recently discovered the need for the *positional_inherit* operator.

I suspect that the real answer to the completeness and adequacy concerns will rely on solving the second problem, namely, that very few computation rules for the calculus have been demonstrated here. The real test of the calculus beyond its ability to express what is necessary is the ability to reason with it, in calculations. Considerably more experience is needed here. Certainly, efficiency concerns will be a driving force. Special consideration of tactics for eliminating *fixed-point* application in the presence of some of the simpler operators will be necessary. This will require at the very least that the transformations applied be analyzable (not boding well for higher-order transformations, I fear). Another area for exploration is the invention of further operators for areas of abstract syntax specification not yet explored. What operators can take advantage of understand the inheritance hierarchy of phyla or the optional presence of fields in an abstract syntax tree record?

These issues notwithstanding, the present formulation of operators provides a higher level of specification for transformation applications than other alternatives presently available.

7 ACKNOWLEDGEMENTS

I sincerely thank members of IFIP WG2.1 for their encouragement in this endeavor, especially Richard Bird, Jeremy Gibbons, Lambert Meertens, and Doaista Swierstra, and observer, Johan Jeuring. I am deeply indebted to one reviewer of this paper for providing the most comprehensive review I have ever seen. He fixed myriad typos, helped me with Haskell conventions, supplied a proof for the relabeling theorem based on a category theory theorem and suggested the other operators I referred to above.

8 BIBLIOGRAPHY

Bird, R.S. (1987) An introduction to the Theory of Lists. in *Logic of Programming and Calculi of Discrete Design* (ed. M. Broy), Springer-Verlag, 3-42.

Donzeau-Gouge, V., Kahn, G., Lang, B., and Mélèse, B. (1984) Document structure and modularity in Mentor. in *Proceedings of the ACM SIGSOFT/SIGPLAN Software Symposium on Practical Software Development Environments*, 141-148.

Gibbons, J. (1991) *Algebras for Tree Algorithms*. Ph.D. Thesis, Programming Research Group, Oxford University.

Gibbons, J. (1993) Upwards and downwards accumulations on trees. in LNCS 669: *Mathematics of Program Construction* (eds. R. S. Bird, C. C. Morgan, and J. C. P. Woodcock), Springer-Verlag, 122-138.

Gibbons, J. (1994) An initial-algebra approach to directed acyclic graphs. in *Mathematics of Program Construction*, ed. B. Möller, LNCS 947, Springer-Verlag. 122-138.

Goldman, N. M. (1989) Code walking and recursive descent: a generic approach. in *Lisp and Functional Programming Conference*.

Heckmann, R. (1988) A functional language for the specification of complex tree transformations. in *Proceedings of the 2nd European Symposium on Programming*. Springer-Verlag, 175-190.

Hudak, P., Jones, S. P., and Wadler, P. (1992) Report on the programming language Haskell. Yale Computer Science report YALEU/DCS/RR-777.

Huet, G. and Lang, B. (1978) Proving and applying program transformations expressed with second-order patterns. *Acta Informatica* **11(1)**. 31-55.

Jeuring, J., and Swierstra, S. D. (1995) Constructing functional programs for grammar analysis problems. in *Proceedings of a Conference on Functional Programming Languages and Computer Architecture,* La Jolla, CA, USA, 259-269.

Jones, G. and Gibbons, J. (1993) Linear-time breadth-first tree algorithms: an exercise in the arithmetic of folds and zips. IFIP Working Group 2.1 working paper 705: WIN 2, University of Auckland Computer Science Report No. 71.

Kibler, D. (1978) *Power, Efficiency, and Correctness of Transformation Systems.* Ph.D. Thesis. University of California, Irvine.

Lieberherr, K. (1995) *Adaptive Object-Oriented Software: the Demeter Method with Propagation Patterns*. PWS Publishing Company, Boston.

Malcolm, G. (1990) Data structures and program transformation. *Science of Computer Programming* **14**. 255-280.

Meertens, *L.* (1988) First steps toward the theory of rose trees. IFIP Working Group 2.1 working paper 592: ROM 25, CWI, Amsterdam.

Meertens, L. (1992) Paramorphisms. In Formal Aspects of Computing **4**. 413-425.

Paulson, *L.* (1983) A higher-order implementation of rewriting. in *Science of Computer Programming* **3,** 119-149.

Reps, *T.* (1982) Optimal-time incremental semantic analysis for syntax-directed editors. in *Ninth Annual ACM Symposium on the Principles of Programming Languages*, 169-176.

Runciman, C. (1989) Another look at labeled trees. IFIP Working Group 2.1 working paper 621: JVL 2, University of York.

Wile, D. *S.* (1986) Organizing programming knowledge into syntax-directed experts. in *Proceedings of an International Workshop on Advanced Programming Environments*, WG2.4, Trondheim, Norway, June.

Wile, D. *S.* (1988) Definitions toward the theory of labeled tree expressions. IFIP Working Group 2.1 working paper: CHM 8, USC/Information Sciences Institute.

Wile, D. *S.* (1991). *Popart Manual.* USC/Information Sciences Institute. 1991.

Wile, D. *S.* (1996) Abstract syntax from concrete syntax. Working Group 2.1 working paper, Rancho Santa Fe, CA. (To appear in ICSE 97).

9 BIOGRAPHY

After receiving his Computer Science from Carnegie-Mellon University in 1974, Dr Wile joined Information Sciences Institute. His interests span the programming process, from domain-specific language designs for problem specification and programming, through the specification and optimization design processes, to the programming environments and software architectures for developing and integrating these designs.

Dr. Wile is an editor for IEEE Transactions on Software Engineering and is a member of SIGSOFT, SIGPLAN, the Association for Computing Machinery, and IFIP's Working Group 2.1 on Algorithmic Languages and Calculi.

Discussion Session
Wednesday morning

Armando Haeberer: I would like to begin with some motivation for my discussion topic. The Achatz and Partsch paper contains the sentence "Transformational programming is short for a methodology of constructing programs from formal problem specifications". The Pettorossi and Proietti paper says: "There are various methodologies for developing programs from specifications". If you look around the literature, you also have the CIP method, the VDM and Z methods, Squiggol (the Bird-Meertens formalism), and so on. Now the categorical mafia is bringing programming in the large into WG2.1. We should be careful because there are other things that are claimed to be methods: Shlaer-Mellor, Booch, the Rise method, and so on. So the question is: what is or is not a method or methodology? And do these methods and calculi have any connection to the meaning in, say, the Runge-Kutta method, or the Solvay method in chemistry, or other methods in mathematics and logic?

Jim Boyle: One might characterize object-oriented things as a method for developing programs, but most of the ones I have seen are not what I would call a formal method. There are no axioms and the manipulations are not supported by a well-developed theory.

Dave Wile: A basic idea of a useful calculus is that induction is a nasty thing. Program verification is difficult because it involves induction. The solution is to add higher-order operators to datatypes and to establish their properties once and for all. By expressing their programs in terms of these operators, users can reason in terms of the equational properties of the operators, properties like distributivity, commutativity, and so on.

Alberto Pettorossi: I don't think we should enter a terminological debate. What is more important is the objective of a calculus.

Jeremy Gibbons: The way I have always understood the terms, a calculus is a collection of notations and laws, while a method tells you how to use these things. For example, folding and unfolding are semantics-preserving transformations, and Darlington and Burstall's unfold-fold method tells you how to apply these transformations to obtain new programs.

Jim Boyle: I would like to change the topic slightly. The first two talks illustrated different points on the spectrum of approaches to transformation. Partsch's talk was about a large transformation that could be used in many situations provided all the requirements could be verified. Pettorossi's talk was more at the level of the basic rules of calculation, and therefore potentially more mechanizable. The disadvantage is that every time you encounter a similar specification you prove essentially the same theorem over and over.

I would be interested in a discussion of the relative advantages of the two approaches.

Richard Bird: The difference between basic rules and larger theorems is common in mathematics. For example, compare the chain rule for differentiation with a theorem that says that under certain conditions a differential equation has a certain closed-form solution. There is no reason to prefer one kind of result over the other, they are simply aspects of the same theory expressed at different levels.

Jim Boyle: While in a sense I agree, my experience is that if one wants to do automatic transformation, then it is better to work at the rule level. The higher-level theorem requires a lot of verification of the attendant hypotheses. You gain flexibility by doing things in small steps, even though you pay a price in terms of extra work.

Michel Sintzoff: As a human being, I would like to use those excellent ideas expressed as theorems. I am waiting for the kind of organized body of knowledge in our field as exists in classical mathematics. Although we have made good progress over five or ten years, I am not sure that my students are able to use these systems and theories. I give them selected papers from you guys, and can tell you that sometimes their reactions are very interesting! They can survive courses in classical mathematics, but not in algorithmic calculi.

Alberto Pettorossi: Terminological discussion is not really useful. I do not care whether this is a table or a desk, but I do care whether this object is what I need when writing a paper or attending a lecture. I want to specify that the object is stable and does not move when I am writing.

Doug Smith: Is there a formal definition of a calculus? We know now what an algebra is and we can talk about transformations between algebras. There is a formalization of what a logic is with institutions, and that allows us to talk about morphisms between logics. You see now work on operations that are institutionally independent, so you can have machine support for theorem proving that is independent of the logic you are working in. In the Specware system we have been using that as a basis for code generation. I am not sure what the benefits of formalizing a design calculus would be, but you can imagine some calculus-independent operations.

Steve Schuman: A long time ago we were taught by some people here that a calculus was something that could be done by purely syntactic manipulation. During one period, when there were summer schools in the Netherlands, people were quite enthusiastic about the idea; they felt the beginnings of progress, and also as much of what was needed as a formal definition of a calculus. I don't think we should be in a hurry to lose that potential, a potential that might interest and impact the outside world, and should not try to come up with a formal definition of what a calculus is.

Dave Wile: It seems to me that the key issue is what you can express, what you can prove in the language, without using induction. How much of the space can you cover without using induction?

Tom Maibaum: There is more to a calculus than just a formal framework. It is not quite having a goal because the same calculation may support different goals. Method introduces goals and can be both formal and non-formal. For example, people knew how to put metal things round wheels before they understood the science. They knew you had to heat the metal up, put it on the wheel, and let it cool down so it would fit tightly. But they could not explain why they did it, nevertheless, it was a perfectly effective informal method. Engineers, on the other hand, want formal methods. They want the things that they do to be explainable in terms of calculations even if such calculations are not actually done in most situations. So, electronic engineers design filters by using an informal notation – the tent and poles method – but there is a close correlation between this visual representation and the differential equations that it represents. If you asked them, some can produce the differential equation representation and do calculations instead of manipulations in the visual model.

14

Principled strength reduction

*Yanhong A. Liu**
Computer Science Department, Indiana University
201E Lindley Hall, Bloomington, IN 47405, U.S.A.
Email: liu@cs.indiana.edu, Tel: (812)855-4373, Fax: (812)855-4829

Abstract

This paper presents a principled approach for optimizing iterative (or recursive) programs. The approach formulates a loop body as a function f and a change operation $\oplus$, incrementalizes f with respect to $\oplus$, and adopts an incrementalized loop body to form a new loop that is more efficient. Three general optimizations are performed as part of the adoption; they systematically handle initializations, termination conditions, and final return values on exits of loops. These optimizations are either omitted, or done in implicit, limited, or *ad hoc* ways in previous methods.

The new approach generalizes classical loop optimization techniques, notably strength reduction, in optimizing compilers, and it unifies and systematizes various optimization strategies in transformational programming. Such principled strength reduction performs drastic program efficiency improvement via incrementalization and appreciably reduces code size via associated optimizations. We give examples where this approach can systematically produce strength-reduced programs while no previous method can.

Keywords

program optimization, incrementalization, strength reduction, caching intermediate results, maintaining auxiliary information, initialization, termination condition, loop optimization, iteration, recursion

1 INTRODUCTION

Strength reduction (Aho, Sethi & Ullman 1986, Allen 1969, Allen, Cocke & Kennedy 1981, Cocke & Kennedy 1977, Cocke & Schwartz 1970, Grau, Hill & Langmaac 1967, Gries 1971, Steffen, Knoop & Rüthing 1991) is a classical loop optimization technique in optimizing compilers. The idea is to replace certain operations in loop bodies by faster operations. For example, a multiplication involving an induction variable can sometimes be transformed into an addition. Finite differencing (Paige & Schwartz 1977, Paige 1983, Paige

*This work was supported by ONR under grant No. N00014-92-J-1973, NSF under grant No. CCR-9503319, and Indiana University under a junior-faculty start-up grant.

& Koenig 1982) generalizes strength reduction to languages with expressions composed of aggregate operations like set operations. Basically, a set of finite differencing rules are developed to transform aggregate operations in loop bodies into more efficient incremental operations. The essence of these optimizations is **incrementalization** of computations in loop bodies, *i.e.*, computing each iteration based on the result of the previous iteration. Such optimizations are crucial for performance.

This paper presents a principled approach for optimizing iterative (or recursive) programs, by explicitly formulating from them problems of incrementalization, using a general systematic approach to do the incrementalization, adopting the resulting incremental programs to form more efficient iterations (or recursions), and performing associated optimizations. This approach allows us to achieve optimizations such as strength reduction and finite differencing, as well as more drastic efficiency improvements. We call it **principled strength reduction**. There are at least two motivations for it: first, to achieve greater incrementality than allowed by a fixed set of strength-reduction or finite-differencing rules, and second, to provide a general and systematic approach following which new rules can be developed for both existing and new languages.

We have previously proposed a general systematic approach to incrementalization (Liu 1996, Liu, Stoller & Teitelbaum 1996). Given a program f and an input change operation $\oplus$, the approach aims to obtain an **incremental program** that computes $f(x \oplus y)$ efficiently by making use of $f(x)$ (Liu & Teitelbaum 1995b), the intermediate results computed in computing $f(x)$ (Liu & Teitelbaum 1995a), and auxiliary information about $f(x)$ that can be inexpensively maintained (Liu et al. 1996). Since every non-trivial computation proceeds by iteration (or recursion), the approach can be used for achieving efficient computation by computing each iteration using an appropriate incremental program. However, until now, a key issue was unaddressed: Given an iterative (or recursive) program, how exactly to determine the appropriate programs f and operations $\oplus$ on which to apply the incrementalization method, and how to adopt the resulting incremental programs to form new iterations (or recursions) that are more efficient?

This paper addresses this key open issue. The approach includes automatic transformations for formulating the incrementalization problem and for adopting the incremental programs. These transformations cleanly handle the initializations before iterations and the conditions for termination. To take full advantage of the incremental programs, three associated optimizations are performed: **folding initialization** and **replacing termination condition** are based on equality analysis; **minimizing maintained information** uses dependence analysis and is based on the idea that seemingly important values are not necessarily maintained in each iteration. Some of these optimizations are often seen as programmers' tricks, and they are particularly subtle and error-prone when done in *ad hoc* fashions. We, for the first time, unify and systematize these optimizations, together with incrementalization, to achieve principled strength reduction. Once formulated around the idea of incrementalization, these optimizations and the overall principled strength reduction become simple and clear.

We give examples where our approach can systematically produce strength-reduced programs while no previous method can. These examples are in VLSI design, array processing, *etc.*

This paper is organized as follows. Section 2 prepares preliminaries. Section 3 presents a principled approach to speeding-up iterations using appropriate incremental programs. Section 4 describes optimizations in adopting incremental programs to form more efficient iterations. Section 5 discusses extensions and applications of the approach. Section 6 gives examples. Finally, Section 7 discusses related work and concludes.

2 PRELIMINARIES

Our incrementalization method (Liu 1996, Liu et al. 1996) has been described using a first-order, call-by-value functional programming language. The expressions of the language are given by the following grammar:

$e ::= v$	variable
$\mid\ c(e_1, ..., e_n)$	constructor application
$\mid\ p(e_1, ..., e_n)$	primitive function application
$\mid\ g(e_1, ..., e_n)$	function application
$\mid\ \textbf{if } e_1 \textbf{ then } e_2 \textbf{ else } e_3$	conditional expression
$\mid\ \textbf{let } v = e_1 \textbf{ in } e_2$	binding expression

In particular, <> denotes a tuple constructor, and primitive functions $1st$, $2nd$, $3rd$, ... select the first, second, third, ... elements, respectively, of a tuple.

A program f is a set of mutually recursive function definitions of the form $g(v_1, ..., v_n) = e$ and a function f that is to be evaluated with some input $x = \langle x_1, ..., x_n \rangle$.* Figure 1 gives some example definitions.

An input change operation $\oplus$ to a program f combines an old input $x = \langle x_1, ..., x_n \rangle$ and a change $y = \langle y_1, ..., y_m \rangle$ to form a new input $x' = \langle x'_1, ..., x'_n \rangle = x \oplus y$, where each x'_i is some function of x_j's and y_k's. For example, an input change operation to the functions *cmp*, *odd*, *even*, *sum*, and *prod* of Figure 1 may be $x' = x \oplus_1 y = cons(y, x)$; an input change operation to the function *update* may be $x' = x \oplus_2 y = \langle n, m, i \rangle \oplus_2 \langle\rangle = \langle n, update(n, m, i), i - 1 \rangle$, even using *update* itself. Input change operation is an important notion. It describes how a new input to f differs from an old input, and thus affects how the new output can be computed efficiently using the old output. In

*Note that <> is a tuple constructor in the language, but $\langle\rangle$ is only a tuple notation used in the presentation of the paper.

$cmp(x)$: compare sum of odd and product of even positions $cmp(x) = sum(odd(x)) \leq prod(even(x))$ $odd(x) =$ **if** $null(x)$ **then** nil **else** $cons(car(x), even(cdr(x)))$ $even(x) =$ **if** $null(x)$ **then** nil **else** $odd(cdr(x))$ $sum(x) =$ **if** $null(x)$ **then** 0 **else** $car(x) + sum(cdr(x))$ $prod(x) =$ **if** $null(x)$ **then** 1 **else** $car(x) * prod(cdr(x))$	$update(n, m, i)$: update m by $\pm 2^i$ according to $n - m^2$ $update(n, m, i) =$ **let** $p = n - m^2$ **in** **if** $p > 0$ **then** $m + 2^i$ **else if** $p < 0$ **then** $m - 2^i$ **else** m

Figure 1 Example function definitions.

an iterative (or recursive) program where the loop body is formulated as a function f, an input change operation should capture how the iterative (or recursive) computation proceeds so that we can determine how one iteration can be computed incrementally using the previous iteration.

We use an asymptotic cost model for measuring time complexity and write $t(f(v_1, ..., v_n))$ to denote the asymptotic time of computing $f(v_1, ..., v_n)$. Of course, maintaining additional information takes extra space. Our primary goal is to improve the asymptotic running time of the incremental computation. We attempt to save space by maintaining only information useful for achieving this.

Given a program f and an operation $\oplus$, we can use the approach in (Liu 1996, Liu et al. 1996) to derive (i) a program $\tilde{f}(x)$ that extends $f(x)$ to return also useful additional information about x, (ii) a program $\tilde{f}'(x, y, \tilde{r})$ that incrementally computes $\tilde{f}(x \oplus y)$ when $\tilde{r} = \tilde{f}(x)$, and (iii) a function Π that projects $f(x)$ out of $\tilde{f}(x)$ and projects $f(x \oplus y)$ out of $\tilde{f}'(x, y, \tilde{r})$.* For the function cmp in Figure 1 and operation $\oplus_1$, the intermediate results $sum(odd(x))$ and $prod(even(x))$ and auxiliary information $sum(even(x))$ and $prod(odd(x))$ are also returned, in components 2, 3, 4, 5, respectively, and the functions $\widetilde{cmp}$ and $\widetilde{cmp}'$ in Figure 2 and the projection function $\Pi = 1st$ are obtained.

Using the above functional language, we can directly simulate an imperative language with assignment, sequence, conditional, and loop statements, with functions and procedures, with basic data constructions, such as records, but without arrays or pointers. This paper considers iterative programs written in such an imperative language. Pieces of the programs that need to be incrementalized are translated into the above functional language. For simplicity, only structured programs are considered.

*While $f(x)$ abbreviates $f(x_1, ..., x_n)$, and $f(x \oplus y)$ abbreviates $f(\langle x_1, ..., x_n\rangle \oplus \langle y_1, ..., y_m\rangle)$, $f'(x, y, r)$ abbreviates $f'(x_1, ..., x_n, y_1, ..., y_m, r)$. Note that some of the parameters of f' may be dead and eliminated (Liu & Teitelbaum 1995b).

$cmp(x) = 1st(\widetilde{cmp}(x))$.
For x of length n,
  $\widetilde{cmp}(x)$ takes time $O(n)$;
  $cmp(x)$ takes time $O(n)$.

If $\widetilde{cmp}(x) = \tilde{r}$,
  then $\widetilde{cmp}'(y, \tilde{r}) = \widetilde{cmp}(cons(y, x))$.
For x of length n,
  $\widetilde{cmp}'(y, \tilde{r})$ takes time $O(1)$;
  $\widetilde{cmp}(cons(y, x))$ takes time $O(n)$.

$$
\begin{aligned}
\widetilde{cmp}(x) \;=\; & \textbf{let } v_1 = odd(x) \textbf{ in} \\
& \textbf{let } u_1 = sum(v_1) \textbf{ in} \\
& \textbf{let } v_2 = even(x) \textbf{ in} \\
& \textbf{let } u_2 = prod(v_2) \textbf{ in} \\
& < u_1 \le u_2,\ u_1,\ u_2, \\
& \quad sum(v_2),\ prod(v_1) >
\end{aligned}
$$

$$
\begin{aligned}
\widetilde{cmp}'(y, \tilde{r}) \;=\; & < y + 4th(\tilde{r}) \le 5th(\tilde{r}), \\
& \quad y + 4th(\tilde{r}),\ 5th(\tilde{r}), \\
& \quad 2nd(\tilde{r}),\ y * 3rd(\tilde{r}) >
\end{aligned}
$$

Figure 2 Resulting function definitions.

Example We use the derivation of an efficient binary integer square root algorithm for VLSI design (O'Leary, Leeser, Hickey & Aagaard 1994) as a running example. The initial specification of the algorithm is given in Figure 3(a). Given a binary integer n of l bits, where $n > 0$ (and l is usually 8, 16, ...), it computes the binary integer square root m of n using the non-restoring method (Flores 1963, O'Leary et al. 1994), which is exact for perfect squares and off by at most 1 for other integers. In hardware, multiplications and exponentials are much more expensive than additions and shifts (doublings or halvings), so the goal is to replace the former by the latter. We will obtain the program in Figure 3(b).

```
n := input; m := 2^(l-1);
for i := l - 2 downto 0 do
    p := n - m^2;
    if p > 0 then
        m := m + 2^i
    else if p < 0 then
        m := m - 2^i;
output(m)
```

(*a*)

```
p := input; v := 0; w := 2^(2*(l-1));
while w >= 1 do
    if p > 0 then
        p := p - v - w; v := v/2 + w; w := w/4
    else if p < 0 then
        p := p + v - w; v := v/2 - w; w := w/4
    else v := v/2; w := w/4;
output(v)
```

(*b*)

Figure 3 Non-restoring binary integer square root example.

3 A PRINCIPLED APPROACH

This section shows how to formulate a problem of incrementalization from an iterative program and how to use a derived incremental program to form a new iterative program. For simplicity, this section considers only single loops; extensions are discussed in Section 5.

3.1 Step 1: Formulating the incrementalization problem

Each loop consists of initialization, termination condition, and loop body, where loop body includes updates to the induction variables. To formulate the incrementalization problem, we regard computations in the loop body as forming a function f, and we regard the update to the input of f, including in particular the update to the induction variables, in each iteration as forming an input change operation $\oplus$. Note that the update to the input of f in each iteration is a result of update of the state by f itself.

Consider a loop statement. Let s be a tupling of the variables that are defined before the loop and are used in either the termination condition or the loop body. Then, any single loop can be transformed into a **while** loop of the form:

$$\begin{array}{ll} s := s_1; & \text{-- initialization} \\ \textbf{while } c(s) \textbf{ do} & \text{-- termination condition} \\ \quad s := b(s) & \text{-- loop body} \end{array} \tag{1}$$

from which we directly formulate a function f and an input change operation $\oplus$:

$$f(x) = b(x) \quad \text{and} \quad x \oplus y = b(x) \tag{2}$$

Example Transforming the **for** loop into a **while** loop, the program in Figure 3(a) is transformed into:

```
[1]   n := input;
[2]   m := 2^(l-1);
[3]   i := l - 2;
[4]   while i >= 0 do
[5]       p := n - m^2;
[6]       if p > 0 then
[7]           m := m + 2^i
[8]       else if p < 0 then
[9]           m := m - 2^i;
[10]      i := i - 1;
[11]  output(m)
```
(3)

The part of the program between lines 1 and 10 is then transformed into a **while** loop of form (1):

$$\begin{array}{l} <n,m,i> \ := \ <input, 2^{l-1}, l-2>; \\ \textbf{while } i \geq 0 \textbf{ do} \\ \quad <n,m,i> \ := \ <n, update(n,m,i), i-1> \end{array} \tag{4}$$

where assignments to the tuple elements are parallel and function *update* is as defined in Figure 1. From the loop body, we obtain the function f and operation $\oplus$:

$$f(n,m,i) = <n, update(n,m,i), i-1> \text{ and } \langle n,m,i\rangle \oplus \langle\,\rangle = \langle n, update(n,m,i), i-1\rangle \quad (5)$$

3.2 Step 2: Incrementalization

Given a functional program f and an input change operation $\oplus$, using the approach in (Liu 1996, Liu et al. 1996, Liu & Teitelbaum 1995a, Liu & Teitelbaum 1995b), we can derive an incremental program that computes $f(x \oplus y)$ incrementally by using the return value (Liu & Teitelbaum 1995b), the intermediate results (Liu & Teitelbaum 1995a), and certain auxiliary information (Liu et al. 1996) of $f(x)$, *i.e.*, we obtain a program $\tilde{f}$ that computes $f(x)$ and necessary additional information, a program $\tilde{f}'$ that incrementally computes $f(x \oplus y)$ and maintains the additional information, and a constant-time projection function Π that projects the value of f out of $\tilde{f}$ and $\tilde{f}'$. The derived programs $\tilde{f}$ and $\tilde{f}'$ and projection function Π satisfy: if $f(x) = r$, then

$$\Pi(\tilde{f}(x)) = r \quad \text{and} \quad t(\tilde{f}(x)) \leq t(f(x)) \quad (6)$$

and if $f(x \oplus y) = r'$ and $\tilde{f}(x) = \tilde{r}$, then

$$\Pi(\tilde{f}'(x,y,\tilde{r})) = r', \;\; \tilde{f}'(x,y,\tilde{r}) = \tilde{f}(x \oplus y), \text{ and } t(\tilde{f}'(x,y,\tilde{r})) \leq t(f(x \oplus y)) \quad (7)$$

i.e., the programs $\tilde{f}$ and $\tilde{f}'$ preserve the semantics and compute asymptotically at least as fast as long as the original program terminates.

For the program f and operation $\oplus$ formulated in (2), the parameter y is not used, *i.e.*, $x \oplus y = x \oplus \langle\rangle$. In addition, the parameter x, if necessary, can always be included in the return value of $\tilde{f}(x)$. Therefore, the corresponding program $\tilde{f}'$ actually uses only the parameter $\tilde{r}$. We obtain specialized forms of (6) and (7): if $f(x) = r$, then

$$\Pi(\tilde{f}(x)) = r \quad \text{and} \quad t(\tilde{f}(x)) \leq t(f(x)) \quad (8)$$

and if $f(x \oplus \langle\rangle) = r'$ and $\tilde{f}(x) = \tilde{r}$, then

$$\Pi(\tilde{f}'(\tilde{r})) = r', \;\; \tilde{f}'(\tilde{r}) = \tilde{f}(x \oplus \langle\rangle), \text{ and } t(\tilde{f}'(\tilde{r})) \leq t(f(x \oplus \langle\rangle)) \quad (9)$$

Incrementalization *per se* is not the subject of this paper. Thus, we explain the methods of (Liu 1996, Liu et al. 1996, Liu & Teitelbaum 1995a, Liu & Teitelbaum 1995b) only on the running example.

Example For the function f in (5), components 1 and 3 of its return value are trivially updated by the operation $\oplus$ in (5). Thus, we consider only the function *update* in component 2. Incrementalizing *update* under $\oplus$, as done in (Liu et al. 1996), we obtain the functions $\widetilde{update}$ and $\widetilde{update}'$, explained below, and the projection function $\Pi = 1st$.

$$\widetilde{update}(n,m,i) = \begin{array}{l} \textbf{let } p = n - m^2 \textbf{ in} \\ \textbf{if } p > 0 \textbf{ then} \\ \quad \textbf{let } u = 2^i \textbf{ in } < m+u,\ p,\ u,\ 2{*}m{*}u,\ u^2 > \\ \textbf{else if } p < 0 \textbf{ then} \\ \quad \textbf{let } u = 2^i \textbf{ in } < m-u,\ p,\ u,\ 2{*}m{*}u,\ u^2 > \\ \textbf{else } < m,\ 0 > \end{array} \tag{10}$$

$$\widetilde{update}'(\tilde{r_1}) = \begin{array}{l} \textbf{if } \tilde{r_1}.p > 0 \textbf{ then} \\ \quad \textbf{let } p = \tilde{r_1}.p - \tilde{r_1}.v - \tilde{r_1}.w \textbf{ in} \\ \quad \textbf{if } p > 0 \textbf{ then} \\ \quad\quad \textbf{let } u = \tilde{r_1}.u/2 \textbf{ in } < \tilde{r_1}.m+u,\ p,\ u,\ \tilde{r_1}.v/2+\tilde{r_1}.w,\ \tilde{r_1}.w/4 > \\ \quad \textbf{else if } p < 0 \textbf{ then} \\ \quad\quad \textbf{let } u = \tilde{r_1}.u/2 \textbf{ in } < \tilde{r_1}.m-u,\ p,\ u,\ \tilde{r_1}.v/2+\tilde{r_1}.w,\ \tilde{r_1}.w/4 > \\ \quad \textbf{else } < \tilde{r_1}.m,\ 0 > \\ \textbf{else if } \tilde{r_1}.p < 0 \textbf{ then} \\ \quad \textbf{let } p = \tilde{r_1}.p + \tilde{r_1}.v - \tilde{r_1}.w \textbf{ in} \\ \quad \textbf{if } p > 0 \textbf{ then} \\ \quad\quad \textbf{let } u = \tilde{r_1}.u/2 \textbf{ in } < \tilde{r_1}.m+u,\ p,\ u,\ \tilde{r_1}.v/2-\tilde{r_1}.w,\ \tilde{r_1}.w/4 > \\ \quad \textbf{else if } p < 0 \textbf{ then} \\ \quad\quad \textbf{let } u = \tilde{r_1}.u/2 \textbf{ in } < \tilde{r_1}.m-u,\ p,\ u,\ \tilde{r_1}.v/2-\tilde{r_1}.w,\ \tilde{r_1}.w/4 > \\ \quad \textbf{else } < \tilde{r_1}.m,\ 0 > \\ \textbf{else } < \tilde{r_1}.m,\ 0 > \end{array} \tag{11}$$

Function $\widetilde{update}(n,m,i)$ extends $update(n,m,i)$ to return also the intermediate results p and u and auxiliary information $2{*}m{*}u$ and u^2.* The intermediate results are directly computed in $update(n,m,i)$. The auxiliary information is obtained by unfolding $update(\langle n,m,i\rangle \oplus \langle\rangle)$ and analyzing the resulting expression. In particular, *update* computes an intermediate result $n-m^2$, and $\oplus$ updates m to be $m \pm u$ ($+$ or $-$ depending on the condition in *update* in $\oplus$); thus, to compute $n-(m \pm u)^2$, which equals $n-m^2 \mp 2{*}m{*}u - u^2$, two expensive pieces of auxiliary information $2{*}m{*}u$ and u^2 are maintained, in additional to the intermediate result $n - m^2$. Of course the equality above depends on properties of $+$, $-$, and $*$. The analyses and transformations in our incrementalization methods (Liu 1996, Liu et al. 1996, Liu & Teitelbaum 1995a, Liu & Teitelbaum 1995b) first exploit all such intermediate results and auxiliary information and then prune out the ones not used in the incremental computation. For example, the value of m^2 is also an intermediate result, but it is not used separately, and thus is not maintained.

---

*Such additional values are returned only in branches where they are computed; in other branches, they could be denoted using a placeholder _, which can be safely eliminated when they are at the rightmost positions of a tuple (Liu et al. 1996, Liu & Teitelbaum 1995a).

Function $\widetilde{update}'(\tilde{r_1})$ uses the extended return value of $\widetilde{update}(n, m, i)$ to compute $\widetilde{update}(\langle n, m, i\rangle \oplus \langle\rangle)$. For readability, we name the five components of the return tuple as m, p, u, v, w, respectively, and use these names rather than the corresponding selectors $1st$, $2nd$, $3rd$, *etc.* Under each of the three different conditions on p in $update(n, m, i)$ in $\langle n, m, i\rangle \oplus \langle\rangle$, m is updated differently and is used to compute the new value of p; under each of the three different conditions on the new value of p, the new return tuple is maintained differently. For example, in the first branch of (11), where $\tilde{r_1}.p > 0$ and $p > 0$, the fourth component is $2{*}m'{*}u'$, where $m' = m{+}u$ and $u' = u/2$, and is transformed into $2{*}(m{+}u){*}(u/2) = 2{*}m{*}u/2 + 2 * u^2/2 = \tilde{r_1}.v/2 + \tilde{r_1}.w$.

Now, going back to f, we obtain

$$\tilde{f}(n,m,i) = <n, \widetilde{update}(n,m,i), i-1>, \ \tilde{f}'(n,\tilde{r_1},i) = <n, \widetilde{update}'(\tilde{r_1}), i-1>, \ \text{and} \quad \Pi(<n,\tilde{r_1},i>) = \ <n, 1st(\tilde{r_1}), i>. \tag{12}$$

Obviously, if we use $\tilde{f}'$ instead of f to form a new loop body, then all multiplications and exponentials in the looping part are replaced by additions and shifts.

3.3 Step 3: Adopting the incrementalized program

With the derived programs $\tilde{f}$ and $\tilde{f}'$ and projection Π, we can obtain a new loop that computes its iteration using the incremental program $\tilde{f}'$. To use notations corresponding to those used in the original program (1), let

$$\tilde{b}(s) = \tilde{f}(s) \quad \text{and} \quad \tilde{b}'(\tilde{s}) = \tilde{f}'(\tilde{s}). \tag{13}$$

We transform the original program (1) into

$$
\begin{array}{l}
s := s_1; \\
\textbf{if } c(s) \textbf{ then} \\
\quad \tilde{s} := \tilde{b}(s); \\
\quad \textbf{while } c(\Pi(\tilde{s})) \textbf{ do} \\
\quad\quad \tilde{s} := \tilde{b}'(\tilde{s}); \\
\quad s := \Pi(\tilde{s})
\end{array}
\tag{14}
$$

where in the first "iteration", the extended function $\tilde{b}$ computes the additional information while computing the result of b.

Theorem 1 *If the program in (1) terminates in a state s, then the program in (14) terminates in the same state s and is asymptotically at least as fast.*

Proof: It follows from the equations in (2) and (13) and the correctness results about the functions $\tilde{f}$, $\tilde{f}'$, and Π in (8) and (9). □

To implement the assignments in (14), new variables are needed to store the additional information in $\tilde{s}$ over s. Moreover, since the assignments to $\tilde{s}$ are parallel, additional temporary variables may be needed to make the assignments sequential. A naive algorithm could create a temporary variable v_{tmp} for each v in $\tilde{s}$, assign all the new values of v's to v_{tmp}'s, and then copy all the values of v_{tmp}'s back to v's. Yet, the number of additional copy statements and the number of additional temporary variables can sometimes be reduced substantially by carefully ordering the assignment statements.

The problem of minimizing the number S of additional copy statements is NP-complete (Garey & Johnson 1979, Sethi 1973), but good heuristics exist (Sethi 1973). We can use an algorithm that easily decides an appropriate order of assignments when no additional temporary variables or copy statements are needed and reduces the problem to the problem of minimizing S otherwise. Basically, it builds a directed graph G representing the dependencies in the given assignments, solves the assignment problem for each of the strongly connected components (SCC) of G, and puts the resulting assignments for each of the SCCs together according to a topological order of the SCCs. Thus, if each SCC contains a single node, then no additional temporary variables or copy statements are needed, and a topological order of all the nodes determines an appropriate order of the sequential assignments.

Example For the running example, we have

$$\tilde{b}(n,m,i) = \; <n, \widetilde{update}(n,m,i), i-1> \quad \text{and} \quad \tilde{b}'(n,\tilde{r_1},i) = \; <n, \widetilde{update}'(\tilde{r_1}), i-1> . \quad (15)$$

The termination condition is still $i \geq 0$. We can obtain a new program of form (14) using these resulting functions.

The orders of the return components in the parallel assignments using $\tilde{b}$ and $\tilde{b}'$, respectively, are also topological orders according to the dependencies in the assignments, with the exception that, in the assignments using $\tilde{b}$, the first return component of $\widetilde{update}$ should be assigned last. Thus, using the algorithm above, assignments to all the components are sequentialized without using additional temporary variables or copy statements. We simply use p and u for the intermediate results in components 2 and 3, respectively, and v and w for the auxiliary information in components 4 and 5, respectively.

4 OPTIMIZING THE INCREMENTALIZED LOOP

This section discusses three associated optimizations that further improve the strength-reduced programs: folding the initialization, replacing the termination condition, and minimizing the maintained information. These optimizations benefit from the use of incrementalization.

4.1 Step 4: Folding the initialization

Additional information is often used by $\tilde{b}'$ for the incremental computation of a loop body. In (14), that information is initialized by $\tilde{b}$ before entering the loop. The code $\tilde{b}$ for initialization may often be saved by folding it into the loop body $\tilde{b}'$.

Given the initial state s_1, loop body b, and termination condition c as in (1), we look for a state s_0 such that $b(s_0) = s_1$ and $c(s_0) = true$. If b has an inverse b^{-1}, then a candidate state for s_0 is $b^{-1}(s_1)$. Note that s_0 is not necessarily unique and does not need to be. With such a state s_0, the original program (1) can be transformed into

$$
\begin{array}{l}
s := s_0; \\
\textbf{while } c(s) \textbf{ do} \\
\quad s := b(s)
\end{array}
\qquad (16)
$$

and thus the resulting program (14) can be transformed into

$$
\begin{array}{l}
\tilde{s} := \tilde{b}(s_0); \\
\textbf{while } c(\Pi(\tilde{s})) \textbf{ do} \\
\quad \tilde{s} := \tilde{b}'(\tilde{s}); \\
s := \Pi(\tilde{s})
\end{array}
\qquad (17)
$$

It is easy to see that, in the resulting program (17), the part of the initial state $\tilde{s}$ that corresponds to s just equals s_1. Thus, the initialization in (17) needs to compute only the part of $\tilde{s}$ that corresponds to the additional information for s_1. In general, we look for a state $\tilde{s_1}$ that extends s_1 with appropriate additional information, *i.e.*, $\Pi(\tilde{s_1}) = s_1$ and, if $\tilde{b}(s_1) = \tilde{s}$, then $\tilde{b}'(\tilde{s_1}) = \tilde{s}$, and that can be initialized asymptotically as fast as s_1. Then, the computation of $\tilde{b}$ in (14) can be replaced with $\tilde{b}'$, which can be folded into the loop body of (14), yielding the simplified program:

$$
\begin{array}{l}
\tilde{s} := \tilde{s_1}; \\
\textbf{while } c(\Pi(\tilde{s})) \textbf{ do} \\
\quad \tilde{s} := \tilde{b}'(\tilde{s}); \\
s := \Pi(\tilde{s})
\end{array}
\qquad (18)
$$

The correctness of program (17) follows from Theorem 1 and properties of s_0; the correctness of program (18) then follows from properties of s_1.

Because of their neat effect in reducing code size, such optimizations are often performed by programmers. Albeit seemingly simple, they are prone to errors when done in an ***ad hoc*** fashion. Our method can find a state $\tilde{s_1}$ by inspecting the original program (1) (finding s_0) and deducing the corresponding additional information for the incrementalized program (computing

$\tilde{b}(s_0)$), rather than directly inspecting the resulting program (14), which is often more complicated.

Similar optimizations for the preprocessing code are discussed by Cai and Paige (Cai & Paige 1988/89), whose programs are written in a very-high-level language based on sets. While they can obtain simplified programs by exploiting properties of sets, our optimizations apply also to programs written in lower level languages.

It is worth noting that folding the initialization may increase the absolute running time of a program, but by at most a constant amount. So the asymptotic running time here is not increased, but there can be a trade-off between the code size and the absolute running time of a program. To gain some possible speedup, an optimizing compiler may prefer to unfold the first iteration of program (18). However, the actual running time also depends on the machine cache behavior, which is partly affected by the code size. Also worth noting is that, for a particular machine, the initial values of certain variables may be the default values on the machine and their initialization can be saved. Our method is independent of particular machines.

Example For the running example, the initial state s_1 is $<n, m, i> \; = \; <input, 2^{l-1}, l-2>$. We find a preceding state

$$s_0 = \; <input, 0, l-1>$$

such that $b(s_0) = s_1$ and $c(s_0) = true$. Computing the initial state $\tilde{s_1} = \tilde{b}(s_0)$, where $\tilde{b}$ is as in (15), we obtain

$$\tilde{s_1} = \; <input, <2^{l-1}, \underline{input}, 2^{l-1}, \underline{0}, \underline{2^{2*(l-1)}}>, l-1>. \qquad (19)$$

We will see in the next two subsections that the components not underlined are redundant and will be eliminated by appropriate optimizations in Steps 5 and 6. Thus, in the final program in Figure 3(b), only the underlined components, which correspond to variables p, v, and w, are initialized.

This optimization would have saved a level in the 2-level proofs in (O'Leary et al. 1994). Also, while we obtain this optimization based on the original program (1), they discover the transformation from the resulting program (14), which is more complicated and harder to reason about.

4.2 Step 5: Replacing the termination condition

Certain values in the state s are maintained by a loop solely for testing the termination condition. This becomes unnecessary if the termination condition can be replaced by an equivalent test using other values, in particular, the values maintained in the additional information in $\tilde{s}$. The new condition $\tilde{c}$ must satisfy

$$\tilde{c}(\tilde{s}) = c(s) \quad \text{and} \quad t(\tilde{c}(\tilde{s})) \leq t(c(s)). \tag{20}$$

Thus, such a condition $\tilde{c}$ can be obtained based on the original condition c and the relationship between $\tilde{s}$ and s, which is encoded in the function $\tilde{b}$.

For additional information in $\tilde{s}$ that is computed and maintained only in some but not all branches of $\tilde{b}$ and $\tilde{b}'$, if it can be inexpensively computed and maintained in those other branches as well, then we simply add the computation and maintenance of such information to those other branches. This allows such information to be used in the termination condition regardless of which branches are taken in any iterations.

Since the original termination condition often uses values of induction variables, this optimization generalizes the elimination of induction variables in classical strength reduction (Aho et al. 1986, Allen et al. 1981, Cocke & Kennedy 1977) to the elimination of all replaceable variables.

Example Consider the running example. It is obvious that the variable i is maintained only to test the termination condition, since i is used in the new loop body $\tilde{b}'$ in (15) only for updating itself.

Consider the additional information computed in the loop body, as shown in functions $\widetilde{update}$ in (10) and $\widetilde{update}'$ in (11). In particular, u, $2*m*u$, and u^2 are computed in the first two branches of every conditional but not in the third. Yet they can be inexpensively maintained in each of the third branches as well. We obtain the functions $\widetilde{update_1}$ and $\widetilde{update_1}'$ below:

$$\begin{array}{ll}\widetilde{update_1}(n,m,i) = & \textbf{let } p = n - m^2 \textbf{ in} \\ & \textbf{if } p > 0 \textbf{ then} \\ & \quad \textbf{let } u = 2^i \textbf{ in } < m+u, p, u, 2{*}m{*}u, u^2 > \\ & \textbf{else if } p < 0 \textbf{ then} \\ & \quad \textbf{let } u = 2^i \textbf{ in } < m-u, p, u, 2{*}m{*}u, u^2 > \\ & \textbf{else let } u = 2^i \textbf{ in } < m, 0, u, 2{*}m{*}u, u^2 > \end{array} \tag{21}$$

$$\begin{array}{ll}\widetilde{update_1}'(\tilde{r_1}) = & \textbf{if } \tilde{r_1}.p > 0 \textbf{ then} \\ & \quad \textbf{let } p = \tilde{r_1}.p - \tilde{r_1}.v - \tilde{r_1}.w \textbf{ in} \\ & \quad \textbf{if } p > 0 \textbf{ then} \\ & \quad\quad \textbf{let } u = \tilde{r_1}.u/2 \textbf{ in } < \tilde{r_1}.m+u,\ p,\ u,\ \tilde{r_1}.v/2+\tilde{r_1}.w,\ \tilde{r_1}.w/4 > \\ & \quad \textbf{else if } p < 0 \textbf{ then} \\ & \quad\quad \textbf{let } u = \tilde{r_1}.u/2 \textbf{ in } < \tilde{r_1}.m-u,\ p,\ u,\ \tilde{r_1}.v/2+\tilde{r_1}.w,\ \tilde{r_1}.w/4 > \\ & \quad \textbf{else let } u = \tilde{r_1}.u/2 \textbf{ in } < \tilde{r_1}.m,\ 0,\ u,\ \tilde{r_1}.v/2+\tilde{r_1}.w,\ \tilde{r_1}.w/4 > \\ & \textbf{else if } \tilde{r_1}.p < 0 \textbf{ then} \\ & \quad \textbf{let } p = \tilde{r_1}.p + \tilde{r_1}.v - \tilde{r_1}.w \textbf{ in} \\ & \quad \textbf{if } p > 0 \textbf{ then} \\ & \quad\quad \textbf{let } u = \tilde{r_1}.u/2 \textbf{ in } < \tilde{r_1}.m+u,\ p,\ u,\ \tilde{r_1}.v/2-\tilde{r_1}.w,\ \tilde{r_1}.w/4 > \\ & \quad \textbf{else if } p < 0 \textbf{ then} \\ & \quad\quad \textbf{let } u = \tilde{r_1}.u/2 \textbf{ in } < \tilde{r_1}.m-u,\ p,\ u,\ \tilde{r_1}.v/2-\tilde{r_1}.w,\ \tilde{r_1}.w/4 > \\ & \quad \textbf{else let } u = \tilde{r_1}.u/2 \textbf{ in } < \tilde{r_1}.m,\ 0,\ u,\ \tilde{r_1}.v/2-\tilde{r_1}.w,\ \tilde{r_1}.w/4 > \\ & \textbf{else let } u = \tilde{r_1}.u/2 \textbf{ in } < \tilde{r_1}.m,\ 0,\ u,\ \tilde{r_1}.v/2,\ \tilde{r_1}.w/4 > \end{array} \tag{22}$$

The termination condition tests $i' \geq 0$ after assignments of $u = 2^i$, $w = u^2 = 2^{2*i}$, and $i' = i - 1$ by the function $\tilde{b}$. We have

$$i' \geq 0 \quad \text{iff} \quad i \geq 1 \quad \text{iff} \quad u \geq 2 \quad \text{iff} \quad u^2 \geq 4 \quad \text{iff} \quad w \geq 4. \tag{23}$$

Therefore, the test on the induction variable i can be replaced by a test on u or w; the value of i becomes redundant and can be eliminated. We will see the value of u is not needed for any other purpose but the value of w is. Thus, in the final program in Figure 3(b), the test on w is used in the termination condition. Due to the folding done at the end of Step 6, which will be explained in the next subsection, the test is $w \geq 1$ instead of $w \geq 4$.

In the design work in (O'Leary et al. 1994), the termination condition is not handled formally, and elimination of the induction variable i is deferred to transformations in the hardware implementation. Our method yields a cleaner strength-reduced version that maps into hardware more directly.

4.3 Step 6: Minimizing the maintained information

The entire final state is not necessarily needed on exit of the loop. Using a backward dependence analysis, starting from the "output" or "export" statements of the original program, we can determine the part that is needed. We denote that part as s_{exit}. For the running example, s_{exit} is m.

The main observation is that, even though the value of s_{exit} must be available on exit of the loop, it is not necessarily needed in each iteration. If the value of s_{exit} can be retrieved, on exit of the loop, from other values, in particular, the values maintained in the additional information in $\tilde{s}$, and if maintaining these other values does not need s_{exit}, then the value of s_{exit} does not need to be maintained by the loop. The power of this novel optimization goes beyond any direct dependence analysis; it is enabled only because the addition information for the incrementalization is explicitly maintained by the loop and the relationship between such information and the state of the original program is explicitly recorded. Also note that this optimization does not move any code out of the loop; it removes the unnecessary code. As in the previous subsection, appropriate additional information computed only in some but not all branches is added to those other branches as well.

The optimization is composed of three sub-steps. We first analyze the program $\tilde{b}$ to trace how the value of s_{exit} can be retrieved from what pieces of additional information in $\tilde{s}$ without the need to maintain s_{exit}. Once such pieces s_{retr} of additional information are found, we analyze $\tilde{b}'$ to determine all the values that are needed in computing s_{retr}, using a backward dependence analysis. We then prune computations not needed for computing s_{retr}, including in particular the computation of s_{exit}, out of $\tilde{b}$ and $\tilde{b}'$, and adjust the projection function Π accordingly. By pruning in the backward dependency graph, this optimization always produces programs that compute faster and use less space. This optimization can be surprisingly powerful, since seemingly important values can be completely eliminated from the loop.

In general, we can retrieve the final value from additional information maintained in the loop only if the loop body is executed at least once. So, a conditional is needed. However, if the loop is obtained after folding the initialization, then the additional information is appropriately initialized even if the loop body is not executed and, thus, we can omit the conditional. A last associated optimization is to fold the statement for retrieval into the loop body, if possible. This can be determined by testing the equality between the retrieved state and the state following the final state of the loop. In other words, such folding can be done if the final return value can be computed using one more iteration based on the maintained additional information.

The backward dependence analysis needed for this optimization can use the one developed in (Liu & Teitelbaum 1995a).

Example For the running example, the value that is needed on exit of the loop, *i.e.*, the value of m, is the first component computed by $\widetilde{update}_1$. Analyze (21). This value depends on (i) the value of p, (ii) the value of m in the previous computation, and (iii) the value of u. Since, right after the exit of the loop, we have the "opposite" conditions of (23), *i.e.*, $i' = -1$ iff $i = 0$ iff $u = 1$, we know that (ii) is retrievable from $v = 2 * m * u$ by $m = v/2$ and (iii) is 1. The retrieval is:

$$\textbf{if } p > 0 \textbf{ then } m := v/2 + 1 \textbf{ else if } p < 0 \textbf{ then } m := v/2 - 1 \textbf{ else } m := v/2 \tag{24}$$

Analyzing dependencies for the function $\widetilde{update}_1{}'$ in (22), we obtain all components in the maintained state that are needed to compute components p and v. They are components p, v, and w. Since the original return value in m, the first component, is not needed anymore, different branches induced by conditional tests on p can be merged. Pruning the functions $\widetilde{update}_1$ and $\widetilde{update}_1{}'$ yields:

$$\begin{aligned} \widetilde{update}_2(n,m,i) = \; & \textbf{let } p = n - m^2 \textbf{ in} \\ & \textbf{let } u = 2^i \textbf{ in } < p, 2{*}m{*}u, u^2 > \end{aligned} \tag{25}$$

$$\begin{aligned} \widetilde{update}_2{}'(\tilde{r_2}) = \; & \textbf{if } \tilde{r_2}.p > 0 \textbf{ then} \\ & \quad < \tilde{r_2}.p - \tilde{r_2}.v - \tilde{r_2}.w,\; \tilde{r_2}.v/2 + \tilde{r_2}.w,\; \tilde{r_2}.w/4 > \\ & \textbf{else if } \tilde{r_2}.p < 0 \textbf{ then} \\ & \quad < \tilde{r_2}.p + \tilde{r_2}.v - \tilde{r_2}.w,\; \tilde{r_2}.v/2 - \tilde{r_2}.w,\; \tilde{r_2}.w/4 > \\ & \textbf{else } < \tilde{r_2}.p,\; \tilde{r_2}.v/2,\; \tilde{r_2}.w/4 > \end{aligned} \tag{26}$$

The three components computed by $\widetilde{update}_2$ correspond to variables p, v, and w. In the final program in Figure 3(b), they are computed incrementally in the loop body as in the function $\widetilde{update}_2{}'$.

We fold the retrieval (24) into the loop body by finally retrieving the value of m from v and changing the termination condition from $w \geq 4$ to $w \geq 1$ (since w is updated by $w/4$, $w \geq 4$ equals $w/4 \geq 1$). We obtain the final program in Figure 3(b).

Similar optimization is needed in (O'Leary et al. 1994) but is done implicitly; it is never said explicitly or proved formally how the desired value is finally returned. This is another subtle and error-prone optimization.

5 EXTENSION AND DISCUSSION

So far, we have limited ourselves to considering only iterative programs with only single loops. This section discusses extensions and other issues about applying the approach.

5.1 Multiple iterations

In a structured program, multiple loops are either disjoint or nested. If the loops are disjoint, then we incrementalize each one separately. If the loops are nested, we handle the innermost loop first. Such an approach is based on the the assumption that, in common programming style, the inner iterations form a piece of computation whose states are updated more continuously following one another. Of course, given programs could be arbitrary. We may need to develop special program analysis to recognize such continuity and perform loop interchanging transformations, similar to those used for enhancing parallelism and data locality (Banerjee 1990, Wolf & Lam 1991a, Wolf & Lam 1991b). Section 6 gives examples with nested loops.

5.2 Recursive programs

For a recursive program, determining an input change operation that corresponds to how the recursion proceeds is not always simple.

If the recursion is linear, not necessarily being a tail recursion, then it can be handled in a similar way as iteration, since it straightforwardly corresponds to an iteration: the base case corresponds to the initialization; the condition that distinguishes base case from recursive case corresponds to the termination condition; and the recursive case corresponds to the loop body.

If the recursion is not linear, then there is no direct correspondence of it to an iteration. In fact, it is known that the **while** scheme is equivalent to flow chart, which is strictly less expressive than the recursive scheme (Greibach 1975). Simple heuristics exist for recognizing how recursions proceed on the argument, e.g., for an integer argument, a change operation may be $x' = x+1$; for a list argument, a change operation may be $x' = cons(y, x)$. Section 6 gives examples with non-linear recursions.

5.3 Applying the approach

Steps 1 and 3 can be fully automated. They are simply transformations between a simple functional language and an imperative language that uses the corresponding constructs. Of course, how to handle more complicated program constructs needs to be further studied. Steps 2 and 4-6 are systematic but are parameterized with equality reasonings and dependency analyses. These analyses may exploit various properties of the program constructs. Thus, their degrees of automation depend on the power we require from such analyses.

In general, the approach has a spectrum of applications. First, by limiting the analyses to use fully automatable techniques, it can be used in optimizing compilers. Second, through interacting with the user or a theorem prover, it can be used for semi-automatic transformational programming. Third, used off-line on paper, it supports a general methodology for systematic program efficiency improvement, which is one of the most important issues in program development and maintenance. A prototype implementation for semi-automatic use is under development (Liu 1995). To scale up the method for application to larger problems, we can select only expensive subcomputations in an iteration to be strength reduced.

5.4 How good is the resulting program

Even though it is not always possible to analyze the cost of executing an arbitrary program, it is important to guarantee that a transformed program P' is at least as efficient as the original program P. Our method guarantees that P' is asymptotically at least as fast as P. Further study is needed to guarantee that P' is in practice at least as fast as P or that P' is (asymptotically) faster than P. Further study is also needed on space efficiency. For the square root example, since, in hardware, multiplications and exponentials are much (asymptotically, in a sense) slower than additions and shifts, replacing the former by a few of the latter indeed results in a much faster program. Also, examining Figure 3, the original program (a) uses five units of space (n, m, l, i, p), but the new program (b) uses only four (p, v, w, l).

As with usual compiler optimization techniques, the effectiveness of our techniques depends on the original programs. Section 6 illustrates this. In any case, it is the incrementalization that can give the drastic speedup. The associated optimizations give only linear speedup, but they can save much space and appreciably reduce code size. For the square root example, incrementalization replaces multiplications and exponentials with additions and shifts; associated optimizations reduce the eight units of space (n, m, l, i, p, u, v, w) used in (14) to four (p, v, w, l) in (18), and reduce the size of code in (14), which uses (10) and (11), to (18), which uses (26).

6 EXAMPLES

This section gives more examples, including some with nested iterations and some with non-linear recursions. In particular, we show that different ways of writing the original programs result in different optimized programs. We also show that the general principles underlying our approach apply to programs that use arrays, though detailed analyses and transformations for arrays are worked out elsewhere (Liu & Stoller 1997).

6.1 Non-restoring binary integer square root

The running example is taken from VLSI circuit design (O'Leary et al. 1994), which transforms the original specification into a strength reduced version and further into a hardware implementation. The strength-reduced program was manually discovered and proved correct using Nuprl (Constable et al. 1986).

As discussed above, the optimizations used in (O'Leary et al. 1994) either incurred extra levels of proofs or were not handled formally. Another drawback is that there was no formal treatment of cost. As mentioned in (Liu et al. 1996), the final program in (O'Leary et al. 1994) contains an unnecessary shift.

We have showed through the presentation how our method is used to systematically derive a strength-reduced program, which automates and simplifies the VLSI circuit design process. Many similar programs, such as various versions of real/integer division/square-root algorithms (Dershowitz 1983), can also be derived using our method.

6.2 Minimum-sum section problem

This example is taken from (Gries 1984). Given an array $a[1..n]$ of numbers, where $n \geq 1$. A minimum-sum section of a is a non-empty sequence of adjacent elements whose sum is a minimum. A naive algorithm takes $O(n^3)$ time to compute such a minimum. Some ways of writing the loops enable easy improvement to $O(n^2)$, while others enable easy improvement to $O(n)$.

From the $O(n^3)$ time program on the left, we obtain the program on the right that takes $O(n^2)$ time:

```
min := a[1];
for i := 1 to n do
  for j := i to n do
    sum := 0;
    for k := i to j do
      sum := sum + a[k];
    min := min(min, sum)
```

```
min := a[1];
for i := 1 to n do
  sum1 := 0;
  for j := i to n do
    sum1 := sum1 + a[j];
    min := min(min, sum1)
```
(27)

The transformation proceeds as follow. First, consider the innermost loop L_k

only. Since each iteration of L_k adds a new number, L_k remains unchanged. Next, consider the middle loop L_j, which contains the loop L_k. Since each iteration of L_j first repeats computation in the previous iteration, L_j is incrementalized: the value of *sum* is maintained in a variable sum_1 after each iteration by adding only a new number; sum_1 is initialized to 0 (obtained with the optimization of folding initialization) before L_j starts; and the loop L_k is eliminated. Finally, consider the outermost loop L_i, which now contains the new middle loop L_j. Unfortunately, L_i can not be incrementalized since its iteration goes destructively, *i.e.*, as i increases, the interval from i to n decreases. This suggests that, if j loops from i down to 1 instead of to n, we may be able to incrementalize L_i. This is indeed the case.*

From the $O(n^3)$ time program on the left, which is the same as the one on the left of (27) except that j goes from i down to 1 instead of to n, we obtain the program on the right that takes $O(n)$ time:

```
min := a[1];
for i := 1 to n do
  for j := i downto 1 do
    sum := 0;
    for k := i to j do
      sum := sum + a[k]
    min:= min(min, sum);
```

```
min := a[1];
for i := 1 to n do
  sum1 := 0;
  for j := i downto 1 do
    sum1 := sum1 + a[j];
    min:= min(min, sum1)
```

```
min := a[1];
min1 := 0;
for i := 1 to n do
  min1:= min(min1+a[i], a[i]);
  min := min(min, min1)
```

(28)

The transformations on the innermost and the middle loops are similar to those for (27), and we first obtain the program in the middle of (28), which is the same as the one on the right of (27) except that j goes from i to 1 instead of to n. Next, consider the outermost loop L_i, which now contains the new middle loop L_j. Using properties of min:

$$\begin{aligned}\min\{\Sigma_{k=j}^{i+1} a[k] \mid j = i+1..1\} &= \min\{\min\{\Sigma_{k=j}^{i+1} a[k] \mid j = i..1\},\ a[i+1]\} \\ &= \min\{\min\{\Sigma_{k=j}^{i} a[k] \mid j = i..1\} + a[i+1],\ a[i+1]\},\end{aligned}$$

L_i is incrementalized: the value of *min* is maintained in a variable min_1 after each iteration using the above equation; min_1 is initialized to 0 (obtained with the optimization of folding initialization) before L_i starts; and the loop L_j is eliminated.

We have studied automatic techniques for incrementalizing array computations (Liu & Stoller 1997), and they can be applied in obtaining the program on the right of (27) from that on the left and obtaining the program in the middle of (28) from that on the left. To obtain the program on the right of (28) automatically, we need to extend our techniques to identify the functionality of min over a loop and use the equation above.

*We are mainly showing that different ways of writing the original programs end up in different optimized programs, not that how one way can be transformed into another that has a better optimized program. The latter is a problem that needs further study.

6.3 Fibonacci function and path sequence problem

The Fibonacci function fib is improved from an exponential time program to a linear time program $fib(x) = 1st(\widetilde{fib}(x))$ in (Liu & Teitelbaum 1995a), by considering fib as a function f, $x' = x + 1$ as an operation $\oplus$, and using the derived constant time function f' to form a new recursion:

$$fib(x) = \textbf{if } x \leq 1 \textbf{ then } 1 \; \textbf{else } fib(x-1) + fib(x-2) \qquad \widetilde{fib}(x) = \begin{array}{l} \textbf{if } x \leq 1 \textbf{ then } <1> \\ \textbf{else if } x = 2 \textbf{ then } <2,1> \\ \textbf{else let } \tilde{r} = \widetilde{fib}(x-1) \textbf{ in} \\ \quad <1st(\tilde{r})+2nd(\tilde{r}),\ 1st(\tilde{r})> \end{array} \tag{29}$$

The resulting program $\widetilde{fib}$ had an additional conditional that seemed unnecessary but it was not clear how it could be eliminated as a result of systematic procedure. Such elimination falls out of the optimizations in this paper. In particular, folding the initialization by maintaining an additional value 1 in the branch where $x \leq 1$ and folding the branch where $x = 2$ into the recursive case, we obtain a simpler program:

$$\widetilde{fib}(x) = \begin{array}{l} \textbf{if } x \leq 1 \textbf{ then } <1,1> \\ \textbf{else let } \tilde{r} = \widetilde{fib}(x-1) \textbf{ in} \\ \quad <1st(\tilde{r})+2nd(\tilde{r}),\ 1st(\tilde{r})> \end{array} \tag{30}$$

Bird's path sequence problem generalizes Dijkstra's longest up sequence problem and the longest common subsequence problem (Bird 1984). Given a directed acyclic graph, as a predicate arc, and a string l whose elements are vertices in the graph, the function llp below computes the length of the longest subsequence in l that forms a path in the graph (Bird 1984):

$$\begin{array}{l} llp(l) = \\ \textbf{if } null(l) \textbf{ then } 0 \\ \textbf{else } \max(llp(cdr(l)), 1+g(car(l), cdr(l))) \end{array} \qquad \begin{array}{l} g(n,l) = \\ \textbf{if } null(l) \textbf{ then } 0 \\ \textbf{else if } \mathrm{arc}(n, car(l)) \textbf{ then} \\ \quad \max(g(n, cdr(l)), 1+g(car(l), cdr(l))) \\ \textbf{else } g(n, cdr(l)) \end{array} \tag{31}$$

This program is improved from exponential time to square time in (Liu et al. 1996) (and also incorrectly in (Bird 1984), but corrected in (Bird 1985)), and the resulting program is $llp(l) = 1st(\widetilde{llp}(l))$, where $\widetilde{llp}$ is

$$\begin{array}{l} \widetilde{llp}(l) = \\ \textbf{if } null(l) \textbf{ then } <0> \\ \textbf{else if } null(cdr(l)) \textbf{ then } <1,<0>> \\ \textbf{else let } \tilde{r} = \widetilde{llp}(cdr(l)) \textbf{ in} \\ \quad \textbf{let } v_2 = \tilde{g}'(car(l), cdr(l), 2nd(\tilde{r})) \textbf{ in} \\ \quad <\max(1st(\tilde{r}), 1+1st(v_2)),\ v_2> \end{array} \qquad \begin{array}{l} \tilde{g}'(i,l,\tilde{r_1}) = \\ \textbf{if } null(cdr(l)) \textbf{ then} \\ \quad \textbf{if } \mathrm{arc}(i, car(l)) \textbf{ then } <1,<0>> \\ \quad \textbf{else } <0,<0>> \\ \textbf{else let } v_1 = \tilde{g}'(i, cdr(l), 2nd(\tilde{r_1})) \textbf{ in} \\ \quad \textbf{if } \mathrm{arc}(i, car(l)) \textbf{ then} \\ \qquad <\max(1st(v_1), 1+1st(\tilde{r_1})),\ \tilde{r_1}> \\ \quad \textbf{else } <1st(v_1),\ \tilde{r_1}> \end{array} \tag{32}$$

Optimizing this resulting program by folding the initialization for $\widetilde{llp}$ and then $\tilde{g}$, *i.e.*, maintaining an additional value <> in the branch where $null(l)$ is true and folding the branch where $null(cdr(l))$ is true into the recursive case, we obtain a simpler program:

$$
\begin{array}{ll}
\widetilde{llp}(l) = & \tilde{g}'(i,l,\tilde{r_1}) = \\
\textbf{if } null(l) \textbf{ then } <0,<>> & \textbf{if } null(l) \textbf{ then } <0,<>> \\
\textbf{else let } \tilde{r} = \widetilde{llp}(cdr(l)) \textbf{ in} & \textbf{else let } v_1 = \tilde{g}'(i, cdr(l), 2nd(\tilde{r_1})) \textbf{ in} \\
\quad \textbf{let } v_2 = \tilde{g}'(car(l), cdr(l), 2nd(\tilde{r})) \textbf{ in} & \quad \textbf{if } \mathrm{arc}(i, car(l)) \textbf{ then} \\
\quad <\max(1st(\tilde{r}), 1+1st(v_2)),\ v_2> & \qquad <\max(1st(v_1), 1+1st(\tilde{r_1})),\ \tilde{r_1}> \\
 & \quad \textbf{else } <1st(v_1),\ \tilde{r_1}>
\end{array}
\qquad (33)
$$

7 RELATED WORK AND CONCLUSION

Strength reduction (Allen et al. 1981, Cocke & Kennedy 1977) is a classical compiler optimization technique that can be traced back to recursive address calculation for early ALGOL 60 compilers (Grau et al. 1967, Gries 1971). As discussed in (Steffen et al. 1991), it is syntactic (ignoring semantic equivalences between syntactically different terms), locally updating (thus not guaranteeing safety or speedup), and structurally restricted (only working on induction variables and region constants). **Composite hoisting-strength reduction** (Joshi & Dhamdhere 1982a, Joshi & Dhamdhere 1982b) is also syntactic and locally updating. Although it can handle more program terms, these terms are still of limited structures. Our method is general; it exploits program semantics to reduce computation strength, utilizes program analyses to guarantee correctness and efficiency, and is not limited to particular term structures. In fact, we can reduce the computation strength for a loop body as a whole. In particular, eliminating induction variables (Allen et al. 1981) is a special case of one of our optimizations.

Optimal code motion (Steffen, Knoop & Rüthing 1990) is a principled method for optimal placement of computations within a program with respect to the Herbrand interpretation. It is adopted for strength reduction by exploring the additional availability obtained from properties, such as distributivity, of numeric operators (Steffen et al. 1991), and it improves over conventional methods. Our method is also a principled approach, based on the idea of incrementalization. It exploits properties of more primitive operators, data structures, and conditionals, and thus is a more comprehensive exploration of availability. In fact, their method would not perform any strength reduction on the square root example (Knoop 1994). Of course, the complexity of our algorithm is larger. We plan to further study the complexity issues.

Inductively computable constructs in very-high-level languages (Fong 1977, Fong 1979, Fong & Ullman 1976) generalize conventional strength reduction and the elimination of induction variables to set-based languages. **Finite differencing** (Paige & Schwartz 1977, Paige 1983, Paige & Koenig 1982) and **fixed point recomputation** (Cai & Paige 1988/89) systematically reduce strength of programs that use fixed point iteration and set-theoretic notations as the initial program specification. These techniques do not handle function abstractions, conditionals, or data types other than sets, as we do. In general, they apply only to programs written in very-high-level languages like SETL; our method applies also to lower-level languages.

Maintaining and strengthening loop invariants has been advocated by Dijkstra, Gries, and others (Dijkstra 1976, Gries 1981, Gries 1984, Reynolds 1981) for almost two decades as a standard strategy for developing loops. As discussed in a previous paper (Liu et al. 1996), its underlying principle is essentially incrementalization. But their work stresses mental tools for programming, rather than mechanical assistance, so no systematic procedures were proposed for automatic or semi-automatic uses.

Transforming recursive functions in CIP (Bauer, Möller, Partsch & Pepper 1989, Broy 1984, Partsch 1990) uses a collection of optimization strategies, including memoization, tabulation, relocation, precomputation, differencing, *etc.* They are essentially all subsumed by principled strength reduction, which is one method that is composed of step-by-step analyses and transformations, rather than a collection of strategies that needs to be applied by prudent judgment, and thus is more unified and more systematic. Other work on transformational programming for improving program efficiency, including the **extension technique** (Dershowitz 1983), the **promotion and accumulation strategies** (Bird 1984, Bird 1985), and finite differencing of functional programs in KIDS (Smith 1990), can also be further automated with principled strength reduction.

Principled strength reduction improves over previous approaches for program efficiency improvement. It systematically handles program constructs and operations that were not handled systematically before. Also, it systematically handles initializations and termination conditions, which are often particularly error-prone. Our three optimizations are either omitted, or done in implicit, limited, or *ad hoc* ways in previous methods. This unified approach also opens up a number of directions for further study. Its potential application is widespread.

REFERENCES

Aho, A. V., Sethi, R. & Ullman, J. D. (1986). *Compilers, Principles, Techniques, and Tools*, Addison-Wesley, Reading, Massachusetts.

Allen, F. E. (1969). Program optimization, *Annual Review of Automatic Programming*, Vol. 5, Pergamon Press, New York, pp. 239–307.

Allen, F. E., Cocke, J. & Kennedy, K. (1981). Reduction of operator strength, *in* S. S. Muchnick & N. D. Jones (eds), *Program Flow Analysis*, Prentice-Hall, Englewood Cliffs, New Jersey, chapter 3, pp. 79–101.

Banerjee, U. (1990). Unimodular transformations of double loops, *Proceedings of the Workshop on Advances in Languages and Compilers for Parallel Processing*, pp. 192–219.

Bauer, F. L., Möller, B., Partsch, H. & Pepper, P. (1989). Formal program construction by transformations—Computer-aided, intuition-guided programming, *IEEE Transactions on Software Engineering* **15**(2): 165–180.

Bird, R. S. (1984). The promotion and accumulation strategies in transformational programming, *ACM Transactions on Programming Languages and Systems* **6**(4): 487–504.

Bird, R. S. (1985). Addendum: The promotion and accumulation strategies in transformational programming, *ACM Transactions on Programming Languages and Systems* **7**(3): 490–492.

Broy, M. (1984). Algebraic methods for program construction: The project CIP, *in* P. Pepper (ed.), *Program Transformation and Programming Environments*, Springer-Verlag, Berlin, pp. 199–222.

Cai, J. & Paige, R. (1988/89). Program derivation by fixed point computation, *Science of Computer Programming* **11**: 197–261.

Cocke, J. & Kennedy, K. (1977). An algorithm for reduction of operator strength, *Communications of the ACM* **20**(11): 850–856.

Cocke, J. & Schwartz, J. T. (1970). Programming Languages and Their Compilers; Preliminary Notes, *Technical report*, Courant Institute of Mathematical Sciences, New York University.

Constable, R. L. et al. (1986). *Implementing Mathematics with the Nuprl Proof Development System*, Prentice-Hall, Englewood Cliffs, New Jersey.

Dershowitz, N. (1983). *The Evolution of Programs*, Vol. 5 of *Progress in Computer Science*, Birkhäuser, Boston.

Dijkstra, E. W. (1976). *A Discipline of Programming*, Prentice-Hall Series in Automatic Computation, Prentice-Hall, Englewood Cliffs, New Jersey.

Flores, I. (1963). *The Logic of Computer Arithmetic*, Prentice-Hall, Englewood Cliffs, New Jersey.

Fong, A. C. (1977). Generalized common subexpressions in very high level languages, *Conference Record of the 4th Annual ACM Symposium on POPL*, Los Angeles, California, pp. 48–57.

Fong, A. C. (1979). Inductively computable constructs in very high level languages, *Conference Record of the 6th Annual ACM Symposium on POPL*, San Antonio, Texas, pp. 21–28.

Fong, A. C. & Ullman, J. D. (1976). Inductive variables in very high level languages, *Conference Record of the 3rd Annual ACM Symposium on POPL*, Atlanta, Georgia, pp. 104–112.

Garey, M. R. & Johnson, D. S. (1979). *Computers and Intractability: A Guid to the Theory of NP-Completeness*, W. H. Freeman and Company, New York.

Grau, A. A., Hill, U. & Langmaac, H. (1967). *Translation of ALGOL 60*, Vol. 1 of *Handbook for automatic computation*, Springer, Berlin.

Greibach, S. A. (1975). *Theory of Program Structures: Schemes, Semantics, Verification*, Vol. 36 of *Lecture Notes in Computer Science*, Springer-Verlag, Berlin.

Gries, D. (1971). *Compiler Construction for Digital Computers*, John Wiley & Sons, New York.

Gries, D. (1981). *The Science of Programming*, Springer-Verlag, New York.

Gries, D. (1984). A note on a standard strategy for developing loop invariants and loops, *Science of Computer Programming* **2**: 207–214.

Joshi, S. M. & Dhamdhere, D. M. (1982a). A composite hoisting-strength reuction transformation for global program optimization—part I, *International Journal of Computer Mathematics* **11**: 21–41.

Joshi, S. M. & Dhamdhere, D. M. (1982b). A composite hoisting-strength reuction transformation for global program optimization—part II, *International Journal of Computer Mathematics* **11**: 111–126.

Knoop, J. (1994). Private comminication.

Liu, Y. A. (1995). CACHET: An interactive, incremental-attribution-based program transformation system for deriving incremental programs, *Proceedings of the 10th Knowledge-Based Software Engineering Conference*, IEEE Computer Society Press, Boston, Massachusetts, pp. 19–26.

Liu, Y. A. (1996). *Incremental Computation: A Semantics-Based Systematic Transformational Approach*, PhD thesis, Department of Computer Science, Cornell University, Ithaca, New York.

Liu, Y. A. & Stoller, S. D. (1997). Optimizing aggregate array computations, *Technical Report TR 477*, Computer Science Department, Indiana University, Bloomington, Indiana.

Liu, Y. A., Stoller, S. D. & Teitelbaum, T. (1996). Discovering auxiliary information for incremental computation, *Conference Record of the 23rd Annual ACM Symposium on POPL*, St. Petersburg Beach, Florida, pp. 157–170.

Liu, Y. A. & Teitelbaum, T. (1995a). Caching intermediate results for program improvement, *Proceedings of the ACM SIGPLAN Symposium on PEPM*, La Jolla, California, pp. 190–201.

Liu, Y. A. & Teitelbaum, T. (1995b). Systematic derivation of incremental programs, *Science of Computer Programming* **24**(1): 1–39.

O'Leary, J., Leeser, M., Hickey, J. & Aagaard, M. (1994). Non-restoring integer square root: A case study in design by principled optimization, *in* R. Kumar & T. Kropf (eds), *Proceedings of the 2nd International Conference on Theorem Provers in Circuit Design: Theory, Practice, and Experience*, Vol. 901 of *Lecture Notes in Computer Science*, Springer-Verlag, Berlin, pp. 52–71.

Paige, B. & Schwartz, J. T. (1977). Expression continuity and the formal differentiation of algorithms, *Conference Record of the 4th Annual ACM Symposium on POPL*, pp. 58–71.

Paige, R. (1983). Transformational programming—Applications to algorithms and systems, *Conference Record of the 10th Annual ACM Symposium on POPL*, pp. 73–87.

Paige, R. & Koenig, S. (1982). Finite differencing of computable expressions, *ACM Transactions on Programming Languages and Systems* **4**(3): 402–454.

Partsch, H. A. (1990). *Specification and Transformation of Programs—A Formal Approach to Software Development*, Springer-Verlag, Berlin.

Reynolds, J. C. (1981). *The Craft of Programming*, Prentice-Hall, Englewood Cliffs, New Jersey.

Sethi, R. (1973). A note on implementing parallel assignment instructions, *Information Processing Letter* **2**: 91–95.

Smith, D. R. (1990). KIDS: A semiautomatic program development system, *IEEE Transactions on Software Engineering* **16**(9): 1024–1043.

Steffen, B., Knoop, J. & Rüthing, O. (1990). The value flow graph: A program representation for optimal program transformation, *Proceedings of the 3rd ESOP*, Vol. 432 of *Lecture Notes in Computer Science*, Springer-Verlag, Berlin, pp. 389–405.

Steffen, B., Knoop, J. & Rüthing, O. (1991). Efficient code motion and an adaption to strength reduction, *Proceedings of the 4th International Joint Conference on TAPSOFT*, Vol. 494 of *Lecture Notes in Computer Science*, Springer-Verlag, Berlin, pp. 394–415.

Wolf, M. & Lam, M. (1991a). A data locality optimizing algorithm, *Proceedings of the ACM SIGPLAN '91 Conference on PLDI*, pp. 30–44.

Wolf, M. & Lam, M. (1991b). A loop transformation theory and an algorithm to maximize parallelism, *IEEE Transactions on Parallel and Distributed Systems* .

BIOGRAPHY

Y. Annie Liu is assistant professor of computer science at Indiana University in Bloomington. She received a BS from Peking University (1987), an ME from Tsinghua university (1988), and an MS and a PhD from Cornell University (1992, 1996), all in computer science. She was a post-doctoral associate at Cornell University from 1995 to 1996. Liu's primary research interests are in the areas of programming languages, compilers, and software systems. She is particularly interested in general and systematic approaches to improving the efficiency of computations. Liu has strong other interests in database management, document processing, information management, and distributed computing.

15

The Formal Reconstruction and Speedup Of The Linear Time Fragment Of Willard's Relational Calculus Subset *

Deepak Goyal and Robert Paige
Department of Computer Science, New York University
251 Mercer Street, NY, NY-10012
email: {deepak,paige}@cs.nyu.edu

Abstract

We demonstrate how several programming language concepts and methods can be used economically to obtain an improved solution to a difficult algorithmic problem. The problem is to compile a subset RCS of Relational Calculus defined by Willard (1978) in a novel way so that efficient run-time query performance is guaranteed. Willard gives an algorithm to compile each query q belonging to RCS so that it executes in $O(n \log^d n + o)$ steps and $O(n)$ space, where n and o are respectively the input and output set sizes, and d is a parameter associated with the syntax of query q. Willard's time bounds are based on the assumption that hashing unit-space data takes unit time.

In this paper we use a set-theoretic complexity measure and formal transformational techniques to reconstruct the linear time fragment of RCS in a simplified way. In doing this, we show how complexity can be determined by language abstraction and algebraic reasoning without resorting to low level counting arguments. This approach shortens Willard's proofs considerably, and facilitates an implementation. Finally, we show that the implementation can be typed in a restricted form of a set-theoretic type system based on Cai *et al.* (1991) and Keller and Paige (1995), which guarantees that each hash operation used to implement RCS can be simulated in real-time on a pointer machine model of computation. This improves Willard's linear expected time result to linear worst case time, and demonstrates for the first time how type theory can be used as a tool to obtain an order of magnitude algorithmic speedup.

---

*This research was partially supported by Office of Naval Research Grant No. N00014-93-1-0924, and National Science Foundation grant CCR-9616993. Part of this work was done while Paige was visiting DIKU at the University of Copenhagen.

1 INTRODUCTION

This paper follows a long-term investigation of Willard's Relational Calculus Subset (RCS), a database query language proposed in his thesis (Willard 1978), and developed further in Willard (1983) and Willard (1990), a part of which recently appeared in JCSS (Willard 1996). Under the assumption that hashing unit-space data takes unit time, Willard defined broad subclasses of Relational Calculus queries that could be executed in linear space and low expected time $O(n \log^d n + o)$, where n and o are the input and output set sizes, and d is a parameter associated with the syntax of the queries. Willard's result is algorithmic rather than complexity-theoretic, since no lower bound is implied for any problem that cannot be expressed in RCS.

Our interest in Willard's fascinating work is motivated by a number of issues. RCS is a rare comprehensive investigation of query translation for the Relational Calculus (Codd 1970), which is regarded as more difficult to implement than the Relational Algebra (Codd 1970). Willard's work is one of the earliest investigations that link a substantial language to low order run-time query complexity for a main memory model. Willard's investigation is also one of the earliest nontrivial examples of output-sensitive algorithmic analysis. Although other languages that are bound to low order run-time complexities (e.g., Hunt *et al.* (1977) , Arnold and Crubille (1988), Cleavaland and Steffen (1992) , and Anderson (1994)) may have greater expressive power, RCS is unusual in its richness and its run-time requirements. Consequently the RCS query processing algorithm is a combinatorial challenge, which makes its implementation a formidable task left open by Willard.

We make two contributions that integrate solutions to algorithmic and software problems. First we detail how to implement Willard's linear time fragment of RCS (which we call LRCS) using semantics-preserving source program transformations. Second, we show how type theory can be used to improve the run-time performance of LRCS from linear expected time to linear worst case time.

A problem shared by the database and algorithmics communities is the lack of notation and notational calculi to formally map perspicuous problem specifications into efficient implementations. Our approach to obtain an implementation of LRCS is to use a wide spectrum set-theoretic language capable of specifying both high level user queries and their efficient (but still abstract) implementations. Program transformations that preserve familiar set-theoretic semantics are used to derive efficient implementations from high level queries.

By itself Willard's compilation of RCS queries is a model of sophistication that works in two phases. The first phase, called the decomposition phase, transforms a query into a sequence of efficient lower level queries. The second phase, which we call the back-end implementation, transforms each efficient query into a sequence of element-at-a-time operations (e.g., loads, stores, retrievals), many of which require hashing.

We abide by most of Willard's ideas in the first phase, and contribute an abstract implementation in a convenient set-theoretic language. It is in the back-end implementation where we use set-theoretic expressions tied to implicit implementations in order to reuse redundant low level constructions found in Willard's proofs. Hence, we obtain a perspicuous implementation, and a proof that replaces Willard's repeated low level counting arguments by simpler logical and algebraic reasoning.

We go on to show that Willard's time bound (for run-time query execution) in the expected case can be achieved in the worst case without degrading space utilization. This is achieved by demonstrating that the translated form of each query in LRCS is typable in a variant of the set-theoretic type system described in Cai *et al.* (1991), Keller and Paige (1995). This type system guarantees the real-time simulation of primitive set operations on a pointer RAM, which means that each primitive set operation (*e.g.* membership testing $x \in S$) can be implemented in unit worst case time on a pointer RAM (Knuth (1973), Tarjan (1979)). Thus, we immediately show that each query in LRCS can be translated into pointer machine code that runs in linear worst case time. Our analytic analysis is also carried out using formal proof rules. The brevity of these formal proofs makes it tempting to pass them through a mechanical proof checker, and, hence, formally verify a difficult query compiler.

Currently we are involved in a research project involving translation of a strongly typed version of SETL2 (Snyder 1990) to C. This translator, which will incorporate the efficient read method of Paige (1994), Paige and Yang (1997), is expected to provide an efficient implementation for LRCS.

2 NOTATION

This section describes the notation used for a high level set-theoretic functional language that is capable of representing both RCS and its abstract implementation. We say that a language is *computationally transparent* if it is amenable to algorithmic analysis. In the following subsections, we will show how to make this language computationally transparent under both a hash-based model of computation (assuming hashing of unit-space data in unit expected time) used by Willard and a pointer RAM (Knuth (1973), Tarjan (1979)) model of computation.

We use a set-based language that, besides the usual elementary data types, includes built-in data-types for finite sets, maps and tuples. A set is an unordered collection of distinct values, while a tuple is an ordered collection of values. A map is a set of ordered pairs that may be a single or multi-valued binary relation.

The primitive set-theoretic operations and expressions correspond closely to finite set theory (Suppes 1972) and SETL (Schwartz (1974), Schwartz *et al.* (1986), Snyder (1990)). Expression $\#S$ is used to denote the cardinality of

Table 1 High level Setl Operations

$\cup/S$	$=$	$\bigcup_{x \in S} x$
domain R	$=$	$\{x : [x, y] \in R\}$
range R	$=$	$\{y : [x, y] \in R\}$
R^{-1}	$=$	$\{[y, x] : [x, y] \in R\}$
$R\{x\}$	$=$	$\{y : [u, y] \in R \mid u = x\}$
$R[S]$	$=$	$\{y : [x, y] \in R \mid x \in S\} = \bigcup_{x \in S} R\{x\}$

set S. In its most general form, set comprehension is written in the following set former notation,

$$\{e(x_1, ..., x_k) : x_1 \in S_1, x_2 \in S_2(x_1), ..., x_k \in S_k(x_1, ..., x_{k-1}) | K(x_1, ..., x_k)\},$$

and denotes the set of element values $e(x_1, ..., x_k)$ evaluated over all k-tuples $[x_1, ..., x_k]$ belonging to the search space satisfying the condition,

$$x_1 \in S_1 \wedge x_2 \in S_2(x_1) \wedge ... \wedge x_k \in S_k(x_1, ..., x_{k-1}),$$

and also satisfying the boolean-valued qualifier $K(x_1, ..., x_k)$, which may itself contain an arbitrary sequence of bounded *existential* and *universal* quantifiers. Set former $\{[x_1, \ldots, x_k] \in \times_{i=1}^{k} S_i | K(x_1, \ldots, x_k)\ \}$ denotes a short form for set comprehension expression $\{[x_1, \ldots, x_k] : x_1 \in S_1, \ldots, x_k \in S_k | K(x_1, \ldots, x_k)\}$. When the qualifier subpart $K(x_1, ..., x_k)$ of a set former is the constant *true*, it may be elided.

We also use the unconventional SETL interpretation of maps as finite functions or multi-valued binary relations. Let R be a map, and let S be a set. Then Table 1 defines some of the high level set operations on sets and maps.

The language also includes conventional *let* expressions.

2.1 Real-Time Simulation

In order to make the high level queries described in the beginning of Section 2 computationally transparent, we associate each query with an operational definition in a lower level imperative set machine language containing primitive, element-at-a-time set operations with precise run-time complexities

Table 2 Primitive Set Machine Operations

Operation		Time
Q **with** $:= x$ *	set element addition	$O(1)$
Q less $:= x$ *	set element deletion	$O(1)$
$Q := \{\}$	initialization	$O(1)$
$Q \cup := T$ *	set union	$max(1, O(\#T))$
$x \in Q$	set membership test	$O(1)$
$g\{x\}$	$\{y : [u, y] \in g \| u = x\}$	$O(1)$
$g(x)$	y, if g{x}= {y}; Ω (undefined), otherwise	$O(1)$
for $x \in Q$ **loop** $Block(x)$ **end loop**	execute *Block* for each element x belonging to Q	$O(\#Q \times cost(Block(x)))$
$Q := T$	copy set T to set Q	$O(1)$

as described in Table 2. For example, the high level query $Q = \{K_1(x) : x \in X | K_2(x)\}$ can be implemented in set machine language as follows:

$$
\begin{array}{l}
Q := \{\} \\
\text{for } x \in X \text{ loop} \\
\quad \text{if } K_2(x) \text{ then} \\
\quad\quad Q \textit{ with} := \; K_1(x) \\
\quad \text{end if} \\
\text{end loop.}
\end{array}
\tag{1}
$$

If every element of Q has unit space, then each primitive operation in (1) can be simulated in real time under the assumption that unit-space data x can be hashed in expected unit time. Hence, each operation can be implemented to run in the time associated with it in Table 2 , *e.g.* the run-time cost of (1) can be seen as $O(\#X)$ expected time if $K_1(x)$ and $K_2(x)$ are constant time computations. The time complexity of a high level query is thus easily determined from the time complexity of its implementation.

The decomposition phase of the query translation process involves converting the LRCS queries (formulated as high level set expressions) into a sequence of efficient lower level queries. By translating each of the low level queries obtained at the end of the decomposition phase into a set machine implementation, we obtain an expected linear time implementation of LRCS under the hash-based model of computation used by Willard.

However, we go beyond that, and show how we can use our type and subtype system (derived from Cai *et al.* (1991), Keller and Paige (1995), Paige (1989)) to perform real-time simulation of primitive operations on a pointer RAM. That is, we implement each set operation in Table 2 on a pointer RAM where

*These operations are performed destructively.

the run-time complexities given in Table 2 are in the worst case. For example, code block (1) can be typed in our type system to give a worst case $O(\#X)$ time implementation. We will show that the low level queries obtained at the end of the decomposition phase of LRCS translation are typable in our type system. Since the type system guarantees the real-time simulation of set primitives on a pointer RAM, we immediately get an implementation for LRCS that runs in linear worst case time on a pointer RAM, an improvement over Willard's linear expected time solution.

We provide a brief informal description of our type system below. In Section 2.2 we formalize the notion of associating each primitive set operation with a worst case run-time complexity on a pointer machine by providing inference rules specifying conditions under which real-time simulation of these operations is possible.

Each type τ represents a set $val(\tau)$ *e.g.* type **INT** stands for the set of integers. If τ_1 and τ_2 are types, then $set(\tau_1)$ represents the set of finite subsets of $val(\tau_1)$, $smap(\tau_1, \tau_2)$ and $mmap(\tau_1, \tau_2)$ represent the set of finite, partial, single-valued (respectively multi-valued) maps from domain $val(\tau_1)$ to range $val(\tau_2)$. Type variable B is called a *base* type (after Schwartz (1975a), Schwartz (1975b)), and is uniquely associated with a subtype constraint of the form $B < \tau$ (where τ is any type except a base type, though it may contain occurrences of base types), indicating that each distinct value of type B can be coerced into a distinct value of type τ in constant time. Each distinct program variable v of type τ is restricted to values that belong to $val(\tau)$ throughout the execution of the program. Such a program invariant is specified by a type assignment $v : \tau$.

Besides representing specific sets, each type is also used to model specific data structures needed to implement set and map operations efficiently. For this purpose the type system allows bases to appear in two forms, called weak and strong, and denoted by B and $B - strong$ respectively. Each base type B with a subtype constraint $B < \tau$ is implemented as a set R_B of records. Each record in R_B has a key field that stores a distinct value of type τ. A weakly based set S, denoted by the type assignment $S : set(B)$, is implemented as a doubly linked list of pointers to records in R_B whose key fields store the elements of this set (see Figure 1). Weakly based maps, denoted by $smap(B, \tau_1)$ and $mmap(B, \tau_1)$, have similar linked list implementations for their domains. A strongly based set T is denoted by the type assignment $T : set(B - strong)$. Similarly strongly based maps are denoted by $smap(B - strong, \tau_1)$ and $mmap(B - strong, \tau_1)$. The records of R_B have a distinct field for each set or map that is strongly based on B. If T is a strongly based set, its corresponding field is used to store a doubly linked list that connects the set of records in R_B whose key fields store the elements in T (see Figure 1). The domains of strongly based maps are implemented in a similar way. This representation supports unit-time associative access operations for strongly based sets and strongly based maps.

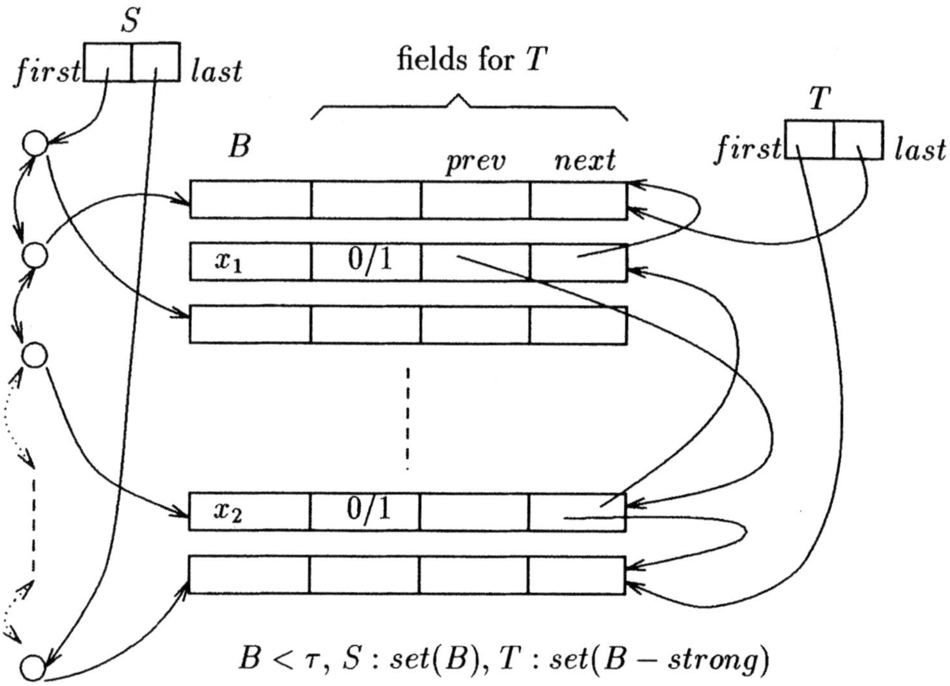

Figure 1 Weakly and Strongly based sets

For example, consider the following code fragment

$$
\begin{array}{l}
\text{for } x \in S \text{ loop} \\
\quad\quad \text{if } x \in T \\
\quad\quad\quad \ldots \\
\quad\quad \text{end if} \\
\text{end loop}
\end{array}
\qquad (2)
$$

where S and T are sets having elements of the same type. In order to simulate this fragment of code in real time, the associative access operation $x \in T$ should be executed in unit time. Consider the following type assignment, $x : B$, $S : set(B)$, and $T : set(B - strong)$, where B is a *base* type. Base type B is implemented as a set R_B of records, one corresponding to each element of $val(B)$. The *weakly* based set S is implemented as a doubly linked list of pointers to records in R_B whose key fields store the elements of set S. Since T is a *strongly* based set on base B, the records in R_B have a distinct field for set T. This field has three subfields, a membership field with a value 0 or 1, and the *prev* and *next* pointers of a doubly linked list linking the elements of set T (see Figure 1). Thus, given an element x in set S in the form of a pointer to the corresponding record in R_B, the test $x \in T$ can be performed in unit time by looking at the membership field for T in the record corresponding to x.

In addition to the weakly and strongly based data structures, we also consider *unbased* data structures. An unbased set is a set whose elements are not of a base type. An unbased set is implemented as a doubly linked list of element values. An unbased map is a map whose domain element type is not a base type. Its domain is implemented as a doubly linked list of element values. Each image set is stored separately, and is accessible from its corresponding domain value by a pointer. We store *first* and *last* pointers to the first and last list cells implementing unbased and weakly based sets and the domains of unbased and weakly based maps. We also store pointers to the first and last records in R_B linking the elements of strongly based sets and domain elements of strongly based maps.

Furthermore, in order to obtain efficient implementations for the primitive operations, non unit-space data objects such as sets and maps are accessed indirectly through pointers. For assignments involving unit-space data (such as boolean, integer *etc.*), we assume copy value semantics, *i.e.* an assignment statement with unit-space data on the *right hand side* is implemented by copying or incorporating the data into the object on the *left hand side*. However, in order to perform assignments involving non unit-space data in $O(1)$ time, they are implemented using pointer semantics by just copying or incorporating the pointer to the non unit-space data into the object on the *left hand side*. For example, the assignment $S := T$, where T corresponds to non unit-space data, is implemented by copying the pointer to the data associated with T into S. Similarly, S *with* $:= T$ is implemented by incorporating the pointer into set S.

Note that this implementation could potentially lead to the violation of copy value semantics if we tried to modify a non unit-space data object that has more than one object pointing to it. For example, if the statement $S := T$ were followed by the statement T *with* $:= x$, then after the execution of the first assignment statement, S points to the same object as T, and the execution of the second assignment would cause a side effect to the value of S. However, we do not need to consider this problem as it is quite easy to verify that our implementation of LRCS is free of such side effects. Thus we have an implementation which efficiently implements assignments involving non unit-space data by pointer semantics, but still preserves the clarity of copy value semantics.

Finally, it is important to note that the real-time simulation of the primitive set and map operations is *not* performed at the expense of degradation of space complexity. The amount of space used to evaluate each LRCS query $S_{k+1} = f(S_1, \ldots, S_k)$ is also always linear in the cardinalities of the input and output sets $S_1, \ldots, S_{k+1}$.

2.2 Time Complexity on a Pointer Machine

In this section we associate the primitive operations with worst case run-time complexities for implementation on a pointer RAM. Next, we show how to use these primitive operations to implement the queries in our high level language, which allows us to determine the worst case run-time complexities of these queries on a pointer RAM.

We first give inference rules in Table 3 that take the type and subtype system into account to give asymptotic run-time complexities for implementation of primitive set operations (Table 2) on a pointer RAM. The judgment

$$\Gamma \vdash \{A\}\ S,\ O(p)\ \mathit{time}$$

can be read as " *In the type environment* Γ, *if the precondition* A *is satisfied then* S *can be executed in* $O(p)$ *worst case time*", where S could be either a statement or an expression, in which case we also assign a type to the computed expression. If the predicate A is *true* then it may be elided. In the judgments in Table 3, τ may be any type except a strong base, and x is unit-space data computable in $O(1)$ time.

We shall not formally prove the soundness of the rules in Table 3 but will try to informally establish their correctness on the basis of the arguments provided below and in Section 2.1. A further detailed description of a closely related type system and the simulation of set operations on a pointer machine can be found in Cai *et al.* (1991), Keller and Paige (1995), and Paige (1989).

In Rule (3), x is an element of type τ that is either an unbased type or a weakly based type. Hence, $Q : set(\tau)$ is implemented as a doubly linked list of element values or pointers to element values, and precondition $x \notin Q$ ensures that the operation $Q\ with := x$ only involves unit-time insertion of unit-space data into a doubly linked list. Similarly in Rule (6), type τ is again an unbased or weakly based type, and, hence, $Q : set(\tau)$ and $T : set(\tau)$ are both implemented as doubly linked lists. Thus, the precondition $Q \cap T = \phi$ ensures that the operation $Q \cup := T$ just involves linking together two doubly linked lists. Since each set that is implemented as a doubly linked list also has *first* and *last* pointers pointing to the first and last elements of the list, then two doubly linked lists can be linked together in $O(1)$ time.

In Rules (4), (5), and (7), x is an element of a base type, and Q is a strongly based set. On the basis of the description of strongly based sets in Section 2.1, we see that insertion, deletion, and membership operations can be implemented in $O(1)$ time. Similarly in Rules (8) and (9), we have single and multi-valued strongly based maps, which allows map application to be done in $O(1)$ time. Note that $g\{x\}$ returns the pair of *first* and *last* pointers to a doubly linked list implementation of a set that corresponds to the image of x in the multi-valued map g.

In Rule (10) we state that an unbased or weakly based set can be initialized

Table 3 Formal Complexity Rules

$$\Gamma\{x:\tau, Q:set(\tau)\} \vdash \{x \notin Q\}\ Q\ with := x,\ O(1)\ time \quad (3)$$

$$\Gamma\{B<\tau, x:B, Q:set(B-strong)\} \vdash Q\ with := x,\ O(1)\ time \quad (4)$$

$$\Gamma\{B<\tau, x:B, Q:set(B-strong)\} \vdash Q\ less := x,\ O(1)\ time \quad (5)$$

$$\Gamma\{Q:set(\tau), T:set(\tau)\} \vdash \{Q \cap T = \phi\}\ Q \cup := T,\ O(1)\ time \quad (6)$$

$$\Gamma\{B<\tau, x:B, Q:set(B-strong)\} \vdash (x \in Q):Bool,\ O(1)\ time \quad (7)$$

$$\Gamma\{B<\tau, x:B, g:mmap(B-strong, \tau_1)\} \vdash g\{x\}:set(\tau_1),\ O(1)\ time \quad (8)$$

$$\Gamma\{B<\tau, x:B, g:smap(B-strong, \tau_1)\} \vdash g(x):\tau_1,\ O(1)\ time \quad (9)$$

$$\Gamma\{Q:set(\tau)\} \vdash Q := \{\},\ O(1)\ time \quad (10)$$

$$\Gamma\{B<\tau, Q:set(B-strong)\} \vdash \{\#Q = n\}\ Q := \{\},\ O(n)\ time \quad (11)$$

$$\Gamma\{x:\tau, Q:set(\tau)\} \vdash \text{for } x \in Q \text{ loop } Block(x) \text{ end loop},\ O(\#Q \times cost(Block(x)))\ time \quad (12)$$

$$\Gamma\{Q:set(\tau)\} \vdash \#Q:int,\ O(1)\ time \quad (13)$$

$$\Gamma\{Q:set(B-strong)\} \vdash \#Q:int,\ O(1)\ time \quad (14)$$

$$\Gamma\{B<\tau, x:B, y:B\} \vdash (x=y):Bool,\ O(1)\ time \quad (15)$$

$$\Gamma\{B<\tau, x:B\} \vdash x:\tau,\ O(1)\ time \quad (16)$$

$$\frac{\Gamma \vdash \{P\}\ A:Bool,\ O(m)\ time \qquad \Gamma \vdash \{P \wedge A\}\ B,\ O(n)\ time \qquad \Gamma \vdash \{P \wedge \neg A\}\ C,\ O(n)\ time}{\Gamma \vdash \{P\} \text{ if } A \text{ then } B \text{ else } C,\ O(m+n)\ time} \quad (17)$$

in $O(1)$ time (simply by initializing the first and last pointers to null values) while in Rule (11) we state that re-initialization of a strongly based set requires time equal to the number of elements in that set. This is because the base records corresponding to each element in the set must be modified*. The correctness of Rules (13) and (14) is easy to see, as we maintain a count with each set of the number of elements in that set, and modify the count suitably whenever the set is modified. Note that this adds only a constant cost to the cost of operations such as insertion and deletion. In Rules (16) and (15) we

*We also have a more complicated $O(1)$ time implementation of re-initialization for strongly based sets and maps; but this is only of theoretical interest.

state that for a base type B and the subtype constraint $B < \tau$, a value x of base type B can be coerced into a value of type τ and compared to another value y of base type B in $O(1)$ time. This is because x is implemented as a pointer to a base record whose key field contains the value of type τ. Furthermore, x and y are equal *iff* they point to the same base record.

We assume that the body of the *for loop* in Rule (12) does not modify the value of Q, so that the number of iterations through the loop is $\#Q$. Furthermore, $cost(Block(x))$ denotes the maximal computation time for the body of the loop. Thus the total time taken by the *for loop* cannot exceed $O(\#Q \times cost(Block(x)))$. Finally, in Rule (17) we again assume that the computation of the boolean expression A causes no side effects that may affect the computation times for B and C. Hence the worst case time to execute the *if statement* is no more than the sum of the time taken to compute the boolean valued expression A and the worst case time to execute either of the two branches. These rules for the *loop* and *conditional* statements are essentially similar to the rules used in Nielson (1984) and Nielson (1987) to show how a Hoare-like proof system for total correctness could be extended to prove the properties of computation time. Nielson showed her proof system to be sound and complete.

Rules (3)–(17) are used as axioms in our algorithmic analysis to establish the worst case linear run-time complexity of LRCS. Furthermore, these rules are used to derive additional inference rules (listed in Appendix 1) for the time complexity of high level set expressions. Again we shall not formally derive these inference rules, but show by means of an example how the time complexity for the high level typed set expressions can be derived algebraically from the complexities of their set machine implementations.

For example, consider Inference Rule (30) in Appendix 1

$$\frac{\Gamma\{x:\tau\} \vdash K_1 : B,\ O(1)\ time \qquad \Gamma\{x:\tau\} \vdash K_2 : Bool,\ O(1)\ time}{\Gamma\{S : set(\tau)\} \vdash \{K_1 : x \in S | K_2\} : set(B - strong), O(\#S)\ time.}$$

Using the inference rules (3)-(17) and implementing $\{K_1 : x \in S | K_2\}$ as

```
for x ∈ S loop
        if K2 then
                Q with := K1
        end if
end loop,
```

it is easy to derive the $O(\#S)$ time complexity.

Finally, we also include some other simple rules in Appendix 1 for which correctness is easily verified and which we find useful in the complexity analysis of expressions in our set-theoretic language. The list of rules in Appendix 1 is not complete, but is intended to show how augmenting expressions with their types and subtypes (thus defining precise data structures for their low level implementation) allows us to reason algebraically about their run-time complexity.

3 LINEAR TIME QUERY LANGUAGE

LRCS includes two kinds of queries, namely *count* queries

$$Q = \{ [x_1, \#\{x_2 \in X_2 | \ e(x_1, x_2)\}] : \ x_1 \in X_1\}, \tag{18}$$

which maps each element $x_1 \in X_1$ into the number of elements $x_2 \in X_2$ that satisfy predicate $e(x_1, x_2)$, and *find* queries

$$Q = \{ [x_1, \ldots x_n] \in \times_{p=1}^{n} X_p \ |\Theta_{n+1} x_{n+1} \in X_{n+1}, \ldots, \Theta_m x_m \in X_m | \ e(x_1, \ldots, x_m) \}, \tag{19}$$

which evaluates the subset of an n-way cross product of sets $X_1, \ldots, X_n$, qualified by an arbitrary number $(m - n)$ of leading bounded quantifiers $\Theta_{n+1} \ldots \Theta_m$, and satisfying the predicate $e(x_1, \ldots, x_m)$ formed from atomic predicates and logical connectives *or*, *and*, and *not*. Willard's result came as a big surprise when he showed that a very broad class of these queries that satisfied the acyclicity condition (described later) could be efficiently computed without actually evaluating the cross product, in time proportional to just the sum of the cardinalities of the input sets and the final output set.

We call $x_1, \ldots, x_m$ the free variables of predicate e within the queries (18) and (19). LRCS includes the following broad categories of atomic predicates, which makes the language powerful enough to express a large proportion of queries that arise in database applications :

1. Boolean constants *true* and *false*.
2. Equality and inequality predicates (also called *joins* and *anti-joins*) *e.g.* $f_1(x) = f_2(y)$, $f_1(x) \neq f_2(y)$, where x and y are free variables of predicate e.
3. Unary Comparison Predicates *e.g.* $f_1(x) = c$, $f_1(x) \neq c$,$f_1(x) > c$, $f_1(x) = f_2(x)$ and $f_1(x) > f_2(x)$, where x is a free variable of predicate e and c is any constant.
4. Unary List Predicates *e.g.* $\exists y \in Y$: $f_1(y) = f_2(x)$ and $\forall y \in Y : f_1(y) = f_2(x)$, where x is a free variable of predicate e.
5. Tabular Predicates *e.g.* $(\exists \ z \in Z : f_1(x) = f_2(z) \wedge f_3(y) = f_4(z))$, where x and y are free variables of predicate e.

Here, all the expressions of the form $f_i(w)$ are assumed to be computable in $O(1)$ time. Also the expressions $f_i(w)$ appearing in tabular predicates are further restricted to be *few-to-one* *i.e.* the sizes of the preimages of f_i are uniformly bounded by a constant.

We define the query graph for *Find* query (19) as having variables $x_1, \ldots, x_m$ as vertices, and having an edge from x_k to x_l *iff* there is a two-variable atomic predicate on x_k and x_l in the expression $e(x_1, \ldots, x_m)$, where x_k appears to the *left* of x_l in query (19). **Find query (19) is in LRCS *iff* the query graph for the query is a forest. In other words the in-degree of every vertex should be no more than 1.**

The rest of the paper will be concerned with proving that the *count* and *find* queries in LRCS can be transformed into a sequence of simpler queries, and can be shown to run in linear time (*i.e. linear in the sum of the cardinalities of the input and output sets*). We shall first show how to decompose the general *find* query (19) into a sequence of *count* queries and a union $\cup_{1=1}^{m} Q_i$ where m is a function of the syntax of the query but independent of its value, and Q_i's are *find* queries whose qualifiers are conjunctions of atomic predicates and their negations with no leading quantifiers. Next we turn each Q_i into a nest of joins, $\bowtie_{i=1}^{q_i} P_{ij}$ where each value q_i is again just a function of the syntax of the query (19). Also each P_{ij} is a query of the form

$$\{[x_1, x_2] \in X_1 \times X_2 \mid e(x_1, x_2)\ \}, \tag{20}$$

where predicate $e(x_1, x_2)$ is a conjunction of atomic predicates and their negations. We shall call queries such as (20) *simple find* queries. Willard's decomposition incorporates a subtle step that forces the sizes of the intermediate outputs P_{ij} to be no more than the sizes of the outputs Q_i. This step is crucial to the the linear time result.

We have adhered to the essentials of Willard's decomposition steps but have simplified his arguments and fleshed out details for an actual implementation. In the back-end phase however, we make a much more significant contribution. We give semantics-preserving transformations that transform *count* and *simple find* queries into simpler queries that can be typed in our type system to give an implementation that runs in worst case linear time on a pointer machine.

The first step in the decomposition of the general *find* query is *Quantifier Elimination.*

3.1 Quantifier Elimination

In this section, we show how to decompose a general *find* query

$$Q = \{\ [x_1, x_2, \ldots, x_n] \in \times_{p=1}^{n} X_p \mid \Theta_{n+1} x_{n+1} \in X_{n+1}, \ldots, \Theta_m x_m \in X_m \mid e(x_1, \ldots, x_m)\ \}$$

into a sequence of *count* queries and a quantifier–free find query of the form

$$Q' = \{ [x_1, x_2, \ldots, x_n] \in \times_{p=1}^{n} X_p \mid e'(x_1, \ldots, x_n)\}.$$

We shall successively eliminate each quantifier from right to left *i.e.* innermost to outermost. We first consider the case when the innermost (rightmost) quantifier is an *existential* quantifier and use the following two rules :

1. $\exists\, x_i : (f(x_i) \vee g(x_i)) \iff (\exists\, x_i : f(x_i)) \vee (\exists\, x_i : g(x_i))$.
2. $\exists\, x_i : (f(x_i) \wedge h) \iff (\exists\, x_i : f(x_i)) \wedge h$, where x_i does not appear free in h.

Converting the expression $e(x_1, \ldots, x_m)$ (appearing in the general *find* query) into *Disjunctive Normal Form (DNF)*, we get:

$$e(x_1, \ldots, x_m) \;=\; e_1(x_1, \ldots, x_m) \vee e_2(x_1, \ldots, x_m) \vee \ldots e_l(x_1, \ldots, x_m)$$

Then by Rule 1, the predicate $\exists x_m : e(x_1, \ldots, x_m)$ can be replaced by

$$\exists x_m : e_1(x_1, \ldots, x_m) \vee \ldots \vee \exists x_m : e_l(x_1, \ldots, x_m).$$

Variable x_m can occur in an atomic predicate with at most one other variable, since, otherwise, the vertex x_m will have in-degree greater than one, which violates the *forest* property.

Suppose the in-degree of x_m is 1, *i.e.* the query graph has exactly one edge coming into x_m, say from x_k. This implies that the atomic predicates involving x_m are either single–variable atomic predicates, or two–variable atomic predicates involving x_k and x_m. The case when the in-degree for x_m is 0, *i.e.* it appears only in single–variable atomic predicates is a trivial special case of the case being considered, and is omitted.

Dividing each e_i for $i = 1, \ldots, l$, into predicates involving x_m versus the predicates not involving x_m and using Rule 2, we get

$$\exists x_m : e_i(x_1, \ldots, x_m) = e_i^1(x_1, \ldots, x_{m-1}) \wedge \exists x_m : e_i^2(x_k, x_m)$$

where $e_i^2(x_k, x_m)$ is a conjunction of one and two–variable atomic predicates on x_k and x_m, and the expression $e_i^1(x_1, \ldots, x_{m-1})$ does not contain any atomic predicates involving x_m. If we compute *count* query

$$C_i \;=\; \{ [x_k, \#\{x_m \in X_m : e_i^2(x_k, x_m)\}] \;:\; x_k \in X_k \},$$

then predicate $\exists x_m : e_i^2(x_k, x_m)$ can be replaced by $C_i(x_k) > 0$.

We can compute l such *count* queries, one for each e_i and replace each test $\exists x_m : e_i^2(x_k, x_m)$ by $C_i(x_k) > 0$, for $i = 1, \ldots, l$. Thus, our initial query

$$Q = \{ [x_1, \ldots, x_n] \in \times_{p=1}^{n} X_p \mid \Theta_{n+1} x_{n+1} \in X_{n+1}, \ldots, \Theta_{m-1} x_{m-1} \in X_{m-1}, \\ \exists x_m \in X_m | e(x_1, \ldots, x_m) \}$$

is transformed into

$$\begin{aligned} &\text{let} \\ &\quad C_1 = \{ [x_k, \#\{ x_m \in X_m : e_1^2(x_k, x_m)\}] : x_k \in X_k \} \\ &\quad \vdots \\ &\quad C_l = \{ [x_k, \#\{ x_m \in X_m : e_l^2(x_k, x_m)\}] : x_k \in X_k \} \\ &\text{in} \\ &\quad Q_1 = \{ [x_1, \ldots, x_n] \in \times_{p=1}^{n} X_p | \Theta_{n+1} x_{n+1} \in X_{n+1}, \ldots, \Theta_{m-1} x_{m-1} \in X_{m-1} | \\ &\qquad (e_1(x_1, \ldots, x_{m-1}) \wedge C_1(x_k) > 0) \vee \ldots \vee (e_l(x_1, \ldots, x_{m-1}) \wedge \\ &\qquad C_l(x_k) > 0) \} \end{aligned}$$

The case when the innermost quantifier to be eliminated is a *universal* quantifier is almost identical except that the expression $e(x_1, \ldots, x_m)$ is first converted into *Conjunctive Normal Form (CNF).*

The preceding technique for eliminating the innermost quantifier is applied repeatedly until all leading quantifiers are removed.

Theorem 31 *If the count and quantifier–free find queries are linear time queries, then the general find query is also a linear time query*

Proof: As seen from the transformation described above, the number of count queries generated is some constant that depends on the syntax of the query but is independent of the database size N. The number of quantifiers in the query is also independent of the database size. Hence the total number of count queries generated during the quantifier elimination process is some constant. Furthermore each count query is *input-bounded i.e.* the size of the output is bounded by the size of the input. Hence if each count query is a *linear time query,* then the time taken for their execution is linear in the size of their input sets. At the end of quantifier elimination, we are also left with exactly one quantifier–free find query. If we assume that the count and quantifier–free find queries are linear time queries, then the total running time for the general find query is bounded by the sum of the sizes of the input and output sets (up to a constant factor). Hence, the general find query is a linear time query. □

Consider the quantifier–free find query of the form

$$Q' = \{ [x_1, x_2, \ldots, x_n] \in \times_{p=1}^{n} X_p | e'(x_1, \ldots, x_n) \}.$$

Converting $e'(x_1, \ldots, x_n)$ to *DNF* we get

$$e'(x_1, \ldots, x_n) = e_1(x_1, \ldots, x_n) \vee \ldots \vee e_j(x_1, \ldots, x_n).$$

Then it can be seen that $Q' = \cup_{i=1}^{j} Q_i$, where

$$Q_i = \{ [x_1, x_2, \ldots, x_n] \subset \times_{p=1}^{n} X_p | e_i(x_1, \ldots, x_n) \}.$$

The sets Q_i may not be mutually disjoint but multi-set discrimination (Cai and Paige 1995) can be used to perform the above union in linear time.

The number of such queries Q_i may be exponential in the syntactic length of Q', but it is still a constant independent of the data base size N. Therefore it is sufficient to show that each of the queries Q_i are linear time queries in order to show that Q' is a linear time query.

In order to show that the queries Q_i are linear time, we next describe transformations to decompose these queries into a constant number of *simple find* queries of the form (20). Finally, we show that all *count* and *simple find* queries can be transformed to run in linear time.

3.2 Join Decomposition

We now look at queries of the form

$$Q = \{ [x_1, x_2, \ldots, x_n] \in \times_{p=1}^{n} X_p | e(x_1, \ldots, x_n) \} \tag{21}$$

where e is a conjunction of atomic predicates and their negations.

Definition 32 Projection: *Given a set Q (Equation 21) containing tuples from $\times_{i=1}^{n} X_i$, the projection of Q onto sets $X_1, \ldots, X_j$, denoted by $\Pi_{X_1,\ldots,X_j} Q$, is a subset of $\times_{i=1}^{j} X_i$ consisting of the restriction of the tuples of Q to the sets $X_1, \ldots, X_j$;* i.e.,

$$\Pi_{X_1,\ldots,X_j} Q = \{[x_1, x_2, \ldots, x_j] \in \times_{p=1}^{j} X_p \mid \exists x_{j+1} \in X_{j+1}, \ldots, \exists x_n \in X_n | e(x_1, \ldots, x_n) \}$$

Definition 33 Natural Join: *Let Q_1 be a subset of $\times_{i=1}^{k} X_i$ and Q_2 be a subset of $\times_{i=k}^{j} X_i$. The natural join of Q_1 and Q_2, denoted by $Q_1 \bowtie_{X_k} Q_2$, is a subset of $\times_{i=1}^{j} X_i$ resulting from the concatenation of tuples in Q_1 and Q_2 that have identical values for X_k;* i.e.,

$$Q_1 \bowtie_{X_k} Q_2 = \{[x_1, \ldots, x_j] \in \times_{i=1}^{j} X_i \mid [x_1, \ldots, x_k] \in Q_1 \wedge [x_k, \ldots, x_j] \in Q_2\}$$

Then we have two simple lemmas that will be used to prove that Q is a linear time query.

Lemma 34 *Let Q be the query defined in (21) and $T = \Pi_{X_1,\ldots,X_j} Q$ where $j \leq n$. Then $\#T \leq \#Q$.*

The proof is trivial, and is omitted.

Lemma 35 *Let Q be the query defined in (21) and $T_1 = \Pi_{X_1,\ldots,X_j} Q$, $T_2 = \Pi_{X_1,\ldots,X_k} Q$ and $T_3 = \Pi_{X_k,\ldots,X_j} Q$ where $1 \leq k \leq j$ and*

$$e(x_1, \ldots, x_n) = e_1(x_1, \ldots, x_k) \;\wedge\; e_2(x_k, \ldots, x_n)$$

i.e. *the predicate $e(x_1, \ldots, x_n)$ does* **not** *contain any two–variable atomic predicates on variables u and v such that $u \in \{x_1, \ldots, x_{k-1}\}$ and $v \in \{x_{k+1}, \ldots, x_n\}$. Then $T_1 = T_2 \bowtie_{X_k} T_3$*

Proof: Proving $T_1 \subseteq (T_2 \bowtie_{X_k} T_3)$ is trivial, and is omitted. To prove that $(T_2 \bowtie_{X_k} T_3) \subseteq T_1$, we consider a tuple $[x'_1, x'_2, \ldots, x'_j]$ that belongs to $(T_2 \bowtie_{X_k} T_3)$. Then, by Definition 33, we know that $[x'_1, x'_2, \ldots, x'_k] \in T_2$, and $[x'_k, x'_{k+1}, \ldots, x'_j] \in T_3$. Also, by Definition 32, $[x'_1, \ldots, x'_k] \in T_2$ implies that $\exists x'_{k+1}, \ldots, x'_n | e_1(x'_1, \ldots, x'_k) \wedge e_2(x'_{k+1}, \ldots x'_n)$, which implies $e_1(x'_1, \ldots, x'_k)$. By similar reasoning, $[x'_k, \ldots, x'_j] \in T_3$ implies that $\exists x'_{j+1}, \ldots, x'_n | \, e_2(x'_k, \ldots, x'_j, x'_{j+1}, \ldots, x'_n)$. Hence, $\exists x'_{j+1}, \ldots, x'_n | e(x'_1, \ldots, x'_n)$. From Definition 32 we see that $[x'_1, \ldots, x'_j] \in T_1$. Therefore, $T_2 \bowtie_{X_k} T_3 \subseteq T_1$. □

Consider again the query Q given by (21). The query graph for Q is a subgraph of the original query graph, and hence, is also a forest. An important consequence of this is that, for every directed edge (x_k, x_j) in the forest, there exists a permutation $[x_k, x_j, x_{p_1}, \ldots, x_{p_{n-2}}]$ of variables $[x_1, x_2, \ldots, x_n]$, such that the query graph for the query

$$Q_{(x_k, x_j)} = \{ [x_k, x_j] \in X_k \times X_j | \exists x_{p_1} \in X_{p_1}, \ldots, \exists x_{p_{n-2}} \in X_{p_{n-2}} | \; e(x_1, \ldots, x_n) \}$$

is also a forest. We can get such an ordering of vertices by first reversing the direction of edges on the path from the *root* (of the tree containing x_k) to x_k in the query graph for Q. As a result x_k becomes the new root and the variables other than x_k and x_j can then be ordered in the same order as the *breadth first search sequence* from x_k.

We generate such a query $Q_{(x,y)}$ for each directed edge (x, y) in the query graph. The number of edges is a small constant depending on the query but independent of the database size. Since for each edge (x, y), $Q_{(x,y)} = \Pi_{X,Y} Q$, we have $\#Q_{(x,y)} \leq \#Q$. We perform *natural joins* (*i.e.* the $\bowtie$ operator) on the queries $Q_{(x,y)}$ to compute Q. We select two queries corresponding to two edges in the query graph such that the conditions of Lemma 35 are satisfied and perform a natural join. The two edges are replaced by an edge corresponding to the result, which, as a consequence of Lemma 35, is also a projection of Q. It is easy to see that if we choose one of the edges to be a leaf edge (*i.e.* one of its vertices is a leaf), and the other to be another edge with which it shares a vertex, then the conditions of Lemma 35 are satisfied. After performing the natural join operation, the two edges are merged into a single edge, and we continue performing the natural joins by selecting another suitable pair of edges. Finally, we are left with singleton edges (corresponding to each different connected component in the original forest), and taking a cross product of each of the sets corresponding to these edges, we get Q.

Since each of the the results of the natural joins are projections of Q (from Lemma 35), the size of each the intermediate outputs from the natural joins is bounded by the size $\#Q$ of the final output.

Theorem 36 *If each of the queries $Q_{(x,y)}$ is a linear time query, and* **join** *is a linear time query, then Q is a linear time query.*

Proof: Q is computed by first computing each of the queries $Q_{(x,y)}$, and then performing *join* operations in a suitable order such that the conditions of Lemma 35 are satisfied for each join. If each $Q_{(x,y)}$ is a linear time query, then its running time is bounded (up to a constant factor) by the sum of its input and output sizes, and hence by the sum of the input size and the size of the final output Q (because $\#Q_{(x,y)} \leq \#Q$). Also the linear running time for the *joins* implies that their running times are bounded (up to a constant factor) by the sum of *their* input and output sizes, and hence by the size of the final output because the intermediate input and output sizes for each join are bounded by the final output size. So the time to compute Q is bounded (up to a constant factor) by the sum of the input set sizes and the final output size, thus proving that Q is a linear time query. □

Furthermore, each $Q_{(x,y)}$ can be transformed into a sequence of *count* queries and a *simple find* query (*i.e. a two–variable quantifier–free find* query) of the form

$$Q'_{(x,y)} \quad = \quad \{\ [x,y] \in X \times Y | e'(x,y)\ \},$$

by using the quantifier elimination technique described in Section 3.1. Thus each $Q_{(x,y)}$ is a linear time query if the *count* and *simple find* queries are linear time queries.

Furthermore a natural join operation is just a very small variation of the *simple find* query

$$\{[x',y'] \in X' \ \times \ Y'|(f(x') = g(y'))\ \}.$$

It is easy to see that X' and Y' can be the two relations (sets containing tuples) participating in the natural join, and x' and y' iterate over the *tuples* in X' and Y'. Predicate $f(x') = g(y')$ can then represent the condition that the tuples x' and y' agree on the value of the set common to the two relations.

4 COUNT AND SIMPLE FIND QUERIES

In this section we turn our attention to *count* queries

$$Q = \{[x, \#\{y \in Y | e(x, y)\ \}] : x \in X\}, \tag{22}$$

and *simple find* queries

$$Q = \{[x, y] \in X \times Y | e(x, y)\ \}, \tag{23}$$

where $e(x, y)$ is just a conjunction of atomic predicates and their negations.

Willard showed that *count* and *simple find* queries could be implemented in expected linear time by studying increasingly more general variants of the predicate $e(x, y)$ appearing in (22) and (23), which he called classes E-1 through E-8 of enactment expressions. He gave algorithms to decompose queries in a more general class E-(i+1) into queries in class E-(i). He describes low level operations to construct indexes and other auxiliary data structures used to compute the simple find queries efficiently. Similar constructions are used to calculate several different forms of simple queries, and are described in detail each time a different case is considered. The low level constructions are analyzed by detailed and sometimes complex counting arguments repeated for each different case.

We use a set theoretic language with expressions specifying data structures and implementations, which eliminates redundancy found in Willard's proofs both in query evaluation and algorithmic analysis. Simply put, our notations provide us with larger, more abstract building blocks that are easily combined by composition and parameter substitution to form queries. This allows us to replace low level counting arguments by more algebraic and logical reasoning in our algorithmic analysis. Consequently, we can focus on the key ideas involved in decomposing difficult queries into simpler queries in terms of high level transformations that are easy to understand and prove correct. Furthermore, the transformations themselves and the order in which they are applied have been carefully tailored to allow the resulting program to be well typed. Since the type system ensures that each hash operation can be implemented to run in $O(1)$ time on a pointer machine, we get a worst case linear time implementation for LRCS.

In Section 2.2 and Appendix 1 we illustrate how inference rules can be used to determine the asymptotic run-time complexities of typed expressions.

Appendix 3 contains a sample complexity derivation for the query in *case 1*. We also provide a sample proof of correctness for *case 1* in Appendix 2. For the sake of brevity, the remaining cases will be described informally.

Theorem 41 *The count queries and simple find queries are linear time queries.*

Proof: The argument for proving the linear time result will be inductive on the number of atomic predicates in the predicate $e(x, y)$. We shall provide transformations in which each step will eliminate one or more atomic predicates. The base case for our inductive proof corresponds to the queries

$$Q = \{[x, \#\{y \in Y | true\}] : x \in X\} \tag{24}$$

and

$$Q = \{[x, y] \in X \times Y | true\}, \tag{25}$$

for the *count* and *simple find* queries respectively. Both of these can be trivially seen to be linear time queries. Note that the find query in (25) is linear in the size of the output.

We shall prove the induction step by looking at different cases corresponding to different kinds of atomic predicates. In each case we provide transformations that eliminate one or more atomic predicates from the query. For each case, under the inductive assumption that the generated queries with a lesser number of atomic predicates are linear time queries, we shall prove that the original query is also a linear time query. There is one more subtle point to be considered. The linear running time result depends on the order in which transformations are applied to eliminate different kinds of atomic predicates. So, the cases that we consider are ordered in the order that the transformations must be applied. For example, while considering *case 2*, we shall assume that all atomic predicates corresponding to *case 1* have already been eliminated by repeated applications of the transformations described in *case 1*.

In each of the following cases, the types $B_1, B_2, \ldots$ represent base types. X is a set of elements of base type B_1 and Y is a set of elements of base type B_2. Predicate $K_1(x, y)$ represents a conjunction of atomic predicates and their negations (only the kind that have not yet been eliminated in the previously considered cases).

Case 1. Simple unary predicates and their negations:

$$Q = \{[x, y] \in X \times Y | K_1(x, y) \wedge K_2(x)\},$$

where $\forall x\ Cost(K_2(x)) = O(1)$ and $K_2(x) : Bool$.

Query Q is transformed into :

```
let
```

$Q_1 = \{ x \in X | K_2(x) \}: set(B_1)$

`in`

$Q_2 = \{[x, y] \in Q_1 \times Y | K_1(x, y) \}.$

The correctness of this transformation is obvious. The number of atomic predicates in query Q_2 is one less than the number in query Q. So under the inductive assumption that query Q_2 is a linear time query, we prove that query Q also runs in linear time. We do so by using the inference rules listed in Section 2.2 and Appendix 1, as described below.

Using Rule (31) we have

$$\frac{\Gamma\{x : B_1\} \vdash K_2(x) : Bool,\ O(1)\ time}{\Gamma\{X : set(B_1)\} \vdash \{x \in X \mid K_2(x)\} : set(B_1),\ O(\#X)\ time.}$$

Furthermore, from Rule (40) we have

$$\#\{x : B_1 \in X : set(B_1) \mid K_2 : Bool\} \leq \#X,$$

and finally, using Rule (38) we have

$$\frac{\begin{array}{c} Q_1 = \{x \in X \mid K_2(x)\} : set(B_1),\ O(\#X)\ time \\ Q_2 = \{[x, y] \in A \times Y | K_1(x, y)\},\ O(\#A + \#Y + \#Q_2)\ time \end{array}}{\begin{array}{c} \text{let } Q_1 = \{x \in X \mid K_2(x)\} \text{ in} \\ Q_2 = \{[x, y] \in Q_1 \times Y | K_1(x, y)\},\ O(\#Q_1 + \#Y + \#Q_2)\ time \end{array}}$$

Informally the proof can be understood as follows. Query Q_1 can be computed in time $O(\#X)$. If query Q_2 is a linear time query (*i.e.* computable in time $O(\#Y + \#Q_1 + \#Q_2)$ time) then our original query can be computed in $O(\#Y + \#Q_1 + \#Q_2 + \#X)$ time. Then, from $\#Q_1 \leq \#X$ and $\#Q_2 = \#Q$ we see that query Q can be computed in $O(\#Y + \#X + \#Q)$ time, and is therefore a linear time query.

The transformation for *count* queries is similar. The case when the unary predicate involves y instead of x is symmetric.

Case 2. Unary list predicates and their negations:

$$Q = \{ [x, y] \in X \times Y | K_1(x, y) \wedge (\exists z \in Z | K_2(z) = K_3(x)) \},$$

where $\forall z, x$: $Cost(K_2(z)) = O(1)$, $Cost(K_3(x)) = O(1)$, $Z : set(B_3)$ and $K_2(z), K_3(x) : B_4$, with B_3 and B_4 being base types.

Query Q is transformed into :

`let`

$Q_1 = \{ [K_2(z), z] : z \in Z \} : mmap(B_4 - strong, B_3)$

$Q_2 = \{ [K_3(x), \#Q_1\{K_3(x)\}] : x \in X \} : smap(B_4 - strong, int)$

`in`

$$Q_3 = \{ [x, y] \in X \times Y | K_1(x, y) \wedge Q_2(K_3(x)) > 0 \}.$$

Query Q_3 can now be further transformed as in *case 1* to get a query with a decreased number of atomic predicates.

The cases for minor variations such as $\neg\exists z \in Z$, $\forall z \in Z$ and $\neg\forall z \in Z$ are similar and are omitted. So are the cases where the unary list predicate involves y instead of x. The transformation for *count* queries is similar.

The correctness of the transformation can be seen as follows. Query Q_1 is the inverse map of K_2 restricted to the elements of set Z *i.e.* $Q_1 = K_2^{-1}|_Z$. Then, in our SETL like notation, the expression $\#Q_1\{K_3(x)\}$ denotes the number of elements in the image of $K_3(x)$ in the multi-valued map Q_1. Then for any $x \in X$, the expression $Q_2(K_3(x))$ equals $\#\{z \in Z | K_2(z) = K_3(x)\}$. So the predicate $\exists z \in Z | K_2(z) = K_3(x)$ can be replaced by the predicate $Q_2(K_3(x)) > 0$.

The arguments for linear time complexity are as follows. Using Rule (34) we see that query Q_1 takes $O(\#Z)$ time. Next, using Rule (16) we get that the expression $\#Q_1\{K_3(x)\}$ can be computed in $O(1)$ time, and hence, using Rule (35) we get that query Q_2 can be computed in $O(\#X)$ time. Next, using Rule (9) we get that the predicate $Q_2(K_3(x)) > 0$ can be evaluated in $O(1)$ time. So, if query Q_3 is a linear time query, then so is query Q.

Case 3. Negated tabular predicates:

In this case the transformations for the *count* and the *find* queries are different, so both are presented. The *find* query is of the form:

$$Q = \begin{array}{l} \{ [x, y] \in X \times Y | K_1(x, y) \wedge \neg\exists z \in Z | (K_2(z) = K_3(x) \wedge \\ \quad K_4(z) = K_5(y)) \}, \end{array} \tag{26}$$

and the *count* query is of the form:

$$C = \begin{array}{l} \{ [x, \#\{y \in Y | K_1(x, y) \wedge \neg\exists z \in Z | (K_2(z) = K_3(x) \wedge \\ \quad K_4(z) = K_5(y))\}] : x \in X \}, \end{array} \tag{27}$$

where $\forall\ x, y, z$: the cost for $K_2(z), K_4(z), K_3(x)$ and $K_5(y)$ are all $O(1)$ and K_3, K_5 are few–to–one. In addition, $Z : set(B_3)$ and $K_2(z), K_3(x) : B_4$ and $K_4(x), K_5(y) : B_5$, where B_3, B_4 and B_5 are base types.

Find query (26) is transformed into :

let

$$Q_1 = \{ [K_3(x), x] : x \in X \} : mmap(B_4 - strong, B_1)$$
$$Q_2 = \{ [K_5(y), y] : y \in Y \} : mmap(B_5 - strong, B_2)$$
$$Q_3 = \{ [K_2(z), K_4(z)] : z \in Z | K_2(z) \in \text{domain}(Q_1) \wedge K_4(z) \in \text{domain}(Q_2) \}$$
$$: mmap(B_4 - strong, B_5)$$

in

$$Q_4 = \{ [x, y] \in X \times Y\ | K_1(x, y)\} - \biguplus_{[p,q] \in Q_3} (Q_1\{p\} \times Q_2\{q\}).$$

The correctness of the transformation can be seen as follows. Queries Q_1 and Q_2 represent the inverse maps for K_3 and K_5 restricted to sets X and Y respectively. The pairs in Q_3 correspond to those $z \in Z$, for which there exist pairs $[x, y] \in X \times Y$ satisfying the tabular predicate

$$\exists z \in Z | (K_2(z) = K_3(x) \land K_4(z) = K_5(x)).$$

Since none of such pairs $[x, y]$ must appear in Q, we compute all the pairs $[x, y]$ that satisfy the condition $K_1(x, y)$ and remove from this set, the pairs, $[x, y] \in Q_1\{p\} \times Q_2\{q\}$, for all $[p, q] \in Q_3$ *i.e.* those pairs that satisfy the tabular predicate.

We show that query Q is a *linear time query* under the inductive assumption that query $Q' = \{[x, y] \in X \times Y | K_1(x, y)\}$, which has a lesser number of atomic predicates than Q, is a linear time query. It is easy to see that queries Q_1, Q_2 and Q_3 take $O(\#X)$, $O(\#Y)$ and $O(\#Z)$ times respectively. Since K_3 and K_5 are few–to–one functions (*i.e.* the number of values mapped to a single value are bounded by a constant), queries Q_1 and Q_2 are one–to–few maps. The number of pairs $[x, y]$ satisfying the tabular predicate (and hence deleted from the output of Q') is bounded by $O(\#Z)$. Thus, the output size of query Q' is bounded by $O(\#Q_4 + \#Z)$. Assuming that Q' is a linear time query, we see that it takes $O(\#Q_4 + \#X + \#Y + \#Z)$ time to compute Q'. Then the run-time complexity for the original query Q is $O(\#Q_4 + \#X + \#Y + \#Z)$, thus showing that it is a linear time query.

Count query (27) is transformed into :

let

$C_1 = \{ [x, \#\{y \in Y | K_1(x, y)\}] : x \in X \}$:*smap*(B_1 − ***strong***, ***int***)

$C_2 = \{ [x, \#\{y \in Y | K_1(x, y) \land \exists\ z \in Z |\ (K_2(z) = K_3(x) \land K_4(z) = K_5(y))\}] : x \in X \}$:*smap*(B_1 − ***strong***, ***int***)

in

$C_3 = \{ [x, C_1(x) - C_2(x)] : x \in X \}$.

The argument for correctness is similar to that for *find* queries. Also it is easy to see that if queries C_1 and C_2 are linear time queries, then so is query C because query C_3 can be computed in $O(\#X)$ time. Note that there is no circularity in the argument because the proof of linear running time for tabular predicates (*Case 4*) will not assume linear running time for negated tabular predicates (*Case 3*).

Case 4. Tabular Predicates:

$$Q = \{ [x, y] \in X \times Y | K_1(x, y) \land K_2(x, y) \},$$

where predicate $K_1(x, y)$ does not contain any tabular predicates and predicate $K_2(x, y)$ is a conjunction of k (a constant) tabular predicates and is of the form:

$$\land_{i=1}^{k} (\exists\ z_i\ \in\ Z_i\ | f_1^i(z_i) = f_2^i(x)\ \land\ f_3^i(z_i) = f_4^i(y)),$$

where $\forall\ x, y, i, z_i$: the computation costs for all $f_1^i(z_i)$, $f_2^i(x)$, $f_3^i(z_i)$ and $f_4^i(y)$ are $O(1)$ time. Also for all $i = 1, \ldots, k$, $f_1^i(z_i) : B_1^i$ and $f_3^i(z_i) : B_2^i$, with B_1^i and B_2^i being base types. Furthermore we assume that for all $i = 1, \ldots, k$, f_2^i and f_4^i are few–to–one. In addition, for each i, at-least one of f_1^i and f_3^i is few to one. In the following transformation, we shall assume that all f_1^i are few–to–one without loss of generality.

Query Q is transformed into :

let

$$Q_1 = \{\ [f_1^1(z), f_3^1(z)] : z \in Z_1\ \} :mmap(B_1^1 - strong, B_2^1)$$
$$Q_2 = \{\ [f_1^2(z), f_3^2(z)] : z \in Z_2\ \} :mmap(B_1^2 - strong, B_2^2)$$
$$\vdots$$
$$Q_k = \{\ [f_1^k(z), f_3^k(z)] : z \in Z_k\ \} :mmap(B_1^k - strong, B_2^k)$$
$$D_1 = \{\ [f_2^1(x), x] : x \in X\ \}$$
$$D_2 = \{\ [f_4^1(y), y] : y \in Y\ \}$$

in

$$Q' = \biguplus_{[p,q] \in Q_1}\ \{\ [x, y] \in D_1\{p\} \times D_2\{q\} |\ K_1(x, y) \wedge (\wedge_{i=2}^{k}\ [f_2^i(x), f_4^i(y)] \in Q_i)\ \}.$$

The correctness of the transformation can be seen as follows. Maps D_1 and D_2 are the inverse maps of f_2^1 and f_4^1 restricted to the sets X and Y respectively. For each pair $[p, q] \in Q_1$, the elements $x \in D_1\{p\}$ and $y \in D_2\{q\}$ satisfy the first *tabular predicate*. Any other pair $[x, y]$ does not satisfy the first tabular predicate and can not be in the output for query Q. In query Q', we consider all the pairs $[x, y]$ that satisfy the first tabular predicate, the rest of the tabular predicates and the predicate $K_1(x, y)$.

The linear running time may be seen as follows. Maps D_1 and D_2 are one–to–few maps because f_2^1 and f_4^1 are few–to–one. Hence for any pair $[p, q] \in Q_1$, $\#(D_1\{p\} \times D_2\{q\})$ is bounded by a constant. Since $\#Q_1$ is bounded by $\#Z$, then $\#Q'$ is bounded by $O(\#Z)$. For each pair $[x, y]$ in Q', the evaluation of the predicate $K_1(x, y)$ (containing only equality and inequality predicates) takes constant time. Also since f_1^i are few–to–one, the maps Q_i are one–to–few. Since each of these maps Q_i is strongly based on its domain, the predicate $[f_2^i(x), f_4^i(y)] \in Q_i$ can be implemented as the predicate $f_4^i(y) \in Q_i\{f_2^i(x)\}$ in constant time since the image of any element in the strongly based map Q_i has only a few (no more that a constant) elements. Thus, the total running time is $O(\sum_{i=1}^{k} \#Z_i + \#X + \#Y)$.

The transformation for the case of *count* queries is similar.

Case 5. Equi-joins:

$$Q = \{\ [x, y] \in X \times Y | K_1(x, y) \wedge K_2(x) = K_3(y)\ \},$$

where $\forall x, y$: $Cost(K_2(x)) = O(1)$, $Cost(K_3(y)) = O(1)$, and $K_2(x), K_3(y) : B_3$, with B_3 being a base type.

Query Q' is transformed into :

let

$Q_1 = \{ [K_3(y), y] : y \in Y \} : mmap(B_3 - strong, B_2)$

$Q_2 = \{ [K_2(x), x] : x \in X | K_2(x) \in \text{domain } Q_1 \} : mmap(B_3 - strong, B_1)$

in

$Q_3 = \biguplus_{z \in\ domain(Q_2)} \{ [x, y] \in Q_2\{z\} \times Q_1\{z\} | K_1(x, y) \}.$

Again the correctness of the transformation is easy to see. Query Q_1 is the inverse map of K_3 restricted to set Y, and query Q_2 is the inverse map of K_2 restricted to set X', where $X' = \{ x \in X | \exists y \in Y | K_2(x) = K_3(y) \}$. The predicate $K_2(x) \in$ domain Q_1, which occurs in query Q_2, ensures that domain $Q_2 \subseteq$ domain Q_1. Clearly the only pairs $[x, y]$ that satisfy the *equality* predicate $K_2(x) = K_3(y)$ are those that belong to $Q_2\{z\} \times Q_1\{z\}$, for some $z \in$ domain Q_2. So, for each $z \in$ domain Q_2, we compute the subset of $Q_2\{z\} \times Q_1\{z\}$ that satisfies the predicate $K_1(x, y)$. The final result is the union of these queries.

The linear running time can be seen as follows. The running time for queries Q_1 and Q_2 is $O(\#Y)$ and $O(\#X)$ time respectively. Since query Q_1 is the inverse of a function, for any two distinct elements w_1 and w_2 in domain Q_1, $Q_1\{w_1\} \cap Q_1\{w_2\} = \phi$. The same is true for Q_2. Since domain $Q_2 \subseteq$ domain Q_1, none of the sets $Q_1\{z\}$ or $Q_2\{z\}$ is empty for any $z \in$ domain Q_2. If for each $z \in$ domain Q_2, the sub-queries $\{ [x, y] \in Q_2\{z\} \times Q_1\{z\} | K_1(x, y) \}$ are linear *i.e.* are computed in time $O(\#Q_1\{z\} + \#Q_2\{z\} + \#Output_z)$ (where $Output_z$ denotes the output for this sub-query), then the time taken for Q_3 is $O(\sum_{z \in \text{domain}(Q_2)} \#Q_1\{z\} + \#Q_2\{z\} + \#Output_z)$ which is bounded by $O(\#X + \#Y + \#Q)$. Hence, the running time for Q is linear in the sum of the sizes of the input and output sets.

Case 6. Anti-joins:

In this final case for anti-join predicates, the transformations for the *count* and *simple find* queries are also different. We first present the transformations for the *count* query:

$$C = \{ [x, \#\{y \in Y | K_1(x, y) \wedge K_2(x) \neq K_3(y)\}] : x \in X \},$$

where $\forall x, y$: $Cost(K_2(x)) = O(1)$, $Cost(K_3(y)) = O(1)$ and $K_2(x), K_3(y) : B_3$, with B_3 being a base type.

Query C is transformed into :

let

$C_1 = \{ [x, \#\{y \in Y | K_1(x, y)\}] : x \in X \} :smap(B_1 - strong, int)$

$C_2 = \{ [x, \#\{y \in Y | K_1(x, y) \wedge K_2(x) = K_3(y)\}] : x \in X \} :smap(B_1 - strong, int)$

in

$C_3 = \{ [x, C_1(x) - C_2(x)] : x \in X \}.$

The correctness is obvious. C_2 is further transformed using the transformation described in *case 5*. Then, assuming that the queries with a lesser number of atomic predicates are linear, C is also a linear time query.

The anti-join case for the *simple find* queries is a little more involved. This transformation is applied when all other kinds of predicates have been eliminated. So the query looks like

$$Q = \{\ [x, y] \in X \times Y \mid \bigwedge_{i=1}^{k}\ g_i(x) \neq f_i(y)\ \},$$

where for all $i = 1, \ldots, k$, $g_i(x), f_i(y) : B_i'$ and B_i' is a base type.

Query Q is transformed into :

let

$Crit_i = \{\ z \in range(f_i) \mid \# f_i^{-1}\{z\} \geq \# Y/2k\ \}{:}set(B_i' - strong)$, for $i = 1, \ldots, k$.

$A_0 = \{\ x \in X \mid \wedge_{i=1}^{k} (g_i(x) \notin Crit_i)\ \}$

$C_0 = \{\ [x, y] \in A_0 \times Y \mid \wedge_{i=1}^{k} g_i(x) \neq f_i(y)\ \}$

$C_i = \bigcup_{z \in Crit_i} \{\ [x, y]{:}\ x \in (g_i^{-1}\{z\} - \cup_{j=1}^{i-1} g_j^{-1}[Crit_j]),\ y \in (Y - f_i^{-1}\{z\}) \mid \wedge_{j=1, j \neq i}^{k}\ g_j(x) \neq f_j(y)\ \}$ for $i = 1, \ldots, k$

in

$Q = \bigcup_{i=0}^{k} C_i$.

We provide a proof outline for the correctness and the linear running time. For $i = 1, \ldots, k$, let us define the expression

$$A_i = g_i^{-1}[Crit_i] - \cup_{j=1}^{i-1} g_j^{-1}[Crit_j]. \tag{28}$$

Then, it is easy to see that A_0 satisfies $A_0 = X - \cup_{i=1}^{k} A_i$ and hence, $X = \bigcup_{j=0}^{k} A_j$. To prove correctness, we claim that for each $i = 0, \ldots, k$,

$$C_i = \{\ [x, y] \in A_i \times Y \mid \wedge_{j=1}^{k} g_j(x) \neq f_j(y)\ \}. \tag{29}$$

The proof for C_0 follows trivially from its definition. Let us use predicate $K(x, y)$ as an abbreviation for the predicate $\bigwedge_{j=1, j \neq i}^{k}\ g_j(x) \neq f_j(y)$. Then query $\{\ [x, y] \in A_i \times Y \mid \bigwedge_{j=1}^{k} g_j(x) \neq f_j(y)\ \}$ is the same as $\{\ [x, y] \in A_i \times Y \mid (g_i(x) \neq f_i(y)) \wedge K(x, y)\ \}$.

For any element $z \in Crit_i$, the elements $x \in g_i^{-1}\{z\}$, satisfy the predicate $(g_i(x) \neq f_i(y))$ only for elements $y \in Y - f_i^{-1}\{z\}$. Also the expression A_i given in (28) can be rewritten as

$$A_i = \cup_{z \in Crit_i} (g_i^{-1}\{z\} - \cup_{j=1}^{i-1} g_j^{-1}[Crit_j]).$$

Then it is easy to see that our claim for C_i given by (29) holds.

Furthermore, from (29) we have

$$\cup_{i=0}^{k} C_i = \{ [x, y] \in X \times Y \mid \wedge_{j=1}^{k} g_j(x) \neq f_j(y) \},$$

which proves the correctness of the transformation.

The following is a proof outline that query Q runs in linear time .

Consider any element $x \in A_0$. Then, by the definition of A_0, $g_i(x) \notin Crit_i$ for all $i = 1, \ldots, k$. By the definition of $Crit_i$, this implies that for any $x \in A_0$,

$$\#\{y \in Y | (g_i(x) = f_i(y))\} \leq \#Y/(2 \times k),$$

which would further imply that

$$\#\{y \in Y \mid \vee_{i=1}^{k} (g_i(x) = f_i(y))\} \leq \#Y/2,$$

or

$$\#\{y \in Y \mid \wedge_{i=1}^{k} (g_i(x) \neq f_i(y))\} \geq \#Y/2.$$

Thus,

$$\#C_0 \geq \#A_0 \times \#Y/2.$$

The running time for query C_0 is clearly bounded by $\#A_0 \times \#Y$ which is no more than twice its output size. Also, the output of query C_0 is a part of the final output. Hence, C_0 runs in time linear in the size of the final output.

Besides C_0, we have k other queries C_i for $i = 1, \ldots, k$. Each of the C_i is further split up into a union of queries for each $z \in Crit_i$. By a simple application of the pigeon hole principle, $\#Crit_i < 2 \times k$. Then clearly we have at-most $2 \times k^2$ queries corresponding to all the C_i's. Each such query has only $k-1$ anti-join predicates, and hence, if we make the induction assumption that each query with $k-1$ anti-join predicates is a linear time query, then we can see that the running time for the query with k anti-join predicates is bigger by no more than a factor of $2 \times k^2$, which is independent of the database size N. The base case with no anti-join predicates can be trivially seen to be linear time. An inductive argument proves that the query Q is a linear time query.

This completes our inductive proof showing that count queries and simple find queries are linear time queries. □

5 CONCLUSION

In this paper we have demonstrated how programming language concepts and methods can be used to shorten, simplify, and, finally, speedup an algorithmic result. As a bonus, we even obtain an implementation and its transformational proof. This work leads to four tempting new directions. First, the complexity based language work in Cai and Paige (1987) and Cai and Paige (1992) should be redone more formally from the type theoretic foundations provided here. Second, it would be interesting to see if the whole of RCS can be improved from complexity in the expected sense to complexity in the worst case sense. Our LRCS translation is simple enough to consider a practical project to mechanically check its correctness. Of course, its correctness must include verification of the linear run-time complexity of translated queries. Finally, it would be interesting to find out if typability can be inferred mechanically or semi-automatically, in order to make our type system a more useful tool for algorithmic speedup.

6 ACKNOWLEDGEMENTS

We would like to thank Archisman Rudra for helpful discussions as we began this research. We are grateful to Dan Willard for many stimulating discussions regarding his work. We are especially grateful to Zhe Yang for many valuable suggestions that helped improve the paper.

REFERENCES

Anderson, H. R. (1994). Model checking and boolean graphs. *Theoretical Computer Science*, 126(1):3–30.

Arnold, A. and Crubille, P. (1988). A linear algorithm to solve fixed point equations on transition systems. In *Information Processing Letters*, volume 29, pages 57–66.

Cai, J., Facon, P., Henglein, F., Paige, R. and Schonberg, E. (1991). Type transformation and data structure choice. In B. Moeller, editor, *Constructing Programs From Specifications*, pages 126–164. North-Holland, Amsterdam.

Cai, J. and Paige, R. (1987). Binding performance at language design time. In *Proc. Fourteenth ACM Symp. on Principles of Programming Languages*, pages 85 – 97.

Cai, J. and Paige, R. (1992). Languages polynomial in the input plus output. In M. Nivat, C. Rattray, T. Rus, and G. Scollo, editors, *Algebraic Methodology and Software Technology*, Workshops in Computing, pages 287–302. Springer-Verlag. Conference Record of the Second AMAST.

Cai, J. and Paige, R. (1995). Using multiset discrimination to solve language processing problems without hashing. *Theoretical Computer Science*, 145(1-2):189–228. URL http://cs.nyu.edu/cs/faculty/paige/papers/hash.ps.

Cleavaland, R. and Steffen, B. (1992). A linear-time model-checking algorithm for the alternation-free modal-calculus. Technical report, Computer Science Dept., North Carolina University.

Codd, E. F. (1970). A relational model of data for large shared data banks. *CACM*, 13(6):377–387.

Hunt-III, H. B., Szymanski, T. G., and Ullman, J. D. (1977). Operations on sparse relations. *CACM*, 20(3):127–132.

Keller, J. and Paige, R. (1995). Program derivation with verified transformations – a case study. *CPAM*, 48(9-10).

Knuth, D. E. (1973). *The Art of Computer Programming, Vol 1: Fundamental Algorithms.* Addison-Wesley.

Nielson, H. R. (1984). *Hoare Logic's for Run-time Analysis of Programs.* PhD thesis, University of Edinburgh, Scotland.

Nielson, H. R. (1987). A Hoare-like Proof System for Run-time Analysis of Programs. *Science of Computer Programming*, 9.

Paige, R. (1989). Real-time simulation of a set machine on a ram. In N. Janicki and W. Koczkodaj, editors, *Computing and Information*, volume II, pages 69–73. Canadian Scholars' Press, Toronto.

Paige, R. (1994). Efficient translation of external input in a dynamically typed language. In B. Pehrson and I. Simon, editors, *Technology and Foundations - Information Processing 94*, volume 1 of *IFIP Transactions A-51*, pages 603–608. North-Holland, Amsterdam. Conference Record of IFIP Congress 94.

Paige, R. and Yang, Z. (1997). High level reading and data structure compilation. 24th Annual ACM SIGPLAN-SIGACT Symposium on Principle of Programming Languages, pages 456-469.

Schwartz, J. (1974). *On Programming: An Interim Report on the SETL Project, Installments I and II.* New York University, New York.

Schwartz, J. (1975a). Automatic data structure choice in a language of very high level. *CACM*, 18(12):722–728.

Schwartz, J. (1975b). Optimization of very high level languages, parts i, ii. *J. of Computer Languages*, 1(2, 3):161–218.

Schwartz, J., Dewar, R., Dubinsky, E. and Schonberg, E. (1986). *Programming with Sets: An Introduction to SETL.* Springer-Verlag, New York.

Snyder, K. (1990). The SETL2 programming language. Technical Report 490, Courant Insititute, New York University.

Suppes, P. (1972). *Axiomatic Set Theory.* Dover.

Tarjan, R. (1979). A class of algorithms which require nonlinear time to maintain disjoint sets. *Journal of computer and System Sciences*, 18:110–127.

Willard, D. E. (1978). *Predicate Oriented Database Search Algorithms.* PhD thesis, Harvard.

Willard, D. E. (1983). Predicate retrieval theory. Technical Report 83-3, SUNY Albany.

Willard, D. E. (1990). Quasi-linear algorithms for processing relational data base expressions. In *Proceedings of the 9th ACM SIGACT-SIGMOD-SIGART Symposium on Principles of Database Systems*, pages 243–257.

Willard, D. E. (1996). Applications of range query theory to relational data base join and selection operations. *J. Computer and System Sci.*, 52:157–169.

APPENDIX 1 ADDITIONAL INFERENCE RULES

Additional Inference Rules for Time Complexity of Expressions

$$\frac{\begin{array}{c}\Gamma\{x:\tau\} \vdash K_1 : B,\ O(1)\ \mathit{time} \\ \Gamma\{x:\tau\} \vdash K_2 : \mathit{Bool},\ O(1)\ \mathit{time}\end{array}}{\Gamma\{S:\mathit{set}(\tau)\} \vdash \{K_1 : x \in S | K_2\} :\ \mathit{set}(B-\mathit{strong}), O(\#S)\ \mathit{time}} \tag{30}$$

$$\frac{\begin{array}{c}\Gamma\{x:\tau\} \vdash K_1 : B,\ O(1)\ \mathit{time} \\ \Gamma\{x:\tau\} \vdash K_2 : \mathit{Bool},\ O(1)\ \mathit{time}\end{array}}{\Gamma\{S:\mathit{set}(\tau)\} \vdash \{K_1 : x \in S | K_2\} :\ \mathit{set}(B),\ O(\#S)\ \mathit{time}} \quad \text{where } \lambda x.K_1 \text{ is one-one} \tag{31}$$

$$\Gamma\{B < \tau, e : B, Q : \mathit{smap}(B-\mathit{strong}, \tau_1)\} \vdash (e \in \text{domain } Q) : \mathit{Bool},\ O(1)\ \mathit{time} \tag{32}$$

$$\Gamma\{B < \tau, e : B, Q : \mathit{mmap}(B-\mathit{strong}, \tau_1)\} \vdash (e \in \text{domain } Q) : \mathit{Bool},\ O(1)\ \mathit{time} \tag{33}$$

$$\frac{\begin{array}{c}\Gamma\{x:\tau\} \vdash K_1 : B,\ O(1)\ \mathit{time} \\ \Gamma\{x:\tau\} \vdash K_2 : \tau_2,\ O(1)\ \mathit{time} \\ \Gamma\{x:\tau\} \vdash K_3 : \mathit{Bool},\ O(1)\ \mathit{time}\end{array}}{\Gamma\{R:\mathit{set}(\tau)\} \vdash \{[K_1, K_2] : x \in R \mid K_3\} : \mathit{mmap}(B-\mathit{strong}, \tau_2),\ O(\#R)\ \mathit{time}} \tag{34}$$

$$\frac{\begin{array}{c}\Gamma\{x:\tau\} \vdash K_1 : B,\ O(1)\ \mathit{time} \\ \Gamma\{K_1:B\} \vdash K_2 : \tau_2,\ O(1)\ \mathit{time} \\ \Gamma\{x:\tau\} \vdash K_3 : \mathit{Bool},\ O(1)\ \mathit{time}\end{array}}{\Gamma\{R:\mathit{set}(\tau)\} \vdash \{[K_1, K_2] : x \in R \mid K_3\} : \mathit{smap}(B-\mathit{strong}, \tau_2),\ O(\#R)\ \mathit{time}} \tag{35}$$

$$\frac{\forall i \in I :\ C_i,\ O(t_i)\ \mathit{time}}{\biguplus_{i\in I} C_i,\ O(\sum_{i\in I} t_i)\ \mathit{time}} \tag{36}$$

Other Simple Inference Rules

$$\frac{\begin{array}{c} A_1,\ O(t_1)\ time \\ A_2,\ O(t_2)\ time \end{array}}{A_1; A_2,\ O(t_1 + t_2)\ time} \tag{37}$$

$$\frac{\begin{array}{c} A_1 = exp_1,\ O(t_1)\ time \\ A_2 = exp_2(A_3),\ O(t_2)\ time \end{array}}{\text{let } A_1 = exp_1 \text{ in } A_2 = exp_2(A_1), O(t_1 + t_2[A_3/A_1])\ time} \tag{38}$$

$$\frac{\begin{array}{c} A_1,\ O(t_1)\ time \\ t_1 \ = \ O(t_2) \end{array}}{A_1,\ O(t_2)\ time} \tag{39}$$

$$\#\{x : \tau \ \in \ S : set(\tau)\}) \mid K : Bool\} \leq \#S \tag{40}$$

$$\frac{\begin{array}{c} \Gamma\{x : \tau\} \ \vdash \ K : B \\ \Gamma \ \vdash \ R : set(\tau) \\ \Gamma \ \vdash \ C = \{[x, K] : \ x \ \in \ R \ \} : smap(\tau, B) \end{array}}{\Gamma \ \vdash \ \sum_{y \ \in \ range \ C} \#(C^{-1}\{y\}) = \#R} \tag{41}$$

$$\frac{\begin{array}{l} \Gamma\{x : \tau\} \ \vdash \ K_1 : B,\ O(1)\ time \\ \Gamma\{x : \tau\} \ \vdash \ K_2 : \tau_2,\ O(1)\ time \\ \Gamma\{x : \tau\} \ \vdash \ K_3 : Bool,\ O(1)\ time \end{array}}{\begin{array}{c} \Gamma\{R : set(\tau)\} \ \vdash \ C = \{[K_1, K_2] : x \in R \mid K_3 \ \} : \\ mmap_{\text{one-to-few}}(B - strong, \tau_2) \end{array}} \quad \begin{array}{l} \text{where } \lambda x.K_1 \\ \text{is few-to-one} \end{array} \tag{42}$$

$$\frac{\Gamma \ \vdash \ C : mmap_{\text{one-to-few}}(B - strong, \tau)}{\Gamma\{x : \tau\} \ \vdash \ \#C\{x\} = O(1)} \tag{43}$$

APPENDIX 2 SAMPLE PROOF OF CORRECTNESS

We use a *Definition Schema* similar to the one defined in Suppes (1972) for set expressions. This *schema* defines the semantics for a basic set expression.

Definition 21 $y = \{ \ x : \varphi(x) \ \} \iff [(\forall x)(x \in y \iff \varphi(x))]$

Note, that this *definition schema* is a simplified version of the one provided in Suppes (1972). We make the assumption that all sets in the language are finite and well defined, in order to use this simplified definition.

The next *schema* provides a more flexible form of definition by abstraction.

Definition 22

$$\{\tau(x_1,\ldots,x_n) : \varphi(x_1,\ldots,x_n)\} =$$
$$\{y : (\exists x_1)\ldots(\exists x_n)(y = \tau(x_1,\ldots,x_n) \wedge \varphi(x_1,\ldots,x_n))\}$$

Definition 23 *domain* $A = \{x : (\exists y)([x,y] \in A)\}$

and

Definition 24 *range* $A = \{y : (\exists x)([x,y] \in A)\}$

The following theorems will be very useful for our proofs.

Theorem 25 $y \in \{x : \varphi(x)\} \Rightarrow \varphi(y)$

Theorem 26 $(\forall x)(\varphi(x) \iff \psi(x)) \Rightarrow \{x : \varphi(x)\} = \{x : \psi(x)\}$

Using these definitions and theorems, we provide a proof of correctness for the transformation defined in *case 1*. Query $Q = \{[x,y] \in X \times Y | K_1(x,y) \wedge K_2(x)\ \}$ is transformed into

```
let
```
$$Q_1 = \{\ x \in X | K_2(x)\ \}$$
```
in
```
$$Q_2 = \{[x,y] \in Q_1 \times Y | K_1(x,y)\ \}.$$

We show the correctness of the transformation by proving $Q = Q_2$.
Using Definition 22

$$\begin{aligned} & \{[x,y] \in X \times Y | K_1(x,y) \wedge K_2(x)\ \} \\ = \ & \{z : (\exists x)(\exists y)(z = [x,y] \wedge x \in X \wedge y \in Y \wedge K_1(x,y) \wedge K_2(x))\}, \end{aligned}$$

$$\begin{aligned} & \{x \in X | K_2(x)\} \\ = \ & \{x : (x \in X \wedge K_2(x))\} \end{aligned}$$

and

$$\begin{aligned} & \{[x,y] \in Q_1 \times Y | K_1(x,y) \wedge K_2(x)\ \} \\ = \ & \{z : (\exists x)(\exists y)(z = [x,y] \wedge x \in Q_1 \wedge y \in Y \wedge K_1(x,y))\}. \end{aligned}$$

Using Theorem 26, we see that it is sufficient to prove that $\forall z$:

$$\begin{aligned} & (\exists x)(\exists y)(z = [x,y] \wedge x \in X \wedge y \in Y \wedge K_1(x,y) \wedge K_2(x)) \\ \iff \ & (\exists x)(\exists y)(z = [x,y] \wedge x \in Q_1 \wedge y \in Y \wedge K_1(x,y)). \end{aligned} \tag{44}$$

But using Definition 21

$$\begin{array}{ll} & Q_1 = \{x : (x \in X \wedge K_2(x))\} \\ \iff & [(\forall x)(x \in Q_1 \iff x \in X \wedge K_2(x))]. \end{array} \tag{45}$$

Substituting $(x \in X \wedge K_2(x))$ for $(x \in Q_1)$ in the right hand side of (44), we get the result.

APPENDIX 3 SAMPLE COMPLEXITY PROOF

Here we provide a sample complexity derivation for *case 1* where under the assumption that Q_2 is a linear time query, we prove that Q is also a linear time query.

$$\dfrac{\dfrac{\dfrac{\begin{array}{c}\Gamma\{x : B_1\} \vdash K_2 \\ : Bool, O(1)\ time\end{array}}{\begin{array}{c}\Gamma\{X : set(B_1)\} \vdash \\ Q_1 = \{x \in X | K_2(x)\} \\ : set(B_1), O(\#X)\ time\end{array}} \qquad \begin{array}{c}Q_2 = \{[x, y] \in A \times Y | K_1(x, y)\}, \\ O(\#A + \#Y + \#Q_2)\ time\end{array}}{\begin{array}{c}\text{let } Q_1 = \{x \in X | K_2(x)\} \text{ in} \\ Q_2 = \{[x, y] \in Q_1 \times Y | K_1(x, y)\}, \\ O(\#X + \#Q_1 + \#Y + \#Q_2)\ time\end{array}} \qquad \dfrac{\begin{array}{c}\dfrac{\begin{array}{c}\#Q_1 \leq \#X, \\ \#Q_2 = \#Q\end{array}}{\begin{array}{c}\vdots \\ \text{complexity} \\ \text{rules} \\ \vdots\end{array}}\end{array}}{\begin{array}{c}\#X + \#Q_1 + \#Y + \#Q_2 = \\ O(\#X + \#Y + \#Q)\end{array}}}{\begin{array}{c}\text{let } Q_1 = \{x \in X | K_2(x)\} \text{ in } Q_2 = \{[x, y] \in Q_1 \times Y | K_1(x, y)\}, \\ O(\#X + \#Y + \#Q)\ time\end{array}} \tag{46}$$

BIOGRAPHIES

Deepak Goyal is currently a Ph.D. student at the Courant Institute, New York University. He received his Bachelor's degree in Computer Science from the Indian Institute of Technology, at Delhi in India and an M.S. in Computer Science from New York University. His current research interests are in the areas of program transformations, algorithms and distributed computing.

Robert Paige received his Ph.D. in Computer Science in 1979 from New York University, Courant Institute, where he is currently a Professor of Computer Science. His research is in the areas of program transformations, programming languages, compilers, software engineering, and algorithms.

16

Predicative Semantics of Loops

Theodore S. Norvell
Faculty of Engineering
Memorial University of Newfoundland
St. John's NF
A1B 3X5
Canada
theo@engr.mun.ca
www.engr.mun.ca/~theo/

Abstract

A predicative semantics is a mapping of programs to predicates. These predicates characterize sets of acceptable observations. The presence of time in the observations makes the obvious weakest fixed-point semantics of iterative constructs unacceptable. This paper proposes an alternative. We will see that this alternative semantics is monotone and implementable (feasible). Finally a programming theorem for iterative constructs is proposed, proved, and demonstrated. A novel aspect of this theorem is that it is *not* based on invariants.

Keywords

Predicative semantics, fixedpoint semantics, recursion, loops, refinement calculi.

0 FORMALIZATION

0.0 Specifications and refinement

Define **xnat** as the set of all natural numbers (**nat**) joined with an additional object ∞. We will suppose the following properties of ∞: it is larger than any natural number; $\infty + i = \infty - i = \infty$, for all natural numbers i; and $\infty - \infty = 0$.

I will use a 'batch' model for specifications borrowed, in most respects, from (Hehner 1993). Let Σ be any type (a nonempty set). I will call the members of Σ 'states', which is suggestive of imperative programming, but the actual contents of Σ will only be relevant in the examples. *Specifications* are functions of type

$$\Sigma \to \mathbf{xnat} \to \Sigma \to \mathbf{xnat} \to \mathbf{bool} \quad .$$

For example, $(\lambda\sigma : \Sigma, \tau : \mathsf{xnat}, \sigma' : \Sigma, \tau' : \mathsf{xnat} \cdot \tau' \geq \tau \wedge \sigma' = \sigma)$ is a specification.

The variables $\sigma, \sigma' : \Sigma$ and $\tau, \tau' : \mathsf{xnat}$ will be used in writing specifications follows: for any expression E, I write $\langle E \rangle$ for the abstraction of E with respect to these variables. For example, $\langle \tau' \geq \tau \wedge \sigma' = \sigma \rangle$ is an abbreviation for the specification $(\lambda\sigma : \Sigma, \tau : \mathsf{xnat}, \sigma' : \Sigma, \tau' : \mathsf{xnat} \cdot \tau' \geq \tau \wedge \sigma' = \sigma)$. The variables are used as follows: σ and σ' represent the initial and final states while τ, and τ' represent the initial and final times. Thus the specification $\langle \tau' \geq \tau \wedge \sigma' = \sigma \rangle$ specifies that the final time is no less than the initial time and the final state is the same as the initial state.

All boolean operators ($\top$, $\bot$, $\wedge$, $\vee$, $\neg$, $\equiv$, $\not\equiv$, $\Rightarrow$, $\Leftarrow$)lift to the specification level; for example, if P and Q are specifications, $P \Rightarrow Q$ is the specification

$$\langle P.\sigma.\tau.\sigma'.\tau' \Rightarrow Q.\sigma.\tau.\sigma'.\tau' \rangle \quad .$$

I use the symbols $\top$ and $\bot$ as the boolean constants true and false.

Refinement is defined as

$$(P \sqsubseteq Q) \equiv (\forall \sigma, \tau, \sigma', \tau' \cdot P.\sigma.\tau.\sigma'.\tau' \Leftarrow Q.\sigma.\tau.\sigma'.\tau') \quad .$$

Equality of specifications is extensional

$$(P = Q) \equiv (P \sqsubseteq Q) \wedge (Q \sqsubseteq P) \quad .$$

0.1 Discussion

This formalization applies equally to imperative programming and to functional programming. In imperative programming Σ is a set of states and in functional programming Σ is a set of values.

The use of predicates as specifications follows (Hehner 1984), (Hoare 1985), (Hehner 1993), (Hoare 1994), and (v. Karger and Hoare 1994).

The treatment of time is based on (Hehner 1993) and (Hehner 1994). It is necessary to include the infinity value in the time domain in order to deal with infinite loops. Because a statement may sequentially follow an infinite loop, **xnat** is used both for the initial and final states. Time is considered a quantity orthogonal to state; this simplifies the writing of specifications, but as we will see, it complicates the theory somewhat. Using the algebra of **xnat** requires some care, as some laws of **nat** do not hold unconditionally.

The use of predicates is reminiscent of the Z method (Spivey 1989), but the notion of refinement in Z is quite different and much harder to work with. More relevant are refinement calculi based on predicate transformers (Back and von Wright 1990) and (Morgan 1990). Binary predicates ordered by refinement are order isomorphic to the universally conjunctive predicate transformers (Holt 1991).

0.2 Bounds and classes of specifications

A specification P is said to be *progressive* if

$$\langle \tau' \geq \tau \rangle \sqsubseteq P \quad ,$$

and to be *implementable* if

$$(\forall \sigma, \tau \cdot (\exists \sigma', \tau' \cdot P.\sigma.\tau.\sigma'.\tau')) \quad .$$

The term *feasible* is also used in the literature —e.g. (Morgan 1990)— for this property of specifications.

A specification P is called a *condition* if it does not depend on its latter two arguments. An expression B is called a *condition*, if $\langle B \rangle$ is a condition.

A function g of type $\Sigma \to \textsf{xnat} \to \textsf{xnat}$ is called a *bound* of a specification R if

$$\langle \tau' \leq \tau + g.\sigma.\tau \rangle \sqsubseteq R \quad .$$

A specification R is said to be *strongly bounded* if it has a natural bound:

$$(\exists g : \Sigma \to \textsf{xnat} \to \textsf{nat} \cdot \langle \tau' \leq \tau + g.\sigma.\tau \rangle \sqsubseteq R) \quad .$$

Such a specification guarantees termination after a finite amount of time.

For a given specification R, we can consider the set of all bounds:

$$\{g : \Sigma \to \textsf{xnat} \to \textsf{xnat} \mid \langle \tau' \leq \tau + g.\sigma.\tau \rangle \sqsubseteq R\} \quad .$$

This set may be ordered pointwise: $(g \leq h) \equiv (\forall \sigma, \tau \cdot g.\sigma.\tau \leq h.\sigma.\tau)$. For an implementable and progressive R, this set will have a minimum member m_R characterized by

$$m_R.\sigma.\tau = (\max \sigma', \tau' \mid R.\sigma.\tau.\sigma'.\tau' \cdot \tau' - \tau) \quad .$$

Henceforth the subscript on m will be omitted if it is the letter R. The key property of m is that a computation, starting in state σ at time τ, could take as long as $m.\sigma.\tau$:

$$(\forall \sigma, \tau \cdot (\exists \sigma', \tau' \cdot R.\sigma.\tau.\sigma'.\tau' \wedge \tau' = m.\sigma.\tau + \tau)) \quad . \tag{0}$$

If m does not depend on its second argument, we say that R is *time-insensitively bounded.*

Specifications that make no demands about the final state, when the initial time is ∞ are called *reasonable.* We want to allow reasonable specifications to be progressive. Define

$$Z = \langle \tau = \infty = \tau' \rangle$$

a specification R is said to be reasonable iff

$$R = Z \vee R \quad .$$

0.3 Semantics

The semantics of programming constructs is given by defining the simple constructs as specifications and compound constructs as functions from (one or more) specifications to specifications. A program can then be defined as a specification built using only the programing constructs.

Some straight-line programming constructs are defined by:

$$skip = \langle \sigma' = \sigma \wedge \tau' = \tau \rangle$$

$$tick = \langle \sigma' = \sigma \wedge \tau' = \tau + 1 \rangle$$

$$P; Q = \langle \exists \hat{\sigma}, \hat{\tau} \cdot P.\sigma.\tau.\hat{\sigma}.\hat{\tau} \wedge Q.\hat{\sigma}.\hat{\tau}.\sigma'.\tau' \rangle$$

$$\textbf{if } B \textbf{ then } P \textbf{ else } Q = (\langle B \rangle \wedge P) \vee (\neg \langle B \rangle \wedge Q) \quad .$$

In the if-statement, it will be assumed that B is a condition. The *tick* construct is not really a programming construct, but is useful in defining the **while** loop.

It should be noted that these definitions hold for P and Q being any specifications, not only those formed from programming constructs.

For condition B and specification P define a function $w_{B,P}$ by

$$w_{B,P}.Q = \textbf{if } B \textbf{ then}(P; tick; Q) \textbf{ else } skip \tag{1}$$

Let $W_{B,P}$ stand for **while** B **do** P. Henceforth the subscripts on w and W will be omitted where they are the letters B, P. As in (Norvell 1993) and (Norvell 1994) I define the while loop by three axioms

Progression: $\langle \tau' \geq \tau \rangle \sqsubseteq W$
Post-fixed-point: $w.W \sqsubseteq W$

Induction: $((\tau' \geq \tau) \sqsubseteq Q) \wedge (w.Q \sqsubseteq Q) \Rightarrow (W \sqsubseteq Q) \qquad$, for all Q.

This definition of the while-loop is called the *weakest progressive post-fixed-point* definition. The lattice of progressive specifications is complete and thus we may apply the Knaster-Tarski (Tarski 1955) theorem to tell us that W is well defined, that it is a fixed-point:

$$w.W = W \quad , \tag{2}$$

and that it is the weakest of the fixed-points:

$$((\tau' \geq \tau) \sqsubseteq Q) \wedge (w.Q = Q) \Rightarrow (W \sqsubseteq Q) \qquad \text{, for all } Q.$$

As an alternative, but equivalent, definition, it is possible to replace the post-fixed-point and the induction axioms with these last two formula.

0.4 Discussion

It should be noted that the only action among the statements presented so far that is considered to take any time at all is the backward jump of the while loop. The "time" calculated for programs under this model is not proportional to the actual time that an implementation would take. However it does give the correct order for time complexities if all primitive operations are $O(1)$. This is not the only alternative, it is possible to use a semantics that keeps more careful track of time. Further discussion can be found in (Hehner 1994).

The importance of the progression axiom and the corresponding antecedent in the post-fixed-point axiom is that simply taking the weakest fixed-point of the equation

$$W = \textbf{if } B \textbf{ then}(P; \textit{tick}; W) \textbf{ else } \textit{skip}$$

would not result in a construct that is closed under progressiveness. For example, with the current definition we have

$$(\tau' = \infty) \sqsubseteq \textbf{while } \top \textbf{ do } \textit{skip} \quad .$$

However, with the weakest fixed-point semantics, such a loop would not even be progressive. The difference between these approaches is manifested for (potentially) infinite loops, and one may wonder if these are worth the trouble. With the limited notion of observations used in this paper (initial and final states only), the point is arguable. However, for communicating programs, which can be modeled using a slightly richer notion of observations, (potentially) infinite loops are of great importance.

It might seem that it would be easier to simply work within the lattice of progressive specifications or even the semilattice of progressive and implementable specifications. From a semantic point of view, this may be true. But from the point of view of specifying, it is simplest if specifications are simply predicates with no restrictions. Also the progressive specifications are not closed under negation, so this would restrict the ways in which specifications are composed.

1 ESSENTIAL THEOREMS

Compound programming constructs are generally monotonic with respect to refinement and preserve implementability and progressiveness. Both these properties hold for the **while** loop as defined above.

We start by showing monotonicity.

Theorem 0 *For any condition B, and specifications P and Q, if $P \sqsubseteq Q$, then*

$$\textbf{while}\, B\, \textbf{do}\, P \sqsubseteq \textbf{while}\, B\, \textbf{do}\, Q \quad .$$

Monotonicity is not hard to prove and illustrates all three axioms at work.

$$W_{B,P} \sqsubseteq W_{B,Q}$$

$\Leftarrow$ " Induction axiom with Q instantiated by $W_{B,Q}$. "

$$(\langle \tau' \geq \tau \rangle \sqsubseteq W_{B,Q}) \wedge (w_{B,P}.W_{B,Q} \sqsubseteq W_{B,Q})$$

$\equiv$ " Progression axiom ($\tau' \geq \tau \sqsubseteq W_{B,Q}$) and prop. calc. "

$$w_{B,P}.W_{B,Q} \sqsubseteq W_{B,Q}$$

$\Leftarrow$ " Post-fixpoint axiom ($w_{B,Q}.W_{B,Q} \sqsubseteq W_{B,Q}$) and transitivity of $\sqsubseteq$."

$$w_{B,P}.W_{B,Q} \sqsubseteq w_{B,Q}.W_{B,Q}$$

$\equiv$ " Definition of w (1). "

$$\textbf{if}\, B\, \textbf{then}(P; \mathit{tick}; W_{B,Q}) \sqsubseteq \textbf{if}\, B\, \textbf{then}(Q; \mathit{tick}; W_{B,Q})$$

$\Leftarrow$ " Monotonicity of **if** and ; . "

$$P \sqsubseteq Q$$

Next we show that progressiveness and implementability are jointly preserved.

Theorem 1 *For any condition B, and specification P, if*

P is progressive and
P is implementable,

then **while** B **do** P *is progressive and implementable.*

The proof is given in appendix 0. This proof also shows that progressiveness is preserved on its own.

2 A PROGRAMMING THEOREM

Among the most useful of the theorems in a refinement calculus are those of the form "if ... then $R \sqsubseteq c.P_0.P_1.\cdots.P_{n-1}$" where c is a program constructor. For example, in the theory used in this paper $R \sqsubseteq$ **if** B **then**$(\langle B\rangle \Rightarrow R)$ **else**$(\neg\langle B\rangle \Rightarrow R)$ is a useful theorem.

In order to derive programs involving while-loops, we would like to have theorems that conclude with $R \sqsubseteq$ **while** B **do** P. In most refinement calculi, such theorems are usually based on invariants. In (Hehner 1979) the idea of "recursive refinement" instead of invariants is suggested. In this section we propose a theorem based on recursive refinement.

A specification R is said to be *recursively refined* if

$$R \sqsubseteq \textbf{if } B \textbf{ then}(P; \mathit{tick}; R) \textbf{ else } \mathit{skip} \tag{3}$$

It is often true that when (3) is true, it is also true that

$$R \sqsubseteq \textbf{while } B \textbf{ do } P \tag{4}$$

So the question arises of under what conditions (3) implies (4). The next theorem presents one possible set of conditions.

Theorem 2 *For any condition B, and specifications P and R, if*

P is progressive;
R is implementable, strongly bounded, time insensitively bounded, and reasonable; and
R is recursively refined:

$$R \sqsubseteq \textbf{if } B \textbf{ then}(P; \mathit{tick}; R) \textbf{ else } \mathit{skip} \tag{5}$$

then $R \sqsubseteq$ **while** B **do** P.

The proof of this is by induction and is given in appendix 1.

2.0 Discussion

It is informative to look at why additional conditions are required beyond (5) are required.

Here is a simple counter example showing that (5) does not imply $R \sqsubseteq \mathbf{while}\, B\, \mathbf{do}\, P$. Take P to be *skip* and B to be $\top$. We have

$$\bot \sqsubseteq \mathbf{if}\ \top\ \mathbf{then}(\mathit{skip}; \mathit{tick}; \bot)\ \mathbf{else}\ \mathit{skip} \quad .$$

But it is certainly not the case that

$$\bot \sqsubseteq \mathbf{while}\ \top\ \mathbf{do}\ \mathit{skip}$$

as this would mean that the while loop is unimplementable. Yet we know from the Theorem 1 and the fact that *skip* is progressive and implementable that the while loop is also implementable.

In (Hehner 1993) it is suggested that recursive refinement is only a valid programming method for implementable specifications. What if we restrict R to be an implementable specification? Again we are disappointed. Consider the following 'monster'. It is true that

$$\langle \sigma' = 0 \rangle \sqsubseteq \mathbf{if}\ \top\ \mathbf{then}(\mathit{skip}; \mathit{tick}; \langle \sigma' = 0 \rangle)\ \mathbf{else}\ \mathit{skip}$$

and that

$$\langle \sigma' = 1 \rangle \sqsubseteq \mathbf{if}\ \top\ \mathbf{then}(\mathit{skip}; \mathit{tick}; \langle \sigma' = 1 \rangle)\ \mathbf{else}\ \mathit{skip} \quad .$$

Yet, if it were true both that

$$\langle \sigma' = 0 \rangle \sqsubseteq \mathbf{while}\ \top\ \mathbf{do}\ \mathit{skip}$$

and

$$\langle \sigma' = 1 \rangle \sqsubseteq \mathbf{while}\ \top\ \mathbf{do}\ \mathit{skip} \quad ,$$

we would have to conclude that

$$\bot \sqsubseteq \langle \sigma' = 0 \wedge \sigma' = 1 \rangle \sqsubseteq \mathbf{while}\ \top\ \mathbf{do}\ \mathit{skip} \quad .$$

Again this contradicts the implementability of **while** loops.

The problem illustrated in this example occurs basically because the loop is infinite. By adding the requirement of strong bounding, infinite loops are eliminated. The requirements that P be progressive and that the minimum bound is not sensitive to the starting time ensure that the induction goes through.

The requirement that R be reasonable is the most troubling, as it requires one to write specifications in a way that one otherwise would not. This requirement is necessary because the induction does not work when the initial time is ∞. One solution to this problem is to use the ordinal numbers as the time domain rather than **xnat**. The problem with this 'solution' is that the proof of Theorem 1 no longer goes through. Other solutions might involve changing the definitions of refinement or of the programming constructs, or removing the orthogonality of time and state (i.e. treat specifications as binary relations on $(\Sigma \times \mathbf{nat}) \cup \{\infty\}$). Such changes are rather undesirable as the simplicity of these definitions is an important attribute of the predicative programming approach.

A somewhat similar theorem appears in (Sekerinski 1993). However the definition of the programming connectives (e.g. sequential composition) is different and the theorem can only be used to show that a specification is a fixed-point. From a programming point of view, this is less satisfactory as one is not so much interested in whether a while loop equals a given specification, but rather whether it implements the specification at hand.

3 A PROGRAMMING EXAMPLE

In imperative programming, Σ consists of states, which may be considered functions from program variable names to values. This function can be extended to expressions. For any program variable name x, and expression E the assignment statement can be defined as

$$x := E \quad = \quad \langle \sigma'.x = \sigma.E \land (\forall y \in \mathrm{dom}.\sigma \mid x \neq y \cdot \sigma'.y = \sigma.y) \land \tau' = \tau \rangle$$

where $\mathrm{dom}.\sigma$ is the set of variable names.

In this section, for any program variable name such as x, I will use the convention of writing x in specifications rather than $\sigma.x$ and of writing x' rather than $\sigma'.x$. With this convention the assignment is simply

$$x := E \quad = \quad \langle x' = E \land y' = y \land \cdots \land \tau' = \tau \rangle \qquad .$$

where the $\cdots$ depends on what variables are in the domain of the states. We have the following useful substitution law

$$x := E; \langle P \rangle \quad = \quad \langle P^x_E \rangle \qquad , \tag{6}$$

provided P is written with the convention. There is an analogous law for the time variable

$$tick; \langle P \rangle \quad = \quad \langle P^{\tau}_{\tau+1} \rangle \qquad . \tag{7}$$

I will solve a trivial programming example in two ways, illustrating the relationship of recursive refinement to the invariant method. The problem is that of finding the product of the elements in an array A of size N. The specification is

$$S = \langle s' = (\Pi i \in \{0,..N\} \cdot A.i) \wedge \tau' \leq \tau + N \rangle \vee Z$$

I will write $\{i,..k\}$ for the set of all integers j, such that $i \leq j < k$ and $\{i,..,k\}$ for the set of all integers j, such that $i \leq j \leq k$. The "$\vee Z$" part of the specification is required to satisfy the condition of 'reasonableness'. The predicate Z was defined in Section 0.2.

3.0 A solution that does not use an invariant

We can refine S using the substitution law (supposing x is of type $\{0,..,N\}$):

$$S \sqsubseteq s, x := 1, 0; R0 \qquad ,$$

where

$$R0 = \langle s' = s \times (\Pi i \in \{x,..N\} \cdot A.i) \wedge \tau' \leq \tau + N - x \rangle \vee Z \qquad .$$

This is refined by cases

$$R0 \sqsubseteq \mathbf{if}\ x < N\ \mathbf{then} (\langle x < N \rangle \Rightarrow R0)\ \mathbf{else}\ skip \qquad .$$

Now we can refine the remaining specification:

$$\begin{array}{ll} & \langle x < N \rangle \Rightarrow R0 \\ \sqsubseteq & \quad \text{“ Splitting the product. ”} \\ & \left\langle \begin{array}{ll} & s' = s \times A.x \times (\Pi i \in \{x+1,..N\} \cdot A.i) \\ \wedge & \tau' \leq \tau + 1 + N - (x+1) \end{array} \right\rangle \vee Z \\ = & \quad \text{“ Substitution (6) and (7). ”} \\ & s, x := s \times A.x, x+1; tick; R0 \qquad . \end{array}$$

Putting these results together (by the monotonicity of **if**) we get

$$R0 \sqsubseteq \textbf{if } x < N \textbf{ then}(s, x := s \times A.x, x+1; tick; R0) \textbf{ else } skip \quad .$$

Since all the conditions of Theorem 2 are met, we may conclude

$$R0 \sqsubseteq \textbf{while } x < N \textbf{ do } s, x := s \times A.x, x+1 \quad .$$

3.1 A solution using an invariant

It should be noted that nowhere in the above development, nor even in the thinking behind it, did the formula

$$s = (\Pi i \in \{0, ..x\} \cdot A.i)$$

appear. This is the invariant that would be used if the invariant method were used. Recursive refinement does not exclude the use of invariants and, in the development of many loops, it is the simplest method.

Using substitution, and some simplification, we could also refine S by

$$S \sqsubseteq s, x := 1, 0; R1$$

where $R1$ is

$$\langle s = (\Pi i \in \{0, ..x\} \cdot A.i) \Rightarrow s' = (\Pi i \in \{0, ..N\} \cdot A.i) \wedge \tau' \leq \tau + N - x \rangle \vee Z.$$

As with $R0$ we can derive that

$$R1 \sqsubseteq \textbf{if } x < N \textbf{ then}(s, x := s \times A.x, x+1; tick; R1) \textbf{ else } skip \quad ,$$

although the reasoning is a little more involved. Again the Theorem 2 can be applied.

We can recognize that the $R1$ has the form of a precondition $s = (\Pi i \in \{0, ..x\} \cdot A.i)$ and a postrelation $s' = (\Pi i \in \{0, ..N\} \cdot A.i) \wedge \tau' \leq \tau + N - x$, and that the precondition is a loop invariant, but there is no real need to think in these terms.

3.2 Views and refinement by parts

It may seem unpleasant to carry the specification of the time bound around while deriving a recursive refinement. However, it is not necessary to consider all parts of a specification while deriving a refinement for it. If f is a monotone function of specifications, then

$$(T \wedge U \sqsubseteq f.(V \wedge W)) \Leftarrow (T \sqsubseteq f.V) \wedge (U \sqsubseteq f.W) \quad .$$

In particular it may be useful to *derive* a recursive refinement for only the part of the specification that does not deal with time and then *check* that the same recursive refinement applies to the remainder of the specification.

For example $R0$ can be split into two 'views': $R0 = T \wedge U$

$$\begin{array}{rcl} T & = & \langle s' = s \times (\Pi i \in \{x, ..N\} \cdot A.i\rangle \vee Z \\ U & = & \langle \tau' \leq \tau + N - x\rangle \vee Z \end{array}$$

We can then derive that

$$T \sqsubseteq \textbf{if } x < N \textbf{ then}(s, x := A.x, x+1; \textit{tick}; T) \textbf{ else } \textit{skip}$$

and check that

$$U \sqsubseteq \textbf{if } x < N \textbf{ then}(s, x := A.x, x+1; \textit{tick}; U) \textbf{ else } \textit{skip} \quad .$$

This gives us that

$$R0 \sqsubseteq \textbf{if } x < N \textbf{ then}(s, x := A.x, x+1; \textit{tick}; R0) \textbf{ else } \textit{skip} \quad .$$

4 CALCULATING THE LOOPS.

Weakest prespecification (Hoare and He 1987) is defined as

$$S \swarrow U = \langle \forall \hat{\sigma}, \hat{\tau} \cdot U.\sigma'.\tau'.\hat{\sigma}.\hat{\tau} \Rightarrow S.\sigma.\tau.\hat{\sigma}.\hat{\tau}\rangle \quad . \tag{8}$$

The key property of the weakest prespecification is this Galois connection:

$$(S \swarrow U \sqsubseteq T) \equiv (S \sqsubseteq T; U) \quad . \tag{9}$$

Suppose one has an R that is implementable, strongly bounded, time insensitively bounded, and reasonable. The remaining condition on R, that of recursive refinement, is equivalent to the conjunction

$$(R \sqsubseteq \langle \neg B\rangle \wedge \textit{skip}) \tag{10}$$

$$\wedge \quad (((\langle B\rangle \Rightarrow R) \swarrow (\textit{tick}; R) \sqsubseteq P) \tag{11}$$

So one can find a suitable loop implementation for R by first finding a B such that (10) (of course, the stronger this B is, the better) and then using as a loop body $P = \langle \tau' \geq \tau \rangle \wedge (\langle B \rangle \Rightarrow R)_{\swarrow}\!\!/(tick; R)$, which is the weakest, progressive specification satisfying (11). Any refinement method can then be attempted to refine P by a program.

The first step, that of searching for a suitable B, can also be made more calculational. One can start with $\neg R.\sigma.\tau.\sigma.\tau$, which is the strongest solution of (10), and then weaken until a condition is found that is easily implemented.

5 CONCLUSION AND FUTURE WORK.

I have presented a semantics for iteration within a particular version of the refinement calculus. This semantics has been shown to enjoy the properties one would expect and also to give interesting results for infinite loops that suggest applications for communicating processes. From the semantics, I have proved a theorem that allows it to be used in the derivation of programs.

The proofs are done in a calculational and point-free style.

Although the notation used is suggestive of imperative programming, the results are equally applicable to functional programming — program variables are only introduced in the examples.

As mentioned above, one of the prime motivations for the weakest progressive post-fixed-point definition of while loops is to accommodate communicating processes. In this case observations would consist not only of an initial and final state, but also a history of communications. Thus generalizing these results to this more general setting is important.

Once processes may interact, potentially infinite loops become of greater interest and the restriction to strong bounding is too severe. The search for such programming theorems will be the subject of future research.

The work so far has concentrated on while loops, but the results should be extendible to any set of mutually recursive subroutines.

The relationship to (v. Karger and Hoare 1994) is intriguing. In that paper a very abstract calculus of specifications is presented. The principal difference between their calculus and relational calculus is the replacement of the converse operator by a relative converse operator. This prevents the formation of specifications that "undo". This is the same motivation for restricting our attention to the lattice of progressive specifications and forming fixed-points within that lattice.

6 ACKNOWLEDGMENTS

Thanks are due to Eric Hehner for many discussions and comments, to the referees for helpful comments, to NSERC for funding, and to the Faculty of

Engineering, Memorial University of Newfoundland, for equipment, location, and funding.

APPENDIX 0 PROOF OF THE IMPLEMENTABILITY THEOREM 1

(This appendix represents joint work with Eric Hehner.)

Given an implementable and progressive P we must show that

$$W = \mathbf{while}\, B\, \mathbf{do}\, P$$

too is implementable and progressive.

Throughout this appendix specification P will be assumed to be implementable and progressive. Rather than work with P, I will work with $P0 = P; \mathit{tick}$. $P0$ is also implementable and progressive.

By the progression axiom, we know that $W = \mathbf{while}\, B\, \mathbf{do}\, P$ is progressive. The question remains whether it is implementable.

Suppose we can find an implementable Q that is also progressive and such that

$$\mathbf{if}\, B\, \mathbf{then}(P0; Q)\, \mathbf{else}\, \mathit{skip} \sqsubseteq Q \quad .$$

The induction axiom tells us that $W \sqsubseteq Q$. Since any specification that is refined by an implementable specification must itself be implementable, this would imply that W is implementable. Thus the goal becomes: find a Q that is implementable, progressive, and a post-fixed-point.

There must be at least one progressive fixed-point. We know this because W is one example. In the following let S be any progressive fixed-point:

$$\begin{aligned} \tau' \geq \tau &\sqsubseteq S & (12)\\ S &= \mathbf{if}\, B\, \mathbf{then}(P0; S)\, \mathbf{else}\, \mathit{skip} \quad . & (13)\end{aligned}$$

S may or may not be implementable. We define a condition D to identify the initial states for which S accepts no final state:

$$D \equiv \neg(\exists \sigma', \tau' \cdot S.\sigma.\tau.\sigma'.\tau') \quad . \tag{14}$$

Now define Q as

$$Q = S \vee (\langle D \wedge \tau' = \infty \rangle) \quad . \tag{15}$$

It is clear that Q is implementable and progressive. We need only prove that it is a post-fixed-point.

To do this I will use two lemmata to be proved later:

$$\langle B\rangle \sqsubseteq \langle D\rangle \tag{16}$$

$$\langle D\rangle \wedge P0; X = \langle D\rangle \wedge P0; ((\langle D\rangle \wedge X) \quad , \tag{17}$$

for any X. Both follow from the fact that S is a fixed-point and will be proved later.

We prove that Q is a post-fixed-point by considering separately D true and D false. First for D true:

$$
\begin{array}{ll}
 & \langle D\rangle \wedge (\mathbf{if}\ B\ \mathbf{then}(P0; Q)\ \mathbf{else}\ \mathit{skip}) \\
= & \quad \text{“ (16) } \langle B\rangle \sqsubseteq \langle D\rangle \text{. ”} \\
 & \langle D\rangle \wedge (P0; Q) \\
= & \quad \text{“ Defn of } Q\text{. ”} \\
 & \langle D\rangle \wedge (P0; (S \vee \langle D \wedge \tau' = \infty\rangle)) \\
= & \quad \text{“ Distribute ; over } \vee \text{. ”} \\
 & \langle D\rangle \wedge ((P0; S) \vee (P0; \langle D \wedge \tau' = \infty\rangle)) \\
= & \quad \text{“ Lemma (16) } \langle B\rangle \sqsubseteq \langle D\rangle \text{ ”} \\
 & \langle D\rangle \wedge ((\mathbf{if}\ B\ \mathbf{then}(P0; S)\ \mathbf{else}\ \mathit{skip}) \vee (P0; \langle D \wedge \tau' = \infty\rangle)) \\
= & \quad \text{“ } S \text{ is a fixed-point. ”} \\
 & \langle D\rangle \wedge (S \vee (P0; \langle D \wedge \tau' = \infty\rangle)) \\
= & \quad \text{“ Lemma (17). ”} \\
 & \langle D\rangle \wedge (S \vee (P0; \langle \tau' = \infty\rangle)) \\
\sqsubseteq & \quad \text{“ } P0 \text{ is implementable. ”} \\
 & \langle D\rangle \wedge (S \vee \langle \tau' = \infty\rangle) \\
= & \quad \text{“ Propositional calculus. ”} \\
 & \langle D\rangle \wedge (S \vee \langle D \wedge \tau' = \infty\rangle) \\
= & \quad \text{“ Defn of } Q\text{. ”} \\
 & \langle D\rangle \wedge Q
\end{array}
$$

Now for D false:

$$
\begin{array}{ll}
 & \neg\langle D\rangle \wedge (\mathbf{if}\ B\ \mathbf{then}(P0; Q)\ \mathbf{else}\ \mathit{skip}) \\
= & \quad \text{“ Defn of } Q\text{. ”} \\
 & \neg\langle D\rangle \wedge (\mathbf{if}\ B\ \mathbf{then}(P0; (S \vee \langle D \wedge \tau' = \infty\rangle))\ \mathbf{else}\ \mathit{skip}) \\
\sqsubseteq & \quad \text{“ Monotonicity. ”} \\
 & \neg\langle D\rangle \wedge (\mathbf{if}\ B\ \mathbf{then}(P0; S)\ \mathbf{else}\ \mathit{skip}) \\
= & \quad \text{“ } S \text{ is a fixed-point. ”}
\end{array}
$$

$$\begin{array}{ll} & \neg\langle D\rangle \wedge S \\ = & \quad \text{“ Propositional calculus .”} \\ & \neg\langle D\rangle \wedge (S \vee \langle D \wedge \tau' = \infty\rangle) \\ = & \quad \text{“ Defn of } Q. \text{ ”} \\ & \neg\langle D\rangle \wedge Q \end{array}$$

From

$$\langle D\rangle \wedge (\mathbf{if}\ B\ \mathbf{then}(P0; Q)\ \mathbf{else}\ skip \sqsubseteq \langle D\rangle \wedge Q$$

and

$$\neg\langle D\rangle \wedge (\mathbf{if}\ B\ \mathbf{then}(P0; Q)\ \mathbf{else}\ skip \sqsubseteq \neg\langle D\rangle \wedge Q$$

we can conclude

$$\mathbf{if}\ B\ \mathbf{then}(P0; Q)\ \mathbf{else}\ skip \sqsubseteq Q \qquad .$$

It remains to prove the two lemmata. We start with (16)

$$\begin{array}{ll} & \langle B\rangle \sqsubseteq \langle D\rangle \\ = & \quad \text{“ Contrapositive. ”} \\ & \neg\langle D\rangle \sqsubseteq \neg\langle B\rangle \\ = & \quad \text{“ Definition of } D. \text{ ”} \\ & \langle \exists\sigma', \tau' \cdot S.\sigma.\tau.\sigma'.\tau'\rangle \sqsubseteq \neg\langle B\rangle \\ = & \quad \text{“ } S \text{ is a fixed-point. ”} \\ & \langle \exists\sigma', \tau' \cdot (\mathbf{if}\ B\ \mathbf{then}(P0; S)\ \mathbf{else}\ skip).\sigma.\tau.\sigma'.\tau'\rangle \sqsubseteq \neg\langle B\rangle \\ = & \quad \text{“ Definition of } \mathbf{if}\text{ . ”} \\ & \langle \exists\sigma', \tau' \cdot skip.\sigma.\tau.\sigma'.\tau'\rangle \sqsubseteq \neg\langle B\rangle \\ = & \quad \text{“ } skip \text{ is implementable. ”} \\ & \top \end{array}$$

It now remains only to prove (17). This follows easily from

$$\langle D'\rangle \sqsubseteq P0 \wedge \langle D\rangle$$

(D' is D with σ and τ replaced by σ' and τ') which is proved by contradiction. Start with the negation:

$$\exists\sigma, \tau, \sigma', \tau' \cdot D \wedge P0.\sigma.\tau.\sigma'.\tau' \wedge \neg D'$$

$\equiv$ " Rename variables. "

$\exists\sigma, \tau, \sigma'', \tau'' \cdot D \wedge P0.\sigma.\tau.\sigma''.\tau'' \wedge \neg D''$

$\equiv$ " Defn D. "

$\exists\sigma, \tau, \sigma'', \tau'' \cdot D \wedge P0.\sigma.\tau.\sigma''.\tau'' \wedge (\exists\sigma', \tau' \cdot S.\sigma''.\tau''.\sigma'.\tau')$

$\equiv$ " Predicate calculus: $\exists$ over $\wedge$. "

$\exists\sigma, \tau, \sigma', \tau', \sigma'', \tau'' \cdot D \wedge P0.\sigma.\tau.\sigma''.\tau'' \wedge S.\sigma''.\tau''.\sigma'.\tau'$

$\equiv$ " Predicate calculus: $\exists$ over $\wedge$. "

$\exists\sigma, \tau, \sigma', \tau' \cdot D \wedge (\exists\sigma'', \tau'' \cdot P0.\sigma.\tau.\sigma''.\tau'' \wedge S.\sigma''.\tau''.\sigma'.\tau')$

$\equiv$ " Definition of ;. "

$\exists\sigma, \tau, \sigma', \tau' \cdot D \wedge (P0; S).\sigma.\tau.\sigma'.\tau'$

$\equiv$ " Lemma (16). "

$\exists\sigma, \tau, \sigma', \tau' \cdot D \wedge (\textbf{if } B \textbf{ then}(P0; S) \textbf{ else } \textit{skip}).\sigma.\tau.\sigma'.\tau'$

$\equiv$ " S is a fixed-point. "

$\exists\sigma, \tau, \sigma', \tau' \cdot D \wedge S.\sigma.\tau.\sigma'.\tau'$

$\equiv$ " Defn D. "

$\exists\sigma, \tau, \sigma', \tau' \cdot \neg(\exists\sigma', \tau' \cdot S.\sigma.\tau.\sigma'.\tau') \wedge S.\sigma.\tau.\sigma'.\tau'$

$\equiv$ " Predicate calculus: $\exists$ over $\wedge$. "

$\exists\sigma, \tau \cdot \neg(\exists\sigma', \tau' \cdot S.\sigma.\tau.\sigma'.\tau') \wedge (\exists\sigma', \tau' \cdot S.\sigma.\tau.\sigma'.\tau')$

$\equiv$ " Contradiction. "

$\perp$

APPENDIX 1 PROOF OF THE WHILE-LOOP THEOREM 2

We will assume

P is progressive;
R is implementable, strongly bounded, time insensitively bounded, and reasonable; and
R is recursively refined:

$$R \sqsubseteq \textbf{if } B \textbf{ then}(P; \textit{tick}; R) \textbf{ else } \textit{skip} \quad .$$

It must be shown that $R \sqsubseteq \textbf{while } B \textbf{ do } P$.

Throughout this appendix condition B and specification P will be assumed to have the properties stated in Theorem 2.

APPENDIX 1.0 $\langle \tau = \infty \rangle$ or $\langle \tau \in \mathsf{nat} \rangle$

Ultimately I want to prove $R \sqsubseteq W$. I will prove this by cases on $\langle \tau = \infty \rangle$; i.e. by proving $R \sqsubseteq \langle \tau = \infty \rangle \wedge W$ and $R \sqsubseteq \langle \tau \in \mathsf{nat} \rangle \wedge W$. I start with the first

$$
\begin{array}{ll}
 & \langle \tau = \infty \rangle \wedge W \\
\sqsupseteq & \quad \text{“ Progression axiom ”} \\
 & \langle \tau = \infty \rangle \wedge \langle \tau' \geq \tau \rangle \\
= & \quad \text{“ } \mathsf{xnat} \text{ arithmetic”} \\
 & \langle \tau = \infty = \tau' \rangle \\
\sqsupseteq & \quad \text{“ Definition of } Z \text{ and generalization”} \\
 & Z \vee R \\
= & \quad \text{“ } R \text{ is reasonable ”} \\
 & R
\end{array}
$$

APPENDIX 1.1 B or $\neg B$

It remains to prove $R \sqsubseteq \langle \tau \in \mathsf{nat} \rangle \wedge W$. I will prove this by cases on $\langle B \rangle$. The easy case is when B is initially false. We do not need to use the fact that τ is finite.

$$
\begin{array}{ll}
 & \neg \langle B \rangle \wedge W \qquad\qquad\qquad\qquad\qquad\qquad\qquad\qquad (18) \\
= & \quad \text{“ } W \text{ is a fixpoint of } w \text{ (2). ”} \\
 & \neg \langle B \rangle \wedge w.W \\
= & \quad \text{“ Definition of } w \text{ (1). ”} \\
 & \neg \langle B \rangle \wedge \mathbf{if}\ B\ \mathbf{then}(P; \mathit{tick}; W)\ \mathbf{else}\ \mathit{skip} \\
= & \quad \text{“ Definition of } \mathbf{if}. \text{ ”} \\
 & \neg \langle B \rangle \wedge \mathit{skip} \\
= & \quad \text{“ Definition of } \mathbf{if}. \text{ ”} \\
 & \neg \langle B \rangle \wedge \mathbf{if}\ B\ \mathbf{then}(P; \mathit{tick}; R)\ \mathbf{else}\ \mathit{skip} \\
= & \quad \text{“ Definition of } w \text{ (1). ”} \\
 & \neg \langle B \rangle \wedge w.R \\
\sqsupseteq & \quad \text{“ } R \text{ is recusively refined (5) and monotonicity of } \wedge . \text{ ”} \\
 & \neg \langle B \rangle \wedge R \\
\sqsupseteq & \quad \text{“ Specialization. ”} \\
 & R \quad .
\end{array}
$$

On the other hand what about the case when B is initially true?

$$
\begin{array}{ll}
 & \langle B\rangle \wedge \langle \tau \in \mathsf{nat}\rangle \wedge W \qquad (19)\\
= & \quad \text{“ } W \text{ is a fixpoint of } w \text{ (2). ”}\\
 & \langle B\rangle \wedge \langle \tau \in \mathsf{nat}\rangle \wedge w.W\\
= & \quad \text{“ Definition of } w \text{ (1). ”}\\
 & \langle B\rangle \wedge \langle \tau \in \mathsf{nat}\rangle \wedge \mathbf{if}\, B\, \mathbf{then}(P; \mathit{tick}; W)\, \mathbf{else}\, \mathit{skip}\\
= & \quad \text{“ Definition of } \mathbf{if}. \text{ ”}\\
 & \langle B\rangle \wedge \langle \tau \in \mathsf{nat}\rangle \wedge (P; \mathit{tick}; W)\\
= & \quad \text{“ } B \wedge \langle \tau \in \mathsf{nat}\rangle \text{ is a condition. ”}\\
 & (\langle B\rangle \wedge \langle \tau \in \mathsf{nat}\rangle \wedge P); \mathit{tick}; W \quad .
\end{array}
$$

At this point we are a little stuck. It is time to bring out the heavy artillery...

APPENDIX 1.2 The repetend decreases the bound more than it spends time.

Here and below, I will write M for the expression $m.\sigma.\tau$, and M' for $m.\sigma'.\tau'$. As R is strongly bounded, M is a natural number (i.e. not ∞); as R is time-insensitively bounded, it does not depend on τ.

We now use our knowledge of R to conclude that P decreases the bound more than it spends time.

$$
\begin{array}{ll}
 & \quad \text{“ Recursive refinement (5) ”}\\
 & R \sqsubseteq w.R\\
= & \quad \text{“ Definition of } w \text{ (1). ”}\\
 & R \sqsubseteq \mathbf{if}\, B\, \mathbf{then}(P; \mathit{tick}; R)\, \mathbf{else}\, \mathit{skip}\\
\Rightarrow & \quad \text{“ Definition of } \mathbf{if}. \text{ ”}\\
 & R \sqsubseteq \langle B\rangle \wedge (P; \mathit{tick}; R)\\
\equiv & \quad \text{“ } B \text{ is a condition. ”}\\
 & R \sqsubseteq (\langle B\rangle \wedge P); \mathit{tick}; R\\
\Rightarrow & \quad \text{“ As } M \text{ is a bound, } \langle \tau' \le \tau + M\rangle \sqsubseteq R\text{; transitivity of } \sqsubseteq . \text{ ”}\\
 & \langle \tau' \le \tau + M\rangle \sqsubseteq (\langle B\rangle \wedge P); \mathit{tick}; R\\
\Rightarrow & \quad \text{“ } R \text{ could take as much time as } M \text{ . ”} \qquad (20)\\
 & \langle \tau' + M' \le \tau + M\rangle \sqsubseteq (\langle B\rangle \wedge P); \mathit{tick}\\
\equiv & \quad \text{“ } M \text{ does not depend on } \tau \text{ ”}\\
 & \langle \tau' + M' + 1 \le \tau + M\rangle \sqsubseteq \langle B\rangle \wedge P \quad . \qquad (21)
\end{array}
$$

The hint at step (20) is an appeal to computational intuition, but can be fleshed out. To do so, we use the weakest prespecification (8).

It will be helpful to restate (0) using different variable names:

$$(\forall \sigma', \tau' \cdot (\exists \dot{\sigma}, \dot{\tau} \cdot R.\sigma'.\tau'.\dot{\sigma}.\dot{\tau} \wedge \dot{\tau} = \tau' + M')) \quad . \tag{22}$$

We can now calculate:

$$\begin{array}{ll} & \langle \tau' \leq \tau + M \rangle \swarrow R \qquad (23) \\ = & \quad \text{“ Definition of weakest prespecification. ”} \\ & \langle \forall \hat{\sigma}, \hat{\tau} \cdot R.\sigma'.\tau'.\hat{\sigma}.\hat{\tau} \Rightarrow \hat{\tau} \leq \tau + M \rangle \\ \sqsupseteq & \quad \text{“ Specialize to any } \dot{\sigma} \text{ and } \dot{\tau} \text{ that (22) says exist.} \\ & \quad \text{(These variables are dependant on } \sigma' \text{ and } \tau'.) \text{ ”} \\ & \langle R.\sigma'.\tau'.\dot{\sigma}.\dot{\tau} \Rightarrow \dot{\tau} \leq \tau + M \rangle \\ = & \quad \text{“ From (22) we know } R.\sigma'.\tau'.\dot{\sigma}.\dot{\tau}. \text{ ”} \\ & \langle \dot{\tau} \leq \tau + M \rangle \\ = & \quad \text{“ From (22) we know } \dot{\tau} = \tau' + M'. \text{ ”} \\ & \langle \tau' + M' \leq \tau + M \rangle \quad . \end{array}$$

Now we can flesh out step (20):

$$\begin{array}{ll} & \langle \tau' \leq \tau + M \rangle \sqsubseteq (\langle B \rangle \wedge P); tick; R \\ \equiv & \quad \text{“ Galois connection (9). ”} \\ & \langle \tau' \leq \tau + M \rangle \swarrow R \sqsubseteq (\langle B \rangle \wedge P); tick \\ \Rightarrow & \quad \text{“ Calculation (23) and transitivity. ”} \\ & \langle \tau' + M' \leq \tau + M \rangle \sqsubseteq (\langle B \rangle \wedge P); tick \quad . \end{array}$$

This completes the proof of (21). As a corollary we have:

$$\begin{array}{ll} & \quad \text{“ } P \text{ decreases the bound more than it consumes time (21). ”} \\ & \langle \tau' + M' + 1 \leq \tau + M \rangle \sqsubseteq \langle B \rangle \wedge P \\ = & \quad \text{“ } P \text{ is progressive. ”} \\ & \langle \tau' + M' + 1 \leq \tau + M \wedge \tau \leq \tau' \rangle \sqsubseteq \langle B \rangle \wedge P \\ \Rightarrow & \quad \text{“ Monotonicity of } \wedge \text{ ”} \\ & \langle \tau' + M' + 1 \leq \tau + M \wedge \tau \leq \tau' \wedge \tau \in \mathsf{nat} \rangle \sqsubseteq \langle B \rangle \wedge \langle \tau \in \mathsf{nat} \rangle \wedge P \\ = & \quad \text{“ Both } M \text{ and } M' \text{ are naturals ”} \\ & \langle \tau' + M' + 1 \leq \tau + M \wedge \tau \leq \tau' \wedge \tau, \tau' \in \mathsf{nat} \rangle \sqsubseteq \langle B \rangle \wedge \langle \tau \in \mathsf{nat} \rangle \wedge P \\ \Rightarrow & \quad \text{“ Transitivity of } \leq . \text{ ”} \end{array}$$

$$\langle \tau' + M' + 1 \leq \tau' + M \wedge \tau \leq \tau' \wedge \tau, \tau' \in \textsf{nat}\rangle \sqsubseteq \langle B\rangle \wedge \langle \tau \in \textsf{nat}\rangle \wedge P$$

$\Rightarrow$ " **nat** arithmetic. "

$$\langle M' + 1 \leq M \wedge \tau \leq \tau' \wedge \tau, \tau' \in \textsf{nat}\rangle \sqsubseteq \langle B\rangle \wedge \langle \tau \in \textsf{nat}\rangle \wedge P$$

$\Rightarrow$ " Weakening the LHS of the refinement. "

$$\langle M' + 1 \leq M\rangle \sqsubseteq \langle B\rangle \wedge \langle \tau \in \textsf{nat}\rangle \wedge P$$

$\Rightarrow$ " M is natural. "

$$\langle M' < M\rangle \sqsubseteq \langle B\rangle \wedge \langle \tau \in \textsf{nat}\rangle \wedge P \quad . \tag{24}$$

APPENDIX 1.3 The induction

With these results in hand, we will prove that $R \sqsubseteq W$. As we already have $R \sqsubseteq \neg\langle B\rangle \wedge W$, and $R \sqsubseteq \langle B\rangle \wedge \langle \tau = \infty\rangle \wedge W$ it remains to prove $R \sqsubseteq \langle B\rangle \wedge \langle \tau \in \textsf{nat}\rangle \wedge W$. The proof is by complete induction on M, which, because of strong bounding, is a natural expression. Specifically we will prove, for any natural i,

$$R \sqsubseteq \langle M = i\rangle \wedge \langle \tau \in \textsf{nat}\rangle \wedge \langle B\rangle \wedge W$$

follows from the induction hypothesis $R \sqsubseteq \langle M < i\rangle \wedge \langle \tau \in \textsf{nat}\rangle \wedge \langle B\rangle \wedge W$. In light of calculation (18), we can see that the induction hypothesis implies

$$R \sqsubseteq \langle M < i\rangle \wedge \langle \tau \in \textsf{nat}\rangle \wedge W \quad . \tag{25}$$

Calculate

$$\langle M = i\rangle \wedge \langle \tau \in \textsf{nat}\rangle \wedge \langle B\rangle \wedge W$$

$=$ " Calculation (19). "

$$\langle M = i\rangle \wedge (\langle B\rangle \wedge \langle \tau \in \textsf{nat}\rangle \wedge P); \mathit{tick}; W$$

$\sqsupseteq$ " (24). "

$$(\langle B\rangle \wedge P); (\langle M < i\rangle \wedge \langle \tau \in \textsf{nat}\rangle \wedge \mathit{tick}); W$$

$=$ " Time insensitivity. "

$$(\langle B\rangle \wedge P); \mathit{tick}; (\langle M < i\rangle \wedge \langle \tau \in \textsf{nat}\rangle \wedge W)$$

$\sqsupseteq$ " Induction hypothesis (25). "

$$(\langle B\rangle \wedge P); \mathit{tick}; R$$

$=$ " B is a condition. "

$$\langle B\rangle \wedge (P; \mathit{tick}; R)$$

$\sqsupseteq$ " Definition of **if**. "

$$\textbf{if } B \textbf{ then} (P; \mathit{tick}; R) \textbf{ else } \mathit{skip}$$

$$
\begin{array}{ll}
= & \text{“ Definition of } w \text{ (1). ”} \\
& w.R \\
\sqsupseteq & \text{“ } R \text{ is recursively refined (5). ”} \\
& R \quad .
\end{array}
$$

It is interesting that there is no need to break the proof into zero and non-zero cases. The reason is that one falls into the $\neg B$ case before hitting zero.

REFERENCES

Back, R. J. R. and von Wright, J., (1990). Refinement calculus, part 1: Sequential nondeterministic programs. In de Backer, J. W., de Roever, W.-P., and Rosenberg, G., editors, *Stepwise Refinement of Distributed Systems: Models Formalisms, Correctness*, number 430 in Lecture Notes in Computer Science. Springer-Verlag, 1990.

Hehner, Eric C. R., (1979). **do** considered **od**: A contribution to the programming calculus. *Acta Informatica*, 11:287–304, 1979.

Hehner, Eric C. R., (1984). Predicative programming. *Communications of the ACM*, 27(2):134–151, 1984.

Hehner, Eric C. R., (1993). *A Practical Theory of Programming*. Springer-Verlag, 1993.

Hehner, Eric C. R., (1994). Abstractions of time. In Roscoe, A. W., editor, *A Classical Mind*, chapter 12, pages 195–214. Prentice-Hall International, 1994.

Hoare, C. A. R and He, JiFeng, , (1987). The weakest prespecification. *Information Processing Letters*, 24:127–132, 1987.

Hoare, C. A. R., (1985). Programs are predicates. In Hoare, C. A. R. and Shepherdson, J. C., editors, *Mathematical Logic and Programming Languages*, pages 141–155. Prentice Hall, 1985.

Hoare, C. A. R., (1994). Mathematical models for computer science. Technical report, Oxford University Computing Laboratory, Oxford University, August 1994.

Holt, Richard C., (1991). Healthiness versus realizability in predicate transformers. Technical Report CSRI-240, Computer Systems Research Institute, University of Toronto, 1991.

Morgan, Carroll, (1990). *Programming from Specifications*. Prentice Hall International, 1990.

Norvell, Theodore S., (1993). *A Predicative Theory of Machine Languages and its Application to Compiler Correctness*. PhD thesis, University of Toronto, December 1993.

Norvell, Theodore S., (1994). Machine code programs are predicates too. In Till, David, editor, *Sixth Refinement Workshop*, Workshops in Computing, pages 188–204. Springer Verlag, 1994.

Sekerinski, Emil, (1993). A calculus for predicative programming. In *Mathematics of Program Construction 1992*, number 669 in LNCS, pages 302–322. Springer-Verlag, 1993.
Spivey, J. M., (1989). *The Z Notation: A Reference Manual.* Prentice-Hall, 1989.
Tarski, Alfred, (1955). A lattice-theoretical fixpoint theorem and its applications. *Pacific Journal of Mathematics*, 5:285–309, 1955.
v. Karger, Burghard and Hoare, C. A. R, (1994). Sequential calculus. *Information Processing Letters*, 53:123–131, 1994.

BIOGRAPHY

A native of Halifax, Nova Scotia, Theodore Norvell obtained Master's and Ph.D. degrees in Computing Science from the University of Toronto. He has worked in the software development industry and has done postdoctoral work both at the Programming Research Group of Oxford University and at the Software Engineering Research Group of McMaster University. He is currently a professor of engineering at Memorial University of Newfoundland.

His research interests include formal specification and derivation of programs, programming language design, and formal aspects of software and hardware engineering.

Richard Bird: I would like to propose as a discussion topic a question that has been implicit in some previous discussions. Even confining ourselves to the derivation of small programs rather than large systems, why are there so many calculi? Ask yourselves: why do I never use anyone else's calculus, and why does no one ever use mine? While you are thinking about how you might respond to these questions, can I ask Tom Maibaum to reiterate a story he told at lunch today.

Tom Maibaum: It is a story about Newton and Leibniz. We know they both invented the calculus at the same time, but what is less well-known is what happened thereafter. There was a schism and the British refused to use the superior Leibniz notation for purely emotional reasons: it was not invented in the UK. Historians of mathematics, including UK historians, now agree that if you look at this period, mathematics was held back in the UK very substantially by this decision. It is a very good story about how the refusal to use a superior notation for calculation purposes had a significant effect on the advancement of science. As a footnote, one of the people who re-introduced Leibniz's notation into British mathematical education was Babbage. As a student at Cambridge, he and two other students – one of them the son of the Astronomer Royal, Herschel, found the French book, translated and expanded it, and it became the standard textbook about calculus in the UK for much of the last century.

Armando Haeberer: I agree that the reason was emotional. For the same reason the English did not change their calendar for some years, and still drive on the wrong side of the road! By the way, when using analog computers as integrators, it is easier to use Newtonian notation with the dots, because each time you put in an integrator, you take out a dot in the equation. So, notation and the purpose to which it is put are closely related.

Jose Fiadeiro: When you say 'use' a calculus, do you mean to do something other than develop the calculus, to use it to do real things? Can the inventor of a calculus really be said to use it?

Bob Paige: How would you evaluate one calculus versus another? If you get most programmers to choose between different calculi, then it may be that a large number of them will simply head off in one direction or another and that will decide it. It could be because Americans prevail, or Germans, or whatever.

Richard Bird: During this conference, I asked a participant a question "How useful is calculus X?". The reply I got was: "It hides detail, allows relatively index-free formulations, and provides some conceptual unity". These are not culture based criteria are they? They are scientific criteria that can be applied by anyone. I have used three or four different calculi in my work on program derivation. The first was based on imperative notations; then I was influenced by David Turner and used a functional notation because it clearly met the first two criteria above; finally, I was persuaded by Oege de Moor to use a relational calculus in a categorical setting, partly because of the third criterion, and partly because of the large amount of work done by others in the area. Actually, the real question I asked the colleague was: "Does it appear to you that the use of category theory in algorithmics is more important than its use in general systems theory, or about the same?".

Sharon Curtis: We are all individuals, working on different problems, with different kinds of research to do, and with different ideas on how to do it. As a member of one research group, I use a relational calculus common to that group. In fact, this calculus was not able to deal with one kind of problem, so I invented another calculus. Somebody thought of using this calculus to solve a problem that had taken about a fortnight of manpower, and it dropped in two minutes.

Thilo Gaul: The third question seems to me to be like the question one programming language designer asks another: Why don't you use my language? You shouldn't ask such questions.

Oege de Moor: I'd like to disagree with asking these questions at all. The first question – why there are so many calculi – would be relevant if there was a divergence and we saw many more different calculi appearing all the time. I don't think that is true; since the last time I was here there has definitely been a convergence, at least at the conceptual level. Of course, we don't agree about notation but it would be unhealthy to standardize at present. Why do I never use a different calculus? Of course, we do; we use different calculi according to the problem area. If we wanted to modify these questions to make them more relevant, we might try to ask how to increase the rate of convergence towards a unified theory. One way of doing that might be to agree to have a specific area where we look for applications. An obvious candidate would be scheduling algorithms, because Doug Smith has made a lot of progress there. Another area might be the processing of structured information; for example, you could think of compression algorithms used to send structured information over the internet. By focusing on such problems, we might be able to make scientific comparisons between variations of essentially the same calculus.

Doug Smith: Interestingly, I have a completely different set of considerations that go into what kind of calculus I am interested in working with. One is how well you can automate it. To my mind that rules out the fold-unfold technique which I used a long time ago and regard as a nice sort of machine language little thing, but its not going to lead to effective automation. Another issue is the granularity of transformations. It is not economical to make hundreds of design decisions to reach reasonable code. That puts the emphasis on calculi that capture large chunks of programming knowledge. Another aspect is inclusiveness. Can my calculus include, say, all of Bob Paige's work on finite differencing and fixed-point induction, as well as the best aspects of the squiggol work, and so on?. If not, then you are not getting leverage from the best ideas world-wide.

One other comment that comes to mind, thinking about *the* calculus as a paradigm: as I understand it, mechanized support for symbolic integration doesn't use the basic techniques we learned for doing calculus; the Risch algorithm and other techniques use much more sophisticated larger grain chunks of knowledge, vastly outperforming what people can do by hand.

Wolf Zimmermann: For numerical computations I think I would disagree with you that they want relatively index-free formulations. Sometimes they even try to have indexed formulations when computing references.

Richard Bird: But in an earlier discussion it was said that numerical analysts think in terms of matrix notations when they write their Fortran programs.

Fritz Bauer: It is very uneconomical for a numerical analyst to think in such a way for sparse matrices, so they are forced to go into indexing. And then comes references to indices, and so on.

Bob Paige: I don't think you would object to modifying the criterion to read "it allows relatively index-free or indexed formulations". [*Laughter*]

Alberto Pettorossi: What is important is the expressivity of the relevant properties. I would also add decidability properties as an important criterion. It would be a very weak calculus if I cannot decide whether two expressions are equal, or one subsumes the other.

Wim Hesselink: I would like to add one criterion not yet discussed. That is, the possibility that the syntax of expressions give some indication of how to proceed. In Dijkstra's words: let the symbols do the work. I wouldn't say that it is always needed, but it can be a strong point in favour of a calculus.

A related comment on what we have heard concerns Wile's remark that induction was to be avoided because it was so difficult. The theorem prover I am using is often able to find induction hypotheses on the grounds of syntax, and that is one of its strong points.

Jim Boyle: I would like to say in regard to the second question as to why don't I use someone else's calculus, I think that all of the non French speaking people who have tried to use the computers here understand part of the answer to that question. [*Laughter*]

INDEX OF CONTRIBUTORS

KEYWORD INDEX

GPSR Compliance

The European Union's (EU) General Product Safety Regulation (GPSR) is a set of rules that requires consumer products to be safe and our obligations to ensure this.

If you have any concerns about our products, you can contact us on ProductSafety@springernature.com

In case Publisher is established outside the EU, the EU authorized representative is:

Springer Nature Customer Service Center GmbH
Europaplatz 3
69115 Heidelberg, Germany

Batch number: 10755284

Printed by Printforce, the Netherlands